The Economics of the European Union

The Economics of the European Union

Policy and Analysis

FOURTH EDITION

Edited by

Mike Artis and Frederick Nixson

OXFORD
UNIVERSITY PRESS

OXFORD
UNIVERSITY PRESS

Great Clarendon Street, Oxford OX2 6DP

Oxford University Press is a department of the University of Oxford.
It furthers the University's objective of excellence in research, scholarship,
and education by publishing worldwide in

Oxford New York

Auckland Cape Town Dar es Salaam Hong Kong Karachi
Kuala Lumpur Madrid Melbourne Mexico City Nairobi
New Delhi Shanghai Taipei Toronto

With offices in

Argentina Austria Brazil Chile Czech Republic France Greece
Guatemala Hungary Italy Japan Poland Portugal Singapore
South Korea Switzerland Thailand Turkey Ukraine Vietnam

Oxford is a registered trade mark of Oxford University Press
in the UK and in certain other countries

Published in the United States
by Oxford University Press Inc., New York

© Oxford University Press 2007

The moral rights of the authors have been asserted
Database right Oxford University Press (maker)

First published 2001
This edition 2007

British Library Cataloguing in Publication Data
Data available

Library of Congress Cataloging-in-Publication Data
The economics of the European Union: policy and analysis / edited by Mike
Artis and Frederick Nixson. – 4th ed.
    p. cm.
Includes bibliographical references and index.
ISBN 978-0-19-929896-9
1. European Union. 2. European Union countries-Economic policy.
I. Artis, Michael J. II. Nixson, F. I.
HC240.E288 2007
337.1'42–dc22   2007009932

Typeset by Graphicraft Limited, Hong Kong
Printed in Great Britain
on acid-free paper by CPI Antony Rowe, Chippenham

ISBN 978-0-19-929896-9

5 7 9 10 8 6 4

■ CONTENTS

■ LIST OF FIGURES

LIST OF TABLES

■ LIST OF BOXES

■ LIST OF ABBREVIATIONS

AAP	Arable Area Payment
AASM	Association of African States and Madagascar
AC	Average Cost
ACARD	Advisory Council for Applied Research and Development
ACOST	Advisory Council on Science and Technology
ACP	African, Caribbean, and Pacific countries
AMS	Aggregate Measure of Support
AR	Average Revenue
ATC	Agreement on Textiles and Clothing
BAE	Bureau of Agricultural Economics
BEPG	Broad Economic Policy Guidelines
BMBF	Bundesministerium für Bildung und Forschung (Federal Ministry for Research and Technology)
BMWi	Federal Ministry for Economics and Technology
BSE	Bovine Spongiform Encephalitis
BSP	Basic State Pension
BTG	British Technology Group
CAC	Command and Control
CAD	Computer-aided Design
CAP	Common Agricultural Policy
CAPB	Cyclically Adjusted Primary Balance
CBA	Cost Benefit Analysis
CBD	(United Nations) Convention on Biological Diversity
CCIR	International Radio Consultative Committee
CEC	Commission of the European Communities
CEEC	Central and Eastern European Country
CEFTA	Central European Free Trade Association
CEPR	Centre for Economic Policy Research
CET	Common External Tariff
CFCs	Chlorofluorocarbons
CFSP	Common Foreign and Security Policy
CI	Community Initiative or Citizen's Income
c.i.f.	cost, insurance, freight
CJD	Creutzfeldt-Jakob Disease
CMEA	Council for Mutual Economic Assistance
CNC	Computer Numerically Controlled
CNRS	Centre National de la Recherche Scientifique
CO_2	Carbon Dioxide
COAPRI	Official Association of Industrial Property Agents
COMETT	Community Programme on Education and Training for Technology
COP	Cereals, Oilseeds and Protein crops
CQS	Community Quota System
CREST	Comité de la Recherche Scientifique et Technique (Scientific and Technical Research Committee)
CSF	Community Support Framework

CTP	Common Transport Policy
CU	Customs Union
DAC	Development Assistance Committee
DDA	Doha Development Agenda
DFG	Deutsche Forschungsgemeinschaft (German Research Association)
DFI	Direct Foreign Investment
DFID	Department for International Development (UK)
DG	Directorate-General
DOM	Départements d'outre-mer (French overseas departments)
DoT	Department of Transport
DPI	Department of Primary Industry
DPS	EU Development Policy Strategy
DRS	Domestic Rate of Substitution
DRT	Domestic Rate of Transformation
DTI	Department of Trade and Industry (UK)
EADS	European Aeronautic Defence and Space Company
EAGGF	European Agricultural Guidance and Guarantee Fund
EAP	Environmental Action Plan
EBA	Everything But Arms
EBRD	European Bank for Reconstruction and Development
EC	European Community
ECB	European Central Bank
ECE	Economic Commission for Europe
ECJ	European Court of Justice
ECOFIN	Council of Economics and Finance Ministers
ECSC	European Coal and Steel Community
Ecu	European currency unit
EDC	European Defence Community
EDF	European Development Fund
EDP	Excessive Deficit Procedure
EEA	European Economic Area
EEC	European Economic Community
EFC	Economic and Financial Committee
EFTA	European Free Trade Association
EIB	European Investment Bank
ELDO	European Launcher Development Organization
EMCF	European Monetary Cooperation Fund
EMI	European Monetary Institute
EMS	European Monetary System
EMU	European Monetary Union or Economic and Monetary Union
ENA	Ecole Nationale d'Administration (National School of Administration)
EP	European Parliament
EPAs	Economic Partnership Agreements
EPL	Employment Protection Legislation
EPO	European Patent Office
EPU	European Payments Union
ER	Export Refund
ERC	European Research Council
ERDF	European Regional Development Fund
ERM	Exchange Rate Mechanism
ERP	European Recovery Programme

ESA	European Space Agency
ESCB	European System of Central Banks
ESF	European Social Fund
ESPRIT	European Strategic Programme for Research and Development in Information Technology
ESRO	European Space Research Organization
ETUC	European Trade Union Confederation
EU	European Union
Euratom	European Atomic Energy Community
EUREKA	European Research Coordination Agency
FAST	Forecasting and Assessment in Science and Technology
FCCC	(United Nations) Framework Convention on Climate Change
FDI	Foreign Direct Investment
FEAP	Fifth Environmental Action Plan
f.o.b	free on board
FEOGA	Fonds Européen d'Orientation et de Garantie Agricole (EAGGF)
FhF	Fraunhofer Association
FP	Framework Programme
FRT	Foreign Rate of Transformation
FTA	Free Trade Area or Agreement
G&S	Goods and Services
GATS	General Agreement on Trade in Services
GATT	General Agreement on Tariffs and Trade
GDP	Gross Domestic Product
GDR	German Democratic Republic
GEM	Global Economic Model
GNI	Gross National Income
GNP	Gross National Product
GSP	Generalized System of Preference
GVA	Gross Value Added
HDTV	high-definition television
HIPC	Harmonized Index of Consumer Prices
IATA	International Air Transport Association
ICP	International Comparison Project
ICT	Information and Telecommunication Technology
IFIs	International Financial Institutions
IGC	Intergovernmental Conference
IICA	Inter-Institutional Collaborative Agreements
IMF	International Monetary Fund
IPR	Intellectual Property Right
IP	Investment Premium
IT	Information Technology
ITA	Information Technology Agreement
ITCP	International Textiles and Clothing Bureau
JASPERS	Joint Assistance in Supporting Projects in European Regions
JEREMIE	Joint European Resources for Micro to Medium Enterprises
JESSICA	Joint European Support for Sustainable Investment in City Areas
JHA	Justice and Home Affairs
JIT	Just In Time
JRC	Joint Research Centre
JNRC	Joint Nuclear Research Centre

LAC	Long-run Average Cost
LDC	Less-Developed Country
LFAs	Less Favourable Areas
LICs	Low-Income Countries
LTA	Long Term Arrangement
MAC	Marginal Abatement Cost
MB	Marginal Benefit
MBI	Market-Based Instrument
MC	Marginal Cost
MCA	Monetary Compensatory Amount
MDGs	Millennium Development Goals
MDS	Maximum Divergence Spread
MEC	Marginal External Cost
MEP	Member of the European Parliament
MERCOSUR	A CU between Argentina, Brazil, Paraguay and Uruguay
METS	Minimum Efficient Technical Scale
MFA	Multi-Fibre Arrangement
m.f.n.	most favoured nation
MFR	Main Refinancing Rate
MIP	Minimum Import Price
MITI	Ministry of International Trade and Industry, Japan
MMC	Monopolies and Mergers Commission
MNPB	Marginal Net Private Benefit
MPG	Max Planck Institute
MPTC	Marginal Pollution Treatment Cost
MPV	Multi-Purpose Vehicle
MR	Marginal Revenue
MRD	Marginal Reduction in Damage
MSC	Marginal Social Cost
MTO	Medium-Term Objective
NAFTA	North American Free Trade Agreement
NAIRU	Non-Accelerating Inflation Rate of Unemployment
NATO	North Atlantic Treaty Organization
NGACE	Nomenclature Générale des Activités Economiques des Communautés
NGO	Non-Governmental Organization
NIEO	New International Economic Order
NIS	New Independent States
NRDC	National Research Development Corporation
NRP	National Reform Programmes
NSI	National Systems of Innovation
NTB	Non-Tariff Barrier
NUTS	Territorial Units for Statistics
OCAs	Optimum Currency Areas
OCTs	Overseas Counties and Territories
ODA	Official Development Assistance
ODF	Official Development Finance
OECD	Organization for Economic Cooperation and Development
OEEC	Organization for European Economic Cooperation
OFT	Office for Fair Trading
OMC	Open Method of Coordination
OP	Operational Programme

OPT	Outward-Processing Traffic
PAC	Pollution Abatement and Control
PEG	Production Entitlement Guarantee
PFC	Production Flexibility Contract
PP	Precautionary Principle
PPP	Purchasing Power Parity
P-P-P	Polluter Pays Principle
PPS	Purchasing Power Standard
PSE	Producer Subsidy Equivalent (now renamed Producer Support Equivalent)
PSRE	Public Sector Research Establishment
PTAs	Preferential Trading Areas
QMV	Qualified Majority Voting
R&D	Research and Development
RCE	Regional Competitiveness and Employment objective
RDP	Rural Development Plan
RIAs	Regional Integration Agreements
RTD	Research and Technical Development
SADC	Southern Africa Development Community
SAP	Set-Aside Payment
SDI	Strategic Defence Initiative
SEA	Single European Act
SEM	Single European Market
SF	Structural Funds
SFP	Single Farm Payment
SGP	Stability and Growth Pact
SME	Small and Medium-Sized Enterprise
SMI	Single Market Initiative
SMP	Single Market Programme
SMU	Support Measurement Unit
SPD	Single Programming Document
SPRINT	Strategic Programme for Innovation and Technology Transfer
SPRU	Science Policy Research Unit
SSNIP	Small Significant Non-transitory Increase in Price
Stabex	System for the Stabilization of Export Earnings
Sysmin	System for Safeguarding and Developing Mineral Production
T&C	Textiles & Clothing
TEC	Treaty establishing the European Community
TENs	Trans-European Networks
TEU	Treaty on European Union
TFP	Total Factor Productivity
TINA	There Is No Alternative
TIP	Technology Integration Projects
TRIPS	Trade Related aspects of Intellectual Property Rights
UNDP	United Nations Development Programme
UNECE	United Nations Economic Commission for Europe
UNICE	Union of the Industries of the European Community
URA	Uruguay Round Agreement
USA	United States of America
VAT	Value Added Tax
VER	Voluntary Export Restraint
VHSICs	Very High Speed Integrated Circuits

VIL	Variable Import Levy
VLSI	Very Large Scale Integration
VSTF	Very Short Term Financing
WB	World Bank
WTO	World Trade Organization

LIST OF CONTRIBUTORS

Mike Artis	Professor of Economics, Institute for Political and Economic Governance, University of Manchester
Giuseppe Bertola	Professor of Economics, School of Political Science, University of Turin
Robin Bladen-Hovell	Professor of Economics, University of Keele
Simon Bulmer	Professor of Government, University of Manchester; from September 2007, Professor of European Politics, University of Sheffield
David Colman	Emeritus Professor of Economics, University of Manchester
Stephen Martin	Professor of Economics, Krannert School of Management, Purdue University
Richard Morris	European Central Bank
Frederick Nixson	Professor of Development Economics, School of Social Sciences, University of Manchester
Hedwig Ongena	European Central Bank
David Purdy	Formerly of University of Manchester
Joseph Quinlan	Johns Hopkins University
André Sapir	Professor of Economics, University of Brussels
Susan Schadler	International Monetary Fund
Peter Stubbs	Emeritus Professor of Economics, University of Manchester
Gabriele Tondl	Associate Professor of Economics, Research Institute for European Affairs, University of Economics, Vienna
Anthony J. Venables	Professor of Economics, Department of Economics, University of Oxford
Nick Weaver	Teaching Fellow, University of Manchester
Bernhard Winkler	European Central Bank

Introduction

Mike Artis and Frederick Nixson

As this book goes to press, a number of commentators are detecting a crisis in the European Union. It seems clear that the momentum has slowed down; and, if the 'bicycle theory' holds true, a slowing of momentum precedes collapse, or in this case crisis. There are indeed quite a few indicators that the climate has changed, and the ranks of EU ill-wishers are not slow to exploit, exaggerate, and misconceive what is going on.

Still, the list of setbacks is rather a long one. The negative outcomes of the referenda on the European Constitution in France and the Netherlands in 2005 must head the list because of their symbolic significance, but there are other failures to record. These cannot but induce a loss of confidence in the viability of the Union. They include, after all, the failure of the first version of the Stability and Growth Pact, clear for all to see by 2004. In an arrangement such as that of the Union, in which governance relies on coordination, this particular failure—where after all, the need for coordination was endorsed and supported by a separate Treaty—is bound to cut deep. It invites—and has resulted in—a sceptical reception for the reformed version of the Pact. In the same category must come the failure of the Lisbon process where the collision of ambitious promises with ineffective governance also has invited ridicule. Again, the resumption of progress on the Lisbon agenda has received only a sceptical welcome. Meanwhile, there are signs of a new protectionism in which Member States seek to prevent the acquisition of certain business enterprises by non-nationals.

The most recent (2004) enlargement, it is true, took place with surprisingly little difficulty, but it has come at the cost of a violation of the Union's promise of a free labour market, with all but three (the UK, Ireland, and Sweden) of the members of the 'old' EU taking advantage of the possibility of enjoying a seven-year derogation of the requirement to admit workers freely from the new Member States. They have now been joined by one of the three exceptional countries (the UK) in extending the derogation to the two remaining members of the (2007) eastern enlargement—Bulgaria and Romania. Some critics have even gone so far as to suggest that the malaise of the Union extends to its premier achievement, its monetary union, with suggestions that this might fall apart because of the strains of adjustment, most notably affecting Italy. Further, the president of the European Commission has now signalled (September 2006) that the consideration of yet further enlargement—to remaining members of the former Yugoslavia and to Turkey—should be postponed. All this implies a malaise which seems likely to further the sense of disengagement from the EU which substantial portions of the European 'demos' already experience. The UK may be an extreme example of this, yet not a completely isolated one.

It seems ironic that the EU should be suffering from this malaise when the extent of globalization is perceived to be developing apace. After all, one way to manage some of the challenges of globalization is to extend the dwindling of effective sovereignty of individual countries by forming regional, subglobal blocs; although this cannot be a way of avoiding adjustment, it should enable adjustment to be more effective (for a balanced account of the impact of globalization on the EU and an assessment of the EU's best response see Denis *et al.* 2006). Subglobal arrangements will typically involve some surrender of formal sovereignty in exchange for an increase in effective sovereignty—indeed this is the whole point. But for this very reason, the coherence of such blocs and the process of holding them together will not always be straightforward: indeed it is not surprising that, for many, Europeanization is hard to distinguish from globalization. In the late 1980s, after an interest in global policy coordination had been aroused by the celebrated 'Plaza agreement' of 1985, the eminent US economist Richard Cooper warned that even in cases where the incentives for coordination are demonstrably strong, the minutiae of the difficulties involved in giving up, or sharing, control may be such as to delay the process enormously, especially when there are unresolved factual or positive disagreements in the background. His reference was the slow process by which nations came to agree on measures to control the international spread of communicable diseases (Cooper 1987). This caution may apply to aspects of the European Union too. The European Union relies upon coordination of policies across the Member States; it has limited powers of its own (with the major exception of that part of the Union which is coterminous with the Euro-area, where the European Central Bank provides policy centrally); the effectiveness of what it can do through the route of coordination is limited and it is not quick.

Where do these observations lead us? An optimist can find plenty of examples of EU effectiveness and EU progress. There are powerful basic reasons why the Member States should want to cooperate and why they should want to improve their cooperation and individually obtain better results. That the Stability and Growth Pact has been reformed is in itself, for example, a promising sign: though it is possible to criticize aspects of the reform, the reform itself has been conducted with an eye to improvement. The same is true of the re-engagement with the Lisbon process. We do not expect any unravelling of the European Union, but it seems clear that the near future will contain more deepening than widening. This is partly because the next enlargement could only bring the question of Turkey's admission closer. It is not unnatural that this should present a substantial obstacle if only because the balance of power inside the Union would be so greatly affected, as Turkey is a large state. If the next years are tilted towards deepening for this reason, one possible result would be the increased use of 'variable geometry' arrangements to accommodate the more divisive disagreements that would be revealed. The position of the UK might become more tenuous, especially as the UK's position on joining the Euro seems now to have consolidated into one of permanent lack of interest.

This volume contains a large number of chapters devoted to the various policy problems and achievements of the EU. An important policy area, unfortunately not covered in this edition, though, is that of environmental policy. We would like to record our sadness at the untimely death of David Pearce, who had agreed to provide a new version of his previous chapter for this volume. David was one of the world's leading environmental economists and his death is a massive loss from all points of view.

■ **REFERENCES**

Denis, C., McMorrow, K., and Roger, W., (2006), 'Globalization: Trends. Issues and Macro Implications for the EU', *European Economy* no. 254, July.

Cooper, R. (1987), 'International Cooperation in Public Health as a Prologue to Macroeconomic Cooperation', in R. Cooper, B. Eichengreen, C. R. Henning, G. Holtham, and R. D. Putnam (eds.), *Can Nations Agree?* Washington, DC: Brookings Institution Press.

1 | History and Institutions

Simon Bulmer

Introduction

The European Union (EU) formally came into existence on 1 November 1993 after final ratification of the Treaty on European Union (TEU or, colloquially, the Maastricht Treaty). The EU is an actor of huge importance in the global economy. Following its enlargement in January 2007 it comprises twenty-seven Member States with a combined population of almost 500 million inhabitants. Although the EU is primarily an economic actor its Member States work together in other policy areas as well: the environment, foreign policy, and on combating crime, terrorism, and illegal immigration. It was in part as a way of emphasizing this broader range of activities that the term 'European Union' was adopted in preference to the earlier term, the European Community (EC). However, European economic integration has always had political objectives. It is the purpose of this chapter to show that a knowledge of the wider context—historical, political, and institutional—is essential to an understanding of the economic activities.

The peaceful integration of the European national economies has been a development specific to the post-1945 era. The integration of Europe was proposed as early as the fourteenth century, but it was not until the period of economic, political, and military reconstruction following the Second World War that it was put into practice. The form taken by integration was strongly influenced by the historical experiences of its founding fathers. Hence they sought to avoid the excesses of nationalism and of the nation-state system that had been demonstrated by the German Nazi regime. They also sought to open up the national economies as a means of avoiding the protectionism that had characterized inter-war Europe. Poor economic performance was widely perceived to have provided a climate of political instability conducive to the growth of Fascism in Europe.

Economic integration has also been rooted in a particular European geography. This, too, has a historical explanation, namely in the division of Europe through the Cold War. Thus the history of economic integration in the EC, until the 1990s, was *West* European history. Only with the collapse of Communism in Eastern and Central Europe at the end of the 1980s did the EC need substantively to develop economic relations with the other half of the continent. For their part, the new democracies of Central and Eastern Europe regarded accession to the EU as one of their principal objectives and a substantial group of these states joined in May 2004.

If the division of Europe has major contextual importance to economic integration, so in particular does the division of one state, Germany. After the Second World War France was concerned that the revival of the German coal and steel industries might trigger expansionism. The principal objective of the European Coal and Steel Community (ECSC) was to allay fears of a 'military–industrial complex' fuelling renascent German nationalism. The roots of economic integration through what we may call the 'Community method' (see below) thus lay in the need to find a political solution to the turbulent past of Franco-German relations.

There are many other ways in which historical circumstance has shaped the pattern of economic integration. In particular, it can explain the tortuous way in which the UK has come to grips with the integration process, as a reluctant participant seeking to come to terms with its 'descent from power'. Similarly, the persistence of non-democratic forms of government in Greece and on the Iberian peninsula isolated those states from the EC until their domestic political transformation permitted membership, as part of a second wave of enlargement in the 1980s.

Thus history has conditioned the process of economic integration. But what of the politics and institutional framework of economic integration? These, too, are important.

Economic integration has not evolved as the result of functional necessity or logic. Nor has it developed as the result of some 'natural' economic law enforced by Adam Smith's 'invisible hand'. Functional and economic determinism fail to explain both the setbacks to integration and the relaunches; economic integration has not been a smooth process following some scientific logic. Rather, it has been dependent upon political and institutional dynamics, and this chapter aims to outline what these are.

In European integration—from the Schuman Plan creating the ECSC to the present—a package deal satisfying all Member States' national interests has been essential to each individual development. However, where the agreement amounts to a new treaty, even consensus between the member governments may be insufficient. Thus, in 2004 twenty-five Member States approved a 'Treaty establishing a Constitution for Europe'. However in May/June 2005 electorates in France and the Netherlands rejected the treaty, and its ratification was subsequently suspended, perhaps indefinitely. The need to satisfy domestic political concerns was also demonstrated with the Maastricht Treaty—the TEU. The Danes' need to hold a second referendum following the Treaty's initial rejection by a narrow margin of voters in June 1992; a close (but successful) referendum in France; a tortuous ratification process during 1992–3 in the UK House of Commons under John Major's government; and a constitutional court ruling in Germany: these all demonstrated the contingency of treaty amendments on domestic politics. Thus major integrative developments require not only agreement between the member governments but an ability on the part of the latter to ensure domestic approval.

On a more routine level, the day-to-day business of integration may be less publicly politicized. However, the political dynamics of policy-making are no less important. The EU is not like the many other international organizations on the world stage. Uniquely amongst European and international organizations, it has supranational characteristics. These are concentrated overwhelmingly in the institutional arrangements concerning the economic 'pillar' of activity. It has its own body of law which has direct effect in the Member States, and takes precedence over national law. It has institutions with autonomy from the Member States. The most prominent of these are the European Commission, which serves as an executive civil service; a parliamentary assembly, which has been directly elected since 1979; and a European Court of Justice (ECJ), which makes rulings on matters of law. Balanced against these three are two powerful institutions representing the interests of the member governments, namely the Council of Ministers and the European Council. The former is composed of national ministers; the latter of heads of government or state. The EU is not like other international economic organizations in a further respect—namely, in the way that economic integration has been a continuing process of evolving goals from the first steps undertaken with the ECSC to the TEU and beyond.

Above all, however, it must be remembered that economic integration has never been an end in itself. It has always served as a means towards the end of political integration. The ECSC involved the integration of the coal and steel sectors as a means towards Franco-German reconciliation and towards creating a new system of post-war European relations. Similarly, an important motivating factor for some states, in particular France, in negotiating the TEU was to strengthen integration in the context of German unification in 1990. The French government feared that a more powerful Germany might become less predictable in European politics. Enlargement encompassing the new democracies of Central and Eastern Europe has involved a process whereby those states have had to meet targets in terms of political and economic stability but with the ultimate incentive of full accession to the EU. In this way the EU has in effect exported its economic and political model to these new states, assuring the development of peaceful relations in the process. Political objectives such as these set the path followed by the EU apart from those of more modest organizations, such as the European Free Trade Association (EFTA).

In reviewing the history of the EU, we explain the key developments summarized in Table 1.1. To do so, we need to commence with the situation in 1945, at the end of the Second World War.

1.1 Economic integration in historical and political perspective

Why European cooperation and integration?

Although European integration was not an idea new to the post-1945 era, it was propelled initially by a distinctive 'mix' of circumstances and impulses. These comprised:

- the defeat of Nazi Germany and of the Axis powers;
- the wish to avoid a repeat of the excesses of nationalism and of the nation-state system by creating a new system of European international relations;
- the economic dislocation caused by wartime destruction;
- the emergence of two global superpowers with competing political and economic ideologies;
- the division of Europe and the wish in the West for security from the Soviet threat;

Table 1.1 Key stages in the development of the European Union

Year	Key developments
1951	Treaty of Paris is signed, bringing the European Coal and Steel Community into effect from 23 July 1952. Membership comprised Belgium, the Federal Republic of Germany, France, Italy, Luxembourg, and the Netherlands.
1957	Treaty of Rome is signed, bringing into effect the European Economic Community and the European Atomic Energy Community from 1 January 1958.
1965	Merger Treaty is signed, with the effect of merging the principal institutions of the three communities from 1967. Henceforth the three communities are known collectively as the European Community.
1973	Denmark, the Irish Republic, and the UK join the EC on 1 January.
1981	Greece joins the EC on 1 January.
1986	Spain and Portugal join the EC on 1 January. The Single European Act is signed, coming into effect on 1 July 1987, and introduces the first systematic revisions to the founding treaties.
1992	February: Treaty on European Union is signed (following broad agreement in December 1991 at a meeting in Maastricht in the Netherlands). It entails systematic revisions to, and extension of, the existing treaties. Following ratification, the TEU comes into effect on 1 November 1993. Within the European Union, the EC represents one 'pillar' of activities: the others relate to foreign and security policy; and justice and home affairs.
1992	May: the European Economic Area Treaty is signed and comes into effect in January 1994. The EEA extends important parts of economic integration to Member States of the European Free Trade Association, excluding Switzerland, which voted against in a referendum. As of 2006 the EEA includes Iceland, Liechtenstein, and Norway.
1995	Austria, Finland, and Sweden join the EU on 1 January.
1997	Amsterdam Treaty is signed, coming into effect on 1 May 1999.
1999	Stage 3 of Monetary Union, including the launch of the Euro, takes effect.
2000	Treaty of Nice is agreed, and signed in 2001. It comes into effect, following ratification, in February 2003.
2004	May: Cyprus, the Czech Republic, Estonia, Hungary, Latvia, Lithuania, Malta, Poland, Slovakia, and Slovenia join the EU.
2004	June: After preparation over a three-year period, the twenty-five states agree on the Constitutional Treaty, designed comprehensively to consolidate all existing EU treaties. The fate of this treaty is unclear following its rejection in two referenda (in France and the Netherlands, in May/June 2005).
2007	January: Bulgaria and Romania join the EU.

- the need to base Western security and defence on economic reconstruction and well-being; and
- the desire for Franco-German reconciliation as the bedrock of stability within Western Europe.

In short, European integration was motivated by political, economic, and security considerations. As a bulwark against the Communist bloc, it enjoyed support from the USA.

The protagonists of cooperation and integration were by no means of one view on how to address these issues. *Federalists* placed primary emphasis on the superseding of the nation-state by a larger democratic structure. Their roots were in many cases in the European resistance movements, and, in 1944, at a meeting in Geneva, they had already drawn up a plan for a federal European order based on a written constitution.

A second category of protagonists may be termed *functionalists*. Like the federalists, they were strongest in continental Europe, but they lacked the federalists' organization. They shared the federalists' objective of a united Europe but adopted a more pragmatic approach to its realization. They saw the need for economic cooperation as a starting-point for achieving their political goals. The Frenchman Jean Monnet was the most prominent figure in this camp. Other political figures, especially from the Low Countries, shared this approach. By 1944 the exiled governments had already agreed on the establishment of Benelux, a customs union to comprise Belgium, the Netherlands, and Luxembourg.

A third category may be termed the *nationalists*. Although they did not display nationalism in its negative sense, these figures did not see any need to participate in a new political order. The nationalists were strongest in those countries which had either escaped invasion during the Second World War or had remained neutral, and fiercely retained national political traditions. Hence they were strongest in the UK, Scandinavia, the Irish Republic, and Switzerland.

For the UK, the allied victory was seen as the source of heightened pride in national institutions; it had, moreover, galvanized relations with the USA. The resultant 'special relationship', together with the Commonwealth, represented powerful alternative poles of attraction for post-war UK foreign policy. Both the main parties in the UK opposed participation in any integration schemes which would jeopardize national sovereignty.[1] Winston Churchill, regarded in continental Europe as one of the protagonists of a federal Europe, was most supportive of integration when out of power. However, he saw the UK's relations with the strongest protagonists as 'with them but not of them'. The nationalists were prepared to participate in a number of European organizations, but these were characterized by cooperation between sovereign nation-states. It was not until the 1960s that the position began to change, as nationalists came to realize that this approach offered very limited opportunities for joint policy action.

A final set of protagonists—and one which must not be forgotten—comprised *external actors*. Essentially this was the political élite of the USA. The US position was to support cooperation and integration, both through exhortation and through financial and political assistance. The European Recovery Programme (ERP), popularly known as the Marshall Plan, played a major role in facilitating economic reconstruction. US leadership within the North American Treaty Organization (NATO) provided the security framework within which economic integration could flourish.

By the early 1950s a small group of six Member States had emerged that had shared objectives and a willingness to sacrifice national sovereignty to achieve them. These were the states which launched the process of supranational integration (see Table 1.1). A wider group—which also included these six—was willing to cooperate on various economic, political, or security-policy goals. However, states in this group were unwilling to go further. It was the different response to post-war circumstances on the part of the six which led them to favour *supranational integration*, whereas the wider group was unwilling to go beyond *intergovernmental cooperation* between sovereign states. Accordingly, the European organizations established in the post-war period tended in principle either to be limited to cooperation or to entail the formal transfer of sovereignty that characterizes supranational integration.

The international organization of the West European economies

The first attempt to organize the European economies in the post-war period was made with the establishment in 1947 of the Economic Commission for Europe (ECE), created under the auspices of the United Nations. However, its pan-European nature was to be its undoing, for the emergence of the Cold War rendered it unworkable as a body aimed at facilitating the reconstruction of Europe as a whole. From this point onwards we are concerned with Western European integration. The Eastern European economies were brought together in the Soviet-led Council for Mutual Economic Assistance (CMEA), which was set up in 1949.

The emergence of the Cold War overshadowed cooperation and integration at the end of the 1940s. In consequence, this was a period when the USA showed leadership in promoting West European developments. The scene was set when President Truman pledged US support for 'free peoples who are resisting attempted subjugation by armed minorities or by outside pressures'. The specific trigger for the 'Truman Doctrine' had been Communist destabilization in Greece, but the declaration was a broader commitment to contain Communism.

The Marshall Plan was announced in June 1947. The US Administration recognized that the objectives of the Truman Doctrine could best be attained if Europe's democracies were based on sound economies. Hence Secretary of State George Marshall's initiative was a response to the continued economic dislocation and food rationing in Western Europe. Although notionally offered to all European states, Marshall aid was in fact accepted only by those in the West.

In defence policy the counterpart to the Marshall Plan was the signature, in April 1949, of the Atlantic Charter which created NATO as the principal organization for the defence of Western Europe. The USA was to play the leading role in NATO.

US leadership was not confined to the European arena. The principles of *international* monetary cooperation had already been established at the Bretton Woods conference of 1944 which led to the establishment of the International Monetary Fund (IMF) and the World Bank. In October 1947 the General Agreement on Tariffs and Trade (GATT) was created, providing the guiding principles of liberalization in the trade arena, namely through tariff reductions. The economic principles embodied in these organizations were to have an important impact on economic cooperation within Western Europe.

The first step towards economic integration came at the start of 1948 with the creation of the Benelux customs union, complete with the introduction of a common customs tariff. Benelux was to serve as a precursor to the European Economic Community (EEC).

Of wider geographical significance was the foundation, in April 1948, of the Organization for European Economic Cooperation (OEEC). This was the organization entrusted with implementing the Marshall Plan. Disbursement of US aid was very much a matter to be organized by the European states themselves through the OEEC and its key governing body, the Council of Ministers. The OEEC was essentially an intergovernmental organization, characterized by cooperation between states. It ensured fulfilment of the US condition that reconstruction should be coordinated, and that tariff reductions should be implemented. Its activities were concentrated on facilitating the reconstruction of the national economies, and reducing quotas on interstate trade and tariffs. Under its umbrella were established other, more specialized, bodies and arrangements such as the European Payments Union (EPU). Established in 1950, the EPU was designed to facilitate a multilateral system of payments for trade until initial liquidity problems were alleviated.

The OEEC, having overseen the task of reconstruction, was succeeded in 1961 by the Organization for Economic Cooperation and Development (OECD), an agency no longer confined to the West European economies. The OEEC and Marshall aid had facilitated the construction of an economic platform, upon which supranational integration could be founded.

For some states the OEEC was not enough. It neither took on ambitious tasks nor had any aspirations to go beyond a nation-state system. The May 1950 Schuman Plan was an attempt by France to seize the reins of integration and take a different direction. Conceived as a Franco-German scheme, it was nevertheless open to other states to join. However, there was a condition: the principle of supranationalism, that is of relinquishing national power, had to be accepted. This precondition (and other factors) had the effect of ensuring that the UK did not participate in the negotiations.

The Schuman Plan, named after the French foreign minister, had in fact been elaborated by Jean Monnet. Its principal concern was with ensuring that reconstruction in the western part of Germany should not endanger peace. The heavy industries of the Ruhr had been under allied control, but this could not continue indefinitely. The proposed arrangements were also welcomed from the German side, for they offered a route to its regaining control over its key industrial sectors, as well as to international rehabilitation.

Thus the Schuman Plan was an explicitly political proposal; it offered a breakthrough into supranationalism; and it followed a functional approach of sectoral integration but with wider objectives in view. These features have come to characterize the 'Community method' of integration. The plan was favourably received in Belgium, the Netherlands, Luxembourg, and Italy as well as in France and West Germany. These six states (or EC-6) were to be the sole participants in the Community method until 1973 (see Table 1.1).

Before the ink was dry on the April 1951 Treaty of Paris, which established the ECSC, proposals had already been made for further integration in the shape of a European Defence Community (EDC). Conceived at the height of the Cold War, and with an eye upon the hostilities in Korea, the EDC proposal was designed to facilitate the rearmament of Germany through supranational control, since a German contribution was seen as indispensable to West European security. The French National Assembly's failure, in August 1954, to ratify the Treaty represented the first setback to supranational integration. German rearmament was achieved in May 1955, when the intergovernmental Western European Union commenced operations.

Those favouring further supranational integration were undeterred by this setback. The reasons for French non-ratification were varied but did not represent a rejection of supranationalism. Rather, there was a feeling that a supranational defence community was proceeding too far too fast. The death of Stalin and the end of the Korean War had also reduced the urgent need for the EDC. By 1955 new ideas were being floated for developing integration beyond the coal and steel sectors. Milward (1992: 120) points out that these proposals were not an attempt to relaunch integration *after* the failure of the EDC. Moves for a wider European customs union had already been mooted.

The forum for initial discussions on the proposals, which were advanced in particular by the Benelux countries, was to be the Messina conference of June 1955. This was attended by the foreign ministers of the EC-6. The proposed areas for further integration comprised the creation of a common market (i.e. beyond the coal and steel sectors), a common transport policy, and integration in the energy sector. These ideas received broad support, and, in consequence, a committee of governmental representatives was set up, chaired by the Belgian Paul-Henri Spaak.

The UK was invited to participate in the negotiations; it accepted the invitation but then withdrew from the Spaak Committee, once again because of outright opposition to the proposed supranational form of integration. Negotiations between the EC-6 were quite protracted, because of several thorny issues, and some matters were barely resolved by the time the EEC Treaty was finalized. Hence the Treaty contains quite limited indications as to the direction to be taken in the integration of agricultural policy and social policy. Nevertheless, negotiations during 1956 and early 1957 led to the two Treaties of Rome: the EEC Treaty and the Treaty establishing the European Atomic Energy Community (Euratom). They were signed on 25 March 1957. Following ratification, they came into effect from the start of 1958.

One further development must be referred to before examining the three European Communities in more detail. Having withdrawn from the Spaak Committee, the UK government began to reappraise its policy. Following a UK initiative, a committee was set up within the framework of the OEEC to examine the creation of a European free trade area. Although the resultant report deemed such a development feasible, there was considerable suspicion on the part of the EC-6 that the UK initiative was designed to undermine their much more ambitious plans for a common market and a supranational political system to supervise it. It was only once the Treaties of Rome had come into effect, and the EC-6 had gone their own way, that the negotiations on a free trade area gained momentum. They culminated in the signing, on 4 January 1960, of the Stockholm Convention creating the European Free Trade Association (EFTA). The founding members were the UK, Norway, Denmark, Sweden, Austria, Portugal, and Switzerland.

EFTA was a classic intergovernmental forum for economic cooperation. There was no threat to national sovereignty. As such, it suited the instincts of UK politicians. EFTA was centred around trade in industrial goods; agriculture was largely excluded. As a free trade area, each Member State was free to set its own external tariff. This enabled the UK to continue its trading relations with the Commonwealth countries.

Until the 1970s the EC-6 and the 'EFTAns' comprised two distinct camps within Western Europe. With the first EC enlargement of 1973, it was agreed to reduce tariff barriers on industrial trade between the two groupings. By the late 1980s a much closer relationship was proposed: the European Economic Area (see below).

The two camps corresponded quite neatly to the two different political approaches to integration that were identified earlier. The EC-6 comprised those states which were prepared to transcend the nation-state by means of supranational integration. By contrast, EFTA was composed of those states which preferred more limited arrangements and the maintenance of national sovereignty. How, then, did integration through the Community method shape the form of integration pursued by the EC-6?

Integration through the community method

The ECSC

The ECSC, which commenced operations in July 1952, was the starting-point of the Community method of supranational integration. Its provisions were set out in the Treaty of Paris. The ECSC had three key features.

First, it proposed a degree of economic integration that went beyond anything developed in the other existing European organizations. It was concerned not with the lowest level of economic integration (a free trade area), but with the higher goal of a common market, albeit confined to the coal, steel, and related sectors. Nevertheless, given that these sectors were then regarded as the 'commanding heights' of the economy, the ECSC was concerned with core activities of the EC-6. The ECSC's chief aims were to ensure security of supplies through the removal of quotas and customs duties over a five-year transitional period; the rational expansion and modernization of the industries; and the provision of mechanisms for managing serious shortages or gluts. The ECSC sought to restrict Member States' use of discriminatory state subsidies and it provided a common external commercial policy relating to the two sectors.

It is worth pointing out that the economic philosophy behind the Treaty of Paris was more interventionist than that behind the later EEC Treaty. This *dirigisme* owed much to the influence of the French; it was no coincidence that the author of the Schuman Plan, Jean Monnet, was head of the French Commission for Economic Planning. Moreover, the Treaty of Paris spelt out most of the detailed arrangements, thus reducing the need for secondary legislation. The ECSC's activities were financed by levies on coal and steel production.

The second key feature was that these detailed arrangements were subservient to the political goal of providing a framework for Franco-German reconciliation. One indicator of the success of this was the relatively smooth reintegration of the Saar into (West) Germany in 1956, after some ten years effectively under French control.

The third key feature, and central to the Community method, was the set of strong, supranational central institutions associated with the ECSC. These provided a model which was later employed for the EEC and Euratom.

The ECSC comprised five institutions:

- the executive, known as the High Authority (equivalent to the European Commission of today);
- the Council of Ministers, comprising representatives of the member governments;
- the Consultative Committee, consisting of representatives of employers/industry, trade unions, and consumers concerned with the ECSC's activities;
- the Assembly, composed of a total of sixty-eight delegates from the six national parliaments;
- the European Court of Justice (ECJ).

These institutions were all located in Luxembourg, thus explaining why some services of the EU are located there today.

The High Authority had a considerable degree of autonomy in carrying out the tasks entrusted to the ECSC. It was headed by nine members who were appointed from the Member States but were to act independently in carrying out their duties. Fittingly, the first president of the High Authority was Jean Monnet. Beneath the 'members'— equivalent to present-day EU commissioners—the High Authority was staffed by an independent civil service. The independence of the High Authority and its staff from the national governments was a characteristic of the supranational approach to integration.

A Council of Ministers was created to allay the concerns of the Benelux countries. They were worried that the ECSC might be dominated by French and German interests. They were also concerned that the High Authority might pursue an excessively *dirigiste* form of economic policy. The Council of Ministers was thus a check against the realization of these worries. Although a check on supranationalism, the Council could not be compared to similar bodies in, for example, the OEEC. This was because the ECSC Council was able, under specified circumstances, to take decisions by qualified majority voting and simple majority, as well as by the conventional method of unanimity.[2]

The Consultative Committee and the Assembly were much less important institutions, confined to advisory roles. The ECJ, however, had a more important function. It was responsible for adjudicating on disputes relating to the ECSC's activities.

In operation, the ECSC was regarded initially as successful. Production and interstate trade in coal and steel increased markedly, although how much of this could be attributed to the ECSC's existence is open to question. The initial success was followed by a period of less progress. The coal crisis towards the end of the 1950s was caused by falling demand owing to cheap oil imports. The High Authority's attempt in 1959 to declare a 'manifest crisis' in the coal industry, so as to obtain powers of intervention in the market, failed because it could not obtain the necessary majority in the Council of Ministers. The ECSC was regarded as having failed its first real test. This was the first of numerous challenges by national interests to the supranational principles of the Community method. It indicated that the ECSC was not so supranational in practice as it was designed to be.

The ECSC retained its separate existence until implementation of the Merger Treaty in 1967. This resulted in the High Authority's absorption into the EC Commission. The Assembly and the ECJ had already been shared with the other Communities from 1958. The Consultative Committee continues to retain its separate identity. Following the creation of the EEC and the merger of the three European Communities, activities based on the ECSC Treaty have tended to be overshadowed: a development hastened in recent times by the changing profile of the EU's economy.

Euratom

The Treaties of Rome expanded the area of joint activity considerably. Of the two, the Euratom Treaty was of much less significance. It was largely the product of French pressure. France had begun to develop a civilian nuclear programme and saw Euratom as a way of obtaining financial support for its extension and of developing a market for French technology.

In fact, Euratom was rather a failure. Differences between the Member States resulted in Euratom having little control over the development of the nuclear sector. Measures have been undertaken on health and safety in the nuclear industry, to promote joint research, and so on, but the core activities of civilian nuclear power have remained in the hands of the Member States.

The EEC

The establishment of the EEC was a most significant development in supranational integration. The ECSC's model of identifying functional bases for joint policy was continued. European integration retained a political objective, although no longer centrally concerned with fears of renascent German power; and the EEC Treaty followed the supranational model already established, albeit in a moderated form.

The activities and arrangements covered by the EEC Treaty can be seen from a summary of its structure (see Table 1.2). The EEC's policies are considered in detail in succeeding chapters. Remarks here are confined to general observations; an outline of the institutions of the EU is given later in the chapter.

The EEC Treaty was distinctly more market-oriented in ideology, compared with its rather *dirigiste* predecessor, the ECSC. Accordingly, the centrepiece of the Treaty was the creation of the common market. The deadline for removing interstate tariffs was set down in the Treaty as 31 December 1969, but this had already been achieved by 1 July 1968. The deeper integration needed to achieve a common market received a boost with the Single European Market Programme, launched in 1985.

Table 1.2 Contents of the EEC Treaty

Contents		Articles
Preamble		
Part One	Basic Principles	1–8
Part Two	Foundations of the Community	
Title I	Free Movement of Goods, including creation of the customs union, elimination of quantitative restrictions	9–37
Title II	Agriculture	38–47
Title III	Free Movement of Persons, Services, and Capital	48–73
Title IV	Transport	74–84
Part Three	Policy of the Community	
Title I	Common Rules, including on competition policy, state aids, tax provisions, and the harmonization of laws	85–102
Title II	Economic Policy, principally the commercial policy	103–16
Title III	Social Policy	117–28
Title IV	The European Investment Bank	129–30
Part Four	Association of Overseas Countries and Territories	131–36
Part Five	Institutions of the Community	
Title I	Provisions Governing the Institutions	137–98
Title II	Financial Provisions (concerning the EEC budget)	199–209
Part Six	General and Final Provisions	210–28

Note: The details relate to the 1957 EEC Treaty. They do not incorporate changes introduced by subsequent treaty amendments.

If the greater market orientation signalled a decline in French influence on negotiations, this was redressed by the EEC's Common Agricultural Policy (CAP). The French made agricultural provisions a prerequisite for agreement to the Treaty, although this was not their priority from the start, as conventional wisdom has it. It is also worth noting that the agricultural 'title' of the Treaty does not specify the highly regulated and protectionist policy which the CAP became. This was the product of secondary legislation—i.e. subsequent legal acts implementing the principles set down in the Treaty. A further area of the Treaty which particularly reflected French interests was Part Four, conferring associate status on colonies and former colonies of the EC-6. The arrangement ensured minimal disruption to France's existing trading patterns.

One or two policy areas provided for in the EEC Treaty have not had the impact that one might assume from their presence in it (see Table 1.2). Transport-policy developments were minimal until the 1980s. Similarly, the social-policy provisions were of a very limited nature, and it was not until the end of the 1980s that attempts were made to extend their range. Finally, it is worth drawing attention to one of the final provisions of the Treaty, Article 235. This article states: 'If action by the Community should prove necessary to attain, in the course of the operation of the common market, one of the objectives of the Community and this Treaty has not provided the necessary powers, the Council shall, acting unanimously on a proposal from the Commission and after consulting the Assembly, take the appropriate measures.' The importance of Article 235 is that it facilitated EC action beyond the immediate provisions of the Treaty. For example, the EC-12 used Article 235 to agree four environmental-action programmes before they were given explicit constitutional authority to do so in the Single European Act![3]

A final observation relating to the overall shape of the EEC Treaty is that it was principally concerned with setting policy principles. By contrast, the ECSC Treaty itself provided most of the detailed arrangements for the supranational governance of the coal and steel sectors. With the exception of the provisions relating to the establishment of the customs union and to the institutions, the EEC Treaty provided only a framework. Thus a vast amount of secondary legislation has been necessary in order to put into practice the Treaty's objectives.

The 1960s: consolidation and challenge

The period from 1958 to 1969 may be seen as one of consolidation and challenge. The consolidation derived from progress in putting the EEC Treaty into operation. The challenge was provided by General de Gaulle. He became president of the Fifth French Republic in 1958, in the first year of the EEC. Attempting to re-establish French credibility after the instability of the Fourth Republic, he sought to rebuild the prestige of the nation-state. This put him on a collision course with the supranational EEC.

Putting the customs union into operation was achieved early, as already noted. The institutions were put into practice, although the (enlarged) Assembly and the ECJ were shared from 1958 with the ECSC and Euratom. The first president of the EEC Commission, Walter Hallstein, was a forceful individual and gave that institution activist leadership. In 1965 the first constitutional amendment was agreed: the Merger Treaty, which came into effect in 1967.[4] This merged the three Communities, with the creation of a single

Commission being the principal result. The Treaties were not merged, however, and a few features remained distinct, such as the separate budgetary provisions for the ECSC.

A number of important legal developments occurred during the 1960s, also with a consolidating effect. These emerged in judgments on specific cases before the ECJ that had wide-ranging implications and strengthened the EC's supranational character. Two cases were of particular importance. In its 1963 judgment on the *Van Gend en Loos* case, the ECJ established the principle of direct effect, i.e. that EC law confers both rights and duties on individuals that national courts must enforce. The effect of this was to make it possible for private individuals or companies to use the national courts to oblige governments to implement treaty provisions. Had this principle not been established, in what was an expansionist judgment on the part of the ECJ, progress towards the common market would have been much more difficult. The ECJ has made a number of major judgments facilitating the creation of the internal market. However, it cannot make these judgments until a case is referred.

A second important legal principle, that of the primacy of EC law over national law, was also established in the 1960s: a feature which had not been specified in the Treaty. This principle was enunciated in *Costa* v. *ENEL* (case 6/64) and in other ECJ judgments. The effect was to reinforce the supranationalism of the EEC. Added to the earlier case establishing the principle of direct effect, this facilitated a process of integration through law. So, whilst the 1960s are often characterized as a period of resurgence in national interests, as demonstrated by the 1965 crisis (see below), important legal developments were under way which had the opposite effect. They have also been of major importance in the realization of the economic objectives set out in the treaties.

Consolidation was also achieved through the translation of treaty objectives into secondary legislation. This was particularly necessary in the agricultural sector, for the whole regulatory structure of the CAP had to be introduced. Given the level of French interest in this policy area, it is not surprising that this was one of the principal battlefields for de Gaulle's assault on supranationalism.

De Gaulle's policy was based on a nation-state-centred view of world politics, and his particular wish was to strengthen 'French grandeur'. His policy generated three specific flashpoints regarding the development of integration. The first resulted from his proposal for a 'Political Union'. Far from being an attempt to advance supranational integration, this was to be organized along traditional intergovernmental lines. The other Member States regarded it as a threat to the successful supranational Community method. His proposal failed. The second occurred as a result of a reconsideration by the United Kingdom of the merits of membership. The Conservative government of Harold Macmillan had already applied for membership in 1961. Applications were also made by Ireland, Denmark, and Norway. However, in a dramatic move, de Gaulle unilaterally rejected the UK application (and by extension the others) at a press conference in January 1963. De Gaulle was suspicious about British motives and did not want competition from the UK for the leadership of the EEC. His actions irritated the other five governments both procedurally and substantively. In 1967 he vetoed the second UK application, this time made by the Labour government of Harold Wilson.

The third and most dramatic clash came with the 1965 crisis. Its immediate cause was the creation of the system for financing the CAP. Hallstein sought to link this provision with the creation of a self-financing, or 'own resources', EEC budget. For de Gaulle, Hallstein was becoming too much like a government head. In addition, a step towards budgetary autonomy was a further (for de Gaulle, undesired) reinforcement of supranationalism. In the background, but at least as important, was the projected 1966 introduction of qualified majority voting in the EEC Council of Ministers. This was also regarded by de Gaulle as a major threat to national sovereignty, for that would mean that French interests could be overridden in the Council. The result was that in June 1965 France withdrew from the workings of the Council of Ministers. It was not until January 1966 that a solution was found in the so-called Luxembourg Compromise. While this had no status in EC law, it established the convention that, on matters of 'vital national interest' to one or more Member States, discussions would continue until consensus had been reached. The Luxembourg Compromise was important in practice, for it led to integration being dictated by the pace of the most reluctant Member State.

The result of the Luxembourg Compromise was a slowing-down of decision-making in the Council of Ministers. The need to satisfy all national interests contrasted with what was supposed to happen, namely decisions being taken by qualified majority vote. The Commission became less ambitious and the Community's supranationalism was in decline. This situation was not really reversed until the 1980s and the SEA. The Luxembourg Compromise has been superseded in the economic domain of integration.

Revival through summitry

It was not until de Gaulle's resignation in 1969 that the political will of the EC could be revived. Even so, Gaullist ideas continued to influence the policies of his successor as president, Georges Pompidou. Pompidou initiated a meeting with the heads of government of the other five states. Designed to give the EC new momentum, the summit initiated a number of developments:

- the opening of negotiations for enlargement of the EC;
- re-examination of the financing of the budget;
- the creation of a system of foreign policy cooperation; and
- the drafting of proposals for an Economic and Monetary Union.

The enlargement negotiations were successful and, on 1 January 1973, the UK, the Irish Republic, and Denmark joined the EC. Norway, which had negotiated its terms of entry, rejected membership in a referendum held in September 1972. An 'own resources' system was introduced for the EC budget through two treaty amendments (1970 and 1975). The new system was fully operational from 1980. A foreign policy cooperation procedure was set up in 1970 and has developed considerably over the intervening period. Finally, the Economic and Monetary Union initiative was launched as a response to currency instability in the EC at the end of the 1960s. The proposals failed because of the collapse of the Bretton Woods international monetary system in 1971 and the impact of the 1973 oil crisis.

Subsequent summits in 1972 and 1974 were less successful, although providing some initiatives. The 1972 Paris summit, for instance, placed environmental policy on the EC's agenda. The 1974 summit, again held in Paris, was more noteworthy. On the institutional front there were two key achievements. The first of these was agreement to the principle of holding direct elections to the European Parliament (EP). This distinctly supranational step, aimed at giving European parliamentarians their own source of democratic legitimacy, was first put into practice with elections in 1979. The second was the agreement to hold regular summit meetings, known as the European Council, at least twice each year. In the period since 1975 most of the key political decisions in the EC/EU have been taken in the European Council. The main policy decision was agreement on the establishment of the European Regional Development Fund (ERDF).

With two former finance ministers at the heart of the European Council—Chancellor Schmidt of Germany and President Giscard d'Estaing of France—it was scarcely surprising that international monetary affairs should feature strongly at its meetings. Thus in 1978 Schmidt launched the initiative for the European Monetary System (EMS) at the Copenhagen European Council. After elaboration of its operation by a group of three experts, it came into effect in March 1979. It was to be one of the main achievements of this period.

The period from 1979 to 1984 was dominated by the UK budgetary problem. Mrs Thatcher's Conservative government was intent upon achieving a lasting solution to what it perceived as an inequitable system. It had been anticipated from the outset of membership that the EC's own resources budget would not favour the UK. However, the economic recession induced by the oil crisis resulted in few of the predicted trade benefits of membership accruing to the UK. It was only after protracted negotiations that a settlement was reached at the Fontainebleau European Council in 1984, including the creation of the British rebate.

This agreement was part of a typical 'package deal' of EC negotiations. Not only did the meeting provide a solution to the UK budgetary crisis, increase the size of the budget, and provide for limited CAP reform, it also decided to look at the institutional structure of the EC, the start of the process leading to the Single European Act (SEA). A further part of the package was to give approval in principle to Spanish and Portuguese enlargement. The two states joined on 1 January 1986; Greece had joined at the start of 1981. The southern enlargements were motivated essentially by political considerations—namely, the wish to strengthen these new democracies, for the three states' economies were at a relatively low level of development.

The Single European Act (SEA) and renewed dynamism

The SEA was signed in February 1986 and came into effect on 1 July 1987. It had been negotiated within an intergovernmental conference (IGC) under the supervision of the European Council. The SEA's significance was that it amounted to the first comprehensive revision of the treaties. The motivations for it included:

- a recognition of the need to overcome the 'Eurosclerosis' that had characterized the EC economy compared with its global competitors;
- a wish to provide a stimulus to the European economy by means of the liberalization associated with completion of the internal market;

- a wish to bring the treaties into line with actual practice in the EC;

- a wish to relaunch supranational integration because of a realization that decisional weakness had impeded the collective interest; and

- a recognition of the need to make the EC more politically responsive if the Iberian enlargement were not to create political sclerosis.

The content of the SEA can be divided into two parts—namely, the policy and the institutional provisions. The policy developments took two broad forms. Some of the treaty revisions were largely concerned with formalizing the EC's competence—for example, in environmental policy, 'monetary capacity', and research and technology policy. In these cases the treaty revisions gave clearer competence for EC action. The codification of foreign policy cooperation, including enhanced institutional provision, had a similar effect, but this development was contained in a separate part of the SEA. The main contribution of the SEA, arguably, was to making the Single Market Programme achievable. Already agreed to in June 1985, this programme had been set out in a Commission White Paper, *Completing the Internal Market*, drawn up by the UK commissioner, Lord Cockfield. It built upon the earlier dismantling of tariffs between Member States by moving on to the remaining physical, fiscal, and technical barriers to the creation of a common market. In particular, it addressed the fragmentation of the market arising from different technical standards required in each Member State's market. The White Paper was thus based on a threefold strategy:

1. a relatively small legislative programme (fewer than 300 items) aimed at setting the essential requirements, by the end of 1992, for completion of the internal market;

2. reliance on the principle of mutual recognition of national product standards as established in ECJ landmark decisions, especially the 1979 *Cassis de Dijon* case; and

3. the 'new approach' of devolving decisions on creating new European standards from the Council to standard-setting agencies.

The SEA contributed to this programme by including provision for increased use of qualified majority voting in the Council of Ministers, thereby limiting the obstacles to achieving the White Paper's legislative programme.

Other institutional changes comprised increased provision for qualified majority voting in other policy areas, increased powers for the EP, and the creation of the Court of First Instance as a means of alleviating the backlog of work facing the ECJ. Initially regarded as rather modest in nature, the SEA succeeded in developing renewed momentum for integration, not least by the establishment of the 'end of 1992' deadline for completion of the Single European Market (SEM) (see Armstrong and Bulmer 1998).

In the aftermath of the SEA, the European Council became concerned with various 'flanking measures', especially relating to economic and social cohesion. The first of these became important in the negotiations surrounding the 'Delors package'—a set of measures designed to help the less-developed EC economies, and those regions suffering from industrial decline, to contend with the competitive challenges posed by the SEM. Agreement was finally reached at the 1988 Brussels summit to provide the finance for such measures, including through new restrictions on CAP spending. The wish to avoid the SEM being developed at the cost of declining social provision lay behind the so-called Social Charter. This whole area was highly contested, as symbolized by the UK government's refusal to sign the charter at the December 1989 European Council in Strasbourg. Subsequently, in the negotiations leading to signature of the TEU in 1992, the UK secured an opt-out from the Social Protocol, an arrangement designed to put the Social Charter into practice.

The momentum for integration was maintained by a revival of interest in European Monetary Union (EMU), culminating in the June 1988 decision of the European Council to establish a committee under the chairmanship of Jacques Delors to report on its feasibility. The subsequent Delors Report, and the broad support to take discussion of EMU further (a position not shared by the UK government), contributed to the wish to engage in a further round of constitutional reform which culminated in the Maastricht negotiations and the TEU.

The Treaty on European Union (TEU)

Whilst the initial momentum for reform was largely attributable to EMU, this was rapidly joined by other major political impulses. These derived from the collapse of Communism in Eastern Europe and the new role expected of the EC in international relations after the Cold War. There was also a recognition that the number of applications for EC membership would consequently increase, and that work should commence on reforming the institutions to facilitate an effective political process within a Community of some twenty members. German unification in October 1990 reawakened strong concerns about German power. For some states, especially France, the solution lay in containing this power through the deepening of European integration. Hence the support of its government and of President Mitterrand for the goal of EMU. Finally, there was a wish, as with the SEA, to tidy up constitutional provisions and make substantive policy changes beyond EMU.

The resultant Treaty, which was finalized at the Maastricht European Council in December 1991, had been prepared by two parallel IGCs. The structure of the Treaty is usually described as resembling a temple. Hence the 'roof' sets out various broad objectives in the so-called 'common provisions'. The roof is located on three pillars. The first pillar consists of the EC activities, i.e. comprising the three Communities as further enhanced by the TEU itself. The second pillar provides for a Common Foreign and Security Policy (CFSP). The third pillar covers Justice and Home Affairs (JHA): initially covering police cooperation, combating drug trafficking and fraud, regulating immigration from third countries, and similar matters, but it was then revised (see below). The policies contained in the last two pillars were thus given greater prominence than before. They were strengthened but retained an essentially intergovernmental basis under the TEU. Finally, the plinth of the 'temple' detailed relationships with the existing treaties, ratification arrangements, and so on. There were also eighteen protocols (e.g. the UK 'opt-outs' on EMU and the new social-policy provisions) and more than thirty declarations.

The first of these pillars is of principal importance to economic integration. Once again the new provisions can be divided into policy provision and institutional provision. The most prominent policy development concerned the conditions and timetable set for achieving EMU by the end of the 1990s. In return for agreement to this, the economically weaker Member States insisted on the creation of a Cohesion Fund to enable resource transfers to their economies; this was also provided for. The EC-12 had sought to give a treaty base to the substance of the Social Charter. However, the UK opted out of this Social Chapter, thus leaving the other states to legislate under rather messy arrangements. There were numerous other policy developments—for instance, on the EU's infrastructure, consumer protection, and industrial policy.

More widening and deepening: after Maastricht

The TEU provided the EU with a fairly full policy agenda for the rest of the decade, not least with the timetable for EMU. However, there was considerable political fall-out associated with, and arising from, ratifying the TEU. Ratification proved problematic in several states: the Danish people initially rejected the Treaty in a referendum but then approved it after some special provisions were negotiated. A very close referendum vote in France approved the treaty. In the UK the Conservative government of John Major secured parliamentary ratification in 1993 only by making the Treaty a matter of confidence, so that rebels in his own party were forced to choose between approving the Treaty or bringing down their own government. These difficulties raised questions about the EU's legitimacy, about its remoteness, and specifically about how to proceed with one of the TEU's commitments, namely to hold another IGC in 1996 to consider further treaty revisions. This episode heralded a period in which the Commission began to consider being less interventionist. The principle of subsidiarity, which had been embodied in the TEU, came to be observed in practice. Subsidiarity essentially means that the EU should perform only those tasks that the Member States' governments (or subnational governments) are unable to carry out themselves. What this provision means in practice is a reduction of European Commission interventionism in policy areas where its authority is relatively weak rather than attempting to build up new powers.

In March 1996 a new IGC was opened. Its objectives were moderated somewhat and the entire exercise became rather protracted. On the one hand, there was an effort to undertake a more widely consultative exercise to try to pre-empt the questions of legitimacy and remoteness associated with the TEU. On the other hand, the UK government of John Major was politically unable to support significant moves for deeper integration owing to its small majority. Eventually the IGC was extended into mid-1997 so that it was to conclude after the UK general election. The election of the Blair Labour government with a landslide majority facilitated the conclusion of the IGC in Amsterdam.

The Amsterdam Treaty, signed in autumn 1997, was a rather low-key reform compared with the TEU. In terms of policy reforms the main change was the introduction of an employment chapter into the treaty provisions. This development, originating in a Swedish proposal, was seen as offering some counter-balance to a perceived bias in the EMU provisions against concerns with unemployment. Another development was that the Blair government acceded to the Social Chapter, thus eliminating the UK opt-out negotiated by the Major government. Other areas strengthened were environmental policy, public health, and consumer protection (the last two partly in response to the crisis associated with an outbreak of 'mad cow disease' in the UK). Perhaps the key policy emphasis of the

Amsterdam Treaty was on launching a programme towards an 'area of freedom, security, and justice', which involved moving some of the activities introduced in the TEU from the third pillar to the supranational first pillar. The policy changes associated with the Amsterdam Treaty were thus quite slight; arguably the 1996 Stability and Growth Pact (see below), which requires continued fiscal prudence after the commencement of EMU, was of greater significance for the economics of the EU than was the Amsterdam Treaty.

Institutionally, the Amsterdam Treaty made some fairly significant reforms, notably through enhancing the powers of the European Parliament and increasing the provision for majority voting in the Council (see below). However, the member governments failed to reach agreement on reforming the institutions ahead of eastward enlargement. One final change needs to be noted. The Amsterdam Treaty entailed revisions to, and the renumbering of articles in, the Treaty on European Union. In the case of the EC Treaty the revisions and renumbering were more fundamental, creating problems for students of the EU using out-of-date textbooks! The Treaty was ratified over the following twenty months or so, and was put into effect in May 1999.

By the time the IGC had got under way a further wave of enlargement had already occurred, namely the EFTAn enlargement. Austria, Sweden, and Finland left the European Free Trade Association and joined the EU in 1995. Originally the EFTA states had sought to develop a closer relationship with 'core Europe', particularly in light of the single market, through an arrangement known as the European Economic Area, which came into effect in 1994. However, with the end of the Cold War and the break-up of the Soviet Union, these states decided that their historical neutrality would no longer be incompatible with EU membership. In consequence, the EEA has very limited importance, since it comprises only three states (Iceland, Liechtenstein, and Norway), the Swiss having voted in 1992 against joining.

In the subsequent period there has been a further round of both deepening and widening of the EU. The deepening came with agreement on the Nice Treaty in 2001, the widening with the substantial enlargement of May 2004, which brought ten new Member States into the EU. The Nice Treaty was essentially confined to institutional changes designed to enable the EU to continue to function after enlargement. The expected entrance of a significant number of states ranging from a micro-state such as Malta to a medium-sized one like Poland meant that a number of the existing decision-making rules and other institutional provisions needed an overhaul. The rules set down in the Nice Treaty are those which apply at present and will be outlined below. On the policy front there were no real developments in the economic domain; the principal initiative concerned strengthening cooperation within the EU on defence policy. Outside the Nice Treaty, however, an important economic policy initiative was launched in March 2000, namely the so-called Lisbon strategy. This strategy aims to make the EU the most dynamic and competitive economy in the world by 2010. It involves a whole set of policy areas, from research and education to environment and employment, to name only a few. An interesting characteristic of the Lisbon strategy is that it uses a much less interventionist approach to policy, and that is why it was not associated with a set of treaty revisions, unlike EMU or the single market. Instead, national policies are compared; best practice is shared; benchmarking is used; peer pressure is applied. In other words, policy is conducted in a relatively decentralized manner. The overall objectives of the Lisbon agenda are of great importance to the EU's economic competitiveness.

A major challenge for the start of the twenty-first century was the lengthy list of applicants to join the EU. Many of these states were relatively new democracies and, indeed, recently established market economies. The EU had recognized these circumstances in June 1993, when the Copenhagen European Council set down three explicit conditions for membership and one implicit. These conditions specified:

1. stable institutions guaranteeing democracy, the rule of law, human rights, and the protection of minorities;

2. a functioning market economy, including the ability to cope with the rigours of competition in the EU; and

3. the ability to adopt the existing policy inheritance (known as the *acquis communautaire*), including the goals of political, economic, and monetary union.

4. Implicitly, enlargement was also conditional on the EU's ability to absorb new members (itself dependent on reform of a number of policies, such as the CAP).

These conditions recognized not only the major disparities in economic performance between the applicants and the existing states but also the special circumstances that most applicant states had to overcome given the legacy of Communist rule. The implicit condition related to the reforms needed for the CAP and the Structural Funds. The former required reform, because its extension to the applicants—including some with quite agrarian economies—would have been very costly. The latter needed geographical refocusing and agreement with the existing major beneficiaries, such as Spain and Greece. The EU made some advances in this direction in the so-called 'Agenda 2000' reforms, agreed in March 1999 at the Berlin European Council, but the reforms have required phasing over time. Individual negotiations were held with each applicant state. Eventually ten states were deemed fit to join as part of the biggest enlargement ever of the EU in terms of the number of states joining. The countries which joined in May 2004 were: Cyprus, the Czech Republic, Estonia, Hungary, Latvia, Lithuania, Malta, Poland, Slovakia, and Slovenia. Two further states—Romania and Bulgaria—joined in January 2007. For a profile of the current membership line-up of the EU, including which states are in the Eurozone, see Table 1.3.

The dual dynamics of deepening and widening have not ended with enlargement in 2007. In fact, they have continued but we shall return to current integration dynamics at the end of the chapter.

1.2 Economic integration and its policy-making context

Economic integration is heavily dependent on legislation. Legislation takes one of two forms. *Regulations* are used chiefly to legislate on quite technical matters. They have direct effect in the Member States. *Directives* are used where there are different national traditions and it is felt more appropriate just to legislate on the objectives of policy. National

Table 1.3 Member State indicators in the EU of 27

Member State	Accession date[a]	Population (million) 2007	Votes in Council	MEPs 2004–7	In Eurozone
Austria	1995	8.1	10	18	Yes
Belgium	1952	10.4	12	24	Yes
Bulgaria	2007	8.0	10	18	No
Czech Republic	2004	10.2	12	24	No
Cyprus	2004	0.7	4	6	No
Denmark	1973	5.4	7	14	No
Estonia	2004	1.4	4	6	No
Finland	1995	5.2	7	14	Yes
France	1952	59.9	29	78	Yes
Germany	1952	82.5	29	99	Yes
Greece	1981	11.0	12	24	Yes
Hungary	2004	10.1	12	24	No
Ireland	1973	4.0	7	13	Yes
Italy	1952	57.9	29	78	Yes
Latvia	2004	2.3	4	9	No
Lithuania	2004	3.4	7	13	No
Luxembourg	1952	0.5	4	6	Yes
Malta	2004	0.4	3	5	No
Netherlands	1952	16.3	13	27	Yes
Poland	2004	38.2	27	54	No
Portugal	1986	10.5	12	24	Yes
Romania	2007	21.7	14	35	No
Slovakia	2004	5.4	7	14	No
Slovenia	2004	2.0	4	7	Yes
Sweden	1995	9.0	10	19	No
Spain	1986	42.3	27	54	Yes
United Kingdom	1973	59.7	29	78	No
Total EU		486.5	345	785	

[a] Accession to the EC/EU or, for founder members, to the European Coal and Steel Community.

legislation must then be enacted in order to translate these goals into national law. A third legal instrument is the *decision*. This is not so much a method of legislating as one of taking administrative decisions, such as on competition policy cases. A decision of this kind may be no less significant, especially if it imposes a substantial fine on a company in breach of European competition law. Resort to *recommendations* is another option for legislation, but these do not have binding effect; they are not part of EC law. As mentioned above, the Lisbon agenda has introduced techniques from business practice, such as peer review and benchmarking. These are soft, i.e. non-legal, mechanisms similar to recommendations.

To explain how legislation is developed, attention is first of all paid to the various EU institutions. Then brief attention is turned to other policy actors.

The EC's structure comprises three supranational institutions which are independent of the national governments—namely, the Commission, the European Parliament (EP), and the European Court of Justice (ECJ). As a counter-balance there are two powerful institutions comprising representatives of the national governments: the European Council and the Council of Ministers.

The *Commission* consists, following the 2007 enlargement, of twenty-seven members (commissioners), each with a specific portfolio. The commissioners are appointed by the national governments but are then expected to detach themselves from national loyalty. Each commissioner has a group of political advisers to act as his or her 'eyes and ears'; they constitute the commissioner's 'cabinet'. One commissioner is appointed president: for the period 2004–9 José Manuel Barroso, a former Portuguese prime minister, is Commission president. The Commission's officials are organized into twenty-six directorates-general (DGs) as well as nine 'services'. The DGs may be seen as the equivalent of ministries: they are responsible for individual policy areas, such as agriculture, while the 'services' include central tasks such as interpreting. The overall staffing of the Commission is some 25,000, but this figure includes a sizeable translation staff.

In the economic policy domain (the EC 'pillar' of the EU) the functions of the Commission are:

- the proposal of legislation;
- mediating between governments to achieve agreement on legislation;
- management of technical details of policy;
- representing the EU, particularly in commercial policy negotiations (for instance, within the World Trade Organization);
- acting as the defender of collective EU interests;
- acting as guardian of the treaties by ensuring that EC law is upheld.

The Commission's strength has varied over the years but achieved particular influence under the presidency of Jacques Delors (1985–94). The Commission's influence is challenged most when national interests are in the ascendant, and this happened in the aftermath of the Delors presidency. The British Prime Minister, John Major, blocked the appointment of Jean-Luc Dehaene, the Belgian Prime Minister, as the Commission president to succeed Delors. The Luxemburger Jacques Santer was eventually appointed as a compromise candidate to serve from 1995 to 1999. Santer and his team were the first to be subject to parliamentary hearings in the EP as part of the appointment process. Commissioners' appointments were also adjusted to a five-year term in order to coincide with the EP's electoral periods. In the event, the Santer Commission did not serve its full term. In 1999, following concern expressed in the EP, a report of independent experts found evidence of instances of mismanagement, favouritism in issuing contracts, and a general lack of vigilance by Commissioners. The Commissioners—known collectively as the College—resigned *en bloc* before their term had expired. A new Commission was installed under Romano Prodi, a former Italian Prime Minister, and it was given the task of reforming its own organization in addition to its regular policy tasks. President Barroso, who succeeded Prodi in late 2004, has placed the Lisbon agenda and European competitiveness at the heart of the Commission's agenda for his term in office.

The *European Parliament*, originally known as the Assembly, consists of members (MEPs) who, since 1979, have been directly elected by Member States on five-year mandates. Following the 2007 enlargement, the number of MEPs was fixed at 785 (for the composition by Member State, see Table 1.3). Their election takes place at five-year intervals (most recently, June 2004). Turn-out for EP elections remains low by comparison with national elections. The EP's plenary sessions are normally held in Strasbourg. Meetings of its committees, which generally 'shadow' one or more of the Commission's DGs, are held in Brussels.

The EP has ways of calling to account the Commission and, to a much lesser degree, the Council of Ministers. It has the power to dismiss the Commission but has never done so. The EP came closest to dismissing the Commission in early 1999. Only after the Commission president, Jacques Santer, had agreed to the appointment of a special investigating committee was the sting drawn from a parliamentary motion of censure. As the committee's report led to the Commission's resignation, the EP could claim its powers were enhanced by this episode. Its chief contribution to EU policy-making is through the legislative process. However, its influence is dependent on the policy area, for the latter determines the extent of its procedural rights. Under the consultation procedure, which originally applied to all legislation, the EP merely gave its opinion and had no effective sanction over the real decision-making agency, the Council of Ministers. Its main economic policy powers are as follows:

- Under the 1970 and 1975 budget treaties the EP gained important powers in this policy area, including the power to reject the budget outright.
- Under the SEA the assent of the EP is needed in respect of the accession of new Member States and of Association Agreements with third countries. The TEU extended this procedure.
- Following the TEU the EP gained a new co-decision procedure (Article 251, of the consolidated Treaty establishing the EC, TEC). This procedure puts the EP in quite a strong position—as a co-legislator with the Council—and it has the ultimate power to reject legislation. Originally applying to fifteen policy areas following the TEU, it was extended by both the Amsterdam and Nice Treaties.

The picture, as can be seen, is quite complex but reflects a gradual extension to the EP of new powers, which that institution uses to full effect. Nevertheless, the EP's public profile is quite low because the fairly technical nature of its work, as well as its multilingual character, does not encourage media coverage.

The *European Court of Justice* consists of twenty-seven judges: one from each Member State. The ECJ does not formulate policy but, in line with provisions in the treaties for referral, its judgments on matters relating to the interpretation and application of EC law are cumulatively of great importance to the operation of the EU. The ECJ is assisted by a Court of First Instance. The EU is unique amongst international organizations in having a body of law which takes precedence over existing national law.

The *Council of Ministers* consists of ministers of the Member States. It meets about a hundred times per annum but in different guises according to the subject matter. Hence the Council of Agriculture and Fisheries Ministers or the Council of Economic and Financial Affairs Ministers (Ecofin) bring together the twenty-seven national government ministers with responsibility for the respective policy area. Together with the General Affairs and External Relations Council (of foreign ministers), these are the three principal formations in which the Council meets. Meetings are chaired by one of the Member States, which holds the 'presidency' of the Council for a six-month period. For example, the UK held this post in July–December 2005. The presidency has become an important office facilitating the EU's operation. Meetings of the Council are prepared by the Committee of Permanent Representatives and an associated committee system. These meetings are attended by national civil servants and aim to pave the way for political agreement by the Council. A separate Council, i.e. other than Ecofin, deals with monetary policy for the twelve full participants in EMU and operates outside the rules for other Councils: the 'Euro-13 Council'.

The Council is empowered to take decisions by qualified majority rather than unanimous vote in a number of policy areas. This was provided for in the original EEC Treaty but majority voting was rarely practised owing to the Luxembourg Compromise. The *practice* of majority voting increased first from the 1970s, following treaty changes relating to the budget, then following the SEA, the TEU, and the Amsterdam/Nice Treaties. There remains a preference for decision-making with the consent of all governments but the practice of qualified majority voting (QMV) has grown over the years. The dynamism of the Council of Ministers determines the effectiveness of the EU, and the increased provision for majority voting has assisted the EU's decision-making speed. Each Member State has to recognize that it will, on occasion, be in the minority, with a negative effect on its national sovereignty. Complete reliance on unanimous voting in a European Union of twenty-five Member States would result in decisional gridlock.

The exact weighting of the individual Member States under the Nice Treaty is as set out in Table 1.3. As can be seen, small Member States are over-represented in terms of the ratio of Council votes to population size, this being particularly pronounced in the case of 'micro-states' such as Luxembourg and Malta. Seen from the perspective of the 'big four'—France, Germany, Italy, and the UK—Spain and Poland are also over-represented. These weightings have evolved incrementally and have been determined politically. The 'micro-states' have to be over-represented in order to give them greater importance in light of the fact that QMV means the loss of sovereign powers. On the other hand, Spain was effective in articulating its claims to being a 'nearly large' state. Reinforced by the accession of the similarly sized Poland, it has been difficult to rebalance these states' voting weight. Under the prevailing system a qualified majority is reached

- if a majority of Member States (in some cases a two-thirds majority) approve, AND
- if a minimum of 255 votes is cast in favour—which is 73.9 per cent of the total.

In addition, a Member State may ask for confirmation that the votes in favour represent at least 62 per cent of the total population of the Union. If this is found not to be the case, the decision will not be adopted. This last condition has been included because the enlargement of 2004 brought in a series of small to medium countries. The consequence was that a large number of small states could in principle outvote a small number of large states. The population rule is designed to ensure that an adequate majority of both states *and* of the EU's population approves legislation.

The *European Council* has, since its establishment in 1974, become a very powerful body. Comprising the twenty-seven heads of state or government, the twenty-seven foreign ministers, the Commission president, and a vice-president, it has had a hand in all the major EU decisions in the intervening period (agreement on the single market, supervision of the SEA and TEU negotiations, decisions on enlargement, reform of the budget, the launching of EMU, the Lisbon agenda, and so on). The European Council meets at least twice a year. Its decisions are political; transposition into EC law is normally left to the Council of Ministers. The European Council is important to the strategic development of the EU and of other joint activities (i.e. the other two 'pillars' of the TEU). It is the principal institution of the EU, being common to all three pillars of activity. It has become a major 'media event', however, which can detract from its efficiency.

A number of additional institutions also exist. Arguably the most important, by virtue of its influence in a specific policy area, is the European Central Bank, located in Frankfurt and established ahead of the move to the final stage of EMU in 1999. This body, headed by Wim Duisenberg from June 1998 to October 2003 and by Jean-Claude Trichet there-after, is responsible for the day-to-day running of monetary policy under the single cur-rency, including decisions on interest rates for the Eurozone. The Economic and Social Committee, a kind of parliament of interest groups, is consulted on most economic policy legislation but is overshadowed by the EP. The TEU created a Committee of the Regions. Its role reflects the increased involvement of subnational government in EU activities, most notably in regional policy. The Commission has sought to allay concerns that it is a centralizing agency by promoting links with regional authorities, some of which have important powers in their domestic context.

Surrounding the EU institutions are numerous lobby groups. There are some 500 such groups, which chiefly focus their activities on the Commission. The Commission is com-paratively open to such lobbying, not least because it has no field agencies in the Member States; hence it needs information. Thus lobbies are an important part of the decision-making framework.

The result of all this is that policy-making consists of a dense network of contacts. The nature of the contacts depends on the precise form that policy-making takes in the area concerned (e.g. which procedure in the EP; what type of voting in the Council?), as well as on the efficiency of lobby groups (and there may be several in competition with each other). The increasing complexity of policy-making has, since the TEU, led to repeated calls for greater openness and more decentralization of power following the so-called subsidiarity principle.

How do these institutional and policy-making characteristics impact upon determina-tion of economic policy, broadly defined, in the EU? We should note as a prior observa-tion that the term 'governance' has come to be used more generally to explain the political process. In the context of the EU we can apply the term 'economic governance'. The advantage of this term is to move away from formal processes to understand the relationships between institutions and lobby groups, individual firms, and so on. These relationships may be presented as consisting of a network of actors concerned with a particular policy issue. The relationships may also be multilevelled, emphasizing that the supranational institutions need active assistance, not only from national authorities—notably to put policy into practice—but also in a number of policy areas, for example the Structural Funds, from subnational government (regions, local authorities) as well. The term economic governance also has the advantage of joining up the stage of making policy with that of operationalizing it.

In the EU context economic policy is predominantly put into practice through regulation. That is to say, the EU provides a framework for 'steering' the European economy. The treaties and subsequent legislation offer a framework within which the Member States must run their economies. The lack of large-scale supranational budgetary resources reinforces this regulatory approach at the expense of macroeconomic or redistributive activities. Similarly, the absence of EU-owned enterprises removes another potential economic-policy lever. A characteristic of regulatory politics is the conduct of policy-making in relatively closed groups of policy specialists. In some cases these groups are formed around EU agencies, of which the European Central Bank is one. In other cases regulation is undertaken by national officials working with the Commission in a process called 'comitology'.

Despite the characteristic regulatory pattern of governance in the EU, it is possible to identify some different patterns of economic governance.

- *Positive integration* relates to those areas of governance where the supranational institutions have a considerable degree of authority, with the Commission, Court of Justice, and/or the European Central Bank as key players. Positive integration specifically means that a detailed policy template has been provided for at the EU level. National discretion is minimal or must at least be authorized by the supranational institutions. Examples of economic policy operating in this way include European Monetary Union, competition policy, and external trade policy. In theory it should also cover the Stability and Growth Pact, which requires the Member States to adhere to prudent macroeconomic policies on public sector debt and borrowing. In practice, it has operated in a much 'softer' manner (see Chapter 12).

- *Negative integration* relates to those policy areas where the EU simply legislates for the removal of discriminatory Member State legislation. There is no template to which Member States or economic actors must adhere; they simply must not discriminate against entrepreneurs, workers, goods, service providers, or citizens from other EU Member States. Examples of economic policy operating in this way include the single market, corporate governance, and industrial relations.

- *Multilevelled partnership* relates principally to the Structural Funds. In order to secure funding from the EU, subnational and national governments have to form partnerships with Brussels in order to secure funding and then to facilitate the running of subsequent projects. At the project level partnership relationships are normally practised between subnational government and local stakeholders, such as firms.

- *Horizontal cooperation* takes place in those policy areas where the EU has no clear responsibility, in many cases because the member governments have refused to give up powers. This form of economic governance has grown significantly in recent times. Two examples will suffice. The first relates to the Lisbon agenda on European competitiveness. Many of the component parts of this agenda are operating according to patterns adopted from the private sector: benchmarking, peer review, league tables, and the like. The EU has coined a term for this type of cooperation: the Open Method of Coordination (OMC). Thus, the member governments come together in the EU context to compare their national employment action plans. Can lessons be learnt from the practice of a fellow EU state? Which state tops the EU league table for innovation or patenting, and how can the UK or any other state catch up with the leader? The EU's role may typically be confined to providing a venue for the discussions or publishing reports to inform those discussions. In the absence of supranational authority over the detailed conduct of macroeconomic policy, member governments cooperate on Broad Economic Policy Guidelines. In this second example the governments consider the Commission's review of the European economy and consider what action to take. However, this is not carried out in the shadow of possible Commission sanctions—unlike the Stability and Growth Pact. Instead the process is horizontal in recognition of the pattern of coordinating Member State policies.

These four patterns of economic governance are well established in the contemporary EU.

1.3 The EU in the 2000s

This account of the EU's history and institutions has covered the developments that have shaped the EU at the start of 2007. However, as mentioned earlier, other developments have already occurred in respect of both deepening and widening. The principal development in respect of the former had begun already in 2001, when the EU proposed an attempt to rationalize its various treaties into something rather more transparent for the European citizen. For example, the EU's policy responsibilities would be spelt out clearly, thus reducing concerns that the Union's powers tend to expand in a covert manner at the expense of the Member States. In addition, the motivating principles behind the EU would be spelt out as well as citizens' rights. A Convention on the Future of Europe was established to consider the task, comprising MEPs, representatives of national governments, and national parliaments amongst others. It met from 2002 to 2003. In 2003 it submitted to the European Council a Draft Treaty establishing a Constitution for Europe. The traditional practice with treaty changes is that the European Council convenes an IGC to draw up treaty amendments, and it did so once again even though a complicated drafting process had already taken place in the Convention. In June 2004 the European Council finally agreed a draft that the twenty-five governments found acceptable. The next step was to put it to the Member States to ratify according to their various constitutional practices. In some cases ratification takes place in the national parliament; in other cases ratification is by referendum; in yet other cases there is some flexibility in practice. The Constitutional Treaty was designed to:

- consolidate all treaties into a single text;
- create a president of the European Council with a longer term of office than the current six-month period;
- create an EU minister of foreign affairs to give the EU more effective external representation;

- make further changes to the QMV rules;
- extend QMV to fifteen further areas;
- allow national parliaments to invoke a subsidiarity objection to halt draft Commission legislation that intruded into Member States' activities unnecessarily;
- incorporate a Charter of Fundamental Rights; and
- provide Member States with the right to leave the EU.

Ratification commenced from 2004 but, with several states having ratified, the process came to a stop in May/June when referenda in France and then the Netherlands rejected the Constitutional Treaty. As founder Member States, these countries' 'no votes' were seen as potentially fatal to the Treaty. In June 2005 the European Council called for a period of reflection. It remains unclear whether the Treaty will be revived or whether it has to be abandoned because of the lack of any prospect of a 'yes vote' in France and the Netherlands.

In the meantime developments continue with regard to widening. Romanian and Bulgarian accession took place in 2007. Croatia and Turkey are candidates with whom negotiations were agreed to commence in late 2005, although the Turkish case may entail a lengthy process.

The EU has become a much larger organization than it was when founded by six states in the early 1950s. Its policy remit has extended from coal and steel to most areas of domestic and foreign policy as well as home affairs. The EU is no longer a 'one-size-fits-all' organization. Some states are absent from EMU (see Table 1.3); others from defence cooperation, for instance. However, the core remains around the single market, of which all states are full members. The Franco-German relationship is no longer the bedrock of the integration process. The relatively weak economic performance of these two states in the Eurozone has reduced their influence on economic policy within the EU in recent years. Some of the new accession states share a more 'Anglo-Saxon' view of the economy. Concerns about the threat of globalization and 'Anglo-Saxon' policies on the economy played a role in the French 'no vote' on the Constitutional Treaty. The politics and institutions of the EU have evolved considerably over the years and their importance in understanding the economics of the EU remains as important as ever.

■ DISCUSSION QUESTIONS

1. How far has economic integration within the EU been subordinated to the achievement of political objectives?

2. How far has the ceding of sovereignty to supranational institutions influenced the course of economic integration within Europe?

3. 'The shape of the EU's institutions reflects the need to harness national and common interests to the pursuit of specific policy goals.' Do you agree?

4. Should the EU have a constitution?

▓ FURTHER READING

An important source of information on the EU is its own publications, many of which can be obtained free of charge from the London offices of the European Commission or European Parliament. Many of the publications are also now available on the EU's websites, which offer a wealth of information. For accounts of the history of integration, see Dinan (2004). McCormick (2005) provides a good introduction to the EU, whereas Cowles and Dinan (2004) give a good review of current issues, both from a political science perspective. On the institutions, see Hix (2005), which is up to date on the details. Nugent (2006) and Peterson and Shackleton (2006) are other useful sources, although they do not currently reflect the institutional arrangements following enlargement in 2007. For analysis of the policy process in the EU, see Wallace *et al.* (2005); also Peterson and Bomberg (1999). For a review of the relationship of the Member States with the EU and the impact of the EU upon them—the phenomenon known as Europeanization—see Bulmer and Lequesne (2005). For a useful dictionary of the terminology of the EU, see Bainbridge with Teasdale (2004).

Useful websites include:

The Europa server—the gateway to all EU sites:	http://www.europa.eu/
The European Parliament:	http://www.europarl.eu/
The European Commission:	http://www.ec.europa.eu/
The Council of the EU:	http://www.consilium.europa.eu/
The European Court of Justice:	http://www.curia.eu/
The European Central Bank:	http://www.ecb.int/
Debate on the European constitution:	http://europa.eu/constitution/futurum/index_en.htm
Sources of reporting on the EU:	http://www.euobserver.com/; http://www.euractiv.com/.

▓ NOTES

1. The history of Britain's relationship to integration cannot be dealt with in detail here. For an account, see George (1998).

2. Qualified majority voting is a system whereby the importance of larger countries in relation to smaller ones is reflected in voting through the assignment of a weighting. However, the system over-represents smaller states relative to their population. This system continues to operate (see below).

3. In 1999, with the implementation of the Amsterdam Treaty, the EC Treaty was consolidated and renumbered (see below). Article 235 became Article 308. Already, and somewhat confusingly, at Maastricht the EEC Treaty had already been renamed the Treaty establishing the European Community (TEC). Separate treaties remain for the ECSC and Euratom.

4. It is from this date onwards that one can refer to 'the EC', i.e. referring to the three Communities.

▓ REFERENCES

Armstrong, K. and Bulmer, S. (1998), *The Governance of the Single European Market* (Manchester: Manchester University Press).

Bainbridge, T. with Teasdale, A. (2004), *The Penguin Companion to European Union*, 3rd edn (London: Penguin).

Bulmer, S. and Lequesne, C. (eds.) (2005), *The Member States of the European Union* (Oxford: Oxford University Press).

Cowles, M. G. and Dinan, D. (eds.) (2004), *Developments in the European Union*, 2nd edn (Basingstoke: Palgrave Macmillan).

Dinan, D. (2004), *Europe Recast* (Basingstoke: Palgrave Macmillan).

George, S. (1998), *An Awkward Partner: Britain in the European Community*, 3rd edn (Oxford: Oxford University Press).

Hix, S. (2005), *The Political System of the European Union*, 2nd edn (Basingstoke: Palgrave Macmillan).

McCormick, J. (2005), *Understanding the European Union: A Concise Introduction*, 3rd edn (Basingstoke: Palgrave Macmillan).

Milward, A. (1992), *The European Rescue of the Nation-State* (London: Routledge).

Nugent, N. (2006), *The Government and Politics of the European Union*, 6th edn (Basingstoke: Palgrave Macmillan).

Peterson, J. and Bomberg, E. (1999), *Decision-Making in the European Union* (Basingstoke: Palgrave Macmillan).

Peterson, J. and Shackleton, M. (2006), *The Institutions of the European Union*, 2nd edn (Oxford: Oxford University Press).

Wallace, H., Wallace, W., and Pollack, M. (eds.) (2005), *Policy-Making in the European Union*, 5th edn (Oxford: Oxford University Press).

2 The European Economy

Mike Artis and Nick Weaver

Introduction

The primary purpose of this chapter is to provide the reader with a statistical illustration of the basic economic features of the European Union (EU) and its constituent members. It is also instructive to consider how the EU compares with other large economies in the world in key dimensions and we include such comparisons here.

A key event, the introduction on 1 January 1999 of the Euro, the European single currency (replacing its predecessor the Ecu on a one-for-one basis), should be noted. Since then, eleven countries (Belgium, Germany, Spain, France, Ireland, Italy, Luxembourg, the Netherlands, Austria, Portugal, and Finland) have fixed their currencies to the Euro at irrevocable conversion rates, being joined by Greece in January 2001. Euro notes and coins were introduced on 1 January 2002, when use of the Euro became compulsory in these countries and national currencies were progressively withdrawn. This establishment of a single currency in a part of the EU has led to the development of separate data in a range of variables for the Eurozone. These too are presented.

In producing a statistical picture it is always difficult to decide what to include and how it should be presented. Presenting data relating to all variables of interest, for all the countries for all the years, could easily result in information overload. The approach taken here is to present figures and tables illustrating the major economic indicators in the most recent year for which a complete and consistent data set is available. There is a large number of websites from which the interested reader can download additional statistical data. A note of these is given at the end of this chapter.

While such a statistical picture of the European economy is useful, some discussion of economic policy is essential. Policy should be judged in terms of targets. At the European Council held in Lisbon in early 2000, a 'strategic goal' for the coming decade was set. The European Union was 'to become the most competitive and dynamic knowledge-based economy in the world capable of sustainable economic growth with more and better jobs and greater social cohesion'. The European Commission suggested a series of 'structural' indicators relating to employment, innovation and research, economic reform, social cohesion, the general economic background, and the environment which could be used to assess the success, or otherwise, in meeting the Lisbon targets. In addition to these indicators other indicators relevant in particular to the EU's role in an increasingly integrated global economy are shown.

2.1 **Population**

The population of the EU (EU-25) at around 460 million (Eurozone 310 million) as of 2006 is greater than that of either of the other major developed economies; the USA's population is 293 million and Japan's is only 127 million. But it is far less than the population of the two largest and fast-growing economies in Asia: China at 1,288 million and India 1,103 million. The situation is, however, not static as not only is there population

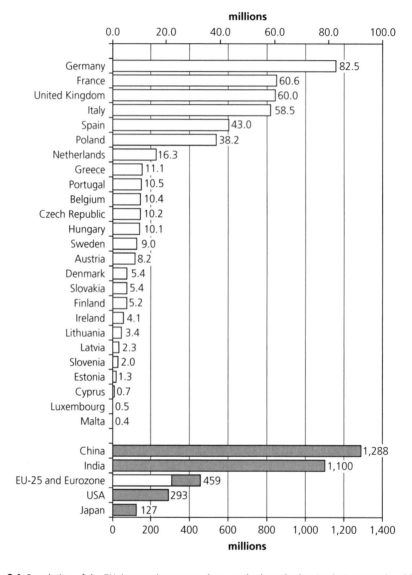

Figure 2.1 Population of the EU, its constituent members, and selected other 'major' economies, 2005

Source: Eurostat, *World Development Indicators*.

growth but also several countries are currently negotiating admittance to the EU. For example, Turkey's accession would add another 72 million.

In terms of population the most notable feature of the EU's constituent members is that most of the population lives in just a few big countries. Roughly 75 per cent of the people live in just six countries: Germany, France, Italy, the UK, Spain, and Poland. The recent round of accessions has meant that the dominance of large countries in terms of population has been reduced. However, Turkey's accession would partially reverse this trend.

It is difficult to make any broad statements about population densities, but it is possible to discern a London–Milan axis around which are areas of relatively high density (more than 100 inhabitants per square kilometre). In contrast, much of the rest of the EU outside the major urban centres is relatively sparsely populated (fewer than 100 inhabitants per square kilometre).

2.2 Dependency rates

A pressing issue in many Member States and for the EU as a whole is the rising old age dependency rate. Dependency rates typically provide a measure of the ratio of the total number of people not working because of age relative to the number of persons of working age. The possible problems arising from a high dependency rate are long term if the high rate is not matched by an increase in the ability and willingness of those employed to support them. In Figure 2.2 we show estimates of current and projected old age dependency ratios where the indicator chosen is the ratio between the number of persons of an age greater than that when people are generally economically active (i.e. aged 65 and over) and the number of those of working age (from 15 to 64). Whilst the ordering of these is interesting, with Italy famously being the country with the highest such rate at present, perhaps most noteworthy is that, according to current predictions, by 2050 all Member States will have a dependency rate far higher than the current highest! This is the so-called 'demographic time-bomb'. It has implications for the way in which pensions are paid. A continuation of the prevalent 'pay as you go' state systems of pension payments must imply higher rates of tax on those working, higher participation rates or burgeoning debt, or a combination of these in the absence of acceleration in productivity growth.

2.3 Gross Domestic Product and Gross National Income

There are various ways of measuring the size of an economy, with Gross Domestic Product (GDP) being the most commonly quoted. The GDP measure includes all goods and services for final consumption which are produced by the economic activity of producer units resident in an economy. It is a territorial measure. Figure 2.3 shows the GDP at market prices for the EU (including the Eurozone,) the USA, Japan, and China for 2005.

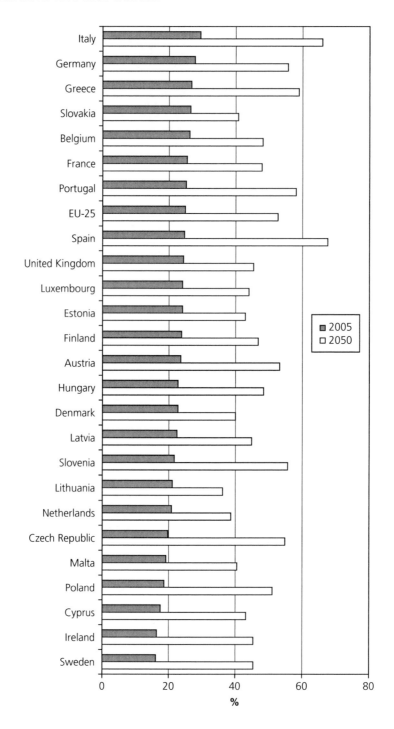

Figure 2.2 Current and projected EU old age dependency ratios

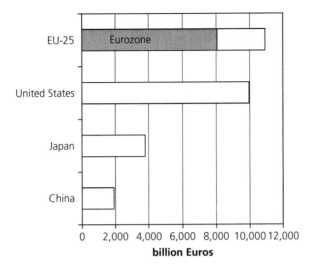

Figure 2.3 Gross Domestic Product, at current market prices, evaluated at current exchange rates, in the EU and selected other major economies, 2005 (billion Euros)

Another measure that is often used is Gross National Income (GNI). This measures the income receivable by resident institutional units regardless of whether they earn their income at home or abroad. GNI equals GDP plus net primary incomes received from the rest of the world.

Whichever measure is used the dominance of the six biggest EU economies—Germany, France, Italy, the UK, Spain, and Poland—is again clear. Together they account for roughly 75 per cent of the total GDP of the twenty-five.

In fact there is generally only a small difference between GDP and GNI for most economies. The countries where GDP is substantially higher than GNI are Ireland and Luxembourg, followed by most of the new entrants from the east, Slovakia, Poland, the Czech Republic, Hungary, and Estonia. The UK has the largest positive proportionate gap between GNI and GDP.

A note of warning needs to be sounded about the use of either GDP or GNI as an unqualified indicator of the size of an economy. Even in countries with advanced statistical services a large part of human activity goes unrecorded. Accounting techniques are not available to measure the value of unmarketed production (such as housework or DIY activities), or to provide estimates of the costs of pollution and environmental destruction. Tax evasion and moonlighting give rise to a substantial 'underground' economy. In 1987 Italy, in response to evidence of the massive extent of underreporting of economic activity, adjusted its estimate of GDP upwards by 18 per cent. Despite the fact that the absence of broader measures has for a long time been recognized as a serious problem, progress in this area is only slowly being made and as yet there is no widely available alternative to GDP and GNI that is consistently reported.

In order to make international comparisons, GDP, which is initially calculated in terms of domestic currency, needs to be re-expressed in terms of some common or *numeraire*

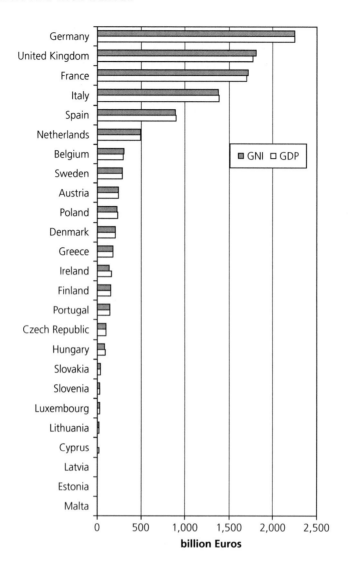

Figure 2.4 Gross National Income and Gross Domestic Product, at current market prices, evaluated at current exchange rates, for the economies in the EU, 2005 (billion Euros)

currency. Internationally this is usually done in terms of the US dollar, although any currency can be used. With the advent of Monetary Union this is increasingly done within the EU in terms of the Euro, as in Figures 2.3 and 2.4.

However, the use of market exchange rates when making international comparisons has been criticized on the grounds that it gives rise to a systematic bias (Gilbert and Kravis 1954). Market exchange rates do not necessarily reflect the amount of goods that can be bought with a currency—that is, the purchasing power of a currency in terms of a volume of goods. This is because the market exchange rate is the result of a whole variety of forces including, not only the supply and demand for foreign exchange required to match the flows of real good and services, but also the speculative activities of foreign exchange dealers, capital flows, and so on. To the extent that these factors do not influence the purchasing power of the currency in a country, the market exchange rate will not be a good measure of the purchasing power of a currency in a country.

Various ways have been proposed to get around this problem. One simple method, proposed by *The Economist*, is the use of the 'Big Mac' index. This uses the relative prices of Big Macs in two countries to construct a new exchange rate. Big Macs are used because they are a standardized commodity whose price is widely known. However, price level differences between countries vary for different commodities and a more sophisticated measure using a similar principle to the Big Mac index but taking into account a larger basket of goods is required. Purchasing power parity estimates attempt to do just this, their aim being to try to eliminate differences in price levels between countries to enable a more accurate comparison of the quantities or volumes that can be purchased.

The measures of purchasing power parity (PPP) used in this chapter, Purchasing Power Standards (PPS), are produced by *Eurostat* (the EU's statistical office) which calculates them using methods established by the International Comparison Project (ICP) of the United Nations. They are calculated on the basis of a list of products chosen for their representativeness and comparability. For each product a price ratio is established and a weighted average across all the products in the list can then be formed for each country. These weighted average price parities give an alternative (PPP) set of exchange rates that can be applied to the original national currency estimates of GDP to give PPP estimates of GDP. A scaling procedure ensures that the EU's total GDP in PPSs is the same as in Euros.

Figure 2.5 shows GDP at current market prices in billions of Euros and in billions of Euros PPS for each of the fifteen countries. It can be clearly seen that a comparison of the relative sizes of the countries is influenced by whether market exchange rates or PPS measures are used.

Scaling GDP by population gives us GDP per capita figures. Figure 2.6 shows GDP per capita in both PPS and Euros. Here the effect of adjusting the GDP figures for PPS is clear. All the countries having a below EU average per capita income are in real (PPS) terms richer than would appear to be the case if market exchange rates instead of some measure of purchasing power parities were used. This is the systematic bias that Gilbert and Kravis (1954) noted. The spread is still considerable with the GDP(PPS) per capita in the richest country—Luxembourg—being roughly five times that in the poorest, Latvia. In terms of the more populous countries, Germany, France, the UK, and Italy are above the EU average and Spain and Poland below it.

2.4 Economic growth

In addition to looking at the static picture that the statistics discussed above provide, it is interesting to consider how the economies have grown. To study the change over time it is again necessary to abstract from price changes so that comparisons in terms of volumes can be made. This is done by adjusting the GDP figures for changes in the level of prices, that is, for inflation. The most appropriate measure of inflation in this context involves a

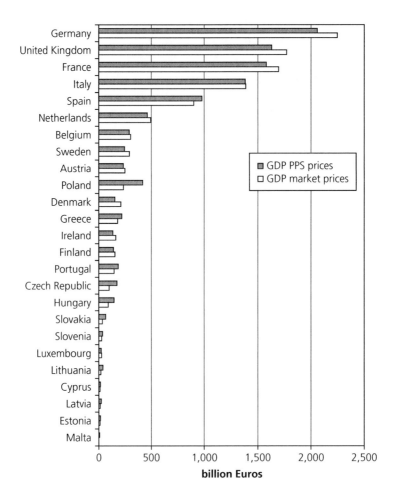

Figure 2.5 GDP at current market prices, evaluated at current exchange rates, and in PPS, EU Member States, 2005 (billion Euros)

weighted basket of the prices of *all* products (not just those purchased by households). This measure of inflation, the GDP deflator, enables nominal GDP which is expressed in current terms to be converted into real GDP expressed in terms of a constant base year.

Since population growth in the EU countries has not been uniform, growth of GDP per capita tells a different story to that of GDP growth per se. Many of the faster growing economies have also been countries with faster growing populations. Even so Figure 2.7 shows how the 'newer' economies have been outperforming the larger developed economies, the UK, Germany, France, and Italy, during this period.

Figures such as these enable us to examine the extent to which the GDP per capita of the EU economies are converging. Here we must be aware that convergence of levels requires divergence in growth rates. Thus for GDP per capita to converge across the economies of the EU, the poorest countries must grow faster than the richer ones.

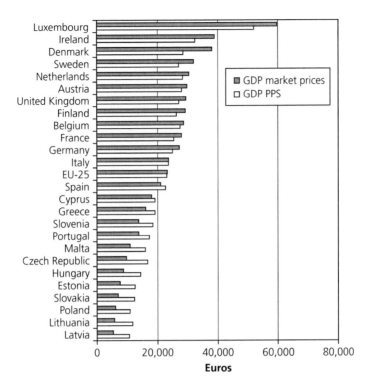

Figure 2.6 GDP per capita at current market prices, evaluated at current exchange rates, and in PPS, EU Member States, 2005 (Euros)

2.5 Income inequality

Looking at aggregate figures of income per head gives us only a very partial view. In addition some measure of the equality or otherwise of the distribution of income is also likely to be revealing. A normal procedure would be to rank households in terms of income received no matter what the source. The most complete description of such a measure is the Lorenz curve which plots households ranked by income against the income they receive. Ideally one would be shown for each country. Data availability and space preclude this. Rather Figure 2.8 shows a simple statistic—a ratio comparing the rich and the poor. The figures are the total income received by the top 20 per cent of the population divided by that of the 20 per cent of the population with the lowest income. For the EU as a whole the figure is 4.5. This indicates that the 20 per cent of the population with the highest income received around 4.5 times as much income as the 20 per cent of the population with the lowest income.

This is an aggregate figure. Different Member States have very large differences in inequality by this measure. Using the data from the most recent year for each country as

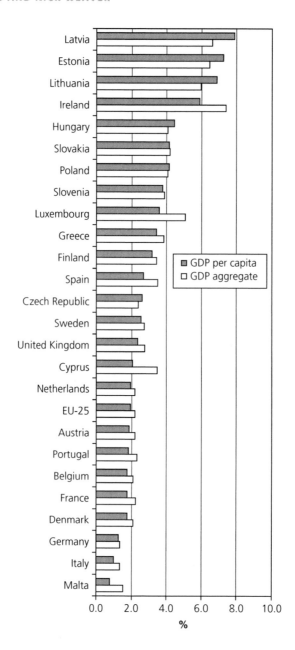

Figure 2.7 Growth in aggregate and in per capita GDP, EU Member States, 1996–2005

a broad generalization, the most equal are in two groups: some of the former socialist countries, Hungary, Slovenia, the Czech Republic, and the Scandinavian countries, all with a ratio of less than four. France is the other economy with a value less than four. The least equal, all with a ratio of greater than five, are the southern countries—Spain, Greece, and Portugal—the UK and Ireland, and two of the Baltic states, Latvia and Estonia.

Figure 2.8 Income inequality, EU Member States, 2003 (ratio achieved by deciding the total income received by the top-earning 20 per cent of the population by that received by the lowest-earning 20 per cent in each Member State)

2.6 Sectoral value added

The total value added in an economy may be found by the summation of the value added of each economic sector. A simple disagregation is as follows

$$GVA = VA \text{ services} + VA \text{ industry} + VA \text{ agriculture}$$

Industry itself is often divided into manufacturing and non-manufacturing.

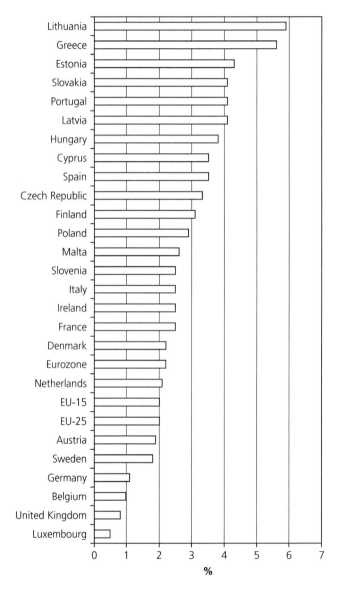

Figure 2.9 Gross Value Added, agriculture, EU Member States, 2004

Eurostat's chosen disaggregation involves six sectors: agriculture; industry (including energy); construction; trade, transport and communication services; business activities and financial services; other services. Of these, the two that are most worth documenting are agriculture and industry.

The countries with the largest shares of Gross Value Added in agriculture are the new members from the Baltic and Eastern Europe and the 'southern' countries of Portugal and Greece. But in no case is the percentage of total value added larger than 6 per cent.

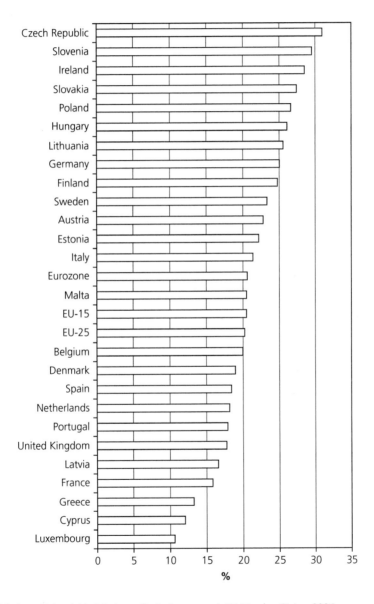

Figure 2.10 Gross Value Added, industry (including energy), EU Member States, 2004

The countries with less than the EU average (2 per cent) include Luxembourg, the UK, Belgium, Germany, Sweden, and Austria.

Industry for the EU as whole contributes 20 per cent to total value added. The countries where industry contributes a higher share than 25 per cent include Ireland, some of the new members from the east—Czech Republic, Slovenia, Slovakia, Poland, Hungary, and Lithuania—and Germany.

2.7 Productivity

Differences in GDP, GNI, and GVA reflect in part differences in productivity. There are various measures of productivity that are used. Here we show two. GDP(PPS) per person employed (no distinction is made for part-time working) relative to the EU average and GDP in Purchasing Power Standards (PPS) per hour worked relative to the EU average.

In terms of productivity per person employed, the EU compares unfavourably with the USA. But whilst the USA's lead is still there in productivity per hour, the effect is substantially lessened when hours of work are taken into account. Within the EU the lower productivity countries by both measures are the Baltic states, the other recently joined members, and Portugal.

A recent study (Denis *et al.* 2005) argues that the EU's productivity problems are related to an 'outdated and inflexible industrial structure' which has been 'slow to adapt to the intensifying pressures of globalisation and rapid technological change'. These, it is argued, result from a combination of factors:

- The 'excessive importance' of low and medium-technology industries which suffer from declining productivity growth rates and a globalization-induced contraction in investment levels.
- The failure of the EU to 'challenge' the USA's domination in large areas of the information and communication technologies (ICT) industry. This is reflected in the relatively small size of the EU's ICT production sector.
- The low rate of diffusion of ICT to other industries in the EU.

2.8 Labour market

The standard procedure when analysing the basic features of the labour market involves distinguishing the population of working age from the total population. The population of working age is then divided into three mutually exclusive and all-encompassing categories—the unemployed, persons in employment, and the inactive. The unemployed plus the employed together are the labour force. From these categories various measures such as employment/population ratios (employment as a percentage of population of working age), activity rates (the labour force as a percentage of the population of working age), and unemployment rates (the number of unemployed as a percentage of the labour

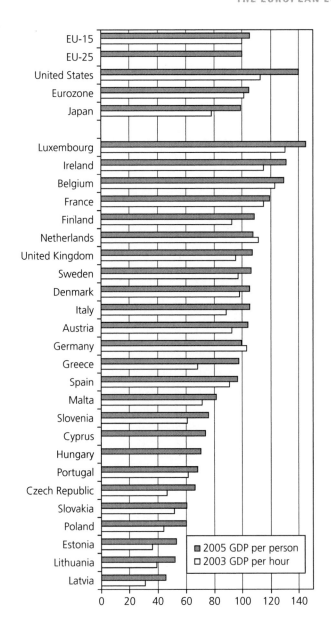

Figure 2.11 Productivity in the EU, USA, and Japan: GDP(PPS) per hour (2003) and GDP(PPS) per person (2005)

force) can be calculated. International comparability is again difficult because countries' statistical services tailor their own data to their national requirements and the political significance of the statistics renders them particularly vulnerable to interference. Eurostat, by adjusting national measures with the help of an EU-wide labour force survey, aims to produce comparable standardized statistics.

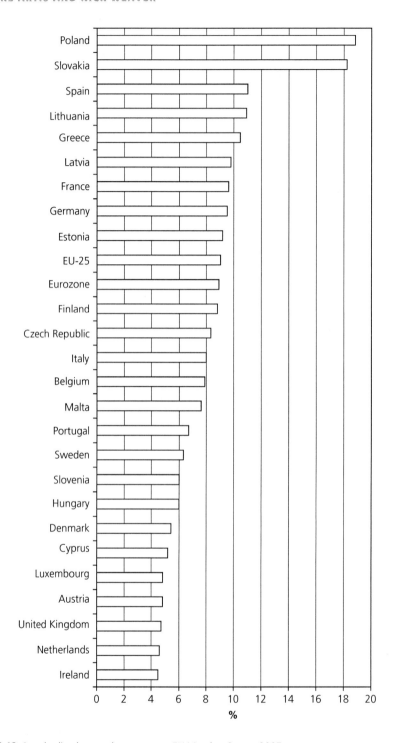

Figure 2.12 Standardized unemployment rate, EU Member States, 2005

2.9 **International trade and the EU**

A measure of the EU's importance in the world economy can be gained from looking at the value of the sum of imports and exports of merchandise trade. Figure 2.13 provides the data on this but also records (in the first column) the total amount of intra-EU trade, which is very considerable when compared with the EU's trade with the rest of the world.

Figure 2.14 shows the world's the top ten trading economies where the members of the EU are treated separately. Here the importance of the some of the major EU members even considered alone is clearly evident.

In addition to the size of these merchandise trade flows we should also look at the direction of trade. Figures 2.15 and 2.16 show the EU's major trading partners. In terms of both imports and exports the importance of the USA is noticeable, but so to are the implied imbalances of trade with both China and Russia.

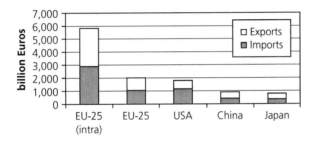

Figure 2.13 EU merchandise imports and exports, 2005 (billion Euros)

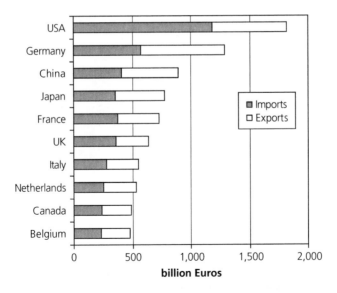

Figure 2.14 The world's top ten merchandise traders, 2005 (billion Euros)

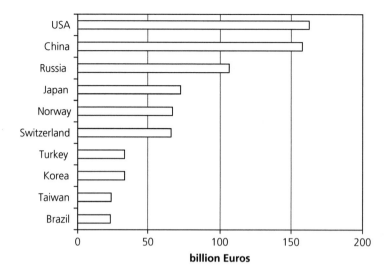

Figure 2.15 The EU's top ten sources of imports (billion Euros), 2005

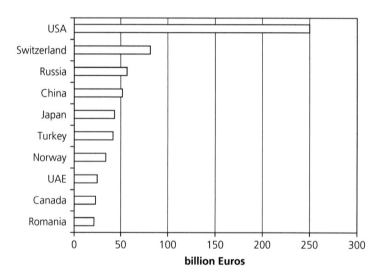

Figure 2.16 The EU's top ten export partners (billion Euros), 2005

2.10 Future enlargement of the EU

The number of countries in the EU has grown considerably since its foundation, and, despite many problems, a number of countries are queuing up to join. At the time of writing most non-EU European countries are viewed as possible future entrants. They are often divided into three distinct groups on the basis of institutional and economic characteristics: Turkey, the former socialist countries, and the European Free Trade Association (EFTA) countries.

The EU Turkey Association agreement of 1963 specifically mentioned the possibility of Turkey's eventual accession to the Community after a twenty-two-year transitional period. As things stand, some of the former socialist countries seem to have pushed into the queue ahead of Turkey.

Bulgaria and Romania headed the list and were admitted early in 2007, but also the former Yugoslav republics and Ukraine are also pushing for entry. All are relatively poor compared with the EU and have until recently had weak institutional links with the EU.

The EFTA countries—Norway, Iceland, Switzerland, and Liechtenstein—are all relatively rich stable countries with economies roughly similar to the richer existing members of the EU. Switzerland and Norway have, for the present, decided against joining the EU. Iceland, owing to fears regarding its fishing interests, and Liechtenstein are unlikely to apply. However, these countries already have most of the benefits of access to the EU's market through their membership of the European Economic Area (EEA). This aims to reduce frontier barriers and to allow the free movement of services, capital, and workers. Agriculture, notably, is excluded.

A Centre for Economic Policy Research (CEPR) (1992) report estimated that there might be some gain in terms of the EU's budget if EFTA countries were to become full members because their GDP per capita was something like 35 per cent higher than the EU average. The EFTA countries could expect to be net contributors and would be unlikely to receive Structural Funds allocated to poor regions. However, the heavy dependence of the EFTA countries on the EU for trade means that there are potentially large gains to be made from participating in the single market. The CEPR report estimated that increased competition would reduce costs and boost productivity, raising EFTA's GDP by up to 5 per cent. Full membership would entail adoption of the EU's Common Agricultural Policy (CAP) by the EFTA countries. This could cause problems for the latter because their agriculture is even more heavily subsidized than the EU's (EU subsidies are roughly equal to 49 per cent of the value of farm output; EFTA countries' subsidies average 68 per cent of farm output and Swiss subsidies as much as 80 per cent).

Within the EEA, the EU's competition policy must be applied to cross-border trade in manufactured goods. Full membership of the EU requires competition policy to be applied to a much wider range of domestic activities. This would restrict much of the state aid to industry and restrictive business practices that are common in the EFTA countries.

■ **DISCUSSION QUESTIONS**

1. What are the main problems involved in making international comparisons of countries' GDP? Illustrate with respect to the Member States of the EU.

2. Describe how you would assess the level of development and the economic strength of an economy. Illustrate your answer by reference to the Member States of the EU.

▒ FURTHER READING

There is a variety of sources of data on the economies of the EU; noteworthy among these would be many of the publications of the OECD, the IMF, and several of the institutions of the UN. However, the statistics produced by Eurostat are non-comparable as far as standardization and inter-country comparability are concerned. The institution, as well as producing a large number of annual, quarterly, or monthly reports, maintains a large statistical database. The most up-to-date source of information on these is the Eurostat home page on the Internet (http://europa.eu.int/en/comm/eurostat). The European Central Bank is perhaps the most useful source of financial and monetary data (http://www.ecb.int/stats/html/index.en.html).

▒ REFERENCES

Anderson, V. (1991), *Alternative Economic Indicators* (London: Routledge).

Barrell, R. (1992) (ed.), *Economic Convergence and Monetary Union in Europe* (Association for the Monetary Union of Europe and the National Institute of Economic and Social Research; London: Sage).

CEPR (1992), 'Is Bigger Better? The Economics of EC Enlargement', *Monitoring European Integration*, 3 (London: Centre for Economic Policy Research).

Denis, C., McMorrow, K., Röger, W., and Veugelers, R. (2005), (Directorate General for Economic and Financial Affairs) 'The Lisbon Strategy and the EU's Structural Productivity Problem', (European Economy. ECONOMIC PAPERS. No. 221. February 2005. European Commission. Brussels. Tab. Free.) KC-AI-04-221-EN-C.

Eurostat (1985), *Purchasing Power Parities and Gross Domestic Product in Real Terms*, Results, 2 (Luxembourg: CEC).

Gilbert, M. and Kravis, I. B. (1954), *An International Comparison of National Products and the Purchasing Power of Currencies: A Study of the United States, the United Kingdom, France, Germany and Italy* (Paris: Organization for European Economic Cooperation).

United Nations and Commission of the European Communitie (UN and CEC) (1986), *World Comparisons of Purchasing Powers and Real Product for 1980; Phase IV of the International Comparison Project: Part I: Summary Results for 60 Countries* (New York: UN).

3 The Economics of Preferential Trading Areas and Regional Integration

Anthony J. Venables

Introduction

Removal of barriers to trade in goods and services is enshrined in the four freedoms of the Treaty of Rome. In 1957 trade between countries was subject to a number of taxes and restrictions, most notably import duties or tariffs, with an average value of more than 17 per cent in France and Italy, and over 10 per cent in Germany and the Benelux countries. These were rapidly eliminated, although other barriers to trade, such as separate currencies, border formalities, and differing tax administration, remained. The European Commission has done much work to reduce these barriers, and one of the Directorates-General of the Commission is devoted to securing completion of the European internal market, an integrated market with completely free trade in goods and services.

As a consequence of the removal of these barriers to trade there has been a massive increase in the volume of trade between EU Member States. A majority of the international trade of EU countries is with other countries of the Union. The impact of membership on trade can be seen most clearly by looking at the reorientation of trade that occurs when a new country joins the EU. The share of a country's trade with other EU members typically rises by 10–15 percentage points, the increase starting slightly before the formal date of entry, and taking ten to twelve years for full adjustment to occur. For example, the share of UK trade that was with just the original six members of the EC increased from around 15 per cent in the late 1960s to a new plateau at around 28 per cent by the mid-1980s.

This chapter analyses the effects of the removal of these barriers—the theory of economic integration. The first set of arguments we develop (section 3.2) is based on the classical gains from trade: countries have a comparative advantage in some goods and disadvantage in others, and trade allows them to specialize and thereby reap the gains from trade. In the context of the EU—or regional trading agreements more generally—the argument is not quite this straightforward. This is because while liberalization takes place between members of the Union, external trade barriers (on imports from countries outside the Union) generally remain in place. This means that there may be both trade

T04117

creation and trade diversion, the latter occurring if countries come to source their imports from a relatively high-cost partner country rather than a lower-cost non-member.

The second set of arguments turns the focus on to firms. One of the effects of trade liberalization is to increase competitive pressure on firms. This is generally a force for good, as monopoly power is diminished. It can also lead to substantial industrial reorganization as some firms expand, others merge, go bankrupt, or establish multinational activities. There may also be the development of new clusters of activity, and the decline of some existing ones. Section 3.3 lays out the arguments.

The final set of issues, presented in section 3.4, deals with the role of trade in determining differences in average income across Member States. Income levels between Member States vary widely, but there are good arguments for thinking that trade integration has, on balance, promoted convergence of per capita incomes.

Before developing the arguments, some introductory definitions (and acronyms) are required. We have already noted that regional integration agreements (RIAs) such as the EU typically cut tariffs (and other trade barriers) internally, but not necessarily externally. They are therefore sometimes known as 'preferential trading areas' or PTAs. External tariffs may continue to be set separately by each Member State, in which case the PTA takes the form of a free trade area (FTA). Alternatively—and as is the case in the EU—they may be harmonized, and set at the same level for all members, giving a customs union (or CU). The difference is more important than it might at first appear. Politically, a CU requires that countries cede decision-taking power over external tariffs to some central authority, and that it has a central budgetary mechanism for handling tariff revenue. Economically, a CU has the great advantage that goods can be allowed to circulate freely within the it. This cannot be allowed in an FTA because any differences in external tariffs would create an incentive for all external imports to enter the FTA through the country with the lowest tariff and then circulate internally. To prevent this, an FTA has to have internal barriers and complex 'rules of origin' to track the internal movement of goods imported from outside the FTA.

While the focus of this chapter is the EU, PTAs are an important worldwide phenomenon, and there are some 250 PTAs notified to World Trade Organization, 130 of these since 1995. Many are small, and many take the form of bilateral affiliations to larger groups. The largest PTAs are the EU, the North American Free Trade Area (NAFTA, composed of Canada, the USA, and Mexico) and, in Latin America, MERCOSUR (a CU between Argentina, Brazil, Paraguay, and Uruguay). There are a number of PTAs in Asia, and intense discussion is proceeding on how to extend and deepen integration in the Asian region.

3.1 Trade creation and diversion

We now turn to setting out the economics of the gains from trade, and of trade creation and diversion. The analysis of trade creation and diversion dates back to Jacob Viner (1950), and we set it out in simple but rigorous form. We then review some of the empirical work that attempts to establish the relative importance of trade creation and diversion in the EU.

Partial equilibrium

First, we rehearse the standard gains from trade argument. This is most easily done in a partial equilibrium framework, that is, looking just at the market for a single good. Figure 3.1 gives the supply and demand curves for this good in the country under consideration. If trade was impossible then the equilibrium would be at point a, with price P_a. However, trade is possible, and the country is able to purchase the good from the world market at price P_W. If there were free trade, then P_W would be the price in the domestic economy, demand would exceed domestic supply, and quantity ds would be imported. Alternatively, the economy might choose to use an import tariff at rate t, so the actual price of the imported good in the domestic economy is $P_W + t$. This price increase cuts demand, increases domestic supply, and causes imports to fall to amount $d's'$.

What is the effect of the tariff on real income? If the tariff were to be removed, then consumers would gain amount $A + B + C + D$; the first terms $(A + B + C)$ are the value of the price fall on the quantity they were previously consuming, while triangle D is the value of the increment in consumption. Government would lose tariff revenue, which is amount $C = t \times d's'$, the tariff rate times the volume of imports with the tariff. Finally, domestic producers would lose amount A; this is the reduction in the price of what they were selling, adjusted for the fact that they have reduced the amount they produce and moved down their supply (= marginal cost) curve. Netting these terms out, the overall gain to the economy of removing the tariff (gain to consumers, minus the loss to government revenue and producers) is $B + D$. B is the production gain—the fact that quantity ss' is now supplied to the economy at price P_W rather than produced domestically at marginal cost greater than P_W. D is the consumer gain—the fact that extra consumption dd' has marginal benefit greater than its cost, P_W.

Figure 3.1 shows that a tariff reduces domestic real income, and it can also be used to establish the gains from trade. If the tariff were to be increased to amount $t = P_A - P_W$, then the two triangles B and D would increase in size until their apexes met at point a. The

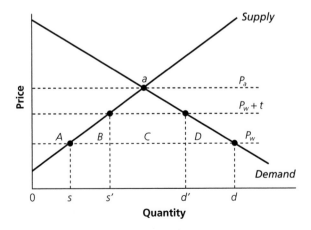

Figure 3.1 Gains from trade

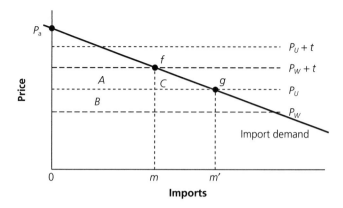

Figure 3.2 Trade creation and diversion

area of this combined triangle is the gain from free trade compared with autarky, that is, tariffs such that there is no trade at all.

In the argument so far there are only two trading partners, the country under study and the rest of the world. The essence of a PTA is that there are (at least) three countries, two members of the PTA, and also the rest of the world outside the PTA. The extra country is added in Figure 3.2. In order to simplify, this figure replaces the separate demand and supply curves of Figure 3.1 by the import demand curve, defined simply as domestic demand minus domestic supply. The world price is as before, P_W, and there is now also supply available from the partner at price P_U. (We assume that this is horizontal—an infinitely elastic supply curve.) The initial situation is one where imports from all sources are subject to a non-preferential tariff at rate t. The equilibrium is at point f, with all imports coming from the lower cost rest of the world (at tariff inclusive price $P_W + t$) rather than the future partner country (which is offering imports at price $P_U + t$).

The PTA means that imports from the partner become duty free. Import demand is met from the cheaper source, that is, the minimum of $\{P_W + t, P_U\}$. As illustrated, consumers find it cheaper to import from the partner, giving equilibrium at point g. What is the value, to real income in the domestic economy, of this change from f to g? Domestic consumers and producers gain by amount $(A + C)$; the argument is similar to the one above, but both consumption and production effects are illustrated together as we are now working with the import demand curve. Domestic government loses tariff revenue, which in the initial situation was equal to $A + B$ (the tariff multiplied by the initial imports). Combining these two elements, the net effect is therefore a real income change of $C - B$. C is *trade creation*, and measures the fact that the marginal benefit of imports mm' exceeds their marginal cost $(= P_U)$. Area B is *trade diversion*, measuring the fact that the economy was previously obtaining quantity $0m$ of imports from the lowest cost source of supply, at cost P_W. However, once it forms a PTA the preferential treatment of imports from the partner means that consumers choose imports from the partner (because $P_W + t > P_U$) even though, once we take into account tariff revenue, the full cost of these imports is greater than the cost of imports from the rest of the world ($P_W < P_U$), giving economic loss measured by area B.

As is clear, trade creation is a source of benefit, while trade diversion brings real income loss. Which is larger? It could go either way, and detailed empirical analysis market by market is required to answer this question. We turn to this in section 3.3, but before this we construct a somewhat wider analysis of trade creation and trade diversion which enables us to investigate the question: which countries are most likely to experience diversion?

The distribution of gains and losses

While the analysis above set out the possibility of trade diversion, it looked just at a single market, for a country assumed to be importing the good under study. What happens in a more general setting, with countries exporting some goods and importing others? Can we say that some countries are more likely to experience trade creation and others trade diversion? To analyse these issues we need to move to a general equilibrium setting, analysing imports and exports simultaneously.

Before setting out the analysis formally, a flavour of the analysis can be given inform-ally. Consider the comparative advantages of two countries—let's call them Germany and Spain—relative to each other and relative to the rest of the world. We might suppose that Germany has a comparative advantage in capital-intensive goods (human and physical capital) relative to Spain and also relative to the rest of the world. Spain has a comparative advantage in labour-intensive goods relative to Germany, but not relative to the rest of the world, compared with which it is quite capital abundant. If Spain and Germany form a PTA, what is the pattern of trade creation and trade diversion? For Spain, there is only trade creation. It imports capital-intensive goods from Germany and, since Germany has a comparative advantage in these goods relative to Spain *and* relative to the rest of the world, there is no trade diversion. However, for Germany there is trade diversion. It comes to import its labour-intensive goods from Spain, in line with intra-PTA compara-tive advantage. However, this is not a global comparative advantage—Germany's imports of these goods have been diverted from the rest of world (which has global comparative advantage in labour-intensive goods) to Spain (which has intra-PTA comparative advant-age but not global comparative advantage in these goods).

With this by way of introduction, we now outline the analysis diagrammatically. The setting will be one in which there are two countries, labelled G and S, that form a PTA, while a third country—the rest of the world—is left outside. Each country produces two goods, which we label A and M. Figure 3.3 has on the axes quantities of goods A and M, consumption of which takes place in fixed proportions, along the consumption line illustrated.[1] The world price of good A in terms of M is p_w.[2]

Production possibilities for countries G and S are illustrated by the solid curves $A_G M_G$ and $A_S M_S$. They are constructed such that both G and S have comparative advantage in good M relative to the rest of the world, but G also has a comparative advantage in M relative to S (think of good M as being capital-intensive manufactures). Thus, with free trade at world prices p_w, countries G and S would produce at points F_G and F_S respectively. They would both export good M, country G more than country S, since it has the more extreme comparative advantage.

The initial situation is not free trade, but a position in which all imports by countries G and S are subject to tariffs at rate t. We set this rate sufficiently high that country S is

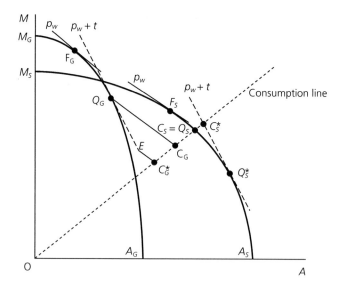

Figure 3.3 Gainers and losers

self-sufficient, neither importing nor exporting. Its production point is therefore on the consumption line, at point $C_S = Q_S$.[3] Country G has the same tariffs, but its more extreme comparative advantage means that it has some trade in the initial situation, and will export good M and import good A. Its equilibrium production is at Q_G and consumption is at C_G. Since it imports good A the domestic price ratio is $p_w + t$, at which Q_G is profit maximizing. The budget constraint holds at world prices, p_w, so country G's trade vector is $Q_G C_G$.

What happens if these two countries form a customs union? Both G and S now have the same internal prices, and we suppose that in the new situation the CU as a whole continues to import A from the rest of the world, so the internal price ratio in each country is $p_w + t$. Production then occurs at points Q_S^* and Q_G. The trade of each of the countries is as follows. Country S has a comparative advantage in good A relative to country G, so trades vector $Q_S^* C_S^*$ with country G, at internal price ratio $p_w + t$. Correspondingly, country G has internal trade vector $Q_G E = Q_S^* C_S^*$. It also has external trade vector $E C_G^*$, this being imports of good A in return for exports of good M, and this trade is conducted at world price p_w, this giving the slope of the line.

The welfare effects of the CU are given by comparison of consumption points. Country S gains from the union as C_S^* is above C_S; it now has some gains from trade, where previously it had none. Notice that this arises despite the fact that country S's production structure has moved in the opposite direction from the way it would go under free trade (moving from producing at Q_S to Q_S^* rather than to F_S). In contrast, country G loses, going from C_G to C_G^*. The reason is trade diversion: it was obtaining all its imports of good A from the rest of the world, and is now obtaining some of them from its higher-cost partner. This shows how the imports of country G (the country with 'extreme' comparative advantage) are diverted to a partner country with comparative advantage between it and the rest of the world. However, for country S (with 'intermediate' comparative advantage), trade with the partner and with the rest of the world are less close substitutes, and therefore less vulnerable to trade diversion.

This diagrammatic analysis provides a rigorous argument, and one that can be generalized, although we pursue it no further here. The point is that patterns of trade creation and diversion can be systematically linked to the comparative advantage of countries relative to each other and relative to the world as a whole. There is a general message here. The country with the 'extreme' comparative advantage (Germany in this example) will experience trade diversion, while the country with the 'intermediate' comparative advantage (Spain) will experience trade creation. Notice that in a PTA between high-income countries, such as the EU, this is a force for convergence of incomes—the richer country is more prone to trade diversion. However, in PTAs between low-income countries the country with the 'extreme' endowment is typically the poorer, so PTA membership leads to the cost of trade diversion being borne by the poorer country. An example is provided by economic integration in East Africa. Kenya, which has a comparative advantage in manufactures relative to Uganda but not relative to the world as a whole, will import agricultural goods from Uganda, in line with Uganda's global comparative advantage. But Uganda will experience trade diversion as it comes to import manufactures from Kenya, rather than importing them from lower-cost countries outside their PTA.

Empirical studies

Do we know whether, in practice, there has been relatively much trade creation or trade diversion in the EU? How might a researcher go about establishing the answer to that question? The problem is a difficult one, because the actual situation (with the CU in place) has to be compared with a counter-factual situation—what would have happened in the absence of the CU. There are two broad ways in which the researcher can construct this counter-factual, neither of which turns out to be very satisfactory in practice.

The first way is by computable general equilibrium modelling. This involves constructing a model of the economies involved, similar to that of the previous section. However, use of the computer means that it can have many more sectors and countries, and that the model can be calibrated to actual country data. The modeller can then undertake experiments, numerically simulating the effects of changing tariffs. Thus, the counter-factual can be constructed by seeing what happens in the model if trade barriers are put back to their initial level. Such models usually show that the gains from trade creation outweigh the costs of trade diversion, although the net benefits are often small—just a fraction of 1 per cent of GDP (see Baldwin and Venables 1997 for a survey of such studies).

The second approach is to use trends in the data to predict what trade flows would have been if the trends had continued without the 'shock' of the CU. This involves using econometric techniques to estimate import equations, typically including a dummy variable which switches on when the CU is formed. The magnitude of this dummy variable measures the shift in the equation that can be attributed to the CU. A number of authors used this approach to assess the effects of the UK joining the EU (see Winters 1987). The consensus finding is that the EU increased members' imports from one another more than it decreased imports from non-members, suggesting that trade creation exceeded trade diversion. Where authors tried to calculate the real income effects associated with these changes, the gains were typically positive but extremely small.

While in practice the two techniques—computable equilibrium models and econometric studies—are quite distinct, we should note that they are both attempts to get as close as possible to an 'ideal' evaluation. Such an evaluation would have all the microeconomic detail of the computable equilibrium models—many sectors and rigorously specified consumer and producer behaviour. It would also use data and econometric techniques to estimate all the parameters of the model—the positions, slope, and curvatures of all the supply and demand curves. In practice this approach is not feasible; there simply is not enough data to obtain good estimates of all the parameters. The approach of computable equilibrium models is to keep the microeconomic detail, but often work with quite poor 'guesstimates' of some of the parameters. The econometric approach uses the data to obtain some of the key parameters, but does not have the microeconomic detail to assess the full general equilibrium effects of the policy change.

Two other remarks are needed concerning these empirical studies. First, it may be possible to have the best of both worlds if the researcher looks at just one sector at a time. It is possible to build a detailed microeconomic model of a single sector and use econometrics to estimate the parameters of the model. The disadvantage of this way of proceeding is, of course, that effects in other sectors—and the general equilibrium interactions between sectors—are ignored. Second, we have seen that the empirical studies typically indicate very small net benefits. The small size of the effects suggests that a number of key economic mechanisms are left out of the traditional trade creation and trade diversion approach. The remainder of this chapter will look at some of these further mechanisms.

3.2 Firms, market structure, and industrial location

The analysis of the preceding section is the classic theory of PTAs, constructed under the assumptions of perfect competition and constant returns to scale, and with trade driven by comparative advantage differences between sectors and countries. However, it became apparent that this approach gives only part of the story of European integration. Much of the growth of trade in the EU took the form of intra-industry trade, such as two-way trade in motor vehicles between countries with quite similar comparative advantages (see Box 3.1). Furthermore, many sectors of the economy are dominated by relatively few large firms that are not operating under conditions of perfect competition. To analyse such trade we need, in addition to the tools of traditional trade theory, a theory of open economy industrial organization, a theory that entered international economics in the 1970s and 1980s, and which we now outline.

Competition and economies of scale

What determines the number of firms in an industry, how much they trade, and where they operate? The benchmark model for addressing these questions is a multicountry

---

BOX 3.1 INTER- AND INTRA-INDUSTRY TRADE

Under the standard assumptions of perfect competition, trade is driven by comparative advantage. There is inter-industry trade, as each country will export output from those industries in which it has a comparative advantage, and will import output from industries in which it has a comparative disadvantage.

Intra-industry trade occurs when the output of a particular industry is both imported and exported by a country. From economic theory, we know that there are two ways to explain intra-industry trade. One is that oligopolistic firms located in different countries all seek to sell in each other's markets—this is just the theory of oligopoly extended to an international setting. The other is that there is product differentiation—e.g. the output of the car industry is highly differentiated, with different varieties of cars. Usually both effects are present, and theory has typically built on both these ingredients to model intra-industry trade.

Intra-industry trade is often measured by the Grubel–Lloyd index, which takes the form

$$GL_i = \frac{(X_i + M_i) - |X_i - M_i|}{(X_i + M_i)}$$

where X_i and M_i are a particular country's exports and imports in industry i (and the vertical straight lines say take the absolute value of the term inside). If either exports or imports are zero, then the index takes value zero. At the other extreme, if $X_i = M_i$ then the index takes value 1; net exports are zero, so all trade is intra-industry.

The index is computed industry by industry, and its value will depend on whether finely disaggregated industries are used, or broad industrial sectors. Measures calculated for each industry can be combined to give an average for the country as a whole, and for the trade of an entire region.

---

extension of the theory of monopolistic competition. We start by reviewing the basic theory, and then discuss how it has been used to assess the effects of trade opening and regional integration.

The theory of monopolistic competition focuses on a single industry, in which there is an endogenously determined number of firms. Each firm operates under increasing returns to scale (i.e. diminishing average costs), implying that marginal cost is below average cost. Each firm also has some degree of market power, so sets its price at a mark-up over marginal cost. The theory shows us how to determine the equilibrium price and output of each firm, and also determines the number of firms in the industry, giving the full industry equilibrium.

The benchmark model is illustrated in Figure 3.4. This figure describes a single firm, so the horizontal axis is its output and the vertical gives unit valuations. Increasing returns are captured in the shape of the cost curves; for simplicity the marginal cost (MC) curve is drawn flat, but the presence of a fixed set-up cost for the firm means that average costs (AC) are declining with volume produced.

The demand curve for the firm's output is drawn downward sloping, and illustrated by the average revenue (AR) curve on the figure. This is downward sloping for two reasons. First, there may be product differentiation, such that each firm is a monopolist over its

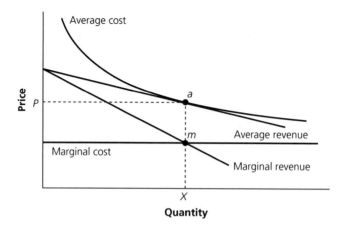

Figure 3.4 Monopolistic competition

own variety of good; selling more units causes the price to fall. Second, each firm is large enough for variations in its output to have a significant effect on the total output produced by the industry, in which case the industry average price falls as output increases. It is important to note that the position of this demand curve for the output of a single firm depends on the total output of all firms in the industry. If other firms all expand (or new firms enter the industry) price will fall, causing the average revenue curve to shift downwards.

Below the average revenue curve lies the marginal revenue (MR) curve, derived in the usual way, that is, equal to price (AR) plus the quantity sold times the change in price associated with selling an additional unit of output. The greater the gap between the marginal revenue and average revenue curve, the steeper is the average revenue curve (since a steeper AR curve means greater price fall when supply is increased). Of course, in the case of perfect competition the two lines collapse into a single horizontal line—the price-taking firm.

Assuming that all firms in the industry are similar, the figure can be used to illustrate the firm *and* industry equilibrium. Equilibrium of each firm is found by noting that a firm maximizes profits by producing where marginal revenue equals marginal cost, and this is the intersection *m* on the figure. The level of profits made by the firm can be checked by comparing average revenue and average cost at that output level; if AR > AC then the firm will be making positive profits, and vice versa. Equilibrium of the industry is found by supposing that new firms enter the industry if profits are positive, or exit if profits are negative, so that in equilibrium the profits of the representative firm are (approximately) zero. In terms of the figure, entry and exit shifts the revenue curves faced by each single representative firm until, at industry equilibrium, average revenue equals average cost at the profit maximizing output level. This is exactly the configuration illustrated on Figure 3.4 in which, at output level *X*, we have both profit maximizing behaviour by the firm (MR = MC) and also zero profits (AR = AC). Of course, the figure does not tell us the number of firms operating in the industry, but since we know the output of each, the price, and the industry demand curve, we have all the information needed to calculate this number.

How is international trade and economic integration added to this standard model of monopolistic competition? The simplest way is to suppose that there are two identical economies, and that initially there is no trade at all between them. What happens if they are allowed to trade? Firms in each country will then export to the other country, this creating intra-industry trade. However, as they do this, so each market becomes more competitive—each market is being supplied by twice as many firms. The effect of this is to flatten the average revenue curve, and therefore also raise the marginal revenue curve and squeeze firms' price–marginal cost margins. This will tend to reduce firms' profits, hence reducing the number of firms operating in the industry, and causing remaining firms to become larger. At the new equilibrium these larger firms have lower average cost—a direct consequence of increasing returns to scale—and prices are lower.

This argument is one of those pieces of analysis where intuition is very simple, but precise analysis requires some maths. To see the intuition, suppose that in the initial situation with no trade each country had three firms in the industry, and that once trade is allowed each just has two. This means that markets are more competitive with trade (each supplied by four firms not three) *and* firms are bigger (four firms in total not six). Prices are lower both because the increase in competition means prices are closer to marginal cost, and because bigger firms have lower average costs. The mathematics is worked out, for a simple case, in Box 3.2.

Notice that the monopolistic competition story generates two distinct sources of real income gain from economic integration, on top of the comparative advantage mechanisms we discussed in section 3.1. First, trade allows firms to reap more of the benefits of increasing returns to scale, this giving them lower average cost. This is a pure efficiency gain; in the data it would show up as an increase in productivity. Second, the fact that each market comes to be supplied by more firms means that, if there is product differentiation, then consumers are benefiting from a wider range of products. The magnitude of this gain is difficult to quantify, but few of us would doubt that new imported varieties of goods have increased consumer choice and welfare.

Two further points need to be made on this approach. The first is that, in practice, working with the notion of a 'representative firm' is quite a poor description of reality. Firms are heterogeneous and have quite widely different efficiency and cost levels. When economies are brought together to trade it tends to be the inefficient firms that are driven out and the efficient ones that remain, often growing by acquiring and making better use of the assets of the less efficient firms. This effect provides an additional boost to the gains from integration.

The second point is to recognize the role of multinational firms in the processes we have been describing. If the number of independent firms operating in a sector falls it might very well be not because of bankruptcy but instead because of merger or takeover, and where this occurs across a border it leads to the creation of a multinational firm. While the qualitative effects are broadly similar to those we have already outlined, the evidence suggests that cross-border merger and acquisition activity has been a very large part of the integration story.

BOX 3.2 INDUSTRIAL CONCENTRATION, FIRM SCALE, AND MARKET INTEGRATION

The effect of market size on competition and firm scale can be derived using a simple model of mono-polistic competition. Consider an industry in which demand is given by the (inverse) demand curve

$$p = a - \sum_{i=1}^{n} x_i / b.$$

The market is supplied by n firms, and the output of the ith firm is x_i, so the summation gives total supply. Price is denoted p, and the parameter a gives the intercept of the demand curve with the vertical axis (the price if there are zero sales). The parameter b gives the size of the market (since if both total supply and b double, then price is unchanged).

A particular firm, say firm j, has profits, π_j, given by

(1) $$\pi_j = x_j(p - c) - F = x_j\left(a - c - \sum_{i=1}^{n} x_i / b\right) - F.$$

This expression is revenue minus costs, where costs have two elements. Marginal production cost is constant at c, and there are fixed costs F. The second equation in (1) substitutes in the demand curve. Each firm chooses its output level to maximize profits, given the output level of other firms. The first order condition for profit maximization is

(2) $$\frac{d\pi_j}{dx_j} = \left(a - c - \sum_{i=1}^{n} x_i / b\right) - x_j / b = 0.$$

To do this differentiation notice that x_j enters (2) twice: outside the brackets, and also as one element of the industry output, in the summation sign. This first order condition is the equality of MR to MC, as can be seen by moving c to the other side of the equation.

We assume that all firms have the same costs and face the same demand so, in equilibrium, all have the same level of output. We can therefore write $x = x_i$ for all firms, and total output is $\sum_{i=1}^{n} x_i = nx$. The first order condition MR = MC (equation 2) can be rearranged to give output of each firm

(3) $$x = b(a - c)/(n + 1).$$

This gives point m on Figure 3.4.

To move from equilibrium of each firm to equilibrium of the industry, we have to see whether firms are making profit or loss, and then determine the value of n—number of firms—that just gives break-even. Using (3) in (1) profits of a representative firm are

(4) $$\pi = b\left(\frac{a - c}{n + 1}\right)^2 - F.$$

There now comes a small sleight of hand. To make algebra easy we pretend that fractional firms may exist and that entry and exit occurs until profits are exactly equal to zero. Setting the expression in (4) equal to zero the number of firms is therefore,

(5) $$n = (a - c)\sqrt{b/F} - 1.$$

Using (5) and (3) total sales are

(6) $$nx = b\left[(a - c) - \sqrt{F/b}\right]$$

continues

BOX 3.2 continued

and hence price is

(7)
$$p = a - nx/b = c + \sqrt{F/b}$$

What do we learn from this? Recall that b is the size of the market, and we can think of trade between two similar economies as being like a doubling of market size. We see that this gives a less than doubling in the number of firms (since n increases with the square root of b, equation 5). Total sales more than double (equation 6 has b both inside and outside the square bracket), meaning that remaining firms have increased in size. Most importantly, equation 7 shows us that the price falls. Price is equal to average production cost, so this says that there is a real efficiency gain as remaining firms have become larger and moved down their average cost curves.

Empirical studies: the Single Market Programme

Empirical application of trade and monopolistic competition models to the EU experience first took place in the late 1980s and early 1990s in response to the Single Market Initiative. In this section we outline what this initiative was, and discuss some of the studies that were undertaken.

By the 1980s it had become clear that, in some sectors at least, achieving truly integrated markets was quite difficult. Even though tariffs had been eliminated decades before, markets remained segmented, with substantial price differentials between countries, and borders still having a strongly negative effect on trade flows. What could be done to make the EU market more like that of the USA—a continent-wide integrated market rather than a set of separate and segmented national markets?

The Single Market Initiative (SMI) was launched in 1986 for completion in 1992, with the objective of eliminating market segmentation and 'completing the internal market'. The economic policy measures introduced fall into four main categories: (1) the simplification or removal of frontier formalities, facilitating and speeding the flow of goods across borders; (2) the simplification of product standards, in particular the adoption of the 'mutual recognition principle', whereby goods approved for sale in any Member State are deemed acceptable in all; (3) the deregulation of transport sectors, allowing for improved efficiency in the internal distribution of goods; and (4) the opening up of public procurement to supply from all Member States. Measures of this type are sometimes referred to as 'deep integration', since they go well beyond the simple elimination of tariffs.

Although individually small, these measures were estimated collectively to reduce the costs of trade across borders by an amount equal to several per cent of the value of goods traded. More importantly, their indirect effects were predicted to lead to gains equivalent to several per cent of EU GDP, as markets became more competitive *and* firms reorganized, increasing their scale to that of the larger integrated market. These predictions were based on exactly the sorts of arguments that we saw in the preceding subsection, but derived from models that were calibrated to particular industrial sectors (see Smith and Venables 1988).

Is there any evidence, *ex post*, on what actually happened? Evidence on actual gains is patchy. The SMI was accompanied by a burst of merger activity, and there is some evidence of further trade creation (Pelkmans 2001). Griffith (2001) in a study of UK manufacturing finds a significant increase in both labour productivity and total factor productivity in establishments in sectors that were particularly affected by the SMI. Increased scales of operation have been attributed to the SMI, particularly in sectors where liberalization of public procurement was important, although the size of firms in the EU remains generally smaller than their US counterparts.

Of course, the Single Market Initiative left countries with different national currencies, until monetary union was introduced for twelve core (Eurozone) currencies in 2002. Part of the motivation for this initiative was to promote price transparency and achieve further market integration, although most of the analysis has surrounded its macroeconomic impact. And, despite the success of the Single Market Initiative, it still has not reached all—or even many of the largest—areas of economic activity. Opening up of service sectors to competition was one of the objectives of the Single Market Initiative, imposing on Member States the obligation to abolish restrictions on the free movement of services and extend mutual recognition to professional qualifications. However, progress remains slow, with differing legal standards and regulatory regimes still impeding cross-border investments and competition. This remains an area where the European Commission is still performing its role of trying to secure further market integration, while encountering stiff opposition from a number of Member States.

Foreign direct investment

In the preceding discussion of theory (section 3.1) we noted that industrial reorganization might involve an increasing number of firms becoming multinational—that is, operating in several countries by means of undertaking direct investment (FDI). This has turned out to be the case. In the world as a whole stocks of FDI have increased faster than both income and trade, and the EU-15 holds around one-third of the stock of inwards FDI. This share surged to more than 40 per cent at the time of the Single Market Initiative, driven by a cross-border merger wave. The importance of FDI for EU economies is vividly illustrated by the fact that 47 per cent of Irish manufacturing employment is in foreign-owned firms, and the foreign-owned share is substantial even in the larger EU countries (France 26 per cent, UK 16 per cent).

Much of the growth of FDI within the EU has been intra-EU investments, which accounts for a majority of the total. Investments from outside the region have also been important as economic integration has allowed outside firms to supply the entire European market from a single EU plant. Indeed, for many suppliers FDI is a much more important means of reaching the European market than is foreign trade. For manufacturing as a whole, sales of goods by US subsidiaries in the EU were, in 1998, 3.75 times larger than EU manufacturing imports from the USA. There is also considerable evidence that some of the inwards Japanese investments of the 1980s were driven largely by EU tariff and non-tariff barriers. These investments are perceived to have important positive effects. Productivity is generally higher in firms that are multinational than in firms that supply only the domestic market (see Barba Navaretti and Venables 2004). Particular importance attaches to FDI in services, since this may be the only means through which foreign competition can enter the domestic market.

Acquired comparative advantage: clustering and external economies of scale

In subsections 3.1–3.3 we saw that reducing trade barriers might trigger industrial reorganization, but we have not asked *where* firms in a particular industry locate following market integration. Are they divided across countries, or do they tend to cluster in a particular country, region, or city? How does economic integration effect the pattern of industrial location?

Empirical motivation for this question was given by from Krugman (1991a) who drew the comparison between the four large US regions (north-east, mid-west, south and west) and the four largest countries in the EU. He showed that the industrial structures of the US regions were considerably more dissimilar from each other than were those of EU countries from each other, and corresponding to this, particular industries in the USA were more spatially concentrated. Table 3.1, drawn from Krugman (1991a), illustrates this for the car industry, showing how the industry was spatially concentrated in the USA, but much more dispersed in Europe.

The same effects can be seen at a more disaggregated spatial and industrial scale. While it is difficult to make precise comparisons because of the inherently different sizes and geographies of the USA and the EU, a somewhat finer comparison can be made by calculating a measure of the spatial concentration of each industry and comparing it with the spatial concentration of industry as a whole. Braunerhjelm *et al.* (2000) compute such measures for eight broad sectors in the USA and the EU. In six of the eight sectors production is more spatially concentrated in the USA than the EU, and the difference does not appear to be declining significantly through time.

How do we explain the location of firms and sectors across countries, and the effect of integration on this location? Part of the explanation lies in comparative advantage—countries specialize in producing and exporting goods from those sectors in which their relative costs are lowest. While this statement is generally true, it is also somewhat incomplete. What determines relative costs? In some sectors we can point to endowments

Table 3.1 Distribution of car manufacturing in large EU countries compared with large US regions, 1990 (per cent)

USA		Europe	
Mid-west	66	Germany	39
South	25	France	31
West	5	Italy	18
North-east	3	England	13
Total	100	Total	100

Source: Krugman (1991a).

of particular types of land, natural resources, climate, or labour skills. In other sectors it is less easy. Why does London specialize in financial services, or Hollywood in movies? It is surely not because of an exogenously determined comparative advantage (e.g. land or climate), but instead because of an *acquired* comparative advantage. The source of this acquired comparative advantage might be simply that it is profitable for firms to cluster together, locating close to other firms in the same industry. In this case there is no intrinsic reason for London to have a comparative advantage in financial services, but once a large number of financial service firms are located there, others choose to locate there also. Integration facilitates this clustering, as it makes it easier to supply the whole market from one or a few locations.

What are the forces that drive this clustering of activity? It arises essentially because of increasing returns that are external to a single firm, and operate within a spatially concentrated industry. These external effects are typically grouped into three categories. The first is knowledge spillovers between firms, as firms in a cluster are able to learn about and imitate the practices of other firms in the industry. Silicon Valley provides an example where knowledge exchange—formal and informal—is quite widespread. The knowledge may be about production methods, marketing skills, or simply knowledge about the location itself. Thus, multinational firms tend to cluster in particular locations, partly because one firm, observing the success (or failure) of another, learns about the quality of the business environment in the location. Hausman and Rodrik (2002) argue that very narrow patterns of specialization in developing countries (for example, a particular town in Pakistan specializing in most of the world's soccer ball production) arise as producers learn about the efficiency of a particular location for producing a particular good.

A second sort of mechanism driving clustering is what are known as 'thick market' effects. For example, in the labour market an industrial cluster brings together workers with industry-specific skills and the firms that use these skills. The matching of workers to firms will be better the larger ('thicker') is the market. Furthermore, incentives to acquire specialist skills are greater if the skills are sought by several firms, so the worker is less likely to be subject to the monopsony power of a single employer.

The third mechanism is linkages between firms at different stages in the vertical production process. Suppliers of specialist intermediate inputs will seek to locate close to the firms that use these inputs. And the firms that use these inputs will benefit from locating close to the intermediate suppliers. This 'positive feedback' between the location decisions of different firms is once again a force for clustering. Suppliers of specialist financial services will locate in the City of London because of the presence of large banks using these services, and the large banks using the services will locate in the City because of the presence of specialist firms and—as in the previous paragraph—the large pool of specialist labour.

These are all clustering forces pulling firms in an industry—or group of related industries —into the same location. But pushing in the opposite direction are dispersion forces. These include congestion costs or high land and house prices associated with urban centres. And they also include the fact that final consumers are likely to be dispersed across different regions and countries. There are costs of shipping goods and services across space and between countries, so it may not be efficient to supply all of Europe's financial services from London or all of its cars from Germany. This is where integration comes in. When trade barriers between countries are high we would expect to see clusters form within countries, but not on an EU-wide level—thus each EU country had its car industry, steel industry, financial services, etc. Economic integration reduces barriers to trade, thereby facilitating clusters at the EU- rather than at the national-level. This can account for the different economic geographies of the USA and the EU that we observed above—the USA has a much longer history of operating as an integrated market than does the EU.

What predictions does this approach offer for the effects of integration? First, integration may trigger a process of spatial concentration of some EU industries. Second, when this occurs it will be a further source of real income benefits. On top of the sources of gain we have already seen—trade creation and firm-level economies of scale—there are also these external economies, and the associated efficiency benefits from clustering firms. However, it should be noted that there may be quite large adjustment costs associated with this process—many countries will cease to have a presence in a number of industries.

Is there any empirical evidence that this process has in fact been occurring in the EU? We can address this by computing a measure of how different each EU country's industrial structure is from that of the rest of the EU, and tracing the evolution of this measure through time.[4] To construct the measure of specialization we calculate the share of industry k in country i's total manufacturing output (gross production value for each industry $x_i^k(t)$) and call this variable $v_i^k(t)$. Corresponding to this, we calculate the share of the same industry in the production of all other EU countries, denoted $\bar{v}_i^k(t)$. We can then measure the difference between the industrial structure of country i and all other countries by taking the absolute values of the difference between these shares, summed over all industries,

$$K_i(t) = \sum_k abs(v_i^k(t) - \bar{v}_i^k(t)),$$

$$\text{where } v_i^k(t) = x_i^k(t)/\sum_k x_i^k(t), \quad \bar{v}_i^k(t) = \sum_{j \neq i} x_i^k(t)/\sum_k \sum_{j \neq i} x_i^k(t)$$

This is sometimes known as the Krugman specialization index (see Krugman 1991a), and it takes value zero if country i has an industrial structure identical to the rest of the EU, and takes maximum value two if it has no industries in common with the rest of the EU.

Values of these indices for each country are given in Table 3.2, computed for each of the fourteen countries reported. They are calculated for four-year averages at the dates indicated, with bold indicating the minimum value attained by each country. The table reports them for each country and, in the bottom row, the average for all the fourteen EU countries.

Looking first at the averages, we see a fall between 1970/3 and 1980/3, indicating that locations became more similar. But from 1980/3 onwards there has been a more or less steady increase, indicating divergence. Turning to individual countries, we see that from 1970/3 to 1980/3 seven out of fourteen countries became less specialized, while between 1980/3 and 1998/2001, all countries except the Netherlands experienced an increase in specialization. That is, they became increasingly different from the rest of the EU. What this indicates, then, is that the economic geography of the EU is reorganizing, perhaps to become more like that of the USA, although the process is slow.

Table 3.2 Krugman specialization index (production data, four-year averages, twenty-six industries), 1970–2001

	1970–3	1980–3	1988–91	1994–7	1998–2001
Austria	0.277	**0.252**	0.271	0.309	0.351
Belgium	**0.263**	0.296	0.318	0.383	0.437
Germany	0.304	**0.294**	0.345	0.352	0.375
Denmark	**0.523**	0.550	0.579	0.569	0.575
Spain	0.386	**0.266**	0.291	0.314	0.299
Finland	0.557	**0.471**	0.511	0.596	0.687
France	**0.122**	0.123	0.156	0.159	0.175
UK	0.195	**0.169**	0.190	0.180	0.227
Greece	**0.512**	0.557	0.626	0.709	0.744
Ireland	**0.679**	0.708	0.767	0.849	0.957
Italy	**0.333**	0.361	0.360	0.429	0.481
Netherlands	**0.479**	0.543	0.536	0.512	0.511
Portugal	0.524	**0.451**	0.559	0.557	0.608
Sweden	0.396	**0.389**	0.401	0.491	0.509
Average	0.396	**0.388**	0.422	0.458	0.495

Note: Bold indicates minimum value attained by each country.

3.3 Trade and income differentials

The mechanisms that we have described in preceding sections indicate that there are gains from integration, but how are these gains distributed across countries? Are regional integration and the associated growth of trade a force for convergence or divergence of incomes between regions of the EU? One of the most striking empirical regularities of the EU is the way in which per capita incomes fall with distance from the centre of the EU—a 'wage gradient' which means that there is a statistically significant negative relationship between distance from the centre of the EU (for example, Luxembourg) and per capita income. Here we simply discuss the impact of trade and market integration on these income differentials. Our analysis will turn on the interaction between two forces. On the one hand, production should relocate towards countries with low factor prices, and this will be a force for equalizing factor prices. On the other, firms will want to locate close to large markets—the centre of the EU—and this can be a force for maintaining wide factor price differences between countries.

Factor price equalization (FPE)

The point of departure for analysis of the effects of trade on differences in real incomes is the 'factor price equalization theorem' of international trade theory. This states that if all countries have the same efficiency levels, all industries are perfectly competitive and operate under constant returns to scale, and trade is perfectly free, then trade in goods should lead to equalization of factor prices. The logic can be seen most readily by noting that in a perfectly competitive constant returns to scale industry price equals average cost. So, if the price of good k in country i is p_i^k, then

$$p_i^k = c_i^k(w_i^1, w_i^2, w_i^3 \dots)$$

where the right-hand side is average cost function, the arguments of which are the country i prices of each input to production, so w_i^1 is the price of factor number 1 in country i, etc. Equations like this hold for each industry (k) that is operating in each country (i). Given values of the output prices, p_i^k, the equations can be solved for the factor prices w_i^j, that is, we can find the factor prices that are consistent with just breaking even in each industry. And if the goods prices are the same in all countries (free trade) and the technologies are the same in all countries (average cost functions are not country specific), then the factor prices that solve these equations will be the same in all countries—factor price equalization. Intuitively the argument is extremely simple. Production will move to a location where factors are cheap, bidding up their prices until, in equilibrium, factor prices are the same everywhere.

The logic of factor price equalization implies that economic integration will tend to bring convergence of factor prices within the EU, yet significant wage differences persist. One reason is that trade frictions—transport costs as well as man-made trade barriers—remain important, and these frictions can give 'central' areas a major advantage over 'peripheral' regions in an integrated economic area.

Centre and periphery

Even within an integrated market, transport and logistical costs remain important barriers to trade. Because of these costs a firm located in Paris or London can access more consumers more cheaply than can a firm in Lisbon. It may also be able to obtain the intermediate goods that it uses in its production more cheaply. These effects can be summarized by looking at the 'market access' of different regions, typically measured by the sum of income in the region and neighbouring regions, weighted by an inverse measure of distance. Given what we know about how fast trade volumes fall off with distance, researchers sometimes use the reciprocal of distance, so the market access of region i is $MA_i = \sum_j Y_j/d_{ij}$ where Y_j is income and d_{ij} is distance from region i to region j. Thus, Paris and London have good market access, while market access in Lisbon is much lower, because the distance terms in the denominator, d_{ij}, are on average much larger.

Market access is quite a powerful force shaping the location decisions of firms, and firms in a location with good market access would, other things being equal, be more profitable than firms in a location with poor market access. (This statement is not quite as obvious as it sounds, because profitability also depends on the number of competitor firms in the location, and an arithmetical example illustrating the basic point is given in Box 3.3.) We can immediately see how a centre–periphery wage gradient can arise. As firms move to locations with good market access so wages in these locations will be bid up, creating the wage gradient that is observed in the data. The centre–periphery wage gap tends to equalize profits everywhere, offsetting the advantages of central locations for firms. But this wage gap also has the effect of making central locations more attractive for workers, suggesting that there may be migration from peripheral regions to central ones. This may create a strongly destabilizing force, as a process of cumulative causation is operating. A location with good market access will be profitable, attracting firms, bidding up wages, which in turn attract inwards migration which further increases the market access of the location. This is a 'positive feedback' which amplifies the differences between locations. It is the destabilizing force that was analysed in Krugman's (1991b) celebrated

BOX 3.3 THE LARGE MARKET EFFECT

Consider the following thought experiment. Suppose that there are two countries, each with the same costs, but with different market sizes. For simplicity, fix the total sales in country 1 at 100 and total sales in country 2 at 200. Suppose furthermore that country 1 has just one firm and country 2 has two. The triples (a: b, b) in the body of Table 3.3 give the sales of each of these three firms, the first element being sales of the country 1 firm, and the second and third the sales of each of the country 2 firms. Columns of the table give firms' sales in markets 1, 2, and, in the final column, each firm's total sales.

The first row of the table is autarky, so the country 1 firm is the only firm supplying country 1, while the country 2 firms divide the larger country 2 market between them. Obviously, each firm ends up with sales of 100. The final row is completely free trade. Each firm then takes one-third of each market, giving sales are as described, and again meaning that each firm's total sales are 100. The middle row is constructed for an intermediate level of trade barriers. The level is set such that each firm does exactly twice as well in its home market as does a foreign competitor. Thus, in column 1, we see that sales in the country 1 market are divided (50: 25, 25) between the domestic firm and each of the foreign firms. In the country 2 market, sales are (40: 80, 80). Adding these, the right-hand column indicates that the country 1 firm—i.e. the firm located in the small market—has lower total sales than do the firms located in the large market, only selling 90 as compared with 105.

Table 3.3 Firms' sales as trade costs change

	Sales of each firm in country 1 (market size = 100)	Sales of each firm in country 2 (market size = 200)	Total sales of each firm (market 1 + market 2)
Autarky	(100: 0, 0)	(0: 100, 100)	(100: 100, 100)
Intermediate	(50: 25, 25)	(40: 80, 80)	(90: 105, 105)
Free trade	(33: 33, 33)	(67: 67, 67)	(100: 100, 100)

This numerical example makes the simple, but rather general point that firms in small economies are particularly disadvantaged at intermediate levels of trade barriers. Since the disadvantage is at intermediate trade costs, it means that in the early stages of integration firms in the small market lose out, with declining sales (100 to 90) and profits. But in the later stages of integration it is firms in the large market that suffer (sales falling from 105 to 100).

The intuition is that there are two opposing forces at work as transport costs fall. On the one hand, firms in the small economy are more dependent on foreign trade than are firms in the large economy, so gain relatively much from trade liberalization. But on the other hand, there are more firms in the large economy than in the small, and each of these firms starts selling into the small market as trade costs come down. In the early stages of liberalization the latter effect dominates (since initial trade volumes are zero), and firms in the small economy lose out to imports. In the latter stages this is reversed, and the benefits of being able to sell into the large market become relatively more important. This emerges as a matter of arithmetic in this example, but is a property of a much wider range of models (see Krugman and Venables 1990).

'core–periphery' model, and which can (under extreme assumptions) lead to concentration of all manufacturing activity in a central location at the expense of the periphery.

Outsourcing, relocation, and wage gradients

The previous subsection noted the possible 'centripetal' forces that can be unleashed by economic integration, drawing both labour and firms into central locations. However, as was noted in Box 3.3, the forces driving this are greatest at 'intermediate' levels of trade costs, and as trade costs become extremely low, so we expect 'factor price equalization' forces to dominate. A further force that is pushing in the direction of factor price equalization is the increasing ease with which firms can outsource part of their activities.

Outsourcing occurs when a firm in one location—let us think of it as a central location within the EU, such as France or Germany—chooses to have some parts of its production process take place in another lower-cost country, say in the Czech Republic. This may be the supply of components, the provision of services (e.g. telephone call centres), or final assembly of the product. The phenomenon has gained increasing importance in intra-EU trade, with the membership of relatively low wage East European economies, and has been extremely important in Asia where international production networks have sprung up.

Analytically, such trade can be thought of using the tools of standard trade theory: labour-abundant economies will attract the labour-intensive parts of the production process, and as this happens, so there will be a tendency towards factor price equalization. However, we should not expect it to lead all the way to factor price equalization. Outsourcing is quite 'transport intensive', as goods may cross borders many times—first as a component part, then embodied in a partially finished goods, then finally in the assembled product, and so on. This means that even quite small transport costs may be consistent with continuing factor price differences and centre–periphery wage gradients.

3.4 Conclusions

Economic integration brings about a reallocation of resources within the economy. Sectors expand or contract in line with (intra-Union) comparative advantage, and in response to clustering and market access forces. There is also reallocation of resources within sectors: integration increases competitive pressure on firms, this leading to changes in the number, size, and type of firms operating. And across countries and regions, there will be forces changing factor prices and income differentials.

The classical theory of trade leads us to expect gains from integration, although the possibility of trade diversion qualifies these benefits. Reallocation of resources between firms within sectors is likely to be a further source of major efficiency gains, since a large integrated market can deliver both more competition and more economies of scale than can separate small segmented markets. However, looking across countries and regions, it is possible that gains may be unequally distributed. The experience of the EU is that there has been significant convergence of income between countries, but with some major regional disparities remaining.

▦ NOTES

1. We could have added indifference curves to the diagram, but to keep it (relatively) simple we make the assumption that the two goods are consumed in fixed proportions.
2. p_w is the world price of A divided by the world price of M, so is the slope of the iso-revenue line illustrated.
3. The internal price ratio in S is given by the gradient of its production possibility frontier at this point, which is steeper than p_w and flatter than $p_w + t$, consistent with there being no trade.
4. This section updates findings reported in Midelfart et al. (2002).

▦ REFERENCES

Baldwin, R. E. and Venables, A. J. (1997), 'International Economic Integration', in G. Grossman and K. Rogoff (eds.), *Handbook of International Economics, vol. III* (Amsterdam: North Holland).

Barba Navaretti, G. and Venables, A. J. (2004), *Multinational Firms in the World Economy* (Princeton: Princeton University Press).

Braunerhjelm, P., Faini, R., Norman, V. D., Ruane, F., and Seabright, P. (2000), 'Integration and the Regions of Europe: How the Right Policies Can Prevent Polarization, Monitoring European Integration 10', Centre for Economic Policy Research.

Flam, H. (1992), 'Product Markets and 1992: Full Integration, Large Gains', *Journal of Economic Perspectives*, 6: 7–30.

Fujita, M., Krugman, P., and Venables, A. J. (1999), *The Spatial Economy: Cities, Regions and International Trade* (Cambridge, MA: MIT Press).

Griffith, R. (2001), 'Product Market Competition, Efficiency and Agency Costs: An Empirical Analysis', IFS Working Paper No. 01/02 (London: Institute for Fiscal Studies).

Hausman, R. and Rodrik, D. (2002), 'Economic Development as Self-Discovery', NBER Working Paper No. 8952 (Cambridge, MA: National Bureau of Economic Research).

Krugman, P. (1991a), *Geography and Trade*, Gaston Eyskens Lecture Series (Cambridge, MA and London: MIT Press; Louvain, Belgium: Louvain University Press).

—— (1991b), 'Increasing returns and economic geography', *Journal of Political Economy*, 99: 483–99.

—— and Venables, A. J. (1990), 'Integration and the Competitiveness of Peripheral Industries', in C. Bliss and C. de Macedo (eds.), *Unity with Diversity in the European Community* (Cambridge: Cambridge University Press).

—— and Venables, A. J. (1996), 'Integration, Specialization and Adjustment', *European Economic Review*, 40: 959–67.

Marshall, A. (1890), *Principles of Economics* (London: Macmillan) (8th edn, 1920).

Midelfart-Knarvik, K. H., Overman, H. G., Redding, S. J., and Venables, A. J. (2002), 'The Location of European Industry', *European Economy*, 2: 216–73.

Pelkmans, J. (2001) *European Integration: Methods and Analysis,* 2nd edn (London: Financial Times and Prentice-Hall).

Porter, M. E. (1990), *The Competitive Advantage of Nations* (London: Macmillan).

Smith, A. and Venables, A. J. (1988), 'Completing the Internal Market in the European Community,' *European Review,* 32: 1501–25.

Viner, J. (1950), *The Customs Union Issue* (New York: Carnegie Endowment for International Peace).

Winters, L. A. (1987), 'Britain in Europe: A Survey of Quantitative Trade Studies', *Journal of Common Market Studies*, 25/4: 315–25.

4 The Common Agricultural Policy

David Colman

Introduction

The Common Agricultural Policy (CAP) of the EU is a remarkably complex assembly of instruments and regulations covering such matters as trade controls, price support, income transfers, production subsidies, investment grants, conservation policies, health regulations, and labelling standards. It entails a huge bureaucracy, most of it at national level, to manage and oversee its operations. Additional complexity continually emerges as the policy as a whole adjusts to the multiple pressures of

- budgetary and consumer costs;
- anguished responses by non-Member States whose trade interests are damaged;
- concerns for the environmental damage caused by modern farming methods;
- the complex requirements of enlarging the EU to admit new members;
- protests about falling farm incomes despite the high costs of the policy.

In response to these pressures the CAP has undergone a number of major changes, with more in prospect at the time of writing as a consequence of the Development Round of Multilateral Trade Negotiations. Indeed this WTO (World Trade Organization) Round and its predecessor Uruguay Round under the auspices of the GATT (General Agreement on Tariffs and Trade) have provided the main pressure for CAP reform, with agricultural policy reform the central area of dispute in both rounds. The Uruguay Round negotiations started in 1986, and brought about the MacSharry CAP reforms from 1992/3 (see section 4.4), named after the then Agriculture Commissioner Ray MacSharry, which paved the way for concluding the Round in 1994 and the implementation of the agreed reforms from 1995 to 2000. These reforms involved a large reduction in EU cereal and oilseed price support levels, and the introduction of a system of direct subsidies in compensation for these price cuts for those farmers prepared to reduce and limit input use. The Doha Development Round of Multilateral Trade Negotiations began in 2000 and may, or may not, be concluded in 2007, with implementation to follow over a period of years. To pave the way for the possibility of a politically successful conclusion to this Round the EU instituted the 'Agenda 2000' reforms for the period 2004/5 to 2007/8 (see section 4.5). These deepened the MacSharry reforms and greatly increased emphasis on environmental protection and public goods output. However, a more dramatic CAP reform, to take advantage of trade policy rules agreed in the Uruguay Round, was the implementation of the Single Farm Payment (SFP) in 2005, which used rules about acceptable and unacceptable policies to move much of the EU's agricultural support into the acceptable category (see section 4.7 below).

This process of change in the CAP has for the most part added new policy instruments to the basic set with which the original six Member States started with in 1957. Thus the chapter starts in section 4.1 by examining the 'old' system of price support, which has survived but with diminished importance, while section 4.2 reviews the pressure for reform which built up by the early 1980s. Section 4.3 charts the moves to introduce output supply controls into the CAP, and the subsequent sections deal with the most recent changes since 2000, including those during the Doha Development Round.

4.1 The original system of CAP

The establishment of an integrated common market for agriculture by its original six Member States was a pivotal task in the formation of the EEC, and is the one which has persistently made the largest demands on its budgetary resources. Article 39 of the Treaty of Rome sets out a number of objectives, including ensuring supplies to consumers at reasonable prices, but the consistent emphasis of the CAP until the mid-1980s was 'to increase agricultural productivity by promoting technical progress' and 'to ensure a fair standard of living for the agricultural community'.

In the post-war period, when the memory of food shortages was relatively fresh, the productivist emphasis of the founding member countries was understandable. The dominant method of agricultural support had been import tariffs, which were an effective means of raising agricultural prices, since, in the early 1960s, the six Member States were net importers of cereals and oilseeds and only just self-sufficient in livestock products. With this background of external protection, the movement to a common external tariff (CET) for agriculture, as required by the Treaty of Rome, was a politically acceptable step towards the creation of a common market when accompanied by the abolition of customs duties on internal trade within the ring-fence of the CET. Importantly, for agriculture, instead of fixed tariffs, the EEC adopted a variable import tariff or levy system (which persisted until July 1995, when fixed upper limits to tariffs were, in principle, introduced—see below). This entailed setting minimum import prices (MIPs) with variable import levies (VILs) equal to the difference between the minimum import price and the *lowest* cost, insurance, and freight (c.i.f.) price offered by importers at the Community's borders. In the case of cereals the MIP is now referred to as the *reference price* in the jargon of the CAP.

Because the MIP for all major products was (with minor exceptions in 1974 and 1978) consistently maintained above the c.i.f. international prices (P_m), at which imports were available, EU market prices of imported commodities have been forced upwards. Figure 4.1 shows the theoretical effects of this. EU supply is increased from S_m to S and demand is depressed from D_m to D. Thus the imported quantity falls from $(D_m - S_m)$ to $(D - S)$. This trade-distorting feature of the policy was, however, exacerbated from the standpoint of non-EU agricultural exporting countries by two attendant facts. One is that import

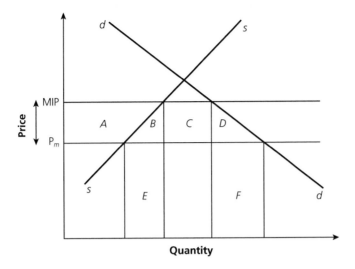

Figure 4.1 Basic system of external protection for imported commodities

demand ($D - S$) became completely inelastic to changes in world prices. As P_m fell the VIL increased to ensure that no imports entered the EU at below the MIP; the EU market was completely insulated from all movements in international prices unless they rose above the MIP. The second is that international market prices are forced downwards; they would rise if EU price support and trade distortion was reduced and EU import demand was higher.

The increase in internal EU prices causes *producer surplus to rise* by the value of area A, as shown in Figure 4.1. *Budgetary revenues* equal in value to C accrue to the EU from import levies/tariffs and may be counted as a gain (less some cost for collection). These two gains ($A + C$) are, however, more than offset by the *loss in consumer surplus* equivalent to areas $A + B + C + D$.[1] In fact, using this neo-classical economic calculus shows an overall *economic welfare loss* to the EU from the policy of $B + D$, reflecting a basic result of comparative static economic theory that free trade is optimal and that trade interventions result in a loss of economic welfare.

This last result can be confirmed by a dual calculation based on Figure 4.1. *Extra resource costs* of $B + E$ are stimulated by the price support to generate output which could be *imported at a cost* of E, thus registering a *welfare loss* B. Consumers have also reduced consumption which they value at $F + D$, but which cost them only F before the imposition of the MIP, resulting in an additional *welfare loss* of D and producing a total economic welfare or 'deadweight loss' of $B + D$.

Because of rapid technical change in agriculture, further stimulated by prices supported above international levels, underlying agricultural supply growth in the EU throughout the 1970s and 1980s continuously exceeded domestic demand growth and resulted in the emergence of excess supply in cereals, beef, dairy products, sugar, wine, and some fruits. This has meant that the internal price support mechanism of *intervention buying*

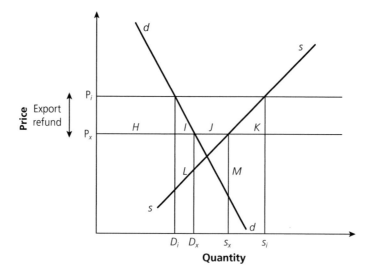

Figure 4.2 Basic system of internal protection for commodities in surplus

(Figure 4.2) played an important role when production of commodities in the EU moved into surplus. This internal support system operates through the process whereby national authorities operating the EU policy offer to buy produce of at least minimum standard quality at certain times of the year at the intervention price P_i. The latter is set in Euros at the community level and is the basis of common pricing throughout the Community. In effect P_i acts as a floor price in the market,[2] and it has been almost always set above the free on board (f.o.b.) export price, P_x which could be obtained by exporting the surplus. This form of price support has not been applied to all commodities covered by the CAP, but applies to wheat, barley, milk in the forms of butter and skimmed milk powder, beef, and wine after distillation. In a modified form it applies to certain fruits, vegetables, and fish, surpluses of which cannot be stored but have to be destroyed.

The effects of the internal price support policy are broadly as shown in Figure 4.2. The higher price and additional output stimulated (from S_x to S_i) results in increased *producer surplus of H + I + J. Consumer surplus is reduced* by $H + I$, as demand is cut from D_x to D_i. The amount by which supply exceeds consumer demand, $S_i - D_i$, is purchased into intervention stores, where it develops into the beef and butter mountains, and wine lakes, as they were often referred to in the media. It is conventional to explain the *budgetary costs* which arise from these intervention surpluses as being equivalent to areas $I + J + K$ in Figure 4.2. This is the cost which would arise if all the surplus $(S_i - D_i)$ is disposed of as exports[3] with the aid of an *export refund*, or export subsidy, equal to $P_i - P_x$; alternatively it is the loss made by the intervention authority from buying the surplus at P_i and selling at P_x. In reality $I + J + K$ underestimates the budgetary cost of surplus management, since it does not allow for the storage costs or for the deterioration and wastage of product while stored. If, however, we accept this measure of budgetary cost and add the consumer surplus loss of $H + I$, it transpires that the producer surplus gain of $H + I + J$ only partially offsets it, and leaves an economic welfare loss of $I + K$. The same result is obtained by setting the increased export revenue $(L + M)$ against the resource cost $(K + M)$ plus the reduction in consumption value $(I + L)$.

A point which should be emphasized is that the system of intervention buying (Figure 4.2) cannot be operated without a minimum import price policy (as in Figure 4.1) if P_i exceeds P_m, which is how the CAP has been operated. Without an MIP in excess of P_i it would be profitable to import at price P_m in order to sell into intervention, which would be a completely unstable and untenable state of affairs. Thus, even though in the 1980s and early 1990s the primary instrument of agricultural price support has been intervention buying, the import-levy/minimum-import-price system has been necessary to protect its operation.[4]

4.2 The pressures for CAP reform

Budgetary pressure

The budgetary costs of the CAP provided a persistent source of pressure leading to the MacSharry reforms of 1992 (see below). They contributed significantly to the need to increase the total tax transfer from 0.77 per cent of the GDP of the nine members in 1980 to 1.03 per cent of the GDP of the twelve members in 1989. This was necessary to permit the expansion of spending on regional and social policy and for the percentage of total EU budgetary expenditure on the CAP to drop from 73 per cent in 1980 to 66 per cent in 1989. This modest change was only achieved by a continuous stream of ad hoc measures, as described in section 4.4 below, to contain agricultural spending, and the periodic effects of a stronger US dollar which reduced the subsidy cost of exporting EU surpluses. The reforms which subsequently occurred have reduced CAP expenditure since 1993 to less than 50 per cent of the total EU budget (see Figure 4.3).

It is the costs of agricultural surplus management which dominate the budgetary expenditure of the European Agricultural Guidance and Guarantee Fund (EAGGF).[5] In the early 1990s export restitution costs alone regularly accounted for more than 30 per cent of total EAGGF expenditure, with the bulk of the 'other expenditure' being on costs for surplus storage and subsidized market disposal within the EU. As can be seen, Guidance Section expenditure on improving the farm structure of agriculture has (despite increases) remained small, with the vast bulk of budgetary resource diverted to market support. As explained below, since 1992 there has been a reduction in export subsidies and large growth in the direct subsidy expenditure by the Guarantee Section.

Some of the ad hoc measures to contain budgetary costs and surpluses prior to the 1992 reform package were very significant, such as the introduction of milk marketing quotas, which are discussed below, and quotas on the number of livestock eligible for subsidies. These measures failed to halt the relentless rise in the budget required for the CAP, and the reforms of 1992 became inevitable. It must be recognized that budgetary costs are *transfers*. Funds are paid as taxes by certain groups in society and paid out or transferred to others. In economic welfare terms, such transfers are not a complete loss of resource; this is evident from the analysis based on Figures 4.1 and 4.2 above, where the triangular

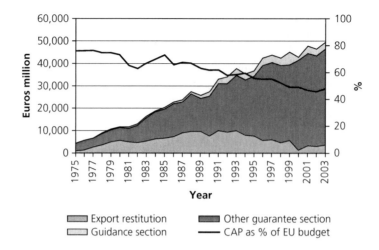

Figure 4.3 EAGGF expenditure on the CAP, selected years (million Euros)

Source: Various issues of the Official Journal of the Commission of the European Communities.

areas of deadweight loss are much smaller than the budgetary and consumer cost transfers. In the case of the budgetary transfers, revenue is raised as a value added tax (VAT) levy at the country level, through direct national budgetary contributions, and through import and sugar production levies; these are transferred to the EU to support the principle of common financing of the Union's costs. These revenues are then used to finance storage and subsidized disposal of surplus products, and also the new forms of agricultural support detailed below. It follows that countries which import more agricultural products tend to contribute more and that there is a net transfer to countries with greater surpluses to store and export. For example, in 1992 the largest net contributors to the CAP budget were (in billions of Euros) Germany (9.7) and the UK (2.4), while the main net gains were made by Greece (3.6), Spain (2.7), Ireland (2.1), and Portugal (2.1).[6] Inevitably it has been the case that some countries have pressed for budgetary reform of the CAP with less enthusiasm than others, and that those which have pushed hardest, such as the UK, have sometimes been accused of lacking 'Community spirit'.

Consumer pressure

All the estimates of the costs of the original CAP system have demonstrated (unsurprisingly, given the assumption that any change in agricultural prices in the EU would be fully transmitted to food consumers) that the estimated transfer costs from consumers to producers are large.

Various estimates have been made of the average cost imposed on EU non-farm families through higher prices and taxes to support the CAP, and these range from €24 to €30 per week for a family of four. Since even non-taxpayers, the poorest members of society, may have to bear perhaps 60 per cent of this cost, and since larger farms and generally wealthier farmers benefit most, the CAP can be legitimately criticized for transferring funds from the poorest members of society (since all must eat) to some who are relatively well off; although there are also poor farmers in the EU. While this fact has been well recognized, the political lobby for consumers' interests has not developed the same weight of influence as the farm and agro-industry lobbies, which have a specified central place in agricultural policy negotiations. Thus it has been largely left to academics, and particularly economists, to argue for CAP reform on the grounds of excessive cost to non-farm families as both consumers and taxpayers (e.g. Josling and Hamway 1972; BAE 1985: ch. 6; Brown 1989).

External pressure: the Uruguay Round of GATT

The CAP gave rise to progressive increases in trade distortion up to 1990. This was not even disguised by the incorporation of new Member States, which, by a process of trade diversion, switched a significant proportion of their agricultural imports from non-member to Member States. (This was particularly true of the accession to the EC of Ireland, the UK, Spain, and Portugal). Table 4.1 confirms this general picture, showing, for several major commodities, either a substantial increase in EC net exports between 1973 and

Table 4.1 Net external trade in selected agricultural products, 1973–2003

Year	Product					
	Wheat[a] (million tonnes)	Other cereals[a] (excl. rice) (million tonnes)	Sugar[a] (million tonnes)	Butter (thousand tonnes)	Cheese (thousand tonnes)	Beef and veal[b] (thousand tonnes)
EC-9						
1973	–	−10.8	−1.1	+204	+41	−913
1977	+0.9	−20.8	+0.1	+140	+84	−210
EC-10						
1981	+10.7	−3.4	+3.3	+373	+213	+389
1986	+11.9	+5.5	+2.6	+220	+269	+714
EC-12						
1989	+18.3	+7.6	+3.3	+332	+324	+589
1993	+20.2	+9.8	+5.7	+118	+415	+697
EU-15						
1995	+10.5	+6.0	+3.3	+144	+446	+718
1999	+12.7	+10.6	+2.9	+64	+252	+550
2003	+7.2	+4.3	+2.7	+202	+334	−66

[a] Wheat, other cereals, and sugar data are for harvest years l973/4 to 1996/7; other commodities data are for calendar years.
[b] Estimated: includes the carcass weight equivalent of trade in live animals.
Notes: Net imports are denoted by a minus (–) sign, and net exports by a plus (+) sign.
Source: CEC, *The Agricultural Situation in the Community, Official Journal of the European Communities* (various issues), and http://europa.eu.int/comm/agriculture/agrista/tradestats/eur15ag.

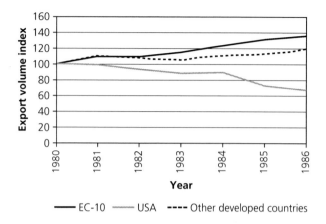

Figure 4.4 Export volume indices of agricultural products, 1980–6 (1980 = 100)
Source: GATT (1988: i, app., table 111).

1992 or, even more strikingly, a switch from being a net importer to a major net exporter. From the standpoint of non-member exporters of temperate zone agricultural products, not only have they suffered a severe contraction of their EU market as a consequence of the principle of Community preference, but they have had to face intensified competition in other markets from the EU's subsidized exports. Australia and New Zealand were particularly badly affected when the UK joined the EC, and the USA (as the world's largest agricultural exporter) suffered particularly in the early 1980s, prior to the inauguration of the Uruguay Round of negotiations on GATT in 1986. As an indication of this, Figure 4.4 displays the dramatic changes in EU and US agricultural export volume in this period.

The USA's concern about the CAP, and about protective policies in Japan and elsewhere, can be gauged from the fact that, although it was at the USA's insistence that agricultural policy was excluded from earlier rounds of GATT negotiations and agreements, it was made the centrepiece of the Uruguay Round. Although agriculture was only one of fifteen negotiating heads, the USA stated that without a satisfactory solution on agriculture it would not sign an agreement. In seeking drastically to reduce agricultural support policies, the USA was backed by the so-called Cairns Group of agricultural exporting countries, which includes Australia and New Zealand.

In order to explain how the GATT negotiations influenced the 1992 reform of the CAP, and how the process has been carried over into the Doha Round, it is helpful to give a simplified account of the negotiating positions of the USA and EU. (These and the positions of other groups are more fully summarized in Rayner *et al.* 1993). At the outset, in 1987–8 the USA demanded

- elimination of all trade-distorting subsidies within ten years;
- elimination of all import barriers, including all health and non-health non-tariff barriers (NTBs);
- changes to policies for individual commodities to permit the agreed phasing-out of government support;

- increased market access; and
- use of an aggregate measure of support (AMS) to establish initial levels of protection and to monitor progress with their elimination.

In the process of negotiation which ensued some key ideas emerged, two of which, *tariffication* and *decoupling*, deserve mention. One aspect of EU policy which was particularly abhorrent to other exporting countries was the variable import levies and export subsidies, since (as noted above) these insulated the EU market almost completely from short-term fluctuations in world prices. The key to tariffication was the expression of non-tariff barriers as tariff equivalents and the combining of these with specific import tariffs to create single, bound (i.e. fixed maximum) tariffs. This placed an upper limit on protection against imports and paved the way for fixed (as opposed to variable) tariffs and their reduction according to a negotiated schedule. In implementing the GATT agreement, however, special conditions affect the way tariff reduction is applied for individual commodities. Tariffs do still change and are not completely fixed.

Given that the central issue is trade distortion, it can reasonably be argued that there is no fundamental cause for international dispute if a country chooses to support its farmers in ways which do not cause supply to exceed competitive free trade levels (S_m and S_x in Figures 4.1 and 4.3). Such payments might be said to be decoupled from supply response and not to be trade distorting. One proposal (Blandford *et al.* 1989) was for the introduction of Production Entitlement Guarantees (PEGs) whereby, for each commodity, farmers would be eligible for fixed payments on a quantity of output less than S_m and S_x in Figures 4.1 and 4.2. In that way, it might be argued, supply at the margin would be influenced only by the free market price and would not be affected by the support payment offered. Another proposal (Tangermann 1991; Swinbank and Tranter 2004) was for an Income Bond, which would be given to farmers to compensate them for removal of all price support; the bond could either be retained as a source of annual income or sold to release capital. It will be seen (below) that the EU and USA have progressively switched to agricultural support measures of these decoupled types.

BOX 4.1 CRITERIA OF DECOUPLED PAYMENTS—(DEFINED ON PAGE 61 OF THE URUGUAY ROUND AGREEMENT)

1. Eligibility for such payments shall be determined by clearly defined criteria such as income, status as a producer or landowner, factor use, or production level in a defined base period.

2. The amount of such payments in any given year shall not be related to, or based on, the type or volume of production (including livestock units) undertaken in any year after the base period.

3. The amount of such payments in any given year shall not be related to, or based on, the prices, domestic or international, applying to any production undertaken in any year after the base year.

4. The amount of such payments in any given year shall not be related to, or based on, the factors of production employed in any year after the base year.

5. No production shall be required in order to receive such payments.

Over the course of the Uruguay Round, the USA was forced to relax its position and it agreed to accept that certain types of support, modelled very much on its own policy at that time, were sufficiently decoupled to be exempt from the reductions in support levels required by GATT; that is, these measures were not included in the aggregate measure of support (AMS) finally agreed for reduction in the final Uruguay Round Agreement. These so-called 'blue box' measures are support payments for which farmers can qualify only by adopting certain supply-restricting measures such as *setting-aside* (taking out of production) a proportion of previously farmed arable land. The acceptance of this blue box category, and agreement to place other environmentally related support payments in the so-called 'green box', proved critical in bridging the gap between the US position and that of the EU, and it led, in November 1992, to the signing of the so-called Blair House Accord, a bilateral agreement between the two negotiating parties.

The Blair House Accord contained three critical elements to be phased into the CAP over the period 1993–9. These were, first, a commitment to *tariffy* all existing border measures and reduce tariff levels by 36 per cent; second, an agreement to reduce internal support measures by 20 per cent from 1986–8 levels (with the 'blue box' compensation payments exempt for the reasons outlined above); third, a commitment to reduce the value of export subsidies by 36 per cent and subsidized export volume by 21 per cent. This accord, which formed the basis of the final GATT Agreement, paved the way for the European Council of Ministers to approve the MacSharry reforms of the CAP in 1992, before the Uruguay GATT Round was concluded, in a way which reduced the impression that the EU had been forced into reform by external international pressure.

The Uruguay Round Agreement (URA) was finally concluded in 1994 with the MacSharry reforms accepted as the basis for honouring the EU's commitments. These commitments, covering the period 1995 to 2000, and implemented by 2000, can be summarized as follows:

- Reduce the AMS of all trade-distorting, 'amber box', measures by 20 per cent. Blue and green box measures to be exempted.

- Reduce existing and new tariffs by 36 per cent on average, and reduce tariffs by at least 15 per cent for each item.

- Reduce expenditure on export subsidies by 36 per cent and the volume of subsidized exports by 21 per cent.

As will be seen, this pattern of reform has to a large extent been carried over into the agreements reached on agriculture prior to completing the WTO Doha Round. Both the USA and EU have used the 'box' definitions to shift much support form the moderately trade-distorting 'blue box' to the 'green box', where it is defined as non-trade-distorting, and to agree to phase out export subsidies, which are unambiguously trade distorting.

Environmental pressure

As agricultural production intensified after 1960, particularly in the northern EU countries, concerns grew about its adverse environmental impacts. Increased use of inorganic fertilizer has resulted in high nitrate and phosphate levels in rivers and lakes with consequent problems of eutrophication. Field sizes have been increased by eliminating hedgerows and removing small woodlands and trees, with a consequent loss of wildlife. Wildlife has also been adversely affected by the heavy use of pesticides and herbicides, some of which cause a damaging build-up of toxic compounds in the food chain. Draining of wetlands and improvement of permanent pasture have caused serious habitat loss to birds, plants, insects, and amphibians. At the same time as these changes have occurred in areas of higher agricultural potential, more remote disadvantaged areas have been struggling to maintain farming systems acknowledged to have high landscape value. For these, the underlying problems are agricultural decline and depopulation of some areas.

To the extent that most of the environmental concerns are the consequence of intensification of production, itself stimulated by EU price support, diverse strong environmental pressure groups have emerged arguing for agricultural policy reform. The Commission's 1984 Green Paper *Perspectives for the Common Agricultural Policy* explicitly recognized that there was a need for agricultural policy to take more account of environmental policy, both as regards the control of harmful practices and the promotion of practices friendly to the environment. However, despite this recognition, environmental measures introduced as part of the CAP prior to the 1992 reforms were limited. They have, however, been strengthened in the Agenda 2000 reforms (see section 4.6 below), and further extended by the major shift to 'green box' support in 2005—the introduction of the Single Farm Payment, which closely resembles the PEG proposal referred to above.

4.3 The start of the reform process: the introduction of supply control mechanisms

Throughout the existence of the CAP, its policy instruments and regulations have been adapted to meet changing economic and political circumstances. For example, during the 1970s, in response to the growing surpluses of some commodities, the EU introduced several new measures to the CAP designed to encourage domestic consumption, including subsidies to certain categories of final consumers, subsidies to industrial users of food products, and even 'denaturing premiums' (whereby product was dyed different colours and in other ways made unfit for human consumption) to encourage the use of grain in livestock feed. Alternatively, the EU attempted to decrease the budgetary cost of an existing policy instrument, intervention buying, by changing its rules of operation; for many commodities supported by this policy instrument, the period of availability of intervention buying was shortened and the quality standards for acceptance were raised, whilst the price received for sales to intervention was reduced to a so-called *buying-in price*, set some percentage points below the relevant intervention price. However, few, if any, of these ad hoc measures did anything substantial to alleviate the mounting pressures for more radical reform of the CAP.

It was not until the early 1980s that more significant changes to the CAP were initiated with the introduction of three new supply control mechanisms—*marketing quotas*, *co-responsibility levies*, and *budgetary stabilizers*. The introduction of these supply control mechanisms essentially marked the end of unlimited price guarantees, with each incorporating what has became known as the 'fourth principle' of the CAP, *producer co-responsibility* for surplus production. For commodities covered by such policy instruments, if production exceeded a certain fixed level (known as the guarantee threshold), action was triggered which ensured that at least part of the cost of the additional surplus disposal was borne by producers. The discussion below focuses on one mechanism, which was retained in the May 1992 CAP reform package, namely marketing quotas. These are set to continue in operation until at least 2014/15.

The economics of marketing quotas

Marketing quotas were first imposed on EU dairy producers in spring 1984 against a background of long-term structural surpluses of dairy products, an extremely depressed world market, and escalating budgetary costs of milk support. Throughout the 1970s and early 1980s the milk regime accounted for the largest proportion of total guarantee expenditure of the CAP, although this fell from 29.7 per cent of EAGGF expenditure in 1984 to 18.2 per cent in 1992.

Prior to the introduction of quotas, in 1981 the EU had introduced a system of maximum guaranteed thresholds intended to operate in such a way that, should milk deliveries in any year exceed the (pre-fixed) quantitative threshold, action would be triggered to offset the additional costs of the regime caused by the excess production. As early as 1983 the guarantee threshold was exceeded by 6.5 per cent. The reduction in intervention price for dairy products which should have been triggered by this surplus was estimated by the Commission to have been in the order of 12 per cent—too large to be politically acceptable. Instead, the EU chose to maintain the level of price support at its existing level and adopt a system of marketing quotas made effective by charging a very high tax, or *super-levy*, on excess deliveries beyond the quota.

Initially, each Member State was allocated a national quota or 'reference quantity' set equal to their 1981 milk delivery levels plus 1 per cent (apart from Italy and Ireland, whose initial reference quantities were based on the quantity of milk delivered during 1983). Quotas were then allocated to individual farmers, again on the basis of their historical production levels.

The welfare implications of quotas as compared with those arising from a straight price support reduction for dairy products are shown in Figure 4.5. Importantly, both sets of welfare effects are measured relative to a base scenario of surplus production and of the EU maintaining a support price at a level significantly above the world price for dairy products. In other words, the base scenario is intended to reflect the situation in the EC dairy industry at the beginning of the 1980s.

A straight reduction in the level of intervention price for dairy products from P_i to P_i' would cause consumers to increase their consumption from D_i to D_i' and farmers to decrease their production from S_i to S_i' by moving down the supply function SS. Consequently, the level of surplus production decreases from $(S_i - D_i)$ to $(S_i' - D_i')$, and the budgetary cost of disposing of the surplus through export refunds falls. A cut in the level of price support would *increase consumer surplus* by area $A + B$, *reduce producer surplus* by the area $A + B + C + D + E$, and *reduce the budgetary cost* of support by $B + C + D + E + F + G + I$, causing overall a net welfare gain relative to the base scenario of $B + G + F + I$.

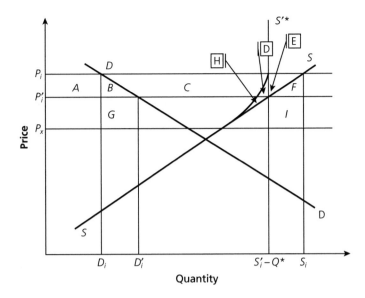

Figure 4.5 Comparison of welfare effects of quotas and support price reductions

In comparison, the imposition of a total quota at Q^* (which, for ease of comparison, is set equal to S_i') shifts the supply curve to SS^*. At output level Q^*, the supply curve is perfectly inelastic, implying that the penalty for surplus production is severe enough to discourage any farmers from exceeding the production threshold and thus incurring the *super-levy*. Consumers are unaffected by the implementation of the new policy instrument —they continue to purchase the same level of output, D_i, at prices significantly above the world price of the commodity, P_x; thus *the change in consumer surplus* is zero. The figure suggests that farmers lose producer surplus equal to area $E + D + H$. Whilst area E is an unavoidable loss of surplus owing to the output-restricting nature of the policy instrument, area $D + H$ is lost because of the manner in which quotas are allocated between individual producers. Distributing quotas purely on the basis of historical production levels rather than efficiency criteria means that some low-cost, efficient production is lost from the industry whilst some high-cost, inefficient production is maintained. If, following the initial allocation, transfer of quota is permitted, then it can be shown that low-cost producers would be willing to purchase or lease quota from high-cost producers and the area $D + H$ can be restored as surplus (Burrell 1989). Assuming that such trade takes place, total *producer surplus loss* to the dairy industry can be reduced to E.[7] The reduction in surplus production by $(S_i - Q^*)$ results in *budgetary savings* relative to the base scenario of $E + F + I$. Thus overall, Figure 4.5 suggests that the implementation of quotas results in a net welfare gain of only $F + I$ which is less than that of a price cut to P_i by $B + G$.

The preceding analysis begs the question: if a straight cut in support prices offered the greatest potential net welfare gains, why did the EU choose instead to implement milk quotas? The answer seems to be that quotas, whilst restraining the budgetary cost of milk support, minimized the dislocation caused to the farm sector. Analysis of previous CAP policy changes has suggested that the weight given to farmers' interests in the decision-making process is far higher than that afforded to consumers or taxpayers (MacLaren 1992) and, in this sense, the choice of milk quotas simply conformed with past precedent. However, the choice of quotas also reflected a widely held belief amongst CAP decision-makers—that, in the short run, reducing the support price of a commodity might not lead to a reduction in output of that commodity but might even cause output levels to increase. Whilst little empirical evidence has been found to support this idea of 'perverse' supply response (Ozanne 1992), it is interesting to contrast the two alternative policy options from a producer's perspective. A straight reduction in price support levels would keep the marginal revenue and average revenue of output perfectly elastic at the new (lower) price and retain the open-ended nature of support. Thus, it can be argued that it would offer individual producers an incentive to reduce costs per unit output but not necessarily their total output level. Surplus production has long been considered by the European Commission as the central problem of the CAP and it was consequently keen to introduce a policy instrument which gave it direct control over aggregate output levels.

The total quota for milk was periodically reduced from 103.7 million tonnes in 1984 to 96 million in 1991/2 for the EU-10. It has subsequently been increased to accommodate the addition of the new Member States. The system, as noted above, has been fairly successful at reducing the budgetary cost of the milk regime, but its success has been possible only because of the way milk is marketed. Virtually all milk is sold from farms to a relatively small number of processing plants. This bottleneck in the marketing chain allows the output of each producer to be monitored and, if necessary, permits enforcement of the quota by charging appropriate individuals the super-levy on excess production. The same policy instrument would be ineffective if applied to the cereals regime, because no equivalent bottleneck in the marketing chain of cereals exists. Instead, during the 1980s, the EU adopted the other two types of supply control methods mentioned above—*co-responsibility levies* and *budgetary stabilizers*—to control the output level and budgetary cost of the cereals regime. Whilst both these mechanisms share the basic characteristics of quotas in that they penalize production in excess of some threshold quantity by imposing some kind of pricing penalty, they offer far less of an incentive to an individual producer to reduce output levels. As explained by Burrell (1987), a rational individual producer will respond to a quantitative threshold on output only if that threshold has been imposed directly on his own production levels. 'Otherwise he is a price-taker, and in spite of the threshold for aggregate output, he perceives the demand for his own output as perfectly elastic at the going price.'

The introduction and gradual increased reliance on supply control mechanisms in the 1980s failed to stifle calls for yet more fundamental reform of the CAP. Thus, in May 1992, the CAP entered into a second stage of reform marked by the Council of Ministers' acceptance of the MacSharry reform package.

4.4 The MacSharry reform package

As intimated above, the MacSharry reform package owed much to the multinational trade negotiations and the pressure from agricultural trading partners to reduce the level of trade distortion caused by the CAP. Whilst the basic price support mechanisms described in section 4.3 above were retained, reductions in the level of support prices significantly reduced their effectiveness. The impact of such price cuts for commodities in surplus can be ascertained by referring back to Figure 4.3. Consumers should benefit (assuming that reductions in the support price of raw agricultural products are passed on in the form of lower food prices); the budgetary cost of disposing of any remaining surplus production should decrease; and the farm sector, in the absence of any countervailing policy action, should suffer a loss in producer surplus. However, to compensate farmers for their potential loss in income, the EU decided to give direct income payments to farmers provided they adhered to certain restraints on input use. For livestock producers, compensation payments were limited to a fixed number of animals based on historical herd sizes and contingent upon a maximum stocking density; whilst for arable producers, compensation came to be paid only if a farmer agreed to *set aside* (take out of production) a proportion of his/her arable land, the exact proportion being determined by the Council of Ministers each year.

By partly replacing price support with direct income payments, the correlation between the amount of support received and the amount of output produced was weakened. In the jargon of the GATT negotiations, the MacSharry reform package marked a move towards *decoupled* farm income support.[8] The main changes to the commodity regimes of the CAP following the 1992 reform agreement are summarized in Table 4.2.

In addition to the changes in the various commodity regimes, a set of 'accompanying measures' were introduced as part of the CAP reforms to encourage farm forestry and farmer retirement, and to generalize and enhance existing agro-environmental policies. Previously, these types of measures were funded under the Agricultural Structures Policy, and they received little budgetary support. However, as part of the reform package, financial support was switched to the Guarantee Section of the CAP's budget and 6.2 billion Ecus, or 5 per cent of the total guarantee budget, was targeted at these issues. In particular, over half was earmarked for policies under the Agri-Environment Programme.

The introduction of the Agri-Environment Programme was significant in that it allowed the implementation of policies at the national level to be flexible, with such policies being co-financed by Member States' governments. By the end of 1994, about 190 programmes had been approved. The changes entailed more emphasis being given to the long-recognized role of the CAP in securing environmental goals. This was consolidated by the subsequent 1993 Treaty on European Union (TEU) requiring all Union policies, including the CAP, to take environmental impacts into account.

The economics of the new arable regime

The 1992 changes to the arable regime of the CAP were particularly significant, not just because of the introduction of land set-aside,[9] but because of the importance of cereals along with oilseeds and protein crops (the so-called COP crops) within the agricultural industry. They were also noticeable as a result of an innovation which has left its mark on subsequent reforms (in the dairy and sugar regimes), namely that producers received compensation for the price support cuts in the form of direct subsidies. This marked a shift of the costs of support from consumers to producers. What these reforms made clear was that the period of reliance of the CAP primarily on market price support was well and truly over.

Table 4.2 Summary of the MacSharry CAP reforms

Commodity	Cuts in support	Compensation and other gains	Production control
Cereals	• Target price cut by 29% from 1991/2 buying-in price. • Price reduction phased in over three years from 1994/95	• Per hectare compensation payments available provided set-aside is implemented. • Producers of less than 92 tonnes of cereals are exempted from set-aside. • Compensation payments based on historical yield levels for regions of the EU. • Co-responsibility levy abolished from 1992/3.	• Annual set-aside required for producers to receive compensation payments. • The minimum percentage of base arable area to be set aside varies from year to year. • Controls over which land can be set aside.
Oilseeds and pulses	• No price support 1993/4 onwards	• Per hectare area payments available but cut from 1992/3 levels. • Linseed added to list of eligible crops.	• Controlled by same set-aside schemes as cereal production.
Sheep	• Payment of ewe premium restricted by producer quota. • Producer quotas based on number of ewe premiums paid in 1991.	• Quota has market value. • Special extensification premiums for reduced stock levels. • Lower feed grain costs.	• If quota sold without land, 15% of quota taxed to national reserve. • No transfer of quota outside existing Less Favoured Areas.
Beef	• Intervention price cut by 15% from 1993/4. • 350,000 tonne limit set on intervention purchases by 1997.	• Beef and suckler cow premium increased but made contingent on stocking rates below minimum level. • Suckler cow quota has marketable value. • Lower feed grain costs.	• Beef premium limited by regional ceiling equal to number of premiums paid in 1991. If exceeded, producer payments reduced pro rata. • Suckler cow premiums restricted by producer quota. • Beef and suckler cow premium payments subject to stocking-rate restrictions.
Dairy	• 5% cut in butter intervention price by 1994/5.	• Milk quota and associated value to last at least to 2000. • Co-responsibility levy abolished from 1992/3.	• Cuts in quota may be made.

Under the new arrangements, each COP farmer in the EU producing more than 92 tonnes of cereals faced a decision over whether (1) to use the whole of his/her arable acreage and receive the new (lower) market price for cereal output, or (2) to comply with the set-aside requirements and thus be eligible for compensation payments in addition to market returns for output from land remaining in production.

For those who adopted the latter strategy and opted into the set-aside scheme (and very few remained outside the scheme), two types of compensation payments can be distinguished: price compensation on land farmed (the so-called arable area payment (AAP)) and set-aside compensation (SAP) on land set aside.

The decision of whether or not to participate in the set-aside scheme depends on the market price of cereals and farms' actual yields. In particular, the decision depends on the value of compensation payments relative to the revenue which could be obtained by planting the area which would be set aside. When cereal prices are high, the opportunity cost of leaving land to stand idle is also high and a farmer is less likely to participate in the scheme. As the market price for cereals falls, the opportunity cost of idling land also falls. At some point, the value of the compensation payments from participating in set-aside will exactly equal the profit that could be earned from planting the additional set-aside area. The price of cereals which gives rise to this equivalence can be called the 'indifference price', since at this price the farmer is indifferent as to whether he opts out of production and into set-aside; either way his total profit level is the same. If the market price of cereals exceeds the indifference price, a rational producer would choose to plant his full area. Alternatively, if the market price for cereals is less than the indifference price, a rational producer would participate in the set-aside scheme in order to be eligible for the compensation payments.

Because farms are not identical, indifference prices will vary among cereal producers. One would expect inefficient, high-cost producers to have a low opportunity cost of idling land and thus a relatively high indifference price. Conversely, one would expect efficient, low-cost producers to have a high opportunity cost of leaving land fallow and thus a relatively low indifference price. Taking such variability into account and aggregating across all producers in the industry, the supply curve for cereals under the new voluntary set-aside scheme would shift from its original competitive level, SS to the kinked curve $S'S$, as shown in Figure 4.6.

In Figure 4.6, P_{ih} and P_{il} represent the highest and lowest indifference price in the industry, respectively. At any price above P_{ih}, the market return for cereals is sufficient to deter *all* farmers from participating in set-aside. Therefore, the total arable area would be utilized and the supply curve would coincide with the competitive supply curve, SS.

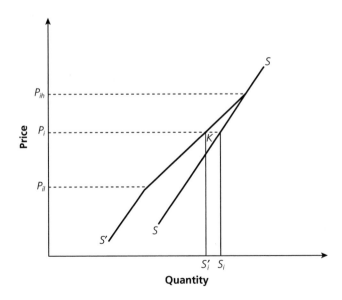

Figure 4.6 Cereal supply curve under voluntary set-aside

However, once the price of cereals falls below P_{ih}, the least efficient, high-cost producers would choose to opt out of full production and into set-aside, idling the required propor-tion of their land and thus causing the supply curve to rotate to the left. As the price falls further, more and more farmers would opt into set-aside and more and more land would be withdrawn from production. Once the price has fallen to P_{il}, all farmers would theoret-ically choose to idle the necessary portion of their land in order to be eligible for com-pensation payments. In practice, market conditions are such that virtually all large arable farmers in the EU have continually participated in the set-aside scheme.

The shift in the supply curve shown in Figure 4.6 allows us to identify the minimum value of set-aside compensation payments necessary to induce a certain reduction of cereal output. For example, if the EU had decided to implement a voluntary set-aside scheme with a fixed compensation payment per hectare *without* reducing the level of price support for cereals from its original level, P_i, Figure 4.6 suggests that enough farmers would opt into the scheme to cause output levels to fall from S_i to S'_i. It can be assumed, since the scheme is voluntary, that this would occur only if there were no overall reduc-tion in producer surplus. In other words, the value of set-aside compensation payments must be at least equal to area K in the figure, which represents the amount of surplus lost from production.

The new supply curve with set-aside, $S'S'$, is replicated in Figure 4.7, where the changes in welfare and transfer effects of the MacSharry reforms of the old cereals[10] regime are investigated. From an initial buying-in price of P_i, the support price for cereals once the scheme is fully implemented falls to P'_i. The price reduction will cause demand to increase to D'_i and supply to decrease to S'_i. One result of this is a *reduction in the consumer surplus loss* of $(A + B) - (A' + B' + J)$, implying that, in principle, EU consumers should have benefited from this element of CAP reform.

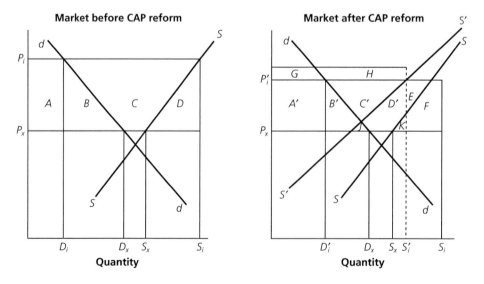

Figure 4.7 The economics of the EU's arable regime, 1992–2005

The welfare effect for producers is less clear cut. From a starting position of producer surplus gain of $(A + B + C)$ under the old regime, their surplus from cereal production is reduced to $(A' + B' + C' + D' + J)$. However, in addition, they received direct compensation payments. As drawn, the new (lower) support price, P'_i, corresponds to the lowest indifference price of the industry. We can, therefore, assume that every eligible cereal producer participated in the set-aside scheme,[11] and that area E is the budgetary transfer that was needed to induce this. Over and above that, the arable area payment (compensation) cost can be represented by areas $G + H$. That is, the cost is represented as a price subsidy averaged over output level S'_i. Thus the total amount of the arable area and set-aside payments can be shown as area $E + G + H$ in Figure 4.7, and the *change in producer surplus gain* (obtained by comparing the two panels in Figure 4.7) is given by $(A + B + C) - (A' + B' + C' + D' + E + J + G + H)$. Whether or not this is positive or negative depends on whether the value of set-aside plus compensation payments is larger or smaller than the loss in producer surplus from reducing support prices to P'_i and output to S'_i. As drawn it is smaller, to reflect the principle that the price compensation was intended to be only partial. However, in some years, such as 1994/5 and 1995/6, market prices remained above support price levels and therefore the 'compensation' was overgenerous.

The impact of this changed policy regime on the budgetary cost of cereal support is also not easily assessed. Whether or not the total budgetary cost of supporting cereal farmers decreases or increases depends upon whether the saving in terms of the disposal of surplus production $(B + C + D) - (B' + C' + D' + J + K)$ is larger or smaller than the value of compensation payments $E + G + H$. As drawn, the figure suggests a fall in the budgetary cost of support. However, in practice, this depends upon the change in the world price for cereals and the extent of participation in the set-aside scheme. It also depends on any additional administrative costs incurred in administering the payments to farmers, something not explicitly represented in the diagram.

The reduction in net welfare loss caused by the policy reform appears less ambiguous (if we ignore administrative costs), and there is a welfare improvement. Taking into account the preceding analysis, the net welfare loss is reduced by $(B + D) - (B' + J + D' + K)$. Importantly, as drawn, the MacSharry reforms reduced but did not eliminate the trade distortion caused by CAP support for cereal producers, with the level of exports falling at $(S'_i - D'_i)$ still remaining above the free trade level of $(S'_x - D'_x)$.

Whilst useful as an indication of the general welfare effects of the post-1992 CAP arable regime, the preceding analysis has ignored the more detailed aspects of the regime which are critical in governing its effectiveness. For instance, no mention has been made of the problem of *slippage*, which is associated with any policy requiring that farmers set aside land. Slippage can be most easily described as the phenomenon whereby a certain reduction in cereal area does not necessarily lead to the same percentage reduction in cereal output. In terms of Figures 4.6 and 4.7, slippage would result in a smaller rotation in the supply curve for cereals to the left. There are many different reasons for slippage, including farmers using inputs more intensively on the land remaining in production, the setting aside of less productive land, and increased fertility of land left to stand fallow, which would result in increased yields once that land is brought back into production. Alternatively, slippage may occur simply because of ineffective policing of set-aside, allowing farmers to plant more hectares than intended under the rules of the new regime.

In addition, producers of fewer than 92 tonnes of cereals (equivalent to around 15 hectares) do not have to participate in set-aside to qualify for area compensation. The analysis has also ignored the fact that the rules of the regime are such that the base arable area of each individual farmer is defined to include land previously sown with oilseeds, potatoes, sugar beet, and protein crops as well as cereals. Thus there will not be a direct correspondence between the change in cereal area and the area of land removed from production under set-aside, even before considering the complications of slippage. Again, the rotation in cereal supply curve shown in Figures 4.6 and 4.7 may be less pronounced than initially implied.[12]

4.5 Agenda 2000 reforms

The changes to the CAP agreed in the MacSharry reforms were basically allowed to run forward to 1999. The set-aside rate was adjusted from year to year, but target and intervention prices for cereals were maintained at the same level from 1995/6 to 1999/2000. There were simplifying modifications to the oilseeds regime, but essentially policy remained unchanged in the crop and livestock sectors.

For 2000/1 a new package of changes was agreed under the title Agenda 2000. For cereals there was a 15 per cent cut in the intervention price in two steps starting in 2000/1, with a partially compensating increase in the AAP and SAP payments. Support was also reduced for oilseeds, with the AAP and SAP payments converging to the cereals' level in 2002/3. For beef, a sector in crisis following the bovine spongiform encephalopathy (BSE) epidemic, the intervention price was reduced by 20 per cent over three years, and the various beef premium (headage) payments were increased in partial compensation. Thus the switch from price support to direct subsidies started in 1992 was deepened.

Surprisingly, the dairy regime survived Agenda 2000 largely unscathed. The milk quota regime was extended, and some countries and regions were granted small increases in quota from 2000/1 and the others from 2005. There were no cuts in intervention prices for butter and skimmed milk powder until 2005, when a phased three-year reduction of 15 per cent began. Significantly, the EU introduced compensation payment for these price cuts, allocated on the basis of quotas operated in 2004/5. This extension of direct subsidies is of considerable significance in relation to the Millenuium WTO Round, as the compensation payments are in the 'green box'.

Agenda 2000 placed more emphasis on environmental objectives, which was another step to shift support for agriculture into the 'green box'. It required Member States by January 2000 to take appropriate environmental measures, by strengthening the environmental criteria for direct support payments; that is, it reinforced *cross-compliance*. It also provided Member States discretion over policy in a number of areas. One of these was for *modulation* (in effect, taxation) of direct payments, and for any savings achieved in this way to be redirected to environmental and other approved schemes such as early retirement.

All states were also required to produce seven year Rural Development Plans (RDPs), formulated with a large degree of discretion within general rules. To illustrate this, England[13] formulated a RDP for 2000–6, which incorporated *modulation* within it. The plan entailed imposing a 'tax' of 2.5 per cent on direct (AAP, SAP, and headage) payments in 2001, and raising this in equal steps to 5.5 per cent in 2006.[14] The Treasury matched this 'saving' pound for pound and put it into the budget for the RDP. By 2006 the plan was to cost £462 million, of which only £81 million was from EU funds, the rest being provided nationally. The general principle underlying this approach to agricultural policy is highly significant. This is the principle of *subsidiarity*, whereby Member States finance an increasing proportion of the cost of support for farmers themselves with less of the funding coming from the EU budget. Any policies funded under this principle have to comply with EU regulations, but, as indicated above, new regulations provide discretion and flexibility about policy details. This discretion applies only to policy instruments which are in the 'green box' and are judged to be decoupled; it does not apply to intervention purchases or export refunds. Thus the discretion to spend more or less on policies in the Rural Development Plans should have minimal distorting effects on intra-EU trade, although no payment can be considered completely decoupled and to have no effect whatever on production.

Agenda 2000 may be seen as representing a step towards reducing central EU funding (and collective financial responsibility) for agricultural support, and a move towards renationalizing agricultural policy.

4.6 **EU enlargement**

In 2004 the EU was expanded to twenty-five members with the accession of Poland, Hungary, the Czech Republic, Slovakia, Slovenia, Estonia, Latvia, Lithuania, Cyprus, and Malta. Further expansion has taken place with Bulgaria and Romania joining in 2007, with issues relating to accession by Turkey, Croatia, and Macedonia still outstanding. Most of these countries are much more heavily dependent on agriculture than existing Member States. The ten new Member States which joined in 2004 added close to 19 per cent to the EU population, but 28 per cent to the agricultural land area,[15] and have in general a greater proportion of their workforce in agriculture than the EU-15 countries, other than Portugal and Greece.

For the new Member States, the terms of accession to the CAP were a major issue, since the attraction of membership of the EU was greatly influenced by whether or not the support system of the CAP would be fully extended to them. The precise terms were negotiated firmly on both sides, in the setting of different categories of quotas, and the schedule for phasing in subsidy payments. Prior to agreement, there were those who questioned the need to offer the same subsidy rates to new member countries, when (for cereals, oilseeds, and milk) those were in significant measure compensation for price support cuts in the EU-15 countries. In the event the principle of a Common Agricultural Policy prevailed and the new Member States were not offered a second-class deal, although it was inevitable that direct subsidy payments would be phased in; starting at 25 per cent the payments are to increase to 100 per cent of the common level by 2013. These commitments have reduced the scope the EU may have had for greater policy reform before 2013, or has at least provided some excuse for not offering more in the Doha WTO Round.

4.7 The WTO Doha Round: additional CAP reforms

In many ways the script for changes in the CAP that would be necessary to secure agreement in the WTO Doha Round was written by the Agreement to the Uruguay Round. It was clear that further cuts in amber box policies would be required, that blue box policies would come under attack, and that a formula approach to reducing tariffs, export subsidies, and support in general would be required if there was to be a successful conclusion. Also it was clear that there would be huge pressure on commodity policy regimes which were particularly trade distorting, such as the EU sugar regime and the USA's cotton regime.

In anticipation of these requirements the EU has responded by making many of the necessary changes ahead of signing any agreement, which will enable it to hang on to the bones of the original CAP, namely a measure of tariff protection across the board, and intervention buying at minimum internal market prices. However, this latter policy instrument is so much weakened by limits placed by the EU on the quantities which can be purchased into intervention, that its effectiveness in the cereals, dairy, and beef sectors is now very limited.

The Single Farm Payment

The most important step taken by the EU to enable it to retain support for farmers' incomes was the consolidation, in 2005, of all direct subsidies into the Single Farm Payment (SFP). In the UK, Ireland, and Sweden this took effect immediately in 2005, but the transition will not be fully completed in other Member States until 2007/8. Prior to 2005 an individual farm might have been receiving, say, an arable area premium plus the set-aside payment, a beef suckler-herd subsidy, and subsidies for sheep. Under the SFP all of these are consolidated into a single payment per farm based on its entitlements at the end of the 2004/5 agricultural year.[16] That entitlement will not change in future, and it does therefore comply with the requirements to be classified as a decoupled payment and placed in the green box. At a stroke, therefore, the EU transferred most of its policy support in the blue box into the green one, where it is treated as non-trade-distorting and therefore acceptable under WTO rules. In doing this the EU followed the USA's shift of its crop subsidy system in 1996 to the Production Flexibility Contract (PFC) payment system, which is also green box compliant, but the EU went further by incorporating both crop and livestock subsidies into the SFP. In these ways both the EU and USA have used the rules devised in the URA for decoupled payment classification, to protect a sizeable element of support for their farmers. The income provided by both the SFP and PFC systems does not require that farmers produce any saleable output, but does demand that they take care of the land. In the case of the EU, set-aside of arable land has been retained.

Export subsidies and the sugar regime

Persistent targets of external pressure on the CAP have been its export subsidies and the massively trade-distorting sugar regime, a key element of which is export subsidies. In 2003, the EU Agriculture Commissioner, Franz Fischler, signalled the EU's preparedness to abandon export subsidies if appropriate reforms and concessions could be agreed with other countries. It was evident that the EU sugar regime would need to be significantly reformed if that was agreed, and in anticipation of agreement reform has been implemented. The EU sugar regime has been unlike those for all other commodities since its inception in 1968, in that it has in principle been self-financing in a budgetary sense. European sugar is produced from sugar beets, and is much more costly to produce than sugar from sugar cane in tropical countries, or in the form of iso-glucose from maize. To protect the European industry very high tariff walls have been in place. Despite having to be reduced by 36 per cent after the URA, according to EU (2004): 'Over recent marketing years, the total protection comprising the fixed duty and additional duty has been around €500 per tonne, which, given shipping costs and a world price of €200 per tonne, offers Community protection of more than €700 per tonne.' Thus the protection against normal commercial imports has been around 250 per cent.

Behind this protective wall a complicated system of production quotas with different support levels and levies has operated with intervention prices per tonne of sugar around €650 per tonne. The high protected prices have consistently meant that the EU farmers have produced an exportable surplus of sugar, requiring large export subsidies, a position exacerbated by the EU's agreements to allow the African, Carribean, Pacific countries, and India tariff-free import quotas for 1.3 million tonnes of sugar which have added to the exportable surplus. At around 5.5 million tonnes the EU is the second largest sugar exporter after Brazil, and it pays an average export subsidy of €223 per tonne (EU 2004).

Given the details sketched out above it is clear that the EU sugar regime could not survive the removal of export subsidies. In 2004/5 production quotas for sugar were cut, and in November 2005, major reform was agreed. The main steps are:

- a 36 per cent price support cut phased in over four years to 2009/10,
- compensation to farmers (to be incorporated into the SFP) of 64.2 per cent of the price cut,
- simplification of the quota system,
- a fund to buy up and thereby eliminate some production quota, and
- a restructuring fund for sugar factories forced to close because of the anticipated reduction in EU sugar production.

It is expected that the reduction in the internal EU price of sugar and sugar beet will cause production in several countries to fall, which will be necessary given the agreement in the WTO Doha Round to eliminate all EU export subsidies by 2013.[17] Nevertheless, protection for the EU sugar market will remain high, as the import tariff cuts of 36 per cent will leave tariffs at a substantial level.

Ironically, the cuts in EU sugar tariffs, while good for developing countries' agriculture as a whole, are damaging to many of the smallest and poorest countries, the Africa, Caribbean, and Pacific (ACP) countries. The EU has a deal with the ACP countries to allow in sugar and other commodities duty free—the 'everything but arms' agreement. This currently gives them a competitive advantage in trade with the EU over other developing countries, such as Brazil, which is the world's largest sugar exporter. Reduction of EU import tariffs therefore reduces the benefits of existing trade preferences for the poor

ACP countries. According to recent research (Winters 2005) the two largest prospective gainers from the projected agricultural trade liberalization in the Development Round are Brazil and Argentina, whilst the macroeconomic and trade gains of the least developed countries as a whole are projected to be small or even negative. Some individual countries (e.g. Bangladesh, Morocco, and Mozambique) are actually projected to lose. This does raise serious questions about the 'development credentials' of the Doha Round.

The outcome of the Doha Round agricultural negotiations

Provisional agreement on some aspects of agricultural trade reforms was finally reached in December 2005, at the ministerial meeting in Hong Kong, possibly paving the way for an eventual conclusion to the Doha Round of WTO negotiations. It was agreed:

- That there would be further cuts in the Aggregate Measure of Support, with larger proportional cuts by countries with the highest support.
- All forms of agricultural export subsidies and equivalent measures were to be eliminated by 2013.
- A 'safe box' will be created to ensure that genuine food aid supplies can be made to poor countries.
- A number of special and differential exemptions were agreed for developing countries, to permit them certain measures of protection.

However, many details remain after the ministerial meeting, such as

- the precise proportions by which tariffs are to be cut,
- the precise proportional cuts in AMS levels,
- restrictions on the scale of 'blue box' payments,
- tightening the rules for 'green box' payments—after the EU and USA have transferred much of their support into the apparently untouchable category, and
- the precise derogations for developing countries.

For more detail, readers are directed to the Draft Ministerial Declaration from the Hong Kong meeting (WTO 2005). However, before agreement can be reached the EU and USA are demanding concessions from developing countries on import access for services and manufactures, while the developing countries remain dissatisfied with the provisional progress on agricultural policy reform by the key developed countries.

4.8 Summary and outlook

Changes which have been made to the CAP in the past fifteen years represent an uneasy compromise between continuing the traditional policies of protecting agriculture, through price supports and income aids, and the various pressures for reform discussed above. By compensating for commodity price reductions through the introduction of direct income payments to farmers, reform has allowed a transfer of some of the cost of support from food consumers to taxpayers, which is socially progressive in reducing food costs to poor non-taxpayers. It also means that the costs of the CAP will be increasingly transparent, being revealed in budgetary accounts rather than being hidden away in the mass of consumer spending. Moreover, the bulk of budgetary expenditure on the CAP is now capped by the fact that the Single Farm Payments (SFPs) are now fixed in total for the future, will be eroded in real value by inflation, and will be 'modulated' (i.e. taxed) to transfer funds to rural development and environmental conservation policies.

Because the SFPs are decoupled, farmers will have to orientate production consistently to market needs and signals. They will not be able to continue to, as has been said, 'farm the commodity subsidies'. While not wholly eliminated, that era is largely over. To the extent that there are direct subsidies (other than the SFP), they will be targeted at conservation, amenity, and environmental outputs. To the extent that there will be 'farming for subsidies', it will be almost wholly for these types of public goods, which are accepted not to be trade distorting.

At the time of writing there has been no signed agreement to the Doha Round. There are obstacles remaining to negotiate, and there are those who question whether the envisaged agreement will be reached. Even if the sceptics are right, reform of the CAP will continue with emphasis on 'green' rather than commodity issues. Nevertheless, there are strong forces within Europe lobbying and working to maintain subsidy support for agriculture, even if that support is in the form of payments to farmers for producing amenity and biodiversity public goods. Such payments may be classified as in the 'green box', but, as long as they keep in business farmers who would otherwise quit, they are not truly decoupled and they do distort trade to some extent. The arguments in favour of public goods are compelling, but logic calls for any subsidies to be targeted at specific areas and farming forms rather than to be an extension of support for all land-based farming.

DISCUSSION QUESTIONS

1. To what extent have the reforms of the CAP been driven by political and economic pressures within the expanding EU rather than by the external trade liberalization agenda set by the USA, the Cairns Group, and developing country exporters of agricultural products?

2. Despite the costs to taxpayers and consumers, are there any justifications for continuing a policy of price support for agriculture?

3. Why will many of the poorest countries, highly dependent on agriculture, lose when the EU and other developed countries reduce agricultural import tariffs?

4. Is there any form of direct subsidy payment to farmers which is truly decoupled and has no trade-distorting effects?

▓ FURTHER READING

Readers wishing to explore issues related to the EU's agricultural policy further might wish to consult the book *The Common Agricultural Policy* edited by Ritson and Harvey (1997), which provides extensive coverage of the political economy of the CAP. Swinbank and Tranter's 2004 book *A Bond Scheme for Common Agricultural Policy Reform* provides extensive insights into the case for decoupled income support to farmers and its limitation.

▓ NOTES

1. This assumes that all increases in the price of agricultural commodities such as wheat are passed through to the retail prices of bread, cakes, flour, etc.

2. For a whole series of reasons (see Colman 1985), the floor is not as rigid as portrayed in Figure 4.2, but it is an acceptable approximation for much analysis.

3. The subsidized export of cereals, dairy products, and sugar have been on a large scale and have been a primary target of attack on the CAP by competing exporting countries outside the EU. At the Hong Kong ministerial meeting of the WTO in December 2005 the EU agreed to phase out all agricultural export subsidies by the end of 2013. This was a major key to paving the way to a Development Round multilateral trade agreement.

4. It may be noted that the position is more complex than this. For example, although the EU is a large exporter of soft wheat, it still has to import more expensive hard wheat for bread making. Import levies/tariffs calculated with respect to soft wheat result in hard wheat entering the EU at prices very much higher than the MIP.

5. This is also known by its French initials FEOGA, which stand for Fonds Européens d'Orientation et de Garantie Agricole.

6. For a fuller analysis of distribution of budgetary and trade gains and losses from the CAP, see Ackrill *et al.* (1994).

7. This assumes that there are no inefficiencies in the quota market.

8. Under 'truly' decoupled income support, a farmer's decisions on levels of output would be based on the free price equivalents of commodities. Since, under the MacSharry arable regime, the decision of whether or not to set aside land depended on the relative size of compensation payments vis-à-vis the lower *support* price for cereals, it was not truly decoupled.

9. The option allowing EU farmers voluntarily to set aside arable land in return for compensation strictly dates from 1988. However, the impact of the initial set-aside scheme was extremely limited, with very low uptake levels in almost all Member States.

10. In fact the set-aside policy applies to cereals plus oilseeds and protein crops (peas and beans), but for simplicity it will be discussed as though it is only applicable to cereals.

11. If this were not the case, it would be impossible to show the value of compensation payments in price/output space, as in Figure 4.5.

12. Yet another complication in measuring the effects of the new arable regime has been caused by farmers planting set-aside land with crops intended for industrial usage (e.g. linseed) or, alternatively, choosing to plant set-aside areas with forage crops, which has implications for other commodity regimes.

13. Because of devolution all four countries in the UK have produced their own plan to meet their own requirements, thus emphasizing both flexibility and *subsidiarity*.

14. The regulations allow for higher rates of modulation.

15. Based on 2004 and 2005 data from Eurostat.

16. The only element of the SFP set to rise over its first few years is the new dairy premium, intended as compensation for the dairy regime support cuts being phased in from 2005/6 to 2007/8.

17. This outcome was agreed at the Hong Kong ministerial meeting in December 2005.

■ REFERENCES

Ackrill, R. W., Suardi, M., Hine, R. C., and Rayner, A. J. (1994), *The Distributional Effects of the Common Agricultural Policy between Member States: Budget and Trade Effects*, CREDIT Research Paper no. 94/1, University of Nottingham.

BAE (Bureau of Agricultural Economics) (1985), *Agricultural Policies in the European Community*, Policy Monograph no. 2 (Canberra, Australia: BAE).

Blandford, D., de Gorter, H., and Harvey, D. R. (1989), 'Farm Income Support with Minimal Trade Distortions', *Food Policy*, 4 (Aug.): 268–73.

Brown, C. (1989), *Distribution of CAP Price Support*, Report no. 45 (Copenhagen: Statens Jordbrugsokonomiske Institut).

Burrell, A. (1987), 'EC Agricultural Surpluses and Budget Control', *Journal of Agricultural Economics*, 38/1: 1–14.

—— (ed.) (1989), *Milk Quotas in the European Community* (Wallingford: CAB International), ch. 8.

Colman, D. (1985), 'Imperfect Transmission of Policy Prices', *European Review of Agricultural Economics*, 12/3: 171–86.

European Union (2004), *The Common Organisation of the Market in Sugar*, http://europa.eu.int/comm/agriculture/markets/sugar/index_en.htm.

GATT (General Agreement on Tariffs and Trade) (1998), *GATT International Trade 87–88* (Geneva: GATT).

Josling, T. E., and Hamway, D. (1972), *Burdens and Benefits of Farm Support Policies* (London: Trade Policy Research Centre).

MacLaren, D. (1992), 'The Political Economy of Agricultural Policy Reform in the European Community and Australia', *Journal of Agricultural Economics*, 43/3: 424–39.

Ozanne, A. (1992), *Perverse Supply Response in Agriculture* (Aldershot: Avebury).

Rayner, A. J., Ingersent, K. A., and Hine, R. C. (1993), 'Agricultural Trade and the GATT', in A. J. Rayner and D. Colman (eds.), *Current Issues in Agricultural Economics* (Basingstoke: Macmillan), 62–95.

Ritson, C. and Harvey, D. (eds.) (1997), *The Common Agricultural Policy* (Wallingford: CAB International).

Swinbank, A. and Tranter, R. (eds.) (2004), *A Bond Scheme for Common Agricultural Policy Reform* (Wallingford: CABI Publishing).

Swinnen, J. (2000), 'Is the Emergence of Agricultural Protectionism in Central Europe Unavoidable?' paper presented to the XXIV International Conference of Agricultural Economists, Berlin, August.

Tangermann, S. (1991), 'A Bond Scheme for Supporting Farm Incomes', in J. Marsh, B. Green, B. Kearney, L. Mahe, S. Tangermann, and S. Tarditi, *The Changing Role of the Common Agricultural Policy* (London: Belhaven), ch. 10.

—— (1996), 'Implementation of the Uruguay Round Agreement on Agriculture: Issues and Prospects', *Journal of Agricultural Economics*, 47/3: 315–37.

—— (2000), 'Eastern Enlargement of the European Union: A General and Partial Equilibrium Analysis', paper presented to the XXIV International Conference of Agricultural Economists, Berlin, August.

Tracey, M. (1993), *Food and Agriculture in a Market Economy: An Introduction to Theory, Practice and Policy*, (La Hutte, Belgium: Agricultural Policy Studies).

Winters, L. A. (2005), 'European Agricultural Trade Policies and Poverty', *European Review of Agricultural Economics*, 32/3: 319–46.

WTO (2005), *Doha Work Programme: Draft Ministerial Declaration*. WT/MIN(05)/W/3/Rev. 2: http://www.wto.org/english/thewto_e/min05_e/final_text_e.htm.

5 Competition Policy

Stephen Martin

Introduction

Since before the Treaty of Rome, competition policy has been seen as an essential element of the ongoing process of European integration. In 1956, the Spaak Report, which laid the groundwork for the Treaty of Rome, envisaged that:

the treaty should provide the means to avoid situations in which monopoly practices block the fundamental objectives of the common market. In this regard, it is appropriate to prevent

- market division by agreement among firms . . . ;
- agreements to limit output or restrict technical progress . . . ;
- the absorption or domination of the market for a product by a single firm . . . (Comité Inter-gouvernemental 1956: 55)

Such provisions appear in Articles 81 and 82 of the EC Treaty.[1]

Article 81(1), which targets collusion, prohibits agreements that affect trade between the Member States and have the object or effect of preventing, restricting, or distorting competition on the ground that they are incompatible with the common market. Article 81(3) allows exceptions to the Article 81(1) prohibition for agreements that improve production or distribution, or promote technical or economic progress, provided among other conditions that a fair share of the benefits generated by the agreement goes to consumers. Historically, the specific permission of the European Commission was required to take advantage of an Article 81(3) exception. From 1 May 2004, the Commission has decentralized the administration of Article 81(3), in ways that will be detailed below.

Article 82 of the EC Treaty prohibits abuse of a dominant market position by one or more firms. Examples of behaviour that have been found to constitute such abuse include restricting output, price discrimination, and using a dominant position in one market to limit competition in another market.

If a firm is found to violate Article 81 or 82, the Commission may impose a fine up to 10 per cent of the firm's annual turnover. The Commission may also order that offending behaviour be ended.

Articles 81 and 82 are concerned with business conduct. The Merger Control Regulation,[2] in contrast, deals with market structure. It gives the European Commission the authority to vet mergers and related types of business combinations that meet specified size and multinationality conditions. Mergers found to create or reinforce either a single-firm dominant position or a position of collective dominance are declared to be incompatible with the common market. Under the Merger Control Regulation, the European Commission may block a proposed merger entirely, or it may permit a merger to go forward on altered terms that are worked out with the firms involved. As we shall see, the Commission's application of the Merger Control Regulation to concentrations that create positions of collective dominance has been controversial. The Court of First Instance[3] has reversed several of the Commission's merger decisions, and the Commission has adapted its procedures accordingly.

Articles 81, 82, and the Merger Control Regulation set rules for different types of business activity. Articles 86, 87, and 88 of the EC Treaty, in contrast, set rules for actions of the Member States towards the business sector. Article 86 specifies that EU competition policy applies to public enterprises and to private enterprises that are given specific missions by a Member State. Article 87(1) prohibits as incompatible with the common market Member State aid to business, if the aid distorts or threatens to distort competition. Article 87(3) allows exceptions to the Article 87(1) prohibition for aid that promotes regional and other specified types of development.

The direct impact of EU competition policy is on market integration. Its deeper role is to maintain public confidence in the fairness of market processes, and therefore public support for integration of all types. The bare bones of the provisions of EU competition policy are given substantive content in decisions of the European Commission, of the Court of First Instance, and the European Court of Justice. That content continues to evolve, as does the economy of the European Union.

These changes are characterized by an increasing emphasis on the economic effects of different kinds of business behaviour. This emphasis reflects the increasing economic sophistication of the European Commission's Directorate-General for Competition and widening acceptance of the viewpoint that the invisible hand of the marketplace—independent decisions taken by independent firms seeking to maximize their own profit—will, over the long run, lead to the best allocation of resources that is attainable in the real world.

In sections 5.1 and 5.2 of this chapter we discuss Articles 81 and 82, respectively, of the EC Treaty, including an examination of the process of market definition, which has considerable importance in all applications of competition policy. Section 5.3 deals with the Merger Control Regulation. Section 5.4 considers a unique but vital aspect of EU competition policy, the control of aid to business by the Member States.

5.1 Article 81

Horizontal cooperation

Cooperation is said to be horizontal if it is between firms that operate at the same level of the production chain—between manufacturers, or between wholesalers, or between retailers. Some horizontal cooperation is virtually always found to violate EU competition policy: explicit collusion to raise price, to reserve particular geographic areas to particular firms (especially when markets are divided along national boundaries), or to raise barriers to entry for firms outside the agreement.

Before the Treaty of Rome, many Member States had an *abuse control* approach to cartels and collusion. Collusion as such was not illegal. Instead, cartels were obliged to register with the government and might be subject to legal action if they were found to have acted in some way contrary to the public interest. Given the contrast between this policy of benign neglect and the prohibition approach of Article 81(1),[4] it is not surprising that many of the most flagrant examples of overt collusion in the history EU competition law appear in the early years of the Community, before businesses had fully adjusted to the changed legal climate.

Overt collusion

An example is the *Franco-Japanese ball-bearings* case.[5] Representatives of Japanese and French trade associations and ball-bearing producers met in Paris in 1972 and agreed that Japanese firms would raise their prices in Europe from a level 15 per cent below the prices of European firms to no more than 10 per cent below, with an eventual increase to only 5 per cent to 8 per cent below the prices of European firms. French participants prepared minutes of the discussions, and these minutes were found in the files by the Commission during the course of its investigation. The result was a decision by the Commission that the agreements violated Article 81(1) of the EC Treaty.

Leniency

While business executives may keep records of collusive agreements, experience quickly teaches them that it is not in their own self-interest to leave minutes of cartel meetings in places where competition authorities can easily find them. An interesting strategy for a competition authority in search of evidence of collusion, therefore, is to sow dissension in the ranks of colluding firms. This is the rationale behind the Commission's *Leniency Notice*.[6]

The Leniency Notice creates incentives for members of a collusive agreement to defect, to disclose its existence, and to provide evidence to competition enforcers. It provides for complete immunity from fines if a firm is the first to provide the Commission with evidence that allows the Commission to prosecute a cartel and for partial reductions in fines if a firm provides evidence that 'represents significant value added with respect to evidence already in the Commission's possession'. The reductions envisaged are 30 to 50 per cent for the first firm to provide such evidence, 20–30 per cent for the second, and up to 20 per cent for the third and subsequent firms. The Leniency Notice thus rewards firms that defect from a cartel, and offers greater rewards to earlier defectors.

The Leniency Notice played a central role in the Commission's prosecution of the *Lysine Cartel* case.[7] This case concerned agreement on prices, sales volumes, and the exchange of firm-specific information in the market for synthetic lysine, an additive used in animal feeds.

The collusive behaviour involved the firms listed in Table 5.1, as well as an industry trade association, Fefana, that was engaged in EU lobbying. The market had historically

Table 5.1 Sales by amino acid conspirators, 1995, and subsequent fines

	Amino acid sales		Fines	
	Worldwide	European Economic Area (million Euros)	USA (million US $)	EU (million Euros)
Archer Daniels Midland (ADM)	202	41	70	47.3
Ajinomoto	239	75	10	28.3
Kyowa	73	16	10	13.2
Daesang	67	15	1.25	8.9
Cheil	52	17		12.2

Source: Commission Decision 2001/418/EC OJ L 152/14.

been supplied by Ajinomoto, Kyowa, and Daesang. They were joined by ADM and Cheil in 1991. ADM entered in a big way, by building a plant that doubled world lysine capacity.

This expansion of capacity on the supply side of the market first triggered contracts among the three Asian firms, to coordinate their response to entry. ADM arranged for representatives of the three Asian firms to tour its plant, for the purpose of convincing them that its facilities were the largest and the most efficient in the world.

When ADM began supplying the market, it did so at low prices. The resulting price war triggered a series of meetings, continuing for years, to fix prices and divide markets.[8]

On 27 June 1995, the US Federal Bureau of Investigation searched the American offices of ADM, Ajinomoto, and Sewon.[9] The Commission's first Leniency Notice was published in July 1996, and shortly thereafter Ajinomoto contacted the Commission to explore the possibility of turning 'state's evidence'. Ajinomoto and the other firms, in varying degrees, eventually cooperated with the Commission's investigation. Ajinomoto and Sewon received 50 per cent reductions in their fines for cooperating, Kyowa and Cheil 30 per cent reductions, and ADM a reduction of 10 per cent.

Tacit collusion

Market structure is itself determined by market forces, and there are some industries[10] for which equilibrium market structure is oligopolistic. The difficulty this creates for competition policy is that when the number of firms supplying a market is relatively small, they may be able to steer the market towards the kind of outcome usually associated with collusion (restricting output, raising price) without engaging in behaviour that the law regards as collusive.[11]

The European Court of Justice's 1993 *Wood Pulp* decision illustrates the issues involved.[12] During the period covered by this case, the European Community was supplied with wood pulp, an input for the production of paper, by firms located in North America and northern Europe. The European Commission relied on several factors to justify its conclusion that the firms involved in the case had violated Article 81(1) by engaging in a concerted practice:

COMPETITION POLICY **109**

- some US producers were members of an export cartel;[13]
- a number of firms were members of a trade association, based in Switzerland, which was the forum for regular meetings at which firms exchanged information about prices and formulated price policies;
- the prices set by different firms had a history of changing by more or less the same amount at more or less the same time, despite the fact that the firms in question were based in many different countries and kept their accounts in many different currencies.

For the Commission, these parallel price movements were decisive evidence of collusion:[14]

The fact that the addressees of this decision have coordinated their market conduct contrary to Article 81(1) of the EEC Treaty is proved by . . . their parallel conduct in the years 1975 to 1981 which, in light of the conditions obtaining on the market . . . cannot be explained as independently chosen parallel conduct in a narrow oligopolistic situation.

The European Court of Justice was unwilling to accept this conclusion. While parallel price changes might have been the result of collusion, they might also have been the result of a combination of a high degree of price transparency—prices widely known and news of price changes circulating rapidly—and the oligopoly structure of the market. For the Court, evidence of parallel pricing in combination with other factors might justify a finding of concertation, but in this instance the other evidence assembled by the Commission was not sufficient.

This is one example of the more general *oligopoly problem* facing competition authorities: when a market has an oligopolistic market structure, firms may be able to obtain collusive outcomes (restricted output, higher prices) without engaging in conduct that is collusive in a legal sense. The oligopoly problem raises at least two difficulties for competition policy. The first is one of proof: even if firms in an oligopolistic market are in fact colluding in a legal sense, it may be difficult to obtain sufficient evidence of that collusion. The Commission's leniency programme seeks to deal with this difficulty.

The second problem is one of remedy. If firms are colluding, they can be ordered not to collude. They can be made subject to large enough fines so that they decide it is in their own best interest not to collude. But firms in oligopolistic industries will often be able to refrain from tough competition without colluding; equilibrium market performance without collusion in an oligopolistic industry may be closer to monopoly than one would like. But if this is the kind of outcome that is produced by independent business decisions, there is not much policy-makers can do to obtain better market performance.[15]

Article 81(3) and the modernization package

At the dawn of the EC, the Commission faced the task of introducing a prohibition-based competition policy to a Community of six Member States, only one of which (West Germany) had a similar national competition policy. The others had either no explicit competition policy or followed an abuse control approach that viewed collusion as a natural and inevitable outcome of market processes. Under these circumstances, the European Commission reserved to itself the right to grant exemptions under Article 81(3).[16] To this end, cooperating businesses were obliged to notify the Commission of their agreement. In theory, such agreements might be permitted or not, depending on whether the conditions of Article 81(3) were or were not met.

In practice, some agreements were not notified to the Commission, and these were condemned if and when the Commission discovered their existence. Otherwise, the Commission was confronted with a flood of notifications that required some response but overwhelmed the resources available. One response was the block exemption system: formal policy statements outlining broad classes of agreements, typically based on market share thresholds and other conditions, that automatically qualified for an Article 81(3) exemption. Another was the issuance of so-called *comfort letters* to notifying firms: statements that on the basis of the information before the Commission, the notified arrangement either did or did not appear to meet the conditions for an exemption under Article 81(3). The Commission issued comfort letters without formal action, and the European Court of Justice held that they did not constitute legally binding decisions.

The notification system, designed to promote reliance on markets as a resource allocation mechanism to a Community of six Member States, became less and less workable as the Community expanded to twenty-five members, and less and less necessary as Member States and businesses reached common views on the rules of the market game. As of 1 May 2004, with Regulation 1/2003,[17] the Commission has abandoned the notification approach, and as part of a general modernization of Community competition policy, allows firms to judge for themselves, in the first instance, whether a contemplated agreement meets the conditions of Article 81(3):

Under the new regulation, agreements that fulfil the conditions of Article 81(3) are legally valid and enforceable without the intervention of an administrative decision. Undertakings will be able to invoke the exception rule of Article 81(3) EC as a defence in proceedings before the Commission, Member States' courts and Member States' competition authorities. (Lowe 2004: 55)

Firms that invoke Article 81(3) may be required to defend that decision by Member State competition authorities or by the Commission. With this in mind, Regulation 1/2003 outlines a division of labour between Member State competition authorities and the Commission, which together make up the European Competition Network, in enforcing this and other aspects of Community competition policy.

Standards for use of the Article 81(3) exemption are set out in a series of regulations and guidelines.[18] These cover vertical cooperation agreements (between a supplier and a customer), specialization agreements, joint R&D agreements, technology transfer agreements, and other types of horizontal cooperation agreements (among actual or potential competitors).[19] The goal is to try to take the good that comes from interfirm agreements while avoiding the bad:

horizontal co-operation between competitors can have both negative and positive effects on the market. On the one hand, horizontal co-operation may lead to competition problems. This is the case if the parties to a co-operation agree to fix prices, output, or share markets, or if the co-operation enables the parties to maintain, gain or increase market power . . .

On the other hand, horizontal co-operation may also often be useful and pro-competitive. . . . Co-operation can be a means to share risk, save costs, pool know-how and launch innovation faster. In particular for small and medium sized enterprises co-operation is an important means to adapt to the changing economic environment. (Lücking 2000: 41–2)

While the details of the specific regulations and guidelines differ, there is a common general approach. Agreements that would serve primarily to eliminate competition cannot be exempted under Article 81(3). This is hardly surprising. The more interesting cases are those in which the realization of efficiency benefits from cooperation inevitably involves some restriction on competition.[20] The approach of the Commission is to set market share thresholds, below which an agreement may take advantage of the Article 81(3) exemption.

The R&D block exemption sets a combined market share threshold of 25 per cent for cooperative R&D by competing firms. The market share threshold for specialization agreements and technology transfer agreements is 20 per cent. The Commission takes the view that if the combined market share of cooperating firms is relatively small, the beneficial effects of cooperation are likely to prevail, since effective competition from other suppliers will limit the exercise of market power.

Market definition

The presence of market share thresholds in block exemptions and guidelines for application of the Article 81(3) exemption lends importance to the process by which markets are defined. Market definition is also critical to Article 82 assessments of the presence or absence of a dominant position, and to decisions under the Merger Control Regulation as to whether a proposed merger would create a single-firm or collective dominant position.

For what might be called backward-looking applications of competition policy—to allegations of collusion or abuses of dominance—market definition may be relatively straightforward. For example, in the *Amino Acids* case, the conduct of the firms involved indicated that the product market was lysine for animal feed and that the geographic market was worldwide. In contrast, decisions about the application of Article 81(3) and the Merger Control Regulation are essentially forward-looking. Assessments of whether or not a cooperative arrangement will generate efficiency gains, whether or not consumers will share in such benefits if they materialize, involve an unavoidable element of speculation about the future. Particularly for forward-looking applications of competition policy, the procedures that are used to define markets and measure market shares therefore assume some importance.

For the Commission,

The main purpose of market definition is to identify . . . the competitive constraints that the undertakings involved face. The objective of defining a market in both its product and geographic dimension is to identify those actual competitors of the undertakings involved that are capable of constraining their behaviour and of preventing them from behaving independently of an effective competitive pressure. (European Commission 1997: 1)

In principle, the Commission emphasizes the demand side when it defines markets (1997: 2): 'A relevant product market comprises all those products and/or services which are regarded as interchangeable or substitutable by the consumer' and (1997: 3) 'Basically, the exercise of market definition consists in identifying the effective alternative sources of supply for customers of the undertakings involved, both in terms of products/services and geographic location of suppliers.' The primary theoretical test that the Commission applies is the SSNIP (Small Significant Non-Transitory Increase in Price), which is based upon how consumers would respond to price changes:

The question to be answered is whether the parties' customers would switch to readily available substitutes or to suppliers located elsewhere in response to an hypothetical small (in the range 5%–10%), permanent relative price increase in the products and areas being considered. If substitution would be enough to make the price increase unprofitable because of the resulting loss of sales, additional substitutes and areas are included in the relevant market. This would be done until the set of products and geographic areas is such that small, permanent increases in relative prices would be profitable. (European Commission 1997: 4)

The Commission also takes supply-side substitutability into account—whether suppliers are (1997: 4) 'able to switch production to the relevant products and market them in the short term without incurring significant additional costs or risks in response to small and permanent changes in relative prices'.[21]

The Commission Notice on market definition suggests applying the SSNIP test 'as a thought experiment'. It may sometimes be possible to carry out sophisticated econometric analyses of demand patterns to reach conclusions about the nature of the market. Often the time and data requirements of such methods will mean that they cannot be used by the Commission when it defines a market. Thus when it defines markets the Commission often looks at practical information about the nature of demand for a class of products (1997: 8–10): historical substitution patterns, the views of customers and competitors, evidence of costs of switching from one brand or supplier to another, whether there are distinctive national preferences.

Vertical cooperation

Cooperation is said to be vertical if it is between firms that operate at different levels of the production chain—between a manufacturer and wholesalers, for example, or between a wholesaler and retailers.

Manufacturers and distributors often agree to contracts that embody vertical restraints, including but not limited to

- exclusive territories (a manufacturer authorizes one and only one distributor for a certain area);
- exclusive purchasing (a distributor agrees to acquire all supplies of a certain product from a specified manufacturer);
- resale price maintenance (the distributor agrees to sell at, or not below, the price designated by the manufacturer).[22]

A manufacturer may also administer a selective distribution system (specifying minimum standards of certain kinds that must be satisfied by a distributor and supplying all or a subset of qualifying distributors). Franchise agreements typically involve some vertical restraints.

Vertical restraints typically restrict competition between dealers of a single brand (intra-brand competition). If a manufacturer finds it profitable to restrict competition between dealers of his brand, it may be because the manufacturer feels that those restrictions will lead the dealers to behave in ways that promote competition between his brand and other brands (inter-brand competition). In such cases, the vertical restraints have both pro- and anti-competitive effects, and the net impact on market performance is ambiguous.[23]

A fundamental purpose of EU competition policy is to promote market integration. The Commission has, therefore, consistently opposed vertical restraints that have the effect of splitting the single market along national boundaries. For example, national resale price maintenance systems do not come under the authority of EU competition law, since they do not affect trade between the Member States.[24] But the Commission has held that existence of a legal national resale price maintenance system cannot be used to block shipments of a manufacturer's product from one Member State to another. If a German record producer supplies a retail distributor in France, the French distributor must be allowed to sell in Germany if it is profitable to do so, even if such sales are at a price below the fixed German retail price.[25]

The *FEG/TU* decision[26] is an example of the not uncommon combination of trade associations and vertical restraints in restricting competition. FEG, the Dutch association of electrotechnical equipment wholesalers, maintained an exclusive dealing system with an association of importers of such goods and with domestic suppliers, all of whom were bound to distribute their products through FEG members. Wholesalers that were not part of FEG were thus subject to artificial restrictions on their ability to obtain supplies; wholesalers located outside the Netherlands were not able to bring their products into the Netherlands using importers that were bound by the exclusive dealing agreement.[27] The Commission ordered that the exclusive dealing agreement be ended and levied fines of €6.5 million.

These cases illustrate the kinds of negative effects that may flow from vertical restraints: raising barriers to entry, foreclosing rivals from distribution channels, facilitating collusion, and impeding effective market integration. Possible efficiency effects include quality control and promoting distributor sales efforts in a way that increases inter-brand competition.[28]

The 1999 vertical restraints regulation[29] adopts an economic effects approach to the treatment of vertical restraints. Minimum resale price maintenance is prohibited. So are airtight exclusive territories: if a dealer receives a request from a customer located outside the dealer's designated territory, the manufacturer must allow the dealer to fill the request. Other types of vertical restraints are permitted under a block exemption if the manufacturer's market share is less than 30 per cent. If a manufacturer's market share exceeds 30 per cent, an exemption under Article 81(3) is possible, taking into account the same general elements of market structure—seller concentration, entry conditions, among others—that come into play for a horizontal cooperative agreement.[30]

The motor vehicle sector has long benefited from exceptional treatment under EU competition policy. A specific regulation[31] permitted car manufacturers to sell only through designated dealers, to assign dealers to specific territories, to require various quality standards (for example, showroom size and post-sales service facilities), and to impose other restrictions. These restrictions on intra-brand competition were said to be justified (¶4) 'because motor vehicles are consumer durables which at both regular and irregular intervals require expert maintenance and repair, not always in the same place'. The regulation also requires car manufacturers to allow a dealer to sell to customers or customers' designated representatives whether or not the customer is resident in the dealer's designated sales area.

Consumer groups long challenged the idea that consumers benefited from the special car distribution regulation. It was seen as contributing to large and persistent car price differences between Member States.[32] Further, car manufacturers did not honour the part of the regulation that requires them to allow dealers to supply customers resident outside the dealer's home territory. In 1995, the European Commission fined Volkswagen AG €102 million on the ground that VW discouraged its authorized dealers in Italy from supplying cars to customers from parts of northern Europe. From 1993 to 1995, exchange rate movements made it attractive for customers in Germany and elsewhere to consider buying cars in Italy. VW structured its dealer programmes so that such sales did not count towards satisfying dealer quotas and did not help the dealer meet requirements for some bonus schemes. VW threatened to end the contracts of some Italian dealers if they sold to customers from outside their territories, and twelve dealerships were in fact cancelled. In July 2000, upon appeal by VW, the Court of First Instance allowed €90 million of the fine to stand.

In April 1999, the Commission suggested that DaimlerChrysler had sought to keep some of its dealers from selling outside their territories. In September 1999, VW was the subject of a second investigation by the Commission for restricting dealers in ways inconsistent with the car distribution regulation. In September 2000, the Commission fined General Motors' Dutch subsidiary €43 million for seeking to block sales by Dutch dealers to EU residents from outside the Netherlands.[33]

A new car distribution regulation was adopted in 31 July 2002,[34] to take partial effect on 1 October 2003 and full effect on 1 October 2005. The Regulation sets out rules intended to open up competition in post-sales service of motor vehicles. At the distribution level, the new regulation requires manufacturers to choose between awarding distributors exclusive territories or using a selective distribution system (excluding non-authorized dealers); after 1 October 2005, it will not be possible to combine the two. Most have opted to maintain selective distribution systems (Lauer 2003). The disappearance of exclusive territories is likely to trigger some consolidation at the distribution level. The impact of the new regulation on market performance, and consumer welfare, remains to be seen.[35]

5.2 Article 82

The *United Brands* decision[36] illustrates the basic principles of EU competition policy towards abuse of a dominant position. The case dealt with conduct in the early 1970s, at which time the United Brands Company (UBC) was the leading banana producer in the world and more particularly in the European Community, with a market share of about 40 per cent. Its operations were vertically integrated from banana plantations through ocean shipping to destination markets. In those markets, it employed networks of banana ripeners and distributors that were subject to vertical restraints. These vertical restraints had the effect of partitioning the EEC into national submarkets. In at least one instance,

UBC cut off supplies from a distributor that had supplied bananas outside its home territory. Prices differed substantially across Member States, although the costs of supplying the different markets were much the same.

A preliminary issue was one of market definition. United Brands argued that the relevant product market was that for fresh fruit, in which UBC's market share was too small to justify a finding that it had a dominant position. The European Commission viewed bananas as the relevant product market, arguing that bananas have distinctive characteristics that separate demand for bananas from the demand for other types of fruit. The European Court of Justice accepted the Commission's arguments and heard the case taking bananas to be the relevant product market.

In the Commission's decision, it characterized a dominant position as:

the power to behave independently without taking into account, to any substantial extent, their competitors, purchasers and suppliers. Such is the case when an undertaking's market share, either in itself or when combined with knowhow, access to raw materials, capital, or other major advantage such as brand loyalty, enables it to determine the prices or to control the production or distribution of a significant part of the relevant goods. ([1978] ECR 207 at 217)

The Commission argued, and the Court of Justice accepted, that UBC had a dominant position in the relevant market, based largely on its market share and the unique vertical integration of its operations. From this dominant position, UBC could maximize profit subject to few constraints from rival banana producers, from vertically related distributors, and from the final consumers of bananas.[37] The Court also found that UBC had abused its dominant position by dint of its conduct towards its distributors. This conduct had the effect of partitioning the EC into submarkets along national boundaries.

The Commission also argued that UBC had abused its dominant position by charging prices that were both discriminatory and unfair. The facts of the case established that prices were in fact substantially different in different Member States. For the Commission, abuse lay in the fact that UBC had 'applied dissimilar conditions to equivalent transactions with the other trading parties, thereby placing them at a competitive disadvantage' ([1978] ECR 207 at 296). The immediate victims of abuse, then, were UBC's distributors in countries where UBC set higher prices. They were, presumably, less able to compete with other types of fruit than UBC's distributors in countries where UBC set lower prices. To sustain these price differences, UBC was obliged to impose restrictions on the resale of green bananas by distributors across national boundaries—otherwise, distributors in low-price countries would export and undersell distributors in high-price countries. The resulting partitioning of national markets was a distinct element of abuse of a dominant position.

The Commission also argued that UBC had abused its dominant position by charging unfair prices. As evidence, the Commission compared the lowest and highest prices set by UBC in different national markets, and argued that if UBC could profitably supply the low-price markets, its prices in the high-price markets must be unfair. The Court accepted the idea that charging unfair prices would be an abuse of a dominant position, but it also found that the Commission should have made a direct investigation of UBC's costs and reached a conclusion about unfairness by comparing costs and prices. Thus the Court set aside the Commission's finding that UBC had abused its dominant position by setting unfair prices.

Price discrimination and partitioning the single market are abuses of a dominant position. Actions that have the effect of making it more difficult for rivals to compete on the merits are also abuse of a dominant position.

For example, in the late 1990s British Airways used incentive schemes for payments to travel agents under which the agents were paid more, the greater the increases in their customers' bookings with BA over the level of the previous year. This loyalty rebate scheme created incentives for travel agents to concentrate bookings on BA, and the incentive payments received by the agents were not directly related to efficiencies or cost savings, if any, generated by the higher booking level.

In its decision regarding the incentive scheme,[38] the Commission defined the relevant market as that for air travel agency services in the United Kingdom. BA disagreed, arguing that the market definition should take account of the fact that some final consumers purchase plane tickets without going through travel agencies (as, for example, directly from the airline over the internet). The Commission found BA to be a dominant customer in the product market (39.7 per cent of 1998 UK airfare sales through travel agents were for travel on BA). It traced BA's position as a dominant purchaser of travel agency services to BA's leading position in passenger air transport and its control of landing slots at major UK airports. The Commission also found that BA's loyalty payment scheme was an abuse of a dominant position, and fined BA €6.8 million. In this case, the nature of the abuse was interference with the ability of rival airlines to compete for the services of travel agencies. BA announced its intention to appeal the decision to EU courts.

The Commission's finding in the BA case is consistent with a long line of decisions which find that a seller with a dominant position may offer prices to consumers that are lower in proportion to lower costs of supplying the consumer, but commits an abuse if it offers lower prices solely for consumer loyalty. The BA decision applies the same logic—interference with the ability of rivals to compete on merit—to the situation of a dominant buyer.

EU competition policy does not seek to limit the ability of dominant firms to compete. It does insist that such competition be based on efficiency rather than strategic anti-competitive behaviour (European Commission 1999b: 38). In this vein, the Commission has applied Article 82 to firms that enjoy a dominant position as a result of Member State legislation. The *Frankfurt Airport* decision[39] involved the market for the provision of airport facilities—services like baggage handling that must be performed for aircraft to land and take off—at the Frankfurt airport. Under German law, the company managing the airport (FAG) had a legal monopoly, hence a dominant position, in the supply of airport facilities at the airport. The Commission determined that the market for the provision of ground-handling services constituted a distinct product market. It found that FAG had abused its monopoly position in the market for airport facilities by reserving the right to supply ground-handling services to itself, and ordered FAG to allow independent firms to supply ground-handling services.[40]

In the Commission's 2004 *Microsoft* decision,[41] it was conceded that Microsoft enjoyed a dominant position in the worldwide market for personal computer operating systems. The Commission found that Microsoft had abused this position by strategically withholding information related to the interoperability of Windows PC operating systems and work group server stations and by bundling its Windows Media Player with its operating system software. Both strategies have the effect of making it more difficult for rivals to compete on merit.[42]

In addition to levying a record €497 million fine, the Commission's decision embodied two remedies:

1. Microsoft was obliged to disclose sufficient information to permit competitors' work group servers to interoperate fully with Windows PCs and servers; and

2. Microsoft was obliged to market a version of its operating system that does not bundle operating system and media player.[43]

This decision is consistent with the general interpretation of Article 82, which is not to punish firms that have a dominant position, but to insist that dominant firms not use their position to shield themselves from competition.

Microsoft appealed the Commission's decision to the European courts. In December 2004, the Court of First Instance refused the company's request to suspend the remedies until after a decision on Microsoft's appeal. In November 2005, the Commission notified Microsoft of the Commission's concern that the company was not complying with the interoperability-related information-disclosure requirements of the March 2004 decision. In July 2006, the Commission fined Microsoft €280.5 million (a penalty of €2 million per day for non-compliance) and raised the daily penalty for continued non-compliance to €3 million.

5.3 Merger control

Our discussion of the oligopoly problem has one clear implication for competition policy. If there are practical difficulties in influencing business conduct in oligopoly markets, competition authorities should take care in policy towards market structure. Proposed mergers should be carefully vetted to ensure that they are privately profitable because they increase efficiency, not because they increase market power.

Merger control came relatively late to the menu of European Community competition policy: control of collusion and of firms with dominant market positions dates to 1957 and the Treaty of Rome, merger control only to 1989. The founding fathers of what has become the European Union were explicitly concerned with preventing collusion and price discrimination along national lines, not with regulating market structure. Indeed, they may well have had some quiet sympathy for the idea of promoting EU champions to operate in world markets. It was only thirty years into the process of EU market integration that political support allowed the European Commission's Directorate-General for Competition to persuade Member State representatives to adopt the Merger Control Regulation.

The original focus of the Regulation, which was subject to technical amendments in 1997,[44] was dominance:

A concentration which creates or strengthens a dominant position as a result of which effective competition would be significantly impeded in the common market or in a substantial part of it shall be declared incompatible with the common market. (Article 2(3))

Whether or not a concentration will create or strengthen a dominant position can be assessed only in the context of a relevant product and geographic market. For merger control, as for other aspects of competition policy, market definition is critical.

The Commission stepped gingerly in the early years of merger control: between 1989 and 1995, only four mergers were blocked. More often, mergers were allowed to go forward, possibly on amended terms that eliminated the Commission's concerns about the creation of a dominant position.[45]

With experience, the Commission has introduced the concept of joint or collective dominance to EU merger control. As we have seen, the Commission has had only limited success in applying Article 81 to situations in which existing market structures allow firms in oligopoly to jointly exercise market power. Use of the concept of collective dominance in merger policy can be seen as an attempt to prevent the emergence of market structures that would allow firms in the post-merger market to exercise market power non-cooperatively.

The nature of post-merger market structure is critical to application of the concept of collective dominance to merger policy. Market characteristics that might lead to a finding of joint dominance are high market concentration as well as 'homogeneous products, transport, high entry barriers, mature technology, static or falling demand, links between suppliers, absence of countervailing buyer power, etc.' (EC Commission 1999b: 51).

Gencor/Lonrho

Collective dominance arose in the Commission's *Gencor/Lonrho*[46] decision. The firms proposing to merge were the leading firms in the world market for platinum and rhodium, with their principal mining operations in South Africa. A third firm, Amplats, would have become the second largest supplier in a highly concentrated market if the merger had gone forward. The European Commission estimated that in the post-merger market, Gencor/Lonrho and Amplats together would have had a combined world market share of 60–70 per cent. This share would have grown to 80 per cent after Russian supplies were depleted. Taking the view that the merger would create a market structure in which the two survivor firms would be able to act as a dominant duopoly, the Commission blocked the merger.

Gencor and Lonrho appealed the Commission's decision to the Court of First Instance, raising three main objections:

- the Commission lacked jurisdiction over the merger;
- the Merger Control does not apply to mergers which create or strengthen a position of collective dominance;
- the Commission was wrong to conclude that the merger would create a position of collective dominance.

With regard to the first objection, the Court had held in many previous decisions that EU competition policy applies to conduct that has an effect on the common market, independent of the location of the firm or firms involved. It applied the same rule to the Merger Control Regulation.

As a matter of principle, it was the second objection that was vital. The Court wrote that

the principal objective set for the Regulation, with a view to achieving the aims of the Treaty . . . is to ensure that the process of reorganising undertakings as a result in particular of the completion of the internal market does not inflict lasting damage on competition

and that

A concentration which creates or strengthens a dominant position on the part of the parties to the concentration with an entity not involved in the concentration is liable to prove incompatible with the system of undistorted competition laid down by the Treaty. Consequently, if it were accepted that only concentrations creating or strengthening a dominant position on the part of the parties to the concentration were covered by the Regulation, its purpose . . . would be partially frustrated.

The Court thus concluded that the Merger Control Regulation does apply to mergers that create a position of collective dominance.

The Commission relied on the following factors, among others, to conclude that the merger would create a position of collective dominance:

- high post-merger market shares of the two leading firms;
- no realistic possibility of entry by new suppliers;
- similar cost structures of the two leading post-merger firms (so that they would have the same views as to the most profitable post-merger price)

The Court set out the general standard that the Commission had to satisfy to reach a conclusion that a merger would create a position of collective dominance:

In assessing whether there is a collective dominant position, the Commission is . . . obliged to establish, using a prospective analysis of the relevant market, whether the concentration in question would lead to a situation in which effective competition in the relevant market would be significantly impeded by the undertakings involved in the concentration and one or more other undertakings which together, in particular because of factors giving rise to a connection between them, are able to adopt a common policy on the market and act to a considerable extent independently of their competitors, their customers and, ultimately, of consumers . . .

The Court considered the firms' objections to each of the Commission's arguments, and concluded that the Commission was justified in reaching its decision.

The firms also argued that the Commission had erred in refusing to accept commitments about the behaviour of the post-merger firm:

- the development of a specified amount of extra capacity;
- the maintenance of output at specified levels;
- the creation of a new supplier in the market.

In affirming the Commission's decision, as regards the first two points, the Court wrote that the purpose of Merger Control Regulation was to control market structure, not business conduct. To permit a merger based on a commitment to maintain output at specified levels would require monitoring the output levels of the post-merger firm, a role for which the Commission was ill-suited. On the third point, the Court found that no evidence had been presented to suggest that a new supplier could be an effective competitive force on the market.

Airtours/First Choice

With the September 1999 *Airtours/First Choice* decision,[47] the Commission sought to push the collective dominance doctrine further by blocking a takeover that would have reduced the number of leading firms in the UK travel operator market from four to three. The Commission estimated the combined 1998 market shares of Airtours and First Choice at 34.4 per cent, with the market shares of the next two leading firms at 30.7 per cent and 20.4 per cent respectively. If these market shares remained unchanged, the post-takeover market would have been one in which the leading three firms had a combined market share of 85 per cent.

The Commission viewed the supply side of the market as an oligopolistic core of large, vertically integrated firms and a fringe of much smaller, non-integrated firms. For the Commission, a takeover of First Choice by Airtours would increase oligopolistic interdependence among the smaller number of core firms and marginalize fringe firms, which would be faced with the necessity of purchasing essential inputs—transportation services —from their larger competitors.

In the Commission's opinion, the merger would make it easier for the large firms to restrict capacity—available tour bookings—about which decisions needed to be made twelve to eighteen months in advance. Capacity restriction would be facilitated even if the large firms did not collude: the takeover would facilitate joint dominance.

The Commission therefore condemned the takeover as incompatible with the common market on the ground that it would create a situation of collective dominance in the UK market for short-haul foreign package holidays. Airtours appealed the Commission's decision to the Court of First Instance.

In its appeal, Airtours complained that

- the Commission had violated legal principles by using a new definition of collective dominance, with respect to earlier decisions; and

- the Commission had not presented adequate proof to conclude that the Airtours–First Choice merger would have created a position of collective dominance.

In dealing with these complaints, the Court first indicated what it was that the Commission had to prove (¶62):

- first, each member of the dominant oligopoly must have the ability to know how the other members are behaving in order to monitor whether or not they are adopting the common policy . . . There must, therefore, be sufficient market transparency for all members of the dominant oligopoly to be aware, sufficiently precisely and quickly, of the way in which the other members' market conduct is evolving; . . .

- second, the situation of tacit coordination must be sustainable over time, that is to say, there must be an incentive not to depart from the common policy on the market . . . each member of the dominant oligopoly must be aware that highly competitive action

COMPETITION POLICY **121**

on its part designed to increase its market share would provoke identical action by the others, so that it would derive no benefit from its initiative . . . ;

- third, to prove the existence of a collective dominant position to the requisite legal standard, the Commission must also establish that the foreseeable reaction of current and future competitors, as well as of consumers, would not jeopardise the results expected from the common policy.

The Court reviewed the Commission's decisions and found factual errors. Among these were that

- the Commission had not provided sufficient evidence to prove its conclusion that the market was highly transparent;
- the Commission had underestimated the inclination and ability of fringe firms to expand output if it should be profitable to do so; and
- the Commission failed to take the implications of relatively low barriers to entry for the creation of a position of collective dominance into account.

For the Court, the Commission had not proved its case, and it annulled the Commission's decision.

Merger Review Package

One element of the institutional modernization of EU competition policy that took effect on 1 May 2004 was a revised Merger Control Regulation.[48] In some ways, Regulation 139/2004 merely fine-tuned features of the previous regulation. In other ways, the new regulation and accompanying changes sought to respond to reversals like those suffered by the Commission in the *Airtours/First Choice* and other[49] decisions.

Like its predecessor, the Merger Control Regulation applies to mergers[50] that have a 'Community dimension': combinations involving firms with sales that are large world-wide, large in the Community, but not concentrated primarily in a single Member State.[51] It aims to minimize the administrative burden on firms in two ways.[52] First, it seeks to combine the 'one-stop shop' and the subsidiarity principles. Mergers should be examined by the most appropriate competition authority: by the Commission if it has a Community dimension, by a Member State competition authority if it will affect mainly the economy of that Member State. The need for firms to subject a proposed merger to the scrutiny of several Member State competition authorities should be minimized. Second, the Commission must deliver a decision within the relatively compact time periods that are specified in the Regulation.

But neither the new regulation nor its complementary reforms are entirely fine-tuning. While the original regulation focused on dominance, the corresponding wording of the new regulation gives attention to dominance, but defines *impeding effective competition* as the critical characteristic that places a proposed merger beyond the pale:

A concentration which would significantly impede effective competition in the common market or in a substantial part of it, in particular as a result of the creation or strengthening of a dominant position, shall be declared incompatible with the common market. (Article 2(3))

The preamble (¶25) to the Regulation makes clear that this evolution of the wording of the Regulation seeks to deal with the oligopoly problem, market structures in which non-cooperative behaviour leads to poor market performance:

under certain circumstances, concentrations involving the elimination of important competitive constraints that the merging parties had exerted upon each other, as well as a reduction of competitive pressure on the remaining competitors, may, even in the absence of a likelihood of coordination between the members of an oligopoly, result in a significant impediment to effective competition . . . In the interests of legal certainty, it should be made clear that this Regulation permits effective control of all such concentrations . . .

Furthermore, the Directorate-General of Competition has created the post of Chief Economist and instituted a process of internal review by an independent panel before decisions are confirmed. The substantive changes in the Merger Control Regulation should enhance Commission control of mergers that would result in collective dominance, and the internal reforms should go far in ensuring that the Commission has its economic and evidentiary houses in order when it makes decisions.

International cooperation

European Union competition policy applies to actions that affect competition in the common market, no matter where those actions take place. As globalization increases the number of markets that have worldwide geographic scope, this means that firms may find their strategic decisions scrutinized by competition authorities of more than one jurisdiction. Since competition authorities enforce different laws, and since business actions that distort competition in one region may not distort competition in another region, it may well happen that a cooperation agreement or merger is given a green light by one competition authority and stopped with a red light by a different competition authority.[53]

To avoid conflict in enforcement of competition laws, in so far as possible, the European Commission has put cooperative arrangements in place with competition authorities of other jurisdictions.[54] The European Commission is also a driving force behind the International Competition Network, an association of competition authorities from around the world that provides a forum for dialogue on enforcement issues.

5.4 State aid

Perhaps the most prominent slippage in the culture of competition that has developed in the European Union is the persistent tendency for Member States to deliver financial support to local firms. Such aid undermines the public faith in a 'level playing field' that is essential for EU integration: businesses in less well-off Member States will not put up for long with tougher competition in their home markets if they have reason to think that rivals from elsewhere in the EU are subsidized by governments of better-off Member States.

Member States have explored a wide variety of ways to deliver aid to business—direct subsidies, capital investment, selective tax breaks, loan guarantees, sales of assets to

Table 5.2 State aid (excluding agriculture, fisheries, transport), EU-15 and EU-25, 2000–4

	EU-15		EU-25	
	Total	% of GDP	Total	% of GDP
Annual average, 2000–2	43.4	0.45	48.5	0.48
Annual average, 2002–4	42.9	0.44	49.0	0.48

Source: European Commission press release, 9 December 2005.

business below a reasonable market price, purchases from the company above a reasonable market price, and so on. The rule for EU competition policy is that state aid is present when public policy directly or indirectly gives a firm an economic advantage it would not otherwise have (Morch 1995). State aid, whatever its form, is forbidden by Article 87(1) of the EC Treaty, provided it distorts competition and affects trade between the Member States. Exceptions may be allowed under Article 87(3) if the aid serves some Community purpose.

General practice is codified and strengthened in the 1999 Regulation on state aid procedures.[55] Member States are required to notify the Commission in advance of aid projects. Aid projects cannot be put into effect unless and until approved by the Commission. Aid that is not notified to the Commission cannot benefit from the possibility of exemption under Article 87(3), and aid that is granted without receiving an exemption is to be recovered.

The 1999 Regulation increases the Commission's investigatory powers and makes clear that legal appeals before national courts are not to delay recovery of aid that has been denied an exemption. But 21 per cent of 1997 aid cases were not notified to the Commission (Sinnaeve 1998: 80). In many instances, firms kept aid after a decision that it was incompatible with the common market: 'Nearly 10% of the recovery decisions are not executed *10 years* after they have been taken, in the majority of cases because of pending procedures before national courts' (Sinnaeve 1998: 80; emphasis in original). Aid continues to be granted at significant levels, and continued Commission efforts will be needed to realize further progress (particularly but by no means only in the new Member States).

5.5 Conclusions

EU competition policy began as the safeguard of the integration process. So it remains, even though the integration process has extended itself to dimensions that were only dreamed of in 1957. One hallmark in the development of EU competition policy is an enhanced role for economic analysis, with business and Member State conduct judged according to its effects in the marketplace, not its legal form. Another is a wave of procedural modernizations that seek to equip competition policy for the larger and more deeply integrated economy that it must serve in the immediate future.

One challenge that must be handled if this modernization is to be successful is to ensure consistent enforcement of horizontal restraint policy under Article 81 as that enforcement moves to the Member State level. Another challenge will be to shackle the tendency of Member States to aid firms that are placed in difficulty by the increased competition that comes with wider and deeper integration.

■ DISCUSSION QUESTIONS

1   Examine the role of market definition in the first merger proposal that was blocked by the European Commission, *Aerospatiale-Alenia/de Haviland*, Commission Decision 91/619/EEC of 2 October 1991, OJ L 334/42 5 December 1991, pp. 327–9.

2   Read Albæk *et al.* (1997). Discuss the role of information in sustaining tacit collusion.

3   Discuss (a) the Court of First Instance *Schneider/Legrand* decision[56] and (b) the European Court of Justice *Tetra Laval* decision.[57] How does the Merger Review Package (*Competition Policy Newsletter*, Special Edition, 2004) respond to the points made by the Courts in these judgments?

■ FURTHER READING

The website of the European Commission's Competition Directorate (http://europa.eu.int/comm/competition/) is the best source for tracking developments in EU competition policy. The *Competition Policy Newsletter* (http://europa.eu.int/comm/competition/publications/cpn/) gives a good overview of Community competition law developments.

■ NOTES

1. The Treaty of Amsterdam renumbered the Articles of the EC and EU Treaties. The Treaty of Nice merged the EC Treaty and the EU Treaty into a consolidated version (Official Journal (OJ) C 325/1, 24.12.2002). Articles 81 and 82 of the consolidated Treaty were originally Articles 85 and 86 of the Treaty of Rome. Throughout this chapter, I have referred to Treaty Provisions by their current numbers, where necessary changing the text of older decisions and documents.

2. First Council Regulation (EEC) No. 4064/89 OJ L 395/1, 30.12.89, amended by Council Regulation (EC) No. 1310/97, OJ L 180, 9.7.1997, now Council Regulation (EC) No. 139/2004 OJ L 24/1, 29.01.2004.

3. Established October 1988.

4. What are now Articles 81 and 82 of the EC Treaty were largely based on Articles 65 and 66 of the Treaty establishing the European Coal and Steel Community, the first versions of which were drafted by Robert Bowie, assistant to the American High Commissioner to Germany, at the request of Jean Monnet. Monnet adopted the US-style approach to competition policy to assuage concerns that the ECSC would be little more than an attempt to revive interwar cartels (Ball 1973: 88; Monnet 1976: 413; Bowie 1989; Spierenburg and Poidevin 1994: 28).

5. OJ No L 343 21 December 1974, pp. 19–26.

6. Commission Notice on immunity from fines and reduction of fines in cartel cases OJ C 45/3 19 February 2002. This notice replaces the first leniency notice (OJ C 207 18 July 1996, p. 4; see Peña Castellot 2001). The leniency programme of US anti-trust authorities dates from August 1993.

7. Commission Decision of 7 June 2000 relating to a proceeding pursuant to Article 81 of the EC Treaty and Article 53 of the EEA Agreement (Case COMP/36.545/F3—Amino Acids). OJ L 152/24 7 June 2001. See, generally, Connor (2001).

8. At a meeting on 30 April 2003 at ADM's facility in Decatur, Illinois (OJ L 152/34 7.6.2001) 'ADM alluded to the importance of a company controlling its sales force in order to maintain high prices, and explained that its sales people have the general tendency to be very competitive and that, unless the producers had very firm control of their sales people, there would be a price-cutting problem.'

9. The eventual penalties in the resulting US anti-trust case included fines for the companies, as indicted in Table 5.1, along with two-year gaol terms and $350,000 fines for two senior ADM executives.

10 Typically those for which efficient operation requires incurring fixed costs that are large in relation to the size of the market.

11. This possibility is suggested by the theory of non-cooperative collusion in repeated games. See, for example, Friedman (1983, chapter 5).

12. OJ L 85/1 26 March 1985, pp. 1–52; *Re Wood Pulp Cartel*: A. Ahlström OY and others v. E.C. Commission [1988] 4 CMLR 901; [1993] 4 CMLR 407.

13. Collusion with respect to the US market is illegal under the Sherman Antitrust Act of 1890. But under the 1918 Webb–Pomerene Act it is not illegal for US firms to collude with respect to export markets. Such conduct, legal under US law, may well be illegal under the law of the target market.

14. OJ L 85/1 26 March 1985 at 16.

15. Around the world, the record of policy-makers in directly regulating markets is not a happy one.

16. Council Regulation No. 17/62 OJ 13/204 21 September 1962, variously amended.

17. Council Regulation (EC) No. 1/2003 of 16 December 2002 on the implementation of the rules on competition laid down in Articles 81 and 82 of the Treaty (OJ L 1/1, 4.1.2003). See Gauer *et al.* (2004).

18. Among which, Regulation (EC) No. 2790/1999 of 22 December 1999 on the application of Article 81(3) of the Treaty to categories of vertical agreements and concerted practices (OJ L 336/21, 29.12.1999); Regulation (EC) No. 2658/2000 on the application of Article 81(3) of the Treaty to categories of specialization agreements (OJ L 304/3, 05.12.2000); Regulation (EC) No. 26659/2000 on the application of Article 81(3) of the Treaty to categories of research and development agreements (OJ L 304/7, 05.12.2000); Guidelines on the applicability of Article 81 of the EC Treaty to horizontal cooperation agreements (OJ C 3/2 6.1.2001); Regulation (EC) No. 772/2004 on the application of Article 81(3) of the Treaty to categories of technology transfer agreements (OJ L 123/11 27.4.2004); Guidelines on the application of Article 81 of the EC Treaty to technology transfer agreements (OJ C 101/2 27.4.2004).

19. Lücking (2000: 41) gives a breakdown of the types of cooperation agreements screened by the Commission: 'A review of the cases dealt with by the Commission under Article 81 showed that around 40% of these cases concerned horizontal co-operation agreements. The majority of these (58%) involved forms of co-operation not covered by any block exemption regulation.'

20. Consider the case of a specialization agreement. If two firms agree that each will specialize in production of particular segments of a line of products, with both firms to offer all segments to final consumers, it may be possible to realize economies of large scale and reduce the overall cost of production. This is an efficiency gain. But an agreement that each firm will specialize in the production of certain types of products is also an agreement that each firm will not compete with the other in production of certain varieties. Thus a specialization agreement, by its nature, eliminates potential competition.

21. See Giotakis (2000) for an example. One might argue that market definition should be based on an assessment of demand substitutability, with supply substitutability a factor to be considered in evaluating entry conditions.

22. Rarely, resale price maintenance has involved the manufacturer specifying a maximum price rather than a minimum price.

23. Vertical restraints may also be part of a collusive scheme. This was a factor in the Commission's *FEG* decision (discussed below) and well as in the rise of the Standard Oil Company in the United States in the late nineteenth century. On the latter, see Granitz and Klein (1996).

24. Thus the EU challenged a resale price maintenance scheme that covered the retail book market in the UK and Ireland but not the separate application of such schemes within national boundaries. More recently, the Commission has challenged resale price maintenance in retail book distribution in Germany and Austria.

25. *Deutsche Grammophon* v. *Metro* [1971] ECR 487.

26. OJ L 39 14 February 2000, p. 1. See also Ferdinandusse (2000).

27. The Commission also found that FEG was the forum for discussions and policies that limited price competition between its members. The Netherlands is one of the Member States in which cartels were legal (but obliged to register) before the EC Treaty, and the Commission suggests that the anti-competitive behaviour at issue in this decision resulted from an agreement that was the descendant of such a cartel.

28. Vertical restraints may eliminate the free-rider problem, which arises if some dealers underprovide sales efforts (from the manufacturer's point of view) and undersell other dealers who provide greater and therefore more costly sales efforts. If unchecked, free riding leads to market failure in the market for distribution services and prevents that manufacturer from obtaining the level of sales efforts it finds most profitable (from independent dealers).

29. OJ L 336 29 December 1999; see also European Commission (2002).

30. See the *Guidelines on Vertical Restraints* (European Commission 2000c) for examples.

31. Regulation 1475/95 OJ L 145 29 June 1995.

32. Degryse and Verboven (2000; Table E1) report that the average price dispersion of about seventy-five car models across EU Member States over the period 1995–2000 ranged from 32 to 39 per cent. After adjusting price differences for differences across Member States in taxes, dealer margins, a right-hand drive surcharge, and for exchange rate fluctuations, there remained a residual price dispersion of about 20 per cent.

33. Commission Decision of 20 September 2000 (Case COMP/36.653—Opel) (OJ L59/1, 28.2.2001). But the Commission cannot condemn unilateral actions by an automobile manufacturer under Article 81(1), since that paragraph deals with agreements that distort competition; see the Judgment of the Court of First Instance of 3 December 2003 in case T-208/01, *Volkswagen AG* v. *EC Commission*.

34. Regulation 1400/2002 OJ L 103/30, 1.8.2002. For discussion, see Tsoraklidis (2002) and Clark (2002).

35. Twice a year, the Commission reports on automobile price differences in the Community (http://europa.eu.int/comm/competition/car_sector/price_diffs/). Data as of 1 November 2004 showed some signs of price convergence, although (in the words of the Commission press release) 'much work needs to be done'.

36. *United Brands Company and United Brands Continental BV* v. *EC Commission* [1978] ECR 207.

37. Like any firm with a position of some market power, UBC would be limited by the ability of its consumers to cease buying the product (la Cour and Møllgaard 2000). Following Lerner (1934), the monopoly price–cost margin is the inverse of the price elasticity of demand.

38. OJ L 030 4 February 2000, pp. 1–24. See also Finnegan (1999).

39. OJ L 72 11 March 1998.

40. In the *Aéroports de Paris* (ADP) decision, the Commission found that the firm operating two Paris airports had abused a dominant position by charging discriminatory fees to airlines that provided their own ground-handling services.

41. Commission Decision of 24 March 2004 C(2004)900 final Brussels, 21 April 2004. For an earlier decision involving similar issues, see *Hilti AG* v. *EC Commission* Case T-30/89 [1990] ECR II-1439; [1990] 4 CMLR 16.

42. For models of the entry-deterring effect of bundling, see Martin (1999) and Nalebuff (2004).

43. Microsoft was not obliged to withdraw the bundled version of its operating system from the market.

44. Council Regulation (EEC) No. 4064/89 OJ L 395/1 30.12.89, amended by Council Regulation (EC) No. 1310/97, OJ L 180, 9.7.1997.

45. This was the result with the 1997 Boeing/McDonnell Douglas merger.

46. Commission Decision of 24 April 1996 Case No. IV/M.619—Gencor/Lonrho (OJ L 11/30); see also Judgment of the Court of First Instance of 25 March 1999.

47. Commission Decision of 22 September 1999 Case IV/M.1524—Airtours/First Choice. See also *Airtours* v. *EC Commission*, Judgment of the Court of First Instance Case T-342/99, 6 June 2002.

48. Council Regulation (EC) No. 139/2004 of 20 January 2004 on the control of concentrations between undertakings (the EC Merger Regulation) (OJ L 24/1, 29.01.2004).

49. See Discussion Question 3.

50. To be precise, 'concentrations'.

51. See Article 1(2) and (3) of the Regulation for the specific numerical standards.

52. Other aspects of the Merger Review Package aim at transparency in the merger review process; the Commission has published a Notice on remedies acceptable in merger cases (OJ C 68/3, 2.3.2001), horizontal merger guidelines (OJ C 31/5, 5.2.2004), a Notice on restraints that are ancillary to concentrations (OJ C 56/24, 5.3.2004), and Best Practices on the conduct of merger proceedings (http://europa.eu.int/comm/competition/mergers/legislation/regulation/best_practices.pdf).

53. Indeed, in July 2001 the European Commission blocked a proposed merger between General Electric and Honeywell that had been approved by US anti-trust authorities. The European Commission decision was challenged by General Electric, but upheld by the Court of First Instance in a December 2005 decision. The Court of First Instance criticized some aspects of the Commission's reasoning, but accepted its conclusion that the merger, if it had gone forward, would have impeded competition in three markets.

54. There is a 1991 US–EC Agreement on the Application of Competition Laws, and in October 2002 a specific 'best practices' agreement for cooperation in merger enforcement was put in place.

55. Council Regulation (EC) No. 659/1999 of 22 March 1999 OJ L 83/1; see also Council Regulation (EC) No. 794/2004 OJ L 140/1, 30.4.2004.

56. *Schneider Electric SA* v. *Commission of the European Communities* T-310/01 Judgment of the Court of First Instance (First Chamber) 22 October 2002.

57. Case C-12/03 P *EC Commission* v. *Tetra Laval* BV 15 February 2005.

▓ REFERENCES

Albæk, S., Møllgaard, P., and Overgaard, P. B. (1997), 'Government-Assisted Oligopoly Coordination? A Concrete Case', *Journal of Industrial Economics* 45/4: 429–43.

Ball, G. W. (1973), *The Past Has Another Pattern* (New York and London: W. W. Norton).

Bowie, R. R. (1989), 'Réflexions sur Jean Monnet', in A. Alphand, *Témoignages à la mémoire de Jean Monnet* (Lausanne: Fondation Jean Monnet pour l'Europe), 81–8.

Clark, J. (2002), 'New Rules for Motor Vehicle Distribution and Servicing', *Competition Policy Newsletter* 3 (Oct.): 3–6.

Comité Intergouvernemental créé par la Conférence de Messine (1956), *Rapport des Chefs de Délégation aux Ministres des Affairs Etrangères (Spaak Report)* 21 Apr. (Brussels).

Connor, J. M. (2001), *Global Price Fixing: Our Customers are the Enemy* (The Netherlands: Springer).

la Cour, L. F. and Møllgaard, H. P. (2000), *'Testing for (Abuse of) Domination: The Danish Cement Industry'*, Department of Economics, Copenhagen Business School, Working Paper no. 10.

Degryse, H. and Verboven, F. (2000), *Car Price Differentials in the European Union: An Economic Analysis* (London: CEPR) (http://europa.eu.int/comm/competition/car_sector/distribution/eval_reg_1475_95/studies/car_price_differentials.pdf)

European Commission (1997), *Notice on the Definition of the Relevant Market for the Purposes of Community Competition Law*, OJ C 372, 9 Dec. (Brussels).

—— (1998), *XXVIIth Report on Competition Policy 1997* (Brussels–Luxembourg).

—— (1999a), *White Paper on the Modernisation of the Rules Implementing Articles 81 and 82 of the EC Treaty*, 28 Apr. (Brussels).

—— (1999b), *XXVIIIth Report on Competition Policy 1998* (Brussels–Luxembourg).

—— (2000a), *Draft Guidelines on the Applicability of Article 81 to Horizontal Cooperation*, 27 Apr. (Brussels).

—— (2000b), *Proposal for a Council Regulation on the Implementation of the Rules on Competition Laid Down in Articles 81 and 82 of the Treaty and Amending Regulations (EEC) No. 1017/68, (EEC) No. 2988/74, (EEC) No. 4056/86 and (EEC) No. 3975/87*, COM (2000) 582 final 27 Sept. (Brussels).

—— (2000c), *Guidelines on Vertical Restraints*, OJ C 291/1, 13 Oct. (Brussels).

—— (2002), *Competition Policy in Europe: The Competition Rules for Supply and Distribution Agreements* (Luxembourg: Office for Official Publications of the European Communities).

Ferdinandusse, E. (2000), 'The Commission Fines FEG, the Dutch Association of Electrotechnical Equipment Wholesalers and its Biggest Member', *Competition Policy Newsletter*, (Feb.): 17–18.

Finnegan, J. (1999), 'Commission Sets out its Policy on Commissions Paid by Airlines to Travel Agents', *Competition Policy Newsletter*, 3 (Oct.): 23.

Friedman, J. (1983), *Oligopoly Theory* (Cambridge: Cambridge University Press).

Gauer, C., Kjolbye, L., Dalheimer, D., de Smijter, E., Schnichels, D., and Laurila, M. (2004), 'Regulation 1/2003 and the Modernisation Package Fully Applicable since 1 May 2004', *Competition Policy Newsletter*, 2: 1–6.

Giotakos, D. (2000), 'The Commission's Review of the Aluminium Merger Wave', *Competition Policy Newsletter*, 2 (June): 8–23.

Granitz, E. and Klein, B. (1996), 'Monopolization by Raising Rivals' Costs: The Standard Oil Case', *Journal of Law and Economics*, 39: 1–47.

Lauer, S. (2003), 'Réforme douce pour la distribution automobile en Europe', *Le Monde*, 30 Sept. (internet edition).

Lerner, A. P. (1934), 'The Concept of Monopoly and the Measurement of Monopoly Power', *Review of Economic Studies*, 1 (June): 157–75.

Lowe, P. (2004), 'Cooperation between the Competition Authorities in the EU: New Challenges for Central and Eastern European Countries', *Law in Transition*, (Apr.): 55–9.

Lücking, J. (2000), 'Horizontal Cooperation Agreements: Ensuring a Modern Policy', *Competition Policy Newsletter*, 2 (June): 41–4.

Martin, S. (1999), 'Strategic and Welfare Implications of Bundling', *Economics Letters*, 62/3: 371–6.

Monnet, J. (1976), *Mémoires* (Paris: Fayard).

Morch, H. (1995), 'Summary of the Most Important Recent Developments', *Competition Policy Newsletter*, Spring: 47–51.

Nalebuff, B. (2004), 'Bundling as an Entry Barrier', *Quarterly Journal of Economics*, 119/1: 159–87.

Peña Castellot, M. Á. (2001), 'An Overview of the Application of the Leniency Notice', *Competition Policy Newsletter*, 1 (Feb.): 11–14.

Sinnaeve, A. (1998), 'The Commission's Proposal for a Regulation on State Aid Procedures', *Competition Policy Newsletter*, June: 79–82.

Spierenburg, D. and Poidevin, R. (1994), *The History of the High Authority of the European Coal and Steel Community* (London: Weidenfeld and Nicolson).

Tsoraklidis, L. (2002), 'Towards a New Motor Vehicle Block Exemption: Commission Proposal for Motor Vehicle Distribution, Adopted on 5 February 2002', *Competition Policy Newsletter* 2 (June): 31–4.

6 | Science and Technology Policy

Peter Stubbs

Introduction

The first and most fundamental issue to address in considering EU science and technology policy is why nation-states and collectivities of nation-states should have a science and technology policy at all. Could we not leave the production and distribution of scientific and technological knowledge to the market mechanism, which, after all, ranges from the humblest individual worker to the largest international firm?

Not surprisingly, scientists and technologists tend to oppose such a proposition. Since Bernard Shaw vilified all professions as conspiracies against the laity, we might suspect self-interest in that opposition; governmental support means more jobs, more prestige, and more money for scientists and technologists. That area of economics known as public choice theory (Mueller 1989) examines the behaviour of interest groups, and acknowledges that bureaucrats have their own agendas, and are not simply dispassionate agents of government (Niskanen 1975). The same is likely to be true of scientists. However, most economists involved have agreed that, objectively, the scientists have a tenable and intellectually respectable case. The most powerful economic support was offered by Kenneth Arrow (1962), who was to become a Nobel laureate in economics in 1972. He observed that there are three categories of economic problems which make it inadvisable to leave the allocation of resources for invention (and, by implication, technological progress) to the market mechanism. They are uncertainty, indivisibility, and inappropriability, and they require some elaboration.

6.1 Reasons for the support of science and technology

Arrow applied neo-classical economic analysis to advocate government financial support for basic research. Basic research is the bedrock of technological progress: its accepted definition is provided by the 'Frascati Manual' as 'experimental or theoretical work undertaken primarily to acquire new knowledge of the underlying foundations of phenomena and observable facts, without any particular application or use in view' (OECD 2002: 29). Clearly, work of this sort is likely to be far removed from the marketplace, yet it has the potential to yield immensely important advances such as the microchip or nanotechnology. For many private investors, including even large corporations, the uncertainty of such research as an acceptable pursuit of financial gain is a severe deterrent. The risks of failure are high, both because the research might lead to a dead end and because there is a risk that, even if it were fruitful, a speedier rival might beat them to the harvest. It also takes many years to recoup the investment, because basic scientific advances usually take much time and money to translate into saleable products or processes. Applying a typical commercial discount rate to compute a net present value for the speculative benefits of long-term basic research tends to disadvantage it when compared with less radical development work with a quicker pay-off.

Governments can pool these risks, since they are bigger than their national companies and may be able to consider longer-term benefits from the social rather than the private point of view: it does not matter to the government whether company *A* or company *Z* exploits the research findings, as long as they are exploited; but, if *A* contemplated doing the research itself, any prospect that *Z*, or *B*, or *C* could exploit it at the expense of *A* would be a disincentive. Notwithstanding, even nation-states can find basic research risky; but the funding of much basic research in most countries is a government responsibility.

There is a further benefit from public funding of basic research. Where a private research body would want to maintain its property rights—that is, 'keep hold' of its research results to cover its costs and make private profits—the public source can be more open. Basic research findings may be more likely to be translated into useful innovations if they can 'spill over' and be adopted and developed by a wide range of innovators. The prevailing ethic among basic researchers is for wide publication and circulation of their findings among their peer group, and this is most likely to be realized where there is no corporate restraint owing to secrecy.

Indivisibilities present problems. Where markets are indivisible, there are problems both in assessing demand and in securing payment. A public health research programme, analogous to a public health investment such as urban drainage, can benefit a whole community, but, given the choice of whether to contribute to its costs, some people could become free-riders, enjoying the benefits without making any contribution to the costs. In this case it is better to fund and operate the project at community level.

There may also be indivisibilities in the process of research itself. Where an industry is atomistic, with many small producers, no single member may be able to afford a worthwhile research and technical development (RTD) facility. In agriculture a multitude of competing farmers are most unlikely to do systematic RTD; individually they lack the assets, the expertise, and the incentive. Centralized RTD, supported by a levy on users, can overcome this problem; this solution can be applied to specific industrial processes or other small-scale industries by establishing research associations. Governments have subsidized these bodies permanently, or temporarily as a pump-priming exercise, until they becoming self-financing.

Inappropriability is a problem because the originator of the invention or technology may be unable to gain due reward, unless he or she can appropriate the returns to the effort. Ideas are easily stolen. If much of the originator's benefit is dissipated through copying and illicit application by others, there is no immediate social loss—indeed there may seemingly be social gain if the innovation is diffused more widely and more cheaply, as happens notoriously in the case of pirated computer software. Indeed, the theft of intellectual property is today a multi-billion dollar industry. But, quite apart from the issue of legality, the loss to the innovator may prove a serious disincentive to the inspiration and hard work which RTD entails: short-run opportunistic gains would then compromise long-run technological progress. Most nation-states, therefore, protect the intellectual property of inventors through patents and copyrights granted upon original works.

A related issue concerns the benefits which accrue to users, as distinct from the innovator. Support for innovation may be given by governments on the grounds that there are social benefits from innovation beyond the private benefits which accrue through payments to the innovator. Empirical studies of specific innovations by Mansfield *et al.* (1976) show that the social rate of return to innovation is usually higher than the private rate, sometimes helped by the spill-over effect noted above. The argument can be pressed further, in suggesting that there are second-order effects in enhancing industrial development and national competitiveness. If so, and the support improves dynamic resource allocation and the responsiveness of the economy, the effects can be subtle, profound, and long lasting. However, it is very problematic to verify these effects in ways rigorous enough to persuade national treasuries to provide funding in the face of other less speculative and more populist claims for finance, though much generally positive evidence has accumulated over the past quarter century.

Beyond these central issues of uncertainty, indivisibility, and inappropriability, there are other motives for government support of technology. It is often asserted that imperfect private capital markets restrict the funds available for RTD, that bankers are unappreciative of the full value of technological opportunities. In response to this view, governments have from time to time established mechanisms targeted at the provision of funds for technology, such as the National Research Development Corporation (NRDC) and its eventual successor, the British Technology Group (BTG), which was later privatized, and other measures in many countries to promote venture capital sources for technological small and medium-sized enterprises (SMEs).

Government may also act as a disseminator of scientific and technological information, and finance arbitration where there are conflicts arising from the use of new technology. Many governments have given support for communications technology, and there are well-known cases where they have funded inquiries into technological matters of public concern, such as the Sizewell B nuclear power station in the UK, or the links between bovine spongiform encephalopathy (BSE) and Creutzfeldt-Jakob Disease (CJD), and instances where authoritative opinion is sought by an anxious public, such as upon Asian bird flu.

Finally, the view may be expressed that economic rationale alone should not rule the allocation of funds for science (in particular) and technology. This view rests on the belief that scientific investigation is a manifestation of advanced civilization with a justifiable ethic of its own, rendering it just as eligible for state support as the arts are. In this context, allocation to science is not simply to be regarded as an investment decision but also involves elements of desirable consumption. Indeed, some of the allocations to basic research face such high degrees of uncertainty and long gestation that it is difficult to apply to them any risk criteria where risk is understood in Frank Knight's sense of 'measurable uncertainty' (Knight 1921). However, even if this viewpoint is given some credit, there are problems of adjudicating between open-ended claims from the science lobby, and of deciding on the total allocation to the science sector. There is a perennial allocative dichotomy between those whom we might characterize as 'scientists', who feel that scientific interest and promise should direct their endeavours, akin to a supply-side pressure or 'science-push', and those administrators and customers who feel that the need for solutions to immediate problems should be the paramount influence, akin to a demand side inducement or 'demand-pull'.

Since Arrow made his contribution, a vast literature has grown as the full complexity of the many issues has emerged. Most contributors have employed a contrasting structuralist-evolutionary approach (Lipsey and Carlaw 1998) reflecting this complexity, though without supplanting Arrow's case for support. Rather, the debate has advanced, to address questions such as: how does RTD actually impact on industry (prompting some revision of its definitions); what form of support is required; and how do different measures perform? Researchers now stress the Schumpeterian pervasiveness of change rather than shifts between neo-classical equilibria, and the emergence of trajectories which map the experience, capabilities, and accomplishments of firms and industries.

In several advanced countries over the past decade, direct state support for science and technology has tended to decline. This arises in part from economic downturns, budget stringency, and a general desire among governments to avoid increasing taxation, but also reflects the sentiment that since industry at large benefits from technological progress, some of its social benefits are internalized in the sector, if not in each firm executing the RTD. Also, the growth of interfirm alliances and international corporate collaboration over high-technology ventures, which we consider later in this chapter, has enabled companies to pursue basic scientific research more enterprisingly than they could have done singly. However, it would be difficult to find many supporters for the proposition of Kealey (1996) that the entirety of scientific funding could and should be left to market forces, even if one concedes to him that grant-seeking scientists are as conscious of the pork-barrel as are any other professions.

6.2 National policies for science and technology

Before the advent of the EC, national policies for science and technology were inevitably separate. Though they shared a common focus of correcting market failures and enhancing scientific and technological performance in the search for improved economic performance and enhanced scientific prestige, there were evident differences between the nations of the Community, their national innovation systems, and their priorities and methods of support. Since there is a wide degree of independence to national policies, we need to examine briefly the national innovation systems and government policies that have developed. In the first edition of this book, we examined Germany, France, and the UK, as the three biggest performers of RTD in the EU (Stubbs and Saviotti 1994: 142–7). In the second edition we examined Italy, the Netherlands, and Sweden. We now cover recent developments in the original three. In aggregate, Member State expenditures on science and technology dwarf EU-level expenditures. Moreover, as M. Claude Allègre, the French Minister for Education, Research, and Technology, noted in 1998, subsidiarity applies in science and technology, so that the EU should operate only in areas too expensive for nation-states to act in alone, and, presumably, where international collaboration might generate strong externalities. Thus national policies remain of paramount importance in the European picture as a whole, though the EU role is now universally accepted and formalized. Some statistics concerning national science and technology performance are shown in Table 6.1 at the end of this section.

United Kingdom

Industrial and technology policies in the United Kingdom have been marked by pragmatism. The only attempt at a highly centralized industrial policy, partly inspired by earlier French planning experience, collapsed within a year in 1966. In the 1960s and 1970s the Ministry of Technology and the Industrial Reorganization Corporation contrived to select national champions, encouraging growth by the merger of large firms, often of doubtful efficiency, which were intended to meet the challenge of the leading foreign firms that, by contrast, had usually grown by internal efficiency. Not surprisingly, the strategy failed dismally.

A right-wing government elected in 1970 dismembered the Ministry of Technology and introduced a 'customer–contractor principle', which sought to inject some market elements into government-funded applied research, decreeing 'the customer says what he wants; the contractor does it (if he can); and the customer pays'. This was to lead to major and lasting changes in the operation of Government Research Establishments (Boden *et al.* 2004). Successive pragmatic interventions under governments of both political colours sought variously and without general success to improve industrial and technological development by interventionist policies under Heath, Wilson, and Callaghan. Moreover, there were long-standing weaknesses in the national technological ethic which governments seemed unable to correct. Walker (1993) suggests that high (and technologically distracting) defence expenditure, poor technological training, short-termism emphasizing immediate profits rather than long-term strategic advantage, and a service rather than a manufacturing culture, all hobbled the optimum application of technology.

By the advent of the Thatcher government in 1979, it was clear that politicians and civil servants alike had lost any confidence they might have had to 'pick winners'—that is, to direct closely through chosen companies as national champions the strategic development of British industrial technology. At the same time, after years of poor performance in the nationalized industries, dogma and pragmatism combined to introduce privatization. Many industrial subsidies were phased out, moribund industries were allowed to disappear, and a more competitive managerial environment was urged. Technology policy saw government expenditure on 'near-market' RTD trimmed back, as this was perceived as more appropriate for firms to fund and conduct; emphasis switched towards collaborative company programmes and longer-term research. Instead of picking company winners, which often meant an enervating relief from all domestic competition, emphasis shifted to generic technologies, such as robotics and microelectronics, which would deploy across a wide range of industries, being adopted by their worthier members. Expert advice was provided by committees such as the Advisory Council for Applied Research and Development (ACARD) and later the Advisory Council on Science and Technology (ACOST).

After the 1992 election, the government created an Office of Science and Technology and proposed changes to the structure of the Research Councils, as well as stressing the need for wealth creation, reaffirming the customer–contractor principle, and urging the need for cross-departmental coordination in science and technology. An important innovation was the Technology Foresight Programme, which brought scientific and industrial communities together in sixteen panels to exchange views and help to explore consensually what future developments might be expected in science and technology.

However, the new market realism brought problems: it was wedded to the minimization of public expenditure, yet the shake-out of employment in inefficient industry placed a heavy financial burden on social services; the collapse of inefficient industries narrowed the base of British-owned manufacturing industry, though foreign direct investment filled the gap in key areas including motor vehicles and consumer electronics. In consequence, there was a steady reduction in government funding of RTD across the 1990s, and in university funding, which eroded their infrastructure for scientific research. RTD intensity declined at all levels of industry—high, medium-high, medium-low, and low technology sectors. RTD as a percentage of GDP fell from 2.13 per cent in 1990 to 1.88 per cent in 2003. The economy was more open than most other countries, with a higher ratio of trade to GDP than the USA, Germany, or France, but it was also more dependent on foreign capital and technology, with more than one-quarter of its business RTD financed by foreign principals in 2003, much more than any of its rivals. Without this foreign injection, the decline in RTD would have been significantly worse. While the UK has some areas of strength, such as pharmaceuticals, defence, oil refining, and services, its innovative performance is weak compared with the USA, Japan, or Germany. An EC survey revealed that fewer British firms introduced innovations than did German ones, though they were ahead of the French and the EU average (Eurostat 2001). Only one-quarter of the innovating British firms conducted formal RTD, and it was observed that large firms were more likely to introduce innovations than small ones.

In 1997 a Labour government was elected under Tony Blair. It pledged to maintain the general primacy of markets, but to emphasize education, health, and technology. It has introduced a wide range of technological initiatives. A second Foresight exercise was launched, following the success of the first, compounding the original sixteen panels into ten, which has now been established as a series of rolling programmes. A Defence Diversification Agency was set up to capitalize on defence RTD. It seeks to make suitable recipients aware of available defence technology suitable for civilian use, draws attention to the Defence Evaluation and Research Agency's laboratories, fosters co-development and adaptation with civil partners, and makes information available to screened recipients of Ministry of Defence needs and on relevant technological trends, thus helping firms to appreciate the military scope for their products. In 1999, following a White Paper on Competitiveness, the Department of Trade and Industry stressed the need for innovation, widespread access to technology, and partnership between industry and the science base. A venture capital fund of £150 million was established, and innovative clusters predicated on California's Silicon Valley and the Cambridge complex in Britain were mooted, with biotechnology as a main focus, including eight enterprise centres to be based on universities. The Teaching Company Scheme was extended, to improve links particularly with small and medium-sized enterprises.

Funding for science has been augmented in a variety of ways. Following growing recognition of the decline in public sector research establishments (PSRE) and university funding, and the consequent inadequacy of funds for laboratory infrastructure, the government set up a Higher Education Innovation Fund with £140 million and a Science Research Investment Fund with £750 million. The first White Paper on science for seven years appeared in 2000 (DTI 2000a), and the science budget for the following three years was set to rise at 7 per cent a year in real terms. PSREs were free to pursue commercial opportunities and to retain their subsequent receipts. Measures were also introduced to attract researchers from overseas, and SMEs were given tax credits for RTD expenditure, as an obvious incentive for the small business sector; but the budget in March 2001 extended the concession to businesses in general, acknowledging that the UK lags behind its competitors in business RTD. Currently, SMEs with fewer than 250 employees can claim 150 per cent tax credit, payable in cash if the company is not in profit; big companies can claim 125 per cent. Areas singled out for support programmes included post-genome medical research, advanced electronic communications, information processing, and nanotechnology.

Initiatives continue, with the Lambert Review of Business–University Collaboration (HM Treasury 2003), a DTI report on innovation in November 2003 (DTI 2003), and an interdepartmental report on the ten-year framework for investment in science and innovation (DTI 2004), the last named, a White Paper in all but name, forming the basis for consultations in the summer of 2006. In May 2006, the Office of Science and Technology was merged with the DTI's innovation group to form the Office of Science and Innovation, to encourage the UK's research base and apply the ten-year investment strategy. Thus there is a clear and concerted array of enhancement policies, to be implemented across a decade with rising government support in real terms, devoted to scientific and innovative performance, and the UK remains the most-favoured location for inward investment in Europe. There is evidence of improvement, yet concerns abound. The UK has a fragile industrial research base, a continuously shrinking manufacturing sector, a lower propensity to patent than its peer countries, and a long and vulnerable tail of SMEs which are not technologically oriented and not readily accessible by current policies. The strength in depth of German manufacturing, with its abler shop-floor workforce, is still lacking in the UK. So while it makes obvious sense to try to compete through technical eminence rather than on low cost, the narrowness of the industrial base is a constraint upon the prospects for the policy, although it is hoped that the positive climate for innovative SMEs may ameliorate past trends.

France

After the Second World War, the French government was more *dirigiste* than its British or German neighbours, directing industrial policy much more closely, and with considerable success at first. From the late 1960s, like the British government, it promoted mergers to foster firms which it hoped would compete with large foreign rivals, of which the United States was perceived as the strongest and most dangerous. It lacked a large and sophisticated capital market, and it was not until the late 1980s that the stock market assumed much importance. The centralist bureaucracy applied equipment procurement policies to encourage selected industries such as telecommunications manufacturing, computers, and nuclear power generation.

Many of the *grands projets* of the 1970s were high-profile successes technically, such as nuclear power and the TGV high-speed train, albeit rather opaque in their economics. But where Britain in the 1980s pursued privatization, deregulation, and the acknowledgement of market forces, the French Socialist government nationalized eight leading French firms as part of a strategy of state-inspired technological advance. The intentions were that continuous state funding would ensure efficient and effective research, and that the state could build bridges between public laboratories and industry, and balance small and big technology programmes. It was thwarted by economic recession, the reality of international market competition, and by the inherent problems which attend such intentions: even today they are still key items on the government agenda. States could no longer carve out industrial territories, as market-led technology spilled out across industries and countries, and swamped many national ambitions. Minitel, the government-led video-link associated with domestic telephones, was outflanked by the privately developed modem that allowed personal computers access to the internet.

In the 1990s French government support for RTD faltered under the combined influences of economic slowdown, high interest rates, falling public expenditure, and cutbacks in defence research. However, the government diagnosed many of the earlier failings of the French innovation system, and set about reform in the latter 1990s. Many problems were identified for treatment. French research was rated good, technology rather less so. RTD was concentrated in high-technology projects in large firms, but was disappointing in information technology and in the service sector. In 1998–9, four major technology programmes were initiated, including life sciences and information technology, and the emphasis for support shifted from large companies, which were urged to finance their own research, to SMEs. Notwithstanding these changes, an authoritative report concluded that 'the framework for innovation is still far from optimal' (OECD 1999*a*: 129). It noted that there was still too much centralization and concentration in the conduct of research. The 1999 Innovation Law set out to make French public research organizations less bureaucratic, and more dynamic and entrepreneurial, through four key policies:

1. by encouraging the mobility of researchers and their freedom to act entrepreneurially,
2. by improving the public research/industry interface,
3. by improving the fiscal regime for innovative companies, especially SMEs, and
4. by simplifying the legal framework for setting up high-technology firms.

A radical reappraisal of innovation policy was undertaken in late 1999 (Majoie and Remy 1999), drawing upon reports from multidisciplinary groups. It recognized that SMEs needed guidance to inform the thrust of their research, possibly after the manner of the British Foresight exercises, and that there was a problem with the ageing profile of the population of researchers in public research organizations. Reforms followed: in April 2000 all state taxes on enterprise creation were eliminated, and new credits provided to enterprises working in new technology areas. The 2001 budget provisions favoured young researchers, and finance was given to help biotechnology, information and communications technology, and aerospace, including the A380 superjumbo Airbus.

Thus French government policy towards science and technology has undergone major, conscious change, consonant with the twenty-first century, and begun to address the problems identified by the OECD. Whether it will escape the traditional centralism of French administration remains to be seen but, interestingly, it has been suggested that a significant proportion of recent graduates of the prestigious civil service training school, the Ecole Nationale d'Administration or ENA, is entering the private sector, partly out of frustration at the rigidities of bureaucracy (*Financial Times*, 7 March 2001, p. 23). Administrative, as well as scientific, labour mobility could be an important asset in France's advance towards the flexibility necessary in a modern economy.

However, the new millennium has posed problems for French policy. The government has been hampered by the Union's requirement to limit budget deficits to 3 per cent of GDP, and has had to restrict its research funding to basic research institutions such as CNRS (Centre National de la Recherche Scientifique): by 2004 it was receiving only 60 per cent compared with its 1993 government funding. Key areas such as genetics and nanotechnology were generally prioritized, but others faced straitened prospects. These pressures, together with the likely reduction in job security betokened by liberalization of labour markets, prompted nationwide strikes in the French science community in 2004. The government aspires to raise RTD expenditure to 3 per cent of GDP by 2010, but to do so it will have to rely heavily on increases from the private sector. Shortages of qualified personnel are also a threat, as young researchers have not been appearing at a rate fast enough to cover a retirement peak among research workers over the period 2005–10. Late in 2005 the government addressed some of these issues (*Research Europe*, 6 October 2005, p. 6), promising to increase its research spending from 19 billion to 24 billion Euros across 2004 to 2010 and listing five objectives:

1. to improve the guidance and evaluation of research by supplying better advice to policy-makers and more transparent evaluation;
2. to encourage competition between laboratories;
3. to raise the international profile of French research;
4. to improve research careers, attracting researchers back from abroad to new 'super-campuses'; and
5. to increase private public cooperation.

Critics have said the funding was more apparent than real because a third would go as tax breaks to industry, and that the plans lacked long-term commitment.

Germany

German industry has long benefited from a strong national tradition of education and scientific research. This has underpinned the impressive performance of its chemical and engineering industries, in which its export performance in the competitive US market has been better than that of its EC partners. In the 1990s it maintained a more positive trade balance in manufactures than France, while the UK and the USA had negative balances across the period 1992–2006. In many respects the German economy appears technologically stronger than its British or French equivalents. It spends proportionately more on RTD than they do, more per head of population, and has almost as many business enterprise personnel engaged in RTD as Britain and France combined. Government support is directed more at science and technology infrastructure, and much less through government procurement, reflecting the lesser role of its defence industry. Its manufactured products are more up-market in their price–quality range, it has a significantly higher propensity to take out European patents, and excels in medium-high technology products. Its industrial strengths lie in industrial chemicals, machinery and electrical machinery, shipbuilding, motor vehicles (which account for 36 per cent of business R&D), and scientific instruments, each with good export performance. GDP per head is well ahead of the British level, but the absorption of East Germany has pulled it back relative to France. It is less dependent on foreign capital than its two rivals, and on foreign technology.

However, there are some points of weakness. Despite success in the medium-high technology sector, it has not performed well in the high-technology sector as such, where it had a negative trade balance in products such as office and computer equipment, as well as radio, TV, and communications equipment. Its corporate research is heavily concentrated in large firms, defined as employing more than a thousand people, and there seems to be unexploited scope for technology-based SMEs which have found it difficult to secure venture capital and skilled human resources, although recent policy measures have sought to remedy this.

Research funding is provided mainly by the federal government, but also by the state governments, or Länder. Federal support has gone mainly to business and private non-profit research institutes, and state contributions to universities. The predominant research institutions are the German Research Association (Deutsche Forschungsgemeinschaft, or DFG), the Max Planck Institute (MPG), and the Fraunhofer Association (FhF), which are supraregional in scope with many out-stations, and for all of which there is extensive government support. The Federal Ministry of Education, Science, Research, and Technology (Bundesministerium für Bildung und Forschung, or BMBF) provided grant finance for a wide range of programmes in high-risk, long-term projects such as aerospace, and public-interest projects such as health and the environment.

After some slippage in research funding in the mid-1990s, by the end of the decade support was increased in real terms, and strategic areas identified for priority projects. These include health and medical research, molecular biology, biotechnology, laser technology and information technology, ecology and climate research, and transport. The Federal Ministry for Economics and Technology (BMWi) was given responsibility for technology-based SMEs, energy research and policy, aviation research, and multimedia issues.

Over the years there have been a number of criticisms of German research performance, notwithstanding the strength of the economy. Keck (1993) suggested that nuclear power research had been undertaken simply to secure research grants, without producing tangible applications, whereas privately funded work led to practical reactors. Later, Beise and Stahl (1999) concluded that while publicly funded research had stimulated some industrial innovation, it was not fully justified by the extent of identifiable transfers. Public research centres were meant to perform more applied research than universities do, emphasizing spin-off to industry, but they tended to concentrate on long-term research, locking in their staff so that there was limited transfer to industry. At a more general level, in a country survey the OECD criticized the government for failing to liberalize its labour markets, and for wasteful investment in the economically depressed east (*Financial Times*, 7 March 2001, p. 1). It highlighted the need for more stringent investment criteria, a more competitive and accountable university sector, and the importance of lifelong training.

In the first years of the new millennium, the German economy appeared to be in the doldrums: it was still suffering indigestion from the absorption of East Germany, state funding for science was cut back, while the federal government and the Länder wrangled over university funding. However, there are signs of improvement, in pursuit of chosen policy goals such as regional innovation clusters, encouragement for high-tech SMEs, and market liberalization. The FUTUR system, like Foresight, helps to prioritize key areas for future research such as nanotechnology and energy. At the start of 2004, the federal government produced its High Tech Master Plan for SMEs, allocating 500 million Euros of public and private finance for venture capital. Clusters of Competence networks are growing, and priority is being given to the best universities. The research institutions mentioned earlier are addressing many key issues in their spheres of interest, and in 2005 were promised 3 per cent annual funding increases until 2010. While it may be difficult for German industry to occupy the technological high ground alongside the USA and Japan, and there are concerns that other European countries have raised their technological profile, the strength in depth of the economy should assure its continued primacy in Europe. However, there remains widespread scepticism that the federal government can realize its stated goal of raising the level of R&D spending to 3 per cent of GDP by 2010.

Table 6.1 shows the national pattern of expenditure on RTD by selected nation-states, as percentages of GDP. Since some of the countries, notably USA, Japan, and Germany, have a much larger GDP than the UK, it is evident that in absolute terms their RTD expenditure is very much higher than that of the UK. UK expenditure on RTD has failed over the years to keep pace with its major competitors, and its positive technological balance of payments of the early 1980s was significantly negative by 1990, yet became positive again later in the decade. Japan has improved greatly, but the USA retains the strongest positive balance of payments on the technology account, partly though not wholly because the US Revenue Service is assiduous in requiring US companies to declare every conceivable element of their technology earnings. Over the years 1998 to 2003 the technological balance payments of the United States has slipped substantially, but those of the other five states have all improved. Germany and France both moved into positive balance during this period. As global industrialization proceeds in countries such as China and India, the market in intellectual property becomes more sophisticated and important. Factories move offshore from Europe, and the sale and supply of technology facilitate that transfer, and point to the importance of research and technological eminence to the member countries.

Table 6.1 Statistics of national science and technology performance, 2003

RTD category	Expenditure on RTD as percentage of GDP					
	USA	Japan	UK	Germany	France	Italy
Gross RTD (GERD)	2.68	3.15	1.88	2.52	2.18	1.16[c]
Civil RTD	2.2	3.1	1.7	2.5	1.9	1.1[d]
Government-funded civil RTD	0.82	0.56	0.59	0.79	0.85	n/a
Defence RTD, % of government RTD funds	55.8	5.1	31.8	5.8	22.7	n/a
Business RTD (BERD)	1.87	2.36	1.24	1.76	1.37	0.55
Industry-financed BERD	1.71	2.35	0.83	1.67	1.11	n/a
Higher education RTD	0.37	0.43	0.4	0.43	0.42	0.38[c]
BERD financed from abroad, %	n/a	0.4	26.0	2.3	10.4	10.3[c]

	Indicators of national size and growth					
	USA	Japan	UK	Germany	France	Italy
GDP (current $bn at PPP[a])	11.679	3,778	1,857	1,228	861	828
GDP growth, 2004/1995	1.61	1.38	1.63	1.31	1.47	1.35
GERD ($bn at PPP)	292.4	112.7	33.7	57.5	38.1	17.7
GERD growth, 2003/1995	1.59	1.37	1.50	1.46	1.34	1.49
Investment in knowledge[b] as % of GDP, 2003	6.6	5.0	4.4	3.9	3.7	2.4
Technological balance of payments (receipts/payments) 2004	2.20	2.65	2.33	1.00	1.60	0.94

[a] PPP = purchasing power parity.   [b] Defined as net expenditure on RTD, higher education, and software.
[c] = 2002   [d] = 2001   n/a = not available.
Notes: Definitional anomalies and rounding can cause seeming inconsistency within national figures.
Source: OECD (2005).

6.3 The development of EU science and technology policy

The original Treaty of Rome in 1957, signed by Belgium, France, Italy, Luxembourg, the Netherlands, and Germany, concentrated on the abolition of customs between the EC-6 and on the adoption of a common external tariff (CET) on goods entering from other countries. Matters such as competition policy, freedom of movement for labour and capital, customs unions, state aid, and the harmonization of national laws fell within the Treaty's area of competence, so that one could say that there were components of an industrial policy but no overall framework, though there was a limited precedent in the experience gained in running the European Coal and Steel Community (ECSC), which had operated since 1951. However, there was no provision in the Treaty for science and technology in the then European Economic Community (EEC), or for the adoption of policy towards them.

However, there was some recognition of a technological issue, albeit very narrow, in respect of civilian atomic energy. At that time, atomic energy was perceived as one of the most dazzling and important frontiers of science, intellectually challenging and exciting. It was expected, in time, to provide very cheap power, which potentially could release Europe from its heavy dependence on coal and imported oil. It was an area where there ought to be economies in conducting RTD collectively. And there was an obvious European dimension, in that the USA and the Soviet Union were committed to nuclear energy programmes, but were secretive about their knowledge because of military security. Against this background, the European Atomic Energy Community (Euratom) Treaty was also signed in 1957.

Nuclear reactor designs and fuel technologies were expected to arise from the work of the Joint Nuclear Research Centre (JNRC), which was set up to conduct a five-year research and training programme. Inspired by the examples of Los Alamos and Oak Ridge in the USA and Harwell in the UK, JNRC was to be established on several sites. As Peterson notes (1991: 269), some commentators at the time foresaw a more influential future for Euratom than for the EEC. Harsh realities soon intruded upon these visionary intentions, however (Ford and Lake 1991); rivalry occurred between the German and French nuclear industries, in the early climate of buoyant demand for nuclear power stations. The JNRC's reactor design, described as 'somewhat eccentric', was unsuccessful. Throughout the 1960s, oil provided increasing rather than shrinking competition, and the JNRC was left with nuclear scientists but little or no nuclear work to do. Gradually it mutated to become the Joint Research Centre (JRC), with its headquarters in Brussels, a main base and administrative directorate at Ispra in northern Italy, with others at Karlsruhe in Germany, Petten in the Netherlands, Geel in Belgium, and, later, Seville in Spain, operating eight research institutes across five sites. The Ispra operation was long criticized for inefficiency. The JRC operation was described as being characterized by 'listlessness, apathy, lack of direction, and lack of conviction' (Ford and Lake 1991: 40). The failure of Euratom was critical: a would-be flagship for European technology seemed to have run seriously aground. In 1993 its mandate was extended to conduct non-nuclear research, and 900 million Ecus were earmarked for it in the Fourth Framework Programme, as part of a strategy to make it more market-oriented and competitive. Since then there has been tangible improvement in the JRC, with major diversification out of its early specialization: currently it has 2,400 staff engaged an a hundred projects, and only 27 per cent of its annual budget of about 300 million Euros now concerns nuclear matters, centred mainly on safety and fusion. Other research themes include food safety, the environment and sustainability, and European competitiveness, with a strong emphasis on interdisciplinary programmes and a conscious attempt to develop know-how clusters in the modern idiom.

The initial failure of this role model for successful collective international research coincided in the 1960s with strongly interventionist national industrial policies in Europe, particularly in France and the UK (though the UK did not enter the EEC until 1972). The publication of an influential book by a French journalist, *Le Défi Américain*, or *The American Challenge* (Servan Schreiber 1967), added to the pressures on governments to boost the capacity of European industries to counter the competition of powerful foreign concerns, typified by IBM, the then dominant US computer giant. The key weapons were mergers and subsidies, which were intended to afford the necessary resource and scale to match foreign competition. There were also several European collaborative initiatives, such as the Anglo-French Concorde airliner project, and the European Space Agency (ESA), independently of the EEC. Concorde was a technical success but a commercial catastrophe from the outset: one commentator noted, 'the advanced technologies of the 1960s provided suitable objects on to which the fantasies of European unity could be projected, while in reality they did not have any substantial long-term significance in contributing to a process of European integration' (Barry 1990, cited by Ford and Lake 1991).

More successful was the Airbus commercial airliner project, in which the original consortium partners were France (38 per cent), Germany (38 per cent), the UK (20 per cent), and Spain (4 per cent). This developed a successful family of airliners which has gained more than half the market share from the USA, though prompting bitter complaints from US manufacturers that it was unfairly subsidized. In the mid-1990s there was growing pressure, in the interests of internal efficiency and transparency of its accounting procedures, for the consortium to set up a public company. Airbus SAS was set up and is now a subsidiary of EADS (European Aeronautic Defence and Space Company): British Aerospace announced in April 2006 that it would sell its 20 per cent stake in Airbus. However, it has shown that European manufacturers can collaborate successfully in a high-technology area and compete head-on with world leaders such as Boeing. In 2001 Boeing announced that it would not compete with the latest Airbus A380 superjumbo, but would develop a radical, smaller, and faster alternative, leaving open the possibility that if they judge the market wrongly, their rival Airbus could monopolize an immense market.

Another technologically successful example in the space sector was not specifically an EC initiative. In 1962 two organizations were established to foster collaboration in space technology: the European Launcher Development Organization (ELDO) and the European Space Research Organization (ESRO). ELDO became a Franco-German initiative after the UK withdrew, but, with the merger of the two bodies in 1973 to form the ESA, a more pan-European stance followed. ESA fared better than its predecessors, for several reasons. First, inter-institutional collaboration was easier because governments and public agencies were the prime contractors; second, the specialized character of the technology led to a closely knit community of policy-makers, engineers, scientists, and industrialists; and, third, its programme was designed so that all the fourteen Member States would share formally in the contracts let by the agency, under *juste retour*. In recent years, however, ESA has been strongly criticized for excessive bureaucracy.

The European Patent Office (EPO), founded in 1977 following the European Patent Convention of 1973, was another significant extra-EC development. It provides a single application process for the grant of a 'European patent', which is valid in all the signatory states for twenty years, and saves the administration and expense of applying individually to them. By 2006 membership comprised thirty-one states. Patent applications grew from 60,000 in 1990 to 118,000 in 2004. It has headquarters in Munich and The Hague, and sub-offices in Berlin and Vienna. The EPO also distributes patent information, which is an important function of any worthwhile patent system, and represents Europe in the World Intellectual Property Organization. A standard Community patent has been proposed, intended to be affordable and comparable in cost to a European patent, but progress is patchy.

Thus by the early 1980s it seemed ironic that the most successful examples of international collaboration were those deriving not from the EC, but from narrower combinations, like the Airbus, or wider ones, like ESA.

The shift of support from firms to generic technologies

Generally, the interventionist policies of support by national governments were seen to be unsuccessful. By the mid-1970s, after the UK had joined the EC, it was apparent that this policy of 'picking winners' was beyond the capacity of governments. If a government selected a firm (sometimes by the merger of former competitors) to be the national champion in an area of technological promise and to endow it with the size and subsidy to compete with the established champion of rival states, the most immediate effect was to remove its domestic competition and give it a comfortable, if temporary, feather-bed on which it might as readily relax as take up the bruising cudgels of foreign competition. However, competitive domestic markets tend to be an important precondition of the vigour required to compete internationally (Porter 1990: chap. 3).

In the 1970s the trend moved from selectiveness towards the identification and support of selected or 'generic' technologies, which might be expected to impact on a wide range of industries: electronics and biotechnology were the leading examples. Again, it was national governments rather than the EC that were prime movers in the new trend, but the first signs appeared of an EC policy towards science and technology.

On 14 January 1974 the Council decided to develop 'a common policy in the field of science and technology'. The scope of the policy was twofold: to coordinate the policies of the Member States and to implement research programmes and projects of EC interest. This sounds simple but is difficult in practice, since the finance available to the EC for implementation was between 1 and 2 per cent of the public funds spent by the Member States on RTD support. Three years later, the Commission produced objectives for the period 1977–80 (CEC 1977):

- securing the long-term supply of resources—namely, raw materials, energy, agriculture, and water;
- the promotion of internationally competitive economic development;
- improvement of living and working conditions; and
- protection of the environment and nature.

These pious if worthy aims posed a number of problems of implementation, apart from the modesty of financial resources already noted. How would Member States cooperate, given the record of national divergence discussed earlier in this chapter? Could EC policy be reconciled with the problems which the states themselves faced in their national science and technology policies? How should science and technology relate to other EC policies?

Criteria for EC support were itemized, four 'general' and eleven 'specific'. The general ones emphasized the need for rationalization and efficiency at EC level, the need for transnational action which would involve several countries, the economic need to spread development costs across several national markets, and the need to meet common national requirements. Specific selection criteria included cases where costs or required

RTD capacity would be too high for a single nation to bear, or where there would be savings through joint efforts; cases where RTD was in an initial phase, where an EC programme would stand a good chance of competing internationally, as in new transport systems; cases where potential is real, such as new sources of energy, and where there was thought to be long-term potential, such as nuclear fusion. The need for standardization of measures and information systems was also noted.

The Scientific and Technical Research Committee (CREST) was responsible for the development of Community RTD policy and coordination at policy level with Member States, and included senior officials from the member countries as well as Commission officials. The Commission established an internally staffed pilot programme of Forecasting and Assessment in Science and Technology (FAST), to collaborate with outside bodies. The FAST programme helped to highlight shortcomings in Europe's capacity to capitalize on basic research, which too seldom produced successful final products. The Commission also acknowledged the importance of evaluating the effectiveness of its research activities and programmes, which we examine later.

Thus by the late 1970s the Commission had begun to address some of the key issues concerning science and technology and establish tentative proposals for action, but these bore the stamp of a hesitant bureaucracy rather than the confidence which once marked the Ministry of International Trade and Industry (MITI) in Japan.

The primacy of US and Japanese technology

Evidence accumulated in the 1980s that the 'technology gap' noted between US and European industry in the 1960s was widening, and that Japan was also outstripping Europe in many critical industries. One of the most visible industries was electronics, because its products could be seen to pervade industrial and domestic use, including the fashionable information technology (IT) sector. The national governments of France, Germany, and the UK had all supported their IT industries throughout the period from the mid-1960s to the early 1980s through subsidy, merger, and procurement preference in government purchases, to little effect (Sandholtz 1992). In 1975 the EC had a positive balance of payments in information technology, but it was in deficit by 1982. Europe's shares of world production in semiconductors and in integrated circuits were declining, foreign penetration of the European market was increasing, and European semiconductor manufacturing was unprofitable. More than four-fifths of the European computer market was held by US firms. Worse still, perhaps, was the fact that the USA and Japan were both pursuing ambitious research programmes in search of future IT supremacy, the former on very-high-speed integrated circuits (VHSIC), while the latter, after its successful very-large-scale integration (VLSI) programme, which had launched Japanese industry into the manufacture of mainstream memory chips in the 1970s, announced an initiative on fifth-generation computers intended, in popular parlance, 'to think for themselves'. Faced with this mounting challenge, a number of leading European IT firms had, with EC encouragement, already begun to collaborate in the late 1970s on 'pre-competitive' research—that is, research on innovations in principle rather than at the level of products for imminent commercial launch. As we shall see later, this concern over US and Japanese technological leadership is a recurrent theme, continuing today.

The emergence of Community programmes

In 1979–80 the Commissioner of DG III, the Directorate-General of Internal Market and Industrial Affairs, Viscount Étienne Davignon of Belgium, invited the heads of Europe's leading IT firms to form a Big 12 Round Table. They commanded more authority than more junior personnel who had attended earlier, less fruitful, discussions, and were well aware of the gravity of their industrial and collective circumstances. Sandholtz (1992) has suggested that 'in general, states will attempt unilateral strategies first and surrender the goal of autonomy only when unilateral means have proved to be impossible or too costly'. The participant national firms knew that unilateralism had failed, and this recognition generated a climate favourable to cooperation, in which Davignon became the champion of new policies (Sharp 1993). Two years of talks failed to establish joint manufacturing companies along the lines of the Airbus consortium, but they did establish a consensus for collaborative research. Moral support also followed from the Gyllenhammer Group, an informal gathering of twenty leading European industrialists, representing Gyllenhammer's Volvo, as well as Pilkington and Philips, which urged an end to national subsidies, intra-European trade barriers, and divided RTD programmes.

There was, however, potential conflict with EC competition policy, which forbids collaboration at the stage of developing products for an immediate market. However, Articles 85 and 86 allow collaboration for 'pre-competitive research'. Davignon's alliance of the EC and heavyweight industrialists, supported by the work of 550 industrial, scientific, and university experts (Sandholtz 1992: 14–15), overcame the doubts of national government officials, and established the European Strategic Programme for Research and Development in Information Technology (ESPRIT). The first outline proposal of September 1980 led to a formal proposal to establish a strategic collaborative IT research programme between the major European companies, together with smaller companies, research institutes, and universities, which was presented in May 1982, and approved by the EC Commission in December, with funding of 11.5 million Ecus (£8.5 million). Contracts under the pilot programme were signed in May, with 38 projects, chosen from over 200 proposals involving 600 companies and institutes, under way by September 1983. The twelve round-table companies won about 70 per cent of the funds. Davignon's gambit of pilot projects with a streamlined application and vetting procedure paid off in overcoming Member State reservations and led to a ten-year 1.5 billion Ecus (£1 billion) programme for 1984–93.

The first five-year phase, ESPRIT I, 1984–8, was to concentrate on pre-competitive research in microelectronics, advanced information processing, and software technology, as well as applications in computer-integrated manufacturing and office systems. There was an enormous response to the first call for proposals in March 1984, with only about one proposal in four winning acceptance. The 227 projects in Phase I involved about 3,000 researchers from 240 companies (of which about 55 per cent were 'small', employing fewer than 500 workers apiece) and 180 universities and research institutes. Three-quarters of the projects involved firms and academic centres in collaborative work. Of the ten-year budget of 1.5 billion Ecus, 1.3 billion had been committed by January 1987. The EC funded up to half of the project expenditure, and firms from at least two Member States had to participate.

The successful reception of ESPRIT I was heartening to Europeans, and the consequences were positive.

- It created a useful European IT network of researchers, and allowed companies to economize on scarce technological personnel. They could commit one or two researchers to an ESPRIT project, and have their efforts geared up by the joint participation of other institutions' workers, with both short- and long-term benefits of collaboration and familiarity.

- Because the research was pre-competitive, collaboration was more open than if it had been near-market, when corporate secrecy would have inhibited the partners.

- Collaboration across national boundaries, required intentionally, meant that the narrow horizons of 'national champions' had to widen.

- In cases of industrial participation, industry met 50 per cent of the costs, thus enjoying effective subsidy from the EC.

- Although the Commission identified priorities and broad areas of research, actual research projects were nominated by the applicants. Thus, within the restriction that they could not be too near-market, projects became more demand-driven.

- Once agreed, each project was timetabled and monitored.

ESPRIT generated a new awareness of Europe's technological strengths, and provided a model for initiatives in other areas of technology. Indeed it helped establish the climate for the 'Framework' programmes, and produced a tribe of acronyms—RACE, BRITE, BRIDGE, BAP, ECLAIR, FLAIR, COMETT, and others.

Another consequence of the success of ESPRIT I was the need to find funds for the remainder of the programme's decade. The Commission brought forward the second phase, ESPRIT II, from 1989 to 1987. The Big 12 Round Table wanted to triple the budget and scope of ESPRIT II, but the proposal fell foul of UK and German government feelings that the EC RTD budget was too high. Compromises were struck over the Framework programme, and in April 1988 ESPRIT II was formally approved for 1988–92 with a budget of 1.6 billion Ecus (£1.07 billion), which was less than originally proposed but more than double the allocation for ESPRIT I. The Commission received about a thousand proposals and agreed to fund about half of them. Three principal areas were emphasized: microelectronics, IT processing systems, and applications technologies. The emphasis on precompetitive research, however, still left the difficulty of how to capitalize at market level, and ESPRIT II went some way to address this issue by emphasizing 'demand driven aspects of the programme' (Sharp 1993), for example, Application Specific Integrated Circuit Technology, and Technology Integration Projects (TIP), which were intended to meld different elements of separate work and show how they linked together. Funds for ESPRIT II were all earmarked by the end of 1990, and the Commission launched ESPRIT III with 1.35 billion Ecus (£645 million) for 1990–4, to exploit seven areas— microelectronics, advanced business and home systems peripherals, high-performance computing and networking, technology for software intensive systems, computer-integrated manufacturing and engineering, open microprocessor systems, and basic research to 'contribute to the programme's main objectives from an upstream position' (DTI 1993: 9).

A further development in the 1980s deserves attention. This is the European Research Coordination Agency, or EUREKA, initiated by France and founded in 1985 as a European response to President Reagan's announcement of the Strategic Defense Initiative (or 'Star Wars' as it became popularly known) in the USA. It extended beyond the EC Member States to include the seven countries of the European Free Trade Association (EFTA), Turkey, and, latterly, Hungary; but it was managed and coordinated by the EC Commission. It was intended to help industry-led, market-driven projects involving the collaboration of at least two organizations from at least two EUREKA member countries. By March 1993 there were 623 projects involving 8.8 billion Ecus (£6.2 billion). No priority areas were specified but the project had to involve technical innovation, and so was closer to the market and more concerned with commercial applications than ESPRIT was allowed to be. In practice, most current projects fell into the following areas: communications, energy, environment, IT, lasers, medical and biotechnology, new materials, robotics and automated production, and transport. Specific concerns included high-definition television (HDTV), which has also been the subject of much Japanese RTD, the Prometheus initiative for automatic car navigation systems, and JESSI, the Joint European Structure on Silicon Initiative.

EUREKA has no central funding, simply acting as an umbrella mechanism for encouraging interfirm collaboration: public funding is granted at the discretion of national governments, which usually follows any approval by the EUREKA programme. Thus EUREKA has a large nominal budget but no actual resource, though in its first twenty years it mobilized more than 24 billion Euros. The partners negotiate the sharing of intellectual property by Member States rather than effective rights (IPRs), for which there are no general rules. EUREKA was conceived as a rival to ESPRIT and other Commission programmes; but, despite occasional overlaps, it became more complementary, partly because its projects can be more applied than the pre-competitive ESPRIT projects. EUREKA and ESPRIT programmes raised the profile for research in the EC by the mid-1980s. Perceptions were also concentrated by the EC-wide acknowledgment of the technology gap, and of problems of the environment, and by a growing appreciation, through experience, of the benefits of interfirm and interinstitutional collaboration. Peterson (1991: 270–1) has argued that 'the interests of public and private actors in promoting new collaborative RTD programmes converged as the Framework programme and EUREKA were launched in 1985'. The instrument which allowed this fuller development of collaborative research was the Single European Act (SEA).

6.4 The SEA of 1987

The 1987 Act contained an additional section, called Title VI—Research and Technological Development, in which it set out in Article 130*f* the following credo:

The Community's aim shall be to strengthen the scientific and technological base of Europe's industry and to encourage it to become more competitive at international level.

In order to achieve this, it shall encourage undertakings including small and medium undertakings, research centres and universities in their research and technological development activities;

it shall support their efforts to cooperate with one another, aiming notably at enabling undertakings to exploit the Community's internal market potential to the full, in particular through the opening up of national public contracts, the definition of common standards and the removal of legal and fiscal barriers to that cooperation.

In the achievement of these aims, special account shall be taken of the connection between the common research and technological development effort, the establishment of the internal market and the implementation of common policies, particularly as regards competition and trade.

The next Articles, 130*g* to 130*l*, spelled out the means. Research, technological development, and demonstration programmes would promote cooperation between businesses, research centres, and universities. Cooperation would also be promoted with third countries and international organizations, as would the 'dissemination and optimization of results'. Training and mobility would also be stimulated. Member States undertook to coordinate amongst themselves policies and programmes carried out at national level, in liaison with the Commission.

The key provision was the adoption of a multi-annual Framework Programme setting out all the EC's proposed activities over a five-year period: it would lay down scientific and technical objectives, prioritize them, set out the main lines of activity and the amount of funding deemed necessary, including detailed rules for EC participation, and its distribution across the appropriate activities. The Framework would comprise specific programmes of fixed duration within each activity. An implementation mechanism worked at two levels: the Framework as a whole had to secure unanimous agreement among the Member States; and sub-programmes were to be adopted by the Council by qualified majority voting after consultation with the European Parliament (EP) and the Economic and Social Committee. Programmes subsidiary to the Framework were permissible involving certain Member States only, which could finance them subject to possible EC participation; and cooperation with third states and international organizations was also feasible.

This was a dramatic advance upon the 1957 Treaty of Rome, since it legitimized EC technology policy—as it did industry policy elsewhere in the Act. In fact, the Framework system had already been subject to discussions for two years when it was launched in 1987, in the hope of an earlier introduction. The motive of both the Commission and the EP was to break out of the stop–start cycle of ad hoc decision-taking and wrangling over the funding of research proposals. The First Framework Programme, now commonly labelled Framework 1, or FP1, was scheduled to run from 1987 to 1991. It was followed by others, with successive increases in funding; the proportionate distributions of activity with the Framework programmes are shown in Table 6.2. In the event, the take-up of funds for programmes was faster than expected; for example, the most important member programme, ESPRIT, overran its budget by 200 million Ecus in 1988, in the face of 'the high quality of the proposals, the industrial commitment underlying them and the urgency of the work proposed' (Peterson 1991: 282–3). A Second Framework Programme had been introduced to run during 1987–91, and by December 1989 the Research Council in Brussels agreed with Research Commissioner Pandolfi to establish a third-generation Framework programme: its funds were topped up in December 1992 from 5.7 billion to 6.6 billion Ecus.

Table 6.2 Framework Programmes of European activities in research and technological development, 1987–2013

Framework Programme	Period	Budget (million Ecus)
FP1	1984–8	3,750
FP2	1987–91	5,396
FP3	1990–4	6,600
FP4	1994–8	13,215
FP5	1998–2002	14,960
FP6	2002–6	17,883
FP7 (forecast)	2007–13	50,521

Source: CEC (1994) and author's estimates for FP5.

The total extent of the European programmes for new technology has been wide, and Table 6.3 lists some of the best known, together with this funding. Programmes often continued through successive generations of Framework—as in the cases of ESPRIT, COMETT, and SPRINT—though the emerging primacy of the Framework Programme has tended to mask the acronyms.

6.5 Evaluations of policy effectiveness

EU-sponsored research is important in both quantity and quality: some system of accountability is obviously necessary. Technically the Commission is accountable to the Council, which is made up of national ministers, and to the European Parliament, which scrutinizes legislation and the drafting and execution of budgets. However, science and technology require expert examination, as do both their scientific and their economic worth, to judge whether the work is worth doing in the first place and whether, once authorized, it has been well accomplished.

Thoroughgoing evaluation is exceedingly difficult (Georghiou and Roessner 2000). Many issues arise, which can be characterized as follows:

- Ambit: how widely do benefits from support occur, through spillovers, research linkages, etc.?
- Horizon: how far into the future should benefits be counted? Can evaluation capture all the long-run effects and ramifications?
- Additionality: can it be demonstrated that support given to RTD raises the total spend, or does some of it merely allow recipients to substitute it for monies that they would have found themselves?
- Counterfactuality: relatedly, what would have eventuated in the absence of official policy? Does the support positively cause change, or simply accelerate it somewhat?

Table 6.3 Major European programmes promoting new technology

Acronym and full name	Period	Budget[a] (million Ecus)	Prime objectives
ESPRIT: European Strategic Programme for RTD in IT	III 1984–8 III 1988–92 III 1992–4 IV 1994–8	750 1,600 1,350	To promote EC capabilities and competitiveness in IT, especially microelectronics systems
RACE: RTD in Advanced Communications Technologies for Europe	Definition 1985–7 RACE I 1990–4 RACE II 1992–4	21 460 489	Help EC competence in broadband communications equipment, standards, and technology
TELEMATICS	1990–4	380	Develop telematics in e.g. health, transport, public administration
BRITE/EURAM: Basic Research in Industrial Technologies/Advanced Materials for Europe	BRITE I 1985–8 EURAM I 1986–8 BRITE/EURAM I 1989–92 BRITE/EURAM II 1992–6 BRITE/EURAM III 1996–	100 450 663 1,487	Support for RTD which upgrades technological or materials base of production
BAP: Biotechnology Action Programme	1985–9	75	Develop infrastructure in biotechnology, esp. research and training
BRIDGE: Biotechnological Research for Innovation, Development and Growth in Europe	1990–3	100	As BAP, but for large projects, e.g. molecular modelling, advanced cell culture
BIOTECH	1992–6	164	Pre-normative research, more basic than BRIDGE, includes safety
ECLAIR: European Collaborative Linkage of Agriculture and Industry through Research	1989–94	80	Applying advanced biotechnology in agro-industrial sector, esp. using raw materials from agriculture
FLAIR: Food Linked Agro-Industrial Research	1989–94	25	As ECLAIR, but food-oriented, in manufacture and processing
COMETT: Community Action Programme for Education and Training for Technology	COMETT I 1987–9 COMETT II 1990–4	30 200 + 30	Training programmes between university and industry, via enterprise partnerships and international staff exchange
VALUE	VALUE I VALUE II 1992–4	66	Disseminate and exploit research results of Community programmes
SPRINT: Strategic Programme for Innovation and Technology Transfer	SPRINT I experiment SPRINT II 1986–9 SPRINT III 1989–94	9 90	Promote innovation and technology transfer, esp. among small and medium-sized enterprises internationally. Merged with VALUE 1994
EURET	1990–3	27	Rail, sea, air transport research
STRIDE: Science and Technology for Regional Innovation and Development in Europe	1990–3	400	DG XVI programme to promote RTD in assisted regions
MONITOR	1989–93	22	Identify RTD policy priorities

[a] The figures shown as budgeted do not include industrial contributions to ESPRIT and other shared cost programmes: in those cases actual expenditure involved in the programmes will approximate twice the budget figure shown above.
Sources: CEC (various publications).

Hall and Van Reenen (2000) surveyed authoritatively the difficulties and findings of studies which attempted to quantify the impact of fiscal incentives for RTD. Results varied widely, but they were able to conclude that 'a tax price elasticity around unity is a good ballpark figure', that is, a reduction in the cost of research invokes an equi-proportionate increase in the amount of RTD conducted. Response to tax credits for RTD tends to be fairly small at first but increases over time. However, the intrinsic problems of cost–benefit approaches are exacerbated in the case of EU support by the complexity of cross-national involvements, so that qualitative review is favoured as more likely to capture major long-term benefits. Luukkonen (2000) suggests that Framework Programmes were important as sources of finance for SMEs, but less so for large companies, for which new exchanges and informal contacts were more important. However, an ideal system of evaluation was a distant hope. The urgent need was to get something started as a discipline.

One early possibility was to employ FAST (Forecasting and Assessment in Science and Technology) in evaluations. But there seemed little enthusiasm at the top of the Commission to involve FAST: its resources were small for such a vast job, and independent outside judgement was deemed desirable (Holdsworth and Lake 1988: 424).

When the Third Framework Programme was adopted, the Council required the Commission to undertake an evaluation of all programmes which operated under the second programme, formally to provide 'an overall appreciation of the current state of execution and achievements of the specific programmes adopted under the second Framework . . . and to set out the principal lessons that have been learned from the execution of these programmes'. The main source of information was the reports of independent evaluation panels commissioned to examine the operations of specific programmes. In addition there were reports from consultants commissioned to examine particular questions, internal Commission reviews drawing on the reports of panels or outside experts, reviews and reports of programme committees, plus findings from specially commissioned studies of the horizontal aspects of the effects of Community RTD programmes. An example of commissioned work was a study of the impact of EC policies for RTD on science and technology in the UK, which was prepared for the UK Office of Science and Technology and the Commission (HMSO 1993).

The findings of these studies were generally positive: they chronicled good work and effective international and inter-institutional collaboration. A report from CREST was submitted to the Council in September 1992, giving an evaluation of the Second Framework Programme (CREST 1992). It addressed three major issues—the quality of programme results and their impact on competitiveness; management and cost-effectiveness of research; and consistency with EC policy and principles. It noted a substantial amount of state-of-the-art research, with a fair balance between incremental and more ambitious research, but intellectual property rights problems were an inhibition on dissemination and exploitation, for which there was, implicitly, more scope. While there were cases of RTD conferring significant technological advantage over international rivals, the most significant impact was felt to be in promoting the idea of collaboration across industry, academia, and the nations of the EC. There remained much scope for developing the harmonization of standards across the EC. Though there was general satisfaction over programme management, sometimes project assessment needed more attention, as did the lags between calling for proposals and beginning the research. Programme objectives could be more clearly defined and there was scope for closer and more transparent links with other DGs responsible for policy in areas such as transport, environment, energy, health, and agriculture. According to Pownall (1995), ESPRIT I raised 'European awareness' but brought less evidence of tangible and marketable results because of the pre-competitive nature of the work, but business and market factors were better considered in ESPRIT II.

With nearly 18,000 collaborative links in Framework 2, the UK was its most active participant. In fact, the UK fared well in the early Framework provisions, according to calculations by the Cabinet Office, reported in earlier editions of this book. UK views on Framework 2 were analysed by questionnaire and interviews among participants in academia and industry (Georghiou *et al.* 1993). Academics were more positive, but two-thirds of industrial firms involved considered the benefits outweighed the costs, against 21 per cent that did not; and more than three-quarters intended to reapply for future participation. It was estimated that about half of EC RTD spending in the UK was 'additional' —that is, adding to the total of publicly financed RTD, and not just funding what would have been undertaken without EC monies. Moreover, EC programmes had a bigger impact than the 6 per cent of publicly funded RTD that they constituted, because they were approved by senior staff, they concentrated on recently established priorities, eased research-funding scarcities, and were geared up by EC participation. However, UK industrial participation in Framework 3 was disappointing in comparison with German and French industry. There were also complaints that project approval rates were low in the third programme and that there was not enough continuity, which is vital to long-term research work (*Research Fortnight*, 30 November 1994, p. 12).

An independent panel of experts also found in favour of EUREKA's benefits (*Outlook on Science Policy* 1993: 73–4). Most partnerships were vertical, between firms, customers, and suppliers, rather than horizontal. Collaboration worked best between partners of similar size, with smaller firms more product-oriented than large ones, which focused on longer-term research projects. More than 40 per cent of participants were found to expect substantial sales increases within three years, reflecting the near-market emphasis of EUREKA compared with Framework.

In the discussions leading to the Fourth Framework Programme, lessons were drawn from earlier experience. The UK government submitted a policy paper in February 1992 (Cabinet Office 1992) drawing together the views of the UK science and technology community. It stressed the need for evaluation of Framework 2, for planning of annual commitments, for emphasis on generic technologies and dissemination of technology from research projects, as well as the need for consultation between DGs. Some of these views were accepted in CREST (1992), but the Fourth Framework proposal was controversially received (Hill 1993: 16).

The programme proposed 13.1 billion Ecus of expenditure, but its adoption required a unanimous decision from the twelve Member States. However, the three biggest contributors to the EU—Germany, the UK, and France—sought against the wishes of the other nine to reduce the Framework budget by at least 1 billion Ecus. One of the difficulties has been that the pay-off to Framework RTD is singularly problematic to assess in financial terms. Since it is not near-market research, it will take time to see clear financial benefit, and the advantages so far ascribed to it by expert analysts are inevitably qualitative rather than measurable in money terms. A cynic might observe that of course firms will welcome, and laud, Framework Programmes if they bring handsome subsidies with them. The EU still seems to be lagging behind its US and Japanese technological competitors in many industries, but this can hardly be laid at the door of the EU programmes, which account for only a very small part of total RTD effort across the companies and countries of the EU. While Framework 4 remained directed, like its predecessors, at pre-competitive research, it was designed to complement national research efforts, and projects are expected to offer practical longer-term advances.

Framework 5 adopted new priorities with greater emphasis on problem-solving in areas of high social concern, with 'key actions' complementing generic research activities. Previous specific programmes were rationalized into four thematic programmes (such as energy, user-friendly information society, competition, and sustainability) and three horizontal programmes (community research, innovation and SMEs, and enhanced human research potential). These were intended to help budgetary flexibility but complicated the switch from Framework 4.

Several countries worried about funding, cost overruns on Framework 4 adding to misgivings. Germany was keen to restrain public expenditure to meet the financial criteria set out in the Treaty on European Union (TEU), and sought concentration on a small number of strategic industries, gaining flexible funding to make programmes more adaptable in the face of emerging needs, and seeking Article 169 'variable geometry' which would allow Member States to opt in or out of individual programmes. Pressure on research funds intensified in most countries: the UK capped its contribution to ESA in 1995, and EU-funded research by UK companies was balanced by a cutback of national government funds, acting as a considerable disincentive to the effort required to bid for them. The growth rate in funding, so pronounced between Frameworks 3 and 4, slowed markedly.

The Framework Programmes across 1994–9 were evaluated by an independent expert panel which reported in July 2000 (CEC 2000*a*). It drew on more than two thousand questionnaire responses from participants in Frameworks 3 and 4, numerous reports from monitoring and assessment panels, and interviews with key figures in the Commission and selected Member States. It assessed past activities positively, praising collaboration, networking, training-related activities, and the increased involvement of SMEs, and recommended continued emphasis on social relevance, collective RTD projects, and excellence and mobility of researchers. It recommended numerous changes to cope with future needs, several of which went beyond their remit but were considered vital. These included:

- simpler, more understandable application procedures;
- encouragement to propose riskier projects;
- a restructured and expanded Framework Programme, but no need for Programme Committees;
- a major review of systems and procedures to determine goals, specify delivery mechanisms, and implement programmes; and
- modification of existing management and admininstration structures and procedures to delegate tasks downwards in the Commission, or externalize them, to avoid needless bureaucracy.

The most important conclusion went beyond Framework, and was accompanied by others:

- Framework alone would not satisfy EU policy goals and a European RTD strategy was needed at the highest political levels;
- science and technology budgets should rise to at least 3 per cent of GDP over the next ten years;
- private sector RTD should be stimulated by indirect measures such as tax incentives;
- urgent action is required to counter foreseeable skills shortages over the next decade;
- centres of research and teaching excellence should be supported, though RTD support for expectant Central and Eastern European entrants to the EU would have to be channelled through existing academies until new competitive science and industry structures emerged; and
- RTD policies among the Member States need to reinforce rather than duplicate each other.

On its inception, Framework 5 met widespread criticism that its attempt to combine thematic elements with horizontal factors spanning innovation, technology, training, and international cooperation would prove too complex to manage effectively, without more preparation. Frameworks have been subject to scrutiny by the European Union every four years and occasionally by independent commentators. This is no mean task as it involves about 15,000 transnational multifunded research actions, prompting some observers to describe the FP as the most comprehensive research funding provision in the world. Official evaluation now involves three exercises:

1. ad hoc evaluation exercises are initiated and managed by research managers within the Directorate-General responsible for the FP, be it thematic, programme specific, or individual in scope;

2. independent experts help the Commission to monitor annually the implementation of research; and

3. a five-year assessment examines the effects and achievements of the FPs over the previous five years, the last such exercise being in 2004. The five-year assessments thus span successive four-year FPs.

Member states can also supplement these exercises with their own impact studies. The Five-Year Assessment Panel was chosen, thirteen strong, with care and is judged to have worked intensively and well (Reeve 2005). But there is scope for improvement, as even the panel chairman confirmed (Ormala and Vernotas 2005), involving simplification, better evidence and utility of results, avoiding fragmentation and overdetermination of low-level areas, and tailoring the assessment to the specific FP concerned. There has also been criticism from the European Union Court of Auditors.

It is perhaps prudent to include some wholly neutral commentators in assessing the programme. One crucial issue concerns 'additionality'—whether the programme stimulates extra research investment, or simply subsidizes work that would have eventuated anyhow, via the principal or other parties. It is a tricky question: do you assess inputs, outputs, behaviour? Polt and Streicher (2005) addressed these complexities before concluding on the basis of 1,700 responses that FP5 generated additionality, often more effectively than national programmes do. Where additionality was somewhat grey, it was often true that the project was enhanced significantly beyond its unsupported status. A few cases arose where support was actually counter-productive, where projects would have fared better without it, which they felt deserved closer scrutiny to avoid future pitfalls, as would the concept of behavioural additionality where benefits transcend immediate input and output benefits, such as enhanced capability to scale technological trajectories. Improvements might follow from better monitoring of outcomes and outputs, *ex ante* analyses to compare more readily with outcomes, and fuller analysis of behavioural additionality. Arnold *et al.* (2005) confirmed in a survey article the general presence of additionality, with the FP as driver or very pronounced accelerator, acting most strongly in long-term projects and those less traditionally accustomed to R&D. They concluded that the FP is a useful, flexible device, stimulating good scientific work, usually producing pre-competitive intermediate outputs rather than final outcomes. (This characterstic was confirmed by Guy *et al.* (2005) who note that knowledge and networking aims scored highest, and strategic goals lowest, among major goals: and that among high-ranking secondary goals was internal use of results, though not spin-offs or the use of patents or copyrights.) But by no means all firms, including some major R&D performers, were involved, and there was scope for improvement in evaluation methods, data, and the neutrality and systematic unity of assessment. An important conclusion was that the Framework Programmes unaided could not deliver the Lisbon goals; greater programme flexibility and other instruments would be required to establish a real European Research Policy.

The assessment included some consideration of Framework 6, which ran from 2003 to the end of 2006, to which we now turn. While it has some detailed aims, such as increasing the disbursement of project funds to SMEs to 15 per cent, the driving ambition has been to establish a European Research Area, with the intention of raising the EU's level of RTD expenditure to 3 per cent of GDP, in line with the Lisbon European Council Declaration of March 2000, in the hope of meeting the technological challenges from the United States, Japan, and elsewhere.

The Commission called for a European Research Area, with a number of priorities (CEC 2000*b*). Broadly, it stressed the need for networking, centres of excellence, and targeted large-scale projects. Further strengthening of SME technology was called for, as well as increased end-user involvement to exploit RTD results more effectively, improvements to research infrastructure including electronic networking, and more open access to national programmes. Human resource development was prioritized, including cross-border mobility for researchers, the recruitment of more women into science, and the attraction of more foreign scientists into the EU. Science should attend dialogue with citizens, in the face of public scepticism, RTD should relate to broad EU goals, and programme and project management should be efficient and transparent, being subjected to systematic appraisal, monitoring, and evaluation, but with easier, decentralized procedures for SMEs. The British Office of Science and Technology generally welcomed the proposals (DTI 2000*b*), but with one or two hard-nosed observations. They noted that selection should concentrate on areas too large-scale for national programmes, and suggested that programmes of 1–2 billion Euros could make a substantial difference to Europe's competitive position in areas such as biosciences, informatics, aeronautics, nanotechnology, quantum computing, agile and intelligent manufacturing technology, and environmental goods and services including renewable energy. They should complement national programmes, and have inputs from 'customer' Directorates-General on programme definition concerning issues such as environment, transport, food safety, and Common Agricultural Policy reform. Networked interdisciplinary centres of excellence were welcome, but 'substantial management and logistic competence' would be needed if tens of millions of Euros would be applied for long periods to some programmes. As the programme unfurled, while singing its praises, the Commission noted (CEC 2004) that it was the victim of its own success, able to support only one application in five, and only half of those considered to be of very high standard. The virtues claimed for FP6's stated objectives are the creation of centres of excellence; the launch of technological initiatives; creativity in basic research through competition between research teams; enhanced attraction of research careers in Europe; growth of new research infrastructures; and improved coordination of national research programmes. Eventually, under Article 169 of the Treaty, the hope is that there will be genuine integration of national programmes, where they apply to research programmes on a particular topic. Integrated projects involving multiple partners are intended to achieve a critical mass of resources which enable major societal needs to be addressed, or major improvements in Europe's international competitiveness to be achieved. The concept of networks of excellence also involves multipartner projects in which networks are established around a joint programme of activities, which will simultaneously advance knowledge and create lasting links that will enable the development of competences with the potential to address emerging needs in the future, beyond the immediate FP funding horizon. Beyond these new emphases, many tried and tested project and action mechanisms remain common to FP5 and 6.

The Lisbon objective has been reaffirmed periodically since, with a target date for accomplishment by 2010 (and been paralleled by identical national goals for France and Germany). The intention is that private industry should source two-thirds of the provision and government one-third. However, the influence that the Commission has over corporate research is very limited, so they may be giving a hostage to fortune: national governments through their basic research strategies and fiscal policies giving corporate tax relief and credits for research are more influential, though even they, as we saw earlier in the cases of France and Germany, can sometimes be hamstrung by the requirements of EU macroeconomic rules. Industry, however, has been shy of deep involvement, perhaps because of concerns over intellectual property rights (Siune *et al.* 2005).

The Euratom Framework 6 accounts for a further 1,230 million Euros, mainly devoted to fusion research.

Until the next five-year assessment, we must be guarded about the performance of FP6. There are recurrent acknowledgements, as there were with Framework 5, that administration and financial rules should be simplified and improved to enhance efficiency and flexibility in the management of instruments. As Siune *et al.* note (2005: 380): 'In spite of efforts to improve procedures in comparison to FP5, the legal, financial and administrative requirements are still overwhelming. However, the EC is aware of the problem.'

Table 6.4 Sixth Framework Programme, 2003–6

Programme area	Budget (million Euros)	% RTD
Life sciences, genomics, and biotechnology	2,514	14.0
Information society technologies	3,984	22.3
Nanotechnology, materials, and new production processes and devices	1,429	8.0
Aeronautics and space	1,182	6.6
Food quality and safety	753	4.2
Sustainable energy, transport, and ecosystems	2,329	13.0
Citizens and governance	247	1.4
Specific activities covering wider research fields	1,409	7.9
Joint Research Centre: non-nuclear activities	835	4.7
Structuring and strengthening the European Research Area	3,201	17.9
Total	17,883	100.0

Source: Cordis website, 2005.

Framework 7 proceeds in embryo, and was approved by the European Parliament in June 2006, albeit to be funded, at 50.5 billion Euros, rather less generously than the Commission's starting bid of 73.2 billion just over a year earlier, which would effectively have doubled FP funding. Germany, France, and the UK were among those taking a tough line on the budget. As it is, there remains a substantial rise. The shares of finance allocated to component parts of the budget remain to be decided, but if they mirrored the early bids, could approximate 60 per cent to 'cooperation', 16 per cent to 'ideas', that is, the European Research Council, and 10 per cent each to 'people' and 'capacities'. The main industrial sectors within 'cooperation' comprise health, food, agriculture and biotechnology, ICT, nanotechnology, energy, environment, transport, security, and space. MEPs wanted to keep the 15 per cent target for SMEs, to establish the European Research Council, to support young researchers, and to approve stem cell research, subject to ethical safeguards.

Evidently the Framework system has evolved into a permanent element in EU policy, and one that is accorded growing importance. As something of an adjunct to Framework 7, a European Research Council is being established to cover a gap in Europe's basic or 'blue skies' research. This is seen as an area of weakness relative to the USA, which Framework itself is not suited to remedy, and takes at least some of its inspiration from that country's National Science Foundation. There, scientific teams compete and flourish: it is hoped that European scientists might emerge from their presently fragmented state, interact, and bid for attractive research carrots which would reflect scientific rather than bureaucratic criteria, in the manner that scientists always relish. A side-benefit of a scientifically excellent institution might be to retain in Europe those ambitious young scientists who currently go west across the Atlantic. The idea is interesting, but already a problem is looming: some countries are talking of fair national shares, or *juste retour*. Yet how can the pursuit of excellence be reconciled with the idea that all participants should be financed, whether good, bad, or indifferent?

6.6 **Policy problems**

Industrial policy is traditionally concerned with matters such as influencing industrial and market structure and competitiveness, and encouraging the modernization of capital stock. It shares uncertain borders with technology and trade policies. For example, the structure of output cannot be decided independently of trade policies. If a country wishes to develop a new industrial sector in which other countries already have capabilities and experience, it may have to invoke the infant-industry argument and offer its industry a period of protection from unrestricted foreign competition. Subsidies to indigenous RTD may also be considered necessary. Technology, industrial, and trade policies clearly overlap here; perhaps the simplest theoretical discriminator is that industry policy emphasizes physical capital, whereas technology policy emphasizes the creation and utilization of knowledge.

However, it is a practical and not just a theoretical dilemma. Technology policy seeks to create productive capability, which often requires public sponsorship of RTD. Such support is only compatible with competition (which is a common goal of industrial policy) if the RTD is pre-competitive; but the boundary between pre-competitive and near-market RTD is fuzzy, at best. The tension between protectionism and enhancing capability is exemplified by European attitudes towards microelectronics and IT. European firms have persistently failed to compete satisfactorily in these sectors in spite of varied forms of protectionism. How long, and by how much, is it necessary to support the development of European potential, before an infant industry can be weaned? Yet is it possible for the EU to achieve adequate economic performance and prospects for the future if these strategic industries are allowed to wither?

The tension between a protectionist Fortress Europa and an open, competitive EU of the sort which Porter (1990) would consider a prerequisite for efficiency, is reinforced by the institutional division of labour which assigns industrial, technology, and trade policies to different DGs. Each DG has its own routines, traditions, and power structure. Programmes, once initiated, are difficult to terminate and attitudes harden. Thus the rigidities and contradictions can persist if they are inherent in the priorities of different interest groups. It takes time and continuous effort to reconcile these conflicting forces and establish an acceptable balance of competition, protection, and capability enhancement. Further, one of the goals of EU policy is to enhance the science and technology capacities of Member States presently less capable in these areas. Resource is transferred via taxation from the advanced, efficient Member States to the disadvantaged. This may be acceptable in times of general prosperity and growth, but can create tensions if the advanced states face competitive pressures from non-Member States. As the EU accepts new members, and others join the queue for entry, additional pressures arise. The secretariat is presently unwilling to reveal how support under the Framework Programmes is distributed among Member States. Admittedly it is not an easy calculation because of all the split receipts among the international projects, but it is feasible; the bureaucratic coyness arises from fears that different countries are likely to object if their contributions run far ahead of their incomes. The principle of *juste retour* which seeks a balance between the two, as applied in ESA, is not applied to the Framework Programmes—hence the sensitivity.

Globalization and corporate alliances

As we have seen, EU technology policy has concentrated on sponsoring different forms of collaboration between European countries. Such forms of collaboration are not generally those which participants would choose spontaneously, otherwise the EU initiatives would have been redundant, having been implemented already by the market. In this context one should note the rise since the late 1970s of inter-institutional collaborative agreements or IICAs (Chesnais 1991; Mytelka 1991). They can be of very different scope, varying from licensing agreements, joint RTD, joint development of new products, and joint ventures in marketing and distribution, with or without joint equity. The Airbus consortium was just one of many possible manifestations.

The growth of IICAs poses a considerable theoretical and practical problem. From a theoretical standpoint, firms are not expected to collaborate. As they grow in size, we might expect them to integrate vertically and develop internal hierarchical organizational forms. Given the realities of market imperfection, firms tend to internalize functions (Coase 1937; Williamson 1975, 1985). Industrial RTD in particular is a function often internalized, because of the difficulties of establishing satisfactory markets in technology, given the complexities of valuation and the need for secrecy to ensure appropriability of returns to technological effort. The development of internalized RTD has been one of the most striking institutional changes of the last century (Schumpeter 1943; Freeman and Soete 1997). In this context, inter-institutional collaboration might be considered an oddity.

Why then do IICAs happen and why have they proliferated? Several authors have suggested contributory factors. One is the growing importance of knowledge in production, revealed by the growth of RTD in GDP and as a proportion of corporate turnover in many industries, and by the growing percentage of non-material investment (Mytelka 1991). Most IICAs are in relatively high-technology industries, such as IT, biotechnology, aerospace, or new materials. Other possible contributing factors were the productivity slowdown of the late 1960s and 1970s, and the observed shortening of product lifecycles, which implies more frequent innovation with its attendant costs and uncertainties. The decline of traditional mass production ('Fordism') and the rise of flexible manufacturing systems also place a premium on technological capability. Collaborative agreements can reduce the heavy fixed costs of entry, as well as facilitating exit by providing a partner to whom an interest might be sold. Another possible motive is a search for monopoly power. IICAs effectively reduce rivalry, and so represent a clandestine increase in concentration. If they enable players to raise their RTD game, they also raise barriers to entry. These have implications for economic welfare, but on the positive side the improved diffusion of knowledge that IICAs entail is valuable and effective. So long as technology continues to grow in complexity and expense, as seems certain, IICAs will figure prominently and, indeed, increase in the corporate landscape.

Collaborative agreements impinge upon technology policies. It might seem that they are in tune with the collaborative tenor of current EU technology policy; but IICAs are driven in opportunistic directions, not those favoured by state or community governments. Possibly the EU programmes may facilitate intra-EU IICAs; but collaboration outside the EU makes it more difficult to evaluate the pay-off to EU technology policy, and Sachwald (1993) showed that major European firms tend to adopt a global rather than a

Eurocentric view of their markets. In this context, it can make more sense for a European firm aspiring to a global presence to seek global, rather than European, partnerships. The 1990s witnessed a strong increase in foreign direct investment, prompting much talk of globalization. Europeans invested in foreign subsidiaries, and foreigners invested in European subsidiaries, as each sought to maximize the returns to their know-how. Provided that Europe maintains a strong science and technology infrastructure, and a dynamic economy, globalization can enhance its science and technology and its economic performance: it is much less a threat than an opportunity which, as Archibugi and Iammarino (1999: 265) put it, 'can allow a country to become an information crossroads, and thus acquire expertise in a wide range of technologies'. There is scant point in reinventing other people's ideas; it is better to understand, adapt, and progress them. Yet it is likely to be difficult to guarantee the primacy of EU research that EU members seek in the face of commercial realities, as developments in China show. China has been seen as a low-cost production location, with a dedicated and able workforce, which began with production of relatively simple products. It proceeded to much more sophisticated products, applying technology accessed through global corporate alliances. It has now, thanks to explosive growth in the numbers of qualified scientists and engineers, developed the capacity and cost-advantage to provide an admirable research base for global companies such as Sony. In April 2006, Astra Zeneca announced that it would spend $100 million over three years to develop a research facility in China, one of more than 200 foreign corporations to do so recently. Thanks to recent salary rises for scientific workers (evidence of a burgeoning knowledge market), China's RTD spending is now second only to the USA having nudged ahead of Japan in 2006, underlining the strength of the challenge. In the words of one commentator, 'it has advanced from a low-cost production base to become a low-cost knowledge base'.

National systems of innovation and EU technology policy

The concept of national systems of innovation (NSI) has gained much attention among leading scholars of technology (Freeman 1987, 1988; Lundvall 1988, 1993; Nelson 1988, 1990, 1993), who seek to interpret the persistence of areas of industrial and technological strength in national economies, and of very specific institutional configurations for very long periods of time. Such areas of industrial strength are chemicals, luxury cars, and machine tools in Germany; cars and consumer electronics in Japan; electronics, aircraft, and biotechnology in the USA. Furthermore, the institutions which control the generation and adoption of innovations in each country show a high degree of national specificity. Thus, not only do the degree of centralization and of state intervention, and the organization of universities and research institutes (to mention just a few factors), differ widely across countries, but these differences persist over time. Finally, what contributes still more to the specifically national character of the innovation system is the pattern of interactions between different institutions. There are powerful networks formed by research laboratories, government departments, and firms, which are extremely important and, again, very specific.

Pronounced differences exist at the level of national institutions; Lundvall (1988, 1993) laid particular emphasis on user–producer relations. These create institutional networks which communicate and interact, and define a system which may be highly country- or even region-specific, as Porter (1990) has noted widely. The role of MITI has been profoundly influential in defining industrial and technological priorities and coordinating firms' actions, stressing the role of forecasting and horizontal flows in organizations as significant elements of the Japanese national system of innovation (Freeman 1987, 1988). In particular, information flows in enterprises improve the relationship between RTD and production, in which the Japanese system has been singularly successful.

However, the observations of Sharp and Holmes (1989: 220–1) remain apposite:

> The degree to which a nation-sate seeks to carve out for itself an area of 'industrial space' which it can dominate is now minimal. The growing interdependence of the economic and industrial systems of the nations of Western Europe means that actions pursued in one country spill over rapidly into others . . . the degree of autonomy available to the individual nation-sate for the pursuit of industrial objectives is severely constrained . . . It is technology as much as political dogma that has put paid to the era of national champions.

Further, even though national systems of innovation have excited such interest, they are difficult to pin down analytically (Edquist 2004). However, the growth of European policies and instruments that we have just examined has prompted the question of whether a European innovation system is emerging, or could emerge. Expert opinion seems to be that it has not done so yet (Borrás 2004), and that national systems remain much more powerful for the moment (Archibugi and Coco 2005), though EU-sponsored forms of inter-institutional collaboration across national boundaries can establish valuable new networks, with links across the entire Union. This prospect prompts several questions. Will the networks be stable? How will they benefit the EU and Member States? Will there be conflicts between an EU and national systems of innovation? Will the Framework Programmes become institutionalized forces for conservatism, in the sense that Banchoff (2002) suggested, with increasingly large and complex programmes absorbing the administrative capacities of the Commission and breeding a clientele devoted to the status quo? And there is the question of opportunity costs: will benefits be equitably distributed and will resources allocated to the EU system of innovation impair the performance of national systems? In essence, this poses the question of subsidiarity on a technological plane. The accession of new entrants, generally poorer, to form a Union of twenty-five states involved some of these issues directly.

Some issues arising from enlargement

The accession of new states into the Union in recent years has been a predominantly political decision, in which pure size and ultimate potential were given primacy over the more immediate goals, which may even be compromised by entry. Even though low labour costs may and do attract EU manufacturing investment to the newcomers, they are not in the vanguard of technology or RTD expenditure. The Lisbon target of achieving research expenditure of 3 per cent of GDP is disturbingly above trend for the big hitters in the European league, but manifestly impossible for the whole team of twenty-five. Von Tunzelmann and Nassehi (2004) have explored some of the implications that arise. The Central and Eastern European (CEE) economies suffered poor networks before and after transition. In particular, since transition new resource links have been dominated by multinational companies to which the economies are more passive suppliers rather than true participants in the creative process, while national systems of innovation have imploded. While some elements of that system were defective, even the competent elements now suffer. The multinationals have no reason to locate there other than cost, and therefore tend to be footloose in the face of emergent lower cost locations. It is therefore vital for these economies to acquire broader competences and networks to raise their attraction and long-term viability. Yet this poses problems for European Policy. Framework Programmes are not subject to *juste retour* provisos, which would assure participant states a proportionate return for their contribution: excellence not equity determines the choice of project for support, and must remain a powerful determinant in a technologically competitive environment. Yet, already, weaker regions in Spain, Portugal, and some of the CEE countries are observing that they want more from FP7 than they have gained from its predecessor. The nurture of the CEE countries is likely to require the emergence of technological, economic, social, and political sustainabilities according to von Tunzelmann, in which the provisions of Framework Programmes may prove to be too wedded to old linear views of the innovation process, with a strong emphasis on technology-push, to afford much comfort to them.

Risk governance in science and technology

Among policy-makers, it is accepted that the development and application of technology are key elements of economic performance in advanced countries. The readiness of the general public to accept and embrace new technology can be influential, positively or negatively. The national enthusiasm to catch up with the West is held to have created a receptive attitude to technological change among the Japanese public (Williams and Mills 1986: 429–30), whereas the Chernobyl nuclear power plant disaster of 1986 strengthened the hands of the opponents of nuclear power in Germany and Sweden to the point where the state decided to phase out nuclear power generation altogether. Fear of untrammelled science is not new, as Mary Shelley's *Frankenstein* in 1818 clearly demonstrates, or as, more chillingly, does Robert Oppenheimer's quotation of Vishnu after witnessing the first atomic bomb test: 'I am become death, the destroyer of worlds.' Recently there have been many alarms involving technology, directly or indirectly, giving rise to legitimate public concern. Three Mile Island, Chernobyl, the Gulf War backwash, salmonella, genetically modified organisms, mad cow disease, a foot-and-mouth epidemic in Britain, and Asian bird flu are incendiary fuel to the worries of the fearful, while para-scientific cults seem, to the scientifically literate, to gain adherents with undeserved ease. There is a danger that the limits of science at its frontiers, which all must acknowledge, may be used to raise unwarranted opposition to science and technology at their proven core. Such fears have been voiced by the British House of Lords, and within the EU itself, such that a major task of any technology policy is to dispel the wilder and more hysterical claims that may be made against science and technology.

Obviously there is a need for objective information about scientific and technological developments. Government officials need to ascertain which public fears are most widely and/or keenly held, how to address them, and what guidance might be offered to politicians and public. A national survey in Britain was commissioned jointly by the Wellcome Trust and the Office of Science and Technology (DTI 2000*a*: 48–97). On the whole there was public support for science and technology, but evident misgivings, as the following data reveal: they represent proportions of respondents who agreed or agreed strongly with propositions on a questionnaire, and exclude those who disagreed, disagreed strongly, or who felt neither way.

- 42 per cent felt science changes too fast;
- 36 per cent felt science was out of control;
- 41 per cent felt science was out of control of the government;
- 64 per cent felt the media sensationalized science;
- 70 per cent felt that scientists would do what they wanted behind closed doors, notwithstanding attempts to regulate them;
- 79 per cent felt that science and technology were important for competitiveness;
- 84 per cent expressed an interest in new medicines.

Interestingly, the leading interest in medicine and health mirrored the results of a French survey conducted about a year earlier, as did a strong interest in pollution and the environment.

Later surveys have confirmed general support for science and technology, though some of them have tendentious overtones. The Office of Science and Technology commissioned MORI to poll the UK public in the 2004 survey *Science in Society*. It reported that 86 per cent of adults thought that science made a good contribution to our lives, 82 per cent expected it to make life easier—both figures higher than in previous polls. The proportion trusting scientists to tell the truth had risen over five years from 63 to 70 per cent, but 72 per cent felt that the media sensationalizes science. Consultation of the public about decisions on the development of science was judged important by no less than 51 per cent, though many doubted that government paid much attention. Areas of particular concern, tending to incur more opposition over time, were GM food, cloning, and radioactive waste.

National concerns may differ in degree, but there is an evident similarity overall in what concerns people. If a central tenet of EU science and technology policy is to do in common what it would be more expensive to do separately, then seeking and disseminating this sort of information is a natural function for it. The Joint Research Centre, which states as its main aim 'to help to create a safer, cleaner, healthier and more competitive Europe' (JRC website 2001), does relevant work.

In recent years the roles of expert advice, risk governance and public participation have attracted understandable attention. Scientific expertise and opinion, which can vary widely, must be supplemented by public participation, as the EU recognizes increasingly: practically all EU documents concerning environment, health and safety, and risk issues include calls for public participation not only in their detection and definition but also in their management (De Marchi 2003). The precautionary principle applies the development of procedures to frame and regulate risk rather than the traditional response of offering compensation after the event, and the EU has adopted this as its guiding principle in environmental matters. It is also influential in health and consumer matters, where the system of scientific consulting was reformed in 1997, culminating in the establishment of the European Food Safety Authority in 2002. Among its charges under Articles 23 and 40 of Regulation 178 are to ensure 'that the public and interested parties receive rapid, reliable objective and comprehensible information'. However, as Gonçalves (2004) notes, public involvement in science and scientific advice has advanced much less than it has with industry. Yet scientific advice, while increasingly consulted, is increasingly questioned; and there is a further area of concern in that science tends by its nature to be in the public domain, while technology, as it is closer to market, may be more concealed because of commercial considerations and hatched before the public can consider issues arising from its application. It may be advisable therefore for the EU to widen the scope for its regulatory intervention in the innovation process as a whole, though it would have to combine commercial sensitivity with lightness of touch if commercial disadvantage in world markets is to be avoided. Above all transparency would seem to be the prime virtue in avoiding the worst pitfalls of untrammelled science and technology, and in assuaging the worst fears of technological Luddism.

6.7 Summary and conclusions

EU science and technology policy has now been in operation for over two decades. It sought to create new interinstitutional links and forms of collaboration, and to establish capabilities in specific industrial sectors. It was bound to be problematic, because the spontaneous development of the market would be unlikely to replicate those links. Yet it can be, and is, argued that the EU level of aggregation is the only possible locus at which adequate technological capacity can be established in certain industries or sectors, and that collaborative benefits and spillovers will occur which the market would ignore, to the cost of society at large.

The principle of subsidiarity still leaves the vast bulk of national RTD outside the authority of the EU, since the dominant Framework Programme is only about 5 per cent of the total RTD expenditure of the Member States, and even with ESA, EUREKA, Cost, etc., less than 15 per cent of the spend is supranational. But it is surely significant that there has been no pressure to abandon the Framework system. It is seen to have brought wide and approved benefits, albeit with an embarrassing abundance of bureaucratic irritations and shortcomings. To that extent it is a perceived if qualified success. EU policy might even seem to be burgeoning, with FP7 granted an enlarged budget over an extended term, and prospects for a European Research Area and a European Research Council which could boost basic research suggesting that the national focus may be redirected given time.

On the other hand, it must be said that most of the policies just mentioned arise from fear, inadequacy, and misgiving. There is widespread dissatisfaction that the EU still trails behind the USA and Japan in technological league tables and innovative scoreboards, and that the gap has widened. In percentage of GDP spent on RTD, in patenting, and in the top ten technological corporations, Europe shows up poorly by comparison. Its research efforts are also more fragmented. Hence the search for improvement, which drove the establishment of a European policy twenty years ago, continues even more critically as Framework 7 approaches. The EU resembles a distance runner, panting in third place along successive laps of the track and failing to make an impression on the two leaders, while behind them all is an intensely fit and impressive newcomer, increasingly confident and gaining ground with every stride.

Certainly, policy and its execution require a continuous scrutiny, both because the interaction of profit-seeking companies will always generate new forms of organization and collaboration, moving more freely than governments and transcending the boundaries of nations and of blocs, and because the growth of EU-directed science and technology activity looks certain to increase in cost, scale, and complexity. Whether it can spearhead a real boost in aggregate European RTD effort, however, and what reactions will follow the likely failure to achieve the Lisbon goals in 2010, remain open if disturbing questions.

▨ DISCUSSION QUESTIONS

1. What sorts of activities in science and technology do you think national governments should support, and why? Illustrate, using specific examples.

2. Why has EU RTD effort lagged behind that of the United States and Japan? Would you expect the EU to enlarge its share of world RTD in the foreseeable future? What factors will impinge upon it?

3. Discuss the pros and cons of *juste retour* if it were to apply to RTD disbursements in the EU.

▨ FURTHER READING

Arrow (1962) is the classic reference justifying the role of government in supporting science and technology. Freeman and Soete (1997) provide a valuable introduction to innovation in the real world, while Dosi *et al*. (1988) put innovation in a theoretical framework. Porter (1990) is an intriguing, if long, analysis of the basis of national competitiveness, and Nelson (1993) examines the importance of national characteristics and policies which underlie performance. Stoneman (1995) collects a number of authoritative contributors to debates in the area on technology, while Dodgson and Rothwell (1994) do the same with a more industrial focus. Problems of evaluation, including Framework, are explored by Georghiou *et al*. (2006). For recent developments and statistics in many official areas, there are very useful websites.

OECD Science, Technology and Industry site: http://www.oecd.org/department/
0,2688,en_2649_33705_1_1_1_1_1,00.html
UK Office of Science and Innovation: http://www.dti.gov.uk/science
Community R&D Information Service: http://cordis.europa.eu/
Eurostat (CEC statistics source): http://eurostat.ec europa.eu/
UK National Statistics: http://www.statistics.gov.uk/.

▒ REFERENCES

Arnold, E., Clark, J., and Muscio, A. (2005), 'What the Evaluation Record Tells us about the European Union Framework Programme Performance', *Science and Public Policy*, 32: 385–97.

Archibugi, D. and Coco, A. (2005), 'Is Europe Becoming the Most Dynamic Knowledge Economy in the World?', *Journal of Common Market Studies*, 43: 433–59.

—— and Iammarino, S. (1999), 'The Policy Implications of the Globalisation of Innovation', in D. Archibugi, J. Howells and J. Michie (eds.), *Innovation Policy in a Global Economy* (Cambridge: Cambridge University Press), 242–71.

Arrow, K. J. (1962), 'Economic Welfare and the Allocation of Resources to Invention', in National Bureau of Economic Research (ed.), *The Rate and Direction of Inventive Activity* (Princeton: Princeton University Press), 609–25.

Banchoff, T. (2002), 'Institutions, Inertia and European Union Research Policy', *Journal of Common Market Studies*, 40: 1–21.

Barry, A. (1990), 'Community and Diversity in European Technology', paper presented at the Science Museum, London.

Beise, M. and Stahl, H. (1999), 'Public Research and Industrial Innovations in Germany', *Research Policy*, 28: 397–422.

Boden, R., Cox, D., Nedeva, M., and Barker, K. (2004). *Scrutinising Science: The Changing UK Government of Science* (Houndmills: Palgrave Macmillan).

Borrás, S. (2004), 'System of Innovation Theory and the European Union', *Science and Public Policy,* 31: 425–33.

Cabinet Office (1992), *United Kingdom Paper on the Fourth Framework Programme* (London: Office of Science and Technology).

CEC (Commission of the European Communities) (1977), 'Common Policy for Science and Technology', *Bulletin of the European Communities*, supplement (Mar.).

—— (1993), *Working Document on the Fourth Framework Programme*, 22 Apr. (Brussels: CEC).

—— (1994), *The European Report on Science and Technology Indicators 1994* (Brussels: CEC).

—— (2000a), *Five-year Assessment of the European Union Research and Technological Development Programmes, 1995–99* (Brussels: CEC).

—— (2000b), *Making a Reality of the European Research Area: Guidelines for EU Research Activities (2002–2006)*, COM (2000) 612 (Brussels: CEC); see also http://www.europa.eu.int/comm/research/area/com2000-612-en.pdf.

—— (2004), *Science and Technology, the Key to Europe's Future: Guidelines for Future European Union Policy to Support Research*, COM (2004) 353 (Brussels: CEC).

Chesnais, F. (1991), 'Techinical Cooperation Agreements between Independent Firms: Novel Issues for Economic Analysis and the Formulation of National Technological Policies', *STI Review*, 4: 51–120.

—— (1993), 'The French National System of Innovation', in R. R. Nelson (ed.), *National Innovation Systems: A Comparative Analysis* (Oxford: Oxford University Press), 192–229.

Coase, R. H. (1937), 'The Nature of the Firm', *Economica*, 4: 386–405.

—— (2003), *Competing in the Global Economy: The Innovation Challenge* (London: DTI).

CREST (1992), *Evaluation of the Second Framework Programme* (Brussels: CREST).

De Marchi, B. (2003), 'Public Participation and Risk Governance', *Science and Public Policy*, 30: 171–6.

Dodgson, M. and Rothwell, R. (eds.) (1994), *The Handbook of Industrial Innovation* (Aldershot: Edward Elgar).

Dosi, G., Freeman, C., Nelson, R., Silverberg, G., and Soete, L. (eds.) (1988), *Technical Change and Economic Theory* (London: Pinter).

DTI (Department of Trade and Industry) (1993), *Innovation: A Guide to European Community RTD Programmes* (London: DTI).

—— (1996), Office of Science and Technology, *Forward Look of Government-Financed Science, Engineering and Technology*, Cm 3257 (London: HMSO).

—— (2000a), *Excellence and Opportunity: A Science and Innovation Policy for the 21st Century*, Cm 4814 (London: HMSO).

—— (2000b), *Making a Reality of the European Research Area: Guidelines for EU Research Activities (2002–2006)—UK response* (London: DTI).

—— (2004), *Science and Innovation: Working towards a Ten-year Investment Framework* (London: HMSO).

Edquist, C. (2004), 'Reflections on the Systems of Innovation Approach', *Science and Public Policy*, 31: 485–9.

Eurostat (2001), *Statistics in Focus—Science and Technology: Community Innovation Survey* (Eurostat website).

Ford, G. and Lake, G. (1991), 'Evolution of European Science and Technology Policy', *Science and Public Policy*, 18: 38–50.

Freeman, C. (1987), *Technology Policy and Economic Performance: Lessons from Japan* (London: Pinter).

—— (1988), 'Japan: A New National System of Innovation?', in G. Dosi, C. Freeman, R. Nelson, G. Silverberg, and L. Soete (eds.), *Technical Change and Economic Theory* (London: Pinter), 330–48.

—— and Soete, L. (1997), *The Economics of Industrial Innovation*, 3rd edn (London: Pinter).

Georghiou, L. and Roessner, D. (2000), 'Evaluating Technology Programs: Tools and Methods', *Research Policy*, 29: 657–78.

—— Cameron, H., Stein, J. A., Nedeva, M., Janes, M., Yates, J., Pifer, M., Boden, M., and Senker, J. (1993), Cabinet Office, *The Impact of European Community Policies for Research and Technological Development upon Science and Technology in the United Kingdom* (London: HMSO).

—— Rigby, J., and Cameron, H. (2006), *Evaluating the Impact of Technology and Research* (Cheltenham: Edward Elgar).

Gonçalves, M. E. (2004), 'Risk Society and the Governance of Innovation in Europe: Opening the Black Box?', *Science and Public Policy*, 31: 457–64.

Guy, K., Amanatidou, E., and Psarra, F. (2005), 'FP5 Impact Assessment: A Survey Conducted as Part of the Five-year Assessment of European Union Research Activities (1999–2003)', *Science and Public Policy*, 32: 349–66.

Hall, B. and Van Reenen, J. (2000), 'How Effective are Fiscal Incentives for RTD? A Review of the Evidence', *Research Policy*, 29: 449–69.

Hill, A. (1993), 'RTD in a Tussle over EC Funding', *Financial Times*, 26 Oct., 16.

HM Treasury (2003), *Lambert Review of Business–University Collaboration* (London: HMSO).

HMSO (1993) *The Impact of European Community Policies for Research and Development upon Science and Technology in the United Kingdom* (London: HMSO).

Holdsworth, D. and Lake, G. (1988), 'Integrating Europe: The New RTD Calculus', *Science and Public Policy*, 15: 411–25.

Kealey, T. (1996), *The Economic Laws of Scientific Research* (London: Macmillan).

Keck, O. (1993), 'The National System for Technical Innovation in Germany', in R. R. Nelson (ed.), *National Innovation Systems: A Comparative Analysis* (Oxford: Oxford University Press), 115–57.

Knight, F. H. (1921), *Risk, Uncertainty and Profit* (New York: Houghton Mifflin).

Lipsey, R. G. and Carlaw, K. (1998), *Taking Schumpeter Seriously on Structuralist Assessment of Technology Policy*, Working Paper (Ottawa: Industry Canada).

Lundvall, B.-Å. (1988), 'Innovation as an Interactive Process: From User–Producer Interaction to the National System of Innovation', in G. Dosi, C. Freeman, R. Nelson, G. Silverberg, and L. Soete (eds.), *Technical Change and Economic Theory* (London: Pinter), 349–69.

—— (ed.) (1993), *National Systems of Innovation: Towards a Theory of Innovation and Interactive Learning* (London: Pinter).

Luukkonen, T. (2000), 'Additionality of EU Framework Programmes', *Research Policy*, 29: 711–24.

Majoie, B. and Remy, B. (1999), *Recherche et Innovation: la France dans la Competition Mondiale* (Paris: Documentation Française).

Mansfield, E., Rapoport, J., Romeo, A., Wagner, S., and Beardsley, G. (1976), 'Social and Private Rates of Return from Industrial Innovations', *Quarterly Journal of Economics*, 91: 221–40.

Mueller, D. C. (1989), *Public Choice II* (Cambridge: Cambridge University Press).

Mytelka, L. K. (ed.) (1991), *Strategic Partnerships and the World Economy* (London: Pinter).

Nelson, R. R. (1988), 'Institutions Supporting Technical Change in the US', in G. Dosi, C. Freeman, R. Nelson, G. Silverberg, and L. Soete (eds.), *Technical Change and Economic Theory* (London: Pinter).

—— (1990), 'Capitalism as an Engine of Progress', *Research Policy*, 19: 193–214.

—— (ed.) (1993), *National Innovation Systems: A Comparative Analysis* (Oxford: Oxford University Press).

Niskanen, W. (1975), 'Bureaucrats and Politicians', *Journal of Law and Economics*, 18: 617–43.

OECD (Organization for Economic Cooperation and Development) (1999a), *Economic Surveys: France* (Paris: OECD).

—— (1999b), *Public Understanding of Science and Technology* (Paris: OECD).

—— (2002), *The Measurement of Scientific and Technological Activities* (Frascati Manual) (Paris: OECD).

—— (2003), *The Sources of Economic Growth in OECD Countries* (Paris: OECD).

—— (2005), *Main Science and Technology Indicators* (Paris: OECD).

Ormala, E. and Vonortas, N. S. (2005), 'Evaluating the European Union's Research Framework Programmes: 1999–2003', *Science and Public Policy*, 33: 399–406.

Outlook on Science Policy (1993), 15 (July–Aug.).

Pavitt, K. and Patel, P. (1988), 'The International Distribution and Determinants of Technological Activities', *Oxford Review of Economic Policy*, 4: 35–55.

Peterson, J. (1991), 'Technology Policy in Europe: Explaining the Framework Programme and Eureka in Theory and Practice', *Journal of Common Market Studies*, 29: 269–90.

Polt, W. and Streicher, G. (2005), 'Trying to Capture Additionality in Framework Programme 5: Main Findings', *Science and Public Policy*, 32: 367–73.

Porter, M. E. (1990), *The Competitive Advantage of Nations* (London: Macmillan).

Pownall, I. (1995), 'The Capture of Internalisation as a Policy Tool: The Case of ESPRIT', *Science and Public Policy*, 22: 39–49.

Reeve, N. (2005), 'On the Evaluation of European Union Research: The 2004 Five-year Assessment', *Science and Public Policy*, 33: 335–8.

Sachwald, F. (1993), *L'Europe et la globalisation: Acquisitions et accords dans l'industrie* (Paris: Masson Éditeur); English edn, *European Integration and Competitiveness: Alliances and Acquisitions in Industry* (Aldershot: Edward Elgar, 1994).

Sandholtz, W. (1992), 'ESPRIT and the Politics of International Collective Action', *Journal of Common Market Studies*, 30: 1–24.

Saunders, C. T., Matthews, M., and Patel, P. (1991), 'Structural Change and Patterns of Production and Trade', in C. Freeman, M. Sharp, and W. Walker (eds.), *Technology and the Future of Europe* (London: Pinter).

Schumpeter, J. A. (1943), *Capitalism, Socialism and Democracy* (London: Allen & Unwin).

Servan Schreiber, J. J. (1967), *Le Défi Américain* (Paris: de Noel); English edn, *The American Challenge* (Harmondsworth: Penguin, 1968).

Sharp, M. (1993), 'The Community and the New Technologies', in J. Lodge (ed.), *The EC and the Challenge of the Future*, 2nd edn (London: Pinter), 200–23.

—— and Holmes, P. (eds.) (1989), *Strategies for New Technologies: Case Studies from Britain and France* (London: Philip Allan).

—— and Pavitt, K. (1993), 'Technology Policy in the 1990s: Old Trends and New Realities', *Journal of Common Market Studies*, 31: 129–51.

—— and Shearman, C. (1987), *European Technological Collaboration* (London: Routledge and Kegan Paul).

Siune, K., Schmidt, E. K., and Aagaard, K. (2005), 'Implementation of European Research Policy', *Science and Public Policy*, 32: 375–84.

Stoneman, P. (ed.) (1995), *Handbook of the Economics of Innovation and Technological Change* (Oxford: Blackwell).

Stubbs, P. and Saviotti, P. (1994), 'Science and Technology Policy', in M. Artis and N. Lee (eds.) *The Economics of the European Union*, first edn (Oxford: Oxford University Press).

Tunzelmann, N. von and Nassehi, S. (2004), 'Technology Policy, European Union Enlargement, and Economic, Social and Political Stability', *Science and Public Policy*, 31: 475–83.

Walker, W. (1993), 'National Innovation Systems: Britain', in R. R. Nelson (ed.), *National Innovation Systems: A Comparative Analysis* (Oxford: Oxford University Press), 158–91.

Williams, R. and Mills, S. (eds.) (1986), *Public Acceptance of New Technologies: An International Review* (London: Croom Helm).

Williamson, O. E. (1975), *Markets and Hierarchies* (New York: Free Press).

—— (1985), *The Economic Institutions of Capitalism* (New York: Free Press).

7 Regional Policy

Gabriele Tondl

Introduction

One of the primary objectives of the European Union (EU) is to assure equal income standards and economic development among Member States and regions. Under this objective the Union introduced in several stages its regional and cohesion policy, implemented through the EU Structural Funds. In 1975, following the first enlargement, the main instrument of EU regional policy was established with the creation of the European Regional Development Fund (ERDF) which was meant to address the increased problem of regional imbalances. In 1986, a common regional policy was created in the context of the Single Market Programme and enshrined in the Community treaties with the Single European Act (SEA). It was designed to meet the rising economic imbalances after the southern enlargement and to assist the new members to offset the burdens of restructuring associated with the single market. The reform of the Structural Funds—the ERDF together with the European Social Fund (ESF) and the European Agricultural Guarantee and Guidance Fund (EAGGF)—in 1988, established the main policy guidelines of EU regional policy which are still valid today.

In the 1990s, EU regional policy continued to gain in importance as it was given the task of assisting the less prosperous Member States, the so-called cohesion countries, to meet the Maastricht convergence criteria while keeping economic development on track. The Cohesion Fund was created, intended to finance large-scale infrastructure, and the total financial resources of EU regional policy were doubled. After two generations of regional policy support programmes, Agenda 2000 laid the policy foundations for EU regional policy for the period 2000–6, with the objective of streamlining policy instruments and improving efficiency. Moreover, there was agreement between the Member States to limit the financial scope of EU regional policy and to keep its financial contribution to the beneficiaries constant.

The 2004 enlargement has brought a substantial reduction of regional policy aid for the old beneficiaries that are at the threshold of overcoming the development gap. The debate for a further policy reform necessary to accommodate the old and new members of the EU after 2006 is currently taking place.

In this chapter we discuss the regional policy of the EU with respect to its objectives, its instruments, its impact on development, and its future prospects. Section 7.1 presents the arguments justifying regional policies in the EU. Section 7.2 presents the policy priorities, institutional procedures, and financial contribution of EU regional policy. This demonstrates that EU regional policies have made a significant contribution to economic development particularly in the cohesion countries, but that their impact is also important in some richer Member States. Section 7.3 focuses on EU regional policy in Objective 1 areas and assesses its contribution to development. Section 7.4 looks at Objective 2 policies. In section 7.5, we consider the current debate on how to reform regional policies for the next programme period after 2006. The appendix (by Artis and Nixson) considers EU Cohesion Policy after 2007.

7.1 The arguments for EU regional policy

Regional income differences in the EU

The essential argument for EU regional policy is the existence of large income disparities in the EU and the insight that balanced economic development is a prerequisite for functioning economic integration, in both economic and political terms.

Before the 2004 enlargement, the EU had only two Member States, Portugal and Greece, with a per capita income level below the threshold of 75 per cent of EU-15 average income, a measure customarily used to indicate the less developed areas. Some ten years previously, Ireland and Spain belonged to that group of countries as well, while at present a substantial part of these two countries is already well above the threshold.

Nevertheless, important income disparities remain within the former EU-15. While they have become less pronounced at the Member State level, where most Member States have an income position of around 80–120 per cent of the EU-25 average per capita GDP (see Table 7.1), regional income disparities are still a reason for great concern. The most prosperous regions in the former EU-15, the centres of economic activity lying on the well-known 'banana' that stretches from northern Italy, southern Germany to Brussels, Île de France, and southern England, have a per capita income from 120 to more than 140 per cent of the EU average.[1] Other dispersed centres, such as Vienna, Hamburg, Uusimaa, and Stockholm, have similarly high income levels. In contrast, there are large areas, particularly in the periphery, that have an income level of around only 80 per cent of the average. This group consists of the eastern German Länder, the north-west and centre of Spain, the Algarve in Portugal, the Athens area, as well as the Aegean Islands and Crete in Greece. A small group of regions remains with a per capita income of about 70–75 per cent of EU average income. Here we find today the southern Italian regions, the south of Spain, and large parts of Portugal and Greece. In contrast, the capital areas of Madrid and Lisbon have reached average income levels. Table 7.1 shows that income disparities exist not only in the poorer Member States but also in the richer ones.

There have been some important changes over time within the group of less developed Community areas. The income gap of all cohesion countries has diminished since 1988. Among those, Ireland is an extreme example which—probably owing to exceptional circumstances and a focused development strategy—saw an increase of its GDP per capita relative to that of the EU from 64 per cent in 1988 to 115 per cent in 2000. In 2003, Ireland had a per capita GDP of 130 per cent of the EU-25 average (Table 7.1). In Spain,

Portugal, and Greece relative income steadily improved from 1988 to 2000. In Spain it rose from 72 per cent of EU average to 82 per cent, in Portugal from 59 to 68 per cent, and in Greece from 58 to 68 per cent (European Commission 2002, 2003). In the former East Germany, as a result of a rapid transformation process and substantial national support for development, per capita income rose from 37 per cent in 1991 to 69 per cent in 2000. Nevertheless, there are also less satisfactory developments. Particularly at the regional level, we see that catching up is not uniform. In southern Italy, relative income rose very modestly in the period under question. The catching-up process of eastern Germany has stagnated since 1997, and in Greece, the improvement in the income position is only a recent development since the mid-1990s, after income had stagnated for almost a decade (see below, 7.3).

The EU's cohesion problem can be best summarized by developments in per capita incomes, although the problem of unequal welfare manifests itself in a number of other indicators, for example, labour market indicators, the quality of public health and other social services, and education (European Commission 2001). It is beyond the scope of this chapter, however, to give a detailed description of socio-economic developments in the EU regions, but it is the case that the issue of cohesion is a continuing problem for the EU. With the accession of ten new members, from Eastern Europe (Hungary, the Czech Republic, Slovakia, Slovenia, Poland, Estonia, Latvia, and Lithuania), Malta, and Cyprus, in 2004, income disparities have become much more substantial in the EU than before. Many of the new members have a GDP per capita of less than 60 per cent of the EU-25 average (Table 7.1).

A large part of the economic integration literature claims that European integration helped to reduce income disparities, for which some empirical evidence exists (for example, Badinger 2001; Crespo-Cuaresma *et al.* 2002). However, there are also a number of counter-arguments from integration and growth theory which propose that income convergence is not at all a clear-cut outcome of European integration. Drawing on the diverse arguments in economic theory, EU policy-makers have found good reason to advocate a regional development policy for the EU. The resources that were spent by the Structural Funds in force under this policy were significant enough to produce some positive effects on income growth in the less developed Community areas (Roeger, 1996; European Commission, 2000a; ESRI, 1997; Beutel, 2002), although recently the effects of the Structural Funds on regional development have been viewed more critically.

The motivation of EU regional policy from the perspective of economic theory and political concerns

This section discusses the main arguments for EU regional policy. First it is necessary to note that the primary reason behind this policy is political. The European Community has set itself the objective of equal standards of living within the European Union (Article 2 EU Treaty) and the existence of income disparities clearly conflicts with this goal. Therefore, assuring equality is one of the primary arguments underlying its regional policy (Article 158 EU Treaty). The EU wishes to portray itself as an institution that is characterized by solidarity between its members and has thus established a regional

Table 7.1 Income disparities in EU-25: relative GDP per capita 2003 (EU-25 = 100, PPS)

Member State	GDP per capita	Regions with highest/ lowest income in country[a]	GDP per capita
EU-15			
Luxembourg	233.9		
Denmark	121.0		
Ireland	134.1	Southern and Eastern	149.2
		Border, Midland & Western	92.5
Austria	120.9	Vienna	170.9
		Südösterreich	102.6
Netherlands	124.8	West-Nederland	137.6
		Oost Nederland	104.6
Belgium	118.1	Brussels	237.6
		Vlaams Gewest	116.9
		Region Wallonne	85.0
Sweden	115.9	Stockholm	157.9
		Norra Mellansverige	99.5
Germany	108.4	Hamburg	184.0
		Hessen	130.8
		Bavaria	128.2
		Baden-Würtemberg	122.8
		Saxony	79.6
		Brandenburg	75.8
		Sachsen-Anhalt	79.6
Finland	112.9	Uusimaa	154.3
		Itä-Suomi	84.1
Italy	107.9	Lombardy	137.4
		Emilia Romagna	133.7
		Nord Est	128.5
		Sud	73.5
		Sicily	73.1
		Campania	72.1
France	111.4	Île de France	173.3
		Centre-Est	107.4
		Est	98.5
		Bassin Parisien	97.2
		Méditerranée	98.4
United Kingdom	116.2	London	175.0
		South-East	127.0
		Eastern	112.1
		Wales	91.6
		Northern Ireland	92.8
		North-East	92.2
Spain	97.4	Madrid	128.8
		Noreste	115.2
		Noroeste	80.4
		Centro	80.2
		Sur	75.4
Portugal	72.9	Lisbon	104.3
		Algarve	78.7
		Centro	61.3

Table 7.1 (*continued*)

Member State	GDP per capita	Regions with highest/ lowest income in country[a]	GDP per capita
Greece	81.1	Attica	86.7
		Nisia Aigaiou, Crete	83.6
		Kentriki Ellada	78.7
New Member States			
Cyprus	79.9		
Slovenia	76.0		
Czech Republic	67.8	Prague	138.2
		Jihozápad	62.0
		Stredni Morava	54.4
Malta	72.7		
Hungary	59.3	Közép-Magyarország	94.9
		Nyugat-Dunántúl	64.5
		Eszak-Alföld	39.0
Slovakia	52.0	Bratislavia	115.9
		Vychodné Slovensko	38.8
Estonia	48.2		
Poland	47.0	Mazowieckie	72.8
		Slaskie	51.2
		Podlaskie	35.7
		Podkarpackie	33.2
Lithuania	45.3		
Latvia	40.9		

[a] This column shows the extent of internal income disparities in the Member States. Hence the NUTS 1 level aggregation is used instead of NUTS 3 if a larger part of the country has similar income levels. *Source*: European Commission (2006).

development policy that follows the principle of redistribution between rich and poor Member States.

Second, there are very important arguments drawn from economic integration theory and growth theory which can be used to justify EU regional policy.

Integration theory offers two major approaches from which conclusions may be drawn about the impact of the establishment of a common market on income convergence. In classical trade theory and customs union theory (Viner 1950), market integration leads to a better allocation of resources and specialization which would benefit all partners, although not necessarily equally. Specialization also requires restructuring which can impose a heavy burden.

New trade theory, in contrast, assuming monopolistic competition and innovation based on product differentiation, suggests that rich countries are likely to gain more benefits from integration. Thus, from the perspective of new trade theory, poor EU members may not be able to improve their income position vis-à-vis rich members. The new economic geography literature (Krugman 1991) also suggests that the rich core in the EU would gain more from integration than would the periphery as a result of agglomeration advantages. This pattern will only be reversed with very low trade barriers and a cost advantage in the periphery that more than offsets the agglomeration advantage of the core.

Finally, growth theory also provides no explicit argument for income convergence. From the perspective of neo-classical growth theory (Solow 1956; Barro and Sala-i-Martin 1995), income convergence is an automatic process if technology is free and capital mobile owing to higher rents in poor regions. New growth theory (Romer 1990; Aghion and Howitt 1992), in contrast, argues that rich regions can enjoy a continuous growth bonus through the generation of technological advance which is based on their better human capital endowment. In summary, therefore, neither trade theory nor growth theory offers an explicit convergence argument. It is rather the case that market integration may in the short term lead to particular adjustment difficulties in poor regions and that long-term gains can only be achieved through improvements in location factors (education, infrastructure). This consideration led the European Union to create and shape EU regional policy.

From a political perspective, the creation of EU regional policy was a delicate power struggle between the rich EU members and the poorer Mediterranean countries, Greece, Spain, and Portugal. The latter requested a redistributive policy that would compensate them for potential losses from the Single Market Programme. The EU had to step in to assist them to alleviate adjustment problems and improve their competitiveness through public investment (Bache 1998). This need, to achieve a balance of power between rich and poor EU members, was repeatedly felt in successive stages of the development of EU regional policy.

The creation of EU regional policy and EU integration can also be viewed from another field of economic theory, namely political economy. From this perspective, integration is considered to be a public good, but the different players, rich and poor members, have different policy goals if their levels of economic development vary. In this context, development support provided by EU regional policy is meant to contribute to the formation of more homogeneous policy interests which are a prerequisite to develop the common good of 'economic integration'. As an illustration, one may consider the case of the common EU trade policy, where the negotiation positions of Member States may differ depending on their economic structures.

The case for EU regional policy received yet another series of economic arguments in the light of the creation of the European Monetary Union (EMU) whereby different levels of economic development mean that these economies would not form an optimum currency area (Mundell 1961), which could severely endanger its functioning. Income differences between members of a monetary union are associated with different product specialization which exposes them to asymmetric shocks. This leads to differences in growth rates and desynchronized business cycles (Bayoumi and Eichengreen 1993; Artis and Zhang 2001). Consequently, the common monetary policy becomes problematic for the members affected by an asymmetric shock. Therefore, the Delors Report, which designed the Monetary Union project, also foresaw the strengthening of EU regional policy to accelerate economic development and thus reduce the potential for asymmetric shocks. Consequently, the Delors II package, enforcing regional policy support, was agreed together with the Maastricht Treaty of 1993 that established EMU. In political terms, the Delors II package can also be viewed as a compensation to the poorer Member

States for the extraordinary efforts they had to make to meet the Maastricht fiscal deficit criteria in order to enter the EMU.

Another argument for EU regional policy arises from the potential of migration under unequal development and the constraints of national social policies in the recipient countries. Richer Member States have feared scenarios of massive immigration from poorer EU members possible under the right of free movement of workers between EU Member States. To prevent this scenario, EU policy-makers supported the idea of a common regional policy that should help to initiate the development of backward areas and thus to eliminate the pressures of emigration. This argument was first raised with the southern enlargement and has become more relevant in view of potential major migration from new Eastern European members.

Finally, in terms of the associated demand effects, EU policy-makers like to emphasize that EU regional policy benefits not only the recipient countries of the Structural Funds, but also the net payers of this policy through imports associated with the development programmes. A considerable share of investment generated in the context of these programmes consists of capital goods produced in the rich Member States. In smaller Member States like Portugal and Greece, up to 40 per cent of the investment funded by the Structural Funds goes to imports from richer Member States (Hall 2003).

In summary, we can state that the European Union has created its regional policy out of the concern that economic theory provides an ambiguous perspective for income convergence and that unequal development endangers the project of European integration. Regional policy set itself the goal of assisting development in the poorer EU members and thus strengthening cohesion. This goal has been reached to some extent, but there are also increasingly critical voices which claim that EU regional policy has not fulfilled its goals and should be nothing more than a central redistribution mechanism which provides income support to less wealthy regions.

7.2 Policy priorities, financial contributions, and institutional procedures of EU regional policy in the programme period 2000–6

Policy priorities

Since the creation of EU regional policy in the Single European Act and its implementation by the reform of the Structural Funds, regional policy has focused on the least developed areas of the Union and has followed a set of policy priorities.

These policy priorities are the well-known 'Objectives' of EU regional policy, each of which addresses a specific priority.

Under *Objective 1*, EU regional policy aims to promote the development and structural adjustment of regions whose development is 'lagging behind'. The beneficiaries of this policy priority are the poor, less developed parts of the European Union with a GDP per capita below the threshold of 75 per cent of average EU income. The Community areas classified as Objective 1 areas in the programme period 2000–6 included southern Italy, the Midlands and Border regions in Ireland, Portugal (except for its capital area), and the major part of Spain, as well as Greece and eastern Germany. As a consequence of catching up, a number of regions were phased out from Objective 1 status in this period, for example, the mid-east and mid-west regions in Ireland, the Highlands of Scotland, Corsica, and Lisbon. Thus Objective 1 areas are generally large territories and traditionally have coincided with Member States. (Note that for the poor Member States, Portugal, Spain, Greece, and Ireland, having largely consisted of Objective 1 areas, the term 'cohesion countries' is also used since they are entitled to transfers from the Cohesion Fund; see below.) There are, however, also a few, smaller regions in richer Member States with Objective 1 status such as west Wales, Cornwall, Merseyside, and South Yorkshire in the UK, the Burgenland in Austria, Hainaut in Belgium, and Flevoland in the Netherlands. Finally, two large territories of the EU, the thinly populated areas of Sweden and Finland (with fewer than eight inhabitants per square kilometre), are assisted under Objective 1, although there is no development problem in the strict sense (given their unfavourable natural location, there is no prospect of a broad economic development). Objective 1 areas are generally defined at the NUTS 2 level, the medium aggregation level of the EU's regional classification.[2]

For Objective 1 areas, almost 70 per cent of the Structural Funds, i.e. 135 billion Euros, were reserved for development assistance in the period 2000–6. Twenty-two per cent of the EU-15's population lives in Objective 1 areas. EU regional policy supports economic development in the Objective 1 areas by funding infrastructure investment, encouraging business investment, and promoting training of students and workers.

In addition to the support through Objective 1 policies, the weakest Member States receive support from the so-called *Cohesion Fund* to finance large-scale infrastructure projects in the transport and environment sectors. The Cohesion Fund was conceived in 1993 to provide additional funds for public investment in order to counter-balance the cuts in budgetary spending required by the Maastricht convergence criteria to enter Monetary Union. It was meant to permit the beneficiaries to continue important projects for economic development while consolidating their budgets. The cohesion countries were defined as countries with a GDP per capita of less than 90 per cent of EU average and originally in 1993 included four countries: Spain, Portugal, Greece, and Ireland (phasing out). In the programme period 2000–6, the cohesion countries received 18 billion Euros from the cohesion fund.

Under its policy priority *Objective 2*, EU regional policy aims to support economic and social conversion in small industrial, rural, urban, or fisheries-dependent areas in the richer Member States, which face structural difficulties. Although an important share of the EU-15 population, namely 18 per cent, lived in Objective 2 areas, support for Objective 2 areas was much less significant than in Objective 1 regions. Only 11.5 per cent of the Structural Funds were reserved for Objective 2 policies in the programme period 2000–6. There are many Objective 2 areas in the United Kingdom, France, Spain, Italy, Finland, and Austria.

Under the third policy priority, *Objective 3*, EU regional policy contributes to active labour market policies outside Objective 1 areas. It co-finances training schemes to upgrade and modernize professional skills in order to fight structural unemployment, youth, and long-term unemployment. Objective 3 is a thematic policy, and it is not confined to certain territories, with 12.3 per cent of EU regional policy funding allocated to Objective 3 measures in 2000–6.

In addition to priority objectives, EU regional policy has established a number of small-scale policy areas, the *Community initiatives*, the *fisheries measures*, and the *innovative actions*.

Financial allocation of Structural Funds to EU-15 Member States

The allocation of the financial resources of the Structural Funds and the Cohesion Fund to policy priorities and the EU-15 Member States, as determined by Agenda 2000, is shown in Table 7.2. We see that the largest share of EU regional support, 50 per cent, has gone to the cohesion countries. Spain received by far the highest share of EU regional policy support with 26.5 per cent of the total, followed by Germany and Italy, which both have large Objective 1 areas, with each receiving 14 per cent of the total. Portugal and Greece received about 10 per cent each of the regional policy budget, with Ireland receiving about 2 per cent, as Objective 1 support was being phased out. Except for the UK and France, which have a number of Objective 1 and Objective 2 territories and thus also a higher share of EU support of about 7 per cent, wealthy Member States received no significant share of the EU regional policy budget. In terms of GDP, the contribution from the Structural Funds amounted to 2.4 per cent in Greece, 2 per cent in Portugal, 1.2 per cent in Spain, but only 0.6 per cent in Ireland. As a proportion of GDP these contributions have decreased to a certain extent with respect to the previous programming period, as regional policy support for old Member States was curtailed with Agenda 2000 to free resources for pre-accession aid to prospective members from Eastern Europe. In the richer Member States, the contribution of EU regional policy accounted for 0.23 per cent in Italy and 0.35 per cent in Germany. In practically all others, the contribution remained below 0.2 per cent of GDP.

Pre-accession aid and the transfer of EU regional policy to new Eastern European members in the period 2000–6

In order to assist the Eastern European candidate countries in catching up, the European Union began to provide financial assistance for restructuring and development. The central instrument, the *Phare* programme, was established in 1989. Originally intended to support new investment in business and infrastructure and social measures, its focus shifted to the improvement of institutions, administration, and public bodies in order to apply Community law correctly, not least with a view to the implementation of the future EU regional policy programmes after accession. The second programme, *SAPARD*, started in 2000 and was designed to prepare the accession countries to join the Common Agricultural Policy. It supported the modernization of agricultural structures, the introduction of EU foodstuff quality standards, the development of rural areas, and the protection of the environment. The third programme, *ISPA*, also initiated in 2000, corresponded to the Cohesion Fund and aimed to co-finance large-scale infrastructure projects in the transport and environment sectors. In total, Agenda 2000 envisaged a pre-accession aid

Table 7.2 Regional transfers to EU-15 Member States, by priority objectives, 2000–6

	Structural Funds and Cohesion Fund 2000–6 total (million Euros)	Average annual contribution 2000–6 (in % of GDP 1999)	Average annual contribution 1994–9 (in % of GDP 1994)	Objective 1*	Objective 2*	Objective 3	Fisheries instrument	Community initiatives	Cohesion Fund	Share of Member State in receipts
				(million Euros)						
Rich EU members										
Belgium	2,037	0.12	0.15	625	433	737	34	209	–	0.9
Denmark	825	0.09	0.14	0	183	365	197	80	–	0.4
Germany	29,764	0.23	0.24	19,958	3,510	4,581	107	1,608	–	14.0
France	15,666	0.18	0.23	3,805	6,050	4,540	225	1,046	–	7.4
Italy	29,656	0.35	0.36	22,122	522	3,744	96	1,172	–	14.0
Luxemburg	91	0.07	0.15	0	40	38	0	13	–	0.1
N/lands	3,286	0.12	0.15	123	795	1,686	31	651	–	1.5
Austria	1,831	0.14	0.15	261	680	528	4	358	–	0.9
Finland	2,090	0.27	0.30	913	489	403	31	254	–	1.0
Sweden	2,186	0.16	0.13	722	406	720	60	278	–	1.0
United Kingdom	16,596	0.18	0.21	6,251	4,695	4,568	121	961	–	7.8
Cohesion countries										
Ireland	3,974	0.64	2.53	3,088	–	–	–	166	720	1.9
Spain	56,205	1.18	1.62	38,046	2,651	2,140	200	2,008	11,160	26.5
Portugal	22,760	2.04	3.87	19,029	–	–	–	671	3,060	10.7
Greece	24,883	2.38	3.34	20,961	–	–	–	862	3,060	11.7
Total	211,850			54,780	17,803	21,910	906	6,630	18,000	100.0

Source: Data from Eurostat, European Commission DG 16 and author's calculations.   * includes transitory assistance.

to the eastern candidate countries of almost 22 billion Euros for the period 2000–6, slightly more than the Cohesion Fund budget for the EU cohesion countries. In addition, some 40 billion Euros were reserved for structural expenditures for the accession countries for the post-accession period 2004–6.

The accession negotiations, completed with the ten candidate countries in December 2002 at the Copenhagen European Council, fixed the framework for extending EU regional policies to the new Member States from their accession in 2004 until 2006. The new members were eligible for Objective 1 policies with the exception of a few areas, namely Prague, Bratislava, and Cyprus. They received 24 billion Euros (at 2004 prices) for their first EU regional policy programmes from the Structural Funds and the Cohesion Fund starting after accession, which meant a payment of 117 Euros per capita. Since a part of the reserved resources in the EU budget for new Member States was reallocated to CAP measures in these countries, this was less than originally foreseen by Agenda 2000. EU regional policies were gradually extended to the new members with a lower support level than that of present Objective 1 areas, accounting for 217 Euros per person (European Commission 2003).

Table 7.3 shows that Poland was expected to receive the lion's share of EU support for this programme period. In terms of GDP, however, the contribution would be highest in the Baltic republics with 2–3 per cent of their respective GDPs. Hungary, Poland, and Slovakia were to receive support of about 1.4–1.8 per cent of GDP, while that of the wealthier Czech Republic, Slovenia, Malta, and Cyprus would remain below 1 per cent. After becoming fully applicable for EU regional policies after 2006, support can be expected to rise to higher levels, despite being restricted by the maximum 4 per cent of GDP support level stipulated in Agenda 2000.

Table 7.3 Structural and Cohesion Fund commitments to new Member States, 2004–6 (in million Euros, 1999 prices)

	Objective 1	Objective 2	Objective 3	Community initiatives	Total Structural Funds	Average annual contribution SF in per cent of GDP	Cohesion Fund
Hungary	1,765.4			87.7	1,853.1	1.40	879–1,108
Czech Republic	1,286.4	63.3	52.2	89.3	1,492.2	0.96	741–932
Slovakia	920.9	33.0	39.9	56.5	1,050.3	1.85	433–586
Poland	7,320.7			314.6	7,635.3	1.74	3,465–4,002
Slovenia	210.1			26.7	236.8	0.41	130–207
Estonia	328.6			13.0	341.6	2.30	219–333
Latvia	554.2			20.6	574.8	3.10	384–537
Lithuania	792.1			30.4	822.5	2.74	467–620
Malta	55.9			3.2	59.1	0.57	12–27
Cyprus		24.9	19.5	5.4	49.8	0.19	32–63
Total	13,234.3	121.2	111.6	647.4	14,114.5	1.52	7,595.5

Source: Author's calculations based on European Commission (2003) and Eurostat.

7.3 Development problems and policy focus in Objective 1 regions

This section looks more closely at the Objective 1 policy of the EU-15. Table 7.4 contains the list of Objective 1 regions in EU-15 which had that status during the 1990s and traces their income position and unemployment.

At the beginning of the 1990s, four different groups of Objective 1 regions could be distinguished.

First, there was a group of wealthier Objective 1 areas with a GDP per capita above 70 per cent of the EU average, comprising Ireland, the Italian Mezzogiorno, Spanish Objective 1 regions, those of the UK, as well as Corsica and the two small Objective 1 regions Hainaut and Flevoland. Despite a relatively well-developed income situation, those Objective 1 areas faced serious unemployment problems in the early 1990s with unemployment rates of 12 per cent in the UK, about 15 per cent in Ireland and Italy, and more than 18 per cent in Spain.

Second, there were the Objective 1 areas in the two poorer cohesion countries, Greece and Portugal, which had showed a relative per capita income of 61 and 65 per cent of the EU average respectively. In general, their unemployment situation was much less of a concern than for the first group. Unemployment reached 3.6 per cent in Portugal and 6.9 per cent in Greece in 1991. A few regions of these countries were already better developed, for example, the Athens and Lisbon areas and the tourist sites of Crete, the southern Aegean Islands, and the Algarve.

Third, the new German Länder had received Objective 1 status after German unification and constituted the least developed parts of the EU in Europe in 1991, with a GDP per capita of barely 40 per cent of EU average. Nevertheless, their unemployment levels were still not much above the EU average, amounting to 10 per cent.

Fourth, the French overseas departments (DOM) and the Portuguese islands of Madeira and the Azores were the least developed Community areas before German unification, with a GDP per capita of 45 per cent of EU average. These French departments faced a serious unemployment situation with unemployment rates of about 30 per cent.

The structural economic weaknesses of the Objective 1 areas were well known when the European Union launched the major development initiative for these regions after the reform of the Structural Funds in 1988 (EC Commission 1991; Tondl 1998, 2001).

Most regions, except for the new German Länder, the UK, and the Belgian and Dutch Objective 1 regions, had a high agricultural employment share of above 10 per cent, with many Greek regions at 20 per cent. An important concern of EU regional policy programmes was to improve the efficiency of agricultural production and of product marketing. At the same time it was clear that the gradual decline of the agricultural sector, which these regions had already witnessed since the 1980s, was a major reason for increasing unemployment.

Consequently, EU regional policy wished to support the modernization of industry and services in order to create alternative income sources to agriculture. A large share of the Structural Funds was therefore used to finance business aid schemes. The creation of new firms and the modernization of enterprises was therefore promoted by investment aid of more than 50 per cent of the investment project.

Objective 1 areas suffered from weak infrastructure in the areas of transport, energy, and other public services. In view of the peripheral location of the Objective 1 areas, this was considered highly problematic for economic development. Therefore the financing of infrastructure was also a major policy focus in Objective 1 areas. The Structural Funds and the Cohesion Fund could co-finance 75–90 per cent of public investment projects in infrastructure. EU regional policy acknowledged that infrastructure would improve the long-term attractiveness of Objective 1 regions as business locations and thus would lead to better economic prospects.

Finally, the population in Objective 1 regions had much lower education attainments than in richer EU regions. In 1992, according to Eurostat data, the average secondary educational attainment rate in the population was 14 per cent in the southern cohesion countries, Spain, Portugal, and Greece, and 22 per cent in Ireland and the Italian Mezzogiorno. In contrast, secondary education attainment rates of the population had reached about 50 per cent in German and Belgian regions. This was considered a major handicap for the creation of modern economic production with specialized skill requirements and a main reason for high unemployment levels. Thus EU regional policy financed education and training measures in the Objective 1 regions with the aim of raising the skill levels of the working population and to secure long-term economic development via an improved human resource base.

The Community Support Framework (CSF) programmes of the Member States with Objective 1 regions addressed these development problems to varying extents. Table 7.5 shows the allocation of the Structural Funds to different policy measures in the programme periods 1994–9 and 2000–6. We see that particularly the Greek, Spanish, and Italian Objective 1 programmes put a strong emphasis on infrastructure development in the first and the second programme periods. Greece aimed to develop the main motorway axes 'Pathe' and 'Egnatia' and the Athens underground system with the help of the Structural Funds. Spain also emphasized large-scale transport projects like the high-speed train link between Madrid and Barcelona. In a detailed investigation of annual Structural Funds commitments by policy priority, Rodríguez-Pose and Fratesi (2003) found an even stronger emphasis of EU regional policy on infrastructure in the countries concerned. Table 7.5 shows that, in contrast, the programmes of Ireland, the UK, eastern Germany, and Portugal placed a much stronger emphasis on the development of the business sector. Major inward investment was promoted with investment aid schemes co-financed from the Structural Funds. The Italian Objective 1 programme equally stressed business investment along with infrastructure. Ireland, which was losing its Objective 1 status, was forced to accept a major cut in its Structural Funds allocation, in particular for business support, in 2000–6.

The third policy measure, the development of human resources, also received different emphasis between Member States' programmes. The Irish programmes stressed human capital development, while the Italian programme put very little weight on training measures in the first programme period, which was problematic in view of the unemployment situation, despite higher Italian educational levels. Although there are still differences between Member States, it is clear that the new support programmes place a stronger emphasis on human resources, an obvious response to mounting unemployment rates in Objective 1 areas (see Table 7.4) and in line with the European employment strategy.

Table 7.4 Development of relative per capita income, growth, and unemployment in Objective 1 regions, 1990s

	GDP per capita (in PPS, EU-15 = 100)			Real growth of GDP	Unemployment rate	
	1991	1993	2000	1991–2000	1991	2000
East Germany (excl. Berlin)	**38**	**55**	**69**	**5.6**	**9.9**	**15.3**
Berlin		73	96	4.2	9.7	13.0
Brandenburg	41	59	69	5.8	9.1	14.7
Mecklenburg-Vorpomm.	39	53	69	5.5	12.0	15.3
Sachsen	38	54	70	5.6	8.6	15.0
Sachsen-Anhalt	38	55	68	4.9	9.9	18.0
Thüringen	34	53	70	6.5	9.9	13.4
Greece	**61**	**64**	**68**	**1.7**	**6.9**	**11.1**
Anatoliki Makedonia, Thraki	56	57	55	1.4	4.8	8.6
Kentriki Makedonia	60	64	68	2.1	5.5	10.7
Dytiki Makedonia	63	60	67	0.2	7.2	14.7
Thessalia	59	58	61	1.2	6.2	12.4
Ipeiros	42	43	47	1.7	8.8	10.6
Ionia Nisia	56	59	59	2.3	3.5	5.1
Dytiki Ellada	52	55	51	1.7	7.8	10.2
Sterea Ellada	71	66	76	0.9	6.3	13.6
Peloponnisos	58	57	58	1.1	5.0	9.3
Attiki	65	72	77	2.3	8.9	12.2
Voreio Aigaio	45	48	66	1.9	7.9	7.4
Notio Aigaio	69	73	80	2.6	3.2	10.5
Kriti	65	68	66	2.1	3.6	6.7
Spain Objective 1	**71**	**69**	**70**	**2.1**	**18.8**	**17.1**
Galicia	62	62	65	2.0	12.3	15.0
Asturias	75	74	71	1.2	16.1	17.9
Cantabria	79	76	80	1.7	15.4	14.2
Castilla y León	71	74	76	1.9	14.5	14.1
Castilla-la Mancha	68	67	67	2.1	13.6	12.7
Extremadura	54	56	53	2.5	24.2	24.8
Comunidad Valenciana	82	76	79	2.2	15.2	11.9
Andalucia	62	58	61	2.0	24.7	25.3
Murcia	76	70	69	1.5	16.5	12.0
Ceuta y Melilla	70	69	68	3.3	29.7	25.5
Canarias	77	76	78	3.1	24.4	14.5
France DOM	–	**48**	**57**	–	**31.0**	**27.2**
Guadeloupe	–	41	58	–	31.1	26.1
Martinique	–	54	67	–	32.1	27.7

Table 7.4 (*continued*)

	GDP per capita (in PPS, EU-15 = 100)			Real growth of GDP	Unemployment rate	
	1991	1993	2000	1991–2000	1991	2000
French Guyana	–	51	54	–	24.0	22.0
Réunion	–	47	50	–	36.9	33.1
Ireland	**78**	**83**	**115**	**6.7**	**14.6**	**4.4**
Border, Midland and western	–	–	84	6.0	–	5.8
Southern and eastern	–	–	126	7.4	–	3.9
Italy Objective 1	**75**	**72**	**71**	**1.3**	**15.2**	**19.0**
Abruzzo	93	87	84	1.1	8.0	7.6
Molise	79	75	79	1.3	12.8	13.6
Campania	71	68	65	0.6	17.8	23.6
Puglia	75	70	67	1.1	13.2	17.6
Basilicata	65	66	73	1.9	17.0	17.4
Calabria	62	60	62	1.5	18.6	27.7
Sicilia	72	69	65	1.1	18.7	24.2
Sardegna	79	78	76	1.4	15.7	20.5
Portugal	**65**	**68**	**68**	**2.2**	**3.6**	**4.1**
Norte	56	60	56	3.0	2.7	4.1
Centro	51	55	54	3.1	2.3	1.8
Lisboa and Vale do Tejo	85	87	91	2.1	4.4	5.4
Alentejo	53	54	54	1.2	9.1	5.7
Algarve	68	71	66	2.4	3.9	3.3
Açores	46	49	52	0.9	3.7	3.4
Madeira	47	51	74	2.6	3.0	2.3
UK Objective 1	**73**	**76**	**72**	**1.7**	**12.1**	**7.7**
Merseyside	73	75	70	1.1	14.9	11.2
South Yorkshire	76	–	75	1.4	11.6	8.1
West Wales and the Valleys	–	70	71	0.9	–	7.4
Cornwall and Isles of Scilly	67	–	65	3.0	9.8	7.1
Highlands and Islands	–	81	75	1.3	8.3	4.1
Northern Ireland	78	80	78	2.8	16.0	8.2
Others						
Corsica	88	84	76	2.3	11.3	12.5
Flevoland (Netherlands)	77	75	80	5.1	5.7	4.0
Burgenland (Austria)	66	72	73	2.7	3.1	3.6
Hainaut (Belgium)	79	84	71	1.4	10.7	13.1
EU-15	**100**	**100**	**100**	**2.2**	**8.2**	**8.4**

Source: Author's calculations based on Eurostat Regio database; Cambridge Econometrics, regional database; European Commission (2000*b*, 2001, 2002, 2003).

Table 7.5 Sectoral allocation of regional assistance, 1994–9 and 2000–6 (per cent of total Structural Funds commitments)

	Greece	Spain	Portugal	France	Italy	Ireland	UK	Germany	Belgium
1994–9									
Infrastructure	45.8	37.1	29.5	29.2	34.7	17.2	20.6	8.0	14.2
Human resources	23.5	24.4	26.6	27.8	14.2	35.7	30.7	26.7	13.3
Production	30.1	30.0	39.3	35.7	50.3	40.0	41.7	62.9	61.2
2000–6									
Infrastructure	43.2	42.4	22.5	29.5	37.2	45.8	22.9	22.7	14.1
Human resources	19.0	25.4	24.3	31.8	20.1	28.1	31.0	28.3	26.5
Production	25.5	28.1	38.1	33.8	39.6	22.6	44.2	44.9	52.4

Note: Remaining share of programmes goes to 'other measures', e.g. technical assistance.
Source: Author's calculations based on data from European Commission (2001).

A number of evaluation studies were carried out for the CSF during 1994–9 that scrutinized the effectiveness of single policy measures. The evaluation study on transport infrastructure in Objective 1 areas (European Commission 2000*c*) showed that the intended investment was on average between 53 and 80 per cent, depending on the transport mode. The new infrastructure improved the link between regions and with other national centres and thus reduced journey times on average by 20–50 per cent. There was a significant employment impact of 2.3 million jobs associated with these public works. However, the report also urged a stronger commitment to complete these projects, especially in Italy and Greece. It pointed out that a sizeable portion of large-scale networks could not yield full benefits since second-order transport links in the regions were missing. A better management of transport flows would improve transport in Objective 1 areas significantly.

With respect to education measures, evaluation studies reported on the number of persons that received training measures financed by the Structural Funds. In Spanish Objective 1 areas 7 million persons (CEET 2003) received training financed by the Structural Funds; however, there is no evidence of the extent to which training measures improved the fit of qualification profiles with labour market requirements and facilitated the integration of the unemployed into the labour market. In contrast, the evaluation report of the eastern Germany Objective 1 programme reported that 950,000 persons benefited from training measures financed by the Structural Funds, mainly young people and older disadvantaged persons. It further found that training improved the employability of the trainees (Stumm and Robert 2003). In Ireland, 150,000 persons participated in training measures but their labour market effects were not reported (Fitzpatrick Associates 2003). The evaluation study for the Italian Objective 1 areas pointed out that although some 380,000 persons enrolled in professional education and universities, and the unemployed benefited from support by the Structural Funds, the measures did not have a clear employment strategy and cooperation with the enterprise sector did not exist (Ismeri Europa 2002). This evidence suggests that SF support made a significant contribution to the improvement of education and enrolment in training schemes. However, the employment effect of these measures may be reduced if training measures are not designed according to labour market requirements.

It also proved hard to raise the level of innovation activity in the Objective 1 regions. In the south of Italy, support for research and development (R&D) benefited universities but could not change innovation activity in the enterprise sector (Ismeri Europa 2002). The same was true of the Spanish Objective 1 programme which pursued an ambitious R&D programme targeted at small and medium-sized enterprises (SMEs) that had to be downsized (CEET 2003). In eastern Germany, where public and private research facilities had largely broken down after German unification, the CSF contributed to the rebuilding of the R&D system and notably helped to give SMEs access to innovation activities through technology transfer centres (Stumm and Robert 2003).

With respect to the programme priority investment support, it must be noted that the effect on regional development depends on the extent to which this aid improves economic structures. Industrial diversification, the creation of advanced manufacturing, and a broad basis of SMEs is needed for regional development. The Objective 1 programmes reached this goal to a varying extent. The Spanish programme made a significant contribution to the set-up of SMEs owing to the creation of new credit instruments (CEET 2003). In eastern Germany, investment support benefited a considerable number of large-scale projects with important job effects and also helped to extend the SME sector. The structural effects of these investments are less clear (Stumm and Robert 2003). In Italy, a large number of industrial investments were subsidized by the CSF, without a selective strategy (Ismeri Europa 2002). In summary, the evaluation documents provide little evidence on the structural effects linked to investment support.

In macroeconomic terms, economic theory suggests that policy measures carried out within the EU regional policy programmes should result in immediate demand effects, associated with private and public investment, and supply side effects related to long-term structural improvements as a result of educational measures and improved infrastructure. The resulting growth effects associated with the EU programmes were calculated in the course of *ex ante* evaluations. Two simulations were carried out with macroeconomic models, the HERMIN model of the Irish ESRI institute and the Commission's QUEST model. In addition, the studies of Beutel (1995) provide the results of an input–output analysis (see Table 7.6). Although resulting in quite different assessments (the HERMIN model forecast as much as 9 per cent of additional GDP in Ireland in the period 1994–9 in contrast to the more modest projections of the QUEST model of 3 per cent), those studies made a valuable contribution to the discussion of the likely effects of Structural Fund spending and the potential growth bonus. According to the QUEST model simulations, the heavy receivers of Structural Funds in the period 1994–9, namely Ireland, Portugal, and Greece, could have realized an additional GDP growth of 2.2–3 per cent over the whole programme period. Beneficiaries with a smaller contribution from the Structural Funds, Spain and Italy, would have realized a somewhat smaller additional GDP growth according to the three studies.

In reality, the actual growth of GDP and per capita incomes in the 1990s lagged behind the potential gains suggested by the evaluation studies. Looking at Table 7.4, we see that from the sixty-one regions having Objective 1 status in 1994, only thirty-five improved

Table 7.6 Projected additional GDP growth associated with EU regional development programmes in *ex ante* evaluations (in per cent relative to baseline scenario without regional programme)

	CSF 1994–9			CSF 2000–6	
	HERMIN	QUEST	Beutel	HERMIN	QUEST
Ireland	9.3	3.0	4.2	1.8	0.5
Portugal	9.2	2.3	4.2	6.0	2.0
Spain	4.3	1.2	4.2	2.2	0.9
Greece		2.2	5.4	6.1	2.4
Mezzogiorno			2.4		
East Germany				4.0	

Sources: Barry *et al.* (1996); European Commission (1996, 2000); Beutel (1995).

their relative income position over the decade. In contrast, twenty-one regions lost in terms of relative income and five were unchanged. A noticeable improvement in income levels was achieved by Ireland and eastern Germany, with average GDP growth rates of 6.7 and 5.6 per cent per annum. In Ireland, relative income rose from 78 per cent in 1991 to 115 per cent in 2000, in eastern Germany from 40 to 70 per cent. Portugal and Greece also improved their income levels to some extent, reaching 68 per cent in 2000, as did the French overseas departments. In contrast, the income levels in Spanish, Italian, and UK Objective 1 areas slightly decreased, with GDP growth rates lying below the EU average. In addition to this not very satisfactory development of income levels in Objective 1 regions under the regional policy programmes, the unemployment situation improved to a noteworthy extent only in Ireland and to some degree in the UK Objective 1 regions. Spanish Objective 1 regions hardly reduced their high unemployment as the rate decreased only from 18.8 to 17.1 per cent. In southern Italy and eastern Germany there was a serious increase of unemployment from 10 to 15 per cent and 15 to 19 per cent respectively. In most other regions unemployment worsened. Only Portuguese regions continued to keep an unemployment level below the EU average. Finally, it should be noted that the unequal performance of Objective 1 regions resulted in an increase of regional income disparities within the respective Member States, while at the same time a general catching up at the country level took place (European Commission 2003).

How should we judge this mixed evidence of the contribution of EU regional policies to regional growth and income convergence? First, as is evident from the above discussion of the policy mix in regional development programmes, policy strategies may not always have been adequately focused on the specific regional problems. Most probably, the neglect of human resources in southern Italian regional programmes contributed to stagnating development. The infrastructure focus of Greek programmes may have neglected the development of other factors important for economic development. A similar view, of unbalanced regional development strategies being responsible for the weak growth effects of EU regional policies, is proposed by Rodriguez-Pose and Fratesi (2003), who argue that in many cases regional programmes failed to improve long-term growth prospects and led rather to short-term demand effects, for example, in the case of large-scale transport infrastructure investment, which would often benefit the core rather than the poorer regions.

Another reason for the mismatch between the projected growth impact and actual growth may be the persistent weaknesses in the financial implementation of EU regional policy programmes. In all programme periods, many regions failed to make full use of the resources committed for regional programmes. In the programme period 1994–9, Objective 1 programmes showed large differences in financial implementation. While Spain, Portugal, Ireland, and eastern Germany had used almost 90 per cent of Structural Fund commitments at the end of the programme, Italian, French, and UK Objective 1 regions had used only about 67 per cent of the available funds. (European Commission 2001; Tondl 2001). Infrastructure projects were implemented at the 90 per cent level in Portugal and Ireland, but only at 66 per cent in southern Italy and 33 per cent in Greece. It should be mentioned that Objective 2 regions faced even more difficulties in implementing EU programmes. Weaknesses in implementation were linked not only to institutional deficits and mismanagement but also to difficulties in creating appropriate investment projects eligible for EU support.

These insights suggest that EU regional policies may not be able to fulfil expectations to reduce regional income disparities as stipulated in the EU treaties. It may be concluded that EU regional policy can have some impact on regional economic development, but it cannot claim to have reduced the cohesion problem in the European Union. It should be clear, therefore, that EU regional policy largely constitutes a redistributive instrument which serves to maintain a socio-political balance between the Member States.

7.4 **Objective 2 policies**

Objective 2 policies—which cover regions with industrial conversion problems, regional problems in rural areas, areas dependent on fisheries, and urban problem areas—primarily address regional problems found in the wealthier EU Member States. Those structural regional problems often have persisted for a considerable time and have been the subject of intensive national regional policy schemes dating back to the 1960s. Support by the EU Structural Funds has become a benefit which the concerned countries do not wish to lose, although the level of assistance from the Structural Funds is much lower than in Objective 1 areas.

Before 2000, regional policies for industrial areas and rural areas were separated under former Objectives 2 and 3. Since industrial conversion and rural areas tend to be small regions and are close to each other, or even found within one NUTS 3 region, when designing the programme period 2000–6 in the Agenda 2000, EU policy-makers clustered these regions under more comprehensive regional development programmes designed for larger territories and including several assisted regions. In addition to the concern for more coherent and comprehensive regional policies, the combination under one objective served to streamline EU regional policy and to make programme management more efficient at the Member State and Community levels.

Among the wealthier EU members, the United Kingdom has a high share of Objective 2 regions. Twenty-four per cent of its population live in Objective 2 areas. Typically, medium-size industrial centres with structural problems are located close to agriculturally dominated areas and subsumed under one Objective 2 programme. Many industrial sites have had conversion problems for a long time. In the Midlands Objective 2 area there are problems with traditional industrial centres, such as in Birmingham, that need to modernize, as well as problems in former coal-field areas and in rural parts. In east Wales, regional problems inherited from mining and other traditional industries persist. The north-west faces problems with declining industries in Greater Manchester as well as sparsely populated rural areas. The north-east suffers from declining industries such as shipbuilding, engineering, and steel in Durham. Further, parts of eastern and western Scotland are Objective 2 regions with partly rural, partly industrial regional problems (engineering, petrochemicals, coal mining).

Given the different regional problems grouped under Objective 2, policy measures have also varied. In industrial conversion areas, the set-up of new businesses in different sectors, the support of SMEs, and the creation of technology transfer and business service centres, together with training measures, are major issues in regional policy. In rural areas, support for the creation of activities linked to the agricultural sector (processing and marketing of own products, agritourism) or of alternative activities outside the agricultural sector with a link to the regional natural heritage (spas and hiking/biking tourism, handicrafts) are important pillars of regional development strategies. In urban problem areas, local social initiatives and support for business start-ups may be important in regional programmes.

With respect to EU regional policy programmes in *industrial conversion areas*, the evaluation study of Bachtler and Taylor (1999) provides some interesting findings concerning policy strategies and effects. In general, in the first programme period 1989–93 most operational programmes for industrial conversion areas proposed a very similar overall policy strategy which emphasized investment support to the business sector (40 per cent of expenditures) including SMEs, technology support and business services, public expenditure for business-related infrastructure (36 per cent of expenditures), and training measures (21 per cent of expenditures). There were, however, some notable dissimilarities. The Belgian, Dutch, Danish, German, and Italian programmes mainly focused on the support of business investment where support to SMEs played a major role. In contrast, the programmes of France, the UK, and Spain prioritized infrastructure investment (physical regeneration of business sites and environment) and training measures. In the programme period 1994–9 the focus shifted significantly away from previous priorities to the support for business investment (45 per cent of expenditures) and human capital (36 per cent of expenditures). The creation of training and retraining facilities to qualify people for jobs in new businesses, such as tourism, innovation, and environment, received much higher attention then before. Support for business investment became based on the approach of indigenous development which favoured, for example, investment in the tourism and environment sectors. Promotion of R&D, support for innovation networks, and technology transfer were emphasized. Strategies became highly complex and sophisticated. Since the regions concerned played a major role in policy formulation, their understanding of structural problems developed significantly in the course of the first two programme periods and they advanced considerably in formulating region-specific development strategies.

7.5 The future of EU regional policy

With the completion of the programme period 2000–6, the European Union has had to extend fully its cohesion policy to the accession countries. Given the income gap of the accession countries, only 42 per cent of EU-25 GDP per capita in 2001, it is clear that the 2004 enlargement constitutes a major challenge for EU regional policy. The share of 'cohesion countries', which previously accounted for one-sixth of the EU population, now constitutes one-third of the population. Under this perspective, a central dilemma arises between the drastic increase of regional development problems and limited financial resources owing to the restriction of the EU budget to 1.27 per cent of EU GDP. Consequently, an intensive debate has started on the future of these policies.

The cohesion countries will no longer be the poorest EU members. In an enlarged Union of twenty-five members, using 2000 figures, Greece, Portugal, and Slovenia show a relative income position of about 75 per cent, Cyprus 83 per cent, and Spain 90 per cent. Most accession countries will show a much lower relative income position, the Czech Republic and Malta of about 60 per cent, Hungary 54 per cent, Poland and Estonia 42–44 per cent, Lithuania 39, and Latvia 34 per cent (European Commission 2003).

Since the cohesion problem of the European Union is defined in relative terms—the European Union is bound by the policy objective of EU regional policy to focus on its least prosperous parts—the cohesion problem will shift to the east. This means that a large number of current Objective 1 areas will lose that status. From the current forty-eight Objective 1 regions, only thirty would retain this status. An additional thirty-six Objective 1 regions will be located in the new Member States (European Commission 2003). From the present Member States with Objective 1 regions, on the basis of 2000 GDP per capita levels, southern and northern Member States would have to withdraw important parts from Objective 1 support. In the south, in Spain, Asturias, Castilla Leon, Valencia, and Murcia would lose Objective 1 status; also Basilicata and Sardinia in southern Italy, Corsica, and Sterea Ellada and Attiki in Greece. Practically the whole territory of eastern Germany would lose Objective 1 status, with the exception of Chemnitz and Dessau. Ireland would completely lose its Objective 1 status, having also to withdraw the Border, Midlands and Western regions. In the UK, Northern Ireland, the Highlands and Islands region, and Wales would lose their Objective 1 status.

The shift of EU regional policy towards the east is not only a consequence of the definition of the cohesion problem in relative terms and the threshold level of 75 per cent for the definition of Objective 1 areas, but is also necessitated by budgetary restrictions in the EU. Retaining the present support for Objective 1 areas in the EU-15 and providing additional assistance to the new Member States in relation to their development gap would dramatically go beyond the limits of the EU budget, as pointed out by, among others, Baldwin and Portes (1997) and Breuss and Schebeck (1999). There is, however, a firm consensus between the richer EU Member States that budgetary resources allocated to regional policies should not exceed the present level of 0.45 per cent of EU GDP.

Nevertheless present Objective 1 areas which are at risk of losing that status argue that their development problems will still be the same even when the reference EU average income value for defining the group of below 75 per cent areas will have changed after enlargement. Among those Objective 1 areas that will be phased out, some regions will be more capable of sustaining their development process than others. Some can already forgo support, for example, the Border, Midlands and Western regions in Ireland or Corsica and Sardinia, while in others the development process risks coming to a standstill if EU support disappears. Thus the problem of phasing out areas calls for a careful and fair solution (Hall 2003).

The reluctance of the net budget contributors to provide additional resources has also led to fixing a 4 per cent of recipient country GDP ceiling for EU regional transfers with the Agenda 2000. Fearing that a proportionate transfer of present regional policy support to significantly poorer Eastern European regions would demand additional financial resources, the argument of limited absorption capacity for development support was put forward, followed by the demand to limit support. It was argued that the Eastern European countries would have serious institutional gaps and thus would face problems in implementing regional policies involving large amounts of transfers. However, there are also those that question these arguments and consider the 4 per cent ceiling as an arbitrary limit. They make the point that the rich Member States in the EU have exhibited severe absorption problems owing to institutional problems and limited ability to design appropriate projects for funding. In addition, they argue that institutional limits in eastern countries are likely to be overcome within a short period. Even the worst performers among the Objective 1 regions, such as southern Italy and Greece, managed to create capable regional administrations under Community pressures and requirements. Furthermore, eastern countries would have already learned a great deal through the management of pre-accession aid and partnerships with institutions in EU Member States.

Given the high costs of EU regional policy and the demand from present and future beneficiary countries to maintain and increase that support, increasing scepticism with respect to the effectiveness of EU regional policy has arisen. Opponents of regional policy claim that it has largely failed to promote economic development and convergence (see above); some even propose that it would counteract market forces, such as agglomeration forces in the sense of new economic geography, and therefore would either harm natural economic forces or be ineffective (Midelfart-Knarvik and Overman 2002). In view of the mixed evidence on the economic effects of EU regional policies, there are also those who demand a reformulation of the goals of EU regional policy. Instead of economic development, they claim to make interregional income redistribution the key objective of EU regional policy.

Another point of debate is the question of how to proceed with Objective 2 policies. One view is that the European Union should completely withdraw from that policy field. In view of the small resources of Objective 2, transfers would be too thinly spread over problem areas to become effective. Furthermore, as we have seen above, Objective 2 policies have often been poorly implemented (Begg 2003). Evidently, Objective 2 areas have more problems in defining projects for regional development than do cohesion countries.

For example, in a small coal-mining area, policy-makers may be less inventive in defining a project that really contributes to conversion. In contrast, policy-makers in cohesion countries usually have a whole array of potential projects that would contribute to development, for example, infrastructure and the improvement of teaching facilities. Therefore, many Objective 2 areas have hardly shown any progress over the past decade in overcoming their regional problems. The growth effects lag behind those in Objective 1 areas. Consequently, EU members such as the UK and the Netherlands have proposed that Objective 2 policies should be re-nationalized and that EU budgets for this policy should be cancelled, leaving the funding as well as the execution to the Member State.

However, the proposal to renationalize Objective 2 policies with respect to policy fine-tuning but keeping EU financing meets considerable opposition. The idea of providing financial means to the rich Member States but allowing them to define and implement regional policies themselves is not always welcome. Although rich Member States have created well-developed procedures for regional policy design and management, not least because of Community regulations, there is no convincing evidence that rich members are more efficient in regional policy implementation so that less control by the EU would be required than for poor Member States.

Another point of debate with Objective 2 policies is the designation of specific areas to this policy. Under the current Objective 2, very different regional problems are addressed, such as rural areas, industrial restructuring, and urban problems. Even between rural areas, say in the south-west of France or in the Alpine areas of Austria, there are big differences in the types of problem and regional policy strategies. Thus the question arises as to whether EU regional policy should keep to the tradition of drawing a map of Objective 2 areas and pursue common policy guidelines. As an alternative it has been suggested that the territorial Objective 2 be replaced by a thematic objective as in the case of Objective 3 (Hall 2003). This means that the EU would identify policy areas of interest, such as innovation, and direct budgetary resources towards them, with Member States responsible for the actual policy measures. Policy coordination would be carried out by exchange of views and review of best practices, similar to the current conduct of the EU's employment strategy. Such practices would leave more freedom to the rich Member States for individual policies and would simplify EU procedures.

Finally, an important issue is the consistency of other EU policies with the goals pursued by cohesion policy. Several policies counteract the efforts of EU regional policy. A prominent example is the area of state aid. Despite the common framework for state aid, rich EU members have larger budgetary resources to finance state aid. This counteracts the efforts of EU regional policy (Tondl 2002). Corporate tax policies are another area of inconsistent policies. Since tax policies are not within Community competence, Member States could design policies that conflict with cohesion policies, for example, a favourable corporate tax rate in a rich Member State could counteract EU-funded investment support in poorer Member States. Other sets of policies, such as transport policies, R&D policies, and labour market policies, may potentially come into conflict with cohesion policies (Molle 2003).

There is no doubt that EU regional policy will continue to play a prominent role in EU policies in the future. The dramatic cohesion problem in an enlarged Union will clearly maintain the demand for this policy. However, any conversion of regional policy into a sizeable redistributive policy within a federal fiscal system at Union level, as could be envisaged in the context of Monetary Union, is not politically feasible. Moreover, it should become clear that EU regional policy is no guarantee for development. In the past, it has not fully met its goal of reducing regional income disparities. There is also no doubt that the practice of EU regional policy will have to change further in simplifying and improving policy management, for both existing and new Member States. Improvements at the institutional level and correct and efficient management of EU regional policies will be vital for securing the support of the rich EU members for a strong future cohesion policy.

▓ NOTES

A version of this paper has been published in Van der Hoek (2004).

1. Note, however, that a number of old declining industrial areas are also found close to prosperous centres on the 'banana', particularly in Rhein-Westphalia, Saarland, Liège, Namur, and Lorraine (Rodríguez-Pose 1998).

2. NUTS 2 corresponds to traditional administrative regional units, such as the Regierungsbezirke in Germany, the Régions in France, the Comunidades Autónomas in Spain, and the Bundesländer in Austria. The next, less aggregated regional level is NUTS 3.

▓ REFERENCES

Aghion, P. and Howitt, P. (1992), 'A Model of Growth through Creative Destruction', *Econometrica*, 60/2: 323–51.

Artis, M. and Z. W. (2001), 'Core and Periphery in EMU: A Cluster Analysis', *Economic Issues*, 6/2: 39–59.

Bache, I. (1998), *The Politics of European Union Regional Policy: Multi-level Governance or Flexible Gatekeeping?* (Sheffield, Sheffield Academic Press).

Bachtler, J. and Taylor, S. (1999), *Objective 2: Experiences, Lessons and Policy Implications* (Strathclyde: European Policies Research Center, University of Strathclyde).

Badinger, H. (2001), *Growth Effects of Economic Integration: The Case of the EU Member States (1950–2000)*, IEF Working Paper no. 40, Research Institute for European Research (Vienna: Wirtschaftsuniversität).

Baldwin, R. and Portes, R. (1997), 'The Costs and Benefits of Eastern Enlargement: The Impact on the EU and Central Europe', *Economic Policy*, 24: 127–76.

Barro, R. J. and Sala-i-Martin, X. (1995), *Economic growth* (New York: McGraw Hill).

Barry, F., Bradley, J., Hannan, A., McCartan, J., and Sosvilla-Rivero, S. (1996), *Single Market Review 1996: Aggregate and Regional Impacts: The Cases of Greece, Ireland, Portugal and Spain*, Report for the European Commission (Brussels).

Bayoumi, T. and Eichengreen, B. (1993), 'Shocking Aspects of European Monetary Integration', in F. Torres and F. Giavazzi (eds.), *Adjustment and Growth in European Monetary Union* (Cambridge: Cambridge University Press), 193–223.

Begg, I. (2003), 'Completing EMU: Rethinking Cohesion Policy', paper presented at the Experts Workshop on 'Cohesion in the European Union', College of Europe, Bruges, Apr.

Beugesdijk, M. and Eijffinger, S. (2003), *The Effectiveness of Structural Policy in the European Union: An Empirical Analysis for the EU 15 during the Period 1995–2001* (Tilburg: Tilburg University Centre).

Beutel, J. (1995), *The Economic Impact of the Community Support Frameworks for the Objective 1 Regions 1994–99* (Brussels).

—— (2002), *The Economic Impact of Objective 1 Interventions for the Period 2000–2006*, Report to the Directorate-General Regional Policies of the European Commission (Constance).

Boldrin, M. and Canova, F. (2001), 'Europe's Regions: Income Disparities and Regional Policies', Economic Policy, 32 (Apr.): 206–48.

Breuss, F. and Schebeck, F. (1999), 'Costs and Benefits of EU Eastern Enlargement', *Austrian Economic Quarterly*, 4/1: 43–53.

Cappelen, A., Castellacci, F., Fagerberg, J., and Verspagen, B. (2001), 'The Impact of Regional Support on Growth and Convergence in the European Union', paper presented at the European Meeting on Applied and Evolutionary Economics, Vienna, Sept.

CEET (Centro de Estudios Económicos Tomillo) (2003), *Member State Report Objective 1 Evaluation 1994–99—Spain*, Report to the European Commission (Brussels: European Commission).

Crespo-Cuaresma, J., Dimitz, M. A., and Ritzberger-Grünwald, D. (2002), *Growth, Convergence and EU Membership*, OeNB Working Paper no. 61 (Vienna: Austrian National Bank).

EC Commission (1991), *Fourth Period Report on the Socio-economic Situation of the Regions in the Community* (Brussels: EC).

Ederveen, S. and Gorter, J. (2002), *Does European Cohesion Policy Reduce Regional Disparities?*, CFB Discussion Paper no. 15 (The Hague: CFB Netherlands Bureau for Economic Policy Analysis).

ESRI (1997), 'The Single Market Review: Aggregate and Regional Impacts: The Cases of Greece, Spain, Ireland and Portugal', in European Commission (eds.), *The Single Market Review*, subseries VI, vol. 2 (Brussels: Office for Official Publications).

European Commission (1996), *European Economy*, Reports and Studies no. 4.

—— (2000a), 'The EU Economy: 2000 Review', *European Economy*, 71 (Brussels: Office for Official Publications).

—— (2000b), *Sixth Periodic Report on the Economic and Social Situation and Development of the Regions of the European Union* (Brussels: European Commission).

—— (2000c), *Thematic Evaluation of the Impact of the Structural Funds on Transport Infrastructure* (Brussels: European Commission).

—— (2000d), *Eleventh Annual Report on the Structural Funds 1999* (Brussels: European Commission).

—— (2001), *Second Report on Economic and Social Cohesion* (Brussels: European Commission).

—— (2002), *First Progress Report on Economic and Social Cohesion* (Brussels: European Commission).

—— (2003), *Second Progress Report on Economic and Social Cohesion* (Brussels: European Commission).

—— (2006), *Third Progress Report on Economic and Social Cohesion* (Brussels: European Commission).

Fitzpatrick Associates (2003), *Ex-post Evaluation of Objective 1 1994–99, National Report of Ireland*, Report to the European Commission (Brussels: European Commission).

Hall, R. (2003), 'The Future of EU Regional Policy', paper presented at the Conference of the Regional Studies Association, Pisa, Apr.

Hooghe, L. (1998), 'EU Cohesion Policy and Competing Models of European Capitalism', *Journal of Common Market Studies*, 36/4: 457–77.

Ismeri Europa (2002), *Ex-post Evaluation of the Objective 1 1994–99, National Report of Italy*, Report to the European Commission (Brussels: European Commission).

Krugman, P. (1991), 'Increasing Returns and Economic Geography', *Journal of Political Economy*, 99: 484–99.

Midelfart-Knarvik, H. and Overman, H. (2002), 'Delocation and European Integration: Is Structural Spending Justified', *Economic Policy*, 17/35 Oct: 323–59.

Molle, W. (2003), 'Are EU Policies Good or Bad for Convergence?', paper presented at the Experts Workshop on 'Cohesion in the European Union', College of Europe, Bruges, Apr.

Mundell, R. (1961), 'A Theory of Optimum Currency Areas', *American Economic Review*, 51/4, Sept.: 657–65.

Rodríguez-Pose, A. (1998), *The Dynamics of Regional Growth in Europe: Social and Political Factors* (Oxford: Clarendon Press).

—— and Fratesi, U. (2003), 'Between Development and Social Policies: The Impact of European Structural Funds in Objective 1 Regions', paper presented at the Experts Workshop on 'Cohesion in the European Union', College of Europe, Bruges, Apr.

Roeger, W. (1996), 'Macroeconomic Evaluation of the Effects of the Community Structural Funds with QUEST II', paper presented at the European Conference on Evaluation Methods for Structural Funds Intervention, Berlin, Dec.

Romer, P. (1990), 'Endogenous Technological Change', *Journal of Political Economy*, 98/5 (part II): S71–S102.

Solow, R. M. (1956), 'A Contribution to the Theory of Economic Growth', *Quarterly Journal of Economics*, 70: 65–94.

Stumm, T. and Robert, J. (2003), *Ex-post Evaluation of Objective 1 1994–99, National Report of Germany*, Report prepared for the European Commission (Brussels: European Commission).

Tondl, G. (1998), 'EU Regional Policy in the Southern Periphery: Lessons for the Future', *South European Society and Politics*, 3/1: 93–129.

—— (2001), 'EU Regional Policy', in M. Artis and N. Lee (eds.), *The Economics of the European Union* (Oxford: Oxford University Press), 180–211.

—— (2002), 'Will the New EU Regional Policy Meet the Challenges of Enlargement?', in J. Cuadrado-Roura and M. Parellada (eds.), *Regional Convergence in the European Union: Advances in Spatial Science* (Heidelberg: Springer), 293–31.

Ward, N. and McNicholas, K. (1998), 'Objective 5b of the Structural Funds and Rural Development in Britain', *Regional Studies*, 32/4: 369–74.

Van der Hoek M. P. (ed.) (2004), Handbook of Public Administration and Public Policy in the European Union (New York: Taylor & Francis).

Viner, J. (1950), *The Customs Union Issue* (London: Stevens and Sons).

EU cohesion policy, 2007–2013

The EU summarizes the values behind its regional policies as *solidarity* and *cohesion*. *Solidarity* is important because regional policy aims to benefit citizens and regions that are economically and socially deprived compared with EU averages. *Cohesion* is important because there are positive benefits for all when gaps in income and wealth between poorer and richer regions are narrowed. It also recognizes that Community priorities have to be better integrated into national and regional development programmes and that, in order to ensure greater 'ownership' of cohesion policy in practice, there needs to be improved policy dialogue between the Commission, Member States, and the regions, and a clearer division of responsibilities between them.

In 2005 the European Council renewed the Lisbon strategy with its focus on growth and jobs. Cohesion policy is thus focused on promoting sustainable growth, competitiveness, and employment creation, with the priorities of improving the attractiveness of regions and cities in the Member States, encouraging innovation, entrepreneurship, and growth in the knowledge economy, and creating more and better jobs. On the basis of these priorities, the Commission has proposed to make Europe and its regions more attractive places to invest and work, to improve knowledge and innovation, create jobs through greater labour market flexibility, worker adaptability, and investment in education and skills (human capital), and to adapt cohesion policy more closely to the particular needs and characteristics of individual regions (the European Territorial Cooperation Objective).

The new convergence objective for 2007–13 (regions where GDP per capita is less than 75 per cent of the 2000–2 EU average) applies to a hundred regions, including sixteen granted transitional 'phasing-out' status (regions where GDP per capita would have been below 75 per cent of the EU-15 average; in EU speak this is termed the 'statistical effect' of enlargement). The new Regional Competitiveness and Employment (RCE) objective applies to the rest of the EU, that is, 155 regions with 61 per cent of the EU-27 population (including Bulgaria and Romania). A further thirteen regions are classified as 'phasing-in' (these are regions currently eligible for Objective 1 not fulfilling the criteria for the Convergence objective even when the statistical effect of enlargement is taken into account).

The most recent data available for the EU-27 indicate that in 2002, the 10 per cent of the EU-27 population living in the most prosperous regions accounted for more than 19 per cent of total EU-27 GDP, while the 10 per cent of the population living in the least wealthy regions accounted for only 1.5 per cent of EU-27 GDP. With respect to employment, the EU still does not meet the Lisbon employment rate target of 70 per cent, and it is estimated that 24 million additional jobs will need to be created in the EU-27 if this target is to be reached. This represents 12 per cent of current employment levels overall, but 25 per cent of current employment levels in the ten new members plus Bulgaria and Romania. This is clearly a huge task.

Table 7.7 Cohesion policy 2007–13: indicative financial allocations (million Euros, 2004 prices)[a]

	Convergence Objective			Regional Competitiveness and Employment Objective		European Territorial Cooperation Objective	Total
	Cohesion Fund	Convergence	Statistical phasing out	Phasing in	Regional Competitiveness and Employment		
Belgium			579		1.268	173	2.019
Czech Republic	7.830	15.149			373	346	23.697
Denmark					453	92	545
Germany		10.553	3.770		8.370	756	23.450
Estonia	1.019	1.992				47	3.058
Greece	3.289	8.379	5.779	584		186	18.217
Spain	3.250	18.727	1.434	4.495	3.133	497	31.536
France		2.838			9.123	775	12.736
Ireland				420	261	134	815
Italy		18.867	388	879	4.761	752	25.647
Cyprus	193			363		24	581
Latvia	1.363	2.647				80	4.090
Lithuania	2.034	3.965				97	6.097
Luxembourg					45	13	58
Hungary	7.589	12.654	1.865			343	22.451
Malta	252	495				14	761
The Netherlands					1.477	220	1.696
Austria			159	0	914	228	1.301
Poland	19.562	39.486				650	59.698
Portugal	2.722	15.24	254	407	436	88	19.147
Slovenia	1.239	2.407				93	3.739
Slovakia	3.433	6.23			399	202	10.264
Finland				491	935	107	1.532
Sweden					1.446	236	1.682
United Kingdom		2.436	158	883	5.349	642	9.468
Bulgaria	2.015	3.873				159	6.047
Romania	5.769	11.143				404	17.137
Not allocated						392	392
Total	61.558	177.083	12.521	10.385	38.742	7.75	308.041

[a] Figures result from the application of the methodology agreed by the European Council in December 2005. They are inclusive of all additional provisions decided by the European Council. Technical assistance at the initiative of the Commission is included in the national allocations. Amounts under the 'European Territorial Cooperation' Objective include the contribution of the ERDF to the financing of the cross-border and sea-basin programmes on the external borders of the Union. Figures for Bulgaria and Romania are without prejudice to the date of accession of these countries.
Source: Europa.

As a result of decisions taken in 2005 and 2006 a cohesion policy budget for the period 2007–13 of 308 billion Euros (equivalent to 0.37 per cent of the EU27 GNI) has been proposed. It is proposed that the new Member States will receive 51.3 per cent of total cohesion policy resources, representing about 3.5 per cent of their GDP. Details are given in Table 7.7.

The Commission has developed new policy instruments to assist Member States and regions and is promoting enhanced cooperation between itself and the European Investment Bank Group and other international financial institutions (IFIs). Specific initiatives include:

- JASPERS (Joint Assistance in Supporting Projects in European Regions): a technical assistance partnership between the Commission, the European Investment Bank (EIB), and the European Bank for Reconstruction and Development (EBRD) designed to assist in the preparation of large projects to be supported by the Cohesion Fund and the European Regional Development Fund (ERDF);
- JEREMIE (Joint European Resources for Micro to Medium Enterprises): to improve access to finance for business development;
- JESSICA (Joint European Support for Sustainable Investment in City Areas): a framework for enhanced cooperation between the Commission, the EIB, and other IFIs to assist in financing projects for urban renewal.

Other priorities and activities include strengthening institutional capacity and the efficiency of public administrations and services; the adoption of new regulations on rural development (supporting innovation and restructuring to improve the competitiveness of European agriculture and forestry, improving the environment and the quality of life in the countryside, and encouraging diversification of economic activity); and financial assistance to areas dependent on fisheries.

Although there is evidence of significant convergence with respect to relative incomes in the EU-15, enlargement poses new and perhaps more intractable problems than those faced in the past. The EU's budgetary allocation to its cohesion policies is modest, and national policies in the areas of health and education, income support, and basic service provision remain pre-eminent. However, the fact that EU cohesion expenditure will be concentrated in those regions most in need of assistance may well produce a catalytic effect, mobilizing other sources of finance and encouraging enterprise.

8 Social Policy

David Purdy

Introduction

Ever since its foundation, the EU has had social policies of one sort or another, but no settled consensus has emerged either about what should be done or about who should do it. This is partly a result of disparities of economic development and differences of policy regime among the Member States, but conflicts of interest and ideological cleavages have also played a part, for governments and other social actors hold divergent views about the 'proper' scope of social policy and the 'proper' division of powers and responsibilities between national and supranational authorities. One of the aims of this chapter is to explain the origins and persistence of these disparities, differences, and disagreements.

To prepare the ground, section 8.1 introduces the study of social policy, elucidates the concept of welfare, and defines the welfare state, invoking the distinction, first formulated by Marshall (1950), between three aspects of citizenship—civil, political, and social. Throughout the argument it is stressed that economy and society form an integrated complex whose various elements need to be considered together if they are to be properly understood. Accordingly, attention is drawn to the ways in which the activities of the business, public, household, and voluntary sectors of the economy interact with and depend on each other, and it is suggested that the broad aim of social policy is to keep the four sectors in balance, though ideas about what this means and how it should be achieved vary greatly from one era or culture to another.

Section 8.2 provides an anatomy of the welfare state, distinguishing between in-kind services and income transfers, and shows how different kinds of tax-transfer system impinge on the distribution of income, work, and power, variously reinforcing or countervailing established social divisions. Nowadays, besides being interdisciplinary, social policy is a comparative study and scholars have devoted considerable—some would say excessive—effort to delineating certain ideal-types or models in an attempt to understand how and why welfare states differ, why these differences persist, and how they affect social stratification and economic performance. The second part of this section outlines and assesses the most widely used typology, proposed by Esping-Andersen (1990), who distinguishes between liberal, conservative (or Christian democratic), and social democratic welfare states, in keeping with the three main traditions that shaped European politics in the twentieth century.

Section 8.3 turns to the role of the EU as a social policy actor and seeks to explain why there is no pan-European welfare state and why successive attempts to redress the asymmetry between market integration and European social policy have foundered. Section 8.4 reviews the ways in which European governments and their social partners are responding to the domestic and global challenges facing welfare states, focusing on the emergence of social pacts as vehicles for welfare reform. Social pacts are primarily national affairs, but the EU can help Member States to pool experience, monitor results, and disseminate good practice, and the chapter concludes by comparing the merits of 'hard' legislation and 'soft' coordination as alternative methods of cross-border governance.

8.1 The study of social policy

Social policy and the concept of welfare

As an academic discipline, social policy stands at the intersection of history, law, politics, economics, sociology, and psychology. It is coeval, but not coextensive with the study of the welfare state. The first nationally organized schemes of poverty relief were introduced in Europe in the early nineteenth century, but the term 'welfare state' did not appear until the 1930s and was not widely used until the 1940s. By the same token, even if the welfare state as we know it were to disappear, students of social policy would still find plenty to occupy them. International comparisons reinforce this point. Even in the poorest countries, action can be taken to improve standards of nutrition, health, and literacy, to restrain population growth, and to help the destitute to support themselves, but welfare states in the strict sense are found only in the world's twenty or so richest countries.

What, then, is meant by 'welfare' and when does a state become a welfare state? These questions can be approached either from the standpoint of human individuals or from that of the political community as a whole. Which political community is relevant depends on the locus of state power, for this is typically the focus of efforts in civil society to change or preserve the prevailing configuration of welfare-determining conditions. In contemporary Europe, the nation-state remains responsible for providing or financing social services and social transfers, the main branches of the welfare state. The role of the EU as a social policy actor is largely confined to regulating the consequences of economic integration for employment and social protection in its Member States.

The word 'welfare' may be applied both to individuals and to groups, and is commonly extended to non-human species with more than minimal levels of sentience. To promote someone's welfare is to establish or maintain conditions that enable them to fare well. There are three ways this can be understood: in terms of subjective preferences, objective circumstances, or personal capabilities. Economists tend to take it for granted that welfare should be assessed from the standpoint of the welfare-experiencing subject. But people's preferences are shaped by a variety of social and psychological forces, from advertising and peer-group pressure to unconscious drives and ingrained habits, and are liable to change as they gain experience and knowledge. We must, therefore, distinguish between raw preferences and informed choice. But if we make the requirements for being informed about our objects of desire sufficiently stringent, we end up with a list of the many different things that enhance human life.

Can an objective account of welfare be reconciled with the diversity of views about what the good life consists of? Rawls (1972) points out that no one can live in accordance with any set of values without prior access to what he calls 'primary goods', the material and cultural prerequisites for becoming a moral agent with the capacity to make one's own choices and decisions. Doyal and Gough (1991) develop this idea into a general theory of human need. Sen (1993), following a different tack, argues that if we are concerned with what people make of their lives, with their various doings and beings, then what matters is not so much the life-chances they enjoy, as the capabilities they cultivate.

Whatever one's conception of welfare, it is important to retain an open mind about what factors promote it. It used to be thought that the experience of happiness was inaccessible to direct measurement. Layard (2005), however, reports a close correlation between self-assessed happiness ratings, the judgements of independent observers, and measurements of electrical activity in the relevant parts of the brain. He concludes that happiness is an objective phenomenon, varying along a single continuum, from the utmost misery to the sheerest joy, and can legitimately be studied by investigators seeking to track changes in the happiness of individuals and groups over time, compare patterns of happiness in different countries, and discover what makes people happy.

The most striking findings of the 'new science' concern the relationship between happiness and income. In all countries, the rich are, on average, happier than the poor. Likewise, up to a per capita income of around $20,000 per year, as poor countries grow richer, their inhabitants become happier. Above this threshold, however, the correlation breaks down: affluent societies do not become happier as they grow richer. In the USA, for example, people are, on average, no happier now than they were in 1950, even though per capita income has more than doubled. There has been no increase in the proportion of 'very happy' people, nor any substantial fall in the proportion who say they are 'not very happy'. The story is similar in the UK where happiness has been static since about 1975.

Whether the greatest overall happiness is the sole or supreme goal of public policy is questionable. For one thing, it may conflict with other social values such as freedom, fairness, order, or efficiency and, when this happens, people may disagree about what matters most, especially in modern, pluralistic societies where no single moral outlook commands universal assent. Furthermore, where the consequences of alternative options are shrouded in genuine uncertainty, as distinct from calculable risk, happiness ceases to be a serviceable criterion for deciding what to do. But if happiness cannot simply be substituted for GDP as the lodestar of public policy, its claims can hardly be disregarded. I return to this issue in section 8.4.

Welfare states and social citizenship

Welfare states come in various shapes and sizes. Abstracting from specific national arrangements, we might define a welfare state as a series of state-sponsored programmes, instituted within the framework of capitalism, and designed to ensure that all national citizens enjoy at least minimum standards of income, health care, education, and housing.

As this formulation makes clear, welfare states arose in countries with developed capitalist economies and strong nation-states. Having undermined earlier systems of mutual support based on family ties, religious precept, and parochial provision, the economic growth unleashed by capitalism created the resources required to pay for nationwide public services administered by the state. At the same time, the idea of the nation as a cultural community, bound together by ties of language, mores, character, and history, created opportunities for political actors, inspired by collectivist ideologies of varying hues, to forge connections between national success (however defined) and social solidarity.

Yet welfare states in capitalist societies are *market-limiting*, not *market-usurping*. To the extent that production and investment continue to be driven by competitive rivalry and the pursuit of profit, the allocation of resources and the distribution of income continue to be determined by market forces, subject to the maintenance of certain minimum social safeguards. This does not preclude the pursuit of more ambitious goals. For example, besides preventing or alleviating poverty, social security systems may be designed to redistribute income across the life-course, to redistribute income vertically from rich to poor, to offset the extra costs or special needs of groups such as disabled people or families with children, or to foster certain shared social norms and identities, notably, those associated with being a citizen. (Walker (2005) provides a full discussion of the aims and objectives of social security.)

The welfare state is bound up with the institution of citizenship as it has developed over the past two centuries. In general, to be a citizen is to enjoy certain rights and to owe certain duties as a member of a political community. In modern democracies, citizenship is an inclusive and egalitarian status, at least in a normative sense. Over the long run, all denizens of the national territory tend to become citizens, though a good deal of variation is evident in the treatment of resident aliens and second-generation immigrants (Brubaker 1990). Similarly, both law and public opinion alike normally condemn breaches of the principle that citizenship is a single status, with no internal gradations.

Historically, these two features imparted a powerful democratic logic to the politics of nation-states, slowly extending not only the scope of the citizen-body, but also the range of the political agenda. Conceptually, the rights (and correlative duties) of citizens can be divided into three broad groups: *civil liberties* comprising the classical liberal freedoms —of thought, conscience, expression, movement, assembly, and association—together with the 'possessive individualist' freedoms of contract and security of property; *political rights*, including the right to stand for public office and to vote in elections for local and national government; and *social entitlements*, such as free education, access to health care, affordable housing, and a guaranteed minimum income.

The three dimensions of citizenship may be unevenly developed. The USA, for example, is proud of its liberties and rights, but lags behind Western Europe on the social front, and even in Western Europe the form and scale of social entitlements continue to be contested, not least because they are harder to secure than civil and political rights and impose heavier demands on taxpayers. Nevertheless, without some assured access to primary goods, the value of citizenship is diminished. Nor do social entitlements benefit only individuals: institutions that bind people together into a (national) community of fate make it easier for society as a whole to cope with difference, diversity, division, and conflict in a context of material scarcity.

Economic activity and the remit of social policy

People engage in economic activity whenever they devote time, energy, and skills to producing objects or serving purposes that are of value to others, regardless of where they work, how their work is controlled, whether they work for pay, and whether they produce for the market. There is no single, correct way of classifying activities. For some purposes it suffices to distinguish between the public and private sectors of the economy, abstracting from the wider social framework. But to deal with the interplay between social institutions, cultural change, economic development, and public policy, we need a broader canvas and some additional categories. At a minimum, we need to distinguish between the *business sector*, in which rival, profit-seeking firms employ waged labour to produce marketed commodities; the *public sector*, in which tax-financed agencies which are not, normally, profit-seeking and which are either directly controlled or contractually engaged by the state, employ waged labour to produce non-marketed goods and services for use by the general public; the *household sector*, in which individuals perform unpaid provisioning and caring work both on their own account and for the benefit of others with whom they cohabit; and the *voluntary sector*, in which a variety of charities, membership organizations, civic associations, and informal networks employ paid staff or volunteers to express shared values, promote shared interests, and cater to social needs that are either not met at all, or not met so well, by commercial, public, or domestic providers.

Each sector helps to keep society going and all are mutually interdependent. Thus, just as the business sector produces commodities, which the others purchase and use in their respective spheres, so their activities in turn help to sustain the production of commodities and the accumulation of capital. The state presides over the legal, policing, and penal systems; regulates banking and finance; provides or supervises essential services such as transport, energy, education, health care, and social security; seeks to maintain macro-economic stability; and normally makes some attempt to manage social conflict and legitimize the social order. Households, for their part, produce people—both from generation to generation and from day to day—not, of course, as mere biological organisms or bearers of labour power, but as fully fledged persons who are more or less equipped to participate in social life and whose own lives, from cradle to grave, are bound up with those of their families, friends, and fellows. And the voluntary sector plays a vital—if, as yet, imperfectly understood—role in building and maintaining communal assets such as mutual trust, civic responsibility, public order, and social cohesion which are not only valuable in their own right, but also benefit the other sectors.

In very general terms, we might say that the aim of social policy is to keep the four sectors in balance, ensuring that none damages the others or, better still, that all work together to promote agreed social goals. What aspects of social life are perceived as problematic and what remedies gain acceptance among political elites and the general public vary greatly from one society and era to another. Cross-national differences of policy regime are examined in the next section. Here it suffices to note the succession of policy paradigms which have influenced governments everywhere since the end of the Second World War.

During the 'golden age' of welfare-capitalism, from 1945 to the mid-1970s, the ethos of public policy was strongly collectivist. The welfare state, it was widely believed, was positively good for business, helping to sustain aggregate demand, improve the quality of the labour force, legitimize capitalism, and abate class conflict. With the onset of severe economic crisis in the mid-1970s and the persistence of 'stagflation', these ideas became discredited and were displaced by neo-liberal doctrines which held that the growth of the public sector in general, and of the welfare state in particular, was largely responsible for the deterioration in economic performance and needed to be reversed in order to restore monetary discipline, lessen the burden of taxation, liberate market forces, and rehabilitate the work ethic. From the early 1990s onwards, there was growing disenchantment with the market revolution, which was widely blamed for causing or failing to prevent the growth of poverty, inequality, and social exclusion, for degrading the environment, and for imposing unacceptable levels of stress on workers, families, and communities. One response, which found particular favour with the Democrats in the USA and with New Labour in Britain, was to forge a 'third way', distinct from both traditional social democracy and neo-liberalism in a bid to reconcile economic dynamism with social cohesion and justice (Giddens 1998, 2000). Proponents of this approach seek to combine monetary discipline, fiscal prudence, and flexible labour markets with welfare reform and supply-side activism, urging governments to help improve the employability of those exposed to the risks of social exclusion and impoverishment, and insisting that all who can support themselves and their families through paid work should do so. Critics retort that, far from imposing human and social priorities on the trajectory of turbo-capitalism, the 'third way' is merely the human face of neo-liberalism (Hall 2003).

In short, social policy is an ideological battleground extending over a wide range of issues. Yet the various issues are interrelated. For example, welfare arrangements designed for an era of quasi-fixed exchange rates, Keynesian economics, industrial employment, regulated labour markets, stable marriages, segregated gender roles, two-parent, one-earner families, and low age-dependency ratios need to be redesigned for a world of global finance, fiscal and monetary rules, service economies, flexible labour markets, rising divorce rates, converging gender roles, diversified family and household forms, and ageing populations. Clearly, whatever one's ideological stance, a coherent response to cumulative change calls for coordinated adjustments on several adjacent policy fronts: macroeconomic management, industrial relations, wage setting, employment policy, taxation, social security, retirement pensions, and provision for families and children.

8.2 Welfare regimes

Social services and social transfers

Social services can be provided in two very different ways: government can establish specialized public agencies which hire labour from the household sector and purchase commodities from the business sector; alternatively, it can outsource provision to private organizations in the business or voluntary sectors, relying on regulation, audit or quasi-markets to ensure equity, efficiency, accountability, and user choice. (In quasi-markets, services continue to be free of charge at the point of use, but service-providers compete for public contracts and service-users can choose among alternative suppliers: see Bartlett *et al.* 1998.) Since the late 1980s, outsourcing has spread across the public sector, but nowhere more than in the social services, where finance and provision, once tied together, have been steadily prised apart. Targets and performance standards continue to be set by central government and, indeed, proliferate, with external audit replacing professional ethics as the preferred means of assuring service quality. Within this centrally imposed framework, hospitals, schools, universities, and other non-government public bodies enjoy greater operational independence than in the past. Their objectives remain different from those of profit-seeking firms, but they have increasingly adopted commercial norms and practices, blurring the public–business boundary and encouraging service-users to think of themselves as customers rather than as citizens.

Tax-financed social transfers account for between 10 and 20 per cent of GDP in EU Member States (OECD 2003). Because the state levies taxes on personal income and pays out social security benefits, it is necessary to distinguish between *original income*—what households get before taking taxes and transfers into account—and *disposable income*—what they end up with afterwards. In most EU countries, about 70 per cent of original income accruing to households consists of wages and salaries paid to employees. Earnings from self-employment account for a further 10 to 15 per cent and payments of rent, interest, and dividends for the remainder.

Both earnings and property income derive from market activity. If there were no social transfers, those who owned no income-yielding assets or were, for whatever reason, unable to obtain gainful employment would have to rely on private transfers from their families or friends, beg for charity, or turn to crime. Most people depend for their livelihood on continuous access to paid work, whether in their own right or as dependants of others who are willing or obliged to support them. Besides being a source of income, regular employment confers various other advantages: experience and skills, friendship and contacts, self-esteem, social identity, public status, and political clout.

Regular jobholders are also covered by *social insurance*. Employers, employees, and self-employed workers are all legally obliged to pay 'contributions' (or social security taxes) into one or more earmarked insurance funds, administered or regulated by the state. Together with their dependants, employees who satisfy the requisite contribution conditions are more or less adequately protected, both against temporary interruptions of earnings resulting from unemployment, sickness, and maternity—outside Scandinavia, scant provision is made for paid paternity and parental leave—and against permanent loss of earnings owing to incapacitation or retirement. People who are not in stable, full-time employment throughout their working lives are less well served by social insurance. Indeed, unless the state provides credited contributions for unpaid work and keeps the threshold of admission to the insurance system low enough to include almost all forms of paid work, they may not be covered at all. The main groups at risk are the long-term unemployed, women who take time out of the labour market to provide child or elder care, and workers of either sex engaged in part-time, temporary, or other forms of 'non-standard' employment.

Welfare states typically provide some kind of safety net outside the framework of social insurance, but *social assistance*—to use a generic name for schemes that vary widely in operational detail—is almost invariably means-tested: entitlements are calculated by assessing how far the combined incomes and savings of the family or household unit fall short of some predetermined standard of 'subsistence'. In addition, able-bodied claimants of conventional working age are normally subjected to some more or less stringent work test. During the 'golden age', unemployed claimants were simply required to show that they were capable of, available for, and genuinely seeking (paid) work. Since the late 1980s, such 'passive' criteria have given way to 'active' measures targeted on specific, disadvantaged groups who are or risk becoming disconnected from the labour market: young people who have never had jobs, older workers experiencing long-term (open or disguised) unemployment, lone parents and disabled people who are classified as 'economically inactive', but could be (re-)integrated into the workforce with suitable help and encouragement.

The general aims of active labour market policy are to reduce welfare dependency by enhancing employability, to combat social exclusion by increasing labour force participation, to furnish employers with a plentiful supply of adequately equipped and motivated workers, to contain or restructure social security spending, and to reassure taxpayers that they are not being exploited by 'scroungers'. Programmes vary in detail, but typically participants are interviewed, assessed, and counselled with a view to building bridges into employment or overcoming the various barriers that block access to it, from educational deficiencies and lack of child care to deviant lifestyles and mental illness. Penalties for non-cooperation are generally matched by measures designed to 'make work pay'.

In the UK, for example, besides introducing a national minimum wage, the New Labour government has converted benefits that used to be provided through the social security system into *tax credits*, administered by employers on behalf of the tax authorities and added to workers' pay packets. Initially confined to low-paid family breadwinners, tax credits are now available to anyone in low-paid work. In addition, working parents with earnings up to a generous threshold can reclaim some of the costs of bought-in child care. The case for tax credits is that they strengthen incentives to enter employment and redistribute income in favour of low-paid workers and hard-pressed families in a way that is more acceptable to taxpayers and less stigmatizing for claimants than traditional social assistance. However, like all income-related transfers, they impose high marginal tax rates on recipients, whose entitlements fall if they earn more, and this may be a disincentive to working longer, working harder, or moving to better paid jobs. Tax credits are also complex and costly to administer, and may cause resentment and hardship if recipients who have benefited from assessment errors are subsequently required to pay money back.

Contributory social insurance is designed to replace lost earnings; social assistance protects those with no earnings; tax credits supplement low earnings. In addition, most welfare states provide *categorical transfers*, designed to meet the extra costs or special needs of designated categories of people. The best-known example is *child benefit*, a cash grant payable to all parents and guardians for every child in their care from the moment the child is born until he or she leaves school. No state has yet introduced a *citizen's income*, a recurrent, lifelong transfer payable to every individual citizen, each in his or her own right, with no means test or work requirement. This idea provoked a lively academic debate in the 1990s, but failed to win mainstream support, though it continues to attract 'real' libertarians and post-materialist critics of the contemporary preoccupation with getting as many people into paid employment as possible (see Purdy 1994; Van Parijs 1995; and Robertson *et al.* 1996). I return to citizen's income in section 8.4.

Besides providing explicit transfers, governments also dispense implicit transfers in the form of *tax expenditures*, sometimes known as 'the hidden welfare state'. Personal tax allowances and reliefs drive a wedge between original income and taxable income. The effect is to raise the disposable incomes of eligible taxpayers just as cash benefits and tax credits raise the disposable incomes of eligible claimants. Tax allowances play a useful role in maintaining work incentives for people on the margins of the labour force and it is, in any case, not worthwhile collecting small amounts of revenue from low-income tax units. Tax reliefs, on the other hand, serve to subsidize favoured forms of expenditure, such as giving to charity, contributing to a private pension scheme, or taking out a mortgage to buy a home of one's own, and since they can seriously distort the markets concerned, while simultaneously narrowing the tax base, they are generally frowned on by policy analysts.

Types of welfare regime

Reacting against earlier, unilinear theories of modernization, students of comparative social policy have focused on the *varieties* of welfare-capitalism. Until the mid-1990s, three main questions dominated the research agenda: How do welfare states differ? Why do these differences exist? And what effect do they have on social stratification and economic performance? More recently, two further questions have come to the fore: How have different welfare states responded to common domestic and global pressures for change? And what are the implications of globalization for social policy both within each nation-state and at the supranational level? Here I consider the first three questions, postponing the last two to section 8.4.

In order to reduce the complexity of their task, researchers have delineated a limited number of models or ideal-types to which actual welfare regimes approximate more or less closely, it being understood that most states are hybrids containing various 'impure' elements and 'intermediate' forms. The empirical validity of the resulting typology can be judged by devising suitable indicators of key characteristics, compiling data for different states, and looking to see whether the data do, indeed, fall into distinct clusters, each with a centre of gravity corresponding to the relevant model.

Employing this procedure in a path-breaking study, Esping-Andersen (1990) distinguished three worlds of welfare-capitalism—the liberal, the conservative (or Christian democratic), and the social democratic—exemplified, respectively, by the USA, Germany, and Sweden. The salient features of his typology are summarized in Table 8.1.

Classical liberalism celebrated property, markets, limited government, and the work ethic. Echoing the early puritan belief that the industrious would be saved and the idle damned, the presumption of liberal social policy is that all who are not incapacitated by age, disability, or illness have a duty to support themselves and their dependants. Those with no private means of their own must, therefore, be drawn or driven into the labour market. To this end, social transfers are targeted, means-tested, work-tested, and—in effect, if not in intention—stigmatizing. Social services are similarly residual and the better off are encouraged to opt out of state welfare, not least through the provision of tax relief on private pensions and health insurance. Thus, liberal regimes impose a sharp line of demarcation between self-reliant citizens and those who depend on the state. Education and health care are marked by class division; social security and social housing are the preserve of the poor; and governments, caught between pressures for increased social expenditure and low levels of tax tolerance, rely on a combination of weak trade unions

Table 8.1 Esping-Andersen's (1990) typology of welfare regimes

	Liberal	Conservative	Social democratic
Origins	classical liberalism	conservative nationalism	democratic class struggle
	nineteenth-century Poor Law	Christian social thought	
Goals	self-reliance	corporatism	decommodification
	poverty relief	social market economy	social citizenship
Social policy			
services	residual public	household/voluntary	universal public
transfers	social assistance	occupational social insurance schemes	national insurance; categorical grants
mode of finance	general taxation	earmarked insurance contributions	mixed
tax burden	low	intermediate	high
Employment policy			
macroeconomic priority	non-inflationary growth	non-inflationary growth	full employment growth
industrial relations	anti-collectivism	social partnership	social partnership
means of adjustment	flexible labour markets	labour supply management	active labour market policy
Outcomes			
redistribution	weak vertical	horizontal	strong vertical
stratification	social dualism	status maintenance	social solidarity
impact on gender division	passively neutral	reinforcing	countervailing
Exemplars	United States	Germany	Sweden

and flexible labour markets to maintain a plentiful supply of low-wage jobs without impairing work incentives.

The watchword of conservative welfare regimes is the social market economy. Capitalism is welcomed as an engine of economic growth, but social transfers are used to compensate market losers, uphold family values, and preserve social cohesion. Significantly, it was Germany, Esping-Andersen's exemplar country, which invented social insurance. The German model is, however, hierarchical. Instead of a unitary and comprehensive national insurance scheme covering all workers and all risks, Germany has a variety of occupational schemes, with health insurance funded and administered separately from retirement pensions and unemployment compensation. Each scheme is jointly managed by representatives of employers and workers, subject to broad requirements laid down by the state. Both for this reason and because insurance benefits are earnings related, not flat rate, the system combines income security with *horizontal* redistribution—*within* rather than *across* occupational boundaries—thereby maintaining the established hierarchy of income and status.

Historically, the conservative model originated in the efforts of Bismarck to pre-empt the appeal of socialism by securing the allegiance of German workers to the newly unified German state. The influence of Christian (Catholic and Protestant) social thought is also evident: in the provision of 'family wage' supplements for (male) breadwinners; in the principle of subsidiarity, which accords a preferential role to the voluntary sector in the provision of social services; and in a system of industrial relations inspired by the principle of 'social partnership' and designed to affirm the dignity of labour, prevent class conflict, and incorporate employee representatives in both enterprise decision-making and national policy-making.

Social democratic regimes are also committed to social insurance and social partnership, but as elements in an egalitarian scheme of social citizenship. In this model, the state is not a second or last resort, but plays a primary role in providing all citizens with the highest attainable degree of income security and a wide range of high-quality services. Esping-Andersen (1990) argues that such arrangements decommodify waged labour in the sense that they protect workers from the vicissitudes of the market. This is true, but should not be taken to imply any antipathy to the wages system or the business sector. The social democratic model remains firmly wedded to employment as the pre-eminent form of paid work and, indeed, promotes it to the extent that the state becomes a major provider or purchaser of services that were once produced informally in the home. Likewise, the model rests on an accord between capital and labour: workers accede to management control over the enterprise in return for business acceptance of the welfare state.

In Sweden, where the Social Democrats have held office, usually as the senior partner in a coalition government, for all but nine years since 1932, social transfers were traditionally designed to foster social solidarity based on a commitment to the ideal of the 'people's home'. All citizens were entitled to a tax-financed basic retirement pension as a matter of right, with supplementary, earnings-related pensions provided through a unitary national insurance scheme. Apart from its symbolic significance, this inclusive arrangement pre-empted the growth of private pensions and insurance. It also raised the ceiling of tax tolerance, making it easier to maintain high income-replacement rates. In recent years, Swedish social democracy, like its counterparts elsewhere, has lost ground and following a fiscal crisis in the early 1990s, the pension system was overhauled with cross-party agreement. The flat-rate citizen's pension was replaced by an income-related minimum pension guarantee and employees were allowed to invest part of their earnings-related insurance contributions in private pension plans. Nevertheless, as we shall see, significant elements of the social democratic legacy survive.

Esping-Andersen's typology has been widely adopted, but it has also been criticized: for mis-specifying the 'Mediterranean' welfare states—Italy, Greece, Portugal, and Spain—as underdeveloped or immature conservative regimes; for assigning the Antipodean welfare states to the liberal category; for concentrating on formal employment and social transfers and failing to consider the household and voluntary sectors; and, more generally, for not paying enough attention to the gender dimension of social policy. Arts and Gelissen (2002) survey the debate and review the modified or alternative typologies that critics have proposed. What seems clear is that no typology is suitable for all parts of the world, all aspects of policy, and all lines of social division, let alone all periods of history.

However, in the absence of some unified, macro-social 'theory of everything', ideal-types offer an overview of the broad characteristics of social formations or historical epochs, and should be seen as complementing case studies of single countries, specific programmes, or specific social divisions.

In any case, the 'three worlds' thesis does help to explain the persistent diversity of welfare states. It also throws light on patterns of continuity and innovation in social policy. Consider responses to the passing of the 'golden age' and the rise in unemployment that all countries experienced in the 1980s. In the UK, a liberal welfare state with 'deviant' social democratic features, the Thatcher governments embraced a radical version of the neo-liberal creed and set about dismantling the post-war settlement, emasculating trade unions, deregulating the labour market, and restricting or recasting social entitlements. In Germany, by contrast, the Christian Democrats resorted to the tried and tested strategy of labour supply management, encouraging women to stay at home, older workers to take early retirement, and foreign workers (*Gastarbeiter*) to return to their countries of origin. By lowering resistance to redundancies, this policy helped domestic firms to retain or regain market shares and profitability through higher productivity rather than lower real wages (Esping-Andersen 1994). Its continued viability depended on the willingness of employers and their remaining employees to accept higher taxes in order to meet the extra costs of family support and extended periods of pension entitlement, and this was sorely tried by the 'solidarity taxes' and high interest rates that were imposed on them in the 1990s as the price of German reunification.

The viability of the Swedish model, with its guarantee of paid work or generous transfers from cradle to grave, depended on the maintenance of full employment, not simply in the technical sense that the labour market continued to clear, but in the more vital sense that participation in the labour force was maximized, while frictional and structural unemployment were minimized. Accordingly, Swedish governments continued to pursue active labour market policies, helping workers made redundant to retrain or relocate, and drawing women into employment by creating new jobs in the public sector. This, in turn, required an active child-care policy combining universal access to affordable day nurseries with paid parental leave. Meanwhile, the task of reconciling permanent full employment with low inflation called for the continued commitment of both employers and trade unions to wage restraint. This proved to be the model's Achilles heel. Tensions surfaced in the early 1980s when Swedish employers rejected trade union demands for a voice in corporate investment decisions in return for observing wage restraint and, as the decade wore on, wage discipline gave way to a sectional free-for-all, exacerbated by the extra tax cost of active labour market measures (Meidner 1993). Finally, in the early 1990s, mounting inflation, deteriorating international competitiveness, and pressure on the exchange rate forced the government to make deep cuts in public expenditure and unemployment rose sharply.

This was not, however, the end of the Swedish model. For one thing, institutionalized solidarity makes it possible to impose even-handed welfare cutbacks on a scale that would be unthinkable elsewhere. Moreover, in 1994 the Social Democrats were voted back into office and, combining fiscal prudence with supply-side intervention, presided over a sustained economic recovery. Thus, whereas the UK went in for regime change, while Germany tried to maintain its social market model in the face of cumulative dysfunctions,

Sweden retained those elements of its welfare state—lifelong learning, labour market activism, child-care support, and social partnership—which held out the prospect of solving social problems and adapting to global pressures within the framework of a renegotiated social contract.

8.3 The EU as a social policy actor

Why is there no European welfare state?

The EU is not a traditional state, with its own armed forces, foreign policy, and fiscal powers, but a loose-knit union of nation-states which have agreed to share legal sover-eignty and establish supranational institutions for certain specified purposes, but which still retain far more autonomy than the constituent units of federal states such as the USA, Canada, and Switzerland. As Leibfried and Pierson (1995) note, an inherent problem with multi-tiered governance is that disputes over what is to be done become intertwined with disputes over who is to do it. This greatly complicates the policy-making process. Policies must always serve two goals—tackling substantive problems and protecting institu-tional interests—and assembling a winning coalition may depend on scaling down policy ambitions so as to keep waverers on board or buying off opponents by horse-trading and side-payments. Such 'decision traps' have been particularly common in the field of social policy because the process of economic integration has continually raised questions about the 'proper' division of powers and responsibilities between national governments and supranational authorities without ever fully resolving them. Cross-border 'market-making' creates pressure for EU-wide 'market-braking', whether to compensate losers, restore the balance between market freedom and social protection that existed previously within each sovereign welfare state, or build up the EU as an alternative to the nation-state. Yet because welfare states came into being long before the EU was established, most of the available policy space is already occupied and national governments would strongly resist any transfer of core welfare functions to the EU, for this would fatally undermine their political autonomy.

Having neither the legal authority, tax-raising powers, nor administrative capacity to carry out ambitious social programmes of its own, the EU is largely confined to the edges of social policy space: that is, to areas that were previously not on the public agenda or where established arrangements have been disrupted, or which are only indirectly connected with social policy such as the CAP or regional policy. The Commission's Directorate-General (DG) 5, which deals with employment, industrial relations, and social affairs, is responsible for cross-border rule-making and agenda-setting, and in both cases it generally employs a light touch. Its preferred legislative instrument is the *Directive*, which prescribes objectives or results, but leaves it up to Member States to decide how best to pursue them. And the bulk of its work consists of 'soft coordination': prioritizing issues, defining terms, standardizing statistics, commissioning research, issu-ing opinions, consulting other policy-actors—including the social partners—building coalitions, and brokering agreements.

Why has this pattern of politics and power persisted? Why has the EU not developed a supranational presence in social policy comparable, say, to the federal social security system that was introduced in the USA during the 1930s as part of the Roosevelt administration's New Deal? One reason is that although the process of economic integration might be seen as adding a European layer to the civil rights of EU citizens, their political and, still more, their social rights continue to be framed in national terms. Nor is there any popular demand for a European welfare state. The EU possesses some of the trappings of statehood—its own anthem, passport, flag, and currency—but it has signally failed to inspire the patriotism that was once evoked by the idea of the nation, binding its members together even as it set them apart from outsiders. The nation as an imagined community may be in decline, but it has not been replaced by any wider, supranational focus of loyalty and political mobilization. Except on occasions when voters or parliaments in Member States are called upon to approve major projects such as entry into the eurozone or the adoption of a new treaty, EU politics is an elite business. The popular coalitions that form around national welfare states scarcely exist at the supranational level, and the link between parliamentary representation and executive power, the keystone of democracy in the nation-state, is missing from the institutions of the EU, a fact that was underlined in 2005 when voters in France and the Netherlands rejected the proposed constitutional treaty and plunged the EU into a full-scale crisis of legitimacy.

Even if there were a flourishing European demos, the emergence of an EU-wide welfare state would be inhibited by the diversity of Europe's welfare regimes which, as we saw earlier, fall into three distinct clusters—four if the 'Mediterranean' regime is counted as a distinct type, or even five if one takes account of the former socialist states of Eastern and Central Europe. This was less of a problem in the early years, when the six founding Member States formed a relatively homogeneous bloc, approximating to the conservative model. Even then, ambitious plans to harmonize social insurance systems came to nothing. In part, this was because although the original EC-6 belonged to the same welfare family, initial discrepancies in coverage, scope, scales, financing, and eligibility rules were too wide to permit easy or rapid convergence. But a more serious problem was that any uniform, Community-wide scheme would have entailed interstate transfers on a scale that Germany, as the principal net contributor, was unwilling to countenance, notwithstanding the desire of its government and people to atone for Nazi crimes and regain the respect of its neighbours. The alacrity and largesse with which, after the fall of the Berlin Wall, the West German government absorbed the social security system of the former GDR provide a striking and instructive contrast.

It can, of course, be argued that despite the diversity of Europe's welfare regimes, there is a distinctive 'European social model' and, in two senses, this is true. From a global standpoint, judged by criteria such as the level of spending, the scope of services, the popularity of specific programmes, and the discourse of citizenship (see Pierson 1998: 159–61), the various European welfare families have far more in common with each other than with their distant cousins in North America and the Antipodes, let alone with the 'Confucian' welfare states of East Asia. Similarly, on the policy front, one can point to the growth of an EU-wide social policy network, bringing together politicians, civil servants, interest group functionaries, academic specialists, and media pundits, who share the same intellectual outlook and approach to policy issues. But macroscopic affinities and 'epistemic communities' are no substitute for common institutions and norms. As Ferrera (1998) notes, even when policy experts in different countries use the same language, by the time buzzwords such as 'targeting', 'welfare dependency', or 'social exclusion' have been translated into the operational idiom of national social security systems, the 'European social model' looks far more heterogeneous than it appears from above.

Market integration and 'Social Europe': a case of uneven development

At various points over the years, attempts have been made to enlarge the remit of EU social policy and extend the range of issues subject to qualified majority voting. The best known was the hard-fought campaign waged by Commission President Jacques Delors in the mid-1980s to invest the Single Market Programme with a 'social dimension'. His efforts culminated in what became known as the 'Social Charter' or, to give it its full title, the *Community Charter of Fundamental Social Rights*. This was an attempt to strike a balance between divergent conceptions of 'Social Europe', establishing a common set of social standards that would satisfy social collectivists and Euro-idealists without antagonizing neo-liberals and organized employers. In truth, the Charter contained more symbolism than substance. Adopted at the Strasbourg Council in December 1989, with the UK as the lone dissenting voice, it subsequently formed the basis of the Social Chapter of the Maastricht Treaty under a compromise which allowed the UK to opt out of its provisions. As a result, three new objectives were attached to Article 117 of the Treaty of Rome: 'proper social protection', social dialogue, and 'the development of human resources to achieve lasting employment'. In addition, the scope of qualified majority voting was extended to cover health and safety, working conditions, information and consultation, sex equality in the labour market, and the integration of persons excluded from the labour market.

Despite the controversy it provoked, the Charter was purely declaratory and had no legal force. Most of its specific principles, such as the right to belong or not to belong to a trade union, had long been observed in Member States or, as in the case of equal treatment for women at work, were actually enshrined in Community law. In addition, the preamble contained a pointed reference to the principle of subsidiarity. This was a coded way of saying that EU standards must be compatible with national traditions. At the time, the non-binding character of the Charter was widely regarded as a setback for EU social policy. But in retrospect, it can be seen as the first step towards the pursuit of social policy by means of 'soft coordination' rather than 'hard law'. It served, for example, as a standing reminder that what we call the 'labour market' is not a market like any other because labour power is not a commodity like any other: the capacity for work is inseparable from the person in whom it is embodied; human beings, unlike machines, care about what happens to them at work; and contracts of employment, unlike regulations governing animal welfare, are continually being adjusted and renegotiated in the process of production. This explains why neo-liberals objected to the Charter on principle and were not simply echoing the complaints of employers that it would add to their costs or limit their options. Particular bugbears were the requirement that the wages of non-standard employees should be set by reference to an equitable benchmark; the potential extension of disclosure rights through the establishment of European works councils; and the

Commission's well-known and long-standing desire to establish EU-wide collective bargaining in transnational companies. Employers were also unhappy that the Commission was authorized to write an annual report on the application of the Charter in each Member State. There is, of course, little point in having a statement of principles without some way of monitoring observance. But recurrent monitoring does enable the Commission and its allies to keep social issues on the agenda.

In fact, the scope for instituting EU-wide social standards by means of legally binding Directives is limited. In certain policy areas, the EU has succeeded in harmonizing national regulations—health and industrial safety, environmental risks, and consumer protection. But in the field of social and employment protection, the conflicts have proved to be too intense to be settled within existing EU institutions. The chief obstacles are disparities of economic development and differences of policy regime. Rich countries or those with generous social standards are reluctant to scale down their workers' entitlements to benefits such as sick pay, annual holidays, or parental leave. But poor EU countries, where output per worker is low, need to keep their wage and non-wage costs low as well if they are to compete in the internal market. Thus, unless the rich countries are willing to help them out, they cannot afford to agree to harmonization through levelling up. But interstate redistribution is never a popular cause and wrangling over the EU budget has intensified with the accession of ten new Member States, all of them poorer than even the poorest of the EU-15.

Several writers have suggested that these obstacles could be overcome if social standards and benchmarks were *graduated* according to national per capita income (Scharpf 1997; Mishra 1999; Purdy 2003). Under such an arrangement, all Member States would be obliged or expected to observe specified minimum standards, but rich countries would accept more demanding standards than poor ones, and as the latter grew richer their standards would automatically rise. Graduated benchmarking has several advantages. It accords with the principle of subsidiarity and cuts with the grain of recent EU development: national governments would retain responsibility for social provision, but work within a negotiated supranational framework. It sets a floor to competition and guards against the risk of a 'race to the bottom': existing Member States would be covered by a common set of regulations without compromising either the ability of rich countries to maintain standards superior to the benchmarks or the ability of poor countries to compete in the internal market. And candidate members would face a less daunting task in qualifying for admission. Contentious issues remain, however. In some cases—say, where public health and safety are involved—there are good reasons for insisting on *uniform* standards. What distinguishes such cases from those where graduation is permissible? At what levels should minimum standards be pitched? And when should standards be legally binding?

In practice, it is worth noting, EU Directives are less stringent than existing national laws. The Working Time Directive, for example, adopted in 1993 (against UK opposition), provides for a maximum working week of 48 hours on average—including overtime—for minimum rest breaks during working hours, and for four weeks' annual paid holiday. These standards are less restrictive than national regulations in every Member State except the UK, which deregulated working time in the 1980s. The Directive also permits numerous exceptions and exemptions. The process of European social dialogue, sometimes described as the 'second pillar' of EU social policy, has been similarly anodyne. Under the provisions of the Social Chapter, the Commission is obliged to consult the social part-ners before framing proposals for social legislation. They may indicate that they wish to negotiate an EU-level agreement on the issue in question, 'bargaining in the shadow of the law', as Bercusson (1992: 185) puts it. If they manage to reach agreement, it is their proposal that is put to the Council of Ministers. Having examined five Directives enacted during the 1990s, Keller and Soerries (1999) conclude that where this procedure worked it did not matter and where it mattered it did not work. In short, neither legislation nor social dialogue has done much to redress the asymmetry between market integration and EU social policy. Can soft coordination do better? This question is considered in the next section.

8.4 Welfare reform and the future

Policy challenges and social pacts

Europe's welfare states face four interconnected challenges: from globalization, the post-industrial order, permanent austerity, and European integration. The options open to national governments and their social partners are tightly constrained by the liberaliza-tion of capital markets, increased trade openness, and intensified competition in product markets. At the same time, the coming of a post-industrial age has transformed the agenda of social policy (Taylor-Gooby 2004). Even in the golden age, no one—with the exception of hereditary monarchs—ever had a 'job for life'. Nevertheless, unskilled male manual workers could expect to find jobs that paid a 'family wage' and were sustained in their role as breadwinners by stable marriages and a traditional sexual division of labour. Nowadays, boys and girls who experience multiple deprivation in early childhood have little chance of faring well in a society which puts a premium on employability and, as they grow older, may well add to the case-loads of the police and social services, imposing costs on society as a whole. Other groups too—lone mothers, older unemployed men, disabled people, and members of ethnic minorities—risk becoming disconnected from the labour market and excluded from mainstream society, while privileged 'insiders' such as well-heeled retirement pensioners reap the benefits of yesteryear's 'democratic class struggle'. Yet contemporary welfare states must contend with these problems in circumstances of 'permanent austerity' (Pierson 2001). Established social programmes, especially for pen-sions and health care, are expensive, popular, and entrenched, whereas newly vulnerable groups are weak and fragmented and governments, constrained by fiscal straitjackets, may be unable to respond effectively to their needs, even when they recognize them.

The uneven development of the EU has made matters worse, weakening the problem-solving capacities of national government without creating supranational substitutes. EMU, for example, removes the options of exchange rate and interest rate adjustments as tools of macroeconomic policy, and the rules of the Stability and Growth Pact inhibit deficit financing. Similarly, in the wake of the 2004 enlargement, fears were voiced that migration from new Member States in the east would lower wages and damage social cohesion in the west, while reactions to the prospect of Turkish accession were tinged with xenophobia. Yet the core institutions of the welfare state remain firmly under national control and European social policy is confined to a peripheral role.

It is sometimes suggested that European welfare states are immune to reform. This is, at best, an exaggeration. In the 1980s, it is true, retrenchment rather than reform was the order of the day. Since then, however, strenuous efforts have been made to recast outdated institutions and launch new initiatives across the whole field of social policy. The process has been slow and painful, and the results have often been uneven or indifferent, but after twenty years of what Visser and Hemerijck (1998) call 'puzzling and learning', policy-makers are better versed in both the substance and statecraft of reform. The learning process began with the Dutch 'Wassenaar Accord' of 1982, which set the pattern for subsequent multilateral agreements on working time, social security, and collective bargaining, and paved the way for the Dutch 'economic miracle' of the 1990s. Rhodes (2001) provides a comprehensive survey of similar social pacts. Alongside the success stories of the Netherlands, Denmark, Ireland, and Sweden, he cites the more chequered history of attempts to reform Italy's systems of collective bargaining and retirement pensions, and the efforts of the Portuguese and Spanish governments to lessen insider–outsider divisions by brokering national agreements designed to prioritize job creation over wage growth.

The importance of social pacts for welfare reform can be gauged by considering three countries which do not appear on this list. In the UK, the New Labour government has been relentless in its efforts to overhaul both social security and the public services, but apart from establishing a tripartite Low Pay Commission to advise on the introduction and updating of a national minimum wage, has shown no sign of wanting to revive social partnership. Why should it? In its first two terms of office, it commanded the political stage, enjoyed amicable relations with employers' organizations, and had no need to court a trade union movement that was weak and disunited. Germany presents the opposite spectacle. Here the political balances are poised, the government cannot afford to take the unions for granted, and although it is no secret that Germany has adjusted badly to the challenges of a post-industrial, global age (Manow and Seils 2000), German employers are reluctant to abandon the country's historically evolved system of social partnership and co-determination. In France, by contrast, social partnership is conspicuous by its absence. The tradition of *dirigisme* continues to cast a long shadow and the efforts of successive governments to reform the system of employment and social protection are regularly derailed by militant street protest (Levy 2000).

Why did social pacts re-emerge in the 1990s and how is it that social actors in countries which appeared to lack the organizational prerequisites for corporate policy bargaining were able to reach agreements and sustain them? Three interrelated factors seem to have been important. First, the prospect of EMU acted as a catalyst, particularly for hard currency latecomers such as Italy, Portugal, and Spain where social pacts offered the functional equivalent of devaluation when the latter was no longer available. Second, with macroeconomic policy redesigned and realigned towards preventing any resurgence of inflation and assuring stable growth, governments and their partners could concentrate on the triple tasks of recasting the welfare state, enhancing national economic performance, and reaching an acceptable compromise between clashing sectional interests. And third, given that the agenda of negotiation stretched across the whole field of social policy, from employment and education to social security and child care, it made sense to extend participation beyond employers' organizations and trade unions to a wider range of stakeholders, including representatives of women, ethnic minorities, and the long-term unemployed.

Welfare reform and soft coordination

Inevitably, the provisions of social pacts contain many contingent features and reflect specific national contexts. Nevertheless, there is widespread agreement about the central themes and broad objectives of welfare reform. These are cogently expounded by Esping-Andersen and his co-authors (2002). Welfare policy, they argue, must be underpinned by strong ethical values capable of attracting support from across the political spectrum. It also requires an expansive framework of social accounting—along the lines of the four-sector model outlined in section 8.1—so as to reveal the hidden costs of family failure or community distress, highlight the potential gains from social investment and balanced development, and resist ill-judged attempts to offload the costs of societal adjustment from public budgets to private individuals and firms. Finally, policies must be long term, joined up, and concerned with the dynamics of personal life-chances at each stage of the life-course: childhood, working life, and retirement. Using this basic approach, Esping-Andersen himself enunciates four precepts for welfare reformers.

First, policy-makers must recognize that families are increasingly fragile, yet the quality of childhood experience is ever more important for subsequent life-chances. Second, while welcome progress has been made towards gender equality, European societies have failed to reconcile motherhood with employment and are currently locked into a low fertility syndrome which not only makes them unduly dependent on inward labour migration, but fails to satisfy individual preferences regarding family size. Third, the primary cause of social exclusion and poverty is lack of access to stable, well-paid jobs. Hence, although the current emphasis on labour supply activation and 'making work pay' is unavoidable as a transitional expedient, in the long run it is better to invest heavily in childhood and youth. Fourth, if European societies are to move towards a fair distribution of the costs and benefits of retirement, both between and within generations, they must: (a) take steps to raise employment rates among the working age population and delay the age of labour market exit; and (b) reorganize their pension systems so that all senior citizens, both now and in the future, can enjoy an extended period of withdrawal from paid work without suffering material hardship.

Hemerijck (2002) considers what the EU can do to promote these precepts and commends what has come to be called the 'open method of coordination' (OMC), whereby intergovernmental committees are charged with framing guidelines, monitoring progress, evaluating results, and disseminating best practice. This is a form of multilevel governance that stands somewhere between intergovernmental negotiation and mutual adjustment: government competencies remain national, but are no longer pursued in isolation. OMC has many advantages: it involves no transfer of authority to Brussels, no extra cost for the EU budget, and no departure from EMU rules. More positively, it focuses on new rather than old risks and is easier for new Member States to accommodate than hard legislation; it enables participants to draw on a wider range of experience and perspectives than is available to each one alone; it encourages policy-makers to adopt a long-term, problem-solving approach to employment and social issues rather than seeking quick results and haggling over perceived national interests; it facilitates initiatives in areas where EU competencies are weak and legal regulation is impracticable; and the process of joint monitoring and peer-review serves to motivate national governments and their social partners, while at the same time sensitizing them to national contexts and helping them to determine whether and how far policies pioneered in one country can be transposed to their own—what might be called *constructive* as opposed to *defensive* subsidiarity.

Originating in the 1990s when the European Council authorized the Commission to draw up guidelines for Member States to pursue national action plans aimed at combating unemployment, the OMC agenda has gradually been extended to the whole range of employment and social protection. Critics complain that the method is opaque and technocratic and that public awareness, media coverage, and parliamentary oversight are negligible. A more fundamental problem concerns the mission rather than the method of welfare reform. The new gospel takes no account of the 'new science' of happiness, as expounded by Layard (2005) and others. It conflates education with training; is obsessed with getting and spending; presumes that human beings and social institutions must adapt to the imperatives of economic growth and competitive prowess, not the other way round; takes it for granted that flexible labour markets, geographical labour mobility, and perpetual workplace reorganization are good for us; and more generally, fails to ask what makes us happy rather than what makes us rich. This critique hardly amounts to an alternative policy paradigm and certainly affords no grounds for complacency, but in a world where boundless growth and prodigal resource use cannot continue without breaching dangerous thresholds, it is likely to become increasingly pertinent.

Pension reform

Social pacts are particularly important in the field of pension reform, where change inevitably takes time and policy-makers have to contend with vested interests and institutional inertia. Retirement in the contemporary sense—an extended period of withdrawal from the labour market financed by savings or deferred earnings on a scale sufficient to make paid work unnecessary—used to be the privilege of the few. During the golden age, access was democratized. Retirement 'wealth' was still skewed in favour of those with higher lifetime earnings, women were still disadvantaged by the sexual division of labour, and a minority of pensioners still lived below the poverty line. Nevertheless, from about 1960 onwards, public policy in all the capitalist democracies ensured that a higher proportion of citizens than ever before could look forward to adequate and secure incomes at the end of their working lives.

The question is whether this achievement will be maintained in the decades ahead. Demographic and social trends have raised the cost of established pension schemes substantially. As a result of continued gains in life expectancy and declining fertility, the ratio of retirees to employees is set to rise steeply, while thanks to early retirement, whether voluntary or policy-induced, employment rates among men over the age of 55 have fallen steadily since the 1980s. In the future, moreover, the public budget is likely to have to bear a higher share of the wider costs of population ageing, for the fraction of the elderly most at risk of ill health and disability—those over the age of 80—is growing faster than the elderly population in general, while the capacity of the traditional pool of unpaid caregivers—wives, daughters, and daughters-in-law—is declining a result of rising female employment rates and the weakening of family ties.

Despite these pressures and despite the continued ascendancy of neo-liberal ideas, the post-war pensions settlement is unlikely to be reversed, for significant pension reform cannot be achieved without consensus among the relevant actors. Even the Bush administration which won re-election in 2004 promising to replace the federal, pay-as-you-go pension scheme by a privatized and pre-funded alternative, was forced to back down in the face of popular opposition. (In a *pay-as-you-go* system, current pensions are financed from current contributions and income is transferred from employees to retirees; in a *pre-funded system*, pooled contributions are invested in financial assets and individuals acquire entitlements in proportion to the size of their accumulated holdings. Retirement pensions in Western Europe are predominantly state-organized, insurance-based, and earnings-related. The main exception is the UK, where private pensions account for 40 per cent of pensioner income and the flat-rate component of the contributory state pension accounts for 90 per cent of public spending on pensions.)

Pension reform is a fraught and complex business and governments cannot hope to build a broad consensus for change unless they consult widely, cultivate allies, and take pains to explain and argue for their plans. In Sweden, for example, after the breakdown of institutionalized pay restraint in the 1980s and the financial crisis of the early 1990s, the pension system was radically overhauled. This would scarcely have been possible without cross-party agreement. On regaining office in 1994, the Social Democrats proceeded to implement the proposals of an all-party commission established by their 'bourgeois' predecessors. In Italy, it was the social partners who played a key role in persuading jobholders to accept the need for change. From 1992 onwards, with the public finances seemingly out of control and the post-war political order collapsing in the wake of corruption scandals, strong employer and trade union organizations helped to legitimize the efforts of 'technocratic' governments to reduce the public deficit, reinvent the republic, and reform a 'patriarchal' pension system that was neither financially sustainable nor morally defensible (Ferrera 1997; Pochet and Fajertag 2000).

A similar lesson can be drawn from the shifting and uncertain course of pension reform in the UK where social partnership remains the practice that dare not speak its name. Historically, the UK has relied on a de facto partnership between employers and the state. Voluntary occupational and personal pensions schemes buttress meagre contributory state pensions, which are topped up by means-tested pension credits, a device introduced by the New Labour government in a vain attempt to tackle the problem of pensioner poverty without discouraging private saving. After the collapse of the stock market boom in 2001, the government's declared intention of shifting the balance of provision towards private pensions began to look forlorn. Private companies started to cut back their pension plans, provoking charges that public sector workers are privileged by comparison. Meanwhile, the proportion of pensioners receiving means-tested benefits rose steadily and currently stands at 40 per cent. To investigate ways of promoting saving for retirement, the government appointed a Pensions Commission, chaired by Adair (Lord) Turner, a former director of the Confederation of British Industry.

Wisely, the commission chose to consider the pension system in the round, taking into account both state and private provision, and having shown that on current trends and policies the incomes of pensioners relative to the rest of society were set to fall, made five main recommendations. First, the state-pension age—already due to rise for women from 60 to 65, the current age for men, between 2010 and 2020—should be raised to 68 by 2050. Second, to ensure that more women qualify for a full state pension, the number of contributing years required to qualify should be reduced from thirty-nine to thirty. Third, there should be a new low-cost national pension saving scheme, in which workers would be automatically enrolled, but with the right to opt out. Fourth, if workers decide to stay in the scheme, as most are expected to do, employers should be obliged to contribute to it. And fifth, taxpayers' money should be used to enhance the basic state pension (BSP). Since 1980 the BSP has been uprated annually in line with prices rather than earnings. The commission called for the earnings link to be restored from 2010.

After months of haggling, a compromise was reached. In a White Paper published in May 2006, the government accepted the commission's main proposals and undertook to restore the earnings link by the end of the next parliament, though this commitment is subject to affordability and will not be implemented until 2012 at the earliest. Despite the delay, the final package offers a more coherent and far-sighted approach to pension reform than the government's previous essays in this field, which allowed tactical expediency to trump long-term strategy and made an already complex system even harder to understand and administer. However, neither the commission nor the government was prepared to countenance the idea of converting the BSP into a tax-financed citizen's pension, payable as of right to all legal residents over pension age and indexed to average earnings. A chance has thus been missed to start reforming the work–income nexus, the complex of unspoken conventions and formal rules that determine which activities count as 'work' and how entitlement to income is established.

The challenge facing rich societies is to engage with the problems of distributional conflict in a context where economic growth—the traditional remedy for material deprivation because it creates employment and boosts tax revenue—has ceased to promote personal happiness and is seriously damaging social cohesion and the natural environment. To meet this challenge, they need to start moving towards a social security system based on citizen's income (CI), as defined in section 8.2 above. Suppose CI were paid on a scale sufficient to enable people to live at the prevailing 'subsistence' level without participating in paid work. If it were feasible, such a *basic income*, as it is usually known, would have major benefits both for individuals and for society as a whole. It would avoid the standard problems of social insurance and social assistance and enhance personal freedom in the labour market; it would counter the prevailing bias in favour of paid employment and commodity production by subsidizing unpaid activities in the household and voluntary sectors; and it would establish an inclusive framework for balancing people's shared interests as citizens against the sectional interests that divide them.

But *would* it be feasible? Would people be willing to pay the requisite taxes, together with the psychic costs, if any, of knowing—or believing—that some people were living on their 'basic income' without doing any 'work'? No one really knows, but in societies where the public realm has become emaciated, tax aversion is normal, the puritan work ethic lingers on, and people habitually conflate 'work' with employment, it seems doubtful. In these circumstances, the responsible approach is to advocate partial, prefigurative reforms that sow the seeds of cultural change. With senior citizens guaranteed a basic income and junior citizens covered by enhanced child benefit, the way would lie open to tackle the problems of extending citizens' income to the population of working age. And once citizenship replaces employment as the pivot of the tax-transfer system, society will be in a better position to build a post-materialist civilization in which people are released from the treadmill of economic growth and acquire the capacity and desire to pursue life projects that do not depend on ever-rising levels of private consumption.

▓ DISCUSSION QUESTIONS

1. The writer Samuel Beckett is said to have urged actors performing his plays to 'fail again, fail better'. Might this injunction also be applied to the ideal of social citizenship and the institutions of the welfare state?

2. What does the experience of the EU teach us about the problems of social policy-making in a multilayered system of governance?

3. How are national governments and their social partners responding to the challenges facing contemporary welfare states? What, if anything, can the EU do to help them?

▓ REFERENCES

Arts, W. and Gelissen, J. (2002), 'Three Worlds of Welfare-Capitalism or More? A State-of-the-Art Report', *Journal of European Social Policy*, 12/2: 137–58.

Bartlett, W., Roberts, J. A., and Le Grand, J. (1998), *A Revolution in Social Policy: Quasi-Market Reform in the 1990s* (Bristol: Policy Press).

Bercusson, B. (1992), 'Maastricht: A Fundamental Change in European Labour Law', *Industrial Relations Journal*, 27/3: 177–90.

Brubaker, W. R. (1990), 'Immigration, Citizenship and the Nation-State in France and Germany', *International Sociology*, 5/4: 379–407.

Doyal, L. and Gough, I. (1991), *A Theory of Human Need* (Basingstoke: Macmillan).

Esping-Andersen, G. (1990), *The Three Worlds of Welfare-Capitalism* (Cambridge: Polity Press).

—— (1994), 'Welfare States and the Economy', in N. J. Smelser and R. Swedborg (eds.), *The Handbook of Economic Sociology* (Princeton: Princeton University Press), 711–32.

—— with Gallie, D., Hemerijck, A., and Myles, J. (2002), *Why We Need a New Welfare State* (Oxford: Oxford University Press).

Ferrera, M. (1997) 'The Uncertain Future of the Italian Welfare State', *West European Politics*, 20/1: 231–49.

—— (1998), 'The Four "Social Europes": Between Universalism and Selectivity', in M. Rhodes and Y. Meny (eds.), *The Future of European Welfare* (Basingstoke: Macmillan), 81–96.

Giddens, A. (1998), *The Third Way: The Renewal of Social Democracy* (Cambridge: Polity Press).

—— (2000), *The Third Way and its Critics* (Cambridge: Polity Press).

Hall, S. (2003), 'New Labour's Double Shuffle', *Soundings* 24 (Nov.): 10–24.

Hemerijck, A. (2002), 'The Self-Transformation of the European Social Models', in G. Esping-Andersen *et al.*, *Why We Need a New Welfare State* (Oxford: Oxford University Press), 173–213.

Keller, B. and Soerries, B. (1999), 'The New European Social Dialogue: Old Wine in New Bottles', *Journal of European Social Policy*, 9/2: 111–25.

Layard, R. (2005), *Happiness: Lessons from a New Science* (London: Allen Lane).

Leibfried, S. and Pierson, P. (1995), 'Multi-Tiered Institutions and the Making of Social Policy', in S. Leibfried and P. Pierson (eds.), *European Social Policy* (Washington, DC: Brookings Institution), 1–40.

Levy, J. D. (2000), 'France: Directing Adjustment?', in F. W. Scharpf and V. A. Schmidt (eds.), *Welfare and Work in the Open Economy, vol. II: Diverse Responses to Common Challenges* (Oxford: Oxford University Press), 308–46.

Manow, P. and Seils, E. (2000), 'Adjusting Badly: The German Welfare State, Structural Change and the Open Economy', in F. W. Scharpf and V. A. Schmidt (eds.), *Welfare and Work in the Open Economy, vol. II: Diverse Responses to Common Challenges* (Oxford: Oxford University Press), 264–307.

Marshall, T. H. (1950), *Citizenship and Social Class and Other Essays* (Cambridge: Cambridge University Press).

Meidner, R. (1993), 'Why Did the Swedish Model Fail?' in R. Miliband and L. Panitch (eds.), *Socialist Register 1993* (London: Merlin Press), 211–28.

Mishra, R. (1999), *Globalization and the Welfare State* (Cheltenham: Edward Elgar).

OECD (2003), *Social Expenditure Database* (Paris: OECD).

Pierson, C. (1998), *Beyond the Welfare State*, 2nd edn (Cambridge: Polity Press).

Pierson, P. (2001), 'Post-Industrial Pressures on Mature Welfare States', in P. Pierson (ed.), *The New Politics of the Welfare State* (Oxford: Oxford University Press), 80–104.

Pochet, P. and Fajertag, G. (2000), 'A New Era for Social Pacts in Europe', in G. Fajertag and P. Pochet (eds.), *Social Pacts in Europe: New Dynamics*, 2nd edn (Brussels: European Trade Union Institute and Observatoire Social Europeen), 9–40.

Purdy, D. (1994), 'Citizenship, Basic Income and the State', *New Left Review*, 208 (Nov.–Dec.): 30–48.

—— (2003), *Eurovision or American Dream? Britain, the Euro and the Future of Europe* (Edinburgh: Luath Press).

Rawls, J. (1972), *A Theory of Justice* (Oxford: Oxford University Press).

Rhodes, M. (2001), 'The Political Economy of Social Pacts: "Competitive Corporatism" and European Welfare Reform', in P. Pierson (ed.), *The New Politics of the Welfare State* (Oxford: Oxford University Press), 165–94.

Robertson, J., Dore, R., Van Parijs, P., and Atkinson, A. B. (1996), 'Debate: Citizen's Income', *Political Quarterly*, 67/1: 44–70.

Scharpf, F. W. (1997), 'European Integration, Democracy and the Welfare State', *Journal of European Public Policy*, 4/1: 18–36.

Sen, A. (1993), 'Capability and Well-Being', in M. Nussbaum and A. Sen (eds.), *The Quality of Life* (Oxford: Clarendon Press), 30–53.

Taylor-Gooby, P. (2004), 'New Risks and Social Change', in P. Taylor-Gooby (ed.), *New Risks, New Welfare: The Transformation of the European Welfare State* (Oxford: Oxford University Press), 1–28.

Van Parijs, P. (1995), *Real Freedom for All* (Oxford: Oxford University Press).

Visser, J. and Hemerijck, A. (1998), *A 'Dutch Miracle': Job Growth, Welfare Reform and Corporatism in the Netherlands* (Amsterdam: Amsterdam University Press).

Walker, R. (2005), *Social Security and Welfare: Concepts and Comparisons* (Maidenhead: Open University Press).

9 The Primacy of the Transatlantic Economy: The EU and the USA

Joseph Quinlan

Introduction

When the economic history of the late twentieth century is written, the globalization of economic activity will undoubtedly stand out as one of the defining precepts of the time. The past decade and a half has been a time of buoyant global trade and robust global capital flows, helped in large part by the inclusion of various nations and regions of the world long on the fringes of the global economy.

Globalization's return heralded the opening of new and untapped markets in Central Europe, Latin America, and the Indian subcontinent. Free market reforms have been the mantra of Poland, Hungary, Brazil, India, and a host of emerging markets for over a decade. At the heart of these reforms are initiatives to promote external trade and investment linkages, thereby integrating more companies, more workers, and more consumers into the global economy. Falling telecommunication and transportation costs, or the 'death of distance', has helped drive this process, giving global firms greater access to new consumers, new resources, and new opportunities to grow sales and revenues.

Yet despite all the hype associated with globalization—or the growing economic interdependence of nations through the increasing volume and variety of cross-border transactions in goods and services—and notwithstanding all the excitement surrounding the emerging markets, notably China, one of the core features of the global economic landscape over the past decade has been the increasing integration and cohesion of the transatlantic economy. The latter remains the most powerful global economic entity in the world owing to the transatlantic convergence in such key areas as industry deregulation (media, energy, and telecoms), technology usage, and financial market liberalization. Bolstered by these dynamics, the majority of US and European foreign investments flows are directed towards each other, rather than to low-cost developing nations.

The primary aim of this chapter is to show that it has been the transatlantic economy that has been at the forefront of globalization. The following pages will offer a clearer picture of the deep integrating forces binding the transatlantic economy together and underscore the following critical point: while exports and imports (a shallow form of integration) are the most common measures of cross-border activity between two nations,

foreign direct investment (a deeper form of integration) and the activities of foreign affiliates are the critical integrating forces of the global economy. Foreign direct investment
and foreign affiliate sales—not trade—drive transatlantic commerce.

9.1 The role of multinationals

Global money managers are considered among the most powerful players on the world
economic stage, and with good reason. With their ability to shift billions of dollars in and
out of various countries each day, global traders can be either a blessing or a curse for a
particular economy. But the world's moneymen share the global stage with an equally, if
not more, influential group of players—global multinationals.

For our purposes, a global multinational is a firm that takes a global approach to foreign
markets and production. The United Nations prefers the term 'transnationals', although
this definition includes firms owned and managed by nationals in different countries
(Royal Dutch Shell, for instance). For purposes of clarity, we prefer to use the multinational
designation in speaking about the global spread of production and service activities.

It has been multinationals, with their far-flung production networks, at the forefront
of globalization, changing the global map of growth, production, and trade. While the
investment of global money managers is often footloose and fickle, multinational investment is more strategic and long term. The latter represents not only a source of capital but
also a source of technology, managerial skills, employment, exports, and other critical
inputs to growth for the host country. While it is difficult to quantify the magnitude of
multinationals, broad macro indicators from the United Nations shed some light on the
global influence of these firms.

Table 9.1 summarizes the global might of multinationals and their affiliates. As of 2004,
the multinational universe included some 70,000 parent firms, with roughly 700,000
foreign affiliates. The comparable figures were 37,000 and 170,000, respectively, in 1990.
The stock of foreign direct investment (FDI), a broad measure of the capital component
of international production, totalled $8.9 trillion in 2004, up from $1.7 trillion in 1990
and just $480 billion in 1980. Sales by foreign affiliates, a measure of the revenues gener-
ated by international production, reached $18.7 trillion in 2004, some 70 per cent greater
than world exports. The large spread between affiliate sales and trade underscores the
point that the production of foreign affiliates easily surpasses trade as the primary mode
by which transnationals deliver goods and services to foreign customers.

The gross product (value added) of foreign affiliates totalled $3.7 trillion in 2004, about
one-tenth of global GDP, compared with 5 per cent in 1982. Exports of affiliates tallied
$3.7 trillion, one-third of the global total. Finally, in terms of employment, foreign affili-
ates employed more than 57 million workers in 2004, more than double the level of 1990
(24.5 million). Taking these figures into account, it is rather clear that multinationals play
a dominant role in the world economy.

What is more, the largest multinationals remain geographically concentrated in just
a handful of countries. In 2004, for instance, just five nations—the United States, Japan,
Germany, France, and the United Kingdom—accounted for seventy-one of the top

Table 9.1 Selected indicators of FDI and international production, 1982–2004

Item	Value at current prices (billions of dollars)			
	1982	1990	2003	2004
FDI inflows	59	208	633	648
FDI outflows	27	239	617	730
FDI inward stock	628	1,769	7,987	8,902
FDI outward stock	601	1,785	8,731	9,732
Cross-border M&As[a]		151	297	381
Sales of foreign affiliates	2,765	5,727	16,963	18,677
Gross product of foreign affiliates	647	1,476	3,573	3,911
Total assets of foreign affiliates	2,113	5,937	32,186	36,008
Exports of foreign affiliates	730	1,498	3,073	3,690
Employment of foreign affiliates (thousands)	19,579	24,471	53,196	57,394

[a] Data are available only from 1987 onward.
Source: UNCTAD, based on its FDI/TNC database (www.unctad.org/fdi statistics)

hundred largest global firms. The United States dominated the list with twenty-five firms, while the European Union alone accounted for fifty. Multinationals from Japan, the third pillar of the global 'triad' of developed nations, totalled nine on the list. More multinationals have emerged from the developing nations, although the world's largest companies—among the key drivers of global economic activity—are based in the developed nations.

Motivations for investing overseas

There is no simple reason behind the global dispersion of multinational activities. The motivations for investing abroad are diverse and complex, and are constantly shifting as a result of prevailing macro- and microeconomics variables, as well as institutional factors. The one constant is that firms venture overseas to enhance their overall competitive position. What motivates firms to invest overseas can be broadly grouped into four types of foreign direct investment.

Resource seekers

As the label implies, resource seekers prowl the world for resources, be they raw materials, semi-skilled labour, or highly trained workers. The motivation of resource-seeking investment is to acquire a specific resource that is either unavailable or in short supply in the home market. The world's top energy and mining firms are one such group of resource seekers, with the recent spike in world commodity prices triggering a rise in foreign investment in countries rich in natural resources. Consumer electronics manufacturers, textile firms, and other companies seeking cheap, semi-skilled labour represent a second group of resource seekers.

Market seekers

The strategic objective of market seekers is either to exploit new market opportunities in a particular country or to protect an existing market presence or position established via exports or other means. Market size and prospects for growth along with per capita income in the host nation are critical factors in the market-seeking investment decisions of multinationals. Import barriers and discriminatory government policies that mandate a local presence are also important. The advantage of market-seeking investment is that local production brings closer proximity to end markets, allowing firms quickly and accurately to adjust products to local tastes and trends. In addition, market seekers become closer not only to their customers but also to their competitors.

Efficiency seekers

Efficiency seekers aim to rationalize an existing structure in such a way as to gain economies of scale and scope. According to John Dunning (1993, p. 58), a leading theorist of transnationals and foreign direct investment flows, efficiency-seeking foreign direct investment takes two principal forms:

The first is that designed to take advantage of differences in the availability and cost of traditional factor endowments in different countries . . . The second kind of efficiency-seeking investments is that which takes place in countries with broadly similar economic structures and income levels and is designed to take advantage of the economies of scale and scope, and of the differences in consumer tastes and supply capabilities.

An example of the first type of investment is rising US technology investment in Ireland, with firms like Intel and Microsoft leveraging low-cost, English-speaking technology workers to their competitive advantage. An example of the second is Wal-Mart's foray into the massive markets of Germany and the United Kingdom, a strategy designed to tap into the wealthy markets of two of Europe's largest economies. In general, Europe's steady march towards economic integration over the past half century has given US firms greater opportunities and scope for increased efficiencies and rationalization.

Strategic asset seekers

Of all the motives underlying foreign direct investment over the past fifteen years, strategic asset seeking is among the most prominent. The intent of the strategic asset seeker is to add to the firm's existing portfolio of assets in a manner that bolsters and buttresses the firm's core competitive advantage. Gaining access to marketing networks, managerial skills, innovation production techniques, and strategic distribution chains are critical objectives. Gathering intangible assets is equally as important. What counts is the availability and accessibility of intangible assets or, in the jargon of the United Nations, 'created assets'. The latter are both tangible (communications infrastructure, educational standards, intellectual capital) and intangibles (attitudes towards wealth creation, the prevailing business culture, managerial competencies). The common denominator is knowledge, which has helped concentrate global foreign direct investment in the knowledge-based, advanced industrialized nations, namely the United States and Europe.

Table 9.2 Selected variables influencing the motives of transnational corporations

Type of FDI	Economic determinants of host country
Resource seeking	• availability of raw materials
	• physical infrastructure (ports, roads, power, telecommunications)
	• labour–skilled and unskilled
	• availability of local partners jointly to promote knowledge and/or capital-intensive resource exploitations
	• government restrictions and investment incentives
Market seeking	• market size and per capita income
	• adjacent regional markets (NAFTA, EU, etc.)
	• market growth
	• government policies
	• quality of material and local infrastructure
	• customer preferences; demographics
Efficiency seeking	• cost of resources and related production-cost variables (labour, materials)
	• presence and competitiveness of related firms: e.g. leading industrial suppliers
	• availability of local service support facilities; quality of infrastructure; degree of educated workforce; and other specialized factors: e.g. science and industrial parks
	• membership in regional integration schemes conducive to the establishment of regional corporate networks
Strategic asset seeking	• availability of knowledge-based assets
	• availability of a pool of skilled labour
	• business culture, entrepreneurial class, managerial competencies
	• risk capital

Source: UNCTAD (1998: 91).

Strategic drivers of foreign direct investment

A number of structural forces have facilitated the way in which firms have established cross-border operations over the decade. In particular, enabling technologies related to transportation and communications have been critical in allowing firms to unbundle production and service activities around the world, resulting in the global dispersion of various economic activities. Because of technological advances, firms now have the wherewithal effectively and confidently to manage far-flung operations that used to be more isolated than integrated. Advanced technology has enabled firms to process, interpret, and disseminate information faster and cheaper anywhere in the world. It has also allowed firms to slice up their global production chains, or transfer various service functions to any place in the world, creating an international division of labour the world economy has never experienced before.

More liberal government policies towards trade, investment, and capital flows have also promoted greater global foreign direct investment. Except for a few reluctant holdouts, the general bias of most governments has been towards trade reform, the promotion of inward foreign direct investment, privatization of various state assets, and reduced capital controls. According to the United Nations (UNCTAD 2005, p. 22), of 271 changes to foreign direct investment regulations in 2004, 235, or nearly 87 per cent, involved steps to open up new areas for foreign investors. In addition, more than twenty nations lowered their corporate incomes taxes in 2004, while the number of bilateral investment treaties and double taxation treaties reached 2,392 and 2,559, respectively, in 2004. Figures for 2004 are representative of the past decade and a half.

Finally, rising levels of foreign direct investment have been driven in part by the actions and strategies of multinationals themselves. Sustaining long-term profitability is a strategic prerequisite of any company, which increasingly entails the global utilization of resources. Firms must go where the skilled labour is located or to markets that have the appropriate technology or critical attributes they desire. Many firms have had to shift labour-intensive production to low-wage areas in order to remain competitive. Rising costs of research and development, coupled with shrinking product cycles, mandate that firms search for more markets, new workers, and pool their competencies with other firms around the world.

9.2 Globalization's return: how the transatlantic economy led globalization

'Globalization' has become an overused term that conveys the impression that the world economy is rapidly becoming one seamless market, aided and abetted by unfettered cross-border movement of goods, capital, and people. Reality is different, however. While global integration has increased over the past decade, and various regions have become more commercially linked, globalization remains tremendously uneven. The level of globalization is deepest between some regions—like the USA and Europe—and shallow between others, Europe and Asia, for instance. In other cases, like Japan, globalization has been relatively asymmetrical—with Japan a key provider or source of global foreign direct investment, yet a minor recipient of foreign capital from multinationals.

The developed nations remain the main sources and destinations of global foreign direct investment. In other words, global investment flows are more 'developed to developed' in nature than 'developed to developing nations'. Numerous economic similarities —in education, per capita incomes, demographics, infrastructure development, technology usage—along with converging macro- and microeconomic policies in the United States, Europe, and to a lesser extent, Japan, have driven global foreign investment flows towards the developed nations, or so-called 'triad' powers. The latter is where the major markets are; it is where the competitive threat comes from; and it is where new technologies are likely to originate. In addition, firms in the developed nations, as opposed to companies from the developing nations, are apt to have the resources (capital, technology) and managerial experience that enable them to invest overseas.

As highlighted in Figure 9.1, global foreign direct investment inflows have long been biased towards the developed nations, notably the United States and Europe. During the

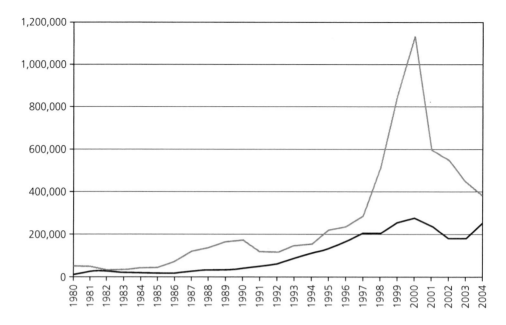

Figure 9.1 FDI inflows: developed v. developing nations, 1980–2004 (millions of US dollars)
Source: UNCTAD 2005.

1990s, for instance, just over 60 per cent of total foreign investment inflows were directed at the developed nations in general, with the United States and the European Union, in particular, accounting for 22.1 per cent and 37.2 per cent, respectively, of the global total.

Among the developed nations, Japan has been an outlier in terms of attracting foreign direct investment. While a significant source of global foreign direct investment, Japan's share of inward foreign investment flows has long lagged behind the United States and Europe. In 2004, for instance, Japan's share of inward foreign direct investment stock as a percentage of the total among the developed nations was less than 1.5 per cent. The relatively low figure reflects both cyclical and structural variables, including Japan's prolonged economic slump of the 1990s, which diminished multinational interest in Japan, and structural and cultural barriers which made it very difficult for foreign multinationals to penetrate the Japanese market. Lately, a rebound in economic growth, combined with market liberalization efforts in Japan, have made the world's second largest economy more attractive to foreign investors, although Japan continues to lag behind the USA and Europe in terms of attracting foreign direct investment inflows.

Meanwhile, the developing nations attracted roughly one-third of global foreign direct investment on average during the 1990–9 period. When China is excluded from the figures, the developing nations' share of global investment inflows drops to just one-quarter of the total.

During the first half of this decade (2000–4), the share of foreign direct investment inflows to the developing nations continued to decline, falling to less than 29 per cent of the total. Excluding China, the developing nations' share of global investment inflows fell to roughly 21 per cent, a much smaller share than is commonly assumed given the widespread perception that transnationals are keen on departing the high-wage developed nations for low-cost destinations in Latin America, Asia, and Central Europe, which has led to myriad fears in the United States, Europe, and Japan about the 'hollowing-out' effect and to the recent political backlash against outsourcing of various service activities.

Many of these fears are not unfounded. Multinationals have increased their productive capacity in the developing nations over the past decade, notably to China, Mexico, and a handful of other nations. On the whole, however, there remain numerous impediments to investing in the developing nations, with an underdeveloped infrastructure—that is, poor roads, inadequate power supplies, the lack of clean water, telecommunication shortfalls—chief among them. Another impediment lies in the sheer number of people living in poverty in the developing nations. The plight of the poor is best illustrated by the fact that some 1.3 billion people, according to the United Nations, still live on less than a dollar a day; that equates to nearly a quarter of the global population that is practically off limits to transnationals. As part of this dynamic, growing income inequalities in many key developing nations are leaving many potential workers and consumers behind. Impressive growth figures in China, for instance, mask huge inequalities and social tensions between urban rich and rural poor. Indeed, urban incomes in China are more than three times greater than the incomes earned in rural areas. In Russia, meanwhile, the richest 10 per cent now earn twenty-three times more than the poorest 10 per cent. At the micro-level, the absence of intellectual property rights, restrictive distribution rights, the lack of transparency, diverging industry standards—all of these variables have impaired and inhibited foreign direct investment flows to the developing nations.

In contrast, most developed nations enjoy good infrastructures, adhere to strong property rights, advocate relatively open trade regimes, possess innovative technological capabilities, encourage high levels of general education, thrive on efficient capital markets, and operate within legal frameworks that are equitable and transparent. Many of these fundamental building blocks are either missing or incomplete in many developing nations, helping to skew foreign direct investment towards the developed nations.

The transatlantic bonds grow stronger, not weaker

The investment options for transnationals from the United States and Europe have never been as large and geographically diverse as in the past decade and a half. Market liberalization measures in India, robust economic growth in China, the economic revival of Central Europe, sweeping privatization measures in Latin America—emerging market prospects, in general, have never looked as promising for the world's global corporate leaders.

American companies invested more capital overseas in the 1990s—in excess of $750 billion—than in the prior four decades combined. But the surge in US foreign investment did not flow to the developing nations for many of the reasons just cited. Rather, the majority of US foreign direct investment in the 1990s, and the first half of this decade, was directed at Europe.

By country, the bulk of US overseas investment in the 1990s was concentrated in the market most similar to the United States—the United Kingdom. The UK accounted for nearly 22 per cent of total US FDI outflows (on a cumulative basis) in the 1990s. To put that number into perspective, the amount of US investment in the United Kingdom in the 1990–9 period ($175 billion) was nearly 50 per cent larger than the total invested in the entire Asia-Pacific region. Additionally, despite all the talk about US investment flows to Mexico courtesy of the North American Free Trade Agreement (NAFTA), US firms ploughed nearly twice as much capital into the Netherlands in the 1990s as they sank into Mexico. Of the top ten destinations of US investments in the 1990s, five countries were in Europe—the United Kingdom (ranked number 1), the Netherlands (3), Switzerland (6), Germany (7), and France (8). Rounding out the top ten were Canada (2), Brazil (4), Mexico (5), Australia (9), and Japan (10).

In the first half of this decade (2000–4), six countries in Europe were among the top ten destinations of US foreign investment. The United Kingdom ranked first again, followed by Canada (2), the Netherlands (3), Switzerland (4), Mexico (5), Ireland (6), Germany (7), Singapore (8), Japan (9), and Italy (10). US investment stakes in Europe have expanded sharply this decade, with Europe attracting nearly 56 per cent of total US foreign direct investment in the first half of the decade. The bias towards Europe runs counter to the hype and angst associated with US outsourcing to such low-cost locales like China and India, and the common belief that it is the low-cost destinations of East Asia that have attracted the bulk of US investment.

US foreign direct investment to China and India has jumped dramatically this decade, notably to China. Total US investment to China, for instance, surged to nearly $11 billion (on a cumulative basis) in the first half of this decade, nearly double US flows to China in the second half of the 1990s. That represents a dramatic rise, although on a comparative basis, US investment in Ireland over the same period ($36 billion) was three times larger. By the same token, while US foreign investment to India doubled in the first half of this decade, to $2.5 billion, US firms ploughed more capital into such smaller European economies like Norway ($3 billion), Denmark ($5 billion), and Belgium ($6 billion) over the same period.

The discrepancy in US investment flows to Ireland, Denmark, and other European nations on the one hand, versus US investment in China and India on the other, reflects many of the impediments to inflows to the developing nations discussed above. Meanwhile, the attraction of Ireland lies with its low-cost, English-speaking labour force, first-class infrastructure, and access to the larger European Union market. US firms have been drawn to Denmark on account of its technological skills, to Norway because of its natural resources, and to Belgium for a variety of reasons, including its world-class infrastructure, access to the EU market, and Brussels' position as the centre of political power within the European Union. In contrast, securing an investment stake in India and China, while attractive on paper, is a much more laborious process, requiring more time, due diligence, and investment capital on account of the many deficiencies still plaguing both nations.

Europe's investment bias towards the United States

The collapse of the Berlin Wall and the demise of Communism opened new markets right in the backyard of Western Europe, and not unexpectedly European transnationals jumped at the opportunity. Europe's leading firms ploughed billions into Hungary, Poland, and the Czech Republic during the 1990s, drawn by the region's cheap labour, raw materials, and new market opportunities. Late in the decade, the prospects of EU enlargement sustained healthy investment inflows to Central Europe.

Yet, despite Western Europe's investment push into Central Europe in the 1990s, the amount of capital sunk in such places as Hungary, Poland, and others pales in comparison to the amount of capital sent across the Atlantic over the same period. After averaging $22.2 billion in the first half of the 1990s, foreign direct investment inflows to the US from Europe soared to an annual average of nearly $110 billion in the second half of the decade, marking one of the most explosive periods of inward foreign investment in US history. For the entire decade, European firms sank nearly $660 billion into the United States, accounting for roughly three-quarters of total US investment inflows in the 1990s. European investors accounted for a similar percentage again in the first half of this decade, with the United Kingdom, Switzerland, and France ranked as the top three foreign investors in the USA over the 2000–4 period.

Many variables lie behind the large and expanding European investment stakes in the United States. As the largest and wealthiest market in the world, the US is considered too important to neglect. As Krish Prabhu, chief operating officer of Alcatel at the time, put it to the *Financial Times*, 'So much of company strategy is driven out of the United States today. No serious player can afford not to have a presence there' (3 Sept. 1999, p. 6). In addition to market access, many European firms have entered the USA to obtain US technological capabilities, or so-called 'created assets'. Other firms have crossed the Atlantic to gain greater market access in US services sectors like utilities, financial services, and telecommunications. Indeed, greater service linkages between the United States and Europe have been at the heart of greater transatlantic deepening.

Deeper transatlantic convergence through services

Cross-border investment in services has been behind the surge in transatlantic investment during the past decade and a half. Once national in character, various service activities in the United States and Europe have been fused and are now more transatlantic in nature. Functions that were once considered non-tradable (data processing, education, medical services) are now being traded regularly. Activities long classified as domestic endeavours (advertising, legal services, consulting) today easily take place across borders. And industries in both the USA and Europe that were once the domain of the public sector (telecommunications, insurance, electric utilities) have been privatized and opened to foreign competition. Both the European Union and Switzerland opened and deregulated their telecommunications markets at the start of 1998, which came on the heels of industry deregulation in such sectors as utilities, insurance, and financial services.

Many of these national efforts to liberalize service activities in both the USA and Europe were encouraged and advanced in part by supporting multilateral trade agreements. The General Agreement on Trade in Services (GATS), for instance, was chief among them. The agreement, reached in 1995, was the first multilateral deal to provide enforceable rights covering trade and investment in the services sector. Meanwhile, under the auspices of the World Trade Organization, GATS and two other seminal multilateral deals—the Information Technology Agreement (ITA) and the Basic Telecommunications Agreement—were concluded in the second half of the 1990s. The ITA helped eliminate tariffs on a range of information technology products and promote trade in computer hardware, software, and semiconductor manufacturing equipment and other products. The Basic Telecommunications Agreement, meanwhile, was the first multilateral tele-communications trade package ever reached and was signed by sixty-nine nations, which accounted for more than 90 per cent of world telecom revenue. In particular, the agreement paved the way for more foreign investment and participation in telecom-munications services and facilities in both the United States and Europe. In general, the Information Technology and Basic Telecommunications agreements helped construct an information highway linking the United States with Europe.

Yet another critical element promoting more transatlantic service linkages was the European Union's Single Market Programme, announced in the second half of the 1980s and implemented in the early 1990s. The programme triggered a wave of EU-wide restructuring and deregulation of services, fostering greater US foreign investment in ser-vices across Europe. Intra-EU services investment also rose as the single market was im-plemented. This helped create even larger and more competitive European service giants that ultimately targeted the United States as a primary source of growth in the late 1990s.

Transatlantic service investment in such sectors as electricity, telecommunications, water, and various business services (like advertising and legal services) soared during the 1990s, with mergers and acquisitions the most widely used mode of entry by trans-nationals. Indeed, massive deal-making between the service giants of the transatlantic economy fuelled the global boom in M&A in the second half of the 1990s. According to the United Nations, 'On average, more than three-quarters of global M&A transactions in the services sector took place among developed countries during 1987–2003. Intra-Western Europe transactions (the bulk of which comprise intra-EU transactions) and transatlantic transactions dominated the picture' (UNCTAD 2004: 111). Led by US and European service leaders, services accounted for sixty-four deals among the top hundred cross-border M&A deals in the 1996–2003 period, versus thirty-six deals of the top hundred in the 1987–95 timeframe. Looked at another way, roughly three-quarters of US foreign investment to Europe in the first half of this decade was in service activities; meanwhile, services accounted for nearly 80 per cent of total European investment in the USA during the same period.

Cross-border investment in various service activities has been bolstered by treaties signed under the aegis of the World Trade Organization. The Telecommunications Agreement, the Information Technology Agreement, and the Financial Services Agreement —all were reached in 1997, opening various service-based activities in telecommunica-tions, information technology, and financial services for multinationals around the world. The agreements came into effect at the end of the decade and have subsequently underpinned robust levels of transatlantic cross-border foreign direct investment in telecommunications, software, semiconductors, scientific instruments, banking, insur-ance, and the securities market.

As the world's leading trade entities, the United States and Europe have a substantial interest in the effectiveness of the World Trade Organization (WTO). However, when it comes to the WTO being a multilateral dispute settlement body, whose rulings are con-sidered binding, the United States and Europe have tended to disregard WTO rulings in many high-profile cases, calling into question the overall effectiveness of the organization.

For example, even though the WTO has ruled that the EU has violated trade rules by refusing the sale of genetically modified foods in Europe, and has ruled that US tax incentives on export income are illegal, both parties have refused to yield to the WTO and have generally disregarded the WTO rulings. Other areas of non-compliance exist, which has made it more difficult for the United States and Europe to push ahead with bilateral trade negotiations. Ongoing transatlantic trade disputes have also made it more difficult to conclude the Doha Round of multilateral trade negotiations. Just as USA–Europe leadership was key in launching the Doha Development Agenda in Qatar in November 2001, so transatlantic leadership is critical in bringing the Doha Round to a successful conclusion.

9.3 Beyond trade: key metrics of transatlantic integration

Conventional analysis of cross-border commerce centres on trade flows, although this trade-only mentality misses and overlooks the strategic role played by foreign affiliates in driving global economic activity. This is particularly true of the transatlantic economy since foreign direct investment and the activities of foreign affiliates represent the commercial backbone of the transatlantic economy. The following metrics, rarely used to analyse bilateral relations, offer a more complete and magnified picture of the transatlantic economy. After examining the following five variables, a clearer picture of the transatlantic economy emerges.

Gross product of foreign affiliates

Foreign affiliates are among the world's top producers of goods and services, with US and European affiliates at the forefront. The total output of US majority-owned foreign affiliates in Europe ($399 billion in 2003) and of European affiliates in the United States ($319 billion) is greater than the total gross output of most nations. On a global basis, the aggregate output of US foreign affiliates topped $700 billion in 2003, with Europe accounting for nearly 57 per cent of the total. The presence of US affiliates in some European nations is particularly noteworthy. The gross output of US affiliates in Ireland, for instance, represented nearly 19 per cent of Ireland's total GDP in 2003. In the United States, European affiliates are major economic producers in their own right. British firms are particularly important—their US output totalled more than $95 billion in 2003. Output from German affiliates totalled $63 billion in the same year, while output from French affiliates was in excess of $41 billion.

Overseas assets of foreign affiliates

Overseas assets of affiliates provide a clear metric to the extent and level of integration between two economies. On that basis, US affiliate assets in Germany—some $366 billion in 2003—were greater than total US assets in all of South America in 2003. In the same year, America's corporate assets in the United Kingdom ($1.8 trillion) exceeded total US assets in the entire Asia-Pacific region. The bulk of US affiliate assets are sunk in the region where US foreign investment roots are deepest—Europe. Roughly 62 per cent of US affiliate assets were located in Europe in 2003. European firms held some $3.9 trillion in US assets in 2003, roughly 75 per cent of total foreign assets in the United States.

Affiliate employment

Conventional wisdom holds that the bulk of corporate America's overseas workforce toils in low-wage nations like Mexico and China. However, most foreigners employed by US affiliates are employed in the industrialized nations, predominantly Europe. US firms employed 4.2 million workers in Europe in 2003, or 42 per cent of the global total. The European workforce of US majority-owned foreign affiliates is almost evenly split between manufacturing and services workers: though the number of manufacturing workers in Europe has levelled off in recent years, US firms still employed roughly 1.9 million of these in 2003. The manufacturing workforce of US affiliates in Germany alone totalled 361,000 in 2003, nearly two-thirds larger than the number of manufacturing workers employed by US firms in China. The employment difference underscores the fact that US multinationals are more interested in leveraging skilled and productive (and therefore more expensive) labour, as opposed to cheap or semi-skilled labour. The same is true of European firms. Despite evidence of European companies leveraging cheaper labour in Central Europe or Asia, most workers employed by European foreign affiliates are in the United States. European majority-owned foreign affiliates directly employed roughly 3.7 million American workers in 2003.

Foreign affiliate sales

Only by analysing foreign affiliate sales does one start to realize the depth of the transatlantic commercial relationship. Where total transatlantic trade amounted to roughly $585 billion in 2003, total transatlantic foreign affiliate sales tallied some $2.5 trillion, more than four times the level of trade. Table 9.3 takes a closer look at the trade versus

Table 9.3 Foreign affiliate sales v. trade, 2003

$ billions	Foreign affiliate sales v. trade
European sales of US-owned affiliates	1545.7
US exports to Europe (G&S)	290.7
German sales of US-owned affiliates	250.4
US exports to Germany	45.7
US sales of European-owned affiliates	1059.5
US imports from Europe (G&S)	385.7
US sales of French-owned affiliates	155.8
US imports from France	31.6

Source: US Department of Commerce, Bureau of Economic Analysis; International Monetary Fund.

affiliate sales comparison by country and region. Note first that US affiliate sales in Europe —$1.3 trillion in 2003—were more than five times greater total US exports; similarly, European affiliate sales in the USA in 2003 ($1.1 trillion) were more than three times US imports from Europe in the same year. By country, the difference between foreign affiliate sales and trade is substantial. French affiliates sales in the United States, for example, were four times greater than US imports from France in 2003. Likewise, US exports to Germany ($46 billion) pale in comparison with US foreign affiliates sales of more than $220 billion. On a global basis, US foreign affiliate sales hit a record $3.4 trillion in 2003, with Europe accounting for half of the total. Sales of US affiliates in Europe were more than double the comparable figures for the Asia-Pacific region. In the end, the key point to remember is that foreign affiliate sales paint a radically different picture of US–Europe commercial linkages from that given by trade.

Foreign affiliate profits

As transatlantic investment linkages have grown during the past decade, so has the importance of the United States and Europe to the bottom line of multinationals on both sides of the ocean. Europe remains the most important region in the world for corporate America when it comes to corporate earnings outside the USA. Similarly, beyond the European Union, the USA is the most important market in the world for European multinationals. In the first half of this decade, Europe accounted for nearly 55 per cent of total US foreign affiliate income, a proxy for global earnings. Corporate America's earnings in Europe were double those in Asia and triple those with NAFTA partners, Mexico and Canada. Meanwhile, given strong real growth in the United States over the past few years, the USA has been a key source of earnings for many European multinationals, offsetting weak growth and earnings in the EU.

Case study—the US recession of 2001 and the effect on the European Union

Trade statistics remain the standard benchmark by which countries measure cross-border commerce. Yet nothing better illustrates the limits of such figures than the US economic recession of 2001 and the widely held belief at the time that Europe, given its limited trade linkages to the United States, was 'immune' to economic problems in the USA.

Not surprisingly, as the US economy decelerated over the course of 2001, America's major trading partners felt the pain, reinforcing the saying 'that when the USA sneezes, the rest of the world catches a cold'. Exporters in Asia and Latin America did catch a cold, with exports falling across both regions, depressing aggregate growth in many export-dependent economies. America's partners in NAFTA, Mexico and Canada, were notably exposed given that their exports to the USA accounted for more than 25 per cent, respectively, of GDP.

Europe was not spared the US recession of 2001 either, but because of Europe's comparatively low level of trade exposure to the USA, many believed Europe was in better shape than other regions to weather the US downturn.

Based on US exports as a percentage of GDP, Europe was hardly in the same league as either Mexico or Canada, with the USA accounting for just 2.2 per cent of total output of the Eurozone. By country, the percentages for Germany, Italy, and Switzerland were 2.6 per cent, 1.9 per cent, and 3.8 per cent, respectively. French exports to the USA as a percentage of GDP were even less—just 1.7 per cent. For the United Kingdom, the figure was higher at 3.3 per cent, but nothing to be overly alarmed about. The lower the percentage, the greater the degree of immunity from a US economic slowdown—or so it seemed.

A trade-only analysis of US–European commercial linkages overlooked the massive investment presence of European firms in the USA. It ignored the fact that Atlantic economic linkages are rooted in foreign direct investment, with trade playing more of a secondary role to investment. As such, the US recession of 2001 was transmitted to Europe not only via the traditional channels of trade, but also through European foreign affiliates operating in the USA. Just as US corporate earnings started to slide over the second half of the 2000, so did the profits of many USA-based European affiliates. Affiliate income earned by European foreign affiliates in the USA fell 4.4 per cent in the second half of 2000 from the same period a year before; the following year the earnings squeeze intensified. German affiliates in the USA actually posted losses in excess of $6 billion in 2001, while Dutch affiliates suffered a 5.1 per cent dive in US affiliate earnings.

All totalled, European affiliates saw their earnings in the USA plunge by 36 per cent in 2001. In turn, deteriorating earnings growth in the USA translated into deteriorating earnings and business conditions for numerous European multinationals back home. Many firms suddenly found themselves saddled with large debt levels, negative rates of return from the USA, and plunging share prices. The level of trade with the United States decelerated as demand in that country slowed. Subsequently, many companies were forced to slash capital spending and employment levels at home and abroad. Consumer confidence in Europe, not surprisingly, fell alongside sagging business confidence, helping to depress real economic growth across Europe. In short, far from being immune to a US economic recession, Europe—via trade and investment linkages—was just as exposed to the US economic conditions as were other regions in the world.

The key point is this: as a yardstick of US–European linkages, foreign affiliate sales reveal a sharply different picture from a trade-only analysis. As nations and regions become more bound together by foreign direct investment, new metrics are needed to measure cross-border linkages.

9.4 The role of related party trade

Given the linear sequence of how companies typically become involved in global markets —exporting first, and then investing locally on a step-by-step basis later—foreign direct investment is often viewed as a substitute for trade. The underlying assumption is that a rise in outward foreign direct investment invariably leads to a corresponding decline in exports of the home country, precipitating a fall in employment and balance of payment pressures. Again, reality is far more complex.

Table 9.4 US related-party trade statistics, 2004

	US imports: 'Related-party trade' as % of total	US exports: 'Related-party trade' as % of total
European Union	57.9	30.4
France	48.9	31.8
Germany	62.1	32.2
Netherlands	53.3	35.9
United Kingdom	58.5	27.7
Other European Union	47.0	27.5

Source: US Department of Commerce, US Census Bureau, Related Party Trade, 2004

While foreign affiliate sales, as opposed to cross-border trade, are the primary means by which transatlantic commerce is conducted, both modes of delivery—affiliate sales and trade—should not be viewed independently of each other. They are more complements than substitutes, since foreign direct investment and foreign affiliate sales increasingly drive and determine trade flows.

A substantial share of transatlantic trade is classified as intra-firm trade or related-party trade, which is cross-border trade that stays within the ambit of the company—for instance, when Siemens of Germany sends parts and components to Siemens of North Carolina, when Dupont of the USA sends a speciality chemical to its affiliate in the Netherlands, or when Michelin of France sends intermediate parts to its foreign affiliate in the Greater Cincinnati area. This type of trade is evident among nations and regions with deep, investment-led linkages, which defines the transatlantic economy. Accordingly, roughly 58 per cent of US imports from the European Union consisted of related-party trade in 2004. The percentage was even higher in the case of Ireland (89.3 per cent) and Germany (66 per cent). Meanwhile, roughly 30 per cent of US exports to Europe in 2004 represented related-party trade.

Against this backdrop, it is hardly surprising that the three-year slide of the US dollar against the Euro has done little to correct America's trade deficit with Europe. From the start of 2002 to the end of 2004, the greenback depreciated by more than 30 per cent against the Euro. Following such a large shift in prices or exchange rates, standard macroeconomic theory would have predicted US export growth to outstrip US import growth, leading to an improvement in the overall trade balance. In fact, the opposite has occurred: America's trade deficit (in goods and services) with the European Union has grown over the past three years, surging 17 per cent in 2004 to a record $104.4 billion. The deficit was in excess of $100 billion again in 2005.

That transatlantic trade flows have failed to adjust to the sizable revaluation of the Euro against the dollar has confounded many on both sides of the Atlantic. Yet what is missing from the conventional analysis is the fact that a large percentage of US imports from Europe are related-party trade. Parent–affiliate trade, and trade among affiliates, is less responsive to shifts in prices or exchange rates and more attuned to domestic demand. While a strong Euro, in theory, would be expected to dampen European export growth to the United States, the fact that many European multinationals produce, market, and distribute goods and services on both sides of the ocean gives firms a high degree of immunity to a dramatic shift in exchange rates. Under this structure, trade flows are driven more by demand in the host nation. As such, when the US economy exhibits strong growth, as it has over the past four years, European affiliates in the United States produce and sell more products, which in turn, generates more demand (imports) for parts and components from the parent company back home, irrespective of exchange rate movements.

In the end, transatlantic trade flows are far more complex than most realize. Trade flows are driven by foreign direct investment, a sign of economic maturity and sophistication. In isolation, a weaker US dollar will not produce a significant rebalancing of transatlantic trade flows. Too much of what Europe exports to America is related-party trade, largely insensitive to exchange rates and more determined by final demand.

9.5 EU enlargement and the transatlantic economy

Foreign direct investment of multinationals has been critical in integrating the ten accession countries of 2004 (Cyprus, Czech Republic, Estonia, Hungary, Latvia, Lithuania, Malta, Poland, Slovenia, and Slovakia) with the European Union in particular and the transatlantic economy in general. Long before the ten nations were formally admitted to the European Union (May 2004), multinationals were busy establishing a local presence in the various accession nations in anticipation of the day when the countries would be full members of the European Union. In this respect, the cases of Poland, the Czech Republic, and Hungary are instructive on how multinationals operate in the global economy.

As the three most attractive nations of the ten accession markets, Poland, the Czech Republic, and Hungary registered massive new capital investment commitments from multinationals shortly after the three nations were invited to the EU negotiating table in the late 1990s. For instance, in 1998, the year accession talks commenced, FDI inflows to Hungary surged by more than 80 per cent in one year, rising from $2.1 billion in 1997 to $3.8 billion in 1998. During the same period, inflows to the Czech Republic nearly tripled, rising from $1.3 billion in 1997 to $3.7 billion the next year. Inflows to Poland surged nearly 30 per cent over the same timeframe. Looked at from a longer-term perspective, while FDI inflows to Hungary averaged $2.2 billion annually in the six years before accession talks were announced, annual inflows averaged $6.1 billion in the following seven years, or during the 1998–2004 period. The same trends were evident in Poland and the Czech Republic: in the former, FDI inflows averaged $2.9 billion in 1992–7, but surged to $6.2 billion from 1998 to 2004. Inflows to the Czech Republic averaged $1.3 billion annually in the six years before the negotiations started, but then soared to an annual average of $5.1 billion during the following seven years.

As Poland, the Czech Republic, and Hungary undertook the institutional adjustments required for EU membership—leading to more policy predictability and a more stable economic backdrop—multinationals responded to this 'euro-convergence' by increasing their level of foreign investment in each country. And the more multinationals became embedded in the accession nations, the more the incentives for both the EU and candidate nations to pursue EU membership. In the end, EU accession talks represented a new starting point in the way in which multinationals viewed Central Europe. As the negotiations produced institutional adjustments in these nations, multinationals responded by raising their level of capital investment in the region, helping to create a virtuous circle of cooperation, macroeconomic stability, and a more favourable environment for all parties involved. As a result, the accession states were already well integrated into the production networks and operating frameworks of multinationals well ahead of the May 2004 accession date.

Low corporate taxes, access to new markets, cheap yet skilled labour, above-average growth prospects—all of these determinants helped boost the stock of foreign direct investment in Central Europe in the past decade. Yet the strategies and motives of multinationals have already begun to shift. In recent years, foreign investment has become more specialized, with labour-intensive activities in locations like Hungary shifting to lower-cost locales like Slovakia and more recent EU candidate nations such as Romania and Bulgaria. More efficiency-seeking investment has flowed to the more developed and skilled markets of Hungary and the Czech Republic. Given that Poland is home to one of the largest consumer markets not only among the accession states, but also in the entire EU, the majority of investment to that nation is market-seeking.

US linkages with the accession states

US multinationals have been very active in the accession states over the past decade, and are already well integrated into Central and Eastern Europe. This is best illustrated by the fact that while US exports were the primary means by which American firms delivered goods to Central Europe in 1990, by the middle of the decade foreign affiliate sales had emerged as the primary mode of delivery of goods and services.

In 1990, US foreign affiliate sales in Central Europe totalled just $500 million, unsurprisingly given corporate America's nominal investment position in the region. US foreign investment to Central Europe rose steadily over the next fifteen years, such that by the end of 2004, the investment stake of US multinationals in the accession nations (roughly $13.5 billion, on a historic cost basis) was nearly on a par with America's investment position in China ($15.4 billion). And as investment levels increased, so did affiliate sales. The latter topped $35 billion in 2003, roughly triple the level of US exports to the region in the same year. No better figure captures the penetration of US multinationals into the region.

9.6 The continued primacy of the transatlantic economy

Deepening the transatlantic bonds, and thereby sustaining the pre-eminence of the transatlantic economy, requires more integration and cooperation across various sectors and subsectors, ranging from aerospace through financial services to pharmaceuticals.

High priority should be given to the liberalization of transatlantic services, a strategy that would help boost bilateral trade and investment between the two partiers, and boost the economic growth and efficiencies of the USA and Europe.

Towards this end, regulatory bodies on both sides of the Atlantic should give more credence and pay more attention to the transatlantic dimensions of domestic policy-making. That means eliminating regulations intended to protect local interests; streamlining and reducing technical standards and regulations across various sectors; and promoting regulatory transparency, thereby creating a level playing field for companies on both sides of the Atlantic. Government procurement programmes should become more open, while both parties should work to increase collaborative efforts in research and development in such cutting edge areas as nanotechnology and hydrogen fuel cell technology.

While transatlantic tariffs are quite low, non-tariff barriers remain important impediments to a free transatlantic marketplace. Remaining non-tariff barriers consist of domestic regulations, including safety norms, different health, environmental, and engineering standards, rules of origin, and labelling requirements. Such measures reflect different societal preferences, but are also a result of lack of coordination and adequate information exchange between regulators and legislators on both sides of the Atlantic, who are subject to different legal mandates and beholden to different constituents. In a bid to streamline and eliminate many barriers to trade and investment, the grand idea of a Transatlantic Free Trade Agreement has been broached in the past, but without much underlying support or success.

Whether through grand design or piecemeal negotiations, the future of the transatlantic partnership will be shaped by continued liberalization and openness on both sides of the Atlantic. As deep and integrated as the transatlantic economy is today, structural reforms would still lead to sizable gains for all parties. According to the OECD, structural reforms that included reduction or elimination of competition-restraining regulations, tariff barriers, and other investment restrictions could lead to a permanent gain in GDP per capita on both sides of the Atlantic of up to 3–3.5 per cent. Other studies have produced similar conclusions—that further transatlantic liberalization would promote mutual economic benefits for both the United States and Europe.

In addition to the above, greater 'out of area' economic cooperation is required of the transatlantic partnership. More cooperation, for instance, is required to promote economic growth and political stability in the Middle East and Africa, with the overriding recognition that more economic growth and a more liberal political backdrop in these two volatile regions is a tool in the war against terrorism and a means to end ethnic violence.

On other fronts, the USA and Europe need to consider joint energy and environmental strategies to reduce the industrialized nations' dependence on fossil fuels and curtail greenhouse gas emissions. In helping to integrate more developing nations in the world economy, ensuring a successful conclusion of the Doha Round on global trade, and future rounds, should be a key priority of both parties. Another transatlantic priority should be the enforcement and protection of intellectual property rights. Homeland security procedures need to be continuously updated and refined on both sides of the ocean. These initiatives and many others are required to preserve the primacy of the transatlantic economy.

9.7 **Conclusions**

Many observers believe the transatlantic partnership has grown weaker since the end of the Cold War in general and, in particular, since the unpopular US-led Gulf War under President George W. Bush. It is fashionable to speak of the transatlantic partnership as past its prime, with the United States and Europe no longer strategic partners in need, free to disengage from each other and free to pursue divergent interests. This view gained even more credence in the post-September 11 environment, when US foreign policy shifted towards more pre-emptive strategies and unilateral initiatives, culminating in the US-led war in Iraq.

Early in the twenty-first century, however, the transatlantic economy remains one of the most integrated and vibrant components of the world economy. Over the past decade, the United States and Europe have set the pace and standards of globalization. A closer look at foreign direct investment flows and foreign affiliate activities reveals the fact that the transatlantic market is among the most open in the world and the most integrated through dense flows of investment, affiliate sales, and related-party trade.

Against this backdrop, one of the most dangerous deficits affecting the transatlantic partnership is not one of trade, values, or military capabilities. Rather it is the deficit in understanding just how integrated and dependent the United States and Europe have become over the past half century.

▓ DISCUSSION QUESTIONS

1. Describe the nature and key trends of global foreign direct investment flows since the collapse of Communism.

2. Explain the motives of multinationals and the key determinants of foreign direct investment.

3. Discuss the key metrics that illustrate the depth and integration of the transatlantic economy.

4. How has EU enlargement affected the transatlantic economy? What role has foreign direct investment played in the enlargement process?

5. What are the long-term risks to the transatlantic economy?

▓ FURTHER READING

For more information and current analysis on the transatlantic economy, two excellent websites to visit are the Center for Transatlantic Relations, Johns Hopkins University, transatlantic@jhu.edu and the Centre for European Policy Studies, info@ceps.be. For more on US investment flows, visit the website of the Bureau of Economic analysis (www.bea.gov). The OECD is another primary source of trade and foreign direct investment data (www.oecd.org). For an excellent analysis of transatlantic trends and policies, see the German Marshall Fund website (www.gmfus.org). Readers wishing to stay abreast of transatlantic issues in relation to the global economy should visit www.theglobalist.com. The site provides outstanding commentary on a number of global topics.

■ REFERENCES

Bergsten, F. C. (2005), *The United States and the World Economy* (Washington, DC: The Institute for International Economics).

Dicken, P. (2003), *Global Shift: Reshaping the Global Economic Map in the 21st Century* (New York: The Guilford Press).

Dunning, J. (1993), *Multinational Enterprises and the Global Economy* (Wokingham, UK: Addison-Wesley).

—— (2000), *Regions, Globalization and the Knowledge Economy* (Oxford: Oxford University Press).

—— (2003), 'Location and the Multinational Enterprise: A Neglected Factor?', *Journal of International Business Studies*, 29/1: 45.

European Commission (2005) The EU Economy 2005 Review, *Rising International Economic Integration—Opportunities and Challenges* (Brussels: Commission of the European Communities, Directorate General).

Hamilton, D. and Quinlan, J. (2004), *Partners in Prosperity: The Changing Geography of the Transatlantic Economy* (Washington, DC: The Center for Transatlantic Relations, Johns Hopkins University).

—— (eds.) (2005a), *Deep Integration: How Transatlantic Markets are Leading Globalization* (Washington, DC, and Brussels Center for Transatlantic Relations/Centre for European Policy Studies).

—— (2005b), *The Transatlantic Economy, 2005: Annual Survey of Jobs, Trade, Investment between the United States and Europe* (Washington, DC: Center for Transatlantic Relations, Johns Hopkins University).

International Investment Perspectives (2005), *Trends and Recent Developments in Foreign Direct Investment* (Paris: OECD).

Lucks, K. (ed.) (2005), *Transatlantic Mergers and Acquisitions: Opportunities and Pitfalls in German–American Partnerships* (Erlangen, Germany: Publicis Corporate Publishing).

Ohame, K. (1985), *Triad Power: The Coming Shape of Global Competition* (New York: The Free Press).

Quinlan, J. (2001), *Global Engagement: How American Companies Really Compete in the Global Economy* (Lincolnwood, IL: Contemporary Books).

—— (2003), *Drifting Apart or Growing Together? The Primacy of the Transatlantic Economy* (Washington, DC: Center for Transatlantic Relations, Johns Hopkins University).

Schnabel, R. A. and Rocca, F. A. (2005), *The Next Superpower: The Rise of Europe and its Challenge to the United States* (Lanham, MD: Rowman and Littlefield).

Scott, A. (1998), *Regions and the World Economy: The Coming Shape of Global Production, Competition, and Political Order* (Oxford: Oxford University Press).

UNCTAD (1995), *World Investment Report* (Geneva: United Nations).

—— (1996), *World Investment Report* (Geneva: United Nations).

—— (1997), *World Investment Report* (Geneva: United Nations).

—— (1998), *World Investment Report* (Geneva: United Nations).

—— (1999), *World Investment Report* (Geneva: United Nations).

—— (2000), *World Investment Report* (Geneva: United Nations).

—— (2001), *World Investment Report* (Geneva: United Nations).

—— (2002), *World Investment Report* (Geneva: United Nations).

—— (2003), *World Investment Report* (Geneva: United Nations).

—— (2004), *World Investment Report* (Geneva: United Nations).

—— (2005), *World Investment Report* (Geneva: United Nations).

Zaborowski, M. (2006), *Friends Again? EU–US Relations after the Crisis* (Paris: European Union Institute for Security Studies).

10 The Creation of EMU

Robin Bladen-Hovell

Introduction

On 1 January 1999 eleven countries from the European Union embarked upon a monetary union, and soon thereafter surrendered their own national currencies in favour of a single currency, the Euro.[1] The move represented the culmination of a twenty-year effort that only six years earlier appeared destined to fail. Few commentators during the currency crises of 1992 and 1993 anticipated that the single currency would emerge to schedule, albeit with some careful interpretation of the rules for membership for some members.

Monetary union entails the surrender of national sovereignty over monetary policy in favour of a single currency adopted across a wider region. As such the formation of a monetary union implies both costs and benefits to potential members. These include amongst other things the loss of control over national monetary policy in return for the potential benefit that accrues from promoting trade and investment by eliminating exchange rate fluctuation and uncertainty across the EU, the net benefit representing the balance of these factors for each country. The rationale and analysis of monetary union is traditionally associated with the so-called optimal currency area literature. Although this literature identifies the source of potential costs and benefits, the outcome for any given country remains an empirical question, with the added complication that the conditions underlying the costs and benefits are themselves endogenous to the process of monetary union formation. We discuss these costs and benefits in section 10.1.

The process of achieving a monetary union within Europe began in earnest with the formation of the Exchange Rate Mechanism (ERM) in 1979. The original intention of creating a zone of monetary stability within Europe was initially balanced by a desire to establish a system that overcame the asymmetric features commonly identified with the Bretton Woods fixed exchange rate system that ERM replaced. Over time, however, the operation of the ERM became increasingly inflexible, until by the end of the 1980s it closely resembled a fully fixed exchange rate system. We describe the key features of ERM and details of its early operation in sections 10.2 and 10.3. The excessive stability of the system subsequently became an important feature in the response of the ERM to the turbulent conditions of the early 1990s. In part these were sparked by the political uncertainty surrounding ratification of the Maastricht Treaty which laid down the formal criteria for monetary union, but also reflected the changed environment brought about by the removal of controls on the international movement of capital across Europe. These issues are addressed in sections 10.4, 10.5, and 10.6. The post-crisis behaviour of the system and the eventual run up to monetary union is subsequently discussed in section 10.7, followed in section 10.8 by a brief description of the key features of the European Central Bank that administers monetary policy across the Euro-area. Finally, in section 10.9, we discuss the position of Britain, Denmark, and Sweden, which chose to opt out of European Monetary Union, and the situation for the twelve new members of the EU, for which membership of EMU is obligatory once the convergence criteria have been met. A brief concluding section completes the chapter.

10.1 The economics of monetary union

A monetary union occurs when a group of countries adopt a single currency and, by implication, implement a common monetary policy. In this sense a monetary union may be thought of as an extreme form of fixed exchange rate regime and, as such, the arguments for its adoption derive largely from the perceived advantage of fixed over flexible rates. In the particular context of the European Union a special emphasis must also be given to the requirement that, to preserve the achievements of the common market, it must not appear that any member country can artificially manipulate its currency to obtain competitive advantage—otherwise the enterprise could unravel.

Traditionally the argument in favour of fixed exchange rates has emphasized their role in eliminating exchange rate uncertainty and reducing transaction costs between countries. Fixing one's exchange rate with respect to a large neighbouring country, for example, eliminates exchange rate variability and reduces the risk and uncertainty that would otherwise affect decisions relating to investment and international trade. Going one step further and adopting the same currency as one's neighbour obviously reduces risk and uncertainty further in so far as the prospect of realignment of the otherwise fixed rate disappears and an important source of transaction costs that arise from the need to exchange currency when transactions cross the international border is also removed. As a result agents in both countries benefit from increased transparency of price setting and greater opportunities for risk pooling.

Generally speaking, the advantage ascribed to fixed rates over flexible rates is considered to be greater, the higher the degree of openness or integration that exists between the countries concerned. For example, the higher the proportion of total output traded between countries, the greater will be the corresponding impact of bilateral exchange rate variability on total output and the greater the benefit that will accrue from fixing the exchange rate. Similarly the ability of central banks to operate independent monetary policy is reduced the more integrated are international capital markets.[2] Countries that are highly integrated in these and other ways potentially constitute an optimal currency area, a region, that is, for which it is optimal to operate a single currency and single monetary policy.

The seminal work on optimal currency areas was undertaken by Mundell (1961), MacKinnon (1963), and Kenen (1969) and this work has subsequently become the dominant framework for discussing of costs and benefits of economic and monetary union. The

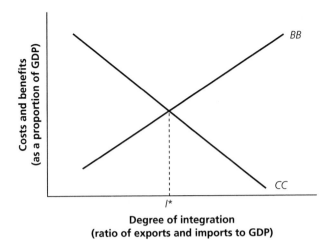

Figure 10.1 The costs and benefits of monetary union
Source: Krugman (1990).

basic idea may be made succinctly with the aid of a framework popularized by Paul Krugman (1990) shown in Figure 10.1. Here we plot the costs and benefits of monetary union, expressed in each case as a proportion of the total output, against the degree of integration between countries, measured by the ratio of total imports and exports to the level of output. In line with our previous argument that the benefit from eliminating transaction costs and exchange rate variability increase with the degree of openness and economic integration, the *BB* schedule is drawn upward sloping. The *CC* schedule on the other hand is downward sloping, reflecting the fact that the main costs of monetary union decline because the effectiveness of monetary policy is lower under the alternative flexible exchange rates regime the more integrated the global economy becomes.

The message from Figure 10.1 is simple. If the benefits from monetary union increase with the degree of integration, and the costs decline, then there is some level of integration *I**, beyond which the benefits will outweigh the costs and at that point monetary union becomes worthwhile.

Economic integration is, of course, multidimensional and various aspects have been discussed in the literature. Mundell (1961), for example, stressed the importance of factor mobility, particularly labour market mobility, for the operation of an optimal currency area. Prior to the adoption of a currency union, regional imbalances in employment may be re-equilibrated through exchange rate adjustment. However, this mechanism is not available under a currency union but may be replaced by a sufficiently high degree of labour mobility and migration flows between the regions. Of course, whether labour markets are sufficiently flexible in practice is an empirical question, though in the European context one suspects that the degree of labour mobility between, say, France and Italy is less than the mobility that exists between Paris and Bordeaux given the language and other cultural differences.

The notion of regional imbalances that lies at the heart of Mundell's argument clearly represents a difficult problem for monetary union. A currency union must by definition

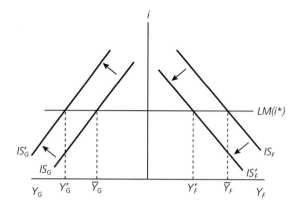

Figure 10.2 Impact of an asymmetric shock

operate the single monetary policy at the union, rather than the sub-union (national) level of output. As a result, countries facing predominantly asymmetric disturbances are unlikely to prove suitable bed-fellows for monetary union.

The essence of this argument is easily made with the assistance of Figure 10.2. Here we represent economic conditions within two countries, France and Germany say, in a currency union by means of the traditional *IS/LM* framework. Goods market equilibrium in France is shown by the downward-sloping schedule *IS$_F$* in the right-hand side of the diagram and by the comparable downward-sloping schedule, *IS$_G$*, for Germany on the left-hand side. The common monetary policy under the monetary union is represented by the horizontal LM schedule drawn at the common interest rate, *i**. For convenience, we presuppose that the initial rate of interest can be set such that both France and the Germany achieve their full employment equilibrium levels of output at $\bar{Y}_F$ and $\bar{Y}_G$ respectively.

Within this framework, an asymmetric shock corresponds to an expansion of demand in Germany and a contraction of demand in France or vice versa, a shock that might occur as a result of non-synchronization of business cycles across the two countries. The result is an upward shift of the German goods market equilibrium schedule to *IS$_G'$* and a downwards shift for the French schedule to *IS$_F'$*. With a policy of unchanged interest rates, new equilibria are established, at Y_G' and Y_F' respectively. As a result of the shock, output is above the full employment level in Germany but below the full employment level in France.

The problem for the monetary union in this situation is, of course, that level of the interest rate doesn't suit the requirements for each country simultaneously. Interest rates need to rise in order to curtail the excess demand in Germany but fall to restore full employment in France—an outcome that will not occur if the central bank targets output at the union level.

It is commonly thought that the problem of asymmetric shocks can be addressed by individual members of a currency union retaining control over fiscal policy. In our example, France should adopt an expansionary budget whilst Germany pursues a contractionary fiscal policy. Unfortunately, it is far from clear just how independent fiscal policy will be under monetary union. Coordination of fiscal policy targets and instruments may be required across the union in order to ensure that the union maintains a stable relationship with the rest of the world. In addition monetary and fiscal policies are themselves interdependent with the budget deficit of each country having to be financed either by government borrowing (selling public sector debt) or by an increase in the money supply. However, governments lose the ability to finance the budget by changing the money supply within a monetary union and further will be constrained in their ability to sell debt in so far as the price at which the debt may be sold (the rate of interest) is determined by the central bank of the currency union and may be set with an entirely different agenda in mind.[3]

Whether the benefits of monetary union outweigh the costs in any particular situation remains an empirical question: it is therefore unsurprising to find that a considerable number of empirical studies have attempted to quantify the potential costs and benefits in the context of European Monetary Union. Since the EU countries maintain exceptionally high levels of trade between themselves, most of the research has attempted to look at the costs of a monetary union. Bayoumi and Eichengreen (1994) for example, infer significant costs for monetary union within Europe on the basis that disturbances to aggregate output by region and country appear less well correlated within the EU than those within the United States. Bayoumi and Prasad (1997) subsequently examine the role of the labour market as an adjustment mechanism in the face of output disturbances in the EU and the United States. They conclude that, although the overall nature of disturbances is broadly similar, interregional labour mobility appears a much more important element of the adjustment process in the United States than it does in its European counterpart, again adducing a significant cost for EMU.

Of course, drawing inference about the potential success or otherwise for a prospective currency union from evidence gathered from a comparison with an existing currency union is, at one level, of questionable validity. Currency union has existed in the United States for many years and this will itself have promoted integration there. The fact that the United States today is more integrated than Europe today is not an argument against monetary union in Europe.[4] The pattern of trade and the degree of synchronization of business cycles across Europe are endogenous and the degree of integration itself may be enhanced with the adoption of a single currency.[5]

10.2 First steps: the ERM

The European Monetary System (EMS) was established in March 1979 with the intention of creating a 'zone of monetary stability' within Europe. The origins of the system may be traced to the Barre Plan published ten years earlier. The Barre Plan contained two substantive proposals: a call for coordination of economic policies in order to produce convergence in inflation, and the establishment of an automatic and unconditional credit facility to stabilize fixed exchange rates across the EC. However, opinion on these issues was split, with France, in particular, stressing the need for the latter whilst Germany emphasized the former. The French position was eventually adopted in December 1969 with further work being called for on the question of policy coordination. The matter was subsequently taken further with the publication of the Werner Reports in 1970 which called for full economic and monetary union by 1980.

Unfortunately, circumstances of the time led to the original timetable for the Werner proposal being abandoned almost immediately. A further attempt to relaunch the idea of a European zone of exchange rate stability was, however, made in the aftermath of the breakdown of the Bretton Woods system in December 1971. In March the following year the EC countries embarked on an experiment to restrict the range of fluctuation between their currencies to a band of ±2.25 per cent of a central rate.[6] Anticipating imminent accession to the EC, the UK, Norway, Denmark, and Ireland also participated in this scheme, which became known as the Snake. The Snake currencies were free to move against the dollar subject to a wider margin determined by the Smithsonian Agreement. The EC called this wider band, 'the tunnel', hence the nickname for the system, 'Snake in the tunnel'.

Unfortunately, the Snake was unable to withstand the considerable turbulence in the currency markets at that time; some countries left the system quite soon after joining (UK and Ireland), whilst others left and rejoined only to leave again (France). By 1977 only a core group of five countries (Germany, Denmark, the Netherlands, Belgium, and Luxembourg) remained. Nevertheless the desire to stabilize exchange rates between EC members remained strong and agreement on a more effective means for achieving this end was achieved at the Council of Ministers meeting held in Brussels in December 1978.[7] The European Monetary System (EMS) began operation the following March.

The EMS was formally organized around a basket of EC currencies that comprised the European Currency Unit (Ecu). This acted as the numeraire for the Exchange Rate Mechanism (ERM) and the unit of account for all EC transactions. The Ecu was a composite currency that contained specific amounts of the currencies of all Member States, including those countries which chose not to participate in the ERM.[8] In this respect the Ecu consisted literally of so many deutschmarks, so many French francs, so many pounds sterling, and so on. However, the actual weight of each currency in the basket was subject to change because of exchange rate movements and the composition of the Ecu was also subject to periodic review, the review period being set initially as every five years.

The centrepiece of the European Monetary System was the Exchange Rate Mechanism. This provided a 'currency grid': a set of all the bilateral exchange rates between participating countries with a nominated central rate for each currency and a permissible band of fluctuation. As a matter of arithmetic a currency's central rate was re-expressed in terms of the Ecu; but the essence of the ERM was the obligation to maintain bilateral exchange rates within the permitted bands of fluctuation. Prior to the decision to allow ERM currencies to float within a margin of ±15 per cent taken by European finance ministers in August 1992, the size of this band was set at ±2.25 per cent for the majority of participating countries. Italy, however, negotiated a transitional arrangement which initially allowed it to operate within a wider, ±6 per cent, band of fluctuation. Italy eventually adopted the narrower ±2.25 per cent band in January 1990, but the transitional arrangement involving the use of the wider band was extended to three new participants: Spain (June 1989), the United Kingdom (October 1990), and Portugal (April 1992) upon their joining the mechanism.

Central rates were not irrevocably fixed within the mechanism but could be adjusted, or realigned, after consultation among EMS members. One of the principal objectives of the ERM was, however, to keep such realignments to a minimum and especially to prevent devaluation being used as a competitive policy instrument within Europe. To this end, central banks were obliged to intervene in the foreign exchange market in order to keep their currencies within the permitted margins of fluctuation. The intervention rules themselves were relatively straightforward and designed to impose symmetry of adjustment on the system.[9] When a country diverged from its central rate by the amount permitted by its band of fluctuation, the central bank of the strongest and the weakest currency within the system were equally obliged to intervene in order to stabilize the currency. Since any of the bilateral exchange rates could trigger such an intervention, measuring the maximum appreciation and depreciation against the weakest and strongest currency respectively meant that the effective band of fluctuation was narrower than that suggested by the margins representing the permissible band of fluctuation. Moreover, the width of the effective band adjusted continually as the weights of individual currencies in the Ecu changed with exchange rate movements.

In order to enable ERM-participating countries to meet their obligation to defend the bilateral currency bands, a credit facility, the European Monetary Cooperation Fund (EMCF) was established. The very short-term finance (VSTF) facility was the most important of these instruments and provided finance for intervention undertaken in the foreign exchange market when the currency reaches the limit of its permissible band of fluctuation, so-called marginal intervention. This facility took the form of a line of credit extended among the central banks of the system. Since marginal intervention was compulsory and was required in unlimited quantities by the two central banks whose currency had reached their bilateral margin, this credit line was automatic and unlimited.[10]

In principle, the design of the VSTF facility had important implications for monetary conditions in those countries that were pushed to their bilateral margins. The use of the credit line resulted in an increase in the liabilities of the central bank managing the stronger currency and an increase in the assets of the central bank managing the weaker currency. As a result, marginal intervention should have led to a monetary expansion in the country with the stronger currency and a monetary contraction in the country with the weaker currency. In practice, however, the extent to which ERM members allowed their domestic monetary policy to be dictated by the needs of the ERM varied considerably, with Germany, in particular, typically acting to sterilize the monetary effects of ERM intervention.

10.3 The operation of the ERM in practice

Although the ERM was conceived of as providing a framework for monetary stability within Europe, exchange rates were not considered immutably fixed, at least not at first. Adjustments or realignments of the central parities were allowed and the early years of the system, in particular, featured a number of realignments of these central rates. Details of the realignments within the ERM over the period 1979–99, are presented in Table 10.1.

Table 10.1 Realignment of central parities of the ERM

Date	
March 1979	ERM begins with Belgium (B), Denmark (DK), France (F), Germany (D), Ireland (IRE), Italy (I), and the Netherlands (NL) as initial members
September 1979	DK(−3); D(+2)
November 1979	DK(−4.8)
February 1981	I(−6)
October 1981	D(+5.5); F(−3); I(−3); NL(+5.5)
February 1982	B(−8.5); DK(−3)
June 1982	D(+4.25); F(−5.75); I(−2.75)
March 1983	B(+1.5); DK(+2.5); D(+5.5); F(−2.5); IRE(−3.5); I(−2.5); NL(+3.5)
July 1985	B(+2); DK(+2); D(+2); F(+2); IRE(+2); I(−6); NL(+2)
April 1986	B(+1); DK(+1); D(+3); F(−3); NL(+3)
August 1986	IRE(−8)
January 1987	B(+2); D(+3); NL(+3)
January 1990	I(−3.75)
September 1992	B(+3.5); DK(+3.5); D(+3.5); F(+3.5); IRE(+3.5); I(−3.5); NL(+3.5); S(+3.5); GB(+3.5); P(+3.5); S(−5); Italy and UK exit the ERM
November 1992	S(−6); P(−6)
February 1993	IRE(−10)
May 1993	S(−8); P(−6.5)
August 1993	Fluctuation band widened to ±15
March 1995	S(−7); P(−3.5)
November 1996	Italy rejoins ERM
March 1998	IRE(+3)
January 1999	Austria, Belgium, Finland, France, Germany, Ireland, Italy, Luxembourg, the Netherlands, Portugal, and Spain adopt the Euro

Note: Figures show the percentage revaluation (+) or devaluation (−) against the Ecu.

Inspection of the table reveals that three distinct subperiods may be distinguished in the history of the ERM. The first period, the so-called soft-ERM, from March 1979 until December 1986, was characterized by frequent and often sizeable realignments of the currencies within the system. This was followed by a five-year period of relative stability (hard-ERM) in which the system expanded to include the Spanish peseta (June 1989), the British pound (October 1990), and the Portuguese escudo (April 1992), and the only realignment was a technical adjustment that accompanied the Italian decision to adopt narrower intervention limits. This golden age came to an end with the currency crisis of September 1992 which saw the Italian lira and British pound leave the system, and initiated a prolonged period of volatility that led to the eventual widening of the intervention limits to ±15 per cent under the so-called flexible-ERM from August 1993 to December 1999 when the EMS disappears and was replaced by the Euro. Stability returned to the system following the crisis, with realignments limited to the Portuguese escudo and the Spanish peseta. This period of renewed stability also heralded a further phase of expansion of the system with the Austrian schilling joining the ERM in January 1995, the Finnish mark in October 1996, and the Greek drachma in March 1998.

During the early soft-ERM period, the realignment of central rates combined the twin objectives of preserving a degree of nominal exchange rate stability in the short run with relatively constant real exchange rates over the longer term. As the system progressed, however, national inflationary pressures across the EC were brought increasingly under the control of more disciplined domestic policy and the need for realignments diminished. In effect, the ERM began to look and operate increasingly like a fully fixed exchange rate system.

Despite the original intention of making adjustments within the ERM symmetric, considerable evidence has accumulated which suggests that substantial asymmetries remained within the system. Indeed these asymmetries appear to have become increasingly more pronounced as the system progressed. The problem in this respect lay in the dominant position of Germany within the ERM. This arose not only from the fact that Germany represented the largest economy within the EC but also because of Germany's record of low inflation. By committing themselves to a fixed rate with respect to the deutschmark, countries were in a sense able to 'import' Germany's counter-inflationary reputation. This proposition is based upon the notion of a reputational policy of the form described by Barro and Gordon (1983). Here the cost to a country, in terms of the loss of output associated with a counter-inflationary policy, depends crucially upon the ability of the authorities to convince the public that they will not renege upon the policy commitment. By announcing a credible future disinflationary strategy, governments benefit from an immediate reduction in inflationary expectations within the economy. As a result lower inflation is achieved at a lower cost in terms of unemployment than would otherwise be possible.

Of course the decision by countries to pre-commit to the German standard implied that the system would operate in a markedly asymmetric manner. Under German leadership, the Bundesbank independently chose its monetary policy whilst all other members of the ERM 'tied their hands' on monetary policy and simply targeted their exchange rates to the deutschmark. The ERM was de facto a deutschmark zone.

10.4 **The Maastricht Treaty**

With the apparent stability of the ERM increasing during the latter half of the 1980s came the desire to make further progress towards economic and monetary union. In June 1988 the European Council established a committee under Jacque Delors (then president of the EU Commission), and the subsequent Delors Report and the ensuing discussion culminated in the Treaty of Economic Union (TEU) signed at Maastricht in December 1991. The Treaty established a timetable for monetary union and laid down five conditions that prospective members were required to satisfy before they could participate. These conditions involved a country demonstrating:

1. an inflation rate no more than 1.5 per cent above the average of the three best-performing EU countries,

2. long-term interest rates no more than 2 per cent points above the average of the three best-performing EU countries,

3. an exchange rate maintained within the normal bands of the ERM for at least two years immediately prior to accession into the monetary union,

4. public debt of no more than 60 per cent of GDP, and

5. a budget deficit of no more than 3 per cent of GDP.

These criteria differ very clearly from the criteria that underpin the optimal currency area described previously. At Maastricht the focus was on nominal convergence and the fiscal discipline of applicants to the monetary union; the focus of the OCA literature, in contrast, is on real convergence, trade integration, cyclical synchronization, labour mobility, fiscal federalism, and the like. In this sense the criteria laid down by the TEU may be considered arbitrary and divorced from the underlying real factors that determine the ultimate success or otherwise of EMU. At another level, however, it could be argued (see, for example, Artis 2003) that the Maastricht criteria provided clear performance targets which, if met, would ensure that prospective members were ready to participate in a monetary framework that emphasized nominal stability.

The timetable set out in the TEU anticipated that EMU would be achieved in three stages, with the final stage (monetary union) beginning no earlier than 1997 but no later than January 1999. In Stage I, beginning July 1990, barriers to the free movement of capital across the EU were to be dismantled and the economic, monetary, and fiscal policies of Member States were to be reconciled. In Stage II, beginning July 1994, the European Monetary Institute (EMI) was established. The EMI was the forerunner of the European Central Bank (ECB) and was charged with monitoring economic performance against the Maastricht criteria and with establishing operating procedures for the ECB. At the same time the sovereignty of national central banks was strengthened and money financing of excessive deficits was prohibited. Stage III of the process involved the introduction of the single currency, initially as non-cash money among participating Member States, and the transfer of responsibility for the operation of monetary policy to the ECB. During this transitional phase national currencies would continue to circulate although their value was to be irrevocably locked in terms of the single currency. Prices, however, had to be reported in terms of both the national and the single currency, though it remained a matter of choice which currency to adopt for the reporting of accounts.

10.5 Crisis in the ERM

The events in the foreign exchange markets associated with the crisis in the ERM during September 1992 and July–August 1993 have been among the most important since the EC began. Strain on the system had been mounting for some time, reflecting changing global economic conditions. In Germany, reunification in 1989 was accompanied by a significant increase in government borrowing and an associated increase in inflationary pressure and interest rates. In contrast, economic conditions in the United States and the rest of Europe moved into recession. In the United States the response of the Federal Reserve to the developing recession was to reduce interest rates, widening the interest differential with respect to the deutschmark and leading to capital flows from the USA into Germany, producing incipient downward pressure on German rates. Lower interest rates would clearly have benefited France, Italy, and the UK which were also experiencing the onset of depressed economic activity. German leadership, however, delivered the opposite, with the Bundesbank sterilizing the capital inflow and keeping German interest rates high in order to maintain its domestic disinflationary stance with the result that the deutschmark and other ERM currencies appreciated against the dollar. This pressure was further exacerbated by the British government's decision to use the ERM as the mainstay of its own domestic disinflationary strategy and to join the system at a central rate that many commentators suggested was too high. The obvious solution to this problem would have been to devalue sterling, the French franc, and the lira (or revalue the deutschmark) within the ERM—an option that would have been adopted during the soft-ERM period. However, this solution was deemed unacceptable under the hard-ERM on the grounds that it might undermine credibility. As a result tension continued to build.

In the event the immediate trigger for the currency crisis was the political uncertainty that surrounded the referenda on the Maastricht Treaty. Denmark rejected the Treaty in June 1992 and the resultant strengthening of the deutschmark placed considerable pressure on the lira and sterling. For the lira, market concern over the country's high level of public debt and excessive budget deficit contributed to these pressures. In the United Kingdom the continued recession and weak current account position influenced market perceptions that sterling might be devalued within the ERM given the apparent constraints on domestic interest rates. Tension was partially eased by intervention, particularly in support of the lira, during the summer, but by the end of August pressure again began to mount in the run up to the French referendum, fed especially by opinion polls that suggested the French might reject the Maastricht Treaty.[11]

Currency speculation reached a peak in September and massive intervention was required by the middle of the month in order to prevent the lira falling below its ERM floor. The lira was eventually devalued by 7 per cent on 12 September but remained under considerable pressure in the week that followed. At the same time the Spanish peseta fell from the top of its ERM band to the bottom. Comparable levels of intervention were required to prevent sterling falling below its ERM floor on 16 September, yet, despite this and a 2 per cent rise in official interest rates, sterling's membership of the ERM had to be suspended. Because intervention and higher interest rates had failed to keep the lira off its ERM floor, it, too, was suspended on 17 September. After the departure of the lira and sterling from the system, the French franc came under intense pressure, especially after the close (albeit positive) result for the referendum. This was only beaten off by a combined defence operation mounted by the French and German central banks.

After the September crisis, significant pressure re-emerged among the ERM currencies in November. The Spanish peseta and the Portuguese escudo were both devalued by 6 per cent on 22 November. By the end of the year sterling had depreciated by approximately 15 per cent, the Italian lira by 16 per cent, while the French franc and German mark were little changed.

Pressure on the ERM continued throughout much of 1993. The Irish punt was devalued by 10 per cent in February; the Spanish peseta and the Portuguese escudo were devalued by 8 per cent and 6.5 per cent respectively in May, and on 30 July the French and Belgium francs, the Danish krone, the Spanish peseta, and the Portuguese escudo all fell close to their floors against the deutschmark despite substantial intervention by central banks. Only the Dutch guilder remained unscathed. As a consequence, finance ministers and central bankers decided on 2 August that operational changes were required to the structure of the ERM and announced that new margins of fluctuation, amounting to ±15 per cent either side of the central rate, would be permitted within the ERM. Only the Netherlands chose, through bilateral arrangement, to retain the original ±2.25 per cent band against the deutschmark. The European Monetary System had all but collapsed.

10.6 Capital controls

The removal of capital controls during Stage I of EMU is frequently credited with playing a critical role in currency crises of 1992–3. This argument is based upon the idea that, by adopting capital controls, the monetary authorities can avert speculative attacks against their foreign exchange position.

The motivation behind speculative capital flows is one of making a capital gain from anticipated movements in spot rates or interest rates. A risk-neutral currency speculator should be indifferent between holding sterling or deutschmark denominated assets if the sterling interest rate equalled the deutschmark interest rate plus the anticipated depreciation of sterling relative to the deutschmark—the uncovered interest parity condition. If the anticipated sterling depreciation exceeds the sterling interest advantage, holders of sterling assets will switch their portfolio into deutschmarks in expectation of making a capital gain by repurchasing sterling at a lower value in the future. Moreover, irrespective of whether the interest differential offsets the expected currency movement or not, since the value of domestic currency falls with a devaluation, holders of domestic high powered money have an incentive to avoid the loss by selling the domestic currency to the central bank in exchange for foreign currency prior to the devaluation, then buying domestic currency back once the devaluation has occurred. If foreign exchange transactions were costless, the effect of such speculative activity would be to reduce the foreign exchange reserves of the central bank to zero.

The difficulty is that, within a regime of controlled floating, the interest differential required to offset expected currency movements is typically very high. A simple example may help to illustrate the point. Suppose that a discrete devaluation, equivalent to a fall of 5 per cent per annum, was expected next month within an otherwise fixed rate regime. The interest required to offset this would be 5 per cent on comparable one-year bonds. For interest-bearing instruments of shorter maturity, however, the required interest differential would be correspondingly higher: 20 per cent on three-month assets, 60 per cent on one-month assets, and well in excess of 1500 per cent on overnight deposits.[12] Capital controls can protect domestic interest rates from the need to assume such levels when discrete changes in the currency are expected by the market. They do so by prohibiting domestic and foreign residents from borrowing at the domestic rate of interest in order to lend abroad in the expectation of capital gains from the currency movement. Of course, such a prohibition on currency transactions would also have the advantage of preventing speculative attacks on the foreign reserve position of the central bank.

As a result of the progressive reduction in capital controls during Stage I, the potential for capital movements among the ERM countries had increased substantially and this feature brought to the fore the need for much closer coordination of monetary policies. This policy dilemma lay at the heart of what Padoa-Schioppa (1988) termed the 'inconsistent quartet'—the inconsistent set of characteristics of an international monetary system: free trade; free capital movements; national policy autonomy; fixed exchange rates.[13] The difficulty is in reconciling these characteristics within one system. During the first phase of ERM, free movement of capital and fixity of the exchange rate were compromised by the presence of capital controls and frequent realignments of the system. Together these factors allowed members to maintain some degree of policy autonomy.

With the progressive removal of capital controls and the relative stabilization of exchange rates during the latter half of the 1980s, the only means of reconciling the otherwise inconsistent characteristics was by countries sacrificing policy autonomy. In practice this sacrifice was forced upon countries by the developing economic and financial conditions. Monetary autonomy was progressively eroded throughout the 1980s as nominal interest rates among ERM participants converged, with interest rate differentials increasingly tending to reflect the markets' assessment of the expected depreciation for each currency. However, the removal of obstacles to trade and success in maintaining exchange rate stability may fail to generate convergence in other indicators of economic performance unless supported by coordinated policy actions elsewhere in the economy.

10.7 Post-crisis ERM

After the exchange rate crises of 1992 and 1993 the option of returning to the hard version of the ERM vanished. Two countries, Italy and the United Kingdom, had been forcibly ejected from the mechanism and many of the others had been severely shaken by the experience. Although Italy subsequently rejoined the ERM (in November 1996), Britain did not. However, the wider, ±15 per cent, permissible band of fluctuation enabled the mechanism to operate in a more relaxed manner during the latter half of the 1990s and the pace of progress towards monetary union continued to quicken as a result.[14] In March 1998 the Commission adopted the convergence report that recommended eleven countries (Austria, Belgium, Finland, France, Germany, Ireland, Italy, Luxembourg, the Netherlands, Portugal, and Spain) join the single currency. This recommendation was ratified by Council in May 1998. Of the remaining four EU countries, Sweden and Greece did not at the time meet the Maastricht criteria, whilst Britain and Denmark exercised their right under the TEU to opt out.[15] The exchange rates of participating countries were subsequently fixed with respect to the Euro in December 1998 with the Euro formally beginning as a non-cash currency on 1 January 1999. Euro coins began to circulate in the twelve participating countries one year later, with dual circulation of the national currencies and the Euro coming to an end on 21 February 2002: a single currency serving more than 300 million people had successfully been introduced within the EU.

10.8 The constitution of the European Central Bank

The constitution of the European Central Bank (ECB) was drawn up at the same time as the Maastricht Treaty. It has been described as a constitution for the most independent central bank in the world and was originally modelled on the constitution of the Bundesbank but with some features 'hardened'. That the Bundesbank's constitution should be taken as a model is no surprise, from several points of view. First and foremost, the Bundesbank had been adopted as the leader of ERM I by countries anxious to maintain a record of low inflation. Second, the Bundesbank's constitution had been written for a federation and EMU resembled a federation in many respects. Third, the academic literature—following the influential analysis of Barro and Gordon (1983)—had come to place special emphasis on the need for a 'commitment technology' that would reliably produce low inflation; giving independence to the central bank was recognized as a means of achieving this.

The ECB is placed at the head of the European System of Central Banks (ESCB). It is given a mandate in the Treaty which forms the basis of its monetary strategy. The first part of the mandate indicates that the ECB's primary objective is price stability. The second part states that, without prejudice to the primary objective, the ESCB shall support the general economic policies in the Community and includes a long list of desirables including high employment and social protection. However, the ECB is prohibited from taking instructions from any national central bank or organization of the EU, and from lending directly to national governments or institutions of the EU.

The ECB is governed by a Governing Council comprising governors of the national central banks, and members of the Executive Board, namely the president and vice-president, and four other members appointed by the common accord of the EU governments for non-renewable terms. Under the Maastricht Treaty, governors of national central banks must themselves possess a large degree of operational independence from their national governments which serves to insure that the focus of the ECB activities remains on the primary objective of price stability. In addition the ECB is relieved of all prudential regulatory and supervisory duties across European financial markets.

10.9 Opt-outs and pre-ins

The decision of Britain and Denmark to opt out of the single currency, and the failure of Greece and Sweden to meet the convergence criteria in 1998, meant that four EU countries remained outside the Euro-area when it began operation in 1999. Although Greece subsequently joined the Euro in 2001, the number of EU countries outside the Euro-area grew following the expansion of the EU into Central and Eastern Europe.[16] For these accession countries, the opt-out clause exploited by Britain and Demark was unavailable:

like Sweden they are obliged to join the EMU once they meet the Maastricht criteria; in the case of Britain and Denmark, it was anticipated that they would eventually surrender the opt-out and accede to the single currency.

To cater to these 'opt-out' and 'pre-in' countries, a further Resolution was adopted by the European Council at Amsterdam in June 1997 whereby the ERM was replaced from the beginning of Stage III of EMU by a new exchange rate mechanism that linked the currencies of the non-Euro Member States to the Euro. Like its predecessor, ERM II was designed to foster convergence and orient policies towards stability, thereby preparing members for eventual participation in the single currency. Although membership of ERM II was voluntary, the presumption was that all non-Euro-area, EU Member States would eventually join, with two years' membership mandatory for subsequent EMU entry.

In many respects the operating procedures for ERM II represented a simple continuation of the arrangements introduced for the original ERM. A central rate was defined for each participating currency around which a single ±15 per cent permissible band of fluctuation was described. As in ERM I, intervention at the margins was automatic and in principle unlimited, with access to very short-term financing facilities available for countries experiencing difficulty. However, unlike ERM I, there was no attempt to impose symmetry of adjustment on the new system. Central rates were defined in terms of the Euro and primacy was given to the objective of price stability over the maintenance of ERM II rates.

ERM II membership has expanded in four waves. Denmark joined the mechanism on 1 January 1999 and operates the same narrow ±2.25 per cent margins that it maintained throughout ERM I. Following enlargement, Estonia, Lithuania, and Slovenia joined ERM II on 28 June 2004 and although all three countries formally operate the standard ±15 per cent margin, Estonia and Lithuania unilaterally chose to maintain a Euro-based currency board whereby their central banks backed the national currency 100 per cent by the euro. The third wave of ERM II membership occurred on 2 May 2005 when Cyprus, Latvia, and Malta joined. Once again, although the notional margin is set at ±15 per cent for all three countries, Latvia unilaterally maintains the lat within a ±1 per cent margin whilst Malta unilaterally maintains the Maltese lira at the central rate, in effect adopting a fixed exchange rate with respect to the Euro. Finally, Slovakia joined the mechanism on 28 November 2005 and adopted the standard margin in the process. The Euro central rates and compulsory intervention rates for all eight ERM II participating countries as of 28 November 2005 are given in Table 10.2.

Progression from ERM II to the Euro requires participating countries to remain within the intervention margins of ERM II and also fulfil the Maastricht criteria. Satisfying these criteria, however, especially the inflation target, may be problematic for some countries. Although many have undergone huge changes in moving from being centrally planned to free market economies, they remain fragile and inflexible. They are therefore susceptible on two fronts. First, the removal of capital controls when they joined the EU may lead to instability and endanger the exchange rate targets under ERM II. In addition, structural reform and enhanced trade prospects within the EU are likely to give rise to relatively faster productivity growth and high wage increases in the industrial sector which, if transmitted to the low productivity service sector, will result in an increase in the overall rate of inflation. This potentially compromises the ability of the accession countries to achieve the Maastricht inflation target or may require them to deflate and therefore risk an unnecessary recession.

Table 10.2 Euro central rates and compulsory intervention rates for ERM II countries

Country (currency)	Lower rate	Central rate	Upper rate
Denmark (krone)	7.292520	7.460380	7.628240
Estonia (kroon)	13.299600	15.646600	17.993600
Cyprus (CY pound)	0.497483	0.585274	0.673065
Latvia (lats)	0.597383	0.702804	0.808225
Lithuania (litas)	2.934880	3.452800	3.970720
Malta (MT lira)	0.364905	0.429300	0.493695
Slovenia (tolar)	203.694000	239.640000	275.586000
Slovakia (koruna)	32.686800	38.455000	44.223300

Source: European Central Bank press release, 28 November 2005.

10.10 Conclusions

The successful launch of the Euro represents a remarkable achievement for the European Union. The successful replacement of twelve individual currencies by the Euro and the development of a clear framework by which other currencies can join the single currency represent a remarkable achievement that few commentators considered possible at the time of the currency crises in 1992 and 1993. However, not all aspects of the project have been a success. Two members of the EU, Denmark and Sweden, have voted against membership of the single currency in referenda, while a third, Britain, shows little willingness to join in the near future. However, despite these disappointments, the adoption of the single currency has been accompanied by a marked increase in the degree of policy cooperation that can only further increase integration among EU Member States.

■ **DISCUSSION QUESTIONS**

1. Describe the costs and benefits of monetary union.

2. Explain how the problem of opt-outs and pre-ins has been dealt with under ERM II.

3. To what extent should fiscal policy be considered as offering an independent policy instrument within a monetary union?

■ **FURTHER READING**

The subject matter of this chapter occupies several books. Those interested in the history and politics of monetary integration in Europe should consult Crawford (1996) or Gros and Thygesen (1998). The analytical framework of monetary union with particular reference to EMU is described by de Grauwe (2000). Monetary and fiscal policy within the framework of a monetary union is dealt with by Eijffinger and de Haan (2000). For current, up-to-date information on developments of the Euro, see the ECB's Monthly Bulletins and the ECB website at http://www.ecb.int/ and EU Commission's Europa site at http://www.europa.com. Giancarlo Corsetti's site at http://www.ieu.it/RSCAS/Research/Eurohomepage is also worth examining.

■ NOTES

1. In technical terms the countries first formed a monetary union by 'irrevocably' fixing the bilateral exchange rates of their national currencies, then moved on to a currency union by replacing their national currencies by a physically new currency, the Euro. The two terms are, however, used more or less interchangeably in this chapter.

2. Under the conventional Mundell–Fleming framework, for example, domestic monetary policy becomes completely ineffective under fixed exchange rates when international capital flows are perfectly mobile. See Mundell (1963) for details.

3. An interesting discussion in this context relates to the question of introducing a stabilizing role for the EU budget. In the United States, for example, much of the effect of regional disturbances is absorbed through the tax system. Fiscal federalism may therefore be a natural counterpart to currency union. See Eichengreen (1990) for a fuller discussion of these issues.

4. Rockoff (2000), for example, argues that it took 150 years for the United States to meet the criteria for an optimal currency area.

5. See Frankel and Rose (1998) for a discussion of this issue.

6. Under the Smithsonian Agreement European currencies were allowed to move within a ±2.25 per cent fluctuation band with respect to the dollar, implying that EC currencies could move within a band of ±4.5 per cent against the dollar and by twice that amount between themselves.

7. The original members of the EMS were Belgium, Denmark, France, Germany, Ireland, Italy, Netherlands, and the United Kingdom. The United Kingdom, however, initially chose not to participate in the ERM.

8. Sterling, for example, was included in the Ecu from the outset even though Britain did not join the ERM until 1990.

9. Asymmetric adjustment was characteristic of both the Bretton Woods system and the Snake. The loss of foreign exchange reserves by deficit nations placed a greater obligation on countries with weaker currencies to adjust than reserve accumulation did for countries with strong currencies.

10. The repayment period for the very short-term financing facility was initially set at forty-five days following the month in which intervention occurred. However, the repayment period was subsequently extended to seventy-five days by the Basle–Nyborg agreement of September 1987. The Basle–Nyborg agreement also made the VSTF facility available on a voluntary basis for financing intra-marginal intervention, that is, foreign exchange market intervention undertaken before a currency hits the floor or ceiling defined by the currency grid bands.

11. Albeit in the event, the referendum returned a weak endorsement (the 'petit oui') of the plan.

12. On 18 September 1992, for example, overnight interest rates in Ireland were set at 300 per cent; on 26 November the overnight rate was 100 per cent; on 3 August 1993 Danish overnight rates reached 250 per cent.

13. Frankel (1999) refers to the principle of the 'impossible trinity'. This principle says that a country must give up one of three goals: exchange rate stability, monetary independence, or financial market integration. With the progressive increase in financial market integration the choice effectively reduces to that between exchange rate integration and monetary independence.

14. There is some evidence that, in practice, the period after August 1993 was characterized by ERM central banks adopting a policy of committing to a narrow exchange rate target over the long term while tolerating wider fluctuations over the shorter term. See Bartolini and Prati (1998) for an example of how this has been modelled.

15. Denmark rejected Euro-area membership in a referendum on 28 September 2000, a stance subsequently adopted by Sweden also in a referendum on 14 September 2003. Sweden did not possess an opt-out clause under TEU but 'deliberately' failed the convergence tests by not joining the ERM. Greece eventually joined the Euro on 1 June 2001.

16. Ten new Member States joined the EU on 1 May 2004. These were the Czech Republic, Estonia, Hungary, Latvia, Lithuania, Poland, the Slovak Republic, Slovenia, Cyprus, and Malta.

■ REFERENCES

Artis, M. J. (2003), 'Reflections on the Optimal Currency Area (OCA) criteria in the light of EMU', *International Journal of Finance and Economics*, 8/4: 297–307.

Barro, R. and Gordon, D. (1983), 'Rules, Discretion and Reputation in a Model of Monetary Policy', *Journal of Monetary Economics*, 12: 101–21.

Bartolini, L. and Prati, A. (1998), *Soft Exchange Rate Bands and Speculative Attacks: Theory and Evidence from the ERM since August 1993*, IMF Working Paper no. 98/156 (Washington, DC: IMF).

Bayoumi, T. (1994), 'A Formal Model of Optimum Currency Areas', IMF Staff Papers, 41/4: 537–54.

—— and Eichengreen, B. (1994), *One Money or Many? Analyzing the Prospects for Monetary Unification in Various Parts of the World*, Princeton Studies in International Finance no. 76 (Princeton: Princeton University Press).

—— and Prasad, E. (1997), 'Currency Unions, Economic Fluctuations, and Adjustment: Some New Empirical Evidence', *IMF Staff Papers*, 44/1: 36–58.

Crawford, M. (1996), *One Money for Europe? The Economics and Politics of EMU* (New York: St Martin's Press).

De Grauwe, P. (2000), *Economics of Monetary Union*, 4th edn (Oxford: Oxford University Press).

Eichengreen, B. (1990), 'Currency Union', *Economic Policy*, 5, Apr.: 117–87.

Eijffinger, S. C. W. and de Haan, J. (2000), *European Monetary and Fiscal Policy* (Oxford: Oxford University Press).

Frankel, J. (1999), 'No Single Currency Regime is Right for all Countries or at all Times', *Essays in International Finance*, No. 215 (Princeton: Princeton University Press).

—— and Rose, A. (1998), 'The Endogeneity of the Optimum Currency Area Criterion', *The Economic Journal*, 108/449: 1009–25.

Gros, D. and Thygesen, N. (1998), *European Monetary Integration*, 2nd edn (Harlow: Addision Wesley-Longman).

Kenen, P. B. (1969), 'The Theory of Optimum Currency Areas: An Eclectic View', in R. A. Mundell and A. K. Swoboda (eds.), *Monetary Problems of the International Economy* (Chicago: Chicago University Press), 41–60.

Krugman, P. (1990), 'Policy Problems of a Monetary Union', in P. De Grauwe and L. Papademos (eds.), *The European Monetary System in the 1990s* (London: Longman), 48–64.

MacKinnon, R. I. (1963), 'Optimum Currency Areas', *American Economic Review*, 53/4: 717–25.

Mundell, R. (1961), 'A Theory of Optimum Currency Areas', *American Economic Review*, 51/4: 657–65.

—— (1963), 'Capital Mobility and Stabilization Policy under Fixed and Flexible Exchange Rates', *Canadian Journal of Economics and Political Science*, 29 (November): 475–85.

Padoa-Schioppa, T. (1988), 'The European Monetary System: A Long-term View', in Michael Giavazzi *et al.* (eds.), *The European Monetary System* (Cambridge: Cambridge University Press).

Rockoff, H. (2000), 'How Long did it Take the United States to Become an Optimal Currency Area?', *NBER Historical Paper* No. 124 (Cambridge, MA: NBER).

11 The ECB's Monetary Policy

Mike Artis

Introduction

In many ways the achievement of the Euro-area must be rated the European Union's premier success. To create an area over which a single monetary policy pertains, where before there were (as of October 2006) twelve separate currencies and monetary policies is a remarkable achievement. Not long ago, the possession of a national currency might have been treated as the hallmark of an individual country's sovereignty and as something not to be given up lightly. In fact, historically, currency unions that have not coincided with political unions have not survived well. Indeed it must be admitted that even after more than seven years of successful operation, there are eminent observers of the Euro-area (e.g. de Grauwe 2006) who predict that the lack of a coincident political union may prove a fatal flaw for the continued operation of Europe's currency area.

Chapter 10 has laid out the path followed to the creation of the Euro-area and the European Central Bank (ECB). In this chapter we will, first, describe the aims and objectives set out for the European Central Bank (ECB) which is in charge of monetary policy across the Euro-area, then, commenting on the ECB's unique constitutional position, go on to describe its policy framework and the apparent effects of its policy decisions—and more broadly, the effects of having a single currency area on trade and finance. Then we review some of the problems facing the ECB, especially the fact that its monetary policy has to suit a diverse set of countries with differing problems. At the end we will look again at the critical views that can be found concerning the ECB's future. In this respect our own conclusion will be more upbeat than some.

Aims and objectives

The European System of Central Banks, and the European Central Bank at its centre, works to a mandate set out in the Treaty of European Union (Maastricht Treaty) according to which: 'The primary objective of the ESCB shall be to maintain price stability', and 'without prejudice to the objective of price stability, the ESCB shall support the general economic policies in the Community with a view to contributing to the achievement of the objectives of the Community as laid down in Article 2' (Treaty Article 105.1). These objectives include those of high employment and growth. The definition of price stability was left to the ECB itself to refine and it defined it as 'a year on year increase in the Harmonized Index of Consumer prices (HICP) for the Euro-area of below 2 per cent', adding that this objective was to be attained 'in the medium term'. In a subtle amendment in 2003 the Governing Council of the ECB clarified that, in the pursuit of price stability, it aims to maintain inflation rates below, but 'close to' 2 per cent in the medium term. It should be noted that measurement error in the published price indices is generally thought to result in an overestimate of inflation (through an inability to account for quality improvement correctly) of the order of 1.5 per cent or more. This makes the formal definition of a low target *inflation rate* a sensible working equivalent of the injunction to maintain 'price stability'.

Such a statement of objectives accords broadly with the contemporary commitments of other central banks around the world,[1] though in some cases these omit any quantification (as in the case of the US Federal Reserve), or accompany the quantification with a 'band' formulation, as in the case of the Bank of England where, currently, the commitment is to contain inflation within +/−1 percentage point of 2 per cent and, instead of the horizon for the commitment being set at 'the medium term', it is set at two years. (Roger and Stone (2005) provide a survey of 'inflation targeting', indicating that it comes in many forms.) The similarity of the ECB's commitment to an inflation target to those entertained by other central banks has not prevented critical observers from squabbling over the small change of the differences that can be found in the precise terms of the commitment; but revealed practice has, with time, eroded the interest of such quibbles. (See Artis (2007) for further comment on this issue.) More enduring has been criticism of the ECB's constitutional position and its implications and the way in which its monetary strategy has been expressed. We turn first to a brief account of the latter. The issues of accountability and transparency are discussed in the subsequent section.

11.1 Monetary policy strategy

Given that the target is to contain inflation and given that monetary policy measures take time to have effect, it is obvious that a central bank which places primacy on inflation control needs to be able to have a view about the likely future trajectory of inflation in the absence of its intervention, so that it can take the appropriate measures. The ECB has set out its strategy for doing this in terms of two 'pillars', one of which is termed the 'monetary pillar', the other the 'economic pillar'. The first of these pillars refers to the information, considered most relevant for the longer term, provided by the growth rate of a monetary aggregate; the second, considered to be more relevant to the short-term prognosis, refers to everything else that might be relevant to an assessment of the risks to price stability. Critical observers have claimed that this language, and the order in which the information pertaining to the two pillars was initially presented, was unnecessarily confusing: for example, in the initial formulation, information on the monetary pillar was presented first, suggesting that somehow monetary analysis might be given more weight. Then again a monetary growth 'reference rate' was presented as a metric to be revised (in principle) every year. In 2003 the ECB reversed the order of presentation of the pillars and renounced the practice of reviewing each year its 'reference rate' for monetary growth. Criticism aimed at finding defects in the ECB's communication policy has subsided since that time. By and large it is now accepted that the ECB should be regarded as an 'inflation targeting central bank' like (but not the same as) its peers (see Artis 2007).

11.2 Monetary policy instruments

The ECB also acts like other modern central banks in choosing to confine its stock of policy instruments essentially to the setting of one 'policy' rate of interest, the so-called 'Main Refinancing Rate' (MFR).[2] Figure 11.1 shows the course of the MFR since the inception of the Euro-area. The ECB operates through the mechanism of 'repos', repurchase agreements generally of two weeks' length; the interest rate is indicated by the difference between the purchase price of the repo and the par value at which it will be realized after two weeks. By indicating the minimum price at which it will accept bids for the initial purchase, the ECB signals its policy rate. By arbitrage this rate is closely linked to other market-determined short-term interest rates. Longer rates are less closely tied to current movements of the MFR because they tend to reflect the market's assessment of the permanence of the current MFR; if the current MFR is expected to be followed by further rises, longer rates will rise, but if the market expects that a rise in the MFR will prove to be just a blip, long rates will not move much, if at all. The transmission mechanism of monetary policy is the means by which changes in the instrument of monetary policy

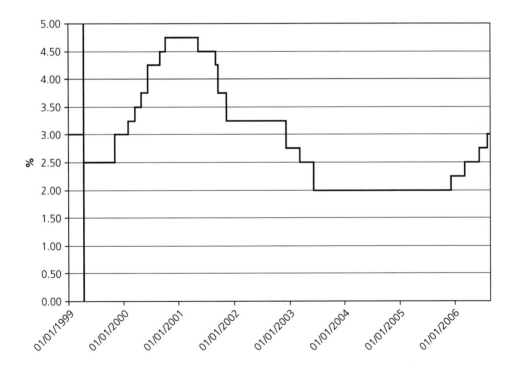

Figure 11.1 The Main Refinancing Rate, 1999–2006

will affect the economy at large. Generally, it is expected that interest rate changes will directly affect activity via their impact on spending decisions and through the effect they may have on the exchange rate and thus on decisions as to whether to buy or sell goods abroad. The transmission mechanism can be expected to vary across countries owing to their different institutions, and this can in principle complicate the ECB's task in setting monetary policy. We return to this issue below after we have examined the policy record. First, however, we turn to discuss the issue of accountability and transparency.

11.3 Transparency and accountability

It is generally reckoned to be in the interests of effective stabilization and low inflation to ensure that the central bank is independent from day-to-day political pressures (Barro and Gordon 1983; Walsh 1998). This independence can be secured in different ways. The statutes governing the operations of the European Central Bank were modelled upon those governing Germany's Bundesbank which were widely regarded as an appropriate model, endowing the central bank with a large degree of independence from the German government. That model was taken to heart in the statutes of the European Central Bank set out in the Treaty of European Union. According to this Treaty the Governing Council of the ECB should be made up of the governors of the individual member central banks (themselves required to be independent) together with a six-person Executive Board to be chosen by 'common consent'. All these individuals are required to act and vote as 'Europeans' and definitely not as country representatives; terms of office are specified as sufficiently long to remove or severely dilute the prospect of a secure job 'back home' tempting an individual to 'vote for his or her country's interests'. Other statutes forbid the ECB from 'bailing out' a member country by open market purchases and forbid it from taking advice from member countries or EU institutions such as the Commission. All this sounds strong stuff. It is worth noting, though, that 'independence on paper' is one thing and effective independence is another; for the latter, an institution like a central bank needs the support of the public based on its track record and firm leadership (Lohmann (1996) points out the difference between paper independence and real independence with exceptional vigour). The Bundesbank enjoyed a position of real independence and was able to fight (and win) on a number of important issues in struggles with the government. The ECB has yet to have its strength tested in this way; it is simultaneously in a stronger and weaker position than the Bundesbank: weaker because its standing with the 'European public' is not developed (as indeed the concept of the European public is not!), and its reliance on the European Parliament is weakened by that institution's own lack of credibility. But the ECB may be stronger because those institutions which might want to control it—the Finance Ministries of the member governments of the Euro-area—are several in number and not likely to agree with each other (whereas the Bundesbank had only one potential opponent—the German government or Finance Ministry, and that opponent could be determined and of one voice).

The formal requirements of accountability falling on the ECB, in the absence of a European government, are that it should report to the European Parliament on a regular basis, something that it has been very keen to do for fear of being pressurized to account, instead or as well, to the Finance Ministries of the member governments which have grouped themselves together as the 'EuroGroup'. This has resulted in a promising 'monetary dialogue' with the relevant committee of the European Parliament (Eijffinger and Mujagic 2004). The ECB's formal independence is underscored by the fact that nothing can be changed without a revision of the Treaty, which is not something that can be arranged easily. These provisions have incurred criticism for the extent to which they remove the bank from democratic pressures, but are lauded by many economists for the freedom from short-sighted government intervention that they also provide. A concomitant is that governments feel quite prepared to criticize the ECB in strong terms, which can lead to an atmosphere of perpetual recrimination that does not seem helpful (see Goodhart 2006).

When formal accountability is lacking it is all the more important for the institution concerned to be transparent in what it does and how it does it.[3] Moreover, by being transparent about the circumstances which lead it to take action (i.e. revealing its 'reaction function'), the central bank can enlist the support of the market rather than working against the grain.[4] Mervyn King, governor of the Bank of England, celebrated this idea by saying that his ambition was for his bank to be so predictable as to be 'boring' (King 2000). The ECB has a strong record on transparency; it has published widely about what it does and why (aside from its *Monthly Bulletin*, see also European Central Bank 2004), and according to relevant research it has become as transparent to the market as other leading central banks. Even so, there have been doubts and criticisms. In the early days of its operations, the ECB several times surprised the markets by its actions; its accounts of its decisions given in press conference by the first president of the ECB were often regarded as opaque; it has decided to take decisions 'by consensus' and discountenanced the prospect of publishing attributed votes in the manner of members of the Bank of England's monetary policy committee (see the debate between Buiter (1999) and Issing (1999) on the voting issue).

11.4 The record

We now turn to an examination of the ECB's policy record. If Figure 11.1 (see above) shows the track of the ECB's principal policy instrument, Figure 11.2 shows the track of its principal objective, the rate of inflation as measured by the annual rate of change of the Harmonized Index of Consumer Prices.

It is clear from the figure that inflation has been more often above than below the target ceiling rate of 2 per cent. Does this mean that the ECB has failed? Such a verdict would be inappropriate or premature for a number of reasons: first, the target is set for the 'medium term', not for a specified horizon; second, when forecasters are asked what their expectations are for inflation in the medium term, they respond by saying 'less than 2 per cent'; third, the infractions of the ceiling rate are neither persistent nor drastic. The ECB has itself recently concluded that 'Euro-area longer term inflation expectations have in recent years been well-anchored at levels consistent with price stability. Survey-based

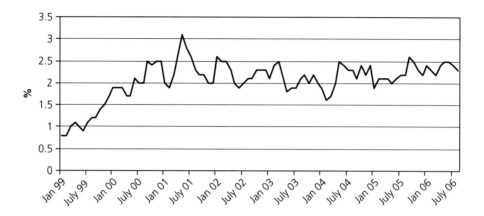

Figure 11.2 Euro-area HICP inflation, 1999–2006 (percentage per annum)

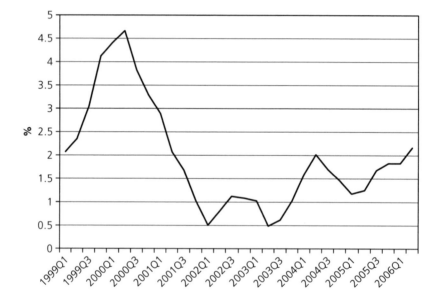

Figure 11.3 Euro-area real GDP growth, 1999–2006

measures of longer-term inflation expectations have been below but close to 2 per cent' (*ECB Monthly Bulletin*, July 2006, p. 67). The emphasis on longer-term expectations indicates that the ECB is relaxed about short-term inflation bursts associated with oil price surges or indirect tax hikes.

All this might lead us to a favourable verdict on the ECB's performance, but it is still important to take a closer look at the record. This would certainly reveal that the Euro-area's record for GDP growth is well below that of, say, the United States.

Figure 11.3 shows how, aside from an early period of rapid growth, the ECB has presided over a long period of low output growth. By contrast, in the USA, output growth—aside from the sharp recession in 2001—has been persistently high. How much of the Euro-area's inferior record should be attributed to mistakes in the setting of monetary policy can be debated, but it seems unlikely that much of the deficiency should be so attributed. Generally, weakness in the GDP growth rate is to be attributed to structural features of the Euro-area economy; moreover, it must be recalled that the ECB's primary objective is that of price stability. The Maastricht Treaty does not invite the ECB to trade off growth-stimulating measures against those designed to ensure price stability—but rather to ensure price stability *first*. Some observers (e.g. Artis and Allsopp 2003) have argued that the ECB should have followed the kind of 'adventurist' policy pursued by the US Federal Reserve through the 1990s, when interest rates were maintained at a lower level than tradi-tional concern for the implications of high growth for inflation might have indicated, with the beneficent result of higher growth and no higher inflation—and it is possible, in fact, that this kind of suggestion was taken to heart by the ECB since, throughout 2004 and 2005, the ECB maintained its interest rate at 2 per cent in the face of persistently higher-than-target inflation.

When the ECB 'opened for business' in July 1998 its first task was to assist in guiding the interest rates of the eleven countries which had then been selected for participation in the Euro-area to come to a common level by the end of the year, for which time it had already been agreed that the 'new' currency, the Euro, would replace the pre-existing Ecu on a one-for-one basis.[5] From then on, all the participating countries would necessarily have the same interest rate, set by the ECB. Some countries entered the new system from a position in which they had upwardly divergent interest rates selected to combat higher inflation and to cool domestic booms; this was notably the case for Ireland, for example, but Finland, Spain, and the Netherlands were also implicated. For these countries the transition to the Euro-area, involving as it did a cut in interest rates, administered an expansionary jolt. Nevertheless this job was done and the ECB set the MFR at 3 per cent for 1 January. This rate was already lower than many had anticipated earlier in 1998, reflecting some caution about the possible deflationary consequences of the south-east Asian foreign exchange crises. The rate was in fact reduced again in April, but it was not long before the ECB adjusted the rate upwards through 1999 and 2001 until May of the latter year, after which interest rate reductions were effected.

Greece joined the Euro-area in 2001 and with effect from the beginning of 2002 the ECB successfully managed the logistically daunting task of introducing the physical new currency; up to that point the EMU had in effect been an exchange rate union, with the Member States maintaining their own currencies in fixed relationship to one another. The conversion rates of the old to the new currencies were of course identical to those implied in the 'irrevocably fixed exchange rates' between the old currencies and the new one (see Box 11.1); the introduction of the common physical currency had important symbolic value and simplified (or should have done) cross-border payments within the Euro-area.

Monetary policy through 2001 and 2002 was dominated by the outfall of the bursting of the 'dotcom' bubble in the United States at the end of 2000. The ECB was slow at first to react to the deflationary implications of this event, which turned out to be considerable, arguing at the time (in line with many other observers) that as the Euro-area approxim-ated a closed economy from the perspective of trade, the implications of a US downturn

---

BOX 11.1 THE IRREVOCABLE EURO CONVERSION RATES: NATIONAL CURRENCY PER EURO

National currency	Conversion rate
Belgian franc	40.3399
German mark	1.95583
Spanish peseta	166.386
French franc	6.55957
Irish punt	0.787564
Italian lira	1936.27
Luxembourg franc	40.3399
Dutch guilder	2.20371
Austrian schilling	13.7603
Portuguese escudo	200.482
Finnish marka	5.94573
Greek drachma	340.750

Note: These conversion rates derived from the decision to make the Euro a one-for-one replacement of the Ecu as of 31 December 1998. The Ecu was a cocktail currency consisting of so many French francs, so many Italian lire, etc.; the value of the Ecu itself was left to be determined by market forces.

The cross exchange rates between the national currencies were fixed for the end of 1998 by the decision to use the currencies' central Ecu exchange rates, whereas the external value of the Ecu and therefore the Euro was determined by the market along with the implied conversion rates reported above.

---

for the Euro-area were not of a first order. As events proved, this turned out to be mistaken appreciation of the strength and significance of the ties between the USA and the Euro-area—which extend well beyond the realm of trade as such—and neglected the fact that a considerable part of the fall in share values associated with the bursting of the bubble directly hit investors outside the USA (including some in Europe). At any rate, the consequences became clear fairly quickly and the ECB reversed its previous policy of raising the MFR, with a cut in May 2001 followed by further decreases throughout the year. Nevertheless the ECB was widely criticized for reacting 'too little too late', and observers drew unfavourable parallels with the more drastic and swifter interest rate cuts promoted by the Federal Reserve. These criticisms may have been too harsh, however, in that the downturn in output was more severe and quicker in the USA (Alesina *et al.* 2001). In fact, in Europe no 'official recession' was ever announced for this period by the CEPR's Euro-area business-cycle dating committee (the European equivalent of the US NBER business-cycle dating committee), in contrast to the situation in the USA. Instead, a period of slow growth set in.

After two cuts in the MFR during 2003, the ECB maintained the MFR 'on hold' at 2 per cent throughout 2004 and virtually all of 2005. Some further increases were made in 2006. The long period of low interest rates coincided with a desire to avoid the phenomenon of 'deflation', with negative inflation and interest rates forced towards the zero bound: this concern had been instilled by the experience of Japan, where nominal interest rates had hit their zero bound. The rewording of the monetary strategy in 2003 in part reflected this same concern. In practice this meant a reluctance to cut rates any further, a reluctance supported by forecasts of growth which in the event proved somewhat optimistic. During 2005 it began to seem evident that the rate of interest was as low as it should be, if not lower. The realization of some of the formerly disappointing growth forecasts, together with some threats to inflation stemming from oil price rises, made it seem prudent late in 2005 to begin a rate-increasing exercise which lasted through 2006.

11.5 The exchange rate

We cannot leave an appreciation of ECB monetary policy without pausing on the topic of the exchange rate, if only because the course of the exchange rate has made fools of the pundits who referred to it as a source of scorn for ECB policy in the early days of the new currency. Figure 11.4 shows the value of the dollar/Euro exchange rate (in dollars per Euro) since the inception of the new currency.

As can readily be seen the period began with a precipitate decline in the value of the Euro. At the outset the market valued the Euro as worth more than a dollar—at an average of $1.16 in fact, during January 1999. The Euro fell more or less continuously after that, reaching a monthly average low of 87 cents in February 2002. This decline was used by many observers as a measure of the extent to which the ECB's policy and/or the structure of the Euro-area economy was inferior to that of the United States. The truth is that it remains hard to explain this period, and the subsequent reversal of fortunes

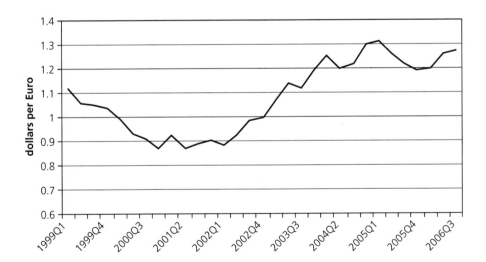

Figure 11.4 The external value of the Euro: the dollar exchange rate, 1999–2006 (dollars per Euro, quarterly averages)

(indeed, more than a reversal) in later years when none of the fundamentals—relative GDP growth or relative interest rates, for example—have changed for any considerable period of time. By the end of 2002, the Euro had recovered to reach a value of more than $1, and thereafter appreciated strongly to levels of $1.20 to $1.30. The initial depreciation of the exchange rate did seem eventually to rattle the policy-makers in the ECB, leading them to intervene directly in the foreign exchange market to support the Euro, despite the earlier claims they had made that 'benign neglect' was the best policy. The interventions, coming in September and November 2000, were coordinated with the Federal Reserve on one occasion and on another not; they appeared to leave little permanent effect and were criticized as to their explanation and execution (see Koen *et al.* 2001). It did the ECB little good.

11.6 Asymmetries

A key desideratum of a common currency area has always been said to be that the member countries of the area should experience broadly common ('symmetric') shocks and business cycles. Otherwise the common monetary policy will be inappropriate for some, and perhaps for all, the countries in the area. Experience in the Euro-area has shown that there are a number of differences between countries which can make them feel uncomfortable with the ECB's policies. The position of those countries which entered the union from a position of higher interest rates has already been mentioned. Inflation rates within the Euro-area continue to show differentials, but their dispersion is not greatly different from the differentials to be found within the states of the USA, although they are more persistent. Figure 11.5 shows a way of measuring the differences between countries (in this case, in 2005) which balances inflation differentials against output gap differentials.

The presentation is described as one of 'Taylor Rule-warranted interest rates' because it is based on the so-called 'Taylor Rule' that John Taylor (1999) advanced as a rule of thumb for describing central bank behaviour. Taylor reasoned that a central bank would aim to reduce inflation and unemployment (or negative output gaps) so far as possible. In practice, he argued, central banks should be found to respond to inflation with a more-than-matching interest rate increase—that is to say, the bank should make sure that the *real* rate of interest rose after the evidence of an increase in inflation. Most central banks would also reduce interest rates when unemployment or spare capacity (the 'output gap') rose. This reasoning has been found to yield a close approximation to many central banks' behaviour. A stylized regression would be as follows:

$$r = \alpha + \beta\pi + \gamma(y - x)$$

where r is the policy rate of interest, π is the rate of inflation, y the (log of the) actual rate of output, and x the (log of the) rate of capacity (or 'trend') output; α, β, and γ are coefficients, of which, in line with the arguments above, we should expect $\beta > 1$ and $\gamma > 0$. Stylized empirical values for β and γ are respectively 1.5 and 0.5, values often approximated in empirical work. The calculations shown in Figure 11.5 are based on a version of

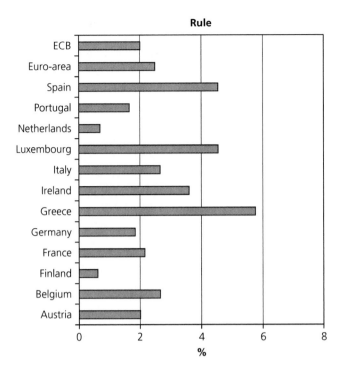

Figure 11.5 Taylor Rule-warranted interest rates, 2005

this where α has been set to zero, γ to 0.5, and the sum of the coefficients on current and one-year lagged inflation (β) come to 1.5. Data for the output gap are taken from the OECD. As the figure shows, the Taylor Rule-warranted rate, calculated at just over 2 per cent for the Euro-area as a whole, is a little higher than the rate set by the ECB (which stayed at 2 per cent almost throughout 2005, only rising on 5 December). The ECB's rate is shown as more or less in line with Germany's needs and those of France, much lower than that warranted by conditions in Greece, Spain, and Luxembourg, and much higher than those called for by conditions in Finland or the Netherlands. Such deviations are certainly to be expected, but there is some evidence that they have declined over time as convergence has improved. The prospect for further improvement may be weakened, however, by the entry of the new Member States into the Euro-area.

The reason for this apprehension can be summed up in the term 'the Balassa–Samuelson effect' (see Balassa (1964) and Samuelson (1964) for the original articles in which this effect was described).[6] It has been widely noticed that countries undergoing structural reform and development regularly undergo a period of appreciation in their real exchange rates. The trigger for this is that, as the countries enter into international trade, their goods export prices must compete with those set in the international market, which they find easy enough to do as productivity and productivity growth in their traded goods sector (generally, manufacturing) accelerates with the onset of the development process in the country. Labour market dynamics tend to ensure that wages rise *throughout* the economy with the rise in productivity in the traded goods sector, causing prices to rise in the (low-productivity) non-traded goods sector. If the exchange rate is flexible, measures of its nominal and real value will show an appreciation; if the exchange rate is fixed, then the real appreciation will show itself in the form of a rise in prices. This process is an *equilibrium adjustment* for the countries concerned, but is indistinguishable from inflation so far as its impact on the price index goes. There has been a fear that after the new Member States enter the Euro-area, a group of high inflation countries will form, which, given that the ECB sticks to its target, must be offset by low inflation performers elsewhere —hence convergence must be delayed. Alternatively, the Balassa–Samuelson effect will contribute to a problem for the new Member States in satisfying the criteria for entry in so far as these are seen as requiring *both* a period of fixed exchange rates *and* a period of low inflation (see Buiter and Grafe 2002).

11.7 The trade effects of monetary union

While the problem of asymmetries may imply a cost for some countries some of the time in belonging to the Euro-area, the formation of the currency union was all along held to convey some benefits, especially the benefits of increased trade, to the participants. The Commission, in its important original study of the matter (CEC 1990) found it natural to view the creation of the common currency area as one of 'completing the market'. Its focus was on the elimination of transactions costs created by the possession of—and the need to exchange—individual currencies; with the introduction of a single currency the costs of exchange from one currency to another would be eliminated and there would be additional benefits to competition from the greater transparency of prices resulting from their quotation in a single currency. The Commission offered some estimates of the trade enhancement effect which, naturally enough, depended on the efficiency of the banking system (more efficient systems for exchanging currency incur less cost), but for a developed country could amount to 0.2 per cent of GDP. This is a small order of magnitude; nor has empirical work delivered reliable evidence that volatile exchange rates deter trade. The profession's sceptical reaction to Andrew Rose's early estimates of very big trade effects (Frankel and Rose 1997, 1998; Rose 2000) was therefore not surprising. Rose deployed panel data estimation, with currency union entering as a dummy variable and (bilateral) trade as the explicandum. The panels involved a large cross-section but a rather weak time dimension. The order of magnitude of the effect initially detected was of the order of 300 per cent. The estimates were faulted as unduly dependent upon monetary unions between small 'postage stamp' countries and larger neighbours, and unduly dependent upon developing economy experience. Even the more modest re-estimates (e.g. Persson 2001), however, continued to be compatible with a large effect. For developed countries the most pertinent example appeared to be that of the break-up of the exchange rate union between the Republic of Ireland and the UK; Thom and Walsh (2001) claimed to find no great decline in Anglo-Irish trade as a result of the Republic joining the Euro-area. The most influential adaptation of the Rose approach, however, came with the paper by Micco *et al.* (2003) which concentrated on the European case and used data which overlapped with the Euro-period. Micco and his colleagues also found large effects from the introduction of the Euro on trade, even if not quite so big as some of Rose's earliest estimates. HM Treasury (2003) updated and replicated the Micco study, reporting a potential increase in trade for the UK following entry into the Eurozone of 50 per cent in total. Since the Treasury's work, there has emerged a number of studies critical of the design of the Micco *et al.* study, among them: Bun and Klaassen (2004) and Baldwin (2005). The common feature of the critical line pursued in these studies is that EMU itself is endogenous to the process of integration, more so among the core economies of Europe than among the peripheral countries. From this the suggestion might be that any dating from which to deduce a 'post hoc ergo propter hoc' 'EMU effect' is largely arbitrary. While this makes it difficult to pursue an econometric estimate with confidence, it does not mean that the countries were wrong to create the Euro-area; rather, on the contrary, seeing the course of further integration and trade enhancement they were right to seek a way of reducing the transactions cost.

11.8 Financial integration effects

In some respects the financial integration effects of creating the Euro-area have been much clearer. The European government bond market is extremely well integrated and larger than that for US bonds; also well integrated are the markets for corporate bonds and there are signs that the equity markets are following suit. It is true that the integration process has not yet spread to retail banking, where central banks are among those guilty of slowing down a process that should make retail banking in Europe significantly more efficient—but this is a promise for the future. Financial integration appears particularly important in a currency union because it permits consumption risk sharing to occur through cross-country portfolio ownership and diversification and easier access to credit. This is of special importance because one of the problems in a monetary union is the unequal sharing of risk that occurs which the common monetary policy necessarily cannot address. In a political union the fiscal system would automatically permit a degree of risk sharing. Suppose that in one region of the country there is a boom whilst in another there is recession. A redistributive fiscal system will automatically raise the effective average rate of tax in the booming region and lower it in the recessionary one. This allows consumption to be protected to some degree from the impact of the primary income changes exemplified in the boom–bust pattern. The Euro-area does not possess a redistributive fiscal system at the level of the Union. But financial integration may do the job. If the citizens of the recession-hit country hold portfolios of assets, some of which are issued from the boom-hit country, then the flow of dividends will help insure consumption levels against the impact of primary changes in income. Some estimates for the USA (see Asdrubali *et al.* 1996) now suggest that in that country these capital market channels are more important than the fiscal ones in spreading consumption risk. For the Euro-area this degree of financial integration has yet to be reached, but it may well be closer to realization than any degree of inter-country fiscal insurance, since the latter waits on political union.

11.9 Conclusions

The Euro-area works and its central bank has proved capable of conducting an effective monetary policy in a world which is prone to shocks, even whilst meeting a number of logistical and strategic challenges—from the replacement of the legacy currencies by the Euro, to planning for the enlargement of the Euro-area as the new member countries eventually joined. The Treaty of European Union does not prescribe any penalty for leaving the Union, and continued membership for any given country depends upon that country continuing to find the prospective balance of benefits and costs to be positive for it. The new member countries have all signed up to the idea of participating in the Euro-area, although to date only Slovenia has succeeded in qualifying. Of the other three countries eligible to join, Denmark, Sweden, and the UK, the last two seem unlikely to join for some time to come, if ever. Denmark, on the other hand, is acting as if it were already a member.

Looking further ahead, though, it is not difficult to see that continued tensions can arise from the continuation of asymmetries and of non-convergence, and that circumstances could present themselves which would exacerbate these. It is in this context that some observers draw attention to the fact that political union offers the salve of common citizenship, which makes shared sacrifices acceptable and institutional innovation practicable that could offer the hope of relieving the worst tensions. What most have in mind here is the introduction of some type of fiscal insurance system. Yet if it is clear that the Euro-area is a long way from a political union of this type, it is equally clear that at the moment it does not need one. It might be possible to imagine that financial integration could proceed far enough and quickly enough to avoid the need to elaborate any inter-country insurance system.

■ DISCUSSION QUESTIONS

1. What is the Balassa–Samuelson effect? Why is it problematic (if it is) for the Euro-area?

2. In what sense does the creation of the Euro-area help to 'complete the single market'? What other effects does the creation of the Euro-area have?

3. Compare the fiscal policy and capital market channels for consumption risk sharing.

■ FURTHER READING

The publications of the European Central Bank itself (especially its *Monthly Bulletin*) and its web site (http://www.ecb.int) are very useful sources of information. A more critical view is offered by the publications in the CEPR's series 'Monitoring the European Central Bank'. These are authored by different collections of observers from issue to issue, but always by prominent authorities.

NOTES

1. In line with the recommendations of modern monetary theory (e.g. Woodford 2003, 2006).

2. Exceptionally, as noted below, the ECB has intervened in the foreign exchange market to influence the Euro exchange rate, but this is not an instrument to which the ECB has had frequent recourse.

3. For a formal treatment of transparency in this context, see Geraats (2002).

4. A number of formal (i.e. econometrically estimated) studies of the ECB's reaction function exist e.g. Gerdesmeier and Roffia (2003), Gerlach-Kristensen (2003), Surico (2003), and Gerlach (2005) which suggest that European monetary policy is guided by consistent and appropriate criteria.

5. Box 1 shows the irrevocable conversion rates established for the participating currencies and includes the rate for Greece which joined later. The decision that the Euro should replace the existing Ecu on a one-for-one basis made for some 'awkward' conversion rates, as can be seen.

6. A standard textbook treatment of the Balassa–Samuelson effect can be accessed in, for example, Krugman and Obstfeld (2003).

REFERENCES

Alesina, A., Blanchard, O., Gali, J., Giavazzi, F., and Uhlig, H. (2001), 'Defining a Macroeconomic Framework for the Euro-area', *Monitoring the European Central Bank*, no. 3 (London: Centre for Economic Policy Research).

Artis, M. J. (2007 forthcoming), 'The Performance of the ECB', in P. Arestis (ed.), *Is There a New Consensus in Macroeconomics?* (Basingstoke: Palgrave Macmillan).

—— and Allsopp, C. (2003), 'EMU Four Years On: The Assessment', *Oxford Review of Economic Policy*, 19: 1–29.

Asdrubali, P., Sorenson, B., and Yosha, O. (1996), 'Channels of Interstate Risk-sharing: United States 1963–1990', *Quarterly Journal of Economics*, 111: 1081–100.

Balassa, B. (1964), 'The Purchasing Power Parity Doctrine: A Reappraisal', *Journal of Political Economy*, 72: 584–96.

Baldwin, R. (2005), 'The Euro's Trade Effects', paper prepared for the ECB workshop 'What Effect is EMU Having . . . ?', Frankfurt, June.

Barro, R. and Gordon, R. (1983), 'A Positive Theory of Monetary Growth', *Journal of Political Economy*, 91: 589–610.

Berger, H., de Haan, J., and Sylvester, S. (2000), *Central Bank Independence: An Update of Theory and Evidence*, CEPR Discussion Paper no. 2353 (London: Centre for Economic Policy Research).

Buiter, W. (1999), 'Alice in Euroland', *Journal of Common Market Studies*, 37: 181–209.

—— and Grafe, C. (2002), 'Anchor, Float or Abandon Ship? Exchange Rate Regimes for the Accession Countries', *Quarterly Review of the Banca Nazionale del Lavoro*, 122: 1–32.

Bun, M. J. G. and Klaassen, F. J. G. M. (2004), 'The Euro Effect on Trade is not as Large as Commonly Thought', revision of 'The Importance of Accounting for Time Trends when Estimating the Euro Effect on Trade', Tinbergen Institute, DP 03-086/2, University of Amsterdam, downloadable from http://www1.fee.uva.n/pp/klaassen/.

Commission of the European Communities (CEC) (1990), 'One Market, One Money', *European Economy*, 44 (October).

De Grauwe, P. (2002), 'Challenges for Monetary Policy in Euroland', *Journal of Common Market Studies*, 40/4: 693–718.

—— (2006), 'Monetary Integration since the Maastrict Treaty', *Journal of Common Market Studies*, 44/4: 711–30.

Eijffinger, S. (1997), 'Central Bank Independence: Theory and Evidence', in S. Eijffinger (ed.), *Independent Central Banks and Economic Performance* (Cheltenham: Edward Elgar).

—— and Mujagic, E. (2004), 'An Assessment of the Monetary Dialogue on the ECB's Accountability and Transparency: A Qualitative Approach', *Intereconomics*, 39/4: 190–203.

European Central Bank (2004), *The Monetary Policy of the ECB* (Frankfurt am Main: European Central Bank).

Frankel, J. and Rose, A. (1997), 'Is EMU More Justifiable Ex-post than Ex-ante?', *European Economic Review*, 41: 753–60.

—— —— (1998), 'The Endogeneity of the Optimum Currency Area Criteria', *Economic Journal*, 108: 1009–25.

Geraats, P. M. (2002), 'Central Bank Transparency', *Economic Journal*, 112: F532–65.

Gerdesmeier, D. and Roffia, B. (2003), 'Empirical Estimates of Reaction Functions for the Euro Area', *ECB Working Paper* no. 206 (Frankfurt: European Central Bank).

Gerlach, S. (2005), *Interest Rate Setting by the ECB; Words and Deeds*, CEPR Discussion Paper no. 4775.

Gerlach-Kristensen, P. (2003), *Interest Rate Reaction Functions and the Taylor Rule in the Euro Area'*, ECB Working Paper no. 258.

Goodhart, C. A. E. (2006), 'The ECB and the Conduct of Monetary Policy', *Journal of Common Market Studies*, 44/4: 757–78.

HM Treasury (2003), *UK Membership of the Single Currency: An Assessment of the Five Economic Tests*, CM 5776 (London: HMSO).

Issing, O. (1999), 'The Eurosystem: Transparent and Accountable or "Willem in Euroland"', *Journal of Common Market Studies*, 37/3: 503–20.

—— (2002), 'On Macroeconomic Policy Coordination in EMU', *Journal of Common Market Studies*, 40/2: 345–58.

King, M. (2000), Address to the Joint Luncheon of the American Economic Association and the American Finance Association, 7 Jan, http://www.bankofengland.co.uk/publications/speeches/2000/speech67.htm.

Koen, V., Boone, L., de Serres, A., and Fuchs, N. (2001), *Tracking the Euro*, OECD Economics Department Working Papers no. 298 (Paris: OECD).

Krugman, P. and Obstfeld, M. (2003), *International Economics: Theory and Policy* (New York: Addison-Wesley).

Lohmann, S. (1996), 'Quis custodiet ipsos custodies? Necessary Conditions for Price Stability in Europe', in H. Siebert (ed.), *Monetary Policy in an Integrated World Economy* (Tubingen: J. C. B. Mohr) (Paul Siebeck).

Micco, A., Stein, E., and Ordonez, G. (2003), 'The Currency Union Effect on Trade: Early Evidence from EMU', *Economic Policy*, 37: 317–56.

Persson, T. (2001), 'Currency Unions and Trade: How Large is the Treatment Effect?', *Economic Policy*, 16: 433–48.

Pisani-Ferry, J. (2006), 'The Debate over the Economic Governance of the Euro Area', *Journal of Common Market Studies*, 44/4: 823–44.

Roger, S. and Stone, M. (2005), *On Target? The International Experience with Achieving Inflation Targets*, IMF Working Papers no. WP/05/163 (Washington: International Monetary Fund).

Rose, A. (2000), 'One Money, One Market: The Effect of Common Currencies on Trade', *Economic Policy*, 30: 7–46.

Samuelson, P. (1964), 'Theoretical Notes on Trade Problems', *Review of Economics and Statistics*, 46 (May): 145–54.

Surico, P. (2003), 'Asymmetric Reaction Functions for the Euro Area', *Oxford Review of Economic Policy*, 19: 44–57.

Taylor, J. B. (1999), 'An Historical Analysis of Monetary Policy Rules', in J. B. Taylor (ed.), *Monetary Policy Rules* (Chicago: University of Chicago Press).

Thom, R. and Walsh, F. (2001), 'The Effect of a Common Currency on Trade: Ireland before and after the Sterling Link', University College Dublin, mimeo.

Walsh, C. (1998), *Monetary Theory and Policy* (Cambridge, MA: MIT Press).

Winkler, B. (2002), 'Which Kind of Transparency? On the Need for Effective Communication in Monetary Policy Making', *Ifo-studies*, 48: 401–27.

Woodford, M. (2003), *Interest and Prices: Foundations of a Theory of Monetary Policy* (Princeton: Princeton University Press).

—— (2006), 'Rules for Monetary Policy', *NBER Reporter*, Spring, 17–22.

12 Fiscal Policy

Richard Morris, Hedwig Ongena, and
Bernhard Winkler*

Introduction

At the core of the fiscal policy framework for the Economic and Monetary Union (EMU)
is the requirement of achieving fiscal discipline to join the Euro-area and of maintaining
it once the single currency has been adopted. The underlying reasoning is that fiscal discipline strengthens the conditions for price stability and for sustainable growth conducive
to employment creation. Under this framework, fiscal policy remains the responsibility of
national policy-makers but is constrained by rules and procedures.

The framework for fiscal policy-making is established in Article 104 of the Treaty and
in the Protocol on the excessive deficit procedure. The provisions of Article 104 were
elaborated further in the Stability and Growth Pact (SGP). The provisions set out in the
Treaty and the SGP apply to all countries of the European Union (EU), but they are more
stringent for the countries that participate in the monetary union.

This fiscal policy framework has been implemented in full since the adoption of the
single currency on 1 January 1999. There are now more than eight years of experience
with the implementation in practice of this framework. During this period, the Council
of Ministers of Economic Affairs and Finance (ECOFIN Council) examined nine sets of
stability and convergence programmes submitted by the EU Member States and adopted
opinions on them. The Council has also adopted numerous decisions and recommendations with a view to preventing and correcting excessive deficits. This 'jurisprudence' and
the agreed interpretations that have been established so far need to be taken into account
when assessing the effectiveness of the rules, procedures, and practices governing fiscal
policy-making in the EU and in the Euro-area.

Since the start of EMU, there have also been several debates between policy-makers
on the interpretation of the rules set out in the Treaty and the SGP. These debates helped
to clarify the provisions of the Treaty and the SGP, but also led to open disagreements
between the ECOFIN Council and the European Commission. These culminated in a
crisis in November 2003 when the Council decided not to implement further steps in
excessive deficit procedures against Germany and France, and the Commission challenged this decision at the European Court of Justice. To restore the credibility of the
framework following these events, the Commission and the Council decided to reform
the SGP. After several months of negotiations, the SGP was reformed in March 2005 and

its implementation since then has so far proceeded quite smoothly, albeit in a context of favourable economic conditions.

The aim of this chapter is to explain why a rules-based framework for fiscal policy-making is necessary in a monetary union and what the main features are of the framework that was set up for the EU and the Euro-area. Section 12.1 surveys the main theoretical building blocks underlying the debate over the fiscal arrangements in EMU between those primarily concerned about preserving flexibility and freedom of action of policy-makers and those stressing the need to limit the scope for discretion in the interest of credibility and longer-term stability. Against this background, section 12.2 sets out in more detail the institutional framework that has been set up in the European Union. This section examines the rules and procedures that have been established under the Maastricht Treaty and the Stability and Growth Pact in order to promote sound public finances in the European Union and in the Euro-area. It also explains the main changes that were introduced when the SGP was reformed in 2005. Section 12.3 looks at the main experiences with the implementation of the EU fiscal policy framework, and section 12.4 offers concluding remarks and some thoughts on future challenges.

12.1 **Theoretical background**

The Maastricht framework for macroeconomic governance is based on two cornerstones: the assignment of price stability as the primary objective of monetary policy entrusted to the independent European Central Bank and a set of rules to ensure sound public finances with responsibility for fiscal policies and other economic policies remaining largely at the national level. The focus on medium-term stability and fiscal discipline is partly a result of the policy experiences of the 1970s and 1980s which called into question the earlier confidence in the ability of monetary and fiscal policy-makers to fine-tune macro-economic developments. This led to a shift in emphasis away from concerns over short-term macroeconomic stabilization to the need for institutional mechanisms to safeguard stability over the medium to longer term which also reflects developments in economic theory. At the risk of oversimplifying, broadly speaking Keynesian economics has been associated with a more optimistic view of the desirability and ability of 'activist' macro-economic policy interventions to stabilize economic fluctuations and address market failures. By contrast, new classical economics as well as public choice or political economy approaches to economic policy-making have tended to espouse a more pessimistic view, stressing the potential for government failure and the virtue of 'non-activist' or rule-based policy-making.

The basic philosophical divide between these two schools of thought has shaped the discussions about EMU in general and the role of fiscal policy in particular. First, from a Keynesian perspective, monetary union suggests a greater need for flexibility of national fiscal policies as the only national macroeconomic stabilization tool remaining. Second, from a neo-classical viewpoint, persistent budget deficits and the accumulation of public debt lead to an increase in equilibrium real interest rates, crowding out of private invest-ment, and, therefore, to a lower capital stock. Against this background the case for some form of constraints on national fiscal policy rests on the presence of domestic 'government failure', such as a deficit bias inherent in the political process. Third, the case for fiscal constraints also rests on the presence of 'market failure' to the extent that financial markets on their own are seen to provide insufficient incentives for sustainable public finances. Fourth, the case for supranational mechanisms to ensure fiscal discipline in a monetary union has to rely on the existence of relevant spillovers across countries. In particular, there can be spillovers relating to national fiscal policies in a monetary union, e.g. excessive deficits drawing on a common pool of savings might lead to higher real interest rates in the area as a whole, or concerns about fiscal insolvency in one country may have cross-country implications for financial stability and corresponding risk premia. Fifth, spillovers can result from the interaction of multiple fiscal authorities with the single monetary policy. An increased propensity to build up public debt can make the task of monetary policy to maintain price stability more difficult.

Optimum currency areas and fiscal stabilization in a monetary union

The natural starting-point for a discussion of the role of fiscal policy in a monetary union is the literature on optimum currency areas (OCAs) pioneered by Mundell (1961). His model is based on the traditional Keynesian assumption of fixed prices and wages. In such circumstances a region or country taking part in a monetary union, which is hit by an exogenous shock (say, reducing its export demand) can—by definition—no longer rely on its own monetary and exchange rate policy to counteract such a shock (i.e. by lowering interest rates and depreciating its exchange rate). From this perspective the question of whether a collection of countries constitutes an optimum currency area will, in the first instance, depend on how important asymmetric shocks are, that is economic shocks that affect different regions differently. It also depends on the degree of wage and price rigidities in the economy. If prices and wages are very flexible, the economy might be able to adjust to economic shocks by itself and without the need for policy intervention. Finally, factor mobility, that is the ability of labour and capital to move freely across the currency zone, has also been stressed as an important criterion for an optimal currency area, in particular in the absence of sufficient price and wage flexibility.

With regard to labour mobility as well as price and, particularly, wage flexibility, European countries are usually argued to score quite badly, especially when compared with the USA. From an OCA perspective this suggests a need to retain flexibility and an active role for national fiscal policies in monetary union. Moreover, unlike when monetary union was first considered in the 1960s and 1970s, proposals for a centralized fiscal system or a significantly expanded EU budget—which would offer some sort of automatic insurance against asymmetric shocks—were not seriously considered this time round.

An active role for national fiscal policies in a monetary union, from the OCA perspective, may, however, be less pressing to the extent that integrated financial markets provide private agents with lending and borrowing opportunities in order to achieve consumption-smoothing over time on their own account. The evidence provided by Sørenson and Yosha (1998) indicates that capital market integration within the EU is less than that within the USA. To the extent that there are obstacles to risk-sharing by private agents, a general case can be made for government policies to provide income stabilization on their behalf, be it at the national or the European level. However, there is evidence that EMU itself is contributing to progress with financial market integration (Capiello *et al.*, 2006). In general, enhancing the efficient functioning of goods, labour, and capital markets will promote the resilience of economies to economic shocks and enhance their adjustment capacity. This reduces the general need for government policy to perform a sizeable stabilization function.

Moreover, as noted above, earlier experience casts doubts on the effectiveness of fiscal policy for Keynesian demand management going beyond the operation of built-in automatic stabilizers, in particular in view of uncertainty about the transmission and the lags involved in the decision process. Thus there is evidence that in the past unconstrained fiscal policies have only made a limited contribution to smoothing the economic cycle (if not at times behaving pro-cyclically), which suggests that the costs of imposing deficit limits in terms of foregone stabilization would not be sizeable either (Artis and Onorante 2006). Moreover, the traditional Keynesian transmission channel from fiscal expansion has also been questioned on theoretical grounds and on the basis of empirical studies. Under *Ricardian equivalence* forward-looking taxpayers do not spend extra income that they may receive from debt-financed transfer payments since they anticipate an equivalent higher future tax burden in order to pay for the temporary debt build-up by the government (Barro 1974). Empirical evidence on Ricardian effects has been mixed, but there have been several episodes, when credible fiscal consolidation appeared to provide an economic stimulus in particular in the presence of high debt levels (see Box 12.1). In particular, output could be stimulated by fiscal retrenchment if budgetary consolidation restores confidence in public finances over the longer term (Giavazzi and Pagano 1990; Bertola and Drazen 1993).

The need for fiscal discipline

From the perspective of the early literature on optimum currency areas discussed in the previous section, a monetary union entails the loss of one important tool of national macroeconomic stabilization policy which would need to be compensated by greater reliance on a second such tool, namely national fiscal policies. During the 1970s and 1980s neo- and new classical schools of thought came into the ascendancy, which questioned the effectiveness of Keynesian-inspired stabilization policies and highlighted the need to provide appropriate incentives and institutions in order to improve policy-making.

In particular, the benefits associated with sound public finances were recognized more widely. Over the medium to long term, budget deficits lead to higher real interest rates crowding out investment with a negative impact on capital formation and growth. Available empirical evidence seems to confirm these effects. For example, Easterly *et al.* (1994), using a cross-section sample of more than fifty countries covering the period from 1965 to 1990, found a positive relation between growth in GDP per capita and budget surpluses. Ardagna *et al.* (2004) provide evidence on significant interest rate effects of national public debt and deficits for sixteen OECD counties; Paesani *et al.* (2006) confirm the finding of interest rates rising in response to higher debt, looking at the case of Germany, Italy, and the USA.

BOX 12.1 NON-KEYNESIAN EFFECTS[a]

In the traditional Keynesian model, with a focus on nominal rigidities and short-term effects, a loosening of fiscal policy has an expansionary effect on economic activity, while a fiscal tightening reduces aggregate demand. The fiscal multiplier is positive, although its size can vary considerably owing to 'crowding out effects' which depend on several factors such as how close the economy is to full capacity and how interest rates and the exchange rate respond to changes in the fiscal stance. In dynamic models, which incorporate a broader range of potential transmission channels from fiscal policy to economic activity, the sign of the fiscal multiplier is ambiguous. Indeed, in such models, fiscal expansions may even turn out to be contractionary owing to so-called 'non-Keynesian effects'.

The possibility that a fiscal loosening may not have an expansionary effect on aggregate demand was first raised by Barro (1974) who introduced the concept of 'Ricardian equivalence'. In his seminal paper, Barro argued that a debt-financed fiscal expansion may fail to stimulate private consumption because consumers discount the future increase in the tax burden required to service and repay the increase in debt. Since then, numerous theoretical models have been developed in which fiscal retrenchment can have expansionary effects on private consumption. This is particularly the case if consumers expect that, by restoring sound public finances, fiscal consolidation will increase their lifetime income. Fiscal retrenchment may also stimulate aggregate demand and hence economic activity through other channels, for example by reducing the likelihood of sovereign default, which would reduce interest rate risk premia and thereby stimulate investment as well as having positive wealth effects. By contrast, fiscal expansions which generate uncertainty about the future course of fiscal policy and are perceived as jeopardizing the sustainability of public finances are likely to have an adverse impact on confidence and economic activity.

In recent years numerous empirical studies have attempted to find evidence of expansionary effects of fiscal consolidation. Approaches vary from the estimation of fiscal multipliers using macroeconomic model simulations to case studies of individual consolidation episodes. Overall, while the evidence for strong non-Keynesian effects (i.e. fiscal consolidations that lead to higher growth in the short term) is limited, most studies find that positive fiscal multipliers tend to be small and that they decline or even turn negative over time. Analysis by the European Commission, for example, has found 'non-Keynesian features' to be commonplace in fiscal consolidation episodes in Europe. Many studies have examined the importance of the size of the adjustment and the initial state of public finances, although the empirical evidence in this regard is, on the whole, inconclusive (Afonso 2006). One problem that arises when attempting to identify non-Keynesian effects is the need to disentangle such effects from the influence of other factors such as exchange rate depreciation or the growth-enhancing impact of structural reforms. This is all the more so since many 'success stories' (e.g. Ireland since the late 1980s) occurred after the country concerned adopted a comprehensive economic strategy combining fiscal consolidation with structural reforms. In this context, there is a considerable degree of consensus that the composition of fiscal adjustment is important, with various studies showing that expenditure-based adjustments tend to be more growth friendly and long lasting than tax-based adjustments (e.g. Alesina and Perotti 1996).

[a] For an overview of the theoretical and empirical literature regarding non-Keynesian effects, see Briotti (2005).

Rules versus discretion

The seminal papers by Kydland and Prescott (1977) and later Barro and Gordon (1983) reflected the rational expectations revolution in macroeconomic modelling. Their papers highlighted the role of expectations and the value of pre-commitment as an answer to the problem of *time inconsistency* in discretionary policy-making. They showed that if policy-makers are left free to reconsider their policy plans at each point in time—i.e. act in a discretionary manner—this can lead to suboptimal outcomes compared with a situation where policy-makers tie their hands and pre-commit to implement an *ex ante* optimal plan.

Most prominently, the problem of time inconsistency has been applied to monetary policy. Here governments are seen as subject to an *ex post* incentive to surprise-inflate in order to stimulate output and employment. For example, once social partners have concluded wage agreements, higher than anticipated inflation will reduce *ex post* real wages and thus increase output and employment. Such incentives to inflate will, however, be understood *ex ante* by a rational public who adjust their inflation expectations accordingly. As a result, output and employment remain unaffected but inflation is suboptimally high. This so-called *inflation bias* of monetary policy has been proposed as an explanation for the high inflation rates observed in the 1970s and early 1980s when monetary policies were no longer constrained by the Bretton Woods system of fixed exchange rates.

Problems of time inconsistency can also arise in the context of fiscal policy. In particular, a capital levy provides a non-distortionary form of taxation *ex post*, while the anticipation of such a levy would destroy the incentives to invest and accumulate capital *ex ante*. A similar argument can be made with respect to inflation, which can be seen as a tax on money holdings or as a capital levy on the stock of accumulated (nominal) government debt. In particular, a government that has run up a high stock of debt fixed in nominal terms will be subject to a strong temptation to reduce the real value of the debt burden through inflation. The general message from this type of literature is that discretionary monetary and fiscal policies—rather than providing solutions to market inefficiencies—could themselves become a source of additional inefficiencies or instability. In such circumstances it can become beneficial to restrict the freedom of policy-makers. In particular, the time inconsistency problem has been invoked as an argument to grant central banks independence from governments and to focus their mandate on price stability.

Applying this line of reasoning it can be argued that the 'loss' of independent national monetary policy as a stabilization tool in a monetary union can actually represent a benefit to the extent that the new institutional set-up provides a more credible solution to the inflation bias problem than proved possible to achieve at the national level. A similar case could be made for fiscal policy if the institutions and incentives for fiscal policies which accompany monetary union mitigate inefficiencies in fiscal policy-making at the national level.

The problem of 'deficit bias' and the sustainability of public finances

Apart from the time inconsistency problem *strictu sensu* (relating to the capital levy or the inflation tax), inefficiencies in fiscal policy-making can result from the institutions governing the political process. One example of such an inefficiency is provided by theories of a political business cycle, which link economic fluctuations to the electoral cycle. More generally, the political process may pay insufficient attention to the effects of policies that accrue in the distant future or fall on constituencies which are dispersed and not well represented. These issues have long been emphasized by public choice theorists (e.g. Buchanan 1977; Olson 1965). In such circumstances a politically induced 'deficit bias' under discretionary budgetary policy may arise in analogy to the 'inflation bias' that was identified in the case of discretionary monetary policy.

Such a deficit bias may be due to the strength of special interests pushing for public expenditure programmes relative to less-organized taxpayers. Moreover, future taxpayers are not represented at all in the democratic process, which favours the build-up of public debt to be repaid by future generations and may also lead politicians to ignore the negative long-run growth effects of deficits via the crowding out of productive private investment. Government instability and a host of other political and institutional factors can explain why the public finance performance of political systems has differed widely across countries (Roubini and Sachs 1989; Grilli *et al.* 1991; Corsetti and Roubini 1993; Alesina and Perotti 1996).

Indeed, the experience in Europe of the 1970s through to the 1990s seems to lend support to the view that the accumulation of debt in this period cannot be fully explained as the outcome of optimal fiscal policies or tax-smoothing behaviour over time. Instead, in particular in view of demographic trends and unfunded pay-as-you-go pension systems, it arguably represents an excessive burden on future generations. Empirical studies such as Artis and Marcellino (2000) also suggest that in the twenty years or so preceding monetary union many EU countries did not appear to take sufficient heed of the constraint implied by the solvency condition in the intertemporal government budget constraint. Over time the presence of a potential 'deficit bias' or myopia in budgetary policy—whatever the source—contributes to a build-up in government debt, which may ultimately cast doubt on the sustainability of public finances.

This suggests a need to strengthen fiscal discipline in the national budgetary processes. Such a case could be made quite independently of monetary union. To redress such inefficiencies at their source countries might wish to reform their budget procedures or adopt mechanisms of unilateral self-commitment, for example, in analogy to the constitutional balanced budget amendment which has long been under discussion in the United States and is in widespread use at the state level there. However, public finance theory gives little guidance on the 'optimal' level of debt and deficits and the size of any budget deficit bias to be addressed (Krogstrup and Wyplosz 2006). On the one hand, the general requirements of sustainability or government solvency constraints simply state that any given level of debt must be financed by a discounted future stream of revenue. This is difficult to operationalize in practice, even though some indicators of sustainability have been proposed (Michel *et al.* 2006). On the other hand, stricter, more binding simple numerical rules for fiscal policy may be criticized as lacking sufficent economic rationale, but can, in principle, be monitored and enforced more easily compared with more sophisticated approaches (Schuknecht 2005). From the sustainability perspective, the evolution of debt would appear to be the most relevant variable rather than the current deficit (Coeuré and Pisani-Ferry 2006), but in order to reduce the possibility of accounting tricks both variables need to be monitored and reconciled via stock-flow adjustments (Buti *et al.* 2006).

Moreover, unless international multilateral commitment is more credible than unilateral reforms, the adoption of mechanisms to sustain fiscal discipline in conjunction with a move to monetary union must be based on an additional set of arguments (Buiter 2006). In particular, monetary union might render the effects of any domestic deficit bias more damaging, allow fiscal problems to be 'exported' to a greater extent to partner countries inside the monetary union, or have negative side-effects on the single monetary policy. These issues are discussed in the remainder of section 12.1.

The role of the 'no-bail-out clause' and financial markets for fiscal discipline

Monetary union means that countries are moving from a position in which they have both money-creating and taxing powers to one in which they are stripped of the former. In addition, Member States' taxing powers may de facto also become increasingly constrained to the extent that economic integration and liberalization promote the mobility of tax bases. Capital in particular may migrate to jurisdictions offering lower tax rates. From this angle monetary union could pose additional risks for government solvency, which in turn call for additional safeguards to encourage fiscal prudence to be put into place.

Moreover, governments that have accumulated a high stock of debt will—in a monetary union—no longer have available the ultimate recourse to the printing press. This means that governments lose the option of a monetary financing of their debt (i.e. reducing the real value of debt via inflation). All else being equal, this raises the spectre of an increased probability of an outright default on government debt (McKinnon 1994). Any suspicion of such a default could in turn precipitate a run on the government debt in question and provoke knock-on effects on the solvency of financial institutions with large exposures to such debt and contagion effects on the financial system at large. Eichengreen and Wyplosz (1998) regard financial stability concerns as the most serious reason for imposing fiscal constraints. However, they consider alternative approaches, such as strengthening prudential measures to govern financial institutions' exposure to public debt and thus limit knock-on effects, to be more appropriate responses.

As in the earlier discussion of the costs and benefits of losing an independent monetary policy as a macroeconomic stabilization tool, the argument can be turned around. Losing the policy 'option' of a monetary financing of deficits and invoking the dire spectre of bankruptcy should sharpen *ex ante* incentives to avoid getting into an unsustainable fiscal position in the first place. In this context 'divorcing' and protecting monetary policy from the influence of fiscal authorities should have a disciplining effect on fiscal policies. In order for such 'deterrence' to be credible and effective it must not be possible for national fiscal authorities to rely on partner countries or union-wide authorities to help out countries that run into fiscal solvency problems. This is the rationale for introducing a 'no-bail-out' clause.

Central bank independence and a no-bail-out clause would seem to be necessary conditions but not sufficient on their own to provide adequate incentives for fiscal discipline in a monetary union (Beetsma and Bovenberg 2000). Additional rules or constraints may be required if governments judge the risks and consequences of a default as remote or too far into the future to affect current behaviour to a sufficient degree. Moreover, governments may judge a no-bail-out clause as not fully credible if a default has systemic consequences for the financial systems also in partner countries. Indeed, most federal states have some sort of restrictions on borrowing at the state level (Masson 1996).

In general, the effects of monetary union and a single capital market on the incentives for fiscal policy-makers go in opposite directions. On the one hand, the long-run budget constraint facing governments is hardened to the extent that a 'no-bail-out clause' is credible and monetary financing of government debt by the European Central Bank is ruled out (Glick and Hutchison 1993). On the other hand, the short-run budget constraint facing national governments is softened to the extent that access to financing is becoming easier in the unified European capital market and cheaper in particular for countries with high debt and deficits. In a monetary union these countries are no longer subject to country-specific interest rate premia for devaluation and inflation risk. Abolishing national currencies removes the disciplining effect of international currency markets on national fiscal policies and, in addition, detrimental effects from a lack of discipline by national policies will now affect the common currency and thus be shared by all countries inside the monetary union.

If a default risk on government debt were to appear, one might expect bond markets to price that risk (at least in the case where the 'no-bail-out clause' is perceived as credible), which should in turn provide incentives for fiscal discipline. However, as long as countries retain sufficient taxing powers and control of the tax base, the probability of outright default should be very small (Eichengreen and von Hagen 1996). By implication, any default risk premia are unlikely to be sizeable enough to act as an effective deterrent *ex ante*. Evidence shows that spreads on government bonds have narrowed considerably with monetary union, but have then remained at low, but still significant, levels. They have also remained somewhat responsive to major country-specific fiscal developments such as changes in credit ratings (Bernoth *et al.* 2004). However, market reactions and political crises in response to fiscal problems tend to be discontinuous. They provoke a sudden and abrupt withdrawal of confidence which is difficult and costly to deal with *ex post* and thus may provoke attempts to furnish some explicit or implicit bail-out. For all these reasons it remains doubtful that the no-bail-out clause and market discipline on their own would be sufficient. From this perspective, the adoption of pre-emptive fiscal rules should help contain any risks of sovereign default at the national level and of related spillovers with knock-on effects on financial stability in an integrated financial market.

The need for fiscal policy coordination

As discussed in the previous two subsections, the adoption of fiscal rules can be useful as a (second best) discipline device in the presence of domestic policy distortions and insufficient incentives provided by market mechanisms, problems which might both be exacerbated by the move to monetary union. From the new classical perspective the main focus is on the need for contraints on policy, as a kind of negative coordination device to avoid major policy mistakes and related externalities. A further set of motivations for introducing supranational mechanisms for fiscal policy in monetary union relates to a more positive notion of policy coordination in order to address significant spillovers among different national economic policies or across different policy areas (i.e. related to questions of an appropriate 'policy mix'). At the time of the Maastricht negotiations, this had inspired (largely unsuccessful) calls for the establishment of a 'gouvernement économique' at the European level to promote macroeconomic policy coordination and to act as a counter-weight to the single monetary policy (Pisani-Ferry 2006).

A standard Keynesian open economy framework like the Mundell–Fleming model can be used to assess these questions with respect to concerns over macroeconomic stabilization. In this model the effectiveness of fiscal policy is enhanced in a fixed exchange rate regime such as monetary union compared with a situation of floating exchange rates (Agell *et al.* 1996). In the case of a fiscal expansion in one member country under floating exchange rates the expansionary impact on output would be partially offset by negative effects on export demand as a result of an appreciating exchange rate. By contrast, under fixed rates inside monetary union any such counteracting effect would only occur to the extent that a national fiscal expansion impacts on the common external exchange rate.

The flip-side of the enhanced effectiveness of fiscal policy for the purpose of national stabilization under monetary union is the reduced expansionary effect (spillover) from national fiscal policies on partner countries, since the (bilateral) exchange rate channel is removed. Overall the effect on foreign output could become ambiguous since the stimulation via greater import demand from a fiscal expansion might be offset by a dampening effect from higher common interest rates (and a higher common exchange rate) in the monetary union (Eichengreen 1997). From the simple Mundell–Fleming model one could thus conclude that the case for the coordination of fiscal policies is less strong inside a monetary union than outside. Most of the spillovers of fiscal policies are directly related not to monetary union per se but to the degree of trade or financial market integration (Eichengreen and von Hagen 1996). To the extent that monetary union itself enhances economic integration and stimulates additional trade between countries inside the currency area, this increases the size of fiscal leakage over time and thus strengthens the *a priori* case for coordinated policy responses to shocks.

Overall the case for enhanced fiscal coordination for cyclical stabilization purposes is generally regarded as weak (Buiter 2006). In any event, a number of practical obstacles to an effective implementation of more ambitious approaches to macroeconomic policy coordination need to be recognized (Winkler 1999).

First, the relevant spillovers need to be clearly identified. Even within a single model such spillovers are often ambiguous in sign; policy recommendations are even more prone to differ across different models and the empirical evidence may not provide clear-cut answers either. For example, there is not even agreement that fiscal retrenchment necessarily leads to a reduction in domestic output (as discussed in Box 12.1).

Second, all the reservations that apply to the experience with activist demand management policies at the national level as a destabilizing—rather than a stabilizing—influence on the economy apply with even greater force when it comes to attempts to organize such stabilization policies among actors with different interests. Timely agreement, action, and effective enforcement of coordinated policies on a case by case basis are difficult to organize in such circumstances.

Third, a process of policy coordination might tempt policy-makers to shift policy actions or the responsibility for policy outcomes on to partner countries. This might weaken and dilute accountability vis-à-vis national constituencies.

At the same time, countries participating in a monetary union are linked together via a common currency and the consequences of individual national economic policies will—for ill or for good—be shared among countries and reflected in common variables such as market interest rates and the exchange rate. This can give rise to potential free-rider problems and supports the need to regard economic policies as fundamentally 'of common interest' in a monetary union. However, such free-rider problems seem less obvious in the case of concerns over macroeconomic stabilization. Soft forms of coordination would thus appear to suffice in this context, that is an ongoing exchange of views to develop a common understanding of the conjunctural situation as well as on more structural challenges. By contrast the risk of undisciplined public finances over the longer term casting a shadow over area-wide financial, economic, and—ultimately—monetary stability seems to establish a much clearer case for minimal safeguards and a hard-wired set of rules to be put into place.

Free-rider problems of the type described above could in principle be solved by establishing a central authority or some other mechanism to enforce 'coordinated' policies in the common interest. Alternatively, constraints or sanction mechanisms could be imposed on decentralized policies in order to shift incentives in the desired direction on a durable basis. The latter is the basic approach taken by the 'fiscal constitution' embodied in the Maastricht Treaty and the Stability and Growth Pact.

The interaction between monetary and fiscal policy

The clear assignment of monetary and fiscal policy functions to independent actors raises the question of consistency in the interaction of both autonomous, but interdependent, policy areas. With regard to the shorter-term macroeconomic stabilization this points to the issue of the so-called 'policy mix' between monetary and fiscal policy. With regard to long-term consistency it needs to be recognized that monetary and fiscal policy—even if they are determined independently—are nevertheless linked via the intertemporal public sector budget constraint (Buiter 2006). Public sector expenditures in any period can in principle be financed out of current taxes, by issuing debt or via seigniorage revenues arising from inflation as a tax on money holdings. The key question in this context becomes whether, in the case of conflict, the path of fiscal deficits or the path of inflation will ultimately give and adjust in the long run.

The separation of fiscal and monetary policy—while desirable to insulate monetary policy from fiscal pressures as much as possible—can on the other hand give rise to potential problems of consistency and lead to conflicts between both policy areas. Such conflicts could make it more difficult for monetary policy to maintain price stability in the short run, and it may also put a question mark on the ability and determination of monetary policy to guarantee price stability in the face of fiscal instability over the longer run. In other words, additional mechanisms to ensure fiscal discipline may not only be desirable in their own right for the reasons discussed in the previous sections. They may also be seen as an additional safeguard to underpin central bank independence and avoid

---

BOX 12.2 THE MONETARY-FISCAL POLICY GAME

Consider the interaction between monetary and fiscal authorities in the game representation below. In the pay-off matrix, the first number in each cell refers to the utility obtained by the central bank from the particular combination of actions by the two players (on interest rates and deficits, respectively); the second number is the fiscal authorities' pay-off. The numbers are chosen for illustration in order to capture the benefits (e.g. in terms of price stability and growth preformance) of fiscal and monetary policy paths being coordinated in the short run and mutually consistent in the long run. Conversely, if policy-makers are on a collision course pay-offs for both players are much lower. For example, a lax fiscal policy combined with tight money leads to an unbalanced policy mix, high interest rates, currency appreciation, and output losses. Note that both sides have an incentive to fall in line.

Faced with a given lax fiscal policy monetary authorities may in the end accommodate and accept the bottom-right outcome as the lesser evil. Likewise, when facing a tough central bank, fiscal authorities will prefer to 'chicken out' and accept discipline (the top-left outcome) rather than stick with zero pay-offs.

A Game of Chicken

		Fiscal Authorities	
		tight policy	lax policy
Central Bank	tight policy	4, 2	−1, −1
	lax policy	0, 0	1, 3

There are two Nash equilibria in this game, where neither of the players has an incentive to deviate. The central bank would prefer the 'tight' equilibrium (top-left) with tight monetary and fiscal policies, whereas fiscal authorities prefer the 'lax' outcome (bottom-right) with relaxed policies. The pay-offs are as in the standard 'game of chicken' (except here we make the 'tight' equilibrium the socially more attractive one). The two players have an incentive to coordinate their actions but differ over the preferred outcome. Therefore each side would like to pre-commit to a particular action in advance in order to induce its own preferred equilibrium. Depending on which side possesses strategic leadership in this simple game, we can distinguish two regimes, 'monetary dominance' and 'fiscal dominance' in the terminology of Canzoneri and Diba (1996).

---

it being challenged by inconsistent fiscal developments (Beetsma and Uhlig 1999). This suggests a game of strategic interaction as illustrated in Box 12.2.

The game in Box 12.2 can be given economic interpretations both with respect to the long-run or the short-run strategic interaction between monetary and fiscal policy-makers, where each of the players can be seen to act under commitment or under discretion (Kirsanova *et al.* 2005). The long-run interpretation focuses on the intertemporal government budget constraint and the credibility of low inflation and no-bail-out promises.

The short-run interpretation looks at the issue of the appropriate policy mix for macro-economic stabilization. From this perspective fiscal constraints can be seen as an attempt to secure pre-commitment to the monetary dominance regime, that is select the better of the two possible equilibria and in particular to avoid costly conflict (leadership battles) between monetary and fiscal policy.

Introducing constraints on fiscal policy as a commitment device and maintaining a clear separation of responsibilities may lead to an implicit solution to the coordination problem represented in Box 12.2 rather than attempt explicit and discretionary coordination between the two actors (Dixit and Lambertini 2003). Moving in the direction of a joint determination of policies, by contrast, would risk reintroducing all the problems of time-inconsistency and credibility that central bank independence was meant to solve in the first place.

Long-run credibility

Monetary and fiscal policy are linked via the intertemporal government budget constraint, which entails that a stream of expenditures can be financed via taxes, issuing bonds, or printing money. Here a regime of 'fiscal dominance' assumes that the government can pre-commit to a path of net deficits and thus ultimately force the central bank to inflate in order to avoid insolvency as in the 'unpleasant monetarist arithmetic' of Sargent and Wallace (1981) or in the more recent literature on the fiscal theory of the price level (Sims 1994; Woodford 1995, 1998), where the price level may adjust independently of monetary policy to satisfy the solvency constraint in equilibrium. Under 'monetary dominance' the central bank can commit not to inflate (no explicit or implicit bail-out) and thus force the government to adjust its path of spending and taxes.

In order to avoid fiscal and monetary policy being put on a collision course in the long run, constraints on fiscal policy can reduce the risk of explosive or unstable debt dynamics. This can be done by placing a restriction or ceiling on the stock of debt or in the form of a feedback rule on deficits that ensures that current deficits react to a debt build-up in a stabilizing manner.

Short-term credibility and policy mix

In addition to the long-run compatibility of fiscal and monetary policy paths as reflected in the intertemporal government budget constraint, the choice of policy mix also becomes important in short-term macroeconomic management. Conflicts between fiscal and monetary authorities can be very costly, as the episodes of Reagonomics in the early 1980s and developments in the wake of German reunification demonstrate. In both cases an expansionary fiscal policy collided with tight monetary policy and the real economy paid a high price for the re-establishment of the strategic leadership of the monetary authorities. In normal times, when monetary leadership is uncontested, agents should be able to rely on the central bank to keep prices stable over the medium term. This should help to anchor expectations (especially for wage bargaining and financial markets) and contain economic uncertainty in the wake of shocks.

European countries' differing responses to the oil price shocks in the 1970s illustrate the virtue of monetary dominance with respect to fiscal dominance. The long but unbalanced struggle of European economies to regain stability over the course of the 1980s can also be taken to illustrate the costs of an unbalanced policy mix (Allsopp and Vines 1996), resulting from an increase in the credibility of monetary policy (constrained by the European Exchange Rate Mechanism) which was accompanied by still relatively lax fiscal regimes. In general, if confronted with undisciplined fiscal policies (in the aggregate) the central bank would need to keep short-term interest rates higher than otherwise in order to contain inflationary pressures. If the central bank has to reassert its leadership (i.e. a regime of monetary dominance) in conflict with fiscal authorities, this may entail greater real economic costs to society. Alternatively (if fiscal dominance prevails), the central bank may be forced to accommodate and monetary control over the price level may be compromised. Fiscal constraints can be seen as a (blunt) safeguard to limit the extent to which the central bank will be confronted with this dilemma and to avoid central bank independence being tested or contested too severely.

12.2 The institutional framework

The Maastricht Treaty

The deficit and debt criteria

To address concerns that large deficits and rising debt could threaten the smooth functioning of EMU, the Maastricht Treaty introduced a number of rules aimed at disciplining EU Member States' fiscal policies. These include the prohibition of monetary financing of deficits by the European System of Central Banks (ESCB) (Article 101 of the Treaty) and the so-called no-bail-out clause, which states that European institutions or Member States shall not be liable for or assume another Member State's financial obligations (Article 103). The former contributes to a clear separation between monetary policy and fiscal policy, which should ensure that a stability-oriented monetary policy is not compromised by excessive government borrowing. The latter makes clear that in EMU, Member States do not have to bear the cost of financing other Member States' debt, which should encourage financial markets to distinguish between different Euro-area governments' debt instruments, thereby strengthening financial market discipline on fiscal policies.

In addition to these basic safeguards, Article 104 paragraph 1 of the Treaty states that 'Member States shall avoid excessive government deficits'. Compliance with this provision is assessed on the basis of the developments of the general government budget deficit in relation to a reference value of 3 per cent of GDP and by the evolution of the government debt with respect to a 60 per cent of GDP reference value, as specified in Article 104 paragraph 2 and in the Protocol. The deficit criterion is violated when the government deficit ratio exceeds the reference value, unless it has fallen substantially and continuously and comes close to the reference value; or when the excess over the reference value is only exceptional and temporary and the ratio remains close to the reference value. The debt criterion is violated when the government debt ratio exceeds the 60 per cent of GDP reference value, unless the ratio is sufficiently diminishing and approaching the reference value at a satisfactory pace.

The formulation of the criteria indicates that the evolution of the ratios over time must be taken into consideration. To comply with the deficit criterion, a deficit ratio that is above the 3 per cent reference value must show a decline that is substantial and continuous and the ratio must already have reached a level that is close to the reference value. The evolution of the deficit ratio was of major importance in the second stage of EMU,[1] when countries had to bring down their deficit ratios from the past high levels, and is relevant today for some of the 'new' Member States that have joined the EU in recent years. This first exception is relevant in case a country still has a deficit ratio above the 3 per cent reference value when the decision regarding compliance with the convergence criterion on the sustainability of the government financial position is taken. In practice, this exception has not so far been used. However, this clause may play a role when the Council has to decide whether or not a country has corrected its excessive deficit. The second exception says that a deficit ratio above 3 per cent of GDP is not excessive if the excess is 'exceptional' and 'temporary' and the deficit ratio remains 'close to the reference value'. For a deficit ratio in excess of the 3 per cent of GDP limit not to be considered excessive, it is sufficient that only one of the two exceptions applies.

The requirements for the evolution of the debt ratio are less stringent. To comply with the debt criterion, a debt ratio above 60 per cent of GDP must be diminishing sufficiently, but not necessarily continuously (in contrast with the deficit criterion, the term 'continuously' is not used in the definition of the debt criterion), and approach the reference value at a satisfactory pace rather than be already close to it. So far, there has been no further specification of what is a 'satisfactory pace' for approaching the reference value, as it has proved to be very difficult to devise a formal rule covering all possible events. It should be noted that, whereas the SGP provides further detailed specifications regarding the interpretation of the deficit criterion, it remains silent on the debt criterion.

The excessive deficit procedure

Breaches of the reference values result in the initiation of an excessive deficit procedure (EDP) with the aim of examining and, if necessary, correcting the situation (see Figure 12.1 for a schematic overview). For Member States that have adopted the single currency, this procedure can ultimately lead to financial sanctions. However, the procedure as laid down in the Treaty is in no sense mechanistic, and ultimately leaves it to the discretion of the ECOFIN Council to decide whether to take action.

Article 104 paragraph 3 of the Treaty stipulates that the Commission shall prepare a report if a Member State does not fulfil the requirements under one or both of the criteria discussed above. The Commission examines the economic and budgetary situation of the country concerned in its report. Special attention is of course given to the level and the evolution of the government deficit and debt ratios. Moreover, the Commission assesses whether there are 'exceptional circumstances' in the country concerned. The Commission's report also takes into account whether the government deficit exceeds government investment expenditure and all other relevant factors, including the medium-term economic and budgetary position of the Member State. However, the Commission does not yet pronounce in this report on the question whether or not the country is, in its opinion, in excessive deficit.

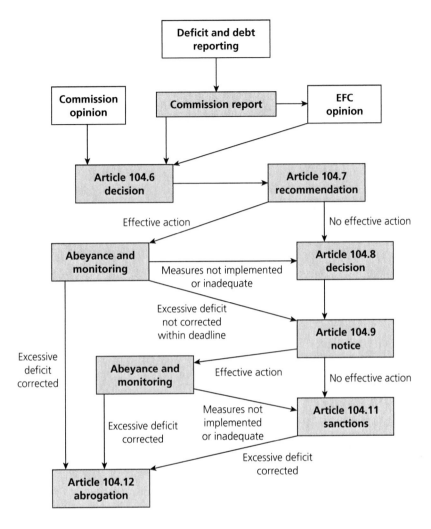

Figure 12.1 The main steps of the excessive deficit procedure

Article 104 paragraph 4 provides that the Economic and Financial Committee (EFC) formulates an opinion on the report of the Commission.[2] Regulation No. 1467/97 says that the EFC must prepare its opinion within two weeks of the adoption of the Commission's report. In this opinion, the EFC gives its view on whether or not an excessive deficit exists.

Article 104 paragraph 5 provides that the Commission addresses an opinion to the Council if it considers that an excessive deficit exists or may occur. When the Commission is of the opinion that an excessive deficit exists, it will address, together with its opinion, a recommendation for a Council decision and a recommendation for a Council recommendation and send these to the Council. However, in case the Commission is of the view that no excessive deficit exists and thus does not submit an opinion and a recommendation to the Council but the Council is of the opposite view, the Council can ask the Commission to prepare a recommendation for a Council decision on the basis of Article 115.

Article 104 paragraph 6 provides that it is up to the Council to decide whether or not an excessive deficit exists. The Council, before taking this decision, shall consider any observations which the country concerned may wish to make. After an overall assessment, it then takes its decision. These provisions imply that the Council should hear the country concerned and carefully weigh all factors. Moreover, these provisions entail that the Council should not take such a decision lightly. This decision, as indeed all decisions in the context of the excessive deficit procedure, is taken on the basis of a 'recommendation' from the Commission. This contrasts with the usual practice in other policy domains where the Council acts on the basis of a Commission 'proposal'. The difference lies in the number of Council votes that is needed to introduce changes to the Commission's text. Whereas a Commission proposal can only be modified on the basis of a unanimous vote in the Council, changes to a Commission recommendation only require the same number of votes as that needed for the Council to act (i.e. a qualified majority).

At the same time as the Council decides on the existence of an excessive deficit, the Council shall make a recommendation to the Member State concerned with a view to bringing that situation to an end within a given period, in accordance with Article 104 paragraph 7. The recommendation must establish two deadlines:

1. a deadline for the Member State to take effective action; and
2. a deadline for the correction of the excessive deficit, which should be completed in the year following its identification, unless there are special circumstances.

In these recommendations, the Council does not need to spell out what specific measures a country should take. In particular, it is not necessary that the Council tells the country concerned to raise certain taxes or to implement cuts in specific expenditure categories. The Council will generally just indicate the results that should be obtained. This is because the composition of the budget and the measures to be taken to achieve a certain deficit or debt position are the full responsibility of the Member States themselves. However, the Council can always welcome the commitments given by the Member State to implement specific measures, in order to give more weight to this commitment.

If the country concerned takes effective action in response to the Council recommendation in application of Article 104 paragraph 7, then the procedure is held in abeyance and the Commission and the Council monitor the situation. If it is established that there has been no effective action within the period laid down, the Council shall decide, in accordance with Article 104 paragraph 8, to make its recommendations public. Such a decision has to be taken immediately after the expiry of the deadline set in the recommendation taken under Article 104 paragraph 7. This decision that no action has been taken is to be based on publicly announced decisions by the government of the country concerned. The reason that it is sufficient for governments publicly to announce action and not yet to implement measures is that it takes time before measures can be effectively implemented and before their results become visible.

After the decision that no action was taken, in the case of Member States that have adopted the Euro, the next step is for the Council to give 'notice' to the Member State concerned to take, within a specified time limit, the measures for the deficit reduction that are judged necessary by the Council in order to remedy the situation in accordance with Article 104 paragraph 9 of the Treaty. In the case of Member States that have not yet adopted the Euro, the procedure can go no further than Article 104 paragraph 8, and so the only course of action available to the Council is to issue a new recommendation under Article 104 paragraph 7. Correspondingly, for decisions to give notice under Article 104 paragraph 9, the voting rights of Member States with a derogation are suspended and only the Euro-area Member States are allowed to vote. As in the case of a recommendation, the Council has to specify in the notice a time limit for action to be taken.

Provided that action is adopted pursuant to the notice given, then once again the procedure will be held in abeyance and the Commission and the Council will monitor the situation. If, on the contrary, the Member State does not take any action, then the Council can impose sanctions on the basis of Article 104 paragraph 11. The sanctions consist of a non-interest bearing deposit, which can eventually be turned into a fine after two years if the excessive deficit persists. In addition to requiring the Member State concerned to make a non-interest bearing deposit, the Council may also impose the following non-pecuniary sanctions:

- require the Member State to publish additional information, to be specified by the Council, before issuing bonds and securities; or
- invite the European Investment Bank to reconsider its lending policy towards the Member State concerned.

Article 122 of the Treaty says that paragraphs 9 and 11 of Article 104 do not apply to the Member States with a derogation, that is to those Member States which do not fulfil the necessary conditions for the adoption of the single currency. This means that the Council cannot give a notice or apply sanctions to these Member States.

Once the excessive deficit has been corrected, Article 104 paragraph 12 of the Treaty specifies that the Council can decide to abrogate the procedure, based on a Commission recommendation.

The 'original' Stability and Growth Pact

In the years that followed the signing of the Maastricht Treaty, the 3 per cent reference value served as a simple yardstick of the success of fiscal policy and received considerable prominence in the public debate. Nonetheless, concerns remained that the fiscal rules as set out in the Maastricht Treaty would not provide enough of a 'stick' to ensure fiscal discipline once the 'carrot' of participation in the single currency had been eaten. There were also concerns that mere compliance with the 3 per cent of GDP reference value might not be sufficient to maintain or reduce debt to reasonable levels. Moreover, pro-cyclical fiscal policies would be the result if Member States were forced to increase taxes or reduce spending during recessions in order to keep their deficits below 3 per cent of GDP.

The original proposal for a 'stability pact' originated from the German government, which proposed an automatic sanctioning mechanism outside the standard Treaty framework. Such automatism was considered inappropriate by some Member States, however. Instead, the negotiations, which were concluded in Dublin in December 1996, culminated in a 'Stability and Growth Pact' (SGP) that took the form of EU secondary legislation with decisions to be taken within the standard legislative framework (i.e. Council recommendations or decisions, adopted by qualified majority, on the basis of recommendations by the Commission). The Commission therefore preserved its 'right of initiative', while the Council ultimately retained discretion in taking decisions within an overall rules-based framework.

The legal acts on which the SGP is based were adopted in June 1997.[3] They consist primarily of two Council Regulations, which in accordance with their aims and functions are often referred to as the 'preventive arm' and the 'corrective arm' (or 'deterrent arm') of the Pact. These were backed by a solemn declaration of the European heads of state or government, which expressed Member States' political commitment to implementing the rules in a strict and timely manner.

In order to prevent an excessive deficit occuring, the SGP set up multilateral surveillance mechanisms, the 'preventive arm'. These mechanisms find their legal basis in Article 99 of the Treaty. They go from a regular monitoring of the budgetary situation in the EU Member States via the stability and convergence programmes to recommendations given to avoid an excessive deficit. Thus, these mechanisms gradually increase in severity.

Euro-area Member States submit annual 'stability programmes' while non-Euro-area Member States present 'convergence programmes', which present information regarding their economic and fiscal policies. These programmes include in particular the 'medium-term objective' (MTO) of fiscal policy and, where applicable, the adjustment path towards it. In its original form, the SGP specified that the medium-term objective should be a budget that is 'close to balance or in surplus'. The rationale was to ensure fiscal positions that would be sustainable in the long run while also creating sufficient room for fiscal policy to help smooth output fluctuations in the short run without breaching the 3 per cent of GDP deficit ceiling. The term 'close to balance or in surplus' reflected the fact that while budgets close to balance should, as a rule, be sufficient to ensure sustainable fiscal positions, some countries might wish to target surpluses with a view to reducing debt ratios more rapidly and preparing for the costs of ageing populations.

The Member States' programmes are assessed by the Commission and may be examined by the ECOFIN Council, which can choose to make public its opinion on each programme. The SGP also introduced an early warning mechanism, which finds its legal basis in Article 99 paragraph 4 of the Treaty. In case the Council identifies actual or expected significant divergence of the budgetary position from the medium-term budgetary objective or the adjustment path towards it set out in the stability or convergence programme, it shall address a recommendation to the Member State concerned to take the necessary adjustment measures. The Council gives this early warning in order to prevent the occurrence of an excessive deficit. It gives this early warning on the basis of a recommendation by the Commission. In case the Council in its subsequent monitoring judges that the divergence of the budgetary position from the medium-term objective, or the adjustment path towards it, is persisting or worsening, it can take a second step. In such a case, the Council makes a recommendation to the Member State concerned to take prompt corrective measures.

From a procedural point of view, the Council does not have to give an early warning to a country before applying the excessive deficit procedure. Thus, the excessive procedure can be opened without any earlier action taken. However, from a policy point of view, a close monitoring of the budgetary situation should allow the Commission and the Council to start applying peer pressure via an early warning recommendation well before the point when the 3 per cent of GDP reference value is about to be breached.

The Council can also address a recommendation to a Member State on the basis of Article 99 paragraph 4 for inconsistency with the *'Broad Economic Policy Guidelines'*[4] or for the risk of jeopardizing the proper functioning of EMU. This is a separate procedure, focusing on the conduct of economic policies in general and not targeted specifically at fiscal policies. It is taken directly on the basis of Article 99 paragraph 4 of the Treaty and it is not mentioned in the SGP. The Council could use the option of addressing such a recommendation to the Member State concerned at any stage, if necessary simultaneously with the procedure based on Article 104.

By contrast to the preventive arm, the corrective arm of the SGP relies on stricter and more formal procedures designed to enforce fiscal discipline in countries where deficits have become excessive and are therefore giving rise to greater concern. To this end, the EDP already outlined in the Treaty was clarified and 'speeded up', in particular with regard to the following:

- *'Exceptional circumstances'*: The conditions under which a deficit above 3 per cent could be deemed exceptional and temporary (and therefore not excessive) were defined strictly as cases in which a country experiences an annual fall in real GDP of at least 2 per cent. A fall in real GDP of between 0.75 per cent and 2 per cent could also be deemed exceptional in the light of supporting evidence submitted by the Member State in question regarding the accumulated output loss and the abruptness of the downturn.

- *The deadline for the correction of excessive deficits*: It was specified that the correction of an excessive deficit should be completed 'in the year following its identification unless there are special circumstances', although the nature of such special circumstances was not explicitly defined.

- *The timing of procedural steps*: A timetable with precise deadlines for the various steps of the procedure was laid out whereby, in the event of non-compliance by a Member State with the recommendations and decisions of the Council, the time between the reporting of a deficit above 3 per cent of GDP and the imposition of sanctions should be no more than ten months.

- *The nature of sanctions*: It was clarified that, if the Council were to impose sanctions on a Member State, a non-interest bearing deposit would be required which, in the event of a further two years of non-compliance, would be converted into a fine.

The reform of the Stability and Growth Pact

Discussions on the SGP have taken place ever since its entry into force on 1 January 1999. These discussions were often triggered by the opening of an excessive deficit procedure against a country by the Commission or by adverse budgetary developments. However, at the same time, EU Member States were reluctant to renegotiate the SGP during its first few years of existence. When the Commission released a Communication on 'Strengthening the coordination of budgetary policies' in November 2002 with proposals to 'strengthen the implementation' of the SGP, the ECOFIN Council agreed in March 2003 that there was no need to change either the Treaty or the SGP, or to introduce new budgetary objectives or rules. However, this was changed with the crisis of November 2003, when the Council decided not to implement further steps in the excessive deficit procedure against Germany and France, as the Commission had recommended, and with the subsequent judgment by the European Court of Justice of July 2004 annulling the Council's conclusions (see below). These events led to legal uncertainty as well as to a loss of credibility of the EU fiscal framework. In these circumstances, the Commission and the Council decided that a reform of the SGP was the only option available.

The negotiations on the reform of the SGP started when the European Commission published a Communication on 'Strengthening economic governance and clarifying the implementation of the Stability and Growth Pact' on 3 September 2004. The discussions took place during the second half of 2004 in the EFC as well as in the Eurogroup and in the ECOFIN Council. The latter reached an agreement on the reform of the SGP on 20 March 2005. This agreement was set out in a report from the ECOFIN Council to the European Council on 'Improving the implementation of the Stability and Growth Pact'. The report was endorsed by the heads of state or government during their meeting on 22–23 March 2005. The ECOFIN Council adopted the legal and technical texts implementing the reform in June 2005.[5] The reform adopted by the ECOFIN Council left the structure of the SGP in place, and did not alter the fundamental elements of the EU fiscal framework enshrined in the Treaty, such as the 3 per cent and 60 per cent reference values, which were outside its scope. Within this overall framework, however, the reform did introduce a number of significant changes.

Under the preventive arm, the reform introduced various refinements to the earlier provisions concerning the setting of and progress towards sound medium-term budgetary positions and to the elements that are to be taken into account when assessing Member States' fiscal positions. These include:

- *Definition of the 'medium-term budgetary objective'*: Each EU Member State has to set a country-specific medium-term objective (MTO). These country-specific MTOs may diverge from the requirement of a 'close to balance or in surplus' position. These MTOs will be differentiated between Member States depending on the current debt ratio and potential growth. Implicit liabilities should also be taken into account as soon as the criteria and modalities for doing so are established by the Council. The MTOs should preserve a safety margin with respect to the 3 per cent of GDP reference value for the government deficit ratio, they should ensure rapid progress towards sustainability, and allow room for budgetary manoeuvre, considering in particular the needs for public investment. For Euro-area and ERM II Member States, the range of country-specific MTOs will be, in cyclically adjusted terms and net of one-off and temporary measures, between –1 per cent of GDP and in balance or surplus. MTOs will be revised when a major reform is implemented and in any case every four years.

- *Specifications for the adjustment path to the 'medium-term objective'*: Member States that have not yet reached their MTO should undertake consolidation efforts to achieve it. The adjustment effort should be greater in good times and could be more limited in bad times. Good times are defined as periods when output exceeds its potential level. The Euro-area and ERM II Member States should pursue an annual adjustment in cyclically adjusted terms, net of one-off and temporary measures, of 0.5 per cent of GDP as a benchmark. Member States that do not follow the required adjustment path should explain the reasons for the deviation in the annual update of their stability and convergence programmes. The Commission should issue 'policy advice' to encourage Member States to adhere to their adjustment path.

- *Structural reforms*: When defining the adjustment path towards the MTO or allowing temporary deviations for Member States that have already reached it, the implementation of major structural reforms will be taken into account. Only reforms which have direct long-term cost-saving effects, including by raising potential growth, and therefore a verifiable impact on the long-term sustainability of public finances will be taken into account. A safety margin with respect to the 3 per cent reference value must, however, be preserved and the budgetary position is expected to return to the MTO within the programme period. Special attention will be paid to pension reforms introducing a multi-pillar system that includes a mandatory fully funded pillar. Member States implementing such reforms will be allowed to deviate from the adjustment path to their medium-term budgetary objective or from the objective itself, with the deviation reflecting the net cost of the reform to the publicly managed pillar, under the condition that the deviation remains temporary and that an appropriate safety margin with respect to the 3 per cent of GDP reference value for the government deficit ratio is preserved.

With regard to the corrective arm, the changes introduced go in the direction of introducing more flexibility into the EDP, in particular by relaxing, adding specificity to, or clarifying the availability of various escape clauses. The changes include:

- *New definition of severe economic slowdown allowing an 'exceptional' excess over the reference value*: An excess of the government deficit ratio over the 3 per cent of GDP reference value will be considered 'exceptional' if it results from a severe economic downturn, which is now defined as a negative annual real GDP growth rate or an accumulated loss of output during a protracted period of very low annual real GDP growth relative to potential growth.

- *'Other relevant factors'*: The Treaty specifies that the Commission, in its report triggering the excessive deficit procedure, should take into account 'all other relevant factors' (Article 104 paragraph 3 of the Treaty). It has now been clarified that the 'other relevant factors' should include developments in the medium-term economic position (in particular potential growth, prevailing cyclical conditions, the implementation of the Lisbon agenda, and policies to foster research and development and innovation) and developments in the medium-term budgetary position (in particular fiscal consolidation efforts in 'good times', debt sustainability, public investment, and the overall quality of public finances). Consideration should also be given to any other factors which, in the opinion of the Member State concerned, are relevant, in order comprehensively to assess in qualitative terms the excess over the reference value. Special consideration will be given to budgetary efforts towards increasing or maintaining at a high level financial contributions to fostering international solidarity and achieving European policy goals, notably the unification of Europe, if they have a detrimental effect on the growth and fiscal burden of a Member State. These 'other relevant factors' will also be taken into account at all subsequent stages of the excessive deficit procedure, except for decisions concerning the abrogation of an excessive deficit and the decision to repeat a Council recommendation (on the basis of Article 104 paragraph 7 of the Treaty) or a Council notice (on the basis of Article 104 paragraph 9 of the Treaty). However, these factors should only be taken into account if the double condition that the excess over the reference value is temporary and the deficit remains close to the reference value is satisfied.

- *Pension reforms*: For Member States where the deficit exceeds the 3 per cent of GDP reference value but remains close to it, the Commission and the Council will also take into consideration the cost of a pension reform introducing a multi-pillar system that includes a mandatory, fully funded pillar. In particular, consideration will be given to the net cost of the reform to the publicly managed pillar. This will be done in a regressive manner over a period of five years. Such reforms will also be taken into consideration when assessing whether an excessive deficit has been corrected, if the deficit has declined substantially and continuously and has reached a level that comes close to the reference value.

- *Increasing the focus on debt and sustainability*: There was agreement that the debt surveillance framework should be strengthened by applying the concept of a government debt ratio that is 'sufficiently diminishing and approaching the reference value' in qualitative terms, by taking into account macroeconomic conditions and debt dynamics. However, neither the SGP Regulations nor the revised Code of Conduct have spelled out what this means. For Member States with a debt ratio above the 60 per cent of GDP reference value, the Council will formulate recommendations on the debt dynamics in its opinions in the stability and convergence programmes.

- *Extension of the deadline for the correction of an excessive deficit*: The correction of an excessive deficit should be completed in the year following its identification, unless there are special circumstances. The Member State having an excessive deficit will have to achieve a minimum annual improvement in its cyclically adjusted balance, net of one-off and temporary measures, of 0.5 per cent of GDP as a benchmark. The initial deadline can be revised when the Council recommendation or a Council notice is repeated. Such a repetition can take place if unexpected adverse economic events with major unfavourable budgetary effects occur and if effective action had been taken in compliance with the earlier recommendation or the earlier notice. When specifying these deadlines, the Council will take into account the 'other relevant factors'. The deadlines for each of the steps in the excessive deficit procedure have also been extended: the Council has to decide on the existence of an excessive deficit four months after the reporting by the Member States of their deficit and debt figures; in its recommendation, the Council will give six months to the Member State in which an excessive deficit exists to take effective action; a notice should be given two months after the Council has established that no effective action has been taken; and the Council will give four months to take effective action in its notice.

The reform of the SGP did not, in itself, introduce major changes in the area of governance. In particular, it did not change the basic procedures and voting rules, which in any case would require changes to the Treaty. However, the ECOFIN Council report of March 2005 did make a number of proposals and suggestions for improving governance and strengthening national ownership of the rules. In this context, it called for closer cooperation between Member States, the Commission, and the Council, as well as for improved peer support and peer pressure. It called for the development of complementary national budgetary rules, the continuity of budgetary targets when a new government takes office, and greater involvement of national parliaments. It also stressed the importance of reliable macroeconomic forecasts and budgetary statistics.

12.3 Experience

Overview of fiscal developments in the Euro-area: from the early 1990s to the present

In the years running up to the start of stage three of EMU, the fifteen then EU Member States (EU-15) embarked upon a process of budgetary adjustment, the magnitude of which was quite remarkable. In 1991, the year the Maastricht Treaty was signed, deficit ratios were above 3 per cent of GDP in six of the EU-15, and by 1993, this figure had risen to twelve out of fifteen (see Table 12.3 in the appendix). This situation was subsequently turned around such that, by 1997, the year on which the evaluation of whether countries were fit to join the first wave of Euro-area entrants was based, eleven Member States had achieved deficits below or at 3 per cent of GDP, at least according to the data available and in accordance with the statistical methodology in force at the time.[6] In six of the eleven countries that adopted the Euro on 1 January 1999, debt-to-GDP ratios remained above 60 per cent of GDP, but were deemed to be declining at a satisfactory pace.[7]

By contrast, since the entry into force of the Stability and Growth Pact in July 1998 and the launch of the single currency in 1999, fiscal consolidation in the Euro-area has largely stalled or even gone into reverse. In the early years of the single currency, nominal fiscal balances did generally improve, but this improvement reflected the positive impact of the economic cycle on budget balances rather than an underlying adjustment of fiscal positions. When the European economy subsequently entered a downturn phase, budget balances in most Euro-area Member States deteriorated. More recently, the fiscal position of the Euro-area has started to improve again, but in 2005 the unadjusted Euro-area budget balance was still at around about the same level as in the years immediately prior to stage three of EMU (see Figure 12.2).

Looking beyond headline budget balances, the underlying factors driving fiscal developments in the Euro-area can be better appreciated by examining the evolution of total revenue and primary expenditure adjusted for the economic cycle (see the right-hand panel of Figure 12.2). This allows us to see beyond the influence on budget balances of economic growth and changes in interest rates and to focus on changes stemming from discretionary fiscal policy (i.e. changes in the fiscal stance). According to the current

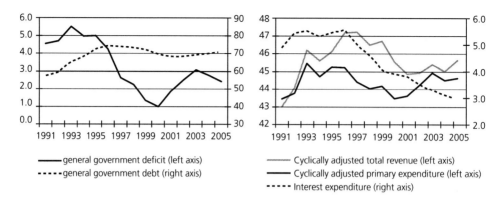

Figure 12.2 Fiscal developments in the Euro-area, 1991–2005 (as a percentage of GDP)

Source: European Commission.

estimates of the European Commission, between 1991 and 1997 the cyclically adjusted primary balance of the Euro-area (i.e. the difference between total revenue and primary expenditure, adjusted for the economic cycle) improved by more than 3 per cent of GDP. This was achieved essentially by increasing revenues as a percentage of GDP, while the primary expenditure ratio and the ratio of interest payments to GDP did not change significantly. Since 1997, the primary expenditure-to-GDP ratio has remained broadly stable, but some of the earlier increase in the revenue-to-GDP ratio has been reversed, with the reduction being broadly equivalent to a reduction in the burden of interest payments. In other words, the fiscal stance of the Euro-area has been loosening as the dividend of lower interest payments has been used to cut taxes rather than to improve the budget balance.

Fiscal (in)discipline under the Stability and Growth Pact

Since the advent of the Euro, aggregate Euro-area fiscal developments have masked different experiences among the participant Member States. Broadly speaking, two main groups of countries can be identified in relation to compliance with the requirements of the Stability and Growth Pact, although even within these groups individual country experiences differ somewhat. The first group consists of six Euro-area Member States that have (more or less) succeeded in achieving and maintaining 'close to balance or in surplus' budgetary positions. Among these, Ireland, Luxembourg, and Finland entered stage three of EMU with budget surpluses. Meanwhile, Belgium, Spain, and Austria started with significant deficits but by 2001 had managed to achieve broadly balanced budgetary positions. For the most part these countries have managed to maintain sound budgetary positions. The second group consists of five countries that have generally struggled to meet the Stability and Growth Pact requirements. Among these, deficits have been continually above 3 per cent of GDP in Greece (although this only came to light some time after the event: see Box 12.3), while deficits have been very close to or above 3 per cent of GDP in Portugal since 2000, in Italy and Germany since 2001, and in France since 2002.

BOX 12.3 REVISIONS OF BUDGETARY STATISTICS IN EMU

The implementation of the EU fiscal rules has been hindered by deficiencies in the collection and reporting of budgetary statistics in some countries. While revisions of economic data are commonplace, the magnitude of revisions of budgetary data in some EU countries has given rise to considerable concern. As can be seen from the table below, particularly large revisions have taken place in the cases of Greece, Italy, and Portugal. The implication of these revisions is that deficits above 3 per cent of GDP have gone undetected, in some cases for a number of years, and that the necessary peer pressure and procedural steps under the Stability and Growth Pact have only been applied after a significant delay. More recently, the Commission and the ECOFIN Council have taken steps aimed at improving the reliability of budgetary data, including a revision of the Council Regulation that governs statistical reporting for the purposes of the excessive deficit procedure. It remains to be seen, however, whether this will yield significant results and in the meantime improving statistical governance remains a priority for bolstering the credibility of EU fiscal policies.

Differences between initially reported and latest deficit estimates

	Notification date	General government budget balance			
		2001	2002	2003	2004
Greece	Initial	−0.4	−1.2	−1.7	−6.1
	Autumn 2006	−5.4	−5.2	−6.1	−7.8
Italy	Initial	−1.4	−2.3	−2.4	−3.0
	Autumn 2006	−3.1	−2.9	−3.5	−3.4
Portugal	Initial	−2.2	−2.7	−2.8	−2.9
	Autumn 2006	−4.3	−2.9	−2.9	−3.2

Source: EDP notifications Spring 2002–Autumn 2006, European Commission.

A country that is more difficult to classify is the Netherlands where the budget balance moved from a surplus to an excessive deficit and then back to a balanced budget, reflecting the high sensitivity of the Dutch budget balance to a relatively volatile economic cycle. Overall, however, it seems appropriate to classify the Netherlands as a country that has complied with the rules, since it has (twice) reached a balanced budgetary position and its excessive deficit was both short lived and corrected promptly.

The different experiences of what we might call the 'good performers' and the 'bad performers' can be aptly illustrated by comparing fiscal outcomes with targets set in successive stability programmes. Panel (a) of Figure 12.3 compares the simple (i.e. unweighted) average actual deficit with the average of the targets set each year by the seven 'good performers' (Belgium, Spain, Ireland, Luxembourg, the Netherlands, Austria, and Finland). Panel (b) does likewise for the five 'bad performers' (Germany, Greece, France, Italy, and Portugal). This shows that in the case of the good performers deviations of

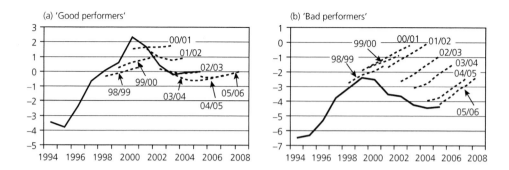

Figure 12.3 Actual general government budget balances versus stability programme targets (as a percentage of GDP)

Sources: European Commission, stability programmes and author calculations.

actual budgetary outcomes from their targeted levels were comparatively small and occurred on both the upside and the downside, depending on whether times were good or bad. By contrast, the fiscal outcomes of the bad performers have been consistently worse than targeted.

A consequence of this divergence in country-level experiences is that EMU has so far failed to bring about a convergence of fiscal positions towards sound and sustainable public finances. In particular, the objective of having debt-to-GDP ratios that converge towards levels safely below 60 per cent is far from being acheived. On the contrary, since the good performers that have succeeded in reaching and maintaining balanced or in surplus budgets have, for the most part, been those that already had relatively low debt levels such as Ireland or Finland, debt reduction in these countries has matched or even outpaced that in high debt countries such as Greece or Italy. Meanwhile in a number of countries, including France and Germany, which had debt ratios that were initially below or close to 60 per cent of GDP, these ratios have increased in recent years (see Table 12.3 in the appendix).

Fiscal stabilization under the Stability and Growth Pact

By guaranteeing fiscal discipline, the Stability and Growth Pact should ensure that Member States maintain sufficient 'room for manoeuvre' to allow the operation of the automatic fiscal stabilizers to cushion the effects of the economic cycle. However, the Pact has been frequently criticized for encouraging pro-cyclical fiscal policies. A closer look at the evidence suggests that this criticism is not justified. Again taking simple averages for the 'good performers' and 'bad performers', Figure 12.4 plots changes in the cyclically adjusted primary balance (CAPB), which captures the fiscal stance, against changes in the output gap, which is a commonly used measure of cyclical conditions.[8] An unchanged CAPB would indicate that the fiscal stance is neutral and that the automatic fiscal stabilizers are being allowed to operate. An upward sloping line (from left to right) indicates a counter-cyclical fiscal policy, that is a tightening (loosening) of the fiscal stance when the change in the output gap is positive (negative), and hence a fiscal policy that is helping

(a) 'Good performers'

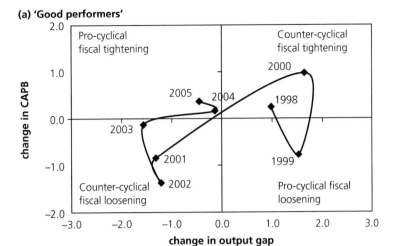

(b) 'Bad performers'

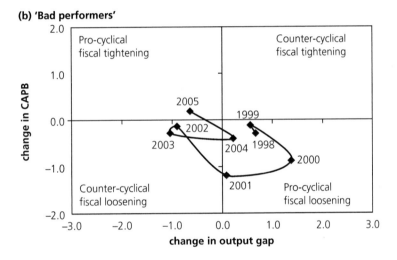

Figure 12.4 Fiscal policy stance

Note: CAPB = cyclically adjusted primary balance excluding the proceeds from the sale of Universal Mobile Telecommunications Systems (UMTS) Licences.
Sources: European Commission and author's calculations.

to stabilize output. A downward sloping line (from left to right) indicates a fiscal policy that is pro-cyclical thereby exacerbating cyclical fluctuations. It can be seen that those countries that struggled to comply with the Pact engaged in a pro-cyclical loosening of fiscal policy in the early years of the single currency. In more recent years, however, fiscal policy in these countries has been broadly neutral and the automatic stabilizers have been allowed to operate (even at the expense of a prompt correction of excessive deficits). Meanwhile, in the countries that have respected the Pact's requirements, fiscal policy has, for the most part, been counter-cyclical.

Nonetheless, an obvious mistake that was made in the early years of the single currency was the failure of some countries to undertake sufficient consolidation in 'good times'. In particular, during the upturn of 1998–2000, underlying budgetary positions were allowed to deteriorate and the room for manoeuvre to avoid excessive deficits in bad times eroded. There are a number of explanations as to why this happened. In some Member States there was certainly an element of 'consolidation fatigue'. As noted above, the fiscal consolidation undertaken in the run-up to EMU was mainly achieved by increasing taxes, which was generally accepted at the time as a price worth paying in order to achieve the objective of Euro-area membership. But in countries where tax levels were already very high by international standards, once in the Euro-area, pressure soon built to relieve some of this increased tax burden. Advocates of tax cuts argued that the impact on the budget balance would be limited since lower tax rates would foster economic growth. In practice, however, this higher growth never materialized and the tax cuts therefore did not prove to be self-financing.

Many policy-makers also appear to have underestimated the extent to which underlying fiscal positions were deteriorating at the time. This may have been partly a result of the fact that too much was read into the improvement of nominal fiscal balances. In theory, the evolution of cyclically adjusted budget balances should have alerted policy-makers to the fiscal loosening that was taking place. In practice, however, estimates of the cyclically adjusted budget balance are prone to error owing to the difficulty of measuring the cyclical position of the economy in real time and the sensitivity to the cycle of some budget items. This is especially true in a situation such as that in the early years of the single currency when estimates of trend or potential output growth for many countries proved to be over-optimistic. In cases where potential growth is overestimated, there will be a bias towards estimating negative output gaps (i.e. concluding that actual output is below potential) and a corresponding tendency to underestimate (overestimate) the cyclically adjusted deficit (surplus). In addition, methods used for the cyclical adjustment of fiscal variables do not always capture all cyclical influences on the budget balance. For example, the impact of asset prices on tax revenues tends not to be well captured by current methods and hence there is a tendency for cyclically adjusted budget balances to paint an overly positive picture of the true state of the public finances during asset price booms such as that related to the 'dotcom bubble' of the late 1990s.

Difficulties enforcing the fiscal framework

Shortcomings in the conduct of fiscal policies in EMU must also be attributed to a less than perfect enforcement of the Stability and Growth Pact. Under the preventive arm of the Pact, there seems to have been a general reluctance to exert 'peer pressure' in favour of tighter fiscal policies when these would have been appropriate. In particular, countries that presented overly optimistic growth and fiscal forecasts or backloaded fiscal consolidation strategies tended to receive at most only very mild criticism of their stability programmes when these were examined by the ECOFIN Council.

When, on occasions, it was decided to apply more explicit pressure on a country to change its policy course, this did not always have the desired effect. A pertinent episode occurred in early 2001 when the Council decided to take a stance against Ireland for what it considered to be a pro-cyclical loosening of Irish fiscal policy. In the 'Broad Economic Policy Guidelines' (BEPGs) of the previous year, the Council had recommended that Ireland should use fiscal policy to prevent an overheating of its economy, which at the time was growing at near double digit levels with inflation at more than 5 per cent. However, the Irish budget adopted in December 2000 introduced a package of tax cuts, in apparent contradiction with the BEPGs. Following a recommendation by the Commission, the Council decided to issue a recommendation to Ireland to correct the inconsistency between its fiscal policy and the BEPGs. But the Irish government resisted the recommendation, arguing that tax cuts were necessary to sustain moderate wage agreements between Ireland's social partners. Ultimately, the Irish government was vindicated as inflationary pressures subsequently eased because of the economic downturn without any change in fiscal policy.

A first indication of the difficulties of implementing the Stability and Growth Pact's 'corrective arm' came in early 2002 when it became clear that both Germany and Portugal were at risk of incurring excessive deficits. The Commission recommended that the ECOFIN Council should issue 'early warnings' to Germany and Portugal to take corrective action. In response, both the German and Portuguese governments reasserted their commitment to avoiding excessive deficits but resisted the early warnings recommended by the Commission. The Council decided that the early warnings were not necessary since the substance of the Commission's concerns had already been addressed by the commitments of the governments concerned. Only a few months later, however, an audit of the public finances in Portugal showed that the Portuguese deficit had already exceeded the 3 per cent of GDP deficit limit in 2001, while Germany also breached the 3 per cent reference value in 2002.

The most serious difficulties arose, however, in the context of excessive deficit procedures initiated against France and Germany for breaching the 3 per cent reference value in 2002 (see Table 12.1). Both France and Germany had received recommendations from the ECOFIN Council to correct the situation by 2004 at the latest. By the autumn of 2003, however, it became clear that the action taken by both countries was not proving effective

Table 12.1 Overview of excessive deficit procedures for Euro-area countries

	Recommendation (Article 104(7))		Notice (Article 104(9))		Status as of 31 March 2007
	Date issued	Deadline	Date issued	Deadline	
Portugal	Nov 2002	2003	–	–	Closed
Germany	Jan 2003	2004[a]	Mar 2006	2007	Abeyance
France	Jun 2003	2004[a]	–	–	Closed
Netherlands	Jun 2004	2005	–	–	Closed
Greece	Jul 2004	2005	Feb 2005	2006	Abeyance
Italy	Jul 2005	2007	–	–	Abeyance
Portugal	Sep 2005	2008	–	–	Abeyance

[a] De facto extended to 2005.

to correct their excessive deficits within this timeframe. The Commission therefore decided to recommend an extension to 2005 of the deadline for correcting the excessive deficits, while at the same time moving forward to the next step of the procedure by recommending that the Council should issue 'notices' to France and Germany under Article 104 paragraph 9 of the Treaty. While there was a general consensus regarding the economic analysis contained in the Commission's recommendations, it proved impossible to find the necessary qualified majority in the Council in favour of adopting the notices. The Council attempted to fill the resulting legal/political vacuum by issuing 'conclusions' in which the procedures were put in abeyance in return for commitments by France and Germany to correct their excessive deficits in 2005. The legality of this approach was challenged by the Commission, however, and the Council's conclusions were later annulled by the European Court of Justice.[9] This procedural impasse ultimately precipitated the debate which led to the reform of the Stability and Growth Pact in spring/summer 2005.

Fiscal policies in the non-Euro-area Member States

While the focus of this section so far has been on the experience of those countries that are part of the Euro-area, a few words are warranted on those countries that are members of the EU but have not yet adopted the single currency. Among these Denmark, Sweden, and the UK have been members of the EU for some years but have so far failed to qualify (or chosen not) to adopt the Euro. In the cases of Deanmark and Sweden, this cannot be attributed to any failing of fiscal policy as both countries have maintained healthy budget surpluses since the late 1990s. The UK also achieved budget surplus in 1999–2001, but this strong position has since given way to renewed deficits above 3 per cent of GDP. While this deterioration can be partly attributed to the downturn of the early 2000s, it is primarily a result of the British government's stated policy of borrowing in order to finance (increasing) public investment.

Among the ten 'new' Member States that joined the EU on 1 May 2004, the Czech Republic, Cyprus, Hungary, Malta, Poland, and Slovakia entered with deficits above 3 per cent of GDP and immediately became the subject of excessive deficit procedures. Slovenia's deficit was slightly below 3 per cent of GDP, Latvia and Lithuania had relatively small deficits, and Estonia had a budget surplus. The fiscal positions of the new Member States thus differ significantly, but for most of them the priority was (and remains) to reduce deficit ratios with a view to meeting the Maastricht convergence criteria for entry into the Euro-area. In this regard, the situation in the new Member States is not dissimilar to that of many of the EU-15 Member States in the mid- to late-1990s, although two notable differences are that the new Member States generally benefit from much lower debt-to-GDP ratios (only Cyprus and Malta have debt ratios above 60 per cent of GDP) and that their interest rates are closer to the level currently prevailing in the Euro-area. These two differences imply that, contrary to the experience of many of the first wave of Euro-area entrants, the saving in terms of interest payments to be derived by these countries' eventual participation in the single currency will not be sizeable.

Since their entry into the EU, fiscal balances in most of the new Member States have been improving. At the same time, many of the new Member States have benefited from a favourable economic environment during this period, so the extent to which this reflects an improvement of underlying fiscal positions is difficult to ascertain. In particular, it has to be borne in mind that, owing to the lack of a sufficiently long time series for many relevant variables, measures of underlying fiscal positions for these countries are subject to even greater margins of error than for the EU-15.

A comparative view: fiscal policies in the Euro-area, Japan, and the United States

In order to put fiscal policies in EMU in a broader context, it is useful to compare developments in the Euro-area with those in other (non-European) industrialized countries. Table 12.2 presents some summary statistics regarding the current fiscal situation and recent experience in the Euro-area compared with that in Austalia, Canada, Japan, New Zealand, and the United States. The current fiscal position of the Euro-area is broadly comparable to that of the United States, is much more favourable than that of Japan, while being much less favourable than that of Australia, Canada, and New Zealand. In particular, the latter three countries have all succeeded in maintaining budget surpluses in recent years leading to significant reductions in their debt-to-GDP ratios, which in Australia and New Zealand have already reached very low levels.

As a rough indicator of the responsivness of fiscal policy to cyclical developments in these countries, the last column in Table 12.2 reports the correlation between the change in the budget balance and the change in the output gap. Higher values of the correlation coefficient are indicative of a counter-cyclical fiscal policy, with above-trend output being accompanied by an improvement of the budget balance and vice versa. On this score, the experience of the Euro-area seems to be comparable to that of the United States, as well as to that of Australia and Canada, where it appears that fiscal policy has been counter-cyclical. By contrast, fiscal policies in Japan and New Zealand do not appear to have played a stabilizing role.

Table 12.2 Fiscal developments in selected industrialized countries (in % of GDP)

	2005		1999–2005		
	Budget balance	Gross debt	Average budget balance	Change in debt	Correlation ΔBB / ΔOG*
Euro-area	−2.4	70.8	−2.1	−1.2	0.83
Australia	2.3	10.5	1.2	−11.6	0.54
Canada	1.7	84.8	1.1	−26.8	0.71
Japan	−6.5	158.9	−7.2	30.0	−0.27
New Zealand	3.9	23.0	2.0	−10.8	−0.39
United States	−3.7	64.6	−2.1	0.2	0.84

* Correlation between the change in budget balance and the change in the output gap.
Sources: European Commission, IMF, OECD.

Experience following the reform of the Stability and Growth Pact

A major issue for Euro-area fiscal policy at this juncture is whether the reform of the Stability and Growth Pact that took place in 2005 will lead to improved compliance with the EU fiscal rules and thereby a convergence towards sound fiscal positions in all EU Member States. At the time of writing, experience since the reform is rather limited and there are some encouraging as well as some more worrisome signs.

On the positive side, following several years of 'disappointing' news, fiscal outcomes in 2005 were actually a welcome surprise. The Euro-area deficit of 2.4 per cent of GDP in 2005 was significantly better than that projected by most forecasters, including the Commission, IMF, and OECD, which as late as autumn 2005 were forecasting a deficit in the order of 2.8 per cent of GDP. It seems premature to attribute this positive surprise to the reform of the SGP, however. Budgets for 2005 were adopted already before the Pact reform and the better than expected outcomes were due to a variety of non-discretionary factors (such as unexpectedly buoyant revenues from profit-related taxes) rather from actual policy actions.

As regards fiscal objectives and targets, the MTOs presented by Member States in their stability and convergence programme updates submitted at the end of 2005 are in compliance with the revised rules. But Member States with large deficits generally fail to specify when these MTOs will be achieved. Moreover, the adjustment path towards the MTO remains backloaded in many countries. This points to a risk of a repetition of past mistakes when the opportunity to use 'good times' to step up consolidation efforts was squandered. In the context of the Pact's corrective arm, a number of decisions in the context of excessive deficit procedure have been taken since the reform without any signs of a repetition of the procedural impasse that occurred in November 2003. At the same time, the flexibility of the new rules has been used to the full to extend deadlines for Germany, Italy, and Portugal to correct their excessive deficits. Moreover, even compliance with these more 'realistic' targets is still far from assured in some cases. Hence, at best, it will take some time before it can be established that the revised rules are working more effectively.

12.4 Conclusions

The framework for fiscal policy-making that has been set up in EMU is unique as it leaves the responsibility to the governments of the EU Member States but subjects these to detailed rules and procedures. A large body of rules and procedures, supplemented by common agreements and 'jurisprudence', has been built up.

From a theoretical perspective, the adoption of fiscal rules can be useful for a number of reasons. They can serve as as an external discipline device in the presence of domestic policy distortions and insufficient incentives for sound public finances provided by market mechanisms alone. In principle, such inefficiencies could be addressed at source by improving policy institutions and regulation at the national level. At the same time, such national deficiencies can be exacerbated in a monetary union and, more importantly, are likely to exert spillover effects on partner countries and on the single monetary policy, thus fundamentally becoming a matter of common concern. From a new classical perspective the main focus to address such spillovers is on the need for constraints on policy, as a kind of negative coordination device to avoid major policy mistakes. This emphasis on rules rather than discretion underpins the basic thrust of the fiscal framework adopted in Maastricht and in the Stability and Growth Pact. At the same time, the framework stopped short of automatic procedures, but acknowledged the need to exercise judgement in the interpretation and case-by-case application of the common rules which ultimately has to rely on peer pressure in decision-making.

The experience with the Maastricht fiscal framework and the Stability and Growth Pact to date has been mixed. While the Maastricht fiscal criteria were a crucial device in promoting convergence in the run-up to monetary union, since the introduction of the single currency fiscal consolidation has slowed or even gone into reverse in many countries. While approximately half of the Euro-area countries have succeeded in complying with the rules of the Stability and Growth Pact, the remainder have squandered the opportunity presented by a lower interest rate burden in EMU. Five of the twelve Euro-area Member States, including the three largest (France, Germany, and Italy) have had deficits close to or above 3 per cent of GDP for several years and debt-to-GDP ratios have increased or failed to decline at a satisfactory pace in these countries. A major shortcoming of fiscal policy in these countries has been the failure to undertake sufficient consolidation in 'good times', which has also contributed to a pro-cyclical fiscal stance in some countries. By contrast, in those countries that have complied with the EU fiscal rules, fiscal policy appears to have played an effective counter-cyclical role.

While the fiscal imbalances that emerged in some Euro-area countries in the context of the economic downturn of 2001–3 placed considerable strains on the original Stability and Growth Pact, it remains to be seen whether the revised version adopted in 2005 will provide an impetus for renewed progress towards sound fiscal positions in all Member States. The reform has extended the list of extenuating country-specific circumstances to be taken into account in the application of the rules and, overall, has enhanced the scope for judgement in the process. In this context it also sought to place greater emphasis on the cyclically adjusted fiscal position and the longer-run requirements for fiscal sustainability. As such the reform represents a step away from the notion of simple rules, which are intended to be easier to monitor and apply, to a more sophisticated and more demanding notion of constrained discretion. The basic challenge remains to induce those in charge of public finances to take into account the interests of future generations and to live up to the broader shared responsibility for macroeconomic stability within monetary union.

DISCUSSION QUESTIONS

1. Why does a monetary union require both greater discipline and greater flexibility of national fiscal policies? In which way have the Maastricht Treaty and the Stability and Growth Pact reconciled these two requirements?

2. Is there a need for greater fiscal policy coordination among the countries of the Euro-area or some kind of 'European economic government'?

3. How do you assess the reform of the Stability and Growth Pact in spring 2005? Give possible reasons why this reform did not have any substantial effects on financial markets, e.g. on government bond spreads?

FURTHER READING

Brunila, A., Buti, M., and Franco, D. (eds) (2001), *The Stability and Growth Pact: The Architecture of Fiscal Policy in EMU* (New York: Palgrave).

Buti, M. and Franco, D. (2005), *Fiscal Policy in Economic and Monetary Union: Theory, Evidence and Institutions* (Cheltenham: Edward Elgar).

Morris, R., Ongena H., and Schuknecht L. (2006), *The Reform and Implementation of the Stability and Growth Pact*, ECB Occasional Paper Series no. 47.

Useful Internet addresses: http://www.ecb.int for publications and press releases of the European Central Bank; http://europa.eu.int is the home page of all European Union institutions. From there, there is a link to the website of the European Commission. The site of the Directorate General for Economic and Financial Affairs http://europa.eu.int/comm/economy_finance provides access to publications on EMU.

NOTES

* The views expressed in this chapter are those of the authors and do not necessarily reflect those of the European Central Bank.

1. EMU was achieved in 3 stages: the first stage (1990–1993) ensured the free movement of capital and the closer coordination of economic and monetary policies; the second stage (1994–1998) focused on the convergence of economic and monetary policy and the creation of the European Monetary Institute (which became the ECB in 1998); in the third stage (1999–2002) the single currency was finally introduced.

2. The Economic and Financial Committee is a committee composed of high-level experts from the administrations and national central banks of the EU Member States, the Commission, and the ECB. Its role is to advise the Commission and the ECOFIN Council on economic and financial matters.

3. The 'original' Stability and Growth Pact consisted of Council Regulation (EC) No. 1466/97 of 7 July 1997 on the strengthening of the surveillance of budgetary positions and the surveillance and coordination of economic policies, published in the Official Journal (OJ) L209 of 2 August 1997, p. 1; Council Regulation (EC) No. 1467/97 of 7 July 1997 on speeding up and clarifying the implementation of the excessive deficit procedure, published in OJ L209 of 2 August 1997, p. 6; and Resolution of the European Council on the Stability and Growth Pact of 17 June 1997, published in OJ C236 of 2 August 1997, p. 1.

4. The 'Broad Economic Policy Guidelines' are the central tool for the overall coordination of economic policies in the EU. Revised annually, they consist of general recommendations for the conduct of economic policies in the EU as a whole as well as specific recommendations issued to each Member State.

5. The changes are laid down in two new Council Regulations, No. 1055/2005 and No. 1056/2005 amending Council Regulations 1466/97 and 1467/97 respectively.

6. As a consequence of the shift from ESA 79 to ESA 95 accounting rules in February 2000 as well as various ad hoc statistical revisions, the deficit estimates for 1997 of Greece, Portugal, and Spain have since been revised to above 3 per cent of GDP.

7. Greece also adopted the Euro on 1 January 2001, despite having a debt ratio well above the 60 per cent reference value and a deficit ratio which, while at the time deemed to be below 3 per cent of GDP, has since been revised upwards substantially. Slovenia adopted the Euro on 1 January 2007, having complied with both the deficit and debt criteria in 2005. In this section, the data for the 'Euro-area' pertain to the Euro-area as it was composed between 1 January 2001 and 31 December 2006 (i.e. the original eleven members plus Greece).

8. A positive (negative) change in the output gap implies that the economy is growing above (below) its potential or trend growth rate.

9. In its ruling, the Court reaffirmed the right of the ECOFIN Council to have a different analysis and thereby deviate in its decisions from the substance of the recommendations issued by the Commission. However, the Council cannot step outside the formal procedures foreseen in the Treaty and the Stability and Growth Pact.

■ REFERENCES

Afonso, A. (2006), *Expansionary Fiscal Consolidations in Europe: New Evidence*, ECB Working Paper no. 675 (Frankfurt: European Central Bank).

Agell, J., Calmfors, L., and Jonsson, G. (1996), 'Fiscal Policy when Monetary Policy is Tied to the Mast', *European Economic Review*, 40: 1413–40.

Alesina, A. and Perotti, R. (1995), 'The Political Economy of Budget Deficits', *IMF Staff Papers* 42, 1–32.

—— —— (1996), *Fiscal Adjustments in OECD Countries: Composition and Macroeconomic Effects*, NBER, Working Paper no. 5730 (also in *IMF Staff Papers*, 44/2, 1997).

Allsopp, C. and Vines, D. (1996). 'Fiscal Policy and EMU'. *National Institute Economic Review* 158, 4/96, 91–107.

Ardagna, S., Caselli, F., and Lane, T. (2004), *Fiscal Discipline and the Cost of Public Debt Service: Some Estimates for OECD Countries*, ECB Working Paper no. 411.

Artis, M. and Marcellino, M. (2000), 'The Solvency of European Government Finances', in *Fiscal Sustainability*, Banca d'Italia, Rome, 2000.

—— and Onorante, L. (2006), *The Economic Importance of Fiscal Rules*, CEPR Discussion Paper no. 5684.

—— and Winkler, B. (1998) 'The Stability Pact: Safeguarding the Credibility of the European Central Bank', *National Institute Economic Review*, Jan: 87–98.

Barro, R. (1974), 'Are Governments' Bonds Net Wealth?', *Journal of Political Economy*, 82/6, 1095–117.

—— and Gordon, D. (1983), 'A Positive Theory of Monetary Policy in a Natural Rate Model'. *Journal of Political Economy* 91, 585–610.

Bayoumi, T. and Eichengreen, B. (1995), 'Restraining Yourself: The Implication of Fiscal Rules for Economic Stabilization', *IMF Staff Papers* 42, 32–48.

—— and Masson, P. (1995), 'Fiscal Flows in the United States and Canada: Lessons for Monetary Union in Europe', *European Economic Review* 39, 253–274.

Beetsma, R. and Bovenberg, L. (2000), 'Designing Fiscal and Monetary Institutions for a European Monetary Union', *Public Choice* 102, 247–269.

—— and Uhlig, H. (1999), 'An Analysis of the Stability Pact', *Economic Journal* 109, 546–571.

Bernoth, K., von Hagen, J., and Schuknecht, L. (2004), *Sovereign Risk Premia in the European Government Bond Market*, ECB Working Paper no. 369.

Bertola, G. and Drazen, A. (1993), 'Trigger Points and Budget Cuts: Explaining the Effects of Fiscal Austerity', *American Economic Review* 83, 11–26.

Bini Smaghi, L. (2004), 'What Went Wrong with the Stability and Growth Pact?', paper prepared for the conference on 'Monetary Union in Europe: Historical Perspectives and Prospects for the Future', Copenhagen.

Blanchard, O. J. and Giavazzi, F. (2004), *Improving the SGP through a Proper Accounting of Public Investment*, CEPR Discussion Paper no. 4220.

Briotti, M. G. (2004), *Fiscal Adjustment between 1991 and 2002: Stylised Facts and Policy Implications*, ECB Occasional Paper no. 9.

—— (2005), *Economic Reactions to Public Finance Consolidations: A Survey of the Literature*, ECB Occasional Paper no. 38.

Buchanan, J. (1977), *Democracy in Deficit. The Political Legacy of Lord Keynes* (New York: Academic Press).

Buiter, W. (2006), 'The "Sense and Nonsense of Maastricht" Revisited: What Have we Learnt about Stabilization in EMU?', *Journal of Common Market Studies*, 44/4: 687–710.

—— and Grafe, C. (2004), 'Patching up the Pact: Some Suggestions for Enhancing Fiscal Sustainability and Macroeconomic Stability in an Enlarged European Union', *Economics of Transition*, 12/1: 67–102.

Buti, M. (2005), *The Stability Pact Pains: A Forward-Looking Assessment of the Reform Debate*, CEPR Working Paper no. 5216.

—— (2006), *Will the New Stability and Growth Pact Succeed? An Economic and Political Perspective*, European Commission Economic Papers no. 241.

—— and Sapir, A. (eds.) (1998), *Economic Policy in EMU—A Study by the European Commission Services* (Oxford: Oxford University Press).

—— Franco, D., and Ongena, H. (1998), 'Fiscal Discipline and Flexibility in EMU: The Implementation of the Stability and Growth Pact', *Oxford Review of Economic Policy*, 14/3.

—— Eijffinger, S., and Franco, D. (2003), *Revisiting the Stability and Growth Pact: Grand Design or Internal Adjustment?*, CEPR Working Paper no. 3692.

—— Nogueira Martins, J., and Turrini, A. (2006), *From Deficits to Debt and Back: Political Incentives under Numerical Fiscal Rules*, CEPR Discussion Paper no. 5809.

Calmfors, L. (2005), 'What Remains of the Stability Pact and What Next?', *Swedish Institute for European Policy Studies*: 8.

Canzoneri, M. and Diba, B. T. (1996), *Fiscal Constraints on Central Bank Independence and Price Stability*, CEPR Discussion Paper no. 1463.

Capiello, L., Hartmann, P., Hördahl, P., Kadareja, A., and Manganelli, S. (2006), *The Impact of the Euro on Financial Markets*, ECB Working Paper no. 598.

Codogno, L., Favero, C., and Missale, A. (2003), 'Yield Spreads on EMU Government Bonds', *Economic Policy*, 37 October: 503–27.

Coeuré, B. and Pisani-Ferry, J. (2005), 'Fiscal Policy in EMU: Towards a Sustainability and Growth Pact', *Oxford Review of Economic Policy*, 21/4, 598–617.

Corsetti, G. and Roubini, N. (1993), 'The Design of Optimal Fiscal Rules for Europe after 1992', in F. Torres and F. Giavazzi (eds.), *Adjustment and Growth in the European Monetary System* (Cambridge: Cambridge University Press), 46–82.

Deroose, S. and van Langedijk, S. (2005), *Improving the Stability and Growth Pact: the Commission's Three Pillar Approach*, European Economy Occasional Papers no. 15.

Detken, K., Gaspar, V., and Winkler, B. (2004), *On Prosperity and Posterity: The Need for Fiscal Discipline in a Monetary Union*, ECB Working Paper no. 420.

Deutsche Bundesbank (2005), *The Changes to the Stability and Growth Pact*, Monthly Report, Apr.

Dixit, A. and Lambertini, L. (2003), 'Symbiosis of Monetary and Fiscal Policies in a Monetary Union', *Journal of International Economics*, 60/2: 235–47.

Easterly, W., Rodriguez, C., and Schmidt-Hebbel, K. (eds.) (1994), *Public Sector Deficits and Macroeconomic Performance* (Oxford: Oxford University Press).

Eichengreen, B. (1997), 'Swing Europe's Automatic stabilizers, *National Institute Economic Review*, 159/1: 92–8.

—— and von Hagen, J. (1996), 'Fiscal Policy and Monetary Union: Federalism, Fiscal Restrictions, and the No-Bailout Rule', in H. Siebert (ed.), *Monetary Policy in an Integrated World Economy* (Tübirgen: Mohr (Paul Siebeck)), 211–231.

—— and Wyplosz, C. (1998), 'The Stability Pact: More than a Minor Nuisance?', *Economic Policy*, 26, pp. 65–115.

Eijffinger, S. and de Haan, J. (2000), *European Monetary and Fiscal Policy* (Oxford: Oxford University Press).

European Central Bank (1999), The Templemention of the Stability and Growth Pact, May: 45–72.

European Commission (2001), *The Economic Policy Framework in EMU*, Nov.: 51–65.

—— (2002), *The Operation of Automatic Stabilizers in the Euro-area*, Apr.: 33–46.

—— (2003), 'Public Finances in EMU', *European Economy* no. 3.

—— (2005), 'Public Finances in EMU', *European Economy* no. 3.

—— (2005), *The Reform of the Stability and Growth Pact*, Aug.: 59–74.

—— (2006), 'Economic Forecasts—Spring 2006', *European Economy* no. 2.

—— (2006), *Fiscal Policies and Financial Markets*, Feb.: 71–85.

Fatás, A., von Hagen, J., Hughes-Hallet, A., Sibert, A., and Strauch, R. (2003), Stability and Growth in Europe: Towards a Better Pact, CEPR–ZEI Monitoring European Integration no 13 (London: Centre for Economic Policy Research/Bonn: Centre for European Integration Studies).

Feldstein, M. (2005), *The Euro and the Stability Pact*, NBER Working Paper no. 11249.

Giavazzi, F. and Pagano, M. (1990), 'Can Severe Fiscal Contractions Be Expansionary? Tales of Two Small European Countries', *NBER Macroeconomics Annual*, 75–111.

Glick, R. and Hutchison, M. (1993), 'Fiscal Policy in Monetary Unions: Implications for Europe'. *Open Economies Review* 4, 39–65.

Grilli, V., D. Masciandaro, and Tabellini, G. (1991), 'Political and Monetary Institutions and Public Financial Policies in the Industrial Countries', *Economic Policy* 13, 341–392.

Gros, D., Mayer, T., and Ubide, A. (2004), *The Nine Lives of the Stability and Growth Pact: A Special Report of the CEPS Macroeconomic Policy Group* (Brussels: Centre for European Policy Studies).

von Hagen, J., Hughes Hallet, A., and Strauch, R. (2001), *Budgetary Consolidation in EMU*, Economic Papers no. 148 (Brussels: European Commission).

—— Hallerberg, M., and Strauch, R. (2004), *Budgetary Forecasts in Europe: The Track Record of Stability and Convergence Programmes*, ECB Working Paper no. 307.

Hughes Hallett, A., Hutchison, M., and Hougaard Jensen, S. (eds.) (1999), *Fiscal Aspects of European Monetary Integration* (Cambridge: Cambridge University Press).

Inman, R. P. (1996), 'Do Balanced Budget Rules Work? US Experience and Possible Lessons for EMU', in NBER Working Paper No. 5838.

Kirsanova, T., Stehn, S. J., and Vines, D. (2005), 'The Interaction between Fiscal Policy and Monetary Policy', *Oxford Review of Economic Policy*, 21/4: 532–64.

Koen, V. and van den Noord, P. (2005), *Fiscal Gimmickry in Europe: One-off Measures and Creative Accounting*, OECD Economics Department Working Papers no. 417 (Paris: OECD).

Krogstrup, S. and Wyplosz, C. (2006), *A Common Pool Theory of Deficit Bias Correction*, CEPR Discussion Paper no. 5866.

Kydland, F. and Prescott, E. (1977), 'Rules Rather than Discretion: The Inconsistency of Optimal Plans', *Journal of Political Economy* 85, 473–491.

Masson, P. (1996), 'Fiscal Dimensions of EMU', *Economic Journal*, 106: 996–1004.

McKinnon, R. I. (1994), 'A Common Monetary Standard or a Common Currency for Europe? Fiscal Lessons from the United States', *Scottish Journal of Political Economy*, November, 337–357.

Michel, P., von Thadden, L., and Vidal, J.-P. (2006), *Debt Stabilizing Fiscal Rules*, ECB Working Paper no. 576.

Morris, R., Ongena, H., and Schuknecht, L. (2006), *The Reform and Implementation of the Stability and Growth Pact*, ECB Occasional Paper Series no. 47.

Mundell, R. (1961), 'A Theory of Optimal Currency Areas', *American Economic Review* 51, 657–665.

Olson, M. (1965), *The Logic of Collective Action*, (Cambridge, MA: Harvard University Press).

Ongena, H. (2004), 'Comment on Article 104 of the Treaty', in H. von der Groeben and J. Schwarze (eds.), *Vertrag über die Europäische Union und Vertrag zur Gründung der Europäischen Gemeinschaft* (Baden-Baden: Nomos Verlag).

Paesani, P., Strauch, R., and Kremer, M. (2006), *Public Debt and Long-term Interest Rates: The Case of Germany, Italy and the USA*, ECB Working Paper no. 656.

Perotti, R. (1999), 'Fiscal Policy in Good Times and Bad', *Quarterly Journal of Economics* 114, 1399–1436.

Pisani-Ferry, J. (2006), 'Only One Bed for Two Dreams: A Critical Retrospective on the Debate over the Economic Governance of the Euro-area', *Journal of Common Market Studies*, 44/4: 823–44.

Poterba J. M. (1995), 'Capital Budgets, Borrowing Rules and State Capital Spending', *Journal of Public Economics*, 56, 165–187.

Roubini, N. and Sachs, J. (1989), 'Political and Economic Determinant of Budget Deficits in the Industrial Democracies', *European Economic Review* 33, 903–938.

Sargent, T. and Wallace, N. (1981), 'Some Unpleasant Monetarist Arithmetic', *Quarterly Review*, Federal Reserve Bank of Minneapolis (Fall), 1–17.

Schuknecht, L. (2005), 'Stability and Growth Pact: Issues and Lessons from Political Economy', *International Economics and Economic Policy*, 2: 65–89.

Sims, C. (1994), 'A Simple Model for Study of the Determination of the Price Level and the Interaction of Monetary and Fiscal Policy', *Economic Theory*, 4/3: 381–99.

Sørensen, B. E. and Yosha, O. (1998), 'International Risk-Sharing and European Monetary Unification', *Journal of International Economics* 45, 211–238.

Stark, J. (2001), 'Genesis of a Pact', in A. Brunila, M. Buti, and D. Franco (eds.), *The Stability and Growth Pact: The Architecture of Fiscal Policy in EMU* (Basingtoke: Palgrave), 77–105.

Winkler, B. (1999), 'Coordinating Stability: Some Remarks on the Respective Roles of Monetary and Fiscal Policy under EMU', *Empirica* 26, 287–295.

Woodford, M. (1995), 'Price Level Determinacy Without Control of a Monetary Aggregate', *Carnegie-Rochester Conference Series on Public Policy*.

—— (1998), 'Control of the Public Debt: A Requirement for Price Stability?' in G. Calvo and M. King (eds.), *The Debt Burden and its Consequences for Monetary Policy*, International Economic Association Conference Volume, no. 118 (New York: St Martin's Press, Basingstoke: Macmillan Press), 117–154.

Wyplosz, C. (2005), 'Fiscal Policy: Institutions versus Rules', *National Institute Economic Review*, 191: 64–78.

■ APPENDIX

Table 12.3 Net lending (+) or net borrowing (−), general government, 1991–2005 (as a percentage of GDP)

	1991	1992	1993	1994	1995	1996	1997	1998	1999	2000	2001	2002	2003	2004	2005
Austria	−2.9	−1.9	−4.1	−4.8	−5.6	−3.9	−1.7	−2.3	−2.2	−1.8	0.0	−0.5	−1.6	−1.2	−1.5
Belgium	−6.0	−6.8	−7.0	−4.7	−4.4	−3.8	−2.0	−0.8	−0.5	0.1	0.4	0.0	0.0	0.0	−2.3
Germany	−3.2	−2.7	−3.4	−2.5	−3.2	−3.3	−2.6	−2.2	−1.5	−1.1	−2.8	−3.7	−4.0	−3.7	−3.2
Greece	−11.4	−12.6	−13.6	−9.9	−10.2	−7.4	−6.6	−4.3	−3.4	−4.0	−5.4	−5.2	−6.1	−7.8	−5.2
Finland	−1.4	−5.6	−7.8	−6.0	−6.2	−3.5	−1.2	1.7	1.6	6.9	5.0	4.1	2.5	2.3	2.7
France	−2.0	−3.8	−5.6	−5.6	−5.5	−4.1	−3.0	−2.6	−1.7	−1.5	−1.6	−3.2	−4.2	−3.7	−2.9
Ireland	−2.2	−2.4	−2.3	−1.5	−2.0	0.0	1.3	2.4	2.7	4.6	0.8	−0.6	0.3	1.5	1.1
Italy	−9.7	−9.2	−9.1	−8.8	−7.4	−7.0	−2.7	−2.8	−1.7	−2.0	−3.1	−2.9	−3.5	−3.4	−4.1
Luxembourg	1.5	0.6	1.3	2.3	2.4	1.2	3.7	3.4	3.4	6.0	6.1	2.1	0.3	−1.1	−1.0
Netherlands	−2.7	−3.7	−3.1	−3.6	−4.3	−1.9	−1.2	−0.9	0.4	1.3	−0.2	−2.0	−3.1	−1.8	−0.3
Portugal	−5.5	−2.7	−5.6	−5.6	−5.2	−4.5	−3.4	−3.0	−2.7	−3.2	−4.3	−2.9	−2.9	−3.2	−6.0
Spain	−4.2	−3.9	−6.6	−6.0	−6.5	−4.8	−3.3	−3.1	−1.3	−0.9	−0.5	−0.3	0.0	−0.2	1.1
Euro-area	**−4.5**	**−4.7**	**−5.5**	**−5.0**	**−5.0**	**−4.2**	**−2.6**	**−2.2**	**−1.3**	**−1.0**	**−1.8**	**−2.5**	**−3.1**	**−2.8**	**−2.4**
Denmark	−2.4	−2.2	−2.8	−2.5	−2.0	−1.1	0.4	1.0	2.2	3.2	2.2	1.2	1.1	2.7	4.9
Sweden	−1.1	−7.3	−11.4	−9.5	−7.0	−2.7	−0.9	1.8	2.5	5.0	2.6	−0.2	0.1	1.8	3.0
United Kingdom	−2.2	−6.0	−7.6	−6.6	−5.7	−4.1	−2.1	0.1	1.1	1.5	0.9	−1.7	−3.3	−3.2	−3.3
EU-15					**−5.1**	**−4.1**	**−2.4**	**−1.7**	**−0.7**	**−0.3**	**−1.2**	**−2.2**	**−2.9**	**−2.6**	**−2.3**
Cyprus									−4.4	−2.3	−2.3	−4.4	−6.3	−4.1	−2.3
Czech Republic									−3.7	−3.7	−6.1	−6.8	−6.6	−2.9	−3.6
Estonia									−3.6	−0.2	−0.3	0.4	1.9	2.3	2.3
Hungary									−5.3	−2.3	−4.1	−9.0	−7.2	−6.5	−7.8
Latvia									−5.3	−2.8	−2.1	−2.3	−1.2	−0.9	0.1
Lithuania									−2.8	−3.2	−2.1	−1.5	−1.3	−1.5	−0.5
Malta									−7.6	−6.1	−6.4	−5.5	−10.0	−5.0	−3.2
Poland									−1.8	−1.5	−4.1	−3.2	−4.7	−3.9	−2.5
Slovakia									−6.4	−11.8	−6.5	−7.7	−3.7	−3.0	−3.1
Slovenia									−2.0	−3.9	−4.7	−2.5	−2.8	−2.3	−1.9
EU-25														**−2.7**	**−2.3**

Source: European Commission, Autumn 2006.

Table 12.4 Gross debt, general government, 1991–2005 (as a percentage of GDP)

	1991	1992	1993	1994	1995	1996	1997	1998	1999	2000	2001	2002	2003	2004	2005
Austria	56.1	55.8	60.5	63.4	67.9	67.6	63.8	64.3	66.5	65.5	66.0	65.8	64.6	63.8	63.4
Belgium	127.1	129.0	133.4	131.5	129.7	126.9	122.2	117.0	113.6	107.7	106.3	103.3	98.6	94.3	93.2
Germany	39.5	42.1	45.8	48.0	55.6	58.4	59.7	60.3	60.9	59.7	58.8	60.3	63.9	65.7	67.9
Greece	82.2	87.8	110.1	107.9	108.7	111.3	114.0	112.4	112.3	111.6	113.2	110.7	107.8	108.5	107.5
Finland	22.2	40.0	55.3	57.8	56.7	56.9	53.8	48.2	45.5	43.8	42.3	41.3	44.3	44.3	41.3
France	36.2	39.8	45.7	48.9	55.1	57.6	58.5	58.7	58.3	56.7	56.2	58.2	62.4	64.4	66.6
Ireland	94.5	91.5	94.1	88.6	81.1	73.0	64.2	53.4	48.4	37.8	35.5	32.2	31.1	29.7	27.4
Italy	98.0	105.2	115.6	121.5	121.2	120.6	118.1	114.9	113.7	109.1	108.7	105.6	104.3	103.9	106.6
Luxembourg	4.1	4.8	6.0	5.5	7.4	7.8	7.7	7.4	6.7	6.4	6.5	6.5	6.3	6.6	6.0
Netherlands	76.1	77.1	78.5	75.6	76.1	74.1	68.2	65.7	61.1	53.8	50.7	50.5	52.0	52.6	52.7
Portugal	57.7	51.7	56.1	59.0	61.0	59.9	56.1	52.2	51.4	50.4	52.9	55.5	57.0	58.6	64.0
Spain	43.4	45.9	57.2	59.8	62.7	66.8	65.3	63.2	61.5	59.2	55.5	52.5	48.7	46.2	43.1
Euro-area	**57.5**	**59.3**	**65.1**	**67.8**	**72.4**	**74.1**	**73.6**	**73.2**	**72.0**	**69.3**	**68.3**	**68.2**	**69.3**	**69.8**	**70.8**
Denmark	62.8	68.0	80.1	76.5	72.5	69.2	65.2	60.8	57.4	51.7	47.4	46.8	44.4	42.6	35.9
Sweden	50.1	63.3	70.7	73.2	73.0	73.0	70.0	67.6	62.2	52.3	53.8	52.0	51.8	50.5	50.4
United Kingdom	33.8	38.5	44.6	47.8	50.9	51.3	49.7	46.6	44.1	41.2	38.0	37.5	38.9	40.4	42.4
EU-15					**69.6**	**71.5**	**69.8**	**68.0**	**67.1**	**63.1**	**62.2**	**61.5**	**63.0**	**63.3**	**64.5**
Cyprus									59.2	59.5	61.4	64.7	69.1	70.3	69.2
Czech Republic									16.4	18.5	25.1	28.5	30.1	30.7	30.4
Estonia									6.0	5.2	4.8	5.6	5.7	5.2	4.5
Hungary									58.9	53.4	50.7	55.6	58.0	59.4	61.7
Latvia									12.4	12.3	14.0	13.5	14.4	14.5	12.1
Lithuania									22.8	23.7	22.8	22.2	21.2	19.4	18.7
Malta									55.7	55.4	61.3	60.1	70.2	74.9	74.2
Poland									39.3	35.9	35.9	39.8	43.9	41.8	42.0
Slovakia									47.5	50.2	48.9	43.3	42.7	41.6	34.5
Slovenia									24.6	27.6	28.3	29.1	28.5	28.7	28.0
EU-25														**62.4**	**63.3**

Source: European Commission, Autumn 2006.

13 Aid, Trade, and Economic Development: The EU and the Developing World

Frederick Nixson

Introduction

The citizens of the EU are more aware of the existence and dimensions of global poverty and inequality at the present time than at any previous time in history. Through the media, tourism, the campaigning activities of pressure groups and non-governmental organizations (NGOs), and the actions of national governments themselves, there is an awareness of poverty and deprivation in low income or less developed countries (LDCs) that even a generation ago would have been inconceivable (Nixson 2002, 2006). The 'Make Poverty History' campaign of 2005 focused attention on issues relating to aid, debt relief, trade, and poverty alleviation, and the UK government used its presidency of the G-8 and its six-month presidency of the EU to focus attention on the problems of sub-Saharan Africa and the need to take urgent action to achieve the Millennium Development Goals (MDGs) by 2015. In 2005, the EU declared that 'Development policy is at the heart of EU external action' and a 'European Consensus' on development was agreed (CEC 2005).

Increasing economic interdependence between national economies has led, and is continuing to lead, to profound changes in both the global economy and in the economic relationships between rich and poor countries. Over the past two decades, the term 'globalization' has been used to describe these changes—the liberalization of international trade, the expansion of direct foreign investment (DFI), and the emergence of massive cross-border financial flows (ILO 2004: 24). National governments, both individually and collectively, have taken policy decisions to reduce national barriers to international transactions, and the development and introduction of new technologies, especially in the fields of information and telecommunications technology (ICT), have created the enabling conditions to make these changes possible. In LDCs, a combination of trade liberalization, privatization, the liberalization of capital account transactions, the deregulation and liberalization of the domestic economy (financial sector liberalization, easier access for direct foreign investment (DFI), the abolition of domestic monopolies and marketing boards, for example), together with a philosophy of market fundamentalism (state minimalism), has led to increasing openness and integration into the global economy.

These changes have often been the result of pressures ('conditionalities') emanating from existing newly empowered global institutions (the World Bank (WB) and the International Monetary Fund (IMF)) and newly created institutions, most notably the World Trade Organization (WTO), which was established in 1995 to replace the General Agreement on Tariffs and Trade (the GATT).

In this chapter, we focus on the twin issues of the EU's aid and trade policies with respect to the LDCs in general and the African, Caribbean, and Pacific (ACP) countries in particular. We consider various aspects of the development assistance policy of both individual members of the EU and of the EU itself. Historical circumstances have left the UK and France, in particular, with a network of economic, political, social, and institutional relationships with a large number of low- and middle-income economies, formalized through a variety of agreements, with the current Partnership Agreement signed in Cotonou (Benin) in June 2000. The development assistance that the members of the EU make available is thus a combination of national (bilateral) aid and assistance programmes, and the multilateral (EU) programmes through which member countries channel a part of their overall aid programmes and assistance. With respect to trade, policies are determined by the provisions of the Cotonou Agreement and more generally by the obligations of membership of the WTO, although as Page (2006) has argued, no clear line can be drawn between trade policy and foreign policy.

13.1 Financial flows to less developed countries

Table 13.1 gives details of total net resource flows from OECD Development Assistance Committee (DAC) member countries and multilateral agencies to aid recipients for the period 1997 to 2004. Prior to this period, between 1991 and 1997, there had been a significant increase in total net resource flows, both private and public, going to low income, less developed economies, but there were equally significant changes in the composition of those flows.

Official development finance (ODF) and official development assistance (ODA) fell in both absolute and relative terms, although there was a rise in both ODF and ODA in 1998. Private flows expanded almost fivefold over the 1991–7 period. DFI rose from US$24.8 billion in 1991 to $106.7 billion in 1997. International bank lending, much of which was short term, rose dramatically up to 1996, fell equally dramatically in 1997, and collapsed spectacularly in 1998. Bond lending demonstrated a similar pattern, although the post-1997 collapse was less dramatic. As Table 13.1 clearly shows, there was a major reduction in net resource flows in 1998.

Patterns of resource flows vary over the period 1997 to 2004. ODF flows fall between 1997 and 2002 and show some recovery in 2003 and 2004, going slightly beyond their 1997 level. As a percentage of total net resource flows, however, ODF accounted for 24.9 per cent, as compared with 23.5 per cent in 1997 (and having risen to 44.7 per cent in 2002). ODA flows rise significantly in absolute terms between 1997 and 2004, although there is little change in their percentage share of total net resource flows. By 2004, therefore, official development assistance (aid) accounted for just less than 25 per cent of

Table 13.1 Total net resource flows from Development Assistance Committee (DAC) member countries and multilateral agencies by type of flow, 1997–2004

	Current billion US dollars								% of total							
	1997	1998	1999	2000	2001	2002	2003	2004	1997	1998	1999	2000	2001	2002	2003	2004e
I Official development finance (ODF)	75.4	89.1	85.9	65.6	68.8	62.8	71.0	76.3	23.5	39.0	27.5	30.3	31.2	44.7	24.4	24.9
1 Official development assistance (ODA)	47.9	50.4	52.1	49.5	51.2	58.1	67.5	75.4	14.9	22.1	16.7	22.9	23.3	41.4	23.2	24.6
of which: bilateral	32.4	35.2	37.8	36.1	35.1	40.8	49.8	54.4	10.1	15.4	12.1	16.7	15.9	29.0	17.1	17.7
multilateral	15.5	15.2	14.3	13.5	16.1	17.4	17.7	21.0	4.8	6.7	4.6	6.2	7.3	12.4	6.1	6.9
2 Official aid (OA)	5.6	7.0	7.8	7.8	6.4	6.4	7.2	8.8	1.7	3.1	2.5	3.6	2.9	4.6	2.5	2.9
of which: bilateral	4.0	4.5	4.9	4.9	3.6	4.5	3.9	4.5	1.3	2.0	1.6	2.3	1.6	3.2	1.3	1.5
multilateral	1.6	2.5	2.9	2.9	2.8	2.0	3.3	4.4	0.5	1.1	0.9	1.3	1.3	1.4	1.1	1.4
3 Other ODF	22.0	31.7	26.1	8.2	11.1	-1.7	-3.7	-8.0	6.8	13.9	8.3	3.8	5.1	-1.2	-1.3	-2.6
of which: bilateral	5.9	12.8	10.4	-1.4	1.5	1.9	-0.8	-4.5	1.8	5.6	3.3	-0.6	0.7	1.4	-0.3	-1.5
multilateral	16.0	18.9	15.6	9.6	9.7	-3.7	-2.9	-3.5	5.0	8.3	5.0	4.5	4.4	-2.6	-1.0	-1.2
II Total export credits	4.8	8.4	4.1	7.8	2.8	-1.5	4.9	6.8	1.5	3.7	1.3	3.6	1.3	-1.1	1.7	2.2
III Private flows	241.4	130.7	222.7	143.0	148.7	79.2	215.1	223.4	75.0	57.3	71.2	66.1	67.5	56.4	73.9	72.9
1 Direct investment (DAC)	102.3	117.1	145.5	124.4	134.8	80.8	86.5	134.7	31.8	51.3	46.5	57.5	61.2	57.5	29.7	43.9
of which: to offshore centres	19.1	20.3	37.9	25.7	32.9	23.2	12.0	23.6	5.9	8.9	12.1	11.9	14.9	16.5	4.1	7.7

2 International bank lending[a]	12.0	−76.3	−21.2	−17.8	−11.4	−12.2	50.0	48.3	3.7	−33.4	−6.8	−8.2	−5.2	−8.7	17.2	15.8
3 Total bond lending	83.7	34.2	30.0	19.7	19.6	18.9	38.7	44.0	26.0	15.0	9.6	9.1	8.9	13.5	13.3	14.4
4 Other (including equities)[b]	37.0	48.4	59.5	7.2	−4.8	−20.3	25.2	−18.5	11.5	21.2	19.0	3.3	−2.2	−14.5	8.7	−6.0
5 Grants by non-governmental organizations	6.4	7.2	8.9	9.5	10.4	12.0	14.6	14.9	2.0	3.1	2.9	4.4	4.7	8.6	5.0	4.9
Total net resource flows (I+II+III)	321.6	228.2	312.7	216.3	220.3	140.5	291.0	306.5	100.0	100.0	100.0	100.0	100.0	100.0	100.0	100.0
Memorandum items (not included)																
Net use of IMF credit[c]	14.4	18.2	−13.0	−10.8	8.0	12.6	1.4	−9.7								
Non-DAC donors (ODA/OA)	1.0	0.9	0.8	1.0	1.0	2.8	3.3	3.1								
For cross reference																
Total DAC net ODA[d]	48.5	52.1	53.2	53.7	52.4	58.3	69.1	79.5								
of which: bilateral grants	31.3	32.5	33.9	33.0	33.5	39.8	50.9	57.3								

Notes:
[a] Excluding bond lending by banks (item III.3.), and guaranteed financial credits (included in II).
[b] Incomplete reporting from several DAC countries (including France, the United Kingdom, and the United States). Includes Japan from 1996.
[c] Non-concessional flows from the IMF General Resources Account.
[d] Comprises bilateral ODA as above plus contributions to multilateral organizations in place of ODA disbursements from multilateral organizations shown above.
[e] Provisional.
Source: OECD (2005: Table 6).

net resources flows to LDCs. The 1980s and early-1990s had been characterized by pro-market and anti-government rhetoric, with major Western donors expressing the desire to substitute private capital flows for ODA (Thorbecke 2000: 47). The 1997 Asian financial crisis in effect prompted a fundamental re-examination of the role of aid, with respect to both bilateral and multilateral institutions, and a new development agenda, with an explicit focus on poverty alleviation, dominated development discussions.

Private flows had reached their peak in 1996 and 1997, fell dramatically in 1998, and after a recovery fell further in 2002, following the Argentina financial crisis. By 2004, they had still to reach their 1997 level. DFI fell in 2002 and 2003, but recovered in 2004. International bank lending (which had peaked at US$ 86 billion in 1996) was negative over the period 1998 to 2002. Bond lending fell significantly over the period 1998 to 2002 and had barely recovered by 2004. It is clear that the liberalization of the financial sector, and capital account liberalization in particular, had led to greater global financial instability.

13.2 Foreign aid and development

Foreign aid or economic assistance consists of transfers of real resources to less developed countries on concessional terms. It excludes, by definition, purely commercial trans-actions, and should also exclude military aid, which, although it is non-commercial and concessional, does not have as its main objective the promotion of economic development. Aid raises a number of fundamental questions about development and underdevelopment and the relationship between rich and poor countries (although not all donor countries are rich: China has made substantial sums of aid available in the past to countries such as Tanzania). These questions include the following:

- Why do donors give aid?
- Why do poor countries accept aid?
- How should aid be given?
  - loans versus grants;
  - tied aid versus untied aid;
  - bilateral versus multilateral aid;
  - project versus programme aid.
- Which countries should be given aid?
- What is the impact of aid on the process of growth and development?
- What is the nature of the aid relationship?

Clearly, simple and straightforward answers cannot be given to these questions, and, even after fifty years of experience of aid, the debate continues (major contributions to the debate include Cassen *et al.* 1986; Mosley 1987; Riddell 1987; more recent contribu-tions are Tarp 2000; World Bank 1998; and OECD 2000). Donors give aid for a number of reasons. Humanitarian motives may dominate, but more usually there are economic, political, and strategic factors that determine the amounts given and the countries selected by donors for assistance.

Equally, poor countries may accept aid for a variety of reasons—the urgency of the problems facing them, the domestic absence or shortage of the resources that aid can provide, the building up of a relationship with a donor or group of donor countries for political reasons, and the role that aid can play in maintaining a particular regime in power and/or consolidating and extending its power.

Aid can be given in various forms—as grants or loans, technical assistance, or commodity (largely food) aid—and with various forms of conditionality attached. Aid may be given for a project (to build a road, for example) or be made available for a programme (e.g. in the transport sector). Bilateral aid is given by the aid agency of one country (the UK Department for International Development, for example) to recipients in another. Multilateral aid (through the EU, the World Bank, or various UN agencies, for example) is usually considered to be superior to bilateral aid, as it avoids the problems that can arise in bilateral one-to-one relationships. Bilateral aid is normally tied (either to a particular project or programme and must be spent in the donor country); multilateral aid may be project- or programme-tied, but, by definition, it cannot be tied to a particular country.

Aid can be tied in various ways (Bhagwati 1967) through formal and informal restrictions, the use of export and import credits, and aid provided in the form of technical services and goods. There is general agreement that tying aid reduces its value to the recipient (lower-cost sources of supply in non-donor countries will not be allowed to bid for aid projects). Tied aid benefits donor-country enterprises and its extensive use has led in the past to allegations that aid policy is subservient to a donor country's commercial interests.

When we consider the effectiveness of aid, it is useful to refer to what Mosley (1987: ch. 5) has called the 'macro–micro paradox'. This refers to the apparent paradox that, whereas the microeconomic evaluation of aid projects is usually positive, there appears to be no statistically significant correlation, either positive or negative, between inflows of aid and the rate of growth of the recipient economy. Mosley (1987: 139–40) and White (1992) suggest various reasons why this situation exists: inaccurate measurement and fungibility within the public sector (that is, if certain conditions are satisfied, aid can never be completely tied to a specific project: see Singer 1965), and backwash effects from aid-financed activities that adversely affect the private sector.

These results have been challenged. The World Bank (1998) argues that financial aid works in a good policy environment; improvements in the economic institutions and policies in the LDCs are the key to the alleviation of poverty and that foreign aid can provide critical support to such improvements; effective aid complements private investment (with sound economic management, foreign aid 'crowds in' private investment); the value of development projects is to strengthen institutions and policies in order to ensure more effective service delivery; the best aid projects change the way the public sector does business and that aid can promote reform in even the most adverse conditions (but it requires patience and a focus on ideas, not money).

OECD (2000: ch. 6) surveys a number of econometric studies which attempt to evaluate aid effectiveness. It concludes that development assistance has had a positive impact on growth, but in some cases it is minor and statistically insignificant. Sound and stable macroeconomic policies reinforce aid's positive effects, but aid is only one of many elements in the complex economic growth process. Hansen and Tarp (2000) argue that the macro–micro paradox is non-existent and that econometric results consistently find that aid increases aggregate savings and investment and that there is a positive relationship between aid and growth. They conclude (Hansen and Tarp 2000: 124): 'the unresolved issue in assessing aid effectiveness is not whether aid works, but how and whether we can make the different kinds of aid instruments at hand work better in varying country circumstances'.

More recent work focuses on the impact of aid on economic growth and poverty reduction. If aid is good for growth and growth is good for poverty reduction then, other things being equal, aid must be good for the poor. Morrissey (2005) examines the relationship between aid and various indicators of economic welfare or human development (various health and educational indicators, for example). There is some evidence that aid is more successful when it is targeted at very specific objectives (the eradication of smallpox, the increased enrolment of girls in primary and secondary schools, for example). Overall, however, 'Aid is only as good as the ability of a recipient's economy and government to use it prudently and productively' (Birdsall *et al.* 2005: 143). This is a timely warning to those who uncritically argue for large increases in the volume of aid to LDCs.

Despite the confidence with which these studies present their conclusions, there is still a great deal that we do not know about the impact of aid on the process of economic development. We cannot prove that aid is either necessary or sufficient for economic and social development, or that the relationship between donor and recipient countries is either advantageous or disadvantageous to the latter. Despite their policy statements, the aid programmes of most major bilateral donors are dominated by political and geo-strategic considerations. If humanitarian factors are not of the highest priority, it should not surprise us if we find it difficult to establish a positive causal connection between aid and development.

13.3 EU development policy

The European Commission and the Council issued a joint statement on EU Development Policy (DPS) in November 2000. The EU's development policies had evolved in a somewhat ad hoc fashion over the years and this was a first attempt to elaborate a DPS that was based on the principles of:

- complementarity of programmes implemented by EU Member States and the European Commission (EC);
- coordination between Member States and the EC on development;
- coherence between EU policies with development objectives; and
- consistency of all external activities of the EU.

The main objective of EU development policy was stated to be the reduction and eventual eradication of poverty, within the context of sustainable, equitable, and participatory human and social development. It was recognized that priorities for action needed to be more clearly defined and more precise sectoral strategies developed. To this end, the Commission drew up a list of six priority areas, namely:

1. establishing a link between development policies and trade and investment policies to ensure that they are complementary and mutually beneficial to one another;

2. supporting efforts at regional integration and cooperation among LDCs;

3. support for stable macroeconomic policies and the promotion of equitable access to basic social services (education and health) consistent with poverty alleviation objectives;

4. the development and maintenance of transport infrastructure;

5. the promotion of food security and sustainable rural development; and

6. supporting and strengthening institutional capacity building (especially in the areas of good governance and the rule of law).

A number of cross-cutting areas were to be mainstreamed in all aid programming: the promotion of human rights, gender equality, children's rights, and the environment. The declaration concludes that, with respect to the allocation of resources, 'the least developed countries and low-income countries will be given priority, in an approach which will take account of their efforts to reduce poverty, their needs, their performance and their capacity to absorb aid . . . To ensure consistency, the objectives of Community development policy will be taken into greater account in the conduct of other common policies' (The European Community's Development Policy—Statement by the Council and Commission, November 2000).

An evaluation of the first four years of the DPS was published in 2005 (European Centre for Development Policy Management 2005). It was concluded that the DPS was a 'valuable document' which performed a variety of useful roles for different stakeholders. However, two major factors had had an impact on development policy since 2000: the UN Millennium Summit (September 2005) and the adoption of the Millennium Development Goals (MDGs) as key guidelines for development cooperation; and the events of 11 September 2001 in the United States which had brought a development perspective on security into the policy mix. With respect to the latter, it was argued that development policy needed to reassert itself as part of the EU's external action policy mix. It is argued by one independent body (BOND 2003: 54) that development policy has become increasingly subordinated to foreign policy post-9/11 and that the gap between rhetoric and reality is striking, especially in the areas of trade and agricultural policy.

In 2005, the 'European Consensus' on development policy was agreed on by the institutions of the EU (CEC 2005), setting out for the first time in fifty years of cooperation 'the framework of common principles under which the EU and its twenty-five Member States will implement their development policies in a spirit of complementarity' (CEC 2005). The primary and overarching objective of EU development cooperation was declared to be the eradication of poverty in the context of sustainable development, including the pursuit of the MDGs (EU 2005). The EU has adopted the timetable for Member States to achieve the goal of an overseas development assistance/Gross National Income (ODA/GNI) ratio of 0.7 per cent by 2015, with an intermediate target of 0.56 per cent by

---

BOX 13.1 A NOTE ON AID STATISTICS: TERMS AND DEFINITIONS

All members of the EU-15 are members of the Organization for Economic Cooperation and Development (OECD). One of the specialized committees of the OECD is the Development Assistance Committee (DAC), the members of which have agreed 'to secure an expansion of aggregate volume of resources made available to developing countries and to improve their effectiveness'.

The Commission of the European Communities (CEC) takes part in the work of the OECD and is a member of the DAC.

Official development finance (ODF) includes:

- bilateral official development assistance (ODA);

- grants and concessional and non-concessional development lending by multilateral financial institutions; and

- other official flows which are considered developmental (including refinancing loans) but which have too low a grant element to qualify as ODA.

'Aid' or 'assistance' refers only to items which qualify as ODA, that is, grants or loans

- undertaken by the official sector,

- with promotion of economic development or welfare as main objectives, and

- at concessional financial terms (if a loan, at least 25 per cent grant element).

Technical cooperation is included in aid. It consists almost entirely of grants to nationals of developing countries receiving education or training at home or abroad and payments to defray the costs of teachers, administrators, advisers, and so on, serving in developing countries.

2010. These commitments should see EU aid double to more than 66 billion Euros in 2010. At least half of this increase will be allocated to Africa. With respect to trade, the 'European Consensus' declares that 'Developing countries should decide and reform trade policy in line with their broader national development plans', within the context of the completion of the Doha Development Round and EU–ACP Economic Partnership Agreements (EPAs) (see below) (EU 2005).

13.4 **The ODA record of EU Member States**

Between 1992 and 1997, aid from DAC member countries to the developing world fell by 21 per cent in real terms. As a proportion of their combined national income, it fell by one-third. As the OECD (2000: 67) noted, these were the largest declines in ODA since the inception of the DAC in 1961. The fall in ODA was halted in 1998. Total net official development assistance rose from US$48.3 billion in 1997 to US$51.9 billion in 1998 (in current prices and exchange rates). This was a rise of 9.6 per cent in real terms, although the rise was smaller in relation to GNP, with the combined ODA/GNP ratio for DAC member countries rising from 0.22 per cent to 0.24 per cent.

This recovery was in part due to the introduction of short-term measures to deal with the 1997 Asian financial crisis, but it also reflected policy decisions by a number of member countries to stabilize or gradually rebuild their aid programmes. However, it was not until 2002 that the DAC total just exceeded the 1993–4 average, and there were further significant rises in 2003 and 2004. Details are given in Table 13.2.

For DAC members as a whole, ODA as a proportion of Gross National Income (GNI) fell during the 1980s from 0.35 per cent in 1982–3 to 0.33 per cent in 1988–9. It fell further during the 1990s, reaching 0.22 per cent in 1997, its lowest level. As can be seen from Table 13.2, there was some improvement in the 2000s, but by 2004 the figure was still only 0.26. In general, the performance of the EU member countries was superior to that of the DAC as a whole (largely because of the very low indicators for the USA and Japan). Burden-sharing indicators are discussed in greater detail below.

The accession to the EU of Austria, Sweden, and Finland in 1995 was seen as a positive move as far as development cooperation was concerned. In 1994 their total ODA amounted to $US2.9 billion, with Sweden alone contributing $US1.8 billion. The Finnish aid programme suffered massive cutbacks in the early 1990s, however, and both Austria and Sweden cut back their aid programmes in the latter half of the 1990s.

A variety of burden-sharing indicators are presented in Tables 13.2 and 13.3. Table 13.2 includes data on ODA as a share of GNI, and we can note that, taking the average for 1993–4, only Denmark, the Netherlands, and Sweden exceeded the UN target of a 0.7 per cent ODA/GNI ratio. By 2004, those three countries had been joined by Luxembourg.

Table 13.3 gives details of a variety of burden-sharing indicators, including the grant equivalent of ODA as a percentage of GNI, and ODA per capita of the donor country. The latter set of figures allows us to make some interesting comparisons. The largest EU donors in absolute terms (Germany, France, and the UK) tend to have low per capita figures. The Netherlands is in the middle of both rankings. The smaller EU donors, especially Denmark, Luxembourg, and to a lesser extent Sweden, have the highest per capita contributions.

Although it is recognized that multilateral institutions have a key role to play in the development process, most donor countries, for the reasons outlined above, prefer to maintain direct control over their aid programmes through bilateral relationships. The early to mid-1970s saw a significant expansion in the role of multilateral aid, including a major expansion of aid from EC members through EC programmes. In the latter half of the 1970s, the proportion of ODA channelled through multilateral institutions levelled off, and in the 1980s the proportion, expressed as a percentage of GNP, actually declined (OECD 1992: 42, Table V-5). In the 1990s, the share of multilateral ODA in total ODA rose in the case of Austria, Finland, Italy, and Sweden. Among the larger donors, it rose in the case of France and fell in the case of Germany. The figure for the UK hardly changed in the 1990s. As of 2003–4, the larger donor countries (France, Germany, and the UK) tend to have low ratios of multilateral ODA as a percentage of GNI, indicating that they still maintain a tight bilateral control over their aid programmes (see Table 13.3).

Table 13.2 Net official development assistance by DAC country, 1988–2004

	Net disbursements at current prices and exchange rates														
	1988–9 average	1993–4 average	2000	2001	2002	2003	2004	1988–9 average	1993–4 average	2000	2001	2002	2003	2004
	(million US dollars)							(% of Gross National Income)						
Austria	292	265	440	633	520	505	678	0.23	0.14	0.23	0.34	0.26	0.20	0.23
Belgium	652	769	820	867	1,072	1,853	1,463	0.43	0.35	0.36	0.37	0.43	0.60	0.41
Denmark	929	1,393	1,664	1,634	1,643	1,748	2,037	0.91	1.03	1.06	1.03	0.96	0.84	0.85
Finland	657	323	371	389	462	558	655	0.62	0.37	0.31	0.32	0.35	0.35	0.35
France	5,632	8,191	4,105	4,198	5,486	7,253	8,473	0.59	0.62	0.30	0.31	0.37	0.40	0.41
Germany	4,839	6,886	5,030	4,990	5,324	6,784	7,534	0.40	0.34	0.27	0.27	0.27	0.28	0.28
Greece	–	–	226	202	276	362	465	–	–	0.20	0.17	0.21	0.21	0.23
Ireland	53	95	234	287	398	504	607	0.18	0.23	0.29	0.33	0.40	0.39	0.39
Italy	3,403	2,874	1,376	1,627	2,332	2,433	2,462	0.40	0.29	0.13	0.15	0.20	0.17	0.15
Luxembourg	18	55	123	139	147	194	236	0.20	0.38	0.71	0.76	0.77	0.81	0.83
Netherlands	2,162	2,521	3,135	3,172	3,338	3,972	4,204	0.96	0.79	0.84	0.82	0.81	0.80	0.73
Portugal	97	269	271	268	323	320	1,031	0.23	0.31	0.26	0.25	0.27	0.22	0.63
Spain	395	1,304	1,195	1,737	1,712	1,961	2,437	0.11	0.28	0.22	0.30	0.26	0.23	0.24
Sweden	1,666	1,794	1,799	1,666	2,012	2,400	2,722	0.91	0.97	0.80	0.77	0.84	0.79	0.78
UK	2,616	3,059	4,501	4,579	4,924	6,282	7,883	0.32	0.31	0.32	0.32	0.31	0.34	0.36
DAC	**46,399**	**57,484**	**53,749**	**52,435**	**58,292**	**69,085**	**79,512**	**0.33**	**0.30**	**0.22**	**0.22**	**0.23**	**0.25**	**0.26**
of which:														
EU	23,413	29,796	25,289	26,388	29,969	37,130	42,886	0.45	0.42	0.32	0.33	0.35	0.35	0.35

Source: OECD (2005: Table 4).

Table 13.3 Burden-sharing indicators, 2003–4 average

			Net disbursements					
	Grant equivalent of total ODA[a] as % of GNI	Multilateral ODA as % of GNI[b]	of which:		ODA per capita of donor country 2003 USD *Memo:*		Aid by NGOs as % of GNI *Memo:*	
			Aid to LICs[c]	Aid to LDCs[d]				
			as % of GNI		1993–4	2003–4	1993–4	2003–4
Austria	0.23	0.04 (0.11)	0.10	0.06	35	68	0.03	0.03
Belgium	0.52	0.05 (0.14)	0.29	0.26	84	152	0.02	0.05
Denmark	0.89	0.27 (0.35)	0.43	0.31	316	330	0.03	0.01
Finland	0.35	0.09 (0.16)	0.13	0.10	79	110	0.00	–
France	0.47	0.05 (0.13)	0.21	0.16	155	122	0.02	–
Germany	0.32	0.06 (0.13)	0.15	0.09	89	82	0.05	0.04
Greece	0.22	0.01 (0.08)	0.05	0.03	–	35	–	0.01
Ireland	0.39	0.06 (0.12)	0.24	0.21	37	130	0.09	0.18
Italy	0.17	0.03 (0.10)	0.07	0.06	63	40	0.01	0.00
Luxembourg	0.82	0.13 (0.21)	0.42	0.29	160	448	0.03	0.02
Netherlands	0.85	0.18 (0.25)	0.29	0.23	198	239	0.08	0.07
Portugal	0.40	0.03 (0.10)	0.36	0.35	35	60	0.00	0.00
Spain	0.25	0.04 (0.10)	0.07	0.04	41	48	0.02	–
Sweden	0.78	0.14 (0.19)	0.32	0.24	230	270	0.07	0.01
UK	0.37	0.06 (0.12)	0.20	0.13	72	110	0.05	0.02
Total DAC	0.29	0.05 (0.08)	0.11	0.08	78	82	0.03	0.04

[a] Equals grant disbursements plus grant equivalent of new loan commitments calculated against a 10 per cent discount rate.
[b] In brackets, including EC. Capital subscriptions are on a deposit basis.
[c] Low-income countries (LICs) comprise LDCs and all other countries with per capita income (World Bank Atlas basis) of $745 or less in 2001. Includes imputed multilateral ODA.
[d] Least developed countries (LDCs) are countries on the United Nations' list. Includes imputed multilateral ODA.
Source: OECD (2005: Table 7).

The percentage of multilateral ODA going through the EU varies widely, although there is no obvious pattern. Some small donors channel the larger part of their multilateral aid through the EU (for example, Portugal and Greece); other small donors channel less (for example, Sweden and Denmark, which focus more on the United Nations agencies). Some big donors, for example, France and Germany, channel 50 per cent or more of their multilateral ODA through the EU. The UK's share is roughly the average for the EU as a whole (see Table 13.4).

As noted above, aid can be either tied or untied. The tying of aid has always been a controversial topic, with critics arguing that tying reduces the value of aid and lowers its 'quality'. The other determinant of the 'quality' of aid is its grant element. This reflects the financial terms of a commitment: interest rate, maturity (interval to final repayment), and grace period (interval to first repayment of capital). The grant element measures the concessionality—that is, the softness—of a loan. The market rate of interest

Table 13.4 ODA from DAC countries to multilateral organizations, 2005 (US$ Million)

	Net Disbursements				
	Total	World Bank Group	United Nations Agencies	of which:	
				EC	EDF
Austria	341	46	27	221	87
Belgium	655	186	47	368	114
Denmark	751	96	307	196	70
Finland	305	38	96	140	49
France	2,787	299	187	1,811	781
Germany	2,635	–	199	2,205	767
Greece	178	5	7	158	41
Ireland	237	31	75	112	22
Italy	2,821	689	305	1,261	415
Luxembourg	69	10	19	25	8
Netherlands	1,432	314	408	432	171
Portugal	159	12	10	128	28
Spain	1,155	150	48	784	193
Sweden	1,106	275	466	198	89
United Kingdom	2,603	683	509	1,180	194
DAC-EU Countries	17,234	2,834	2,710	9,219	3,029
TOTAL DAC	24,644	5,213	5,451	9,216	3,029

Source: OECD www.oecd.org/dataoecd/52/11/1893159.xls

is conventionally taken to be 10 per cent. The grant element of a loan is thus nil for a loan with an interest rate of 10 per cent or higher and, by definition, the grant element of a grant is 100 per cent. The grant element will lie in between these two limits for a soft loan. Although maturity and grace periods are important, it is the interest rate that is the major determinant of the softness of a loan (OECD 1992: A99–100).

As Hjertholm and White (2000) noted, (un)tying performance has tended to change quite markedly over time. The second half of the 1990s witnessed significant untying of bilateral ODA (multilateral aid, by definition, cannot be tied to individual donor countries), and by 2004 (see Table 13.5), bilateral ODA was largely untied except for the smaller EU donors (Austria, Belgium, Greece, and Spain). Changes in policy and performance over time in individual donor countries are a reflection of changes in political administration, changing budgetary priorities, and the result of policy reviews and changing priorities.

The data in Table 13.6 show that EU Member States in general score highly with respect to the concessionality of their aid, with high grant elements in all cases.

The major uses of EU ODA are shown in Table 13.7. Social and administrative infrastructure is the largest sector receiving aid, taking 34.1 per cent of the total in 2003–4 for the DAC as a whole. The directly productive sectors of the economy—agriculture and

Table 13.5 Tying status of ODA by individual DAC members, 2004

| | Commitments (excluding technical cooperation and administrative costs) (million US dollars) | | | | | *Memo:* |
| | Bilateral ODA | | | | | |
	Untied	Partially untied	Tied	Total	Tied ODA as % of total	Technical cooperation
Austria	115	–	105	220	47.8	136
Belgium	724	–	57	782	7.3	488
Denmark	1,251	–	158	1,409	11.2	127
Finland	–	–	–	–		127
France	4,041	–	250	4,291	5.8	2,342
Germany	2,993	–	252	3,246	7.8	2,619
Greece[a]	21	6	64	91	70.5	196
Ireland[a]	370	–	–	370	0.0	12
Italy	–	–	–	–		133
Luxembourg	–	–	–	–		4
Netherlands	1,728	43	219	1,990	11.0	803
Portugal[a]	747	–	6	753	0.8	114
Spain[a]	829	–	395	1,224	32.3	340
Sweden	1,632	223	11	1,865	0.6	96
UK[a]	2,983	–	–	2,983	0.0	751
Total DAC	(30,528)	(375)	(2,793)	(33,696)		20,334

[a] Gross disbursements.
Source: OECD (2005: Table 24).

industry and other production—received less than 6 per cent of total commitments in 2003–4. The share of economic infrastructure has fallen in the period covered in the table. As far as variations between EU members are concerned, of the larger donors, France, Germany, and the Netherlands devote the largest proportion of their aid budgets to social and administrative infrastructure. In the case of the UK, it is clear that there has been a shift in sectoral priorities from industry and other productive activities, agriculture, and economic infrastructure to social and administrative infrastructure.

The final point to be considered in this general overview relates to the geographical distribution of EU aid. The regional distribution is given in Table 13.8. Sub-Saharan Africa remains the major recipient of EU aid and its share of total ODA has risen over the period 1998–9 to 2003–4. It is important to note that these figures are for gross disbursement (the total amount disbursed or spent over a given accounting period), and net disbursements (gross disbursements less any repayments of loan principal during the same period) would be lower.

Concern has been expressed in the Third World that the changes that have occurred in Eastern Europe and the former Soviet Union will cause a diversion of aid from developing

Table 13.6 Financial terms of ODA commitments,[a] 2003–4 average

	Grant element of total ODA Norm: 86%[b]		Grant share of:		Grant element of ODA loans	Grant element of ODA to LDCs[c]	Grant element of bilateral ODA to LDCs
	1993–4	2003–4	Bilateral ODA	Total ODA			
Austria	92.6	100.0	100.0	100.0	–	100.0	100.0
Belgium	99.7	99.7	98.4	99.0	80.9	99.9	99.9
Denmark	100.0	100.0	97.0	98.2	–	100.0	100.0
Finland	99.3	99.9	97.8	98.7	48.6	100.0	100.0
France	93.7	95.5	84.6	88.1	51.1	99.5	99.5
Germany	96.5	96.8	80.6	88.2	65.4	100.0	100.0
Greece	–	100.0	100.0	100.0	–	100.0	100.0
Ireland	100.0	100.0	100.0	100.0	–	100.0	100.0
Italy	98.7	99.5	72.0	91.6	90.6	99.6	99.5
Luxembourg	100.0	100.0	100.0	100.0	–	100.0	100.0
Netherlands	100.0	100.0	100.0	100.0	–	100.0	100.0
Portugal	100.0	92.1	99.7	99.8	61.2	100.0	100.0
Spain	90.7	94.8	66.8	80.6	71.0	94.1	91.7
Sweden	100.0	100.0	99.1	99.3	51.8	99.9	99.8
UK	100.0	100.0	90.4	93.9	–	100.0	100.0
Total DAC	**95.4**	**97.3**	**86.9**	**90.1**	**69.4**	**99.7**	**99.7**

Notes:
[a] Excluding debt reorganization. Equities are treated as having 100 per cent grant element, but are not treated as loans.
[b] Countries of which ODA commitments as a percentage of GNI is below the DAC average are not considered as having met the terms target. This provision disqualified Italy and Portugal in 2004.
[c] Including imputed multilateral grant element.
Source: OECD (2005: Table 20).

countries as conventionally defined. Some of the countries of the former Soviet Union, such as the Central Asian republics, have similar characteristics to developing countries. A small number of countries have been added to the list of aid recipients, including Albania, Kazakhstan, Kyrghizstan (now the Kyrghiz Republic), Tadjikistan, Turkmenistan, Uzbekistan, Armenia, Georgia, and Azerbaijan. From 1993, Central and Eastern European Countries, Newly Independent States of the former Soviet Union (CEEC/NIS), and countries in transition have been included in Part II of a new list of aid recipients (excluding those countries listed above) (OECD 1995: 126–7, A101). In general, DAC members have argued that so far there has been very limited aid diversion and it is difficult to predict how important an issue this will become in the future.

Figure 13.1 lists the top twenty recipients of EU/EC aid for 2001–2. These 'rankings' change from year to year, with new recipients appearing and disappearing according to changing economic and political circumstances. In the late-1990s, for example, Bosnia-Herzegovina, the Palestinian Administered Areas, and South Africa joined the list of major aid recipients, reflecting the political changes that occurred during the 1990s.

Table 13.7 Major aid uses by individual DAC donors, 1983–4 and 2003–4

| | Per cent of total bilateral commitments | | | | | | | | | | | | | | *Memo:* Share of total ODA to / through NGOs[a] |
| | Social and administrative infrastructure | | Economic infrastructure | | Agriculture | | Industry and other production | | Commodity aid and programme assistance | | Emergency aid | | Other | | |
	1983–4	2003–4	1983–4	2003–4	1983–4	2003–4	1983–4	2003–4	1983–4	2003–4	1983–4	2003–4	1983–4	2003–4	2003–4
Austria	29.7	47.7	47.8	2.3	1.6	1.8	7.9	2.6	1.8	0.5	2.2	14.4	9.0	30.7	7.9
Belgium	37.0	27.1	10.1	5.5	7.2	4.1	7.5	0.8	1.4	2.6	0.3	8.4	36.5	51.4	8.5
Denmark	17.6	42.5	26.2	17.6	12.5	6.0	26.9	4.6	1.9	3.5	0.2	0.9	14.7	25.0	4.4
Finland	16.5	46.3	15.5	7.0	17.0	2.2	28.3	1.8	0.6	3.1	2.2	11.5	19.9	28.2	4.3
France	50.6	31.3	16.2	5.6	8.5	2.2	5.3	1.0	6.5	2.0	0.1	7.3	12.7	50.6	0.4
Germany	28.4	39.3	38.1	16.1	9.1	2.9	7.2	1.3	2.9	1.0	0.7	3.2	13.6	36.2	6.9
Greece	–	81.9	–	1.9	–	0.6	–	0.4	–	0.8	–	4.8	–	9.5	4.6
Ireland	–	61.6	–	2.1	–	5.3	–	0.1	–	6.9	–	8.4	100.0	15.6	15.2
Italy	16.5	17.4	22.2	2.4	18.3	1.7	15.6	1.9	6.8	5.8	2.3	7.2	18.3	63.7	2.4
Luxembourg	–	46.4	–	2.4	–	7.8	–	0.7	–	2.1	–	13.0	–	27.6	12.7
Netherlands	28.5	32.8	14.3	10.5	16.6	3.3	6.4	0.9	6.6	4.1	2.3	9.3	25.2	39.1	15.4
Portugal	–	23.6	–	1.2	–	0.5	–	0.3	–	0.7	–	1.8	–	71.8	0.4
Spain	–	36.3	–	16.6	–	5.0	–	2.0	–	0.7	–	6.1	–	33.3	19.6
Sweden	19.3	33.6	10.0	7.9	12.4	2.1	9.3	0.7	1.2	4.5	11.5	20.0	36.3	31.2	13.9
United Kingdom	21.4	38.4	28.3	8.2	11.4	4.1	12.7	1.6	3.7	1.4	0.8	11.3	21.7	35.1	9.7
Total DAC	**26.7**	**34.1**	**18.8**	**13.1**	**11.4**	**3.2**	**8.9**	**2.6**	**12.1**	**4.1**	**1.6**	**9.1**	**20.5**	**33.7**	**5.3**

[a] On a net disbursement basis.   *Source:* OECD (2005: Table 18).

Table 13.8 Regional distribution of ODA by individual DAC donors and multilateral agencies (1993–4, 1998–9, and 2003–4)[a]

Per cent of total gross disbursements

	Sub-Saharan Africa			South and Central Asia			Other Asia and Oceania			Middle East and North Africa			Europe			Latin America and Caribbean		
	1993–4	1998–9	2003–4	1993–4	1998–9	2003–4	1993–4	1998–9	2003–4	1993–4	1998–9	2003–4	1993–4	1998–9	2003–4	1993–4	1998–9	2003–4
Austria	16.6	28.9	39.9	2.9	6.0	9.7	11.2	6.5	4.1	22.9	14.3	12.5	39.0	30.6	26.9	7.3	13.7	6.9
Belgium	57.0	60.6	79.9	6.2	2.0	2.4	16.2	9.8	4.2	6.3	7.9	4.6	0.4	3.0	1.0	13.9	16.7	7.9
Denmark	58.3	56.0	51.9	17.2	16.1	16.2	12.0	11.3	15.5	5.3	6.1	4.8	0.1	0.7	2.8	7.2	9.7	8.8
Finland	43.7	40.6	47.4	11.2	10.6	12.1	20.1	18.2	11.5	6.4	6.2	9.0	4.2	12.8	8.5	14.5	11.8	11.5
France	55.6	45.4	58.3	3.1	1.8	6.9	19.1	23.4	8.7	16.4	20.0	15.8	1.2	2.8	4.5	4.7	6.6	5.8
Germany	26.9	26.8	35.4	12.1	13.0	11.7	20.5	23.6	17.2	15.0	13.2	11.1	13.1	8.8	8.1	12.3	14.7	16.6
Greece	–	3.1	2.3	–	8.8	9.5	–	0.4	0.6	–	9.9	10.4	–	77.1	77.0	–	0.8	0.3
Ireland	85.2	82.4	85.2	2.6	2.4	3.6	4.2	2.8	2.5	1.6	1.8	3.5	4.6	6.8	1.1	1.9	3.9	4.0
Italy	33.3	51.4	52.7	2.6	1.0	5.3	13.9	4.9	6.8	26.9	10.1	17.8	7.8	15.1	7.4	15.5	17.3	10.1
Luxembourg	51.1	42.9	48.5	8.4	5.9	4.6	4.1	10.4	16.0	6.7	7.7	7.8	5.0	10.1	7.0	24.7	23.1	16.0
Netherlands	36.6	36.8	49.1	16.0	13.3	14.7	4.9	8.3	9.6	6.6	6.8	8.7	9.7	9.9	5.6	26.3	24.8	12.3
Portugal	99.0	83.2	89.3	0.0	0.1	0.3	0.2	15.0	6.7	0.3	0.4	2.4	0.2	0.7	1.1	0.2	0.6	0.2
Spain	10.3	21.3	15.0	0.3	1.7	2.8	24.9	8.1	9.0	12.1	15.1	17.4	0.2	6.6	8.3	52.2	47.2	47.5
Sweden	47.1	47.9	50.9	13.9	10.2	11.6	11.4	11.5	9.8	4.0	5.3	5.6	11.2	8.6	9.7	12.5	16.4	12.4
UK	43.2	45.9	51.4	20.8	20.2	29.0	13.7	7.9	5.3	4.2	3.2	8.6	9.3	3.9	1.2	8.9	18.9	4.6
Total DAC	**28.3**	**26.5**	**35.8**	**11.4**	**13.0**	**14.9**	**24.6**	**29.6**	**17.6**	**17.7**	**11.4**	**15.1**	**4.3**	**6.3**	**4.9**	**13.7**	**13.1**	**11.7**
of which:																		
EU members	41.2	40.4	49.8	8.4	9.0	12.0	16.7	16.4	9.8	14.1	12.1	11.2	7.2	7.0	6.0	12.5	15.2	11.2
EC	48.6	38.6	44.3	9.2	7.6	9.2	4.1	5.8	4.7	16.2	20.4	18.9	12.2	14.6	14.1	9.6	13.0	8.8
IFIs[b]	42.4	37.8	43.1	32.5	29.7	31.5	15.1	13.6	11.7	1.3	3.3	1.5	0.8	2.8	3.1	7.9	12.8	9.1
UN Agencies[c]	43.0	36.8	37.7	13.5	15.6	15.0	9.4	10.6	7.3	13.2	20.8	24.9	14.2	2.4	3.9	6.8	13.8	11.2
Overall total	**32.9**	**30.2**	**37.9**	**14.5**	**15.8**	**17.2**	**20.6**	**23.6**	**15.1**	**14.8**	**11.1**	**13.5**	**5.1**	**6.2**	**5.3**	**12.0**	**13.1**	**11.0**

[a] Excluding amounts unspecified by region.   [b] International financial institutions. Includes IDA, regional banks' soft windows, IFAD, and IMF (PRGF).
[c] Includes UNDP, UNICEF, UNRWA, WFP, UNHCR, UNFPA, and UNTA.
Source: OECD (2005: Table 27).

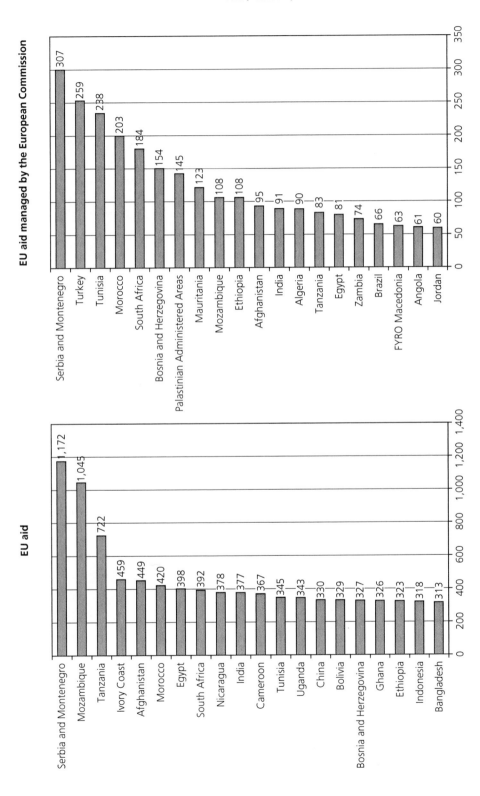

Figure 13.1 Top twenty recipients of EU and EC aid (disbursements, million US dollars, 2001–2 average)

Source: European Commission (2004: 27, Table 18).

By 2001–2, Serbia and Montenegro was the largest recipient, followed by Mozambique, Tanzania, and the Ivory Coast (none of which was a major recipient of EU aid in the later 1990s). It is also the case that not all major EU aid recipients are ACP Member States, emphasizing the point made above that, although most attention is given to ACP Member States, the EU has wider interests which encompass south Asia, the Middle East, and, to a more limited extent, Latin America. The geographical distribution of aid thus reflects a mixture of historical relationships, contemporary geo-political realities, commercial interests, and humanitarian concerns. The EU, as a major multilateral donor, is perhaps less partisan than major bilateral donors (the USA and France, for example), but the geographical distribution of its aid nevertheless reflects its perceptions of regional and global interests. Aid from the non-EU members of the DAC reflects differing interests, with Indonesia, China, Egypt, and Pakistan being the largest recipients in 2001–2 (DAC Online Database, Table 2a).

13.5 The Europe–ACP relationship

Historical background

Table 13.9 details the evolution of the relationship between the EC/EU and the ACP. The evolving EU–ACP relationships reflect not only changes within the EC/EU itself (the accession of new members), but also changes within the global economic and political context—decolonization, the notion of a new international economic order (the Lomé model), the end of the Cold War (updated Lomé IV), and the effects of globalization (the Cotonou Agreement).

When the Treaty of Rome was signed in 1957, most of the countries that now constitute the ACP were still colonies. The Treaty of Rome provided for an element of aid

Table 13.9 Evolution of the Europe–ACP partnership, 1957–2000

Year	Event	No. of countries	
		ACP	Europe
1957	Association System		
1963	Yaoundé, I Convention	18	6
1969	Yaoundé, II Convention	18	6
1975	Lomé, I Convention	46	9
1980	Lomé, II Convention	58	9
1985	Lomé, III Convention	65	10
1990	Lomé, IV Convention	68	12
1995	Lomé, IV Convention Rev.	70	15
2000	Cotonou Agreement	77	15

Source: The Courier (Sept. 2000, Special Issue, p. 12).

to these colonies, however, in the form of an implementing Convention added to the Treaty. It provided for a form of unilateral association between the EC and its Member States and overseas countries and territories (OCTs), through which trade and aid links could be maintained.

The first European Development Fund (EDF) was established in 1958 and gave grants for economic and social infrastructure projects largely in French-speaking OCTs. The 1960s was a decade of decolonization, and in 1963 the Yaoundé (Cameroon) Convention was signed between the EC-6 and eighteen now-independent African countries (including Madagascar). A second EDF was established to give loans as well as grants, and the Convention included provisions for preferential trade arrangements and for the provision of financial and technical assistance. The Second Yaoundé Convention was signed in 1969, with a third EDF.

In January 1973 the UK joined the EC and some twenty Commonwealth countries were included in the protocol to the Act of Accession, opening the way to the negotiation of some form of special relationship with the EC—an opportunity also offered to those independent states in Africa that were neither members of the Commonwealth nor members of the AASM grouping (Association of African States and Madagascar) which had negotiated the Yaoundé Convention. After a period of some uncertainty as to how newly independent ACP countries would view their position vis-à-vis Europe, the first Lomé Convention was signed in February 1975 in Togo, and, in June 1975, forty-six ACP countries institutionalized themselves as a group with a permanent structure.

Lomé I has been described as a 'partnership of equals' and a number of joint institutions were created to administer the Convention. It introduced STABEX and SYSMIN, designed to stabilize agricultural commodity and mineral product earnings respectively, and, at a time of stalemate in the global negotiations aimed at the creation of a New International Economic Order (NIEO), it 'appeared to offer an opportunity for a group of industrialised and developing countries to break out of the impasse . . . to establish a regional arrangement that would incorporate a number of items on the NIEO agenda' (Stevens 1990: 77).

The optimism that characterized Lomé I was shown to be premature by events that followed the first oil price shock of 1973–4. A brief boom in some primary commodity prices was followed by the second oil price shock of 1979–80. The sub-Saharan economies in particular were hard hit by global economic instability and began a period of stagnant or falling per capita incomes from which the majority of African economies have not yet recovered. Lomé II was signed in 1980, with a larger EDF, but was regarded as disappointing by the ACP. Lomé III was signed in 1985, as the 'decade of structural adjustment' (see below) was beginning to emerge. Lomé III made a commitment to 'self-reliant development' on the basis of food security and self-sufficiency, enhanced by a broad-ranging 'policy dialogue' between EC Member States and the ACP states. Policy dialogue increasingly encompassed involvement in macroeconomic policy-making through the provision of resources through programmes of structural adjustment.

Stevens (1990: 84) argued that the first three Lomé Conventions did not lead to a radical transformation in the economies of the ACP. Lomé aid was widely criticized on two counts: first, it had been poorly used, financing projects either poorly designed or whose possibilities of success had been weakened by a hostile policy environment; and second, aid had been badly administered by the donor, with slow rates of disbursement. Donor procedures were allegedly slow and cumbersome, with duplicated appraisal procedures, over-centralization, and 'meddling' by Member States (Stevens 1990: 85).

In addition, it was argued that the aid relationship had changed over time, with the EC attempting to impose a more orthodox donor–recipient relationship than was initially felt either necessary or desirable. 'Policy dialogue' had increasingly come to mean a shift in the balance of power for aid decision-making towards the EC to give it a greater voice in the selection of aid-financed projects and sectoral policies relevant to the success of those projects (Stevens 1990: 84).

The Fourth Lomé Convention was signed in December 1989. For the first time it covered a period of ten years, although the Financial Protocol covered the first five years only with mandatory renewal provided for at the end of that time. The negotiations in 1989 anticipated the possibility of reviewing the actual text of the Convention midway through its term. The mid-term review negotiations opened in May 1994 and were completed in June 1995. The results were formalized in the agreement signed in Mauritius in November 1995.

The 1990 Convention highlighted new areas of development aid policy which had been somewhat neglected in the previous conventions, including protection of the environment, agricualtural cooperation and food security, and cultural and social co-operation (including issues relating to women in development). The review of the Lomé IV provisions in the mid-1990s was classified under four headings: institutional and political; thematic and sectoral; commercial; and financial (*Courier* 1996: 8). With respect to institutional and political issues, emphasis was placed on the recognition and application of democratic principles, the consolidation of the rule of law, and good governance. Thematic and sectoral issues covered a range of activities including cultural and industrial cooperation.

With respect to finance, programmable aid remained the central feature of ACP–EU cooperation within the context of agreed programmes of structural adjustment. In very broad terms, structural adjustment is a set of policies designed to reduce internal and external imbalances in an economy. Whereas stabilization policies are largely concerned with the reduction in aggregate demand, structural adjustment focuses on the increase in aggregate supply. Both sets of policies complement each other and both share many common elements: more liberal trade policy (removal of quantitative restrictions, reduction in tariffs), improved resource mobilization and allocation (through fiscal and monetary reform, removal of subsidies, reform of public enterprises, reform of agricultural sector pricing policies), and institutional reforms.

The Lomé IV provisions that covered structural adjustment emphasized that these policies were intended to promote long-term development in the ACP states, accelerate the growth of output and employment, and be consistent with the political and economic model of the ACP state in question. Adjustment had to be economically viable and socially and politically bearable. These were ambitious objectives, the achievement of which cannot be taken for granted. The record of structural adjustment programmes has been mixed, and, although the EU argued that it would be pragmatic and realistic in its approach, it would be difficult to argue that these programmes have been successful overall.

The revised Lomé IV Convention made reference to the use of structural adjustment resources to encourage regional integration efforts and to support reforms leading to intra-regional economic liberalization. Support was to be given to the harmonization and coordination of macroeconomic and sectoral policies to fulfil the dual aim of regional integration and structural reform at the national level. It is important to bear in mind that trade policy probably has a greater economic impact on the ACP states than development cooperation policy (although see below). The ACP states have enjoyed free access to the EU market for the majority of their agricultural and manufactured products. The revised Lomé IV Convention signalled a change of emphasis, however, focusing on the role of trade in the development process and on measures to enhance the competitiveness of ACP exports both within ACP and EU markets and within wider global markets.

The Cotonou Agreement, 2000

The Cotonou Agreement was signed in Benin in June 2000, between the fifteen Member States of the EU and seventy-seven countries of the ACP Group, together representing almost one billion people and more than half the Member States of the United Nations. The ACP Group currently consists of forty-eight African states, fifteen Caribbean states, and fourteen Pacific states. France, the Netherlands, and the UK have a number of OCTs between them. (The full text of the Cotonou Agreement was published in a special issue of *The Courier* (2000*b*).) The new partnership was for a period of twenty years, with a five-yearly review clause. It enshrined the principle of participative development, extending the partnership concept to a wide range of actors, including civil society, the private sector, and local authorities. Decentralized cooperation was to be an essential aspect of the ACP–EU partnership.

The Commission's new development policy spelt out six key priority areas: trade, regional integration, support for macroeconomic policies with a particular focus on health and education, transport, food security, and institutional capacity building (*Courier* 2000*a*: 2).

In line with the MDGs, the central objective of the ACP–EU partnership was the reduction and eventual eradication of poverty, within a stable macroeconomic framework. Poverty eradication in ACP countries, however, depends on many factors that lie outside the ambit of the ACP–EU agreement, and if the poverty alleviation targets are to be met, the major donor countries will have to increase their levels of ODA in real terms. We noted above (section 13.3) that the EU has (re)committed itself to the achievement of the 0.7 per cent of GNI target.

With respect to trade policy, the objectives of the new agreement were to accelerate the smooth and gradual integration of the ACP states into the global economy, to help them rise to the challenges of globalization and adopt the new conditions of international trade (as being defined by the World Trade Organization (WTO)), and to enhance their production, supply, and trading capacities, and improve their competitiveness. The trade regime of the Lomé Conventions was not compatible with the WTO rules and the preferential treatment extended on a non-reciprocal basis to ACP countries was to be phased out over a ten-year transitional period (*Courier* 2000*a*: 17). The STABEX and SYSMIN arrangements were also phased out. The 2005 review of the Cotonou Agreement was largely confined to technical matters and minor amendments.

13.6 EU–ACP trade

The EU is the world's largest trading bloc, accounting for 20 per cent of global trade. EU trade with the ACP countries totalled more than 55 billion Euros in 2004, with EU imports totalling 28.4 billion Euros and exports totalling 26.5 billion Euros. For most of the ACP countries, and for virtually all the African ACP countries, the EU is the main trading partner. As of 2005, the main imports from ACP countries were petroleum, diamonds, and ships and boats. The main EU exports to the ACP countries were machinery, vehicles, ships and boats, and pharmaceutical products. Agricultural products accounted for 24 per cent of EU imports from the ACP countries and 12 per cent of exports to them. Cocoa, sugar, coffee, and bananas are the main agricultural imports.

The EU trade regime is complex and trade policy towards both the ACP and non-ACP countries overlaps with foreign policy (Page 2006). Page (2006: 116) further argues that trade policy towards developing countries is not of central importance to EU member countries and that is why they are willing to delegate it to the European Commission. The latter in turn is more influenced by important interests (including European agriculture and relations with the USA) than by the needs of economic development. The EU is a key player in the WTO and the European Commission negotiates trade agreements and represents the European interests of member countries under Article 133 of the Europan Community Treaty.

Global trade negotiations have been a major focus of attention since the failure of the third WTO ministerial meeting held in Seattle in 1999. An attempt was made to address the concerns of developing countries with the launch of the Doha Development Agenda (DDA) in 2001, although as of mid-2006 these negotiations have not been completed successfully. The Doha Declaration (see http://www.wto.org) provided a mandate for negotiations on a range of subjects, including:

- agriculture: the establishment of a fair and market-oriented trading system through fundamental reforms including better market access, the phasing out of export subsidies, and substantial reductions in domestic support that distorted trade;
- services: the General Agreement on Trade in Services (GATS) commits member governments to enter into negotiations to liberalize progressively trade in services;
- market access for non-agricultural products: although average tariffs are at very low levels, certain tariffs continue to restrict trade, especially exports from developing countries; 'tariff peaks', (relatively high tariffs on 'sensitive' products) and 'tariff escalation' (in which higher import duties are applied on semi-finished products than on raw materials and are higher still on finished products), remain issues that need resolution;
- trade-related aspects of intellectual property rights: TRIPS relate in part to issues of public health and access to medicines, geographical indications (place names used to indicate products with particular characteristics, for example, Scotch whisky), and biodiversity;

Table 13.10 European Union trade with developing countries, ACP and least developed countries, 2005

	Developing countries	ACP	Least developed countries (billion Euros)
Imports of the European Union			
Machinery and transport equipment	191.5	6.5	1.10
Mineral fuels, lubricants, and related materials	104.5	16.1	3.91
Miscellaneous manufactured articles	100.5	1.5	4.68
Manufactured goods classified, chiefly by material	59.3	10.4	2.43
Food and live animals	35.9	8.0	1.94
Crude materials, inedible except fuels	24.6	5.2	1.41
Chemical and related products	24.1	0.9	0.21
Commodities and transactions	3.7	1.3	0.04
Animal and vegetable oils, fats, and waxes	3.4	0.3	0.05
Beverages and tobbacco	2.4	0.9	0.23
Exports of the European Union			
Machinery and transport equipment	206.5	25.6	6.78
Mineral fuels, lubricants, and related material	9.2	2.3	0.87
Miscellaneous manufactured articles	35.5	3.3	1.03
Manufactured goods classified, chiefly by material	57.7	5.3	1.59
Food and live animals	14.6	3.3	1.72
Crude materials, inedible except fuels	9.9	0.5	0.26
Chemical and related products	50.4	5.6	1.71
Commodities and transactions	5.8	0.6	0.16
Animal and vegetable oils, fats, and waxes	0.6	0.1	0.05
Beverages and tobbacco	4.3	0.8	0.39

Source: http://ec.europa.eu/comm/trade/issues/bilateral/data.htm.

- other issues include ensuring that regional trade agreements remain compatible with WTO rules.

Some progress was made at the Hong Kong ministerial conference (December 2005) on some of these issues. The WTO reaffirmed its commitment to the Doha Declaration, and committed itself to the elimination of export subsidies on cotton by 2013 (of particular interest to a number of low income economies including Benin, Burkina Faso, Chad, Mali, and Senegal), and to reductions in levels of domestic support. However, as of mid-2006, the major issues were still not resolved. The implications of the Doha Round for the EU agricultural sector, and for sugar in particular, are discussed in Chapter 4.

Economic Partnership Agreements with the ACP countries

Economic Partnership Agreements (EPAs) are an integral part of the Contonou 'approach' to development. The negotiation of EPAs is seen as the means by which ACP countries can be more closely integrated into the global economy. Negotiations began in 2002, with the first phase addressing issues of interest to all regions and the second phase focusing on regionally specific issues and commitments. Formal negotiations have been launched with west Africa, central Africa, eastern and southern Africa, the Caribbean, southern Africa/SADC (Southern African Development Community), and the Pacific, with the intention of concluding WTO-compatible agreements by 2007, on time for entering into force on 1 January 2008. As of mid-2006, the 'policy-based trade negotiations', to use Stevens' (2006) terminology, are continuing with no clear outcomes yet in sight.

Regional negotiations have focused on strengthening ACP regional integration efforts through improvements in the business environment, economic governance, and ACP competitiveness. These policies include, *inter alia,* the development of stable, predictable, and transparent rules to lower the costs of doing business, developing competition policy and investment rules, and improving access to the EU market, although the EU has argued that market building rather than market opening is the main priority.

The negotiation of EPAs has proved to be controversial. Critics argue that further trade liberalization, even if it benefits ACP countries in the long run, will impose short-run adjustment costs related to implementation and restructuring, will lead to the loss of fiscal revenue (arising from the reduction or abolition of import duties), the loss of preference margins in the EU market (see below), and the loss of autonomy in designing and implementing national development policies. A review of the studies that have attempted to model the impact of EPAs (ODI 2006) concludes that the liberalization of commodity trade is broadly positive. But the assumptions on which such studies are based and their lack of detail mean that too much weight cannot be given to these conclusions. It has also been argued that further trade liberalization is neither necessary nor sufficient to achieve the goals of economic development and poverty reduction. The work of Chang (2002) has highlighted the importance historically of some degree of protection of domestic markets in order to foster industrialization. Development economists have highlighted the importance of removing supply-side constraints and improving competitiveness, through investment in education and training, infrastructure, and the acquisition and development of new technologies. Such policies imply a degree of intervention by governments (at the very least to overcome key market failures) which has long been out of favour with neo-classical/neo-liberal economists.

Free trade agreements (FTAs) and the EU

The EU has negotiated five free trade agreements with South Africa, Mexico, Chile, MERCOSUR (Argentina, Brazil, Paraguay, and Uruguay), and Egypt and has a customs union agreement in industrial products with Turkey (François *et al.* 2005). In addition, the Euro-Med Association Agreement (replacing the Cooperation Agreement of 1977) is intended to lead to an FTA by 2010 (the 'Barcelona Process'). For the EU, a combination of economic and political factors (greater peace and stability, further trade and investment liberalization, and access to new markets for EU exports) have been the driving forces behind these agreements. For the developing countries, FTAs have provided preferential access to the EU market and the prospect of more aid.

In a detailed analysis of the FTAs, Francois *et al.* (2005) argue that, although FTAs are required to cover 'substantially all trade', they fall far short of achieving this objective. EU restrictions on both product coverage and the rules of origin (which stipulate the conditions under which goods for export are deemed to originate from a particular country) have an adverse effect on trade in agricultural products and labour-intensive manufactured goods. Second, they argue that only the agreements with Mexico, Chile (in services), and Turkey (because it is a candidate for membership of the EU) have provisions beyond those available under WTO agreements (Francois *et al.* 2005: 1563). The trade and production effects of the FTAs are limited, given that many of the EU's imports from these countries were already subject to zero or very low rates of duty or because they already received unilateral preferences under bilateral schemes (Mediterranean countries) or the Generalized System of Perferences (GSP) (Latin America and South Africa).

The EU Generalized System of Preferences (GSP) and Everything But Arms (EBA)

The EU has offered unilateral, non-reciprocal tariff preferences to all developing countries under the GATT-compatible Generalized System of Preferences (GSP) since 1971, under which they were permitted to export manufactured goods tariff-free to the EU up to a certain limit (tariff quota). In 1999 this was replaced by a revised GSP scheme. In 2001, the Everything But Arms initiative (amending the GSP) was introduced, under which all least developed country goods have full duty-free and quota-free access to the EU market, with the exception of arms and bananas (until 2006), rice and sugar (until 2009). The current GSP no longer uses quotas or tariff ceilings to restrict imports of sensitive items. Rather it uses a complex formula to assess a beneficiary's level of industrial development and sectoral specialization, and excludes any beneficiary taking more than 25 per cent of GSP imports for a given product. This excludes certain products from large countries, for example, Brazil, China, India, and Indonesia.

The abolition of the Multi-Fibre Arrangement (MFA)

The establishment of the WTO in 1995 provided for the phasing out of the MFA over a ten-year period (see Box 13.2). Import quotas were removed as required on 1 January 2005. However, under China's WTO Accession Protocol, importing countries were permitted to impose quotas against China until 2008, if imports from China caused or threatened to cause disruption to the importer's domestic market. The first three months of 2005 saw a significant increase in imports of Chinese textiles and clothing into the EU and new quota arrangements were agreed in June 2005 covering the product categories of greatest concern (pullovers, men's trousers, blouses, T-shirts, dresses, etc.). European retailers accelerated their orders and Chinese manufacturers speeded up the shipping of goods intended for the European market. The full year's quotas for seven of the ten categories were used up almost immediately and 80 million items of Chinese garments were stockpiled at European ports. Further negotiations led to a burden-sharing agreement under which the EU agreed to let in all the unlicensed goods that were blocked at EU

BOX 13.2 A SUMMARY OF THE MULTI-FIBRE ARRANGEMENT (MFA)

Origins

Developed countries have sought special arrangements that would allow the negotiation of quantitative restrictions against cheap foreign imports of textiles and clothing (T&C) products since the early 1960s. Negotiations eventually led to the establishment of the MFA (the 'Arrangement') in 1974 which consisted of a comprehensive framework for the negotiation and conclusion of bilateral agreements on quota restrictions covering trade in T&C between individual developed and developing countries.

On 1 January 1995, the Arrangement was replaced by the Agreement on Textiles and Clothing (ATC). The ATC provided a ten-year transitional period for the complete phase-out of quotas imposed by the developed countries on T&C imports from developing countries. Import quotas were subsequently abolished on 1 January 2005.

Rationale/aim

The two stated objectives of the Arrangement are:

1. 'To achieve the expansion of trade, the reduction of barriers to such trade and the progressive liberalization of world trade in textiles products, while at the same time ensuring the orderly and equitable development of this trade and avoidance of disruptive effects in individual markets and on individual lines of production in both importing and exporting countries' (Article 1(2)).

2. 'To further the economic and social development of developing countries and secure a substantial increase in their export earnings from textiles products and to provide for a greater share for them in world trade in these products' (Article 1(3)).

Members

Membership of the MFA varied throughout its existence. Developed countries imposing quotas against T&C exports of developing countries included the USA, the EU, Canada, and Norway. By the end of 1994, most of the developing countries with substantial T&C exports to these developed markets had quotas imposed against them.

Impact

The imposition of import quotas against T&C exports of developing countries has distorted international trade in T&C in the past three decades. In spite of quota protection against cheap foreign imports, production and employment in the T&C industry in both the USA and the EU has declined. For developing countries, highly constrained exporters have upgraded their products and/or subcontracted out some of their lower value-added activities to the less quota-constrained manufacturers by outward-processing arrangements, for example, Hong Kong investment in China and Taiwanese investment in Lesotho.

End of MFA

There is a general consensus that there would be a sizeable increase in global welfare and trade following the abolition of the ATC. However, the distribution of these benefits is likely to be very uneven across countries. The highly constrained Asian countries are likely to benefit the most, particularly China and India. By contrast, exporters that have benefited under the MFA either by becoming an export platform (Lesotho) for quota-restrained countries or by having preferential access to developed countries (Turkey under the EU–Turkey Customs Union) are likely to lose.

borders, 50 per cent of which would be included in the 2006 quota (Harrison 2006 gives full details). Given the importance of the textiles and garments sector in a number of EU countries (France, Greece, Italy, Portugal, and Spain), and given that the imposition of quotas only postpones and does not solve the problem of adjustment in importing countries, this dispute is unlikely to be settled in the near future.

13.7 **Conclusions**

Few countries have had as much experience with foreign aid as the Member States of the EU (Panic 1992). They were large recipients of aid during and after the Second World War (both relief aid and assistance under the Marshall Plan). With post-war reconstruction complete, they became the most important donors of ODA, along with the USA and, later, Japan. As we have argued above, the giving of aid and the relationships between donor and recipient countries raise a number of complex issues and pose problems which have no simple solutions. EU aid is no exception in this respect. The size, nature, and effectiveness of EU aid have been subject to criticism, and allegations of ineffectiveness, incompetence, and malpractice are not uncommon, if not always proved. Over the past two decades, a number of ACP countries have faced aid sanctions, provisional suspension, or the slowing down of aid because of their failure to comply with agreed conditionalities or because of their violations of human rights and/or excessive levels of corruption. Given the political realities of many low-income ACP countries, it would be misleading to presume that such issues can be avoided in the future. By international standards however, the EU is not a 'bad' donor.

Changing development priorities and policies as incorporated in the Millennium Development Goals and the Cotonou Agreement, and in particular the focus on poverty reduction, are highlighted. Even though it might well be the case that the EU has been slow in developing systematic operational strategies for poverty reduction and so-called people-oriented development (Cox and Healey 2000: 37), this is not a shortcoming unique to the EU, given the complexity of the issues raised.

With respect to EU trade policy with the ACP and developing countries in general, the EU has been forced to make its concessional and non-reciprocal trade policies consistent with the requirements of WTO membership. The chosen institutional vehicle as far as the ACP countries are concerned is the negotiation of EPAs. It is too early to evaluate the likely impact on economic development of such arrangements, and debate will continue between economists as to the appropriateness and effectiveness of particular trade regimes as far as development is concerned.

Economic development is the outcome of many factors, both domestic and global, which interact in a complex way that is still not fully understood. The enlargement of the EU, emerging relationships with Russia and the Newly Independent States of the former Soviet Union, the increasing importance of the WTO, and the likely reform of the CAP, along with socio-economic and political change within the ACP countries themselves, will all influence the direction and pace of future development. The bilateral aid programmes of EU Member States will continue to be of importance, alongside the multilateral aid and trade programmes of the EU itself. Much will depend on the quality of the relationship between bilateral donors and recipients and the effectiveness of the EU–EPA partnerships in creating a more favourable context for sustainable development and poverty reduction.

■ DISCUSSION QUESTIONS

1. Compare and contrast the record of the major EU aid donors since the mid-1990s.

2. What are the main factors which influence the 'aid relationship' between EU donors and ACP recipients?

3. Discuss the main changes that have occurred over time in the economic relationships between the EU and the ACP countries. In what ways do the provisions of the Cotonou Agreement reflect changes in development thinking and policy in the 1990s?

4. 'Looking ahead, the EU needs to give higher priority to achieving a coherent relationship with developing countries and (of course) to achieving coherence between its development policy and its trade policy' (Page 2006). Discuss.

■ FURTHER READING

DAC aid statistics are presented in the OECD Development Cooperation Report, published annually. This is the standard reference and also includes discussions of current aid and development issues. Cassen *et al.* (1986), Mosley (1987), and Hansen and Tarp (2000) contain excellent general discussions of aid and its relation to development. The full text of the Cotonou Agreement is to be found in *The Courier* (2000*b*). Cox and Healey (2000) provide a detailed examination of European development cooperation and its impact on poverty reduction. Page (2006) is excellent on the complexities of EU trade policy. François *et al.* (2005) provide a detailed overview and analysis of EU-developing country FTAs.

Useful websites include:
http://www.eadi.org/edc2010
http://www.odi.org.uk
http://www.acp-eu-trade.org/library
http://www.bond.org.uk
http://www.wto.org
http://www.millenniumproject.org
http://www.oecd.org
http://www.europa.eu.int/comm/development/sitemap_ent.ht.

■ NOTE

I would like to thank Barry Lau, Claire Palmer, and Rebecca Shipley for research assistance on this chapter.

▓ REFERENCES

Bhagwati, J. (1967), 'The Tying of Aid', UNCTAD Secretariat, TDI7/Supp. 4, United Nations; repr. in J. Bhagwati and R. S. Eckaus (eds.), *Foreign Aid* (Harmondsworth: Penguin, 1970), 235–93.

Birdsall, N., Rodrik, D., and Subramanian, A. (2005), 'How to Help Poor Countries', *Foreign Affairs*, 84/4: 136–52.

BOND (2003), *Europe in the World: Essays on EU Foreign, Security and Development Policies*, London: BOND.

Cassen, R. *et al.* (1986), *Does Aid Work?* (Oxford: Clarendon Press).

Commission of the European Communities (CEC) (2005), *Proposal for a Joint Declaration by the Council, the European Parliament and the Commission on the European Union Development Policy, 'The European Consensus'* (Brussels: CEC).

Chang, H. (2002), *Kicking Away the Ladder: Development Policy in Historical Perspective* (London: Anthem Press).

Courier (1996), 155 (Jan.–Feb.).

Courier (2000*a*), 181 (June–July).

Courier (2000*b*), Special Issue (September).

Cox, A. and Healey, J. (eds.) (2000), *European Development Cooperation and the Poor* (London: Macmillan for the Overseas Development Institute).

Department for International Development (DfID) (2000), *Eliminating World Poverty: Making Globalisation Work for the Poor*, White Paper on International Development (London: HMSO).

European Centre for Development Policy Management (2005), *Assessment of the EC Development Policy: Development Policy Statement: Final Report* (Maastricht: EC DPM).

European Commission (2004), *EU Donor Atlas: Mapping European Development Assistance* (Brussels: EU).

European Union (EU) (2005), 'The European Consensus on Development', Joint Statement by the Council and the Representatives of the Governments of the Member States Meeting Within the Council, the European Parliament and the Commission (Brussels: EU).

François, J. F., McQueen, M., and Wignaraja, G. (2005), 'European Union–Developing Country FTAs: Overview and Analysis', *World Development*, 33/10: 1545–65.

Hansen, H. and Tarp, F. (2000), 'Aid Effectiveness Disputed', in F. Tarp (ed.), *Foreign Aid and Development: Lessons Learnt and Directions for the Future* (London: Routledge), 103–8.

Harrison, B. (2006), ' "Bra Wars": The Textile Dispute with China', in P. Maunder (ed.), *Developments in Economics*, vol. 22 (Burgess Hill, West Sussex: Economics and Business Education Association), 93–104.

Hjertholm, P. and White, H. (2000), 'Foreign Aid in Historical Perspective: Background and Trends', in F. Tarp (ed.), *Foreign Aid and Development: Lessons Learnt and Directions for the Future* (London: Routledge), 80–102.

International Labor Office (ILO) (2004), *The World Commission on the Social Dimension of Globalization* (Geneva: United Nations).

Morrissey, O. (2005), *Aid and Poverty Reduction*, Wider Angle no. 1 (Helsinki: World Institute for Development Economics Research).

Mosley, P. (1987), *Overseas Aid: Its Defence and Reform* (Brighton: Wheatsheaf).

Nixson, F. (2002), 'Economic Growth and Development in an Unequal World', in G. B. J. Atkinson (ed.), *Developments in Economics: An Annual Review*, vol. 18, (Ormskirk: Causeway Press), 119–35.

—— (2006), 'Economic Growth and Development in an Unequal World Revisited', in P. Maunder (ed.), *Developments in Economics*, vol. 22 (Burgess Hill, West Sussex: Economics and Business Education Association), 1–18.

Overseas Development Institute (ODI) (2006), *The Potential Effects of Economic Partnership Agreements: What Quantitative Models Say*, Briefing Paper no. 5, (London: ODI).

OECD (1992), *Development Cooperation: 1992 Report* (Paris: OECD).

—— (1995), *Development Cooperation: 1995 Report* (Paris: OECD).

—— (2000), *Development Cooperation: 1999 Report* (Paris: OECD).

—— (2005), *Development Cooperation: 2005 Report* (Paris: OECD).

Page, S. (2006), 'Special and Differential Treatment or Divide and Rule? EU Trade Policy towards Developing Countries', in M. Bne Saad and M. Leen (eds.), *Trade, Aid and Development: Essays in Honour of Helen O'Neill* (Dublin: University College Dublin Press), 116–34.

Panic, M. (1992), 'The Single Market and Official Development Assistance: The Potential for Multilateralizing and Raising EU Assistance', *Journal of Development Planning*, 22: 3–17.

Riddell, R. (1987), *Foreign Aid Reconsidered* (London: James Curry).

Singer, H. (1965), 'External Aid: For Plans or Projects?', *Economic Journal*, 75: 539–5; repr. in J. Bhagwati and R. S. Eckaus (eds.), *Foreign Aid* (Harmondsworth: Penguin, 1970), 294–302.

Stevens, C. (1990), 'The Lomé Convention', in K. Kiljunen (ed.), *Region-to-Region Cooperation between Developed and Developing Countries: The Potential for Mini NIEO* (Aldershot: Avebury), 77–88.

—— (2006), 'Trade Policy Leverage: Past, Present and Future Experience in EPAs', paper presented to Overseas Development Institute, London, June.

Tarp, F. (ed.) (2000), *Foreign Aid and Development: Lessons Learnt and Directions for the Future* (London: Routledge).

Thorbecke, E. (2000), 'The Evolution of the Development Doctrine and the Role of Foreign Aid, 1950–2000', in F. Tarp (ed.), *Foreign Aid and Development: Lessons Learnt and Directions for the Future* (London: Routledge), 17–47.

White, H. (1992), 'The Macroeconomic Impact of Development Aid: A Critical Survey', *Journal of Development Studies*, 28/2: 163–240.

World Bank (1998), *Assessing Aid: What Works, What Doesn't, and Why* (New York: Oxford University Press for the World Bank).

Millennium Development Goals

In September 2000 the United Nations Millennium Declaration was signed by 147 heads of state and government, and 189 nations. The Declaration calls for halving, by the year 2015, the number of people who live on less than $1 a day. This effort also aims to find solutions to hunger, malnutrition, and disease, promoting gender equality and the empowerment of women, guaranteeing a basic education for everyone, and support-ing the Agenda 21 principles of sustainable development. Direct support from the richer countries in the form of aid, trade, debt relief, and investment is to be provided to help the developing countries.

The MDGs are formalized in eight explicit goals, each associated with and driven by its own set of targets.

Goal 1: Eradicate extreme hunger and poverty

Goal 2: Achieve universal primary education

Goal 3: Promote gender equality and empower women

Goal 4: Reduce child mortality

Goal 5: Improve maternal health

Goal 6: Combat HIV/AIDS, malaria, and other diseases

Goal 7: Ensure environmental sustainability

Goal 8: Develop a global partnership for development.

Source: http://www.unmillenniumproject.org/goals/index.htm

14 | Europe's Unemployment Problems

Giuseppe Bertola

Introduction

Unemployment is very much a European problem. In Figure 14.1, the current Eurozone members' unemployment rate is shown to have increased sharply and almost continuously since the early 1970s, in parallel with consolidation of an integrated economy whose size and complexity has been approaching that of the USA, and this contrasts sharply with the US experience of fluctuating and broadly declining unemployment. But there is more than one European unemployment problem, as Figure 14.2 illustrates by plotting unemployment data from the Netherlands and Spain along with Figure 14.1's data. The contrast between EU-12 and US experiences is dwarfed by towering Spanish unemployment in the 1980s and 1990s, and unemployment rates in southern Spain are in turn much higher: unemployment is not uniform across regions within each European

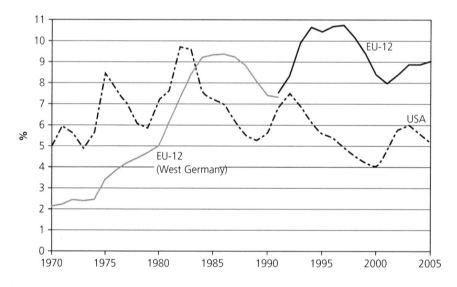

Figure 14.1 Unemployment rate in continental EU and in the USA, 1970–2005

Note: EU-12 are the countries that had adopted the Euro as of 2005.
Sources: Standardized unemployment rates, OECD *Economic Outlook* database.

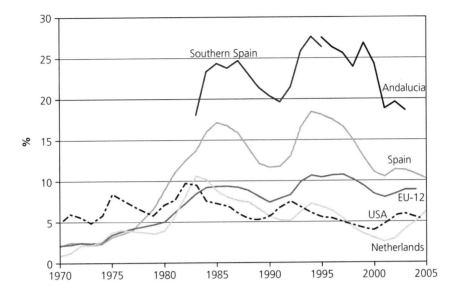

Figure 14.2 Unemployment rate in continental EU, USA, Netherlands, Spain, and southern Spain, 1970–2005

Note: Southern Spain: data available as of 2000, rescaled by the author to redefined aggregate Spanish unemployment.
Source: Standardized unemployment rates, OECD *Economic Outlook* database, except southern Spain and Andalucia (a region of southern Spain): Eurostat REGIO database.

country, and some countries and regions in Europe have lower unemployment than the USA, as Figure 14.2 shows plotting unemployment in the Netherlands. Dutch unemployment tracks its American counterpart downwards after exceeding it in 1982 for the first time, even as unemployment in other European countries remained stubbornly high.

Unemployment problems are also diverse in other respects. The *aggregate unemployment rate* measures the fraction, among those who are willing to work, of those who actively search for a job but are unable to obtain employment. In that respect, the Netherlands and the USA appear very similar in Figure 14.2 over the 1975–2000 period. But Figure 14.3 shows that the levels and dynamics of other labour market indicators are very different in those two countries. *Labour force participation* data in Figure 14.3 show that different fractions of the Dutch and American working-age populations work or seek work in the market (rather than study, work in the home, or enjoy retirement), and that such readiness to work declined in the Netherlands until the mid-1980s, has been constant in the USA since the early 1990s, and grew strongly in both countries in other periods. Another important difference between the two countries' labour markets is shown in Figure 14.3 by wage inequality indicators. In the USA, workers in the top decile of the wage distribution earn some 150 per cent of the wage of workers in the bottom decile in 2000, up from 130 per cent in 1975; in the Netherlands, that indicator grows only from a little less to a little more than 100 per cent, and wage differentials between median and bottom-decile workers are also much smaller in the Netherlands (at some 40 per cent) than in the USA, where they grew from some 70 per cent to over 80 per cent in the period shown.

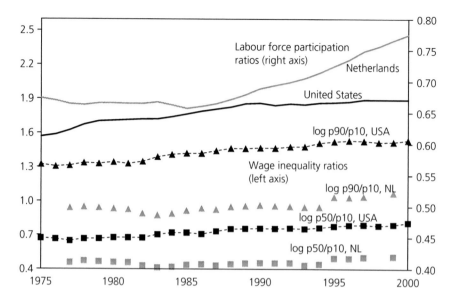

Figure 14.3 Labour force participation and wage inequality in the USA and in the Netherlands, 1975–2000

Note: Logarithm of the 90th- and 50th-percentile hourly wage rates to the 10th-percentile hourly wage rate, computed from the OECD earnings database.
Source: Labour force participation ratio, OECD *Economic Outlook* database.

Labour market participation, wage inequality, regional dispersion, and other disaggregated indicators are all influenced, like aggregate unemployment, by many structural and institutional features, including unemployment benefits, contractual arrangements, and taxation. While the proximate cause of involuntary unemployment is incomplete adjustment of wages to labour demand conditions, the deeper causes of heterogeneous and persistent unemployment in Europe are to be found in institutional features which prevent labour markets from delivering full employment at the same time as they also shape other aspects of employment and wages. Joblessness is not a pleasant experience in general. But employment at very low wages can be just as unpleasant for workers as unemployment, especially if the latter carries an entitlement to monetary benefits as well as leisure. And while flexible wages may reduce unemployment, they need not be universally appealing in other respects. Wage inequality is beneficial for those at the top of the earnings distribution, not for anybody who fears finding him or herself at the bottom of it, and unstable labour incomes are worrisome for families with limited access to loans and other financial market instruments.

This chapter's discussion of Europe's heterogeneous and changing unemployment problems is articulated in three steps. First, it focuses on the interaction of aggregate labour demand shocks with wage-setting behaviour, which is important as a source of high unemployment in many European countries. Second, in order to understand why persistent unemployment has not been reduced by flexibility-oriented reforms, it highlights the distributional implications of institutions that prevent formation of low-wage employment relationships when labour is heterogeneously productive. Finally, it notes the role of stronger product market competition in making high-unemployment labour market configurations increasingly unsustainable in the context of Europe's economic and monetary union process, and reviews how the tension may be resolved by reforms of labour and other markets at the national and European levels.

14.1 Aggregate unemployment

Unemployed individuals, by definition, would like to work and are taking at least some action towards finding a job that suits their wage and working-conditions aspirations. Unemployment is *frictional* when such jobs actually exist, and it is only a matter of time and effort before they are found. But sometimes, and very often indeed when unemployment is as high and persistent as in many European countries, the jobs to which the unemployed aspire do not exist, or are already occupied by workers who have no intention of leaving them vacant. Such mismatch between aspirations and opportunities is the source of *structural* unemployment. We discuss next how labour supply and labour demand may become and remain different at the aggregate level.

Shocks

Why would a labour market ever feature involuntary unemployment? Figure 14.4 illustrates a possible answer, based on the standard approach to the determination of employment levels. Employers maximize their profits when the level of employment, on the horizontal axis, and the wage, on the vertical axis, identify a point on the downward-sloping labour demand relationship plotted in the figure. A labour supply schedule is also

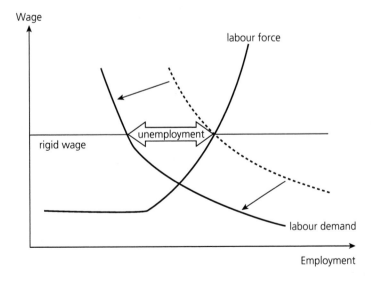

Figure 14.4 Unemployment implications of a labour demand shock when the wage is rigid

plotted, and for our purposes may be interpreted in terms of labour force participation decisions. Nobody is available to work when the wage is lower than the horizontal segment of that schedule; the labour force is positive, and increasingly large, at higher wage levels, because working in the market we are considering entails different opportunity costs across potential workers. Prime-age males, for example, are more readily induced to work than younger individuals, who may prefer to study if the market wage is low, and poor individuals may similarly be less inclined to seek employment than similar individuals with substantial sources of non-labour income. (In reality, the wage commanded in the labour market is also different across individuals, but we postpone a discussion of such heterogeneity to section 14.2 below.)

The wage level drawn in Figure 14.4 is not compatible with full employment, because those who are willing to work (along the labour supply schedule) are more numerous than those who firms find profitable to employ (along the labour demand schedule). The picture offers an explanation for that unemployment: if the labour demand schedule were in the position drawn by a dashed line, the wage would imply full employment; but some negative shock has reduced the number of jobs available at that wage, and the result is lower employment at an unchanged wage—rather than a lower wage rate and full employment of a smaller labour force. In reality, wages do fail to adjust quickly to labour demand fluctuations when they are contracted before labour demand conditions are known with certainty. The interplay of such *wage rigidity* with labour demand *shocks* is important for European unemployment dynamics. When in the early 1970s the first oil shock reduced the amount of labour demanded at any given wage, unemployment began to increase. In Figure 14.1, further episodes of sharply increasing unemployment for the EU aggregate are apparent in the aftermath of the second oil shock in the early 1980s, when macroeconomic policy also imparted negative aggregate demand impulses. Unemployment increases further in the early 1990s, when fiscal and monetary policy were tightened by countries that would otherwise have failed to meet the Maastricht Treaty's criteria.

Macroeconomic and policy shocks that affect unemployment through the mechanism illustrated in Figure 14.4 also matter for inflation. In Figure 14.4, if the wage is measured along the vertical axis in real terms, then lower productivity of labour could be triggered by a negative aggregate demand shock, or by an increase in the price of factors of production other than labour (such as oil), and real wage rigidity could be a result of incomplete information as to the realization or the consequences of such events. Contracts, however, typically pre-specify *nominal* wages, and do so on the basis of expectations of prices, with the implication that real wages turn out to be excessively high when inflation is unexpectedly low. This mechanism underlies Phillips curve relationships between realized inflation and unemployment. If expected inflation were stable over time, then a plot of actual inflation and unemployment should display a downward-sloping relationship, driven by temporary inflation forecast errors; as expected inflation does vary over time, higher inflation expectations result in vertical upward shifts of that relationship.

The top panel of Figure 14.5 displays unemployment and inflation for the EU-12 aggregate. The former tends to increase, as discussed above, and the latter to decline over the thirty years considered in the figure. This may be taken to be an indication of a Phillips curve relationship between the two, but it is important to recognize that while the plot

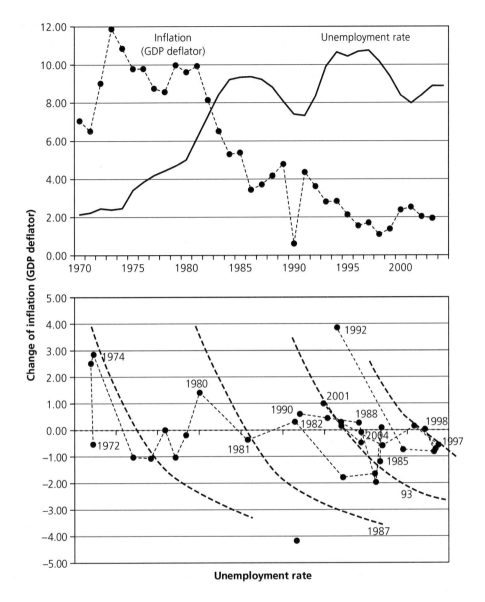

Figure 14.5 'Phillips curves' for the EU-12

Source: Unemployment rate and GDP inflation for the EU-12 aggregate, OECD *Economic Outlook* database.

refers to realized inflation, in Figure 14.4 it is unexpected inflation that explains why pre-set nominal wages turned out to be too high (resulting in unemployment). Inflation expectations are not easy to observe, of course, but were importantly affected at the national level by expectations of exchange rate devaluation during the 1970s and 1980s, when parities between European currencies were not irrevocably fixed. In weak-currency countries, such as Italy, fears of future devaluation would typically lead unions to request steep contractual wage increases, aimed at preventing loss of purchasing power at times of exchange rate realignment. As long as the feared devaluation was not realized, wage inflation reduced competitiveness, and ultimately sowed the seeds of unavoidable devaluation. Imperfect credibility of exchange rate arrangements symmetrically affected strong-currency countries, such as Germany, where both unions and firms would loudly complain about loss of competitiveness when exchange rate crises led to large exchange rate realignments.

The relationship between inflation and unemployment, however, is not affected by inflation expectations only. The simplest way to assess the extent to which inflation is unexpected is based on the idea that past realized inflation may proxy expected inflation: pre-set, rigid nominal wages then support an *accelerationist Phillips curve* relationship between unemployment and *changes* in inflation. From this perspective, the unemployment rate corresponding to stable inflation is that consistent with wage-setting practices, in the absence of unexpected inflation. This *non-accelerating inflation rate of unemployment* (NAIRU) is not constant, and its dynamics underlie the almost continuous increase of European unemployment. The bottom panel of Figure 14.5 plots changes in inflation against unemployment for the EU-12 countries. Inflation did increase and decrease over the 1970s, 1980s, and early 1990s; but while the relationship between inflation changes and unemployment tends to be negative for each such episode, it cannot be described by a single Phillips curve. Four possible such curves are drawn through clouds of points in the figure: their intersection with the horizontal axis (the NAIRU) moves out and to the right until the last few years, when low and stable inflation has been accompanied by slowly decreasing unemployment.

Wage setting

If high unemployment were a result only of unforeseen shocks, then it should be eliminated over time by wage declines. But many *institutions* constrain workers and employers in setting wages and choosing employment in ways that imply that unemployment and wages both remain persistently high. When out-of-work individuals receive unemployment benefits or are bound by legal or contractual wage minima, they will be unwilling or unable to bid for work by accepting lower wages, and will remain unemployed. In Figure 14.6, the wage level is so high as to imply that some willing-to-work individuals fail to obtain employment. In terms of total labour income, however, lower employment is more than compensated by the higher wage paid to those who are employed. If the wage is set collectively rather than individually, in fact, employment should not be a matter of indifference for the marginal worker, as is the case in competitive equilibrium. Rather, the wage should be marked up, as indicated by the vertical arrow, over the opportunity cost (along the labour supply curve) of employment in the market.

The extent to which these considerations reduce employment depends on the shape of the labour demand function, as we will see in more detail below. It also depends on the degree of wage demand coordination across workers, and on the bargaining power of employers—who in the figure simply accept whatever wage is chosen by the union, but in reality may well have more of a say in wage determination. Hence, this perspective on the sources of low employment offers a rich set of reasons why labour market outcomes

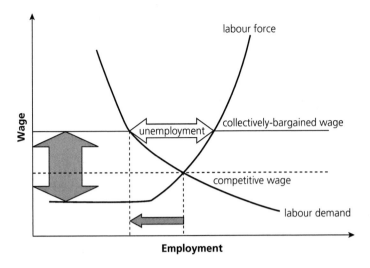

Figure 14.6 Collective bargaining and unemployment

may differ as much as they do in comparisons between EU countries and the USA, where unions and collective wage agreements are much less prevalent, and is also relevant to developments over time. Workers' political power and union activity both increased substantially in the late 1960s and in the 1970s. The *wage push* organized by labour in France and across Europe in 1968–70 took some time to result in lower employment, for reasons considered in the next subsection, but certainly played a role in shaping Europe's unemployment experience, and triggered political support for more generous unemployment benefits. Oil price increases and slower productivity growth in the following years compounded the problem if, as is likely, workers took some time to realize that their real wage aspirations (albeit at the cost of lower employment) could no longer be based on the relatively favourable labour demand conditions of the previous period.

The unemployment implied by high real wage demands accounts for persistently high NAIRU unemployment and, with nominal wage stickiness and poor monetary policy credibility, can also generate inflation. If collective bargaining and other labour market market institutions imply low levels of employment, but unexpected inflation is associated with lower unemployment, there will be a temptation to try to eliminate unemployment through expansionary monetary policy. If such behaviour is expected by wage- and price-setters, then inflation expectations will have to be so high as to remove the temptation for the monetary authorities to generate even higher inflation, and will coincide with realized inflation in the resulting *stagflation* equilibrium, where unemployment and inflation are both high. Similarly, attempts to use fiscal policy to try to boost economic activity above the level determined by structural and institutional features (rather than to stabilize fluctuations around it) can, and did in Italy and other EU countries in the 1980s, result in excessive public debt.

From the collective bargaining perspective of Figure 14.6, persistently high unemployment is the counterpart of high wages. In order to compare wages across countries, one

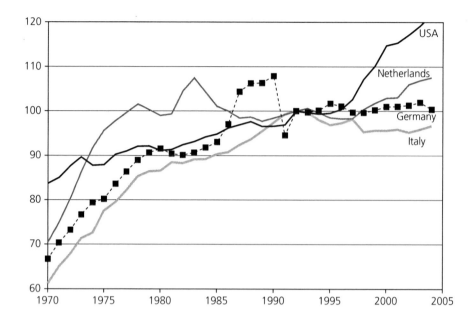

Figure 14.7 Real total compensation per employee, 1970–2005

Note: Real total compensation of employees index (1990 = 100, includes all taxes and contribution, deflated by producer price index).
Source: OECD *Economic Outlook* database.

would need to account for labour productivity differences. We will consider the issue below, but to begin with it is easier to compare real wages over time for the same country, as in Figure 14.7 where real compensation per employee (a measure of employers' costs, which is the relevant wage indicator if employment is determined along the labour demand schedule of Figures 14.4 and 14.6) is displayed for the USA and some European countries. Until 1990, wages in West Germany and in Italy grew much faster than in the USA, paralleling the growth of European unemployment. In the Netherlands, real wages ceased to grow in the early 1980s (like that country's unemployment). To the extent that high wages do to some extent mirror high unemployment experiences, the wage-setting mechanisms illustrated in Figure 14.6 play a role in explaining European experiences. It is interesting to notice that German and Italian wages no longer grow fast in the more recent period, when Dutch (and American) wages grow faster; we will return to these developments when discussing the implications of economic and monetary union below.

Job security

Rigid wages do little to stabilize labour incomes if, as in Figure 14.4, they imply job loss in the aftermath of negative labour demand shocks. *Employment protection legislation* (EPL) serves the purpose of limiting the responsiveness of employment to labour demand fluctuations, mandating that individual dismissals should be motivated (and subject to appeal) and/or that collective dismissals should be negotiated with workers' representatives and with the government. The resulting labour income stability is valuable for workers, especially when underdeveloped financial markets make it difficult for them to smooth out labour income fluctuations. From the point of view of employers, when reducing employment is costly it is no longer optimal to choose employment so as to equate labour's marginal productivity to the wage, as in Figure 14.4. Redundancy payments and legal or administrative expenses imply a smaller reduction of labour costs if employment is reduced. Hence, employers react to negative shocks by firing fewer workers when doing so is costly. Less intuitively, employers behave as if the wage was higher (or labour demand lower) during cyclical upswings: they refrain from hiring many additional workers because doing so would increase the need to reduce employment and pay firing costs in future downturns.

More stringent EPL should therefore be associated with smoother employment dynamics, while its contrasting effects on employers' propensity to hire and fire have ambiguous effects on average employment at given wages. Thus, the unemployment implied by wage rigidity in Figure 14.4 should be less volatile, and more persistent. The scope and stringency of EPL varies widely across countries in ways that are not easy to measure objectively: it is hard to put a price on advance-notice or administrative requirements, and firing costs depend not only on formal legislation but also on the inclination of labour courts to assess dismissals as wrongful, on the likelihood that collective layoffs may result in a serious deterioration of industrial relations, and other subtle issues. Qualitative rankings of EPL, however, do place continental European members of the EU at the top among OECD countries, and the USA at the bottom. Consistently with the theoretical effects of EPL, US unemployment in Figure 14.1 is much more volatile than its EU counterparts. The unemployment impact of oil-price and other shocks was milder in rigid European labour markets than in the USA, where it decreased more quickly and more substantially but, until 1985, was higher than in the EU.

14.2 Distribution and flows

The arguments of the previous section identified reasons why some workers could become and remain unemployed, without focusing on possible differences in the characteristics of employed and unemployed workers, and assuming an identical wage for all employed workers. In reality, employment and wage opportunities are heterogeneous across individuals, who have different productivity and different alternatives to labour market participation, as well as across sectors and firms. This section discusses how European labour market institutions interact with wage distributions and with labour allocation and reallocation.

Wage inequality

Competitive equilibrium implies wage inequality when workers have different skills and wage demands. But low-wage employment may be pre-empted by the availability of unemployment benefits, and by minimum wages (in the UK and other Anglo-Saxon countries) and collective contracts (which are binding regardless of union membership in many continental European countries), as well as by employment taxes: these do not affect labour costs and employment if they are linked to benefits, such as old age and invalidity pensions, which only accrue on the basis of work experience and make lower take-home pay acceptable to workers, but do contribute to eliminating the lowest portion of the pre-tax wage distribution, where net take-home would need to be too low.

When jobs that would pay low wages disappear for these reasons, then employment is lower and wages are both less dispersed and higher on average. Wage compression eliminates many jobs when the labour force is very heterogeneous: in Europe, unemployment tends to be both higher and regionally dispersed in large and heterogeneous countries than in smaller, homogeneous ones (such as Denmark, or Austria). In Figure 14.2 we noticed the high unemployment of Spain's southern regions, where labour productivity is lower but subsidies are the same as in more productive regions of that country. In southern Italy and eastern Germany uniform institutional frameworks similarly prevent wages from adjusting to local labour market conditions. The implications of wage compression may also become more serious, for a given distribution of skills and talents in the labour force, when the labour market tends to pay higher wages to relatively more skilled workers. Trade with less developed countries, where unskilled labour is abundant, and especially technological trends (such as the diffusion of computers and information technology, which also induces 'skill-biased' changes in wage distributions) both can have such effects, and may—but need not be—offset by appropriate upgrading of workers' skills in Europe.

Mobility

In reality, workers lose jobs at the same time as other workers are hired. The time-consuming process of reallocating the labour force from old to new jobs is the source of frictional unemployment, resulting from shifts in relative labour demand regardless of whether aggregate employment is changing. Such shifts would call for wages to adjust so as to equate labour demand and supply in subsets of the whole labour market, such as regions within a country, or industrial sectors. When labour demand decreases in one such market, lower wages would sustain employment, and foster mobility of workers towards higher-wage markets. Mobility is not costless for workers, however, and European labour market institutions tend to protect workers from it. Employment protection legislation reduces labour-shedding by declining firms and sectors and job creation by expanding ones; collective wage-setting agreements reduce the extent to which wages may fluctuate in response to local shocks; and unemployment and non-employment subsidies also tend to reduce workers' incentives to exit depressed segments of the labour market.

Such resistance to reallocation decreases efficiency by reducing the rate at which low-productivity jobs are replaced by high-productivity ones. But its distributional implications are similar to those of a tax on production factors other than labour, and may well be appealing for workers who put less weight on aggregate efficiency than on their own stressful job reallocation. Low flexibility also has implications for the distribution of joblessness across workers. Stringent EPL reduces flows both into and out of employment and lengthens unemployment spells, and also implies higher incidence of youth unemployment: older workers are less likely to lose their jobs, but young labour market

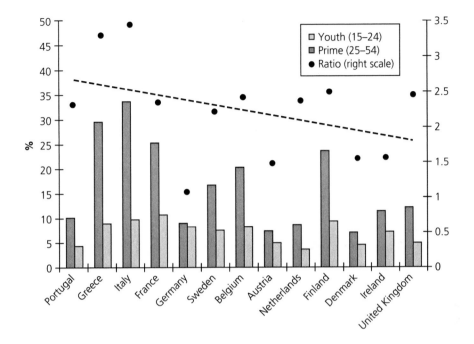

Figure 14.8 Employment protection, and youth and adult unemployment

Note: Countries are ordered on the horizontal axis according to the OECD *Employment Outlook* (1999) index of employment protection legislation stringency. The line interpolates the ratio of youth to adult unemployment rates (in 1999) over this ordering. *Source:* Unemployment rates, OECD *Employment Outlook* database.

entrants still flow into unemployment, and their worse job-finding opportunities lengthen their residence there. Figure 14.8 displays the youth and adult unemployment rates of EU member countries, ordered on the horizontal axis according to the stringency of employment protection legislation. This and other indicators of labour market performance are influenced by many institutional features other than EPL; in particular, the relatively low unemployment rates of German and Austrian youth can be credited to those countries' efficient vocational training systems. But countries with the most stringent EPL, such as Italy, do tend to have higher youth unemployment rates than countries where job security provisions are very mild, such as the United Kingdom.

14.3 Unemployment policy and economic integration

By the arguments of the previous sections, persistent unemployment and low employment rates may both result from policies aimed at increasing the wages of those among workers who are employed. From this perspective, it is hard to see how reforms could reduce unemployment. Eliminating unemployment subsidies could drastically reduce unemployment but only at the cost of increases in poverty and social exclusion; combating regional unemployment by encouraging wage differentiation and geographical mobility could also disturb the existing economic and political equilibrium of large countries. One could be tempted to conclude that European unemployment can hardly be a problem, and certainly not a problem that can ever be solved.

The causes of unemployment, however, differ not only across countries, but also over time. It is important to trace persistent unemployment to its institutional sources and be aware that reducing unemployment is not politically costless. But it is very important to recognize that institutions do need to be reformed when their negative effects (amplified by exogenous structural changes) offset or overwhelm their intended purpose, or that purpose no longer needs to be addressed (for example, because financial market development reduces the need to protect workers from labour income fluctuations). This section reviews from this perspective the changing approaches to the unemployment problem of European countries.

The character of unemployment policies

The sources of unemployment problems are diverse, and so are their remedies. *Passive policies* that simply grant subsidies to the unemployed ameliorate the consequences of joblessness for individuals, but reduce incentives to seek and bid for jobs, and increase joblessness at the market level. By contrast, *active policies* aim at reducing joblessness: job search assistance can help workers find jobs, and training can help them qualify for jobs that pay the wages they aspire to. They are expensive, however, because they require more resources (especially personnel, further contributing to their positive impact on employment rates) than simply paying unemployment subsidies. At one extreme, unemployment may be reduced by direct job creation in the public sector. The costs of activation are of course particularly apparent in this case, and its beneficial effects particularly doubtful if the availability of public jobs reduces wage competition in the private sector and public employees' wages need to be financed by taxing private-sector employment more heavily, enlarging the wedge between employers' costs and employees' take-home pay and decreasing the employment generated by given labour demand and labour supply schedules. Less drastic active policies have qualitatively similar drawbacks. Training is expensive, and may or may not effectively improve employability; forcing unemployed workers drawing benefits to visit job centres and consult with specialized public employees may improve workers' information and job finding rates, but is certainly far from costless for the government, or for the unemployed.

A related but different approach is that of *make-work-pay* policies, which aim at subsidizing employment by reducing the gap between the wage workers aspire to and their productivity. As mentioned, low-wage employment relationships are often not viable because of minimum wage provisions and/or unemployment subsidies. Benefits, even when they not explicitly conditional on non-employment, tend to create *poverty traps* if they are means-tested (i.e. conditional on the absence of other income sources) and are withdrawn as labour income increases. For example, until recently in Germany recipients of unemployment benefits could earn up to 165 Euros per month, but any further earnings led to loss of an equivalent amount of benefits; social assistance benefits were reduced by 85 per cent of amounts earned over about 75 Euros per month. Clearly, 100 per cent or 85 per cent tax rates imply very small incentives to obtain gainful employment. Some countries, including the UK, try to restore employment incentives by moderating the progressivity of the tax rate implicit in entitlement rules: an *earned-income tax credit* can be granted to workers whose labour income, if taxed at the standard rate, would be so low as to threaten benefit loss without net income gains. To make work pay for low-productivity workers, it is also possible to implement negative taxation (subsidization) for low-wage jobs. Like active policies, in-work subsidies can be an expensive way to create additional employment because of *deadweight* effects, whereby subsidies are paid to jobs that they would exist anyway, and through *displacement*, whereby employers replace relatively better-paid workers with subsidized employees with little or no net increase in employment. Waste of subsidies is more problematic if fiscal revenue is scarce. In fact, if maximizing employment was the only policy objective one would want to eliminate all labour income taxation, and perhaps subsidize not only low-wage, but all employment relationships. Eliminating or inverting the tax wedge certainly increases employment but, especially in Europe, making work pay *taxes* is also an important policy objective. And, just as benefits paid only to the unemployed reduce incentives to obtain gainful employment, subsidies paid only to low-wage employment relationships discourage workers and employers from education and training.

National policies, EMU, and reforms

It is not possible here to review in detail how European countries differ in the relevant respects but, to the extent that the costs and benefits of policies meant to address unemployment problems are different across countries, it is not surprising to see that different countries adopt different policy packages. Among the EU-15 countries, the Scandinavian ones (Sweden, Finland, Denmark) and the Netherlands have a tradition of full employment and universal welfare provision with generous unemployment insurance benefits and a very important role for active labour market policies (including job creation in the public sector), while continental countries (Austria, Belgium, France, and Germany) have a Bismarckian tradition of centralized wage determination, stringent employment protection legislation, and contribution-financed occupational pensions, health services, and unemployment benefits. In both groups of countries social assistance safety nets are less important than in the Beveridgian Anglo-Saxon model of the UK and Ireland, where unregulated labour markets feature less generous unemployment insurance, little employment protection, and decentralized wage setting. Southern European countries (Greece, Italy, Portugal, and Spain) have more recent and less precisely defined welfare states, where extended family arrangements still tend to play a non-trivial role, and the central, eastern, and Mediterranean new members add even more heterogeneity to the EU-25 policy landscape.

Much of the heterogeneity of policies and outcomes is accounted for by cross-country differences. For example, we see in the top panel of Figure 14.9 that there are marked differences across European countries in terms of unemployment and of the relevance of unions in wage setting, and that cross-sectional data are far from conforming to the upward-sloping relationship that would be implied (along a given labour demand curve) by larger wage mark-ups and higher unemployment: clearly, the role of unions and the shape of structural relationships are not the same across the countries considered in the

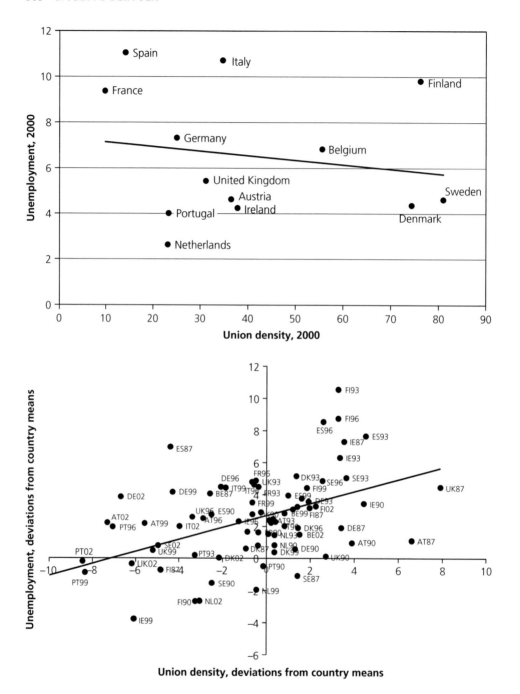

Figure 14.9 Unemployment and unionization, across countries and over time

Sources: Unemployment, OECD *Economic Outlook* database; percentage of workers who are union members, Nickell and Nunziata database.

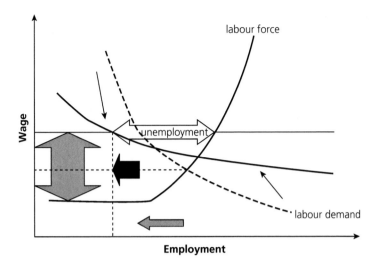

Figure 14.10 Labour market implications of economic integration and more intense competition

figure. Structure and institutions, however, are not stable over time within each country. In the bottom panel of Figure 14.9, for example, we see that unemployment and union-ization have both tended to decline in recent decades, indicating that countries tend to move down and to the right along labour demand schedules such as that drawn in the figures discussed above.

An important source of structural change, in Europe and elsewhere, is the increasing relevance of product market competition, which implies that labour demand is more elastic, that is that wage increases imply larger employment declines. Figure 14.10 shows the implications of a flatter labour demand schedule in the collective bargaining frame-work of Figure 14.6. Since trade and competition improve efficiency, the new demand schedule would imply higher employment and higher wages (along the supply curve) if the labour market were unregulated. But the same mark-up of wages that was supposed to be optimal (at least from the workers' point of view) in Figure 14.6 implies a larger employment decline, and more unemployment, in Figure 14.10. Collective wage setting pays high wages to a core of primary workers, but the resulting wage–employment out-come is not very attractive when that core is very small because firms that pay high wages are driven out of business.

Not only unionization but many other aspects of labour market policies have responded to changing trade-offs between employment and wages. To the extent that collective bargaining, non-employment subsidies, and other institutions are meant to trade off un-employment and higher wages, a more elastic labour demand calls for a smaller mark-up of wages over non-employment opportunities, and should lead to lower unemployment. As we know from Figures 14.2 and 14.7, Dutch wage moderation was associated in the 1980s with a declining unemployment rate and higher employment. It was the result of an agreement, signed at Wassenaar in 1982, exchanging unions' wage moderation and a relaxation of part-time and other work rules, for employers' commitment to employment generation through investment. That agreement was arguably eased by the fact that strong economic links between the Netherlands and Germany, already irrevocably committed to fixed exchange rates and full trade liberalization, made it possible for the Dutch to gain a great deal of employment with relatively small wage declines. But while a more favourable trade-off between wages and employment should make deregulation easier, as shown in Figure 14.10 economic integration and stronger product market integration can actually increase unemployment in the presence of obsolete unreformed institutions. In Figure 14.7, German wages (and other labour costs) kept on growing fast until the early 1990s (the series is broken at the time of German unification). German employment losses resulting from such stiff wage growth can only have been larger as Dutch unions moderated their demands, and production could take place just across the border, than if Germany had been sealed to foreign competition.

The single market (launched in 1992, implemented over the 1990s, and completed in the Eurozone by adoption of a single currency in 1999) made such considerations relevant to interactions between many other European countries which, of course, differ in many respects. As regards policies, concern with high unemployment does produce increasing pressure towards reforms in European labour markets as contractual negotiations and legal requirements at the national (or regional) level face strong deregulatory pressure from *competition between systems*, in the form of lower unionization, wage moderation, increasing wage differentials, and nominal and real wage flexibility. Market integration and macroeconomic policy restraints, however, need not automatically lead to deregulation. Increased market pressure may in fact generate demand for continuing and perhaps increasing the current levels of labour market regulation, particularly for specific socio-economic groups.

In Scandinavian countries, active policies were and remain more prevalent than in continental Europe, but the costs of activation became unbearable in Sweden as unemployment rose from less than 2 to more than 8 per cent in the early 1990s crisis, and government relief jobs and training programmes reached in excess of 6 per cent of the population. As a consequence, the relevant programmes were scaled back quite drastically in the mid-1990s. Similarly, the recent labour market reforms in Germany made that country's largely passive unemployment policies more active and much less generous. Provisions for stronger job search monitoring were introduced by the 'Job-AQTIV' reform of 2002, and the 'Hartz IV' reform package (as of January 2005) improves incentives to take up jobs: on the one hand by reducing (to 70 per cent for 400–700 Euros of monthly earnings) the rate at which benefits are withdrawn as labour income increases; on the other hand, and more importantly, by imposing sanctions on workers who refuse job offers, shortening and tightening eligibility for standard unemployment benefits, and also reducing benefits available in high-unemployment East Germany below those available to more productive West Germans. So far, the most visible results of the reform have been a large increase in the number of unemployed workers, because recipients of social assistance are now supposed to seek work, and a sharp decrease of the government's popularity, resulting in its electoral defeat. In the past, increasing unemployment might have raised calls for more generous subsidies. Now, it is actually a consequence of reforms meant to increase incentives to obtain gainful employment, a politically difficult way to address the unemployment problem, especially if not accompanied by complementary reforms—such as financial market reforms—aimed at reducing households' desire to obtain protection from labour market shocks.

Monetary union is also relevant to national reform incentives, because if national fiscal and monetary policies are restrained or superseded by the Employment and Stability Pact and by adoption of a single currency in the Euro-area, it is no longer possible to target high unemployment by aggregate demand management—which, as mentioned, can only result in high inflation and growing debt when unemployment has structural roots—leaving structural reforms as the only, obvious instrument for unemployment reduction. Lack of national monetary policy may, however, if it eliminates the inflation consequences of national labour market problems, reduce rather than strengthen the incentives to undertake structural reform, which may be further hampered by the inability to use macroeconomic and fiscal policy instruments to smooth adjustment trajectories and buffer the distributional implications, especially across generations. Hence, the national policy reforms mentioned above are, not surprisingly, hesitant, sparse, and politically difficult. And while monetary union does prevent labour market rigidity from generating high inflation, it need not prevent it from generating loss of competitiveness.

In fact, Figure 14.11 shows that since 2000 Dutch and Italian wages both increased much faster than labour productivity. Unit labour costs, the ratio of gross wages to production per worker in manufacturing, remained roughly constant in Germany after monetary unification, and declined strongly in the USA (shown for comparison purposes) as a result of strong output growth and higher productivity. But they increased by some 25 per cent in the Netherlands, where wage growth was no longer as restrained as we saw

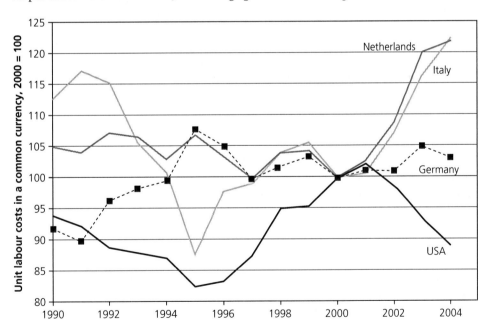

Figure 14.11 Unit labour costs in manufacturing in the Netherlands, Italy, Germany, and the USA, 1990–2004

Source: OECD *Economic Outlook* database.

in Figure 14.7, and in Italy, where wage growth was slower but still faster than in the late 1990s (when Italy's path towards joining EMU was made possible by wage-moderation agreements which, beginning in 1992, broke the wage pressure–devaluation spiral discussed in section 14.2) and productivity failed to keep pace.

Labour market policy in the European Union

Labour demand and macroeconomic policies and developments are both importantly affected by the single market and by monetary unification, but it is difficult to establish a European supranational labour market policy framework. As discussed above, very many structural circumstances and policy instruments interact in complex ways even within each country's labour market, and the policy configuration of European countries is very heterogeneous. Thus, the European constitutional Treaty states that 'a highly competitive social market economy, aiming at full employment and social progress' is a basic objective of the EU, but explicitly rules out supranational legislation in the employment area, where Member States have exclusive competence and only 'exchanges of information and best practices' are suggested. Since 1998, the *Luxembourg process* has envisioned an active role for the European Commission in monitoring and formulating recommendations, on the basis of the annual Joint Employment Report, using criteria meant to address employment problems through 'activation' policies such as training and job finding assistance. In terms of the simple mechanisms illustrated by Figures 14.4 and 14.10, upgrading the labour force through such policies would allow a larger proportion of it to clear the minimum-wage hurdle without removing the legal, contractual, or fiscal features that underlie high labour costs. Similarly, the *Lisbon agenda* agreed in 2000 has focused attention on higher employment rates (rather than lower unemployment rates) as a high-priority objective, placing strong emphasis on productivity enhancement through lifelong learning and knowledge, aimed at aligning worker productivity with wage aspirations.

Lacking legislative powers, EU policies aimed at these objectives are based on discussion and comparison of national policies and outcomes. While this can increase the transparency of policy-making in this field, such open coordination methods have unsurprisingly proved to have no reform-triggering power, especially in the larger and more heterogeneous countries where unemployment is a more serious problem. Labour market policies, like taxation and subsidies, are *subsidiary* in the European Union: their objectives should be achieved at the level of Member States. Since countries are highly heterogeneous, it is in fact difficult to envision agreement in such matters. Binding supranational legislation has proved difficult to harmonize in related areas of shared competence, such as health and safety regulation, which includes work rules: a directive on working time specifies levels less restrictive than national ones in all countries except the UK (which had no law in this area and opposed the introduction of EU-level legislation). Subsidiarity, however, is not appropriate for labour market policies if, as argued above, tighter international integration of product and labour markets makes it difficult for each country to choose its desired wage–employment combination: by flattening the labour demand schedules of the figures encountered in this chapter, international competition removes national degrees of freedom in labour market policies, and tends to enforce deregulation. This is a good thing if regulation is inefficient. But if regulation is in place, it presumably does aim at goals perceived to be important: independent policy choices and competition between systems will fail to maximize collective welfare if it implies that those goals remain unfulfilled.

14.4 Conclusions

Unemployment in Europe may once have been blamed on macroeconomic shocks, or viewed as an acceptable side-effect of desirable labour market institutions. Economic and monetary union has eliminated exchange rate realignments and other sources of macroeconomic instability, and by fostering product market competition has made it increasingly difficult for collective institutions and policies to interfere with laissez faire labour market outcomes. Workers, however, still wish to be protected from labour market shocks. And while national unions and national systems of labour market regulation and social insurance can no longer have the more or less desirable effects reviewed above on the level, composition, and cyclical behaviour of employment, no effective supranational coordination in the relevant area addresses the lack of opportunities for individual insurance in poorly developed financial markets. Concerns about the sustainability of this policy framework are stronger as the EU encompasses countries of Central and Eastern Europe with significantly lower wage costs and different institutional structures. They motivate resistance to completion of the single market in services, disregard of the Stability and Growth Pact's fiscal constraints, and uneasiness with the European Central Bank's independence.

Within a fully integrated European economy, labour market policies would need to be harmonized. It remains to be seen whether EU labour markets will converge in terms of institutional structure and/or in terms of outcomes. The two types of convergence do not imply each other, because the economic and social structure of EU countries is far from homogeneous. To the extent that such structural differences call for different policy approaches, homogeneous policies would result in diverging labour market performances, as in the case of regions within Germany, Spain, and Italy. If the stress generated by international influences on existing institutional arrangements does not result in appropriately harmonized reforms, however, it may well threaten the political sustainability of economic integration itself.

■ DISCUSSION QUESTIONS

1. Which institutional features imply that unemployment increases sharply when labour demand falls? Which ones slow down subsequent declines of unemployment?

2. How do inflation expectations and labour market structure determine shifts of the Phillips curve?

3. What role did productivity growth and wage developments play in determining unemployment in the 1970s, and in the 2000s after adoption of a single currency?

4. Which labour market institutions prevent formation of low-wage employment relationships, and when is this a particularly acute problem?

5. Can active labour market policies reconcile high employment and wage equality?

6. How does economic integration affect the pros and cons of national and international labour market policies?

7. What does 'subsidiarity' mean, and why are most labour market policies excluded from Union competences in the EU Treaty?

■ FURTHER READING

Blanchard (2006) provides a more analytical and very clear review of the history of European unemployment and of changing theoretical and policy approaches to its solution over the past twenty years, with many references. It can be found on the internet at http://www.economic-policy.org, along with an extensive searchable database of policy-oriented, accessible articles dealing with various aspects of labour markets in Europe and elsewhere. The CESifo DICE ('Database for Institutional Comparisons in Europe') at http://www.cesifo.de/DICE offers detailed information on a variety of labour market policies, as well as comparative reports on different countries' institutional structures; Ochel (2005), for example, offers a clear and detailed description of recent German labour market reforms. A more detailed discussion of Phillips curve mechanisms can be found in macroeconomics textbooks. Carlin and Soskice (2006, chapter 3) offer a particularly extensive and advanced theoretical treatment of interactions between monetary policy and unemployment; their chapter 18 reviews unemployment experiences, and section 18.4 discusses EMU. Agell (2002) reviews the theoretical motivations and empirical implications of labour market regulation; Bertola *et al.* (2000) offer a more detailed discussion of national policy frameworks in the context of the European economic integration process.

   Plentiful statistical and institutional information can also be found navigating the websites of the Organization for Economic Cooperation and Development (OECD), http://www.oecd.org, and of the European Union, http://europa.eu.int. For employment and unemployment, http://www.oecd.org/topic/0,2686,en_2649_37457_1_1_1_1_37457,00.html is the appropriate starting-point at the OECD. Detailed information on the European Union's Lisbon policy agenda is at http://europa.eu.int/growthandjobs/index_en.htm. For the employment policy guidelines, and the reports prepared by the member countries on their own situation and strategy, see http://europa.eu.int/comm/employment_social/employment_strategy/index_en.htm.

■ REFERENCES

Agell, J. (2002), 'On the Determinants of Labour Market Institutions: Rent Seeking vs Social Insurance', *German Economic Review* 3/2: 107–35.

Bertola, G., Jimeno, J. F., Marimon, R., and Pissarides, C. (2001), 'EU Welfare Systems and Labour Markets: Diverse in the Past, Integrated in the Future?', in G. Bertola, T. Boeri, and G. Nicoletti (eds.), *Welfare and Employment in a United Europe* (Cambridge, MA: MIT Press), 23–122

Blanchard, O. (2006), 'European Unemployment: The Evolution of Facts and Ideas', *Economic Policy*, 45: 7–59.

Carlin, W. and Soskice, D. (2006), *Macroeconomics* (Oxford: Oxford University Press).

Ochel, W. (2005), 'Hartz IV: Welfare to Work in Germany', *CESifo DICE Report* 3/2: 18–25.

15 | The Challenges of Enlargement

Susan Schadler

15.1 The 2004 enlargement

On 1 May 2004 ten new members acceded to the European Union—eight Central European, formerly centrally planned countries (Czech Republic, Estonia, Hungary, Latvia, Lithuania, Poland, Slovakia, and Slovenia) and two Mediterranean countries (Cyprus and Malta). This enlargement was in many respects the boldest of the five enlargements to date. It brought in more countries and increased the population of the Union by more than any previous enlargement. And most importantly, eight of the ten new members not only had substantially lower income levels than the existing members, but also were just emerging from a legacy of almost fifty years of central planning.

The 2004 enlargement accordingly represented a leap in the diversity of EU membership, presenting the Union with a range of new issues: how to maintain the Union's commitment to supporting the development of the most disadvantaged regions; how to cover the costs of upgrading institutions, environmental standards, and infrastructure deficiencies essential to integrating the economies of the new and old members; how to deal with migration pressures stemming from large differences in wage levels between members; how to ensure that large capital inflows—consequent to the opening of capital accounts required for EU accession—do not open the door to risky foreign exposures; and how to pave the way for each new member to fulfil its commitment to adopt the Euro as its national currency. The enlargement also presented opportunities for the old members to benefit from the opening of new channels for competition and from the expansion of opportunities for lowering costs of production through outsourcing and offshoring of production.

Since the 2004 enlargement, two other candidates, Bulgaria and Romania, completed negotiations on the implementation of the *acquis communautaire*—the existing body of EU law—and acceded to the EU in January 2007. As for the new members before them, these negotiations involved agreeing on transitional periods for implementing the laws of the European Union fully and for acquiring full rights under the *acquis*. At present there are three other candidate countries (Croatia, Macedonia, and Turkey), Croatia and Turkey having started negotiations on the *acquis*. Macedonia has not yet been given a date to start negotiations, pending compliance with several economic conditions. Further out on the horizon are possible requests for candidacy from other Balkan countries. This chapter will focus on the 2004 enlargement, but the issues raised will be equally important to future expansions of the Union.

The plan of this chapter is to start, in section 15.2, with a brief description of the key economic dimensions of the 2004 enlargement. Section 15.3 presents a framework for understanding the fundamental economic and structural differences between new and old members and the market forces for labour and capital flows these should unleash. It examines the various channels through which post-enlargement integration will occur and how institutional change will interact with labour and capital flows to accelerate the catch-up of new members' incomes to those in the EU-15. Section 15.4 explains the commitment of each new member to replace its domestic currency with the Euro, the conditions that must be fulfilled for successful Euro adoption and the considerations surrounding the timing of Euro adoption.

15.2 Economic dimensions of enlargement

The 2004 enlargement expanded the EU in many dimensions—most strikingly in terms of geography, population, and living standards. Bringing in ten new Member States increased the land mass of the EU by 23 per cent, the population by about 19 per cent (to 459 million), but GDP (measured at PPP)[1] by only about 10 per cent. The differences between these various dimensions of the enlargement reflect a relatively low population density and a low level of average GDP per capita in the new members (about 50 per cent, weighted by population, of the average of the old members). Looking ahead, population growth in the new members is expected to be slightly slower than in the old members, so that by 2050 the ten new members should represent about 14.5 per cent of the EU population (at existing borders). Populations of new members are younger and are on average ageing more rapidly (although trends vary widely). This is partly because of emigration of younger workers to the EU-15. Nevertheless, new Member States will not significantly mitigate the demographic challenges that lie ahead for the Union as a whole.

The new members are, however, a potentially significant source of dynamism for the Union. Though growth rates vary over a wide range, they have in recent years been substantially above those in the old Member States. During 2004–5, annual average GDP per capita growth in the new members amounted to 7.5 per cent, against 3.5 per cent in the EU-15. During this period, something of a schism developed between the rapid per capita growth rates in the three Baltic countries (averaging about 11.5 per cent a year) and the five Central European countries (averaging 6.5 per cent a year). Reflecting the massive strides in increasing the outward orientation of the new members during the transition, their exports grew by an average of 18 per cent during this period, as compared with 10 per cent in the EU-15. This meant that the share of new Member States' exports in global imports rose from 1.9 per cent to 2.9 per cent, while the trade share of the EU-15 remained steady at about 13 per cent.

Trade ties between the new and old members are strong. Although the previously centrally planned new members had weak trade ties to the EU-15 prior to 1990, the opening of their economies resulted in a rapid reorientation of trade westward. By 2004, trade with the EU-25 as a share of GDP was for most countries at least as great as for the EU-15. And the relatively strong intra-industry trade—that is trade between industries within the same broad type of activity—also points to the linkages between the production structures of the new and old members. Outsourcing and offshoring of inputs to Western industries have been key to the deepening of these linkages.

Macroeconomic and financial structures of the new and old Member States differ profoundly but, in many respects, are complementary. Nowhere is this more evident than in external current account positions. In general, the new members run large current account deficits, in contrast to the approximate balance for the EU-15 as a whole. Notwithstanding the rapid growth of new members' exports since the beginning of transition, imports have grown faster. Another way, however, to look at current account deficits of new members is as the excess of investment over savings.[2] Such an excess is not surprising. With relatively underdeveloped economies, the new members have plentiful investment opportunities. Also, given the scarcity of consumer goods during central planning and desire to smooth consumption in the face of expected future rapid income growth, their savings rates are low (Figure 15.1).

Old members, on the other hand, are generally capital rich—that is, they have high ratios of fixed capital relative to their domestic labour force—and therefore lower investment relative to their GDP. They also tend to save higher shares of GDP than their lower income neighbors. Current account deficits—the excess of investments over saving—in the new members, therefore, have been financed by capital inflows largely from EU-15 countries.

The structure of production in the new Member States is also remarkably different from that of the old members, though differences are diminishing. With wage levels about half the average in the old members, new members tend to have substantially more labour-intensive production structures than the old members. Manufacturing is favoured over services and agriculture (which is substantial only in Poland), although in the past decade, services have claimed a rapidly growing share in production (Figure 15.2).

A third stark difference between new and old members is in the depth of financial markets. On two common measures of financial market depth—broad money relative to GDP and bank credit to the private sector relative to GDP—the financial markets in the new Central European members were by end-2004 some 30–60 per cent the size of those in the EU-15 (Figure 15.3). These gaps reflect financial repression of the central planning era, when banking was generally centralized in large, state-owned unibanks that channelled savings to largely industrial uses. With transition, these banks were broken up into a banking structure patterned after those in the EU-15: central banks (charged with formulating and executing monetary policy and holding official foreign exchange reserves) and privatized commercial banks. Indeed, foreign (for the most part Western European) banks were large-scale purchasers of these new commercial banks with the result that foreign ownership (by assets) at end-2004 ranged from to 30 per cent (Slovenia) to over 90 per cent (Estonia, Czech Republic, Lithuania, Slovakia) of the banking sectors in the new members. Nevertheless, with credit/GDP starting from very low bases and constraints on growth from financial prudence and a minimal lending culture, banking sectors remain underdeveloped.

In one notable respect—macroeconomic stability—most new members show remarkable similarities to the old members (Figure 15.4). Following immediate post-transition bursts in inflation (some of which took several years to quell), each new member now has

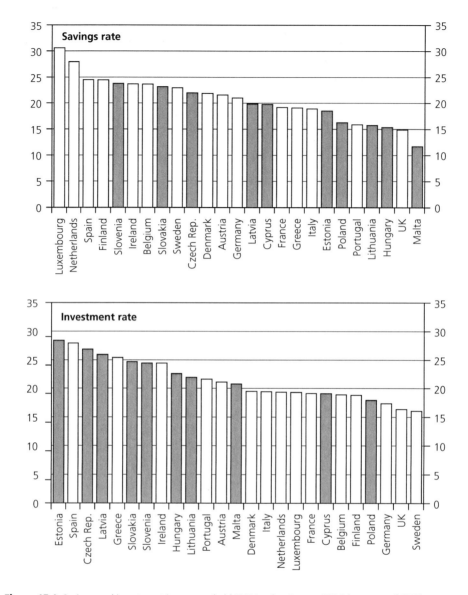

Figure 15.1 Savings and investment in new and old EU Member States, 2004 (per cent of GDP)
Source: IMF, *World Economic Outlook*.

low inflation. Monetary policy frameworks—currency boards or fixed exchange rates in several and inflation targeting with floating exchange rates in the rest—have allowed countries to tame inflation and anchor inflation expectations. For the most part, budget positions, ranging from a surplus in Estonia to moderate deficits in most others, have also converged. Exceptions are Hungary and Poland, where general government deficits crept up to levels above even the highest deficit countries among the EU-15.

Macroeconomic policy issues are clearly in the domain of EU concerns. Members of the EU are obliged to treat economic policy as a matter of common interest and to participate

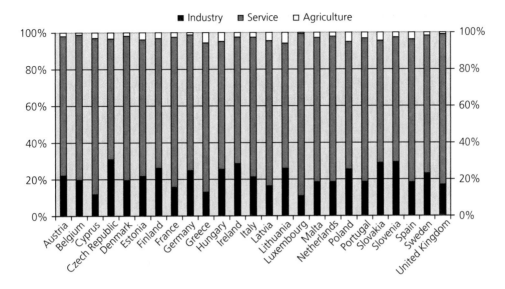

Figure 15.2 Structure of production in new and old EU Member States, 2004 (per cent of GDP)
Source: Eurostat.

in the multilateral coordination and surveillance procedures for macroeconomic polices. This includes submitting to the excessive deficit procedure under the Stability and Growth Pact (SGP)—the set of guidelines to promote sound fiscal policies in the EU. To this end, countries must prepare Convergence Programmes—rolling three-year projections for the economy and projections for public finances. They are also expected to avoid excessive exchange rate fluctuations, competitive devaluations, and exchange rates that are inconsistent with economic fundamentals.

15.3 The challenge of real convergence

This snapshot of the economic dimensions of the 2004 enlargement makes clear that the income gap between new and old Member States is one aspect of a bundle of related economic differences. This section explores the factors that underlie the income gaps and the dynamics that they will produce as integration in an enlarged EU proceeds. All members stand to benefit from this process—new members from catching up to old members' income levels (what is referred to as real convergence) and old members from the dynamic gains in their global competitiveness as they exploit these complementarities. But all countries will need to support the process by ensuring that policies position economies to absorb the change. The objective in this section is to characterize the underlying causes of the income gap and identify the processes that will close it.

The income differential between new and old members is a reflection of three basic gaps. First, workers in the new Member States are matched with much less and poorer

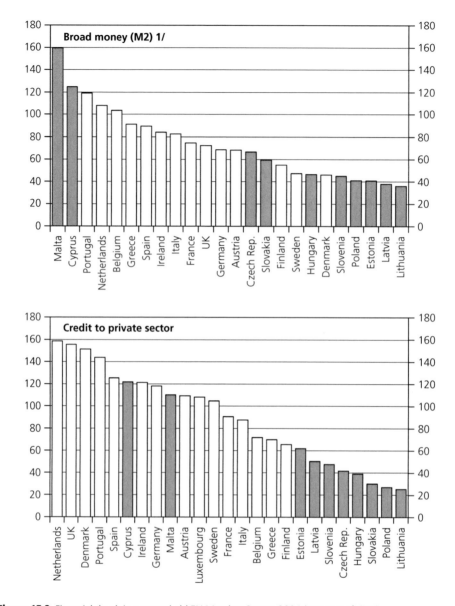

Figure 15.3 Financial depth in new and old EU Member States, 2004 (per cent of GDP)

[a] Broad money is defined as M2 for all countries except Germany and Greece where it is M3.
Sources: IMF, IFS.

quality capital. Second, a smaller share of the working age population in the new members actually works. And third, the environments for doing business are much less hospitable in terms, for example, of the quality of judicial institutions, of infrastructure, of technology, and of the regulatory frameworks. The remainder of this subsection will explore these gaps using a simple production function framework describing the inputs to produce a country's 'bundle' of GDP.

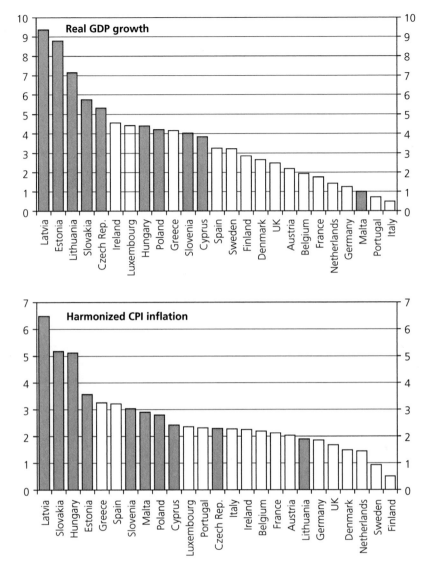

Figure 15.4 Macroeconomic conditions in old and new EU Member States (per cent; 2004–5 average)

Source: IMF, *World Economic Outlook*.

(1)
$$Y = \frac{AK^{\alpha}L^{1-\alpha}}{POP}$$

Here Y is real per capita GDP, K is the capital stock, L is labour input, POP is the population, α is the elasticity of output with respect to capital, and A is 'total factor productivity' (a residual capturing all influences apart from physical capital and labour that contribute to production). Per capita GDP in the new members relative to the old members results

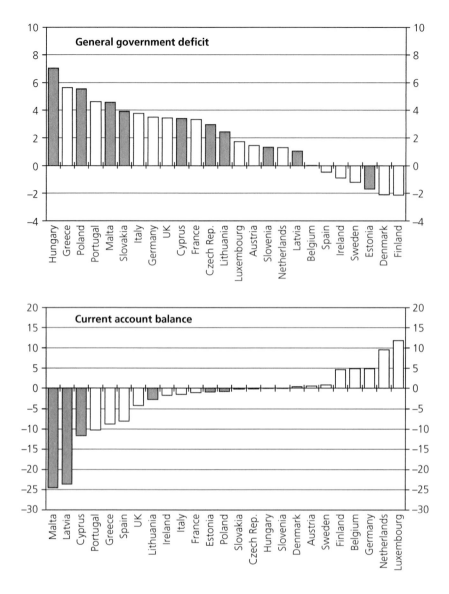

Figure 15.4 (*continued*)

from making a ratio of the function in the new members to that of the old members (assuming the same production technology represented by α).

$$(2) \qquad\qquad\qquad y = ak^\alpha e$$

Here y is the ratio between new and old member real per capita GDP, a is the ratio of A's, k is the capital labour ratio (K/L) in the new members relative to that in the old members, and e is the ratio of the share of the domestic population that is employed (L/P) in new members relative to that in the old members. The gaps between new and old members in

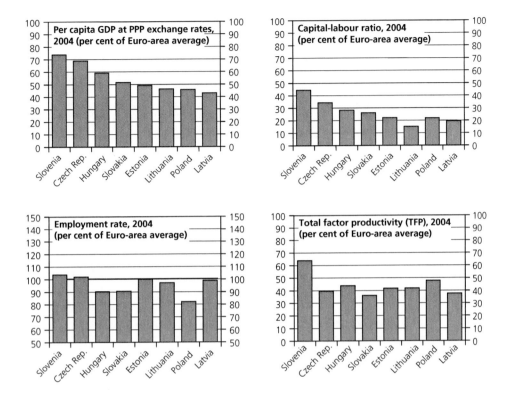

Figure 15.5 Production and inputs to production, 2004

Source: Schadler *et al.* (2006).

each dimension of this simple framework are large (Figure 15.5).[3] Understanding what lies behind these gaps sets the stage for exploring how enlargement is affecting the dynamics of European integration.

First, new members are capital poor compared with old members. Massive forced savings during the era of central planning resulted in large build-ups of capital, much of which proved worthless after the conversion to market mechanisms. Thus, even with relatively high investment rates during the decade and a half since central planning ended, capital–labour ratios in the new members are estimated to be some 15–45 per cent of the average of those in Euro-area countries.

Second, employment rates—the share of the working age population employed—are for several countries low relative to the Euro-area average, itself well below other industrial country standards. Transition entailed, for most countries, waves of job destruction as overstaffed and inefficient enterprises closed or downsized. And although this process has largely run its course, net job creation has been slow to take off. Recorded employment is particularly low in Hungary, Poland, and Slovakia.

Third, total factor productivity (TFP) in most of the new members is estimated at less than half that of the Euro-area average. Reflecting the catch-all nature of TFP, pinning down the causes for this gap is difficult. Recent studies have emphasized the quality of physical infrastructure (for example, roads, other transportation structures, and communication facilities), managerial know-how, and institutions—the 'rules of the game' that determine the incentives for production, investment, and consumption—as among the most important determinants of TFP.[4] Institutions in this sense can be characterized at three levels: (1) organizational entities (such as independent central banks and participation in international trade agreements), (2) regulatory and legal frameworks (such as protections of property rights, laws to guide corporate governance, and limits on politicians' activities), and (3) what might be seen as deep determinants of growth such as political stability, geopolitical influences on a country, and linguistic or religious characteristics.

The combined effects of these three gaps lead to powerful incentives for labour and capital flows between the new members and the EU-15.

Consider first the labour market. We have already seen that real wages in the new members are a faction of those in the EU-15. From the production function framework, it is clear that this reflects the lower productivity of labour in the new members owing to both lower capital per worker and lower TFP.[5] Eventually, investment and TFP growth in the new members will push up the marginal product of labour and therefore wages in those countries. But during the adjustment period (the length of which will depend on policies to support those changes) the real wage differential will constitute a substantial incentive for east to west migration of workers seeking higher paid jobs in EU-15 countries.

A second implication of low capital–labour ratios in the new members—one explored in Lipschitz *et al.* 2005—is that relative rates of return on investment (the increase in output (Y) that results from a given investment (or increase in capital input (K)) stand to be quite high in the new members. This is a reflection of the inverse relationship between capital–labour ratios and the marginal product of capital.[6] Countries with low capital endowments per worker have, all other things equal, high rates of return on investment. This truism has led to what is called the Lucas Paradox: why do global investment funds not flow overwhelmingly to countries with relatively low endowments of capital (Lucas 1990). Most probes of the question point to the tendency for divergences in TFP largely, or even disproportionately, to offset the effect of differences in capital–labour ratios on rates of return. In other words, investment does not flood into countries with weak capital endowments because weak legal, institutional, and physical infrastructure and general managerial know-how hold down the marginal product of capital or rate of return in those countries. And in some instances the negative effect from TFP gaps is so large that it creates the expectation of vastly inferior rates of return on capital even in capital-poor countries. Yet, net capital inflows (roughly equivalent to current account deficits) are large in several of the new members, suggesting that the Lucas Paradox is being overcome at least to some degree.

Why does enlargement matter for these labour and capital flows? The same underlying economic incentives for such flows are present between all relatively rich and relatively poor countries. Is Europe just experiencing the same influences present in the global economy, but writ slightly smaller? In fact, two fundamental aspects of the enlargement stand to have a profound effect on factor flows. First, accession to the EU unleashes some processes that should hasten the narrowing of the TFP gap. And second, enlargement is designed to eliminate economic borders that in other countries impede labour and capital mobility. The rest of this section examines these influences.

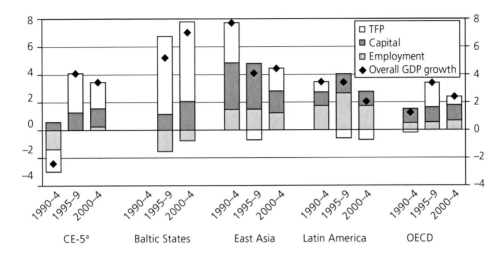

Figure 15.6 Contributions to average GDP growth (per cent), 1990–2004

ᵃ Includes Czech Republic, Hungary, Poland, Slovakia, and Slovenia.
Source: Schadler *et al.* (2007)

Closing the TFP gap

TFP growth in the new Member States has been very rapid by emerging market standards. During the past ten years, contributions of TFP to overall output growth in the new members have consistently exceeded those in other major groups of emerging market countries (Figure 15.6). Indeed, in contrast to the other groups, TFP growth has been by far the largest contributor (of capital, labour, and TFP) to the region's relatively high growth rates.

An obvious question is whether improvements at such a rapid pace can continue. Have the easy gains following the end of central planning been achieved, so a sharp slowdown can be expected? Or does the strong record—one that differentiates the Central European Countries (CECs) from other emerging markets where growth was much more closely related to capital accumulation and, to a lesser extent, increased labour use—presage further gains to come? Without being able to identify the causes of past rapid TFP growth, this question is debatable. Nevertheless, with TFP in the new Central European members at about one-quarter to one-half the average of the EU-15, substantial income catch-up will require large increases in TFP. Entry into the EU should help achieve these gains through two main mechanisms—aligning legal structures with those in the EU and using EU Structural Funds and Cohesion Funds to support improvements in institutions and infrastructure.

The entry negotiations between each prospective member and the European Commission prior to any enlargement entail reaching agreements on how each country adopts the *acquis communautaire*. For the negotiations culminating in the 2004 enlargement, the *acquis* was divided into thirty-one chapters—each encompassing the EU law on a specific area (refer to EU website). Many of these chapters concern issues directly or indirectly influencing institutions that will impact future TFP growth. For example, chapters covering small and medium-sized enterprises, science and research, education and training, justice and home affairs, and financial control address a range of shortcomings that are likely to detract from business environments or otherwise hold back TFP in the new members. Much of the *acquis* has already been implemented, though derogations on both obligations and privileges are numerous. As derogations are lifted, improvements in institutions are likely to continue.

Sizable financial transfers from the EU budget to the new members are a second aspect of enlargement that will hasten TFP convergence.[7] These transfers, which fall under a variety of budgetary objectives, are broadly designed to help offset income differentials in the Union (Common Agricultural Policy instruments and support for farmers in Less Favourable Areas (LFA)), compensate new members who could otherwise be net payers to the EU budget (Compensation Payments), support existing EU policies such as those to administer the borders of the European Union (Internal Policies), or fund programmes (for example, to develop physical or institutional infrastructure) that address the causes of income differentials or of differences in countries' abilities to meet other EU standards (Structural and Cohesion Funds).[8] These last are obviously particularly important for increasing TFP growth. The structure of transfers varies according to the characteristics of the economy (Figure 15.7): countries with lower per capita GDP receive a relatively large share of Structural Funds while richer countries receive a larger share of Compensation Funds. The overall size of transfers is linked to the degree of real income convergence of each member to the EU average (Figure 15.8).

The amount of EU transfers to the new members is set to increase. At the Copenhagen summit in 2002, EU members committed 39.1 billion Euros (1999 prices, around 2 per cent of new members' average annual GDP during 2004–6) for the new members during 2004–6. This commitment was divided between agriculture, structural actions, cash transfers, and other uses. Payments appropriations in the EU budget, however, were only 23.4 billion Euros, and actual transfers during the period were substantially less than

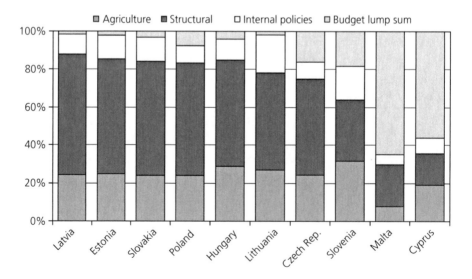

Figure 15.7 Structure of available EU funds, 2004–6

Source: Rosenberg and Sierhej (2007).

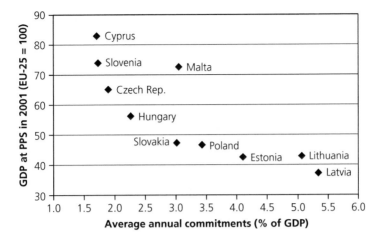

Figure 15.8 EU commitments and real convergence level

Source: Rosenberg and Sierhej (2007).

this amount. This reflected the expectation (based in part on the experience of existing members) that, because almost two-thirds of the commitment was for projects that needed to be planned and implemented before disbursement, countries would not be able to implement all programmes required to receive the full committed amount during 2004– 6. Actual disbursement was some 30 per cent of the Copenhagen commitment at end-2005 but could, according to official estimates, have increased to as much as 60 per cent by end-2006. Disbursement of most of the unused commitment can continue after 2006.

The EU has a new Financial Perspective for 2007–13 which will increase annual commitments for transfers to the new members through the Structural Funds from an average of about 2 per cent of new members' GDP per year during 2004–6 to an average of about 3.5 per cent during 2007–13. Total commitments (including transfers beyond Structural Funds) may be around 5 per cent of average annual GDP. The challenge ahead for the new members will be to increase the efficiency with which they plan and implement projects supported by Structural Funds so that they can raise the relatively low rates of fund usage. These increased commitments would then be a significant boon to the development of infrastructure and institutions and in turn the convergence of TFP.

Eliminating economic borders—labour migration

Higher wages in the EU-15 than in the new members will remain for some time a strong incentive for workers to move from east to west. As the *acquis communautaire* requires free movement of labour within the EU, enlargement should have removed any constraint preventing labour migration from responding to the wage gap. However, responding to fears of a surge in inward migration, all of the EU-15 except Ireland, Sweden, and the UK availed themselves of derogation for up to seven years on the free movement of labour from the new members. On May 1 2006, Finland, Greece, Spain, and Portugal also opened their borders to workers from new members. Thus while the economic incentives for

BOX 15.1 THE STRUCTURE OF EU TRANSFERS[a]

Transfers from the EU budget to members come through a variety of channels (see Figure 15.9). About a third of all transfers to the new members will be through automatic payments set by formula. These include direct payments to farmers, market interventions in agriculture, transfers to support 'internal policies' (which are dominated by costs of administering borders), and compensation for payments to the EU budget that exceed other transfers to the new members. Another (approximately) two-thirds of the commitments are conditional on project implementation in a variety of areas including infrastructure development, environmental standards, and rural development. Structural and Cohesion Funds comprise the most important share of the latter.

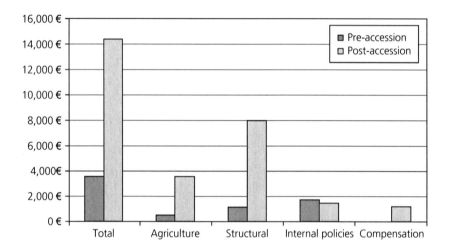

Figure 15.9 Structure of available post-accession funds (annual average, million Euros in 2004 prices)

Source: Rosenberg and Sierhej (2007).

The Structural and Cohesion Funds are the tools of the EU Structural Actions. They are geared towards realizing three broad objectives. The first, and most important in terms of the amount of financial support, is promoting the development and structural adjustment of regions where development has lagged behind the Union average—that is, regions where GDP per capita is less than 75 per cent of the EU average in PPP terms. The second objective is to support economic and social conversion in areas facing structural difficulties—typically regions with falling shares of industry and high unemployment. The third objective is support for modernization of education, training, and employment policies and systems. Cohesion funds support investment in large infrastructure and environmental projects in countries where GDP per capita is less than 90 per cent of the EU average.

[a] This box draws heavily on Sommer (2004).

Table 15.1 Estimates of migration from new Member States, 2004

Population	Counter-factual without enlargement	Actual (May–Dec. 2004) %
Ireland	3,100	31,000
Sweden	6,200	4,000[a]
United Kingdom	12,000	130,000

[a] While this is less than the counter-factual, it is about double the actual 2,100 in 2003.
Source: Boerri (2006).

migration are clear, it is hard to tell yet how large the ultimate migration will be or in turn how large the resulting pressure for wage differentials to narrow will be.

Early estimates, however, suggest migration and its effects on wages even after derogations for all EU-15 end will be modest—far smaller than might be expected from the public protests in some EU-15 countries that motivated the derogation option. Boeri (2006) presents simulations of labour migration with and without restrictions on migration. He finds that with no restrictions on labour flows, net migration from the new members to the EU-15 would have amounted to about 300,000 per year in the first two years after enlargement and then would have fallen gradually to about 100,000 per year within seven years and about 12,000 in the long run. The resulting stock of migrants from the new members in the EU-15 would settle at about 3 million (or less than 1 per cent of the entire EU-15 population). The short experience of Ireland, Sweden, and the United Kingdom without restrictions since May 2004 broadly bears out the conclusion that inward migration will be modest (Table 15.1).

The implications for the new members may be larger and labour shortages could become a problem. With a population of about 78 million, the new Central European members stand to lose some 1 per cent of their working age population each year and in the long run about 10 per cent on a permanent basis. Yet it is worth remembering that the share of these countries' working age population that is not employed is among the highest in Europe. Consequently, migration may be largely matched by increases in labour force participation. Moreover, inflows to these countries from countries further east—Ukraine and Belarus, for example—may largely or fully compensate. Early reports suggest for example that some 8 per cent of the labour force in Latvia—where wage differentials vis-à-vis the EU-15 are largest—currently works in EU-15 countries. This appears to be giving rise to some skill shortages in Latvia. In the Czech Republic, on the other hand, net migration has occurred: more workers are immigrating to the Czech Republic from eastern (non-member) countries than Czech workers emigrating to the EU-15.

Overall, the immediate effect of fully opening borders would likely be modestly lower wages and native employment rates in the EU-15 and higher wages and broadly unchanged domestic employment rates in the new members. These changes also imply distributional effects: workers in receiving countries would lose, while profits of firms in the EU-15 and incomes of migrants would rise. Further dividing labour markets into skilled and unskilled and assuming the majority of migrants are unskilled suggests that unskilled labour would bear the highest costs. In all cases, however, much depends on the flexibility of labour markets—that is, the degree to which labour markets are free of restrictions such as minimum wages or collective bargaining power of unions that would prevent wage changes. The more flexible the labour markets, the more likely that any downward pressure on wages in the EU-15 would elicit investment that over time would push employment and wages back towards pre-enlargement levels. Boerri (2006) shows net impact effects on wages and employment of modest sizes, but points out that over time net effects would be far smaller. A critical consideration in modelling longer-term effects also would be the complementarity or substitutability of labour and capital movements. Specifically, restrictions on labour mobility or, equivalently, reluctance of workers in new members to migrate to foreign countries, may mean that capital mobility will be greater as EU-15 firms take advantage of opportunities to combine their know-how with new members' low wages. Models accounting for this influence in the counterfactual would show smaller net effects from migration. In other words, if workers cannot or will not move to production facilities in the EU-15, EU-15 firms may move production facilities to countries with lower-cost labour.

Eliminating economic borders—capital flows

The injunction in the *acquis communautaire* that all members of the EU allow free movement of capital has required varying degrees of liberalization depending on the extent of initial restrictions and the derogations that individual countries negotiated. At the most liberal end of the spectrum from the outset were the three Baltic countries and the Czech Republic, where financial transactions of both residents and non-residents were virtually free of restrictions well before the negotiations on the *acquis* began. At the more restrictive end of the spectrum were Slovenia, Slovakia, and Hungary, where full liberation of financial flows occurred shortly before May 2004. Poland had relatively few restrictions on financial flows primarily affecting non-bank resident purchases of foreign securities and non-bank non-resident purchases of Polish financial assets and removed them in 2003. Most countries retain some restrictions on other capital flows through derogations that will last up to seven years. In general, these affect purchases of land by foreigners and the share of pension fund portfolios that may be invested in foreign assets.

As with labour migration, it is early days yet to determine how enlargement will ultimately affect capital mobility. Yet, unlike for labour markets, virtually no restrictions on capital flows existed on the part of the EU-15, and most of the new members had at least partially removed restrictions on inflows and outflows several years before accession. So trends in capital flows during the past ten years provide some indication of the potential for capital market integration.

In fact, financial market integration of the new members has increased rapidly over the past decade (Lane and Milesi-Ferretti 2006). For the eight Central European new members (data for Cyprus and Malta are not available), gross capital inflows from all countries have averaged 10 per cent of GDP annually; even gross outflows, at 4.5 per cent of GDP, have been sizable. As a result, the most basic measure of financial integration—the sum of external assets and liabilities relative to GDP—almost doubled during 1995–2004, rising from 80 per cent of GDP to 160 per cent. This increase substantially outpaced that of a group of other emerging market and developing countries, which rose from about 100 per cent to 140 per cent during the same period. Nevertheless, at 160 per cent the absolute measure is well below the 400 per cent in the EU-15 at end-2004.

Equity capital has dominated inflows to Central Europe. Whereas equity capital in Central Europe accounted for only about 10 per cent of total external liabilities—well below the 25 per cent of other emerging market and developing countries—in 1994, it had risen to 50 per cent (as did the ratio in other emerging market and developing countries) by 2004. Thus by 2004, the share of equity capital in total external liabilities exceeded the 35 per cent in the EU-15. The lion's share of the equity capital inflows took the form of foreign direct investment (FDI), also in contrast to the EU15 where equity liabilities and FDI rose in tandem.

This pattern of inflows is not surprising. As we saw earlier, banking systems in the Central European countries remain small relative to the size of the economies and, with a couple of exceptions, fiscal deficits (and the related need for debt financing) have been small. Privatization, however, has proceeded on a substantial scale, offering foreign investors attractive options for diversification, participating in the expansion of the retail sector in new members, and offshoring (the transfer offshore of production facilities for intermediate inputs). The early evidence suggests that companies in Western Europe are indeed realizing substantial rates of return from their FDI in the new members. Marin (2006) examines the experience of Austrian and German companies that placed foreign direct investment in the new members and finds that on average they were able to achieve substantially higher levels of TFP than the average in the host country. This presumably indicates that by bringing in stronger management techniques, foreign firms can achieve higher rates of return than would be expected from a static analysis.

More generally, capital market integration with the EU-15, and in particular with the Euro-area countries, has been strong. Within the category of FDI (which itself has dominated the liability position), funds originating in the EU-15 accounted for more than 80 per cent of the stock as of end-2002: almost all of these liabilities were to Euro-area countries, except in the Baltic countries where Sweden and Denmark account for about 50 per cent of the total. The importance of the EU-15 is slightly less in other liabilities classes (portfolio equity, bank assets, and portfolio debt), but still exceeds 50 per cent of the totals in each subcategory for most countries.

The dominance of the EU-15 and especially of the Euro-area countries raises two key questions. First, is the close link between the Central European countries and Western Europe simply a function of geographical proximity and (probably) related trade ties? Or is there an institutional foundation—that is, the prospect of still closer future linkages from EU enlargement? Second, how much will the elimination of exchange rate risk influence future trends in financial integration with the Euro-area? Although investments —particularly FDI—in a fellow member of the EU has many attractive features stemming from the existence of the single market, exchange rate risk—the risk that a large depreciation of the value of new members' currencies could result in significant losses for investors exposed in foreign currency—remains an impediment. The new members, however, have the opportunity to eliminate this risk by adopting the Euro as their national currency. For countries that succeed in meeting the entry conditions, joining the Euro-area opens the possibility of gaining a significant edge in access to foreign funds and more rapid financial integration with Western Europe.

15.4 **Euro adoption**

Upon entry to the EU, the countries became members of the Economic and Monetary Union (EMU) with a committment to adopt the Euro as their national currency. The path to Euro adoption consists of several steps—selecting a central parity of the country's currency against the Euro and participating in ERMII (Exchange Rate Mechanism) for at least two years, meeting the Maastricht convergence criteria, and final conversion.[9] Countries may decide, based on their national interests, how quickly to attempt to take the preparatory steps (indefinite delay is an option), but they are bound to take them prior to adopting the Euro. Under the principle of equal treatment, new members of the EU aiming to adopt the Euro should neither be confronted with additional hurdles nor allowed to adopt the Euro on looser terms than the twelve existing Euro-area members. EU membership carries no obligation on the timing of joining ERMII, of meeting the Maastricht criteria, or of adopting the Euro.[10]

Maastricht criteria and the new members

The Maastricht criteria are intended as a test of sustainable convergence and consist of four standards.

1. An average rate of consumer price inflation, observed over a one-year period, not exceeding by more than 1.5 percentage points the average rate of inflation in the three 'best performing Member States' in terms of price stability.

2. The year-average nominal interest rate on a ten-year benchmark government security no more than 2 percentage points above the average in the same three countries used in the inflation test.

3. Participation in ERMII for at least two years while the currency trades without severe tensions within the normal fluctuation margins of ERMII and without a devaluation of the central parity. Statements by European Central Bank (ECB) and European Commission officials suggest that this may be interpreted to mean that the exchange rate cannot go below parity (that is, the lower 15 per cent of the band cannot be used) and even sizable depreciations in the top half of the band could be problematic.

4. A fiscal deficit that is not excessive—where excessive is defined as greater than 3 per cent of GDP—and public debt below 60 per cent of GDP. (Exceptions are allowed if the deficit is falling substantially and continually and is close to the reference value, or the excess over the reference value is exceptional and temporary. Exceptions to the debt limit are allowed if the debt ratio is dropping and approaching the reference value at a satisfactory rate.)

EMU members with a derogation from adopting the Euro may request at any time an assessment of their progress in fulfilling the Maastricht criteria. The European Commission and ECB prepare separate convergence reports as inputs to a decision by the Council of Economics and Finance Ministers of the EU (ECOFIN) on whether the country has fulfilled the conditions. In addition to the four criteria, Convergence Reports consider current account developments and prospects, trends in external competitiveness, and the compatibility of national legislation with the Statutes of the European System of Central Banks and the articles of EU treaties concerning the objectives and independence of national central banks.

As of end-2006, seven of the ten new members had joined ERMII with the intention of adopting the Euro at the earliest possible time. Estonia, Lithuania, and Slovenia joined in June 2004; Cyprus, Latvia, and Malta followed in May 2005; and Slovakia in November 2005. In July 2006, the ECOFIN Council assessed the position of Slovenia positively for Euro adoption and it will adopt the Euro in January 2007. Lithuania requested an assessment but its request was denied as its inflation rate was slightly (0.1 percentage point) over the Maastricht reference value (2.6 per cent at the time). Because its inflation rate exceeded the reference value, Estonia did not request a decision and remains in ERMII.

The way in which the Maastricht criteria are applied to the new members has generated some controversy. Several observers have asserted that the criteria, having been formulated for countries with high income levels and at a time when the potential for volatile capital flows was lower than now, are less pertinent for emerging market countries in the process of a substantial income catch-up. Two concerns are dominant.

First, many economists fear that the exchange rate stability criterion effectively turns ERMII into a narrow band arrangement—a framework frequently seen in the literature as prone to speculative attacks. This is of course not a problem for countries that have currency board arrangements (Estonia, Lithuania) or a history of fixed or close to fixed exchange rates (Latvia and Slovenia), but it is potentially a serious consideration for the countries that entered the EU with floating exchange rates (Czech Republic, Hungary, and Poland).

Second, the compatibility of the inflation criterion with the nominal exchange rate stability expected during prospective members' stay in ERMII is questionable. Rapidly growing countries tend to have real appreciations—price inflation faster than that in trading partners when expressed in the same currency. This reflects a variety of influences: faster productivity gains in traded than non-traded goods sectors, which pushes up the relative price of non-traded goods; increasing demand for relatively inelastic non-traded goods as countries become richer; and improvements in quality of non-traded goods not fully captured in measured prices. Whatever the cause, real appreciations are an empirical regularity in rapidly growing emerging markets. Thus, catching-up countries will have either higher inflation than in their more advanced trading partners or nominal appreciation of their currencies against those of more advanced countries. Several estimates put this equilibrium real appreciation at 1–3 per cent per year, the amount depending *inter alia* on the gap between income in the new member and in the EU-15. To get inflation below the Maastricht reference value (which, being 1.5 percentage points above the average of the three lowest inflation rates in the EU, is about equivalent to the Euro-area average) requires either inflation 1–3 percentage points above the Euro-area average or a nominal exchange rate appreciation of about this amount each year. Several analysts have argued that this would be possible for a country that has a short stay in ERMII and some exchange rate flexibility (Wyplotz 2001; Buiter and Grafe 2002; Schadler *et al.* 2005). But it would prove difficult—if not impossible—for the three countries with currency boards or fixed exchange rates. The experience of Estonia and Lithuania, which in mid-2006 met all eligibility criteria except that for inflation, bears out this concern.

When should countries adopt the Euro: benefits and costs

The first step in the new members' decisions about the timing of joining ERMII and then requesting assessments for joining the Euro-area entails reaching a view on the long-term benefits and costs of Euro adoption. The outcome of this assessment does not change the ultimate committment countries have made to adopt the Euro. But an assessment of clear and sizable benefits relative to costs would argue for urgency in undertaking the policy changes and preparations necessary for Euro adoption. A balanced or negative assessment would suggest a slower approach—possibly even an indefinite delay. For example, some have argued that waiting until a threshold degree of real convergence has been achieved would lower costs and raise benefits.

Broadly, the assessment of benefits and costs comes down to a few distinct considerations. Benefits come from gains for trade and growth and the elimination of exchange rate risk; costs stem from the possibility that the monetary policy that is right for the monetary union is wrong for the individual country. This cost could take the concrete form of greater volatility of inflation and growth in the absence of a monetary policy instrument to help absorb idiosyncratic shocks (shocks to an individual country that do not affect—or affect with substantially different strength—the currency union as a whole). Another consideration is the quality of the conduct of monetary policy: even if the ideal monetary policy for an individual country could produce greater stability than the currency union monetary policy, would the country actually have the policy acumen to implement it? Considerable empirical work has attempted to quantify benefits and costs for the new members.

Benefits of Euro adoption

Benefits will come through a number of channels that differ widely in terms of likely strength and amenability to quantification. The most easily measured benefits will come through trade creation and attendant gains in income. Some early estimates of gains from trade and growth from joining a currency union were startlingly large. These came from gravity models of bilateral trade relationships estimated on global panel data sets, including countries that are in and outside currency unions. Gravity models link the volume of trade between two countries to a variety of explanatory variables capturing country size, geographical proximity of the two countries, and institutions, with a dummy variable for membership in a currency union. Rose (2002) examines twenty-four such studies and finds a pooled estimate that currency union membership increases trade by some 85 per cent with currency union partners over a twenty-year period. The increase is shown to be almost entirely through trade creation rather than trade diversion.

A number of studies (Tenreyo and Persson 2001) point to possible upward bias in these estimates. Such a bias could arise from sampling unions that include overwhelmingly poor and/or small countries (sampling bias) and from the importance of existing trade patterns in the formation of currency unions themselves (simultaneity bias). As the actual experience with EMU becomes of sufficient duration to yield meaningful results on this

Table 15.2 Potential long-run gains for trade and per capita output after Euro adoption (per cent)

	Trade[a]	GDP[b]	Trade[c]	GDP[d]
	High estimate[b]		Low estimate[d]	
Czech Republic	60	20	7	2
Hungary	55	18	6	2
Poland	25	8	3	1
Slovakia	59	20	7	2
Slovenia	53	18	6	2

[a] Based on 2002 trade and GDP data.
[b] Assumes currency union increases trade (the sum of exports and imports) with current Euro-area members and the other accession countries by 85 per cent over twenty years. Based on Rose's fixed-effect meta estimates (Rose 2002). Assumes also that trade with other countries rises in line with GDP.
[c] Assumes currency union increases trade with current Euro-area members and the other accession countries by 10 per cent. Estimate drawn from analysis of average five-year gain from EMU experience.
[d] Assumes a 1 per cent increase in total trade/GDP increases real GDP per capita by 0.33 per cent. Estimate drawn from Frankel and Rose (2002).
Sources: Frankel and Rose (2002); Rose (2002); IMF, *World Economic Outlook*; IMF, *Direction of Trade Statistics*; and IMF staff calculations.

question, studies have started to appear based on this more appropriate sample. Faruqee (2004) finds that after five years EMU had produced trade gains of 6–12 per cent for the area as a whole and −3–+13 per cent for individual countries. Whether such trade is likely to persist (so that long-term gains over, say, twenty years would be 24–60 per cent, approximately the prediction of Rose) remains to be seen. Delving into the question of why some EMU countries have experienced larger trade gains than others, Faruqee also finds that these gains show a positive relationship with the degree of a country's structural flexibility. In other words, countries where the structure of production is more responsive to changing trade relationships, prices, or competition from abroad are more likely to experience larger gains from EMU.

Using these studies to calculate possible gains in trade for the new members from joining the Euro-area results in a large range of estimates. Table 15.2 shows estimates of potential gains for trade and GDP growth calculated by applying two sets of parameters to the data of the new members: the upper bounds use parameters from the Rose meta-study and the lower bounds use parameters from Faruqee's study of the actual gains after five years for the initial twelve members of the Euro-area. This suggests that Euro-area membership could increase trade in the new Member States by between 6 and 60 per cent over twenty years, except in Poland where, owing to the smaller share of total trade in GDP than in the other new members, estimates are lower. In fact, because the new members' economies are generally at the most flexible end of the current EMU spectrum, they likely will experience gains for trade towards the upper end of the estimated range.

Links between these gains in trade and GDP growth are imprecise. Frankel and Rose (2002), however estimate—again based on the large global panel data sets—that for every 1 per cent increase in a country's overall trade as a share of GDP, per capita GDP rises by at least 0.33 per cent. The gain presumably comes from increases in efficiency when competition is greater and comparative advantage is given greater play. Combining this estimate with those for trade gains suggests that joining EMU would raise the level of GDP in the new members by some 2–20 per cent after twenty years, with the estimates for Poland again somewhat below this range.

One puzzle left unresolved in these models is what causes increased trade in a currency union. Eliminating exchange rate volatility is an obvious channel, although separate empirical studies of the effect of exchange rate volatility on trade do not unambiguously support that hypothesis (Clark *et al.* 2003). Presumably, therefore, lower transaction costs, greater competition, and transparency of prices must play a role. Perhaps more significant, however, is the effect of removing long-term exchange rate risk on the attractiveness of a catching-up country, in particular, as a platform for foreign investment. Investigating the channels through which currency unions increase trade and growth will be a key area for research in coming years, particularly as longer time series from the EMU experience become available.

Beyond trade creation, Euro adoption should produce other benefits through lower risk premia on borrowing costs and a strong framework for policy discipline (see Schadler and Luengnaruemitchai 2007). Taking this broader range of considerations into account alongside the trade gains, Magyar Nemzeti Bank (2002) concludes that Euro adoption would add 0.6–0.9 percentage points to average GDP growth for Hungary for twenty years—close to the top end of the estimated range in Table 15.2. National Bank of Poland (2004) shows estimates for Poland of about half this range.

Costs of Euro adoption

Gains from Euro adoption come at the expense of relinquishing monetary policy as a stabilization tool. This cost has been assessed in several ways. The most common is to examine how susceptible a country is to asymmetric shocks—so-called optimum currency area (OCA) criteria. This is done by measuring historical correlations of business cycles, the degree to which economies' production structures are integrated (for example, through intra-industry trade), and the similarity of countries' sectoral structures of output. These measures, which show how often a country would have been out of sync with the cyclical position of the currency union, tend to show moderate but rising convergence between cyclical conditions in the new members and the Euro-area. A difficulty in assessing OCA criteria is possible endogeneity, which would make history a poor guide. Specifically, Frankel and Rose (1996) present evidence that entering a currency union starts processes that alter the structure of an economy, making it less susceptible and better able to adapt to asymmetric shocks. Krugman and Venables (1996), however, argue that economic integration creates incentives to exploit economies of scale, resulting in greater specialization and exposure to asymmetric shocks. This debate is unresolved. Historical data, nevertheless, suggest that, on OCA criteria, most of the new Central European members are at least as well suited to Euro-area membership as many existing Euro-area members.

In assessing the costs of losing monetary policy independence, questions must also be raised about the value of the exchange rate as a shock absorber. The OCA analysis starts from the assumption that the exchange rate is a useful tool for smoothing the effects of asymmetric shocks. The presumption is that because exchange rate changes can generate rapid adjustment in relative prices, they are good absorbers of real shocks—that is, shocks that would produce output losses or overheating in the absence of changes in relative prices (usually, more specifically, in real wages). But an exchange rate response may not be optimal for other types of shocks, particularly those from temporary monetary or financial sources that typically do not require relative price changes. Thus, the usefulness of an independent monetary policy (or by extension an exchange rate that can change) is less if the incidence of asymmetric monetary/financial shocks dominates that of real demand shocks. Moreover, a flexible exchange rate buffeted by global market influences may actually be the source of shocks that would be eliminated in a currency union. A final consideration is whether exchange rate changes actually do affect relative prices: in small open economies, the dominance of traded goods together with wage indexing arrangements may mean that exchange rate changes do little other than affect the overall inflation.

While conceptually clear, these issues can only be assessed empirically. The literature is extensive, but a few broad regularities seem to be emerging. Studies of large industrial countries tend to find that the variance of real exchange rates is predominantly linked to real shocks, suggesting that real exchange rates have been reasonable shock absorbers. Other studies—mostly on small open economies and distinguishing between the role of the real and nominal exchange rates—find that monetary/financial shocks explain the bulk of the variability of nominal exchange rates (e.g. Canzoneri *et al.* 1996; Artis and Ehrmann 2000). Early efforts to look at these questions for the Central European new members are yielding mixed results (e.g. Dibooglu and Kutan 2001; Gros and Hobza 2003). Borghijs and Kuijs (2004) apply the most direct test to this question. They find that during periods in which countries allowed a significant degree of exchange rate flexibility, exchange rate changes were linked less frequently to real shocks and more frequently to monetary and financial shocks. They therefore conclude that the value of the exchange rate instrument, particularly for the smaller new members, is not obviously large.

Of course, judgements on the costs of Euro adoption must combine these various possible costs into a single assessment. This requires simulating in a general equilibrium model the response of policies and macroeconomic developments to identical underlying states of the world when a country has adopted the Euro and when it has not. One early such study (European Commission 1990) for the four large EU-15 countries found that, in comparison with a free float, EMU would reduce both inflation and output variability. This results from the elimination of asymmetric exchange rate shocks and greater discipline on wage and price behaviour in EMU, offsetting the effects of an at times suboptimal monetary policy for an individual country. In contrast, however, a simulation study for the UK Treasury (Westway 2003) found that UK inflation and output volatility would be higher if the United Kingdom adopted the Euro than if it did not.

For the Central European countries, early results suggest that net costs will be small. Schadler *et al.* (2005) report results using the IMF Global Economic Model (GEM), developed by Laxton and Pesanti (2003), calibrated (in terms of behavioural parameters and the distribution of shocks) on the Czech Republic. They find that even though exchange rate shocks would be eliminated in EMU, the greater susceptibility to productivity shocks of the typical Central European country than of the existing Euro-area would be problematic. This is because Euro-area monetary policy would not be as effective in countering the effects of such shocks as an ideal independent monetary policy would. They point out, however, that this conclusion holds only if the independent monetary policy is conducted in the most efficient way possible. Moreover, the amount of extra volatility in inflation and output is very small relative to means.

Ultimately, assessments of the net benefits of Euro adoption for any prospective member must take account simultaneously of the likely size of the benefits, the likely frequency of asymmetric shocks, and the effectiveness of an independent monetary policy in countering costs of shocks. As yet no such studies exist. The hurdle to overcome in such an analysis is deriving a metric that allows a direct comparison of the benefits of Euro adoption (measured in terms of a gain in the level of GDP) and the costs of Euro adoption (measured in terms of the volatility of inflation and output)—obviously two different dimensions of welfare that would have to be expressed in comparable terms. Until this is done, the conclusion from available empirical work would suggest that gains for income are potentially large, while costs in terms of increased volatility are likely to be small.

▨ DISCUSSION QUESTIONS

1. Discuss the key economic influences underlying the gap between income per capita in the new Member States and the EU15.

2. What economic processes are these differences producing and how will these processes help close the income gap? In what ways should the enlargement help accelerate these processes?

3. Discuss whether the enlargement was in the economic interest of the EU-15. In what ways will EU-15 countries benefit? What are the actual or perceived costs for the EU-15 countries? If you were an EU-15 politician, how would you sell enlargement to your constituents?

4. Should new members attach much urgency to adopting the Euro as their national currency? Is the case for early Euro adoption different for different countries?

▨ FURTHER READING

For more information on the economies of the new members see the EU website (http://europa.eu.int/comm/enlargement), annual reviews of economic developments on the website of the IMF (www.imf.org), and the annual EBRD transition reports. An extensive review of the costs and benefits, process and policy challenges of Euro adoption in the new members is provided in Schadler *et al.* (2005). Proceedings of an IMF/Joint Vienna Institute/National Bank of Poland conference on labour and capital flows following enlargement (January 2006) cover a wide range of issues concerning the economic underpinnings of labour and capital mobility, the extent to which restrictions on labour mobility will accelerate capital mobility, and the likely effects of factor mobility in Europe. These can be found on the website of the Joint Vienna Institute (www.jvi.org).

■ **NOTES**

1. The purchasing power parity (PPP) exchange rate is the number of local currency units required to buy the same basket of goods that can be bought for one unit of the base currency (Euro in this case).

2. Following the absorption approach to the balance of payments, two identities are key.

$$y = c + i + x - m$$

So that substituting and arranging yields

$$s - i = x - m.$$

Where y is GDP, c is consumption, s is domestic savings (equivalent to $y - c$), i is investment, x is exports of goods and services, and m is imports of goods and services. These identities show that the current account surplus (deficit) equals the excess (shortfall) of domestic savings relative to investment.

3. Owing to the difficulty in obtaining comparable data for some countries, Figure 15.5 and the following discussion compare the eight Central European new members (EU-8) and the twelve Euro-area countries.

4. See, for example, Keefer and Knack (1997), Crafts and Kaiser (2004), and Schadler *et al.* (2006).

5. The marginal product of labour is calculated by taking the derivative of output with respect to labour in the production function (1).

$$\frac{\partial Y}{\partial L} = A\alpha \left(\frac{K}{L} \right)^{\alpha} = \frac{W}{P}$$

where W = the average wage level and P = the price level.

6. The marginal product of capital is calculated by taking the derivative of output with respect to capital in the production function (1).

$$\frac{\partial Y}{\partial K} = A\alpha \left(\frac{L}{K} \right)^{(1-\alpha)} = r$$

where r is the rate of return on capital.

7. This section draws heavily on Rosenberg and Sierhej (2007).

8. A significant portion of Cohesion Funds also supports costs of meeting EU environmental standards.

9. ERMII is an arrangement that links the currencies of prospective Euro-area members to the Euro by establishing a ±15 per cent band for exchange rate fluctuations around an agreed central parity. The Maastricht exchange rate stability criterion, however, may be assessed with respect to a stricter standard than simply remaining in the band.

10. Three EU-15 countries remain outside the Euro-area. Denmark and the United Kingdom are members of EMU with permanent opt-out clauses. Formally, Sweden is required to adopt the Euro when it has fulfilled all the Maastricht entry criteria. But because it has not joined ERMII it cannot fulfil the Maastricht criterion requiring a two-year participation in ERMII. Denmark, on the other hand, participates in ERMII.

■ **REFERENCES**

Artis, M. J. and Ehrmann, M. (2000), *The Exchange Rate: A Shock-Absorber or Source of Shocks? A Study of Four Open Economies*, CEPR Discussion Paper no. 2550 (London: Centre for Economic Policy Research).

Boeri, T. (2006), 'Enlargement, Migration, and Policy Coordination', paper presented at 'Labour and Capital Flows Following European Enlargement', IMF/JVI/National Bank of Poland, Warsaw, Jan. Proceedings posted at http://www.jvi.org.

Borghijs, A. and Kuijs, L. (2004), *Exchange Rates in Central Europe: A Blessing or Curse?*, IMF Working Paper no. 04/2 (Washington, DC: IMF).

Buiter, W. and Grafe, C. (2002), 'Anchor, Float or Abandon Ship: Exchange Rate Regimes for the Accession Countries', *Banca Nazionale del Lavoro Quarterly Review*, 55/221: 111–42.

Canzoneri, M., Vallés Liberal, J., and Viñals, J. (1996), *Do Exchange Rates Move to Address International Macroeconomic Imbalances?* CEPR Discussion Paper no. 1498 (London: Centre for Economic Policy Research).

Clark, P. Tamirisa, N., Shang-Jin, W., Sodikov, A., and Zeng, L. (2003), 'Exchange Rate Volatility and Trade Flows: Some New Evidence', paper presented to World Trade Organization, Washington, DC.

Crafts, N. and Kaiser, K. (2004), 'Long-Term Growth Prospects in Transition Economies: A Reappraisal', *Structural Change and Economic Dynamics*, 15: 101–18.

Dibooglu, S. and Kutan, A. (2001), 'Sources of Real and Nominal Exchange Rate Fluctuations in Transition Economies: The Case of Poland and Hungary', *Journal of Comparative Economics*, 29: 257–75.

European Commission (1990), 'One Market, One Money', *European Economy*, 44 (October): 245.

Faruqee, H. (2004), 'Measuring the Trade Effects of EMU', unpublished paper (Washington, DC: IMF).

Feldman, R. and Watson, M. (2002), *Into the EU: Policy Frameworks in Central Europe* (Washington, DC: IMF).

Frankel, J. A. and Rose, A. (1996), *The Endogeneity of the Optimum Currency Area Criteria*, NBER Working Paper no. 5700 (Cambridge, MA: NBER).

—— —— (2002), 'An Estimate of the Effect of Common Currencies on Trade and Income', *Quarterly Journal of Economics*, 117 (May): 437–66.

Gros, D. and Hobza, A. (2003), *Exchange Rate Variability as an OCA Criterion: Are the Candidates Ripe for the Euro?*, Working Paper no. 23 (San Francisco, CA: International Center for Economic Growth).

Keefer, P. and Knack, S. (1997), 'Why Don't Poor Countries Catch Up? A Cross-National Test and Institutional Explanation', *Economic Inquiry*, 35 (July): 590–602.

Krugman, P. and Venables, A. J. (1996), 'Integration, Specialization, and Adjustment', *European Economic Review*, 40 (April): 959–67.

Lane, P. and Milesi-Ferretti, G. (2006), 'Capital Flows to Emerging Europe', paper presented at 'Labour and Capital Flows Following Enlargement', IMF/JVI/National Bank of Poland, Jan. Proceedings posted at http://www.jvi.org.

Laxton, D. and Pesanti, P. (2003), *Monetary Rules for Small, Open, Emerging Economies*, NBER Working Paper no. 9568 (Cambridge, MA: NBER).

Lipschitz, L., Lane, T. and Mourmouris, A. (2005), 'Real Convergence, Capital Flows, and Monetary Policy: Notes on the European Transition Countries', in *Euro Adoption in the New Members of the European Union: Opportunities and Challenges* (Washington, DC: IMF), 61–9.

Lucas, R. (1990), 'Why Doesn't Capital Flow from Rich to Poor Countries?', *American Economic Review*, 80: 92–6.

Magyar Nemzeti Bank (2002), *Adopting the Euro in Hungary: Expected Benefits, Costs, and Timing*, ed. by A. Csajbok and A. Csermely, NBH Occasional Paper no. 24 (Budapest: NBH).

Marin, D. (2006), 'A Nation of Poets and Thinkers—Less So with Eastern Enlargement? Austria and Germany', Centre for Economic Policy Research, presented at 'Labour and Capital Flows Following Enlargement', IMF/JVI/National Bank of Poland, Jan. Proceedings posted at http://www.jvi.org.

National Bank of Poland (2004), *A Report on the Costs and Benefits of Poland's Adoption of the Euro*, ed. by J. Borowski (Warsaw).

Rose, A. (2002), *The Effect of Common Currencies on International Trade: Where Do We Stand?*, Occasional Paper no. 22 (Berkley, CA: Monetary Authority of Singapore).

Rosenberg, C. and Sierhej, R. (2007), *Interpreting EU Funds Data for Macroeconomic Analysis in the New Member States*, IMF Working Paper (Washington, DC: IMF).

Schadler, S. (ed.) (2005), *Euro Adoption in the New Members of the European Union: Opportunities and Challenges*, proceedings of IMF/Czech National Bank conference, Prague, Feb. 2004 (Washington, DC: IMF).

—— and Luengnaruemitchai, P. (2007), *Do Economists' and Financial Markets' Perspectives on the New Members of the EU Differ?*, IMF Working Paper 07/65 (Washington, DC: IMF).

—— Drammond, P., Kuijs, L., Murgasova, Z., and Van Elkin, R. (2004), 'Euro Adoption in the Accession Countries: Vulnerabilities and Strategies', Paper prepared for the Conference on Euro Adoption in the Accession Countries: Opportunities and Challenges, 2–3 Feb., Czech National Bank.

—— Drummond, P., Kuijs, L., Murgasova, Z. and van Elkan, R. (2005), *Adopting the Euro in Central Europe: Challenges of the Next Step in European Integration*, IMF Occasional Paper no. 234 (Washington, DC: IMF).

—— Mody, A., Abiad, A. and Leigh, D. (2006), *Growth in the Central and Eastern European Countries of the European Union*, IMF Occasional Paper, No. 252 (Washington DC: IMF).

Sommer, M. (2004), 'Financial and Fiscal Implications of EU Accession', internal guidance note, IMF.

Tenreyro, S. and Persson, T. (2001), 'On the Causes and Consequences of Currency Unions', unpublished paper (Cambridge, MA: Harvard University).

Wyplosz, C. (2001), 'Regional Exchange Rate Arrangements: Some Lessons from Europe', paper presented at 'The Role of Regional Financial Arrangements in Crisis Prevention and Management: The Experiences of Europe, Asia, Africa, and Latin America', organized by the Forum on Debt and Development (FONDAD), Prague, 21–22 June.

16 European Strategies for Growth

André Sapir

Introduction

For thirty years, between 1945 and 1975, Europe enjoyed a 'Golden Age' of growth, stability, and social cohesion. The economic and social conditions in Western Europe during this period were truly remarkable. Between 1950 and 1973, the EU-15 (the 15 countries that comprised the European Union before the addition of ten new Member States in May 2004) saw average annual growth rates of 4.6 per cent for GDP and 3.8 per cent for GDP per capita. As a result, Europe's standard of living witnessed a rapid catching-up with the United States: compared with a benchmark of 100 for the USA, GDP per capita (measured at purchasing power parity) in the EU-15 rose from around 40 in 1950 to around 70 in 1973. At the same time, inflation stood on average at 4 per cent and unemployment at 2 per cent.

During the next thirty years the economic conditions in Europe have been less rosy. Potential growth fell by nearly one full percentage point, reaching now only 2 per cent a year, compared with almost 3.5 per cent in the United States, where growth has actually increased. And while it is true that GDP per capita increased at the same rate in Europe as in the United States throughout the period, this actually implies that the income gap between the United States and Europe has remained constant. Hence the rapid catching-up process of the Golden Age actually stopped altogether thirty years ago. At the same time, inflation first rose sharply during the 1970s and then fell steadily during the 1980s and 1990s, staying around 2 per cent since or around 2000. By contrast, unemployment, which also rose rapidly during the 1970s and the early 1980s, never much declined thereafter, hovering instead between 8 and 10 per cent.

The purpose of this chapter is to examine why Europe's growth has declined and what European policies have done to reverse this situation.

16.1 Why has Europe's growth declined?

The question that needs to be addressed is not why European growth came down from the extraordinary levels it had reached during the Golden Age. Clearly the process of catching up with the United States, which provided the main source of European growth,

Table 16.1 GDP per head of population in EU-15, in PPP, 1970 and 2000 (USA = 100)

	1970	2000
GDP per head of population	69	70
GDP per working hour	65	91
Working hours per head of population	106	78
Working hours per person employed	101	86
Persons employed per person of working age	104	88
Persons of working age per head of population	102	103

was bound to be exhausted sooner or later. What needs to be explained, instead, is why the catching-up process stopped more than thirty years ago, when GDP per capita in the European Union had reached only 70 per cent of GDP per capita in the United States.

There are essentially two explanations for what has happened. Both explanations rely on the numbers displayed in Table 16.1, which disaggregate the evolution of GDP per head of population in the European Union compared with the United States between changes in labour productivity (measured as GDP per working hour) and changes in labour input (measured as working hours per head of population).

Blanchard (2004) and Prescott (2004)

The first explanation, best exposed by Blanchard (2004) and Prescott (2004), emphasizes that labour productivity has increased much faster in Europe than in the United States and that it is now roughly the same on both sides of the Atlantic. European productivity, which was only 65 per cent of the level in the United States in 1970, reached more than 90 per cent in 2000. The European problem, therefore, is ascribed entirely to a relative fall in labour input. The figures in Table 16.1 show that working hours per head of population in Europe, which were higher than in the United States in 1970, have fallen sharply thereafter, reaching less than 80 per cent of the US level in 2000. Blanchard concludes that 'had relative hours worked remained the same, the EU would have roughly the same standard of living as the United States' (2004: 5).

Why have working hours per head of population decreased so sharply in Europe compared with the United States during the past thirty years? The last three rows in Table 16.1 provide some clues. The first conclusion is that differences in demographic evolutions, captured in the last row, play no role whatsoever. The ratio of the population of working age to total population has remained slightly higher in Europe than in the United States. The second conclusion is that the difference between Europe and the United States in labour input is explained equally by differences in the evolution of hours per worker and of the employment rate (the ratio of the population employed to the population of working age). Between 1970 and 2000, the number of hours worked per worker and the employment rate have each decreased by 15 per cent in Europe compared with the United States.

Prescott (2004) and Blanchard (2004) put forward different explanations for the fall in the utilization rate of labour in Europe relative to the United States. According to Prescott, the relative fall in the utilization of labour in the EU is entirely attributable to increased labour taxation in Europe, which also produced the relative increase in labour productivity. By contrast, Blanchard does not see the fall in labour utilization and the rise in productivity as the product of a common factor, such as increased labour taxation. He argues that EU economic reforms have fuelled rapid labour productivity growth, which in Europe has been used to increase leisure.

Blanchard's optimistic view of Europe—a continent where structural reforms generate rapid productivity growth and citizens hold a strong and sustainable preference for leisure—is viewed by many as over-optimistic. Critics have pursued several lines of argument.

First, comparing EU and US labour productivity without taking into account differences in hours worked and employment rates in Europe and in America is basically flawed. Cette (2004) forcefully argues that Europe's productivity performance is artificially boosted by the fact that the average hours worked are much shorter and the employment rate much lower than in the United States. In particular, Europe's lower employment rate results from the fact that only the most productive segment of the population is employed, whereas younger and older persons are often excluded, willingly or not, from the labour market. The point is that part of the rapid growth in European labour productivity was obtained precisely by lowering the number of hours worked and the employment rate, which is quite different from a genuine increase in productivity.

Taking into account returns to hours worked and the employment rate, Cette (2004) estimates what he calls a 'structural' (hourly) labour productivity level for Europe relative to the United States. This structural productivity level is an estimate of Europe's productivity assuming that the hours worked and the employment rate are the same as in the United States. According to this estimate, the European productivity level for 2000 should be revised downwards from the 91 per cent figure reported in Table 16.1 to barely 81 per cent. This suggests that the productivity gap between Europe and the United States remains substantial.

Second, even if one ignores the correction just discussed, one cannot dismiss the fact that a new productivity gap between Europe and the United Stated has opened up since 1995. As Van Ark (2005) has documented, whereas average annual labour productivity growth in the USA accelerated from 1.1 per cent during the period 1987–95 to 2.5 per cent during 1995–2004, EU productivity growth declined from 2.1 to 1.4 per cent. The year 1995 marks in fact a historical break in the evolution of labour productivity growth across the two sides of the Atlantic: after having been consistently higher in Europe for nearly fifty years, it turned steadily in favour of the United States thereafter. There is wide consensus that these opposing trends owe much to the information and communication technology (ICT) revolution. Europe has consistently been lagging behind the United States not only in ICT investment but also in total factor productivity growth in ICT-producing as well as ICT-using industries. Van Ark (2005) and others have pointed out that Europe's counter-performance is related to its structural environment which inhibits innovation and the reallocation of resources to new activities.

Third, ascribing Europe's fall in the utilization rate of labour to individual preference leaves out entirely the incentives that shape individual behaviour. Yet, as Nickell (2003) observes, when confronted with differences (across countries and over time) in labour effort, it is natural to look at the incentives to engage in market work relative to other activities. The conclusion of his investigation is that

> tax rates are a significant factor in explaining differences in the amount of market work under-taken by the working age population in different countries. However, the evidence suggests that tax rate differentials only explain a minority of the market work differentials, the majority being explained by other relevant labour market institutions. Particularly important are probably the dif-ferences in social security systems which provide income support to various nonworking groups including the unemployed, the sick and disabled, and the early retired. (2003: 10)

Fourth, even if one accepts that Europe's fall in the utilization rate of labour is genuinely related to increasing preference for leisure, there is no reason to believe that this situation is sustainable in the face of demographic trends. Europe's population has aged consider-ably in recent decades. Between 1960 and 2000, the average dependency ratio (defined as the number of persons aged 60 or more years per 100 persons aged 15–59 years) for the EU-15 rose from 26 to 35. At the same time, the dependency ratio for the United States remained almost constant at around 25. Unfortunately, the outlook for the coming decades is even grimmer than the previous trend. According to the United Nations Population Division (2002), the dependency ratio in the EU-15 is expected to reach 47 in 2020 and 70 in 2050. The European Commission (2002) estimates that the pure demo-graphic effect of ageing would be an increase in public expenditure (related to pensions and health care) of eight points of GDP between 2000 and 2050. This hardly provides grounds for optimism about the sustainability of the European preference for leisure.

The Sapir Report (2003, 2004)

The other explanation of Europe's growth and catching-up problem attempts to explain why *both* labour utilization and productivity growth have fallen in Europe—both abso-lutely and relative to the United States—since the 1970s. The most comprehensive exposition of this approach is probably the Sapir Report (Sapir *et al.* 2003, 2004). The Sapir Report basically shares the view of Prescott (2004) that developments in labour utilization and labour productivity are two sides of the same coin. However, it does not subscribe to the notion that EU productivity has reached the US level nor does it ascribe concomitant trends in labour utilization and labour productivity to labour taxation. Instead it focuses on a much wider issue, of which increased taxation is just one facet.

In a nutshell, the Sapir Report

> views Europe's unsatisfactory growth performance during the last decades as a symptom of its failure to adapt to a rapidly changing environment. It has now become clear that the context in which economic policies have been developed changed fundamentally over the past thirty years. A system built around the assimilation of existing technologies, mass production generating economies of scale and an industrial structure dominated by large firms with stable markets and long term employment patterns no longer delivers in the world of today, characterised by eco-nomic globalisation and strong external competition. What is needed now is greater mobility within and across firms, more retraining, greater flexibility of labour markets, greater availability of external finance, and higher investment in both R&D and higher education. This requires a massive change in economic policies in Europe. (2003: ii; 2004: v)

16.2 **European strategies**

The quest to improve poor European economic performance has driven EU policy over a long period. The need to combat perceived 'Euro-sclerosis' in the mid-1980s gave rise to the Single Market Programme and the Padoa-Schioppa Report (Padoa-Schioppa *et al.* 1987). A similar perception led to the Lisbon process launched in 2000 and the Sapir Report (Sapir *et al.* 2003, 2004).

The Single Market Programme

The Padoa-Schioppa Report was extremely influential. It laid down the intellectual foundation for the construction of a coherent economic edifice resting on three pillars: the single market, to foster efficiency; an effective monetary arrangement, to ensure macro-economic stability; and an expanded Community budget, to foster territorial cohesion within what had then just become a more heterogeneous EU.

By removing barriers to the mobility of goods, services, labour, and capital, the Single Market Programme (SMP) was intended to foster competition, to boost productivity, and to accelerate growth. Yet, growth has been mediocre during the past two decades. Besides the vast costs of German reunification during the 1990s, there are three main reasons for the failure of the Single Market Programme to deliver higher growth.

First, the SMP was never fully implemented. Since 1993, the single market has been a reality for goods. On the other hand, service markets—including financial markets—remain highly fragmented. Yet efficient provision of services—many of which are vital inputs for producers—is crucial for the growth of a modern economy.

Second, the SMP excluded the liberalization of labour markets, which largely remains the prerogative of Member States. Yet without such reform and greater labour mobility within and across companies, the liberalization of product markets is unlikely to trigger the reallocation of resources necessary to produce higher growth.

Third, the conception and implementation of the SMP were rooted in yesterday's thinking. They were based on the assumption that Europe's fundamental problem was the absence of a large internal market that would allow European companies to achieve big economies of scale. It has now become clear that the problem lay elsewhere. In the modern world, characterized by rapid technological change and strong global competition, what European industry needs is more opportunity for companies to enter new markets, more retraining of labour, greater reliance on market financing, and higher investment in both research and development and higher education.

The Lisbon agenda

In March 2000 the EU-15 leaders held a special meeting in Lisbon 'to agree a new strategic goal for the Union in order to strengthen employment, economic reform and social cohesion as part of a knowledge-based economy'. The Presidency Conclusion of the Lisbon European Council acknowledged that the European Union is confronted with 'a quantum shift resulting from globalization and the challenges of a new knowledge-driven economy' that requires 'a radical transformation of the European economy'.

In Lisbon, the Union set itself an ambitious objective for the next decade: 'to become the most competitive and dynamic knowledge-based economy in the world, capable of sustainable economic growth with more and better jobs and greater social cohesion'.

In order to achieve this goal, the European Council agreed on an overall strategy based on three elements: (1) stepping up the process of structural reform for competitiveness and innovation; (2) completing the single market; and (3) modernizing the European social model, investing in people, and combating social exclusion.

It was also decided that implementation of this strategy would involve applying a new 'open method of coordination' as the means of spreading best practice and achieving greater convergence towards the main EU goals. This method, designed to help Member States progressively to develop their own policies, involves, according to the Presidency Conclusion,

fixing guidelines for the Union combined with specific timetables for achieving the goals which they set in the short, medium and long terms; establishing, where appropriate, quantitative and qualitative indicators and benchmarks against the best in the world and tailored to the needs of different Member States and sectors as a means of comparing best practice; translating these European guidelines into national and regional policies by setting specific targets and adopting measures, taking into account national and regional differences; periodic monitoring, evaluation and peer review organized as mutual learning processes.

The Lisbon strategy can be viewed as an attempt to remedy the three shortcomings of the Single Market Programme identified in the previous section. It seeks to combine reforms of product and capital markets at the EU level, through the Single Market Programme, with reforms of labour markets at the national level, through the open method of coordination.

The case for coordinating product and capital market reforms on one hand and labour market reforms on the other *within each EU country* is fairly strong. The structure of product and capital markets affects the performance of the labour market and, vice versa, the structure of labour markets affects the performance of product and capital markets. Reforms of product and capital markets tend to increase the demand for labour and therefore facilitate reforms in the labour market. Equally, reforms of labour markets tend to facilitate the creation of new firms, thereby facilitating reforms in product and capital markets. Conversely, not reforming one set of markets hinders reforms in the other set.

But what about coordinating product and capital market reforms *at the EU level with national* labour market reforms?

In principle one does not expect spillovers between countries as far as labour market (and national product market regulation) reform is concerned, each country reaping most of the effects of its own reform. However, the situation is different inside the European Union because countries share a common good, namely the single market, which (like national product market regulation) also interacts with national labour markets. The better national labour markets operate the easier it is to reform the single market and vice versa.

There are two ways of solving the chicken-and-egg problem between product and capital market reforms at the EU level (i.e. the completion of the SMP) on one hand, and reforms in national labour markets on the other. One is to concentrate all energy on the EU level, secure product market and capital market liberalization, and hope that this will eventually trigger labour market reforms through a TINA ('there is no alternative') process. The other is to act simultaneously at the EU level, with product and capital market reforms (i.e. completion of the SMP), and at the national level, with labour market reforms. The advantage of the second solution is that it would, in principle, be more efficient and less painful as labour market reforms would benefit from product and capital market reforms, and vice versa.

The Lisbon stategy can be viewed as an attempt to solve this 'coordination failure' between EU and national reforms. Its main objective is to speed up productivity growth by removing barriers in product and capital markets (mostly at the EU level, through the Single Market Programme), and to ensure that labour is used more efficiently by reforming labour markets and social policies (at national level). The twin tracks of EU and national level actions are central to the Lisbon process.

An agenda for a growing Europe

Although the Lisbon agenda gained rapid prominence in European policy circles, its implementation was slow at best. One reason, put forward by FitzGerald (2005), is that:

Unlike the *Single European Market* programme, which had an intellectual basis in the *Cecchini Report*, and the creation of a monetary union, which relied on the *One Market One Money Report*, the Lisbon Agenda was launched without a coherent intellectual basis. This absence of a coherent economic basis to back the launch of the strategy limited its initial appeal. The intellectual excitement and debate that accompanied the previous two major economic reform projects of the EU was very slow to emerge in the case of the Lisbon Strategy. It was only in 2003 that the *Sapir Report* set out the economic logic behind the Agenda. (2005: 1)

According to the Sapir Report, the Lisbon agenda rightly set an ambitious objective, but its implementation was deficient because it rested on a flawed strategy with a multitude of targets and a weak method. The report, entitled *An Agenda for a Growing Europe*, attempted to remedy both problems.

First, it argued that effective implementation of the Lisbon process requires focusing the agenda on growth. Although the Lisbon European Council correctly identified globalization and technological change as fundamental changes that require 'a radical transformation of the European economy', it failed to make the link with growth. Perhaps the greatest contribution of the Sapir Report is precisely to see that failure to transform the European economy led to Europe's declining growth performance. Not only that, but also that faster growth is paramount (1) to ensure the sustainability of the European model, which puts a high premium on social cohesion, and (2) to help integrate the low-income countries of Central and Eastern Europe into the Union. The report warned that '[g]rowth must become Europe's number one economic priority' and that '[f]ailure to deliver on the commitments of the Lisbon Agenda would endanger the present European contract and could lead to its fundamental revision, thereby threatening the very process of European integration' (2003: i; 2004: v–vi).

Second, the report confronted the fact that meeting the Lisbon agenda would be an enormous task—an issue that EU leaders had simply ducked so far. In particular, it made clear that the Lisbon agenda requires above all a high degree of coherence, between

EU policies and instruments on the one hand and between decision-makers at EU and national levels on the other. While recognizing that reforms of national policies (especially in the area of labour market and social policies) are obviously crucial to deliver higher growth, the report—because it was addressed to the president of the European Commission, Romano Prodi, who had commissioned it—nonetheless decided to focus its recommendations on where EU policies and their economic management can make the greatest contribution.

The report put forward a six-point agenda for reforms, four to improve EU policies and two to make their delivery more effective. The four recommendations to improve EU policies were:

1. Making the single market more dynamic. The report argued that a dynamic single market is the keystone to Europe's economic growth. Much progress has been achieved in goods markets, but integration in services and in network industries remains very limited. A truly dynamic single market needs not only more integration, but also better regulation to facilitate entry by new players and the development of risk capital. Intra-EU and extra-EU labour mobility were also viewed as crucial and in need of easier rules.

2. Boosting investment in knowledge. The report considered that full integration of goods, services, and capital markets is only a first step. Innovation is a key driver of growth, calling for not only a dynamic market environment but also major investments in knowledge. EU funding for innovation and research should make a significant contribution here.

3. Improving the macroeconomic policy framework. The report considered that after its success in delivering price stability, Economic and Monetary Union (EMU) and the single currency also needed to help growth. In particular, it recommended that some features of the way in which macroeconomic policy is set should be improved: the monetary and fiscal policy framework of EMU should be made more symmetric over the phases of the cycle; implementation of the Stability and Growth Pact should focus more on long-term sustainability by taking into account both explicit and implicit public liabilities in the assessment of national budgetary positions; and the policy framework for EMU should be upgraded to improve policy coordination between Euro-area countries.

4. Redesigning policies for convergence and restructuring. The report viewed the underdeveloped institutional capacity of the new EU members as a serious handicap to their ability to implement beneficial EU policies or even, in some cases, to draw on all the financial and technical assistance that is available. It risks delaying the catching-up process. Hence, EU cohesion policy should target institution building in these countries. The report also argued that EU funding should promote economic restructuring.

An important theme of the report was that the EU suffers from twin problems: some of its methods of governance are obsolete; and the system as a whole has become too complex and fragmented. Attempts to redress policy failures would make little sense while leaving untouched the procedures and processes through which those policies are designed, decided, and implemented. Policy reforms can be expected to be successful only if implemented in conjunction with a restructuring of the methods of governance.

Instead of a clear separation between the EU and the national remits, as was the case in the early days of the EC, there is an increasing overlap between the EU and the national or subnational domains. EU priorities and policies are thus more and more often part of the varied policy environments in which decisions are taken at various government levels and in different countries, each with distinctive characteristics, as will be even more evident with further enlargement.

Effective implementation of EU policy thus frequently depends not only on the explicit cooperation of various national and subnational government bodies in the implementation of common policies, but also on their willingness to set their own priorities and develop their own agenda in accordance with EU priorities, or to shape their local policies in the light of wider European reference points. The difficulty in implementing the Lisbon agenda is a clear example of this situation.

In order to address this problem, the report made two additional recommendations:

5. Achieving effectiveness. The EU should have more power to oversee the correct application of single market rules. Independent EU bodies should be created in certain specific areas, while more authority could be devolved to decentralized, but coordinated, systems of authorities which would operate within the same legal norms. Extending the scope for qualified majority voting in the economic field would also be vital for improving the overall performance of the EU system.

6. Refocusing the EU budget. The economic component of the EU budget should better reflect the economic priorities the Union has set itself, in particular in the context of the Lisbon agenda. The report argued that budgets during the 2007–13 Financial Perspective should take a radical step and redirect EU funding from agriculture to the goals of creating a dynamic knowledge-based economy. But the EU budget is very small and represents barely 2.5 per cent of total public spending in the European Union. The report, therefore, insisted that the EU budget should act in unison with national budgets and act as a 'facilitator' to help shift the composition of national public expenditure and revenue towards growth-enhancing activities.

The Sapir Report had a profound impact on the intellectual and political debate over Europe's economic future. It is probably fair to say that it succeeded in focusing the debate on the need to raise growth and even influenced a number of policy outcomes. It was influential in the creation of the European Research Council (ERC), the new agency modelled after the US National Science Foundation which has received the mission of sustaining fundamental investigation into all aspects of scientific knowledge and to drive up standards of scientific research across Europe. It played an important role in the redesign of the Stability and Growth Pact initiated by the Prodi Commission in 2004 and adopted by the European Council in 2005. It was also instrumental in the setting up of the Globalization Adjustment Fund proposed by the Barroso Commission to complement national measures in helping those affected by economic restructuring as a result of globalization.

Above all, the Sapir Report was influential in the debate on the EU budget. Its radical proposals sparked huge discussion inside and outside the European Commission, which eventually led to the 2004 proposal by the Prodi Commission, later endorsed by the Barroso Commission, to increase substantially the budget for growth, in particular in the area of R&D and higher education. It was again at the centre of the intellectual debate in June 2005 after the failure of the Luxemburg presidency to reach an agreement on the EU budget, when Prime Minister Blair declared in his speech to the European Parliament at the start of the UK presidency that 'the Sapir report shows the way. Published by the European Commission in 2003, it sets out in clear detail what a modern European Budget would look like.'

Unfortunately, the agreement reached by the European Council in December 2005 dashed the hopes of seeing a modern EU budget before the end of the 2007–13 Financial Perspective. On the positive side, however, the European Council agreed that in view of 'the increasing pace of globalization and rapid technological change . . . the EU should carry out a comprehensive reassessment of the financial framework, covering both revenue and expenditure'. The European Commission was asked to undertake a full, wide-ranging review covering all aspects of EU spending, including the CAP, and of resources, including the UK rebate, and to report in 2008/9. 'On the basis of such a review, the European Council can take decisions on all the subjects covered by the review. The review will also be taken into account in the preparatory work on the following Financial Perspective.'

The revised Lisbon strategy

By 2004 it became clear to all concerned that the original Lisbon strategy ('Lisbon 1') was not delivering. There were two problems with Lisbon 1: ineffective coordination and lack of political ownership. The open method of coordination borrowed from the old 'competition for performance' approach had been used with success in the macro-economic sphere, but could not rely on any strong incentive. To be effective, it would have required at the very least the setting up of a benchmarking framework. Unfortunately this was never done. Even then, this would have been benchmarking with neither sanction nor incentive, and therefore a very weak form of coordination. The second problem with Lisbon 1 was the lack of political ownership by national authorities. Altogether, therefore, Lisbon 1 had commendable goals, and helped the fostering of cross-country comparisons and increasing of public awareness through the publication of statistics. But as regards implementation, it was essentially a low-quality, bureaucratic benchmarking enterprise.

In March 2004 the European Council invited the Commission to establish a High Level Group headed by Wim Kok, the former Dutch prime minister, to carry out an independent review of the Lisbon strategy.

The Kok Report (2004) found that the European Union and its Member States had clearly failed to implement the Lisbon strategy. This disappointing delivery was ascribed to an overloaded agenda and governance issues. In the words of the report, 'Lisbon is about everything and thus about nothing. Everybody is responsible and thus no one.'

The Kok Report proposed to remedy the delivery problem first of all by refocusing the strategy's economic, social, and environmental dimensions on growth and employment. The idea was not to abandon the social and environmental dimensions of the Lisbon agenda, but to recognize that growth and employment are essential 'in order to underpin social cohesion and sustainable development'.

As far governance is concerned, the Kok Report proposed a three-pronged approach. First, Member States were asked to take ownership of the process and to commit themselves to delivering the agreed reforms by presenting national programmes, which should be subject to debate with national parliaments and social partners. Second, the Commission was asked to improve the central elements of the open method of coordination— peer pressure and benchmarking—by delivering 'in the most public manner possible' an annual league table of Member State progress towards key targets. Stronger reliance on 'naming, shaming, and faming' was thus advocated. Third, the EU common policies— including the EU budget—were invited to reflect the Lisbon priorities more closely.

As the title of its Communication to the 2005 Spring European Council—*Working Together for Growth and Jobs: A New Start for the Lisbon Strategy*—amply demonstrates, the Barroso Commission squarely adopted the recommendation of the Kok Report to refocus the Lisbon strategy. The Commission also followed two of the three proposals made by the Kok Report to improve governance. It proposed that Member States present national programmes for growth and jobs, after broad discussion at national level. The Commission also proposed better use of the EU common policies, including the EU budget, in order to help in implementing the Lisbon strategy.

On the other hand, the Commission strongly rejected the proposal to 'name and shame' and nearly abandoned benchmarking altogether. The reason for this was probably that the large Member States (above all France and Germany) were determined—having just succeeded in trimming the wings of the Stability and Growth Pact (SGP)—that Lisbon would not be yet another thorn in their side. The Commission thus decided to stop lecturing the Member States and to embark on a partnership with them instead.

A few months later, the Council dealt a further blow to the Community involvement in the Lisbon strategy, when it rejected the EU budget proposal put forward by Commission, which envisaged a substantial increase in EU funding for research. The prospect of supporting the Lisbon strategy through budgetary incentives was thus abandoned.

The new Lisbon strategy ('Lisbon 2') could have attempted to remedy the two dimensions of the Lisbon 1 problem, seeking to improve both the effectiveness of coordination *and* the degree of political ownership. This is essentially what the Kok Report had suggested. Instead, Lisbon 2 chose to focus on the ownership problem. This approach was implicitly predicated on the assumption that the EU was confronted with a trade-off, and that more political ownership could only be gained at the expense of transparency in performance assessment. If, on the other hand, the implementation of the Lisbon strategy actually requires effective coordination *and* a high degree of political ownership, then the new approach is unlikely to succeed where Lisbon 1 failed.

Pisani-Ferry and Sapir (2006) conducted a study of the new Lisbon strategy. They found that Lisbon 2 does not seem to have succeeded in increasing the political ownership of the Lisbon strategy by national authorities. Although the preparation and adoption of National Reform Programmes (NRPs) is an important and positive step, progress as regards ownership remains insufficient.

Pisani-Ferry and Sapir concluded that: 'we do not consider that Lisbon 2 is on track to succeed. On the contrary, our assessment is that it will fail unless its current shortcomings are addressed as a matter of urgency.' However, they refused to reject the whole Lisbon process, arguing instead that 'Lisbon continues to be crucial for the future of Europe. The Lisbon goals continue to reflect the major challenges that European economies are confronting in this age of accelerated globalisation and technological change. These goals and the recognition of interdependence that they embody still command wide consensus' (2006: 13).

Clearly, the last exit for Lisbon is fast approaching. Failure to improve the Lisbon process further and to match ambitious objectives with equally ambitious instruments and methods would lead to the demise of the Lisbon strategy.

Would the Lisbon agenda, correctly viewed as an agenda for economic and social reforms at the EU and national levels, necessarily succumb if the Lisbon strategy were to be declared defunct? Not necessarily. It all boils down to the value of coordination. One can perfectly share the view that EU reforms (of product and capital markets through the Single Market Programme) *and* national reforms (of labour market and social policies) are essential to foster European growth, but disagree on the merits of the Lisbon coordination process as a means of achieving those reforms.

Take, for instance, Alesina and Giavazzi (2006), who clearly support the view that Europe needs reforms of product and labour markets to foster growth, yet reject the Lisbon process as wasteful at best and dangerous at worst. For them, Lisbon is just another example of centralization where 'the EU institutions are being captured by a type of European mentality that sees government policy as a cure-all in many areas. The need for coordination of policies is vastly over emphasized, perhaps strategically, by EU officials, since they will be the ones involved and empowered by the supranational coordination itself' (2006: 142). This view stands in sharp contrast to the more benign approach put forward in the Sapir Report, which considers that EU institutions should 'play the role of a facilitator in encouraging constructive reforms, while not interfering with national competences' (Sapir *et al.*, 2003: 109; 2004: 140).

16.3 Conclusions

This chapter has argued that Europe has a growth problem and that this problem ultimately reflects Europe's difficulty in adjusting its economic and social structures to an environment characterized by rapid technological change and strong global competition. In doing so, it has ignored an important reality of the European landscape, namely diversity.

Although Europe's overall economic performance has been rather disappointing for more than a decade, not all European countries are equally affected and some are even among the world's best economic performers. Differences in overall economic performance across EU countries obviously reflect a diversity of situations with respect to productivity growth and labour utilization, which in turn reflect differences in product and labour market regulations.

Nicoletti and Scarpetta (2003) document that although all EU countries belong to the single market they display important differences in product market regulations. They also show that these differences play an important role in explaining cross-country differences in productivity performance. The implication is not that the completion of the Single Market Programme should not be a priority for the European Union, but rather that national implementation of the SMP also matters a great deal.

But nowhere is the difference between EU countries more pronounced than in the area of labour market and social policies. As Sapir (2006) has shown, national social models greatly differ in terms of both efficiency (defined in terms of employment rates) and equity (defined in terms of poverty rates). Broadly speaking, however, there exist four clusters of countries having similar situations: a Nordic cluster, with efficient and equitable models; a Mediterranean cluster, with inefficient and inequitable models; a Continental cluster, with equitable but inefficient models; and an Anglo-Saxon cluster, with efficient but inequitable models. The difference between the efficient Nordic and Anglo-Saxon countries and the inefficient Mediterranean and Continental countries lies essentially in the extent of labour market regulation. Countries with flexible labour markets tend to have higher employment rates than countries with rigid markets.

In view of the strong correlation across countries between product market and labour market regulations, it follows that the necessity to implement economic and social reforms mainly falls on the Mediterranean and the Continental countries—although not necessarily on all of them. At the same time, since the combined GDP of these groups of countries accounts for two-thirds of the entire EU (with twenty-seven members) and 90 per cent of the Euro-area, their predicament concerns the entire European Union. A European strategy, with EU institutions facilitating reforms, but not interfering with national competences or blurring national responsibilities, seems therefore desirable.

■ REFERENCES

Alesina, A. and Giavazzi, F. (2006), *The Future of Europe: Reform or Decline* (Cambridge, MA: MIT Press).

Blanchard, O. (2004), 'The Economic Future of Europe', *Journal of Economic Perspectives*, 18: 3–26.

Cette, G. (2004), 'Is Hourly Labour Productivity Structurally Higher in Some Major European Countries than in the United States?', Banque de France, mimeo.

European Commission (2002), *The EU Economy 2002 Review*, European Economy No. 6, (Luxembourg: Office for Official Publications of the EC).

FitzGerald, J. (2005), 'Progress on the Lisbon Agenda', paper presented at the Brussels Economic Forum, Brussels, 21 April.

Kok, Wim *et al.* (2004), *Facing the Challenge: The Lisbon Strategy for Growth and Employment*, Report from the High Level Group (Brussels: European Communities).

Nickell, S. (2003), 'Employment and Taxes', paper presented at the CESifo Conference on Tax Policy and Employment, Venice, 21–23 July.

Nicoletti, G. and Scarpetta, S. (2003), 'Regulation, Productivity and Growth: OECD Evidence', *Economic Policy*, 36: 11–51.

Padoa-Schioppa, T., Emerson, M., King, M., Milleron, J.-C., Paelinck, J. H. P., Papademos, L., Pastor, A., and Scharpf, F. W. (1987), *Efficiency, Stability and Equity: A Strategy for the Evolution of the Economic System of the European Community* (Oxford: Oxford University Press).

Pisani-Ferry, J. and Sapir, A. (2006), *Last Exit to Lisbon* (Brussels: Bruegel). http://www.bruegel.org/doc_pdf_287.

Prescott, E. (2004), 'Why Do Americans Work So Much More than Europeans?', *Federal Reserve Bank of Minneapolis Quarterly Review*, 28: 2–13.

Sapir, A. *et al.* (2004), *An Agenda for a Growing Europe: The Sapir Report* (Oxford: Oxford University Press).

—— (2006), 'Globalisation and the Reform of European Social Models', *Journal of Common Market Studies*, 44: 397–418.

—— Aghion, P., Bertola, G., Hellwig, M., Pisani-Ferry, J., Rosati, D., Viñals, J., and Wallace, H. with Buti, M., Nava, M., and Smith, P. M. (2003), *An Agenda for a Growing Europe: Making the EU Economic System Deliver*, Report of an Independent High-Level Study Group Established on the Initiative of the President of the European Commission, mimeo (Brussels).

United Nations Population Division (2002), *World Population Prospects: The 2002 Revision*, http://www.un.org/esa/population/unpop.htm.

Van Ark, B. (2005), 'Europe's Productivity Gap: Catching Up or Getting Stuck?', paper presented at the International Symposium on Productivity, Competitiveness and Globalisation, Banque de France, Paris, 4 Nov.

■ INDEX